Exploring Premium Media Site

Improve your grade with hands-on tools and resources!

- Master *Key Terms* to expand your vocabulary.
- Prepare for exams by taking practice quizzes in the *Online Chapter Review*.
- Download *Student Data Files* for the applications projects in each chapter.

And for even more tools, you can access the following Premium Resources using your Access Code. Register now to get the most out of ***Exploring!***

- *Hands-On Exercise Videos* accompany each Hands-On Exercise in the chapter. These videos demonstrate both how to accomplish individual skills as well as why they are important.*
- *Soft Skills Videos* are necessary to complete the Soft Skills Beyond the Classroom Exercise, and introduce students to important professional skills.*

*Access code required for these premium resources

Your Access Code is:

Note: If there is no silver foil covering the access code, it may already have been redeemed, and therefore may no longer be valid. In that case, you can purchase online access using a major credit card or PayPal account. To do so, go to **www.pearsonhighered.com/exploring**, select your book cover, click on "Buy Access" and follow the on-screen instructions.

To Register:

- To start you will need a valid email address and this access code.
- Go to **www.pearsonhighered.com/exploring** and scroll to find your text book.
- Once you've selected your text, on the Home Page, click the link to access the Student Premium Content.
- Click the Register button and follow the on-screen instructions.
- After you register, you can sign in any time via the log-in area on the same screen.

System Requirements

Windows 7 Ultimate Edition; IE 8
Windows Vista Ultimate Edition SP1; IE 8
Windows XP Professional SP3; IE 7
Windows XP Professional SP3; Firefox 3.6.4
Mac OS 10.5.7; Firefox 3.6.4
Mac OS 10.6; Safari 5

Technical Support

http://247pearsoned.custhelp.com

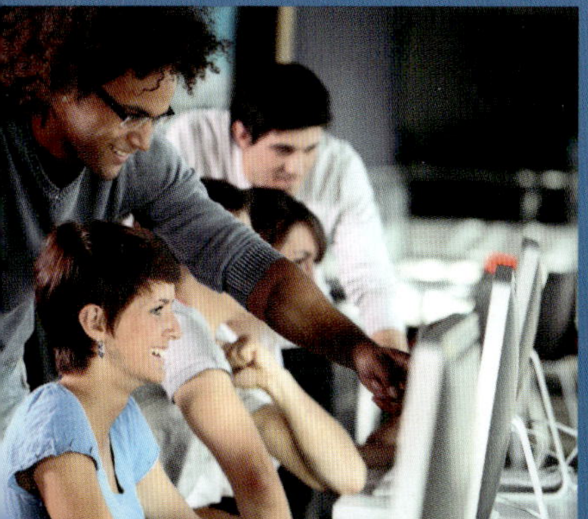

Photo credits: Goodluz/wrangler/Elena Elisseeva/Shutterstock

SERIES

(ex•ploring)

1. Investigating in a systematic way: examining. 2. Searching into or ranging over for the purpose of discovery.

Microsoft®

Excel 2013

COMPREHENSIVE

Series Editor Mary Anne Poatsy

Mulbery | Davidson

Series Created by Dr. Robert T. Grauer

PEARSON

Boston Columbus Indianapolis New York San Francisco Upper Saddle River
Amsterdam Cape Town Dubai London Madrid Milan Munich Paris Montréal Toronto
Delhi Mexico City São Paulo Sydney Hong Kong Seoul Singapore Taipei Tokyo

Editor in Chief: Michael Payne
Senior Editor: Samantha McAfee Lewis
Editorial Project Manager: Keri Rand
Product Development Manager: Laura Burgess
Development Editor: Barbara Stover
Editorial Assistant: Laura Karahalis
Director of Marketing: Maggie Moylan Leen
Marketing Manager: Brad Forrester
Marketing Coordinator: Susan Osterlitz
Marketing Assistant: Darshika Vyas
Managing Editor: Camille Trentacoste
Production Project Manager: Ilene Kahn
Senior Operations Specialist: Maura Zaldivar
Senior Art Director: Jonathan Boylan
Interior Design: Studio Montage
Cover Design: Studio Montage
Cover Photos: Supri Suharjoto/Shutterstock, wavebreakmedia/Shutterstock, Terry Chan/Shutterstock, Csaba Peterdi/Shutterstock
Associate Director of Design: Blair Brown
Digital Media Editor: Eric Hakanson
Director of Media Development: Taylor Ragan
Media Project Manager, Production: Renata Butera
Full Service Project Management: Andrea Stefanowicz/PreMediaGlobal
Composition: PreMediaGlobal

Credits and acknowledgments borrowed from other sources and reproduced, with permission, in this textbook appear on the appropriate page within text.

10 9 8 7 6 5

ISBN 10: 0-13-341218-0
ISBN 13: 978-0-13-341218-5

Dedications

For my husband, Ted, who unselfishly continues to take on more than his share to support me throughout the process; and for my children, Laura, Carolyn, and Teddy, whose encouragement and love have been inspiring.

Mary Anne Poatsy

I dedicate this book in memory to Grandpa Herman Hort, who dedicated his life to his family and to the education field as a teacher and administrator. He inspired a daughter and several grandchildren to become passionate educators and provide quality curriculum to students.

Keith Mulbery

I dedicate this book in loving memory of my grandmother Earline B. Leggett (Nanny). Your kindness, wisdom, and support have been and will always be an inspiration. I couldn't have made it without you.

Jason Davidson

About the Authors

Mary Anne Poatsy, Series Editor

Mary Anne is a senior faculty member at Montgomery County Community College, teaching various computer application and concepts courses in face-to-face and online environments. She holds a B.A. in Psychology and Education from Mount Holyoke College and an M.B.A. in Finance from Northwestern University's Kellogg Graduate School of Management.

Mary Anne has more than 12 years of educational experience. She is currently adjunct faculty at Gwynedd-Mercy College and Montgomery County Community College. She has also taught at Bucks County Community College and Muhlenberg College, as well as conducted personal training. Before teaching, she was Vice President at Shearson Lehman in the Municipal Bond Investment Banking Department.

Dr. Keith Mulbery, Excel Author

Dr. Keith Mulbery is the Department Chair and a Professor in the Information Systems and Technology Department at Utah Valley University (UVU), where he currently teaches systems analysis and design, and global and ethical issues in information systems and technology. He has also taught computer applications, C# programming, and management information systems. Keith served as Interim Associate Dean, School of Computing, in the College of Technology and Computing at UVU.

Keith received the Faculty Senate Faculty Excellence Award for the College of Technology and Computing in 2013, the Utah Valley State College Board of Trustees Award of Excellence in 2001, School of Technology and Computing Scholar Award in 2007, and School of Technology and Computing Teaching Award in 2008. He has authored more than 17 textbooks, served as Series Editor for the Exploring Office 2007 series, and served as developmental editor on two textbooks for the Essentials Office 2000 series. He is frequently asked to give presentations and workshops on Microsoft Office Excel at various education conferences.

Keith received his B.S. and M.Ed. in Business Education from Southwestern Oklahoma State University and earned his Ph.D. in Education with an emphasis in Business Information Systems at Utah State University. His dissertation topic was computer-assisted instruction using Prentice Hall's Train and Assess IT program (the predecessor to MyITLab) to supplement traditional instruction in basic computer proficiency courses.

Jason Davidson, Excel Author

Jason Davidson is a faculty member in the College of Business at Butler University, where he teaches Advanced Web Design, Data Networks, Data Analysis and Business Modeling, and introductory MIS courses. With a background in media development, prior to joining the faculty at Butler, he worked in the technical publishing industry. Along with teaching, he currently serves as an IT consultant for regional businesses in the Indianapolis area. He holds a B.A. in telecommunication arts from Butler University and an M.B.A. from Morehead State University. He lives in Indianapolis, Indiana, and in his free time, enjoys road biking, photography, and spending time with his family.

Rebecca Lawson, Office Fundamentals Author

Rebecca Lawson is a professor in the Computer Information Technologies program at Lansing Community College. She coordinates the curriculum, develops the instructional materials, and teaches for the E-Business curriculum. She also serves as the Online Faculty Coordinator at the Center for Teaching Excellence at LCC. In that role, she develops and facilitates online workshops for faculty learning to teach online. Her major areas of interest include online curriculum quality assurance, the review and development of printed and online instructional materials, the assessment of computer and Internet literacy skill levels to facilitate student retention, and the use of social networking tools to support learning in blended and online learning environments.

Dr. Robert T. Grauer, Creator of the Exploring Series

Bob Grauer is an Associate Professor in the Department of Computer Information Systems at the University of Miami, where he is a multiple winner of the Outstanding Teaching Award in the School of Business, most recently in 2009. He has written numerous COBOL texts and is the vision behind the Exploring Office series, with more than three million books in print. His work has been translated into three foreign languages and is used in all aspects of higher education at both national and international levels. Bob Grauer has consulted for several major corporations including IBM and American Express. He received his Ph.D. in Operations Research in 1972 from the Polytechnic Institute of Brooklyn.

Brief Contents

Contents

CHAPTER EIGHT **Statistical Functions:** Analyzing Statistics 465

CHAPTER NINE **Multiple-Sheet Workbook Management:** Ensuring Quality Control 505

CHAPTER TEN **Imports, Web Queries, and XML:** Managing Data 553

CHAPTER ELEVEN Collaboration and Workbook Distribution: Sharing Data with Others 593

CHAPTER TWELVE Templates, Styles, and Macros: Standardizing Workbooks 643

Application Capstone Exercises

Acknowledgments

The Exploring team would like to acknowledge and thank all the reviewers who helped us throughout the years by providing us with their invaluable comments, suggestions, and constructive criticism.

We'd like to especially thank our Focus Group attendees and User Diary Reviewers for this edition:

Stephen Z. Jourdan
Auburn University at Montgomery

Ann Rovetto
Horry-Georgetown Technical College

Jacqueline D. Lawson
Henry Ford Community College

Diane L. Smith
Henry Ford Community College

Sven Aelterman
Troy University

Suzanne M. Jeska
County College of Morris

Susan N. Dozier
Tidewater Community College

Robert G. Phipps Jr.
West Virginia University

Mike Michaelson
Palomar College

Mary Beth Tarver
Northwestern State University

Alexandre C. Probst
Colorado Christian University

Phil Nielson
Salt Lake Community College

Carolyn Barren
Macomb Community College

Sue A. McCrory
Missouri State University

Lucy Parakhovnik
California State University, Northridge

Jakie Brown Jr.
Stevenson University

Craig J. Peterson
American InterContinental University

Terry Ray Rigsby
Hill College

Biswadip Ghosh
Metropolitan State University of Denver

Cheryl Sypniewski
Macomb Community College

Lynn Keane
University of South Carolina

Sheila Gionfriddo
Luzerne College

Dick Hewer
Ferris State College

Carolyn Borne
Louisiana State University

Sumathy Chandrashekar
Salisbury University

Laura Marcoulides
Fullerton College

Don Riggs
SUNY Schenectady County Community College

Gary McFall
Purdue University

James Powers
University of Southern Indiana

James Brown
Central Washington University

Brian Powell
West Virginia University

Sherry Lenhart
Terra Community College

Chen Zhang
Bryant University

Nikia Robinson
Indian River State University

Jill Young
Southeast Missouri State University

Debra Hoffman
Southeast Missouri State University

Tommy Lu
Delaware Technical Community College

Mimi Spain
Southern Maine Community College

We'd like to thank everyone who has been involved in reviewing and providing their feedback, including for our previous editions:

Adriana Lumpkin
Midland College

Alan S. Abrahams
Virginia Tech

Ali Berrached
University of Houston–Downtown

Allen Alexander
Delaware Technical & Community College

Andrea Marchese
Maritime College, State University of New York

Andrew Blitz
Broward College; Edison State College

Angel Norman
University of Tennessee, Knoxville

Angela Clark
University of South Alabama

Ann Rovetto
Horry-Georgetown Technical College

Astrid Todd
Guilford Technical Community College

Audrey Gillant
Maritime College, State University of New York

Barbara Stover
Marion Technical College

Barbara Tollinger
Sinclair Community College

Ben Brahim Taha
Auburn University

Beverly Amer
Northern Arizona University

Beverly Fite
Amarillo College

Bonita Volker
Tidewater Community College

Bonnie Homan
San Francisco State University

Brad West
Sinclair Community College

Brian Powell
West Virginia University

Carol Buser
Owens Community College

Carol Roberts
University of Maine

Carolyn Barren
Macomb Community College

Cathy Poyner
Truman State University

Charles Hodgson
Delgado Community College

Cheri Higgins
Illinois State University

Cheryl Hinds
Norfolk State University

Chris Robinson
Northwest State Community College

Cindy Herbert
Metropolitan Community College–Longview

Dana Hooper
University of Alabama

Dana Johnson
North Dakota State University

Daniela Marghitu
Auburn University

David Noel
University of Central Oklahoma

David Pulis
Maritime College, State University of New York

David Thornton
Jacksonville State University

Dawn Medlin
Appalachian State University

Debby Keen
University of Kentucky

Debra Chapman
University of South Alabama

Derrick Huang
Florida Atlantic University

Diana Baran
Henry Ford Community College

Diane Cassidy
The University of North Carolina at Charlotte

Diane Smith
Henry Ford Community College

Don Danner
San Francisco State University

Don Hoggan
Solano College

Doncho Petkov
Eastern Connecticut State University

Donna Ehrhart
State University of New York at Brockport

Elaine Crable
Xavier University

Elizabeth Duett
Delgado Community College

Erhan Uskup
Houston Community College–Northwest

Eric Martin
University of Tennessee

Erika Nadas
Wilbur Wright College

Floyd Winters
Manatee Community College

Frank Lucente
Westmoreland County Community College

G. Jan Wilms
Union University

Gail Cope
Sinclair Community College

Gary DeLorenzo
California University of Pennsylvania

Gary Garrison
Belmont University

George Cassidy
Sussex County Community College

Gerald Braun
Xavier University

Gerald Burgess
Western New Mexico University

Gladys Swindler
Fort Hays State University

Heith Hennel
Valencia Community College

Henry Rudzinski
Central Connecticut State University

Irene Joos
La Roche College

Iwona Rusin
Baker College; Davenport University

J. Roberto Guzman
San Diego Mesa College

Jan Wilms
Union University

Jane Stam
Onondaga Community College

Janet Bringhurst
Utah State University

Jeanette Dix
Ivy Tech Community College

Jennifer Day
Sinclair Community College

Jill Canine
Ivy Tech Community College

Jim Chaffee
The University of Iowa Tippie College of Business

Joanne Lazirko
University of Wisconsin–Milwaukee

Jodi Milliner
Kansas State University

John Hollenbeck
Blue Ridge Community College

John Seydel
Arkansas State University

Judith A. Scheeren
Westmoreland County Community College

Judith Brown
The University of Memphis

Juliana Cypert
Tarrant County College

Kamaljeet Sanghera
George Mason University

Karen Priestly
Northern Virginia Community College

Karen Ravan
Spartanburg Community College

Kathleen Brenan
Ashland University

Ken Busbee
Houston Community College

Kent Foster
Winthrop University

Kevin Anderson
Solano Community College

Kim Wright
The University of Alabama

Kristen Hockman
University of Missouri–Columbia

Kristi Smith
Allegany College of Maryland

Laura McManamon
University of Dayton

Leanne Chun
Leeward Community College

Lee McClain
Western Washington University

Linda D. Collins
Mesa Community College

Linda Johnsonius
Murray State University

Linda Lau
Longwood University

Linda Theus
Jackson State Community College

Linda Williams
Marion Technical College

Lisa Miller
University of Central Oklahoma

Lister Horn
Pensacola Junior College

Lixin Tao
Pace University

Loraine Miller
Cayuga Community College

Lori Kielty
Central Florida Community College

Lorna Wells
Salt Lake Community College

Lorraine Sauchin
Duquesne University

Lucy Parakhovnik (Parker)
California State University, Northridge

Lynn Mancini
Delaware Technical Community College

Mackinzee Escamilla
South Plains College

Marcia Welch
Highline Community College

Margaret McManus
Northwest Florida State College

Margaret Warrick
Allan Hancock College

Marilyn Hibbert
Salt Lake Community College

Mark Choman
Luzerne County Community College

Mary Duncan
University of Missouri–St. Louis

Melissa Nemeth
Indiana University-Purdue University Indianapolis

Melody Alexander
Ball State University

Michael Douglas
University of Arkansas at Little Rock

Michael Dunklebarger
Alamance Community College

Michael G. Skaff
College of the Sequoias

Michele Budnovitch
Pennsylvania College of Technology

Mike Jochen
East Stroudsburg University

Mike Scroggins
Missouri State University

Muhammed Badamas
Morgan State University

NaLisa Brown
University of the Ozarks

Nancy Grant
Community College of Allegheny County–South Campus

Nanette Lareau
University of Arkansas Community College–Morrilton

Pam Brune
Chattanooga State Community College

Pam Uhlenkamp
Iowa Central Community College

Patrick Smith
Marshall Community and Technical College

Paul Addison
Ivy Tech Community College

Paula Ruby
Arkansas State University

Peggy Burrus
Red Rocks Community College

Peter Ross
SUNY Albany

Philip H. Nielson
Salt Lake Community College

Ralph Hooper
University of Alabama

Ranette Halverson
Midwestern State University

Richard Blamer
John Carroll University

Richard Cacace
Pensacola Junior College

Richard Hewer
Ferris State University

Rob Murray
Ivy Tech Community College

Robert Dušek
Northern Virginia Community College

Robert Sindt
Johnson County Community College

Robert Warren
Delgado Community College

Rocky Belcher
Sinclair Community College

Roger Pick
University of Missouri at Kansas City

Ronnie Creel
Troy University

Rosalie Westerberg
Clover Park Technical College

Ruth Neal
Navarro College

Sandra Thomas
Troy University

Sheila Gionfriddo
Luzerne County Community College

Sherrie Geitgey
Northwest State Community College

Sophia Wilberscheid
Indian River State College

Sophie Lee
California State University, Long Beach

Stacy Johnson
Iowa Central Community College

Stephanie Kramer
Northwest State Community College

Stephen Jourdan
Auburn University Montgomery

Steven Schwarz
Raritan Valley Community College

Sue McCrory
Missouri State University

Susan Fuschetto
Cerritos College

Susan Medlin
UNC Charlotte

Suzan Spitzberg
Oakton Community College

Sven Aelterman
Troy University

Sylvia Brown
Midland College

Tanya Patrick
Clackamas Community College

Terri Holly
Indian River State College

Thomas Rienzo
Western Michigan University

Tina Johnson
Midwestern State University

Tommy Lu
Delaware Technical and Community College

Troy S. Cash
NorthWest Arkansas Community College

Vicki Robertson
Southwest Tennessee Community

Weifeng Chen
California University of Pennsylvania

Wes Anthony
Houston Community College

William Ayen
University of Colorado at Colorado Springs

Wilma Andrews
Virginia Commonwealth University

Yvonne Galusha
University of Iowa

Special thanks to our development and technical team:

Barbara Stover

Cheryl Slavick

Elizabeth Lockley

Heather Hetzler

Jennifer Lynn

Joyce Nielsen

Linda Pogue

Lisa Bucki

Lori Damanti

Mara Zebest

Susan Fry

Preface

The Exploring Series and You

Exploring is Pearson's Office Application series that requires students like you to think "beyond the point and click." In this edition, we have worked to restructure the Exploring experience around the way you, today's modern student, actually use your resources.

The goal of Exploring is, as it has always been, to go further than teaching just the steps to accomplish a task—the series provides the theoretical foundation for you to understand when and why to apply a skill.

As a result, you achieve a deeper understanding of each application and can apply this critical thinking beyond Office and the classroom.

You are practical students, focused on what you need to do to be successful in this course and beyond, and want to be as efficient as possible. Exploring has evolved to meet you where you are and help you achieve success efficiently. Pearson has paid attention to the habits of students today, how you get information, how you are motivated to do well in class, and what your future goals look like. We asked you and your peers for acceptance of new tools we designed to address these points, and you responded with a resounding "YES!"

Here Is What We Learned About You

You are goal-oriented. You want a good grade in this course—so we rethought how Exploring works so that you can learn the how and why behind the skills in this course to be successful now. You also want to be successful in your future career—so we used motivating case studies to show relevance of these skills to your future careers and incorporated Soft Skills, Collaboration, and Analysis Cases in this edition to set you up for success in the future.

You read, prepare, and study differently than students used to. You use textbooks like a tool—you want to easily identify what you need to know and learn it efficiently. We have added key features such as Step Icons, Hands-On Exercise Videos, and tracked everything via page numbers that allow you to navigate the content efficiently, making the concepts accessible and creating a map to success for you to follow.

You go to college now with a different set of skills than students did five years ago. The new edition of Exploring moves you beyond the basics of the software at a faster pace, without sacrificing coverage of the fundamental skills that you need to know. This ensures that you will be engaged from page 1 to the end of the book.

You and your peers have diverse learning styles. With this in mind, we broadened our definition of "student resources" to include Compass, an online skill database; movable Student Reference cards; Hands-On Exercise videos to provide a secondary lecture-like option of review; Soft Skills exercises to illustrate important non-technical skills; and the most powerful online homework and assessment tool around with a direct 1:1 content match with the Exploring Series, MyITLab. Exploring will be accessible to all students, regardless of learning style.

Providing You with a Map to Success to Move Beyond the Point and Click

All of these changes and additions will provide you with an easy and efficient path to follow to be successful in this course, regardless of your learning style or any existing knowledge you have at the outset. Our goal is to keep you more engaged in both the hands-on and conceptual sides, helping you to achieve a higher level of understanding that will guarantee you success in this course and in your future career. In addition to the vision and experience of the series creator, Robert T. Grauer, we have assembled a tremendously talented team of Office Applications authors who have devoted themselves to teaching you the ins and outs of Microsoft Word, Excel, Access, and PowerPoint. Led in this edition by series editor Mary Anne Poatsy, the whole team is equally dedicated to providing you with a **map to success** to support the Exploring mission of **moving you beyond the point and click**.

Key Features

- **White Pages/Yellow Pages** clearly distinguish the theory (white pages) from the skills covered in the Hands-On Exercises (yellow pages) so students always know what they are supposed to be doing.
- **Enhanced Objective Mapping** enables students to follow a directed path through each chapter, from the objectives list at the chapter opener through the exercises in the end of chapter.
  - **Objectives List:** This provides a simple list of key objectives covered in the chapter. This includes page numbers so students can skip between objectives where they feel they need the most help.
  - **Step Icons:** These icons appear in the white pages and reference the step numbers in the Hands-On Exercises, providing a correlation between the two so students can easily find conceptual help when they are working hands-on and need a refresher.
  - **Quick Concepts Check:** A series of questions that appear briefly at the end of each white page section. These questions cover the most essential concepts in the white pages required for students to be successful in working the Hands-On Exercises. Page numbers are included for easy reference to help students locate the answers.
  - **Chapter Objectives Review:** Appears toward the end of the chapter and reviews all important concepts throughout the chapter. Newly designed in an easy-to-read bulleted format.
- **Key Terms Matching:** A new exercise that requires students to match key terms to their definitions. This requires students to work actively with this important vocabulary and prove conceptual understanding.
- **Case Study** presents a scenario for the chapter, creating a story that ties the Hands-On Exercises together.

- **Hands-On Exercise Videos** are tied to each Hands-On Exercise and walk students through the steps of the exercise while weaving in conceptual information related to the Case Study and the objectives as a whole.
- **End-of-Chapter Exercises** offer instructors several options for assessment. Each chapter has approximately 12–15 exercises ranging from multiple choice questions to open-ended projects. Newly included in this is a Key Terms Matching exercise of approximately 20 questions, as well as a Collaboration Case and Soft Skills Case for every chapter.

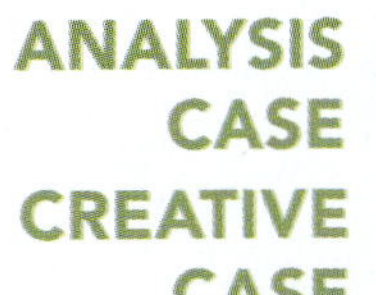

- **Enhanced Mid-Level Exercises** include a **Creative Case** (for PowerPoint and Word), which allows students some flexibility and creativity, not being bound by a definitive solution, and an **Analysis Case** (for Excel and Access), which requires students to interpret the data they are using to answer an analytic question, as well as **Discover Steps**, which encourage students to use Help or to problem-solve to accomplish a task.

- **MyITLab** provides an auto-graded homework, tutorial, and assessment solution that is built to match the book content exactly. Every Hands-On Exercise is available as a simulation training. Every Capstone Exercise and most Mid-Level Exercises are available as live-in-the-application Grader projects. Icons are included throughout the text to denote which exercises are included.

Instructor Resources

The Instructor's Resource Center, available at www.pearsonhighered.com, includes the following:

- **Instructor Manual** provides an overview of all available resources as well as student data and solution files for every exercise.
- **Solution Files with Scorecards** assist with grading the Hands-On Exercises and end-of-chapter exercises.
- **Prepared Exams** allow instructors to assess all skills covered in a chapter with a single project.
- **Rubrics** for Mid-Level Creative Cases and Beyond the Classroom Cases in Microsoft® Word format enable instructors to customize the assignments for their classes.
- **PowerPoint® Presentations** with notes for each chapter are included for out-of-class study or review.
- **Lesson Plans** provide a detailed blueprint to achieve chapter learning objectives and outcomes.
- **Objectives Lists** map chapter objectives to Hands-On Exercises and end-of-chapter exercises.
- **Multiple Choice and Key Terms Matching Answer Keys**
- **Test Bank** provides objective-based questions for every chapter.
- **Grader Projects** textual versions of auto-graded assignments for Grader.
- **Additional Projects** provide more assignment options for instructors.
- **Syllabus Templates**
- **Scripted Lectures** offer an in-class lecture guide for instructors to mirror the Hands-On Exercises.
- **Assignment Sheet**
- **File Guide**

Student Resources

Companion Web Site

www.pearsonhighered.com/exploring offers expanded IT resources and self-student tools for students to use for each chapter, including:

- Online Chapter Review
- Web Resources
- Glossary
- Student Data Files
- Chapter Objectives Review

In addition, the Companion Web Site is now the site for Premium Media, including the videos for the Exploring Series:

- Hands-On Exercise Videos*
- Audio PPTs*

*Access code required for these premium resources.

Student Reference Cards

A two-sided card for each application provides students with a visual summary of information and tips specific to each application.

Office

Office Fundamentals and File Management

CHAPTER 1

Andresr/Shutterstock

Taking the First Step

OBJECTIVES

AFTER YOU READ THIS CHAPTER, YOU WILL BE ABLE TO:

CASE STUDY | Spotted Begonia Art Gallery

You are an administrative assistant for Spotted Begonia, a local art gallery. The gallery deals in local artists' work, including fiber art, oil paintings, watercolors, prints, pottery, and metal sculptures. The gallery holds four seasonal showings throughout the year. Much of the art is on consignment, but there are a few permanent collections. Occasionally, the gallery exchanges these collections with other galleries across the country. The gallery does a lot of community outreach and tries to help local artists develop a network of clients and supporters. Local schools are invited to bring students to the gallery for enrichment programs. Considered a major contributor to the local economy, the gallery has received both public and private funding through federal and private grants.

As the administrative assistant for Spotted Begonia, you are responsible for overseeing the production of documents, spreadsheets, newspaper articles, and presentations that will be used to increase public awareness of the gallery. Other clerical assistants who are familiar with Microsoft Office will prepare the promotional materials, and you will proofread, make necessary corrections, adjust page layouts, save and print documents, and identify appropriate templates to simplify tasks. Your experience with Microsoft Office 2013 is limited, but you know that certain fundamental tasks that are common to Word, Excel, and PowerPoint will help you accomplish your oversight task. You are excited to get started with your work!

Windows 8.1.1 Startup

You use computers for many activities for work, school, or pleasure. You probably have never thought too much about what makes a computer function and allows you to do so many things with it. But all of those activities would not be possible without an operating system running on the computer. An ***operating system*** is software that directs computer activities such as checking all components, managing system resources, and communicating with application software. ***Windows 8.1.1*** is a Microsoft operating system released in April 2014 and is available on laptops, desktops, and tablet computers.

The ***Start screen*** is what you see after starting your computer and entering your username and password. It is where you start all of your computing activities. See Figure 1.1 to see a typical Start screen.

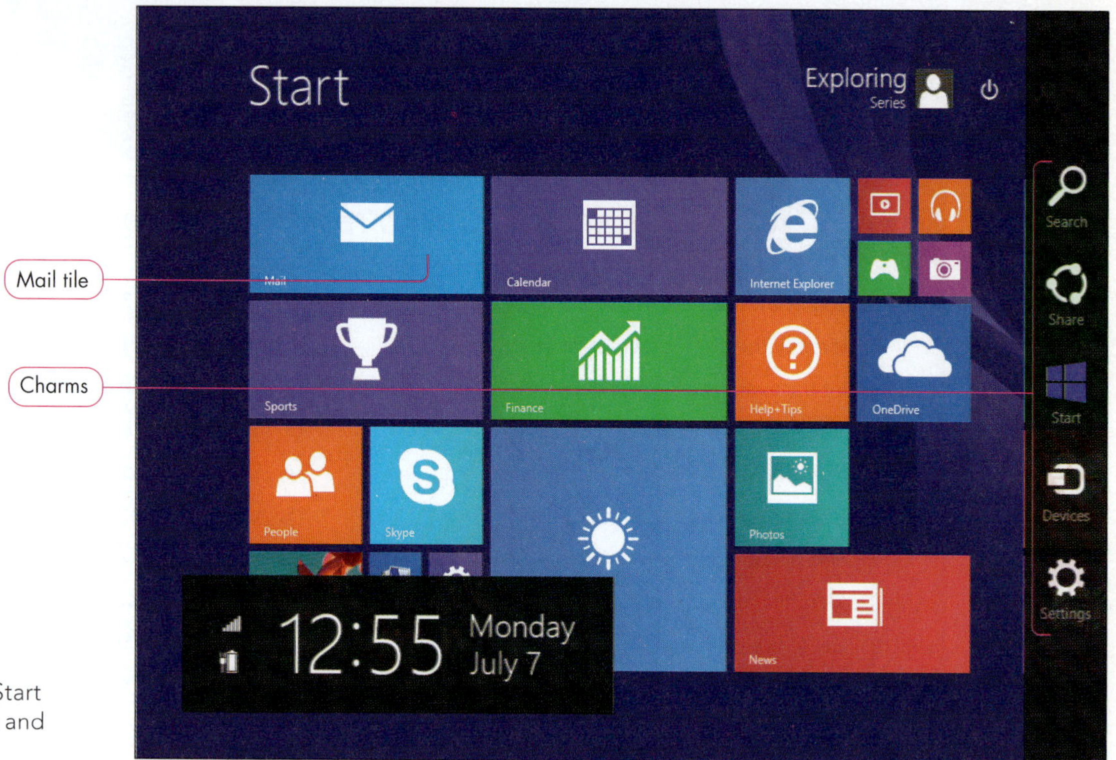

FIGURE 1.1 Typical Start Screen Components and Charms

In this section, you will explore the Start screen and its components in more detail. You will also learn how to log in with your Microsoft account and access the desktop.

Logging In with Your Microsoft Account

Although you can log in to Windows 8.1.1 as a local network user, you can also log in using a Microsoft account. When you have a Microsoft account, you can sign in to any Windows 8.1.1 computer and you will be able to access the saved settings associated with your Microsoft account. That means the computer will have the same familiar look that you are used to seeing. Your Microsoft account will allow you to be automatically signed in to all of the apps and services that use a Microsoft account as the authentication. You can also save your sign-in credentials for other Web sites that you frequently visit.

Logging in with your Microsoft account not only provides all of the benefits just listed, but also provides additional benefits such as being connected to all of Microsoft's resources on the Internet. These resources include a free Outlook account and access to cloud storage at OneDrive. ***Cloud storage*** is a technology used to store files and to work with programs that are stored in a central location on the Internet. ***OneDrive*** is an app used to store, access, and share files and folders. It is accessible using an installed desktop app or as cloud storage using a Web address. Files and folders in either location can be synced. For Office 2013 applications, OneDrive is the default location for saving files. Documents saved in OneDrive are accessible from any computer that has an Internet connection. As long as the document has been saved in OneDrive, the most recent version of the document will be accessible from any computer connected to the Internet. OneDrive allows you to collaborate with others. You can easily share your documents with others or add Reply Comments next to the text that you are discussing together. You can work with others on the same document simultaneously.

STEP 1» You can create a Microsoft account at any time by going to live.com. You simply work through the Sign-up form to set up your account by creating a username from your e-mail address and creating a password. After filling in the form, you will be automatically signed in to Outlook and sent to your Outlook Inbox. If you already have a Microsoft account, you can just go ahead and log in to Outlook. See Figure 1.2 to see the Sign-up page at live.com.

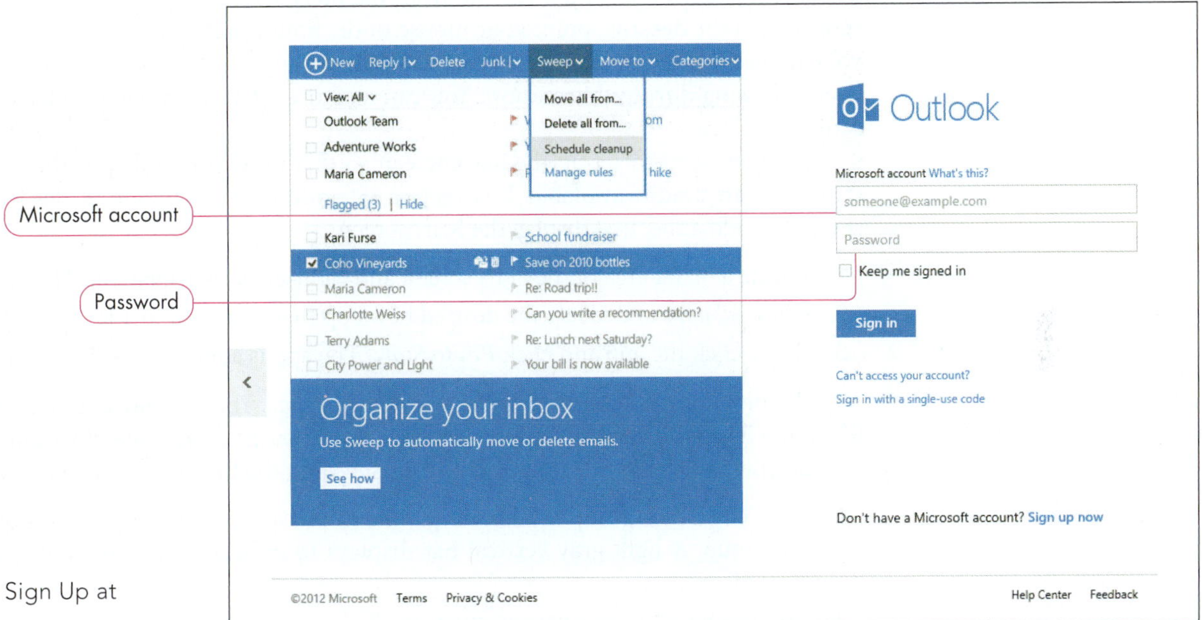

FIGURE 1.2 Sign Up at live.com

Identifying the Start Screen Components

The first thing you will notice when you turn on a computer running Windows 8.1.1 is that the Start screen has a new sleek, clean look and large readable type (refer to Figure 1.1). The user is identified in the top-right corner of the screen. You can click the user's name to access settings such as locking or signing out of the account. You can also change the picture associated with the account here.

You will notice that the Start screen is made up of several colorful block images called ***tiles***. When you click a tile, you will be taken to a program, file, folder, or other ***Windows 8.1.1 app***. Windows 8.1.1 apps are applications specifically designed to run in the Start screen interface of Windows 8.1.1. Some Windows 8.1.1 apps, such as desktop, Mail, and OneDrive, are already installed and ready to use. Others can be downloaded from the Windows Store. The default apps are brightly colored. Tiles for programs that run on the traditional Windows desktop are smaller and more transparent. The look of the tiles is customizable, but all tiles include the name of the app or program. Depending on the number of apps that you have installed, as you move your mouse to the bottom of the screen, you will see a horizontal scroll bar display. This can be used to access any app that does not display within the initial view of the Start screen.

STEP 2» The traditional Start button is not present in Windows 8.1.1. Instead, the ***Charms*** are available (refer to Figure 1.1). The Charms are made up of five icons that provide similar functionality to the Start button found in previous versions of Windows. The icons are Search, Share, Start, Devices, and Settings. Using the Charms, you can search for files and applications, share information with others within an application that is running, or return to the Start screen. You can also control devices that are connected to your computer or modify various settings depending on which application is running when accessing the Setting icon. To display the Charms, point to the top-right or bottom-right corners of the screen. Refer to Figure 1.1 to view the Start screen components and the Charms.

Interacting with the Start Screen

To interact with any tile on the Start screen (refer to Figure 1.1), simply click it. If you have signed in with your Microsoft account, you will automatically be able to access any of the Internet-enabled programs. For example, if you click Mail, you will go straight to your Outlook Inbox. If you right-click a tile, you will see several contextual options displayed. For example, the option to unpin the tile from the Start screen displays. To return to the Start screen from the desktop, point your mouse in the bottom-left corner of the screen. Pointing your mouse to the top-left corner reveals the open applications or programs that you have been accessing during this session. You can also use Charms to navigate back to the Start screen.

You may want to set up the Start screen so that programs and apps that you use most frequently are readily available. It is very easy to add tiles to or remove tiles from the Start screen. To add a tile, first display the Start screen.

1. Locate a blank area of the Start screen and right-click to display the *All apps* icon.
2. Click *All apps* and locate the desired new app that you want to add.
3. Right-click the app and click *Pin to Start.* The app is added to the Start screen.

The new app's tile is added at the end of your apps. You can move tiles by dragging the tile to the desired location. You can remove a tile from the Start screen by right-clicking the tile and clicking *Unpin from Start.* You can also group the tiles and name the groups:

1. To create a new group of tiles, drag a tile to the space to the left or right of an existing tile group. A light gray vertical bar displays to indicate where the new group will be located.
2. Add more tiles to this new group as needed.
3. To name the group, right-click any blank area of the Start screen and click Name groups. Type in the space provided to name a group. If a name is not entered for a group, the horizontal Name group bar disappears.

Accessing the Desktop

Although the Start screen is easy to use, you may want to access the more familiar desktop that you used in previous versions of Windows. The Desktop tile is available on the Start screen. Click the tile to bring up the desktop. Alternatively, you can be pushed to the desktop when you click other tiles such as Word. In Windows 8.1.1, the desktop is simplified to accommodate use on mobile devices where screen space is limited. However, on a laptop or desktop computer, you may want to have more features readily available. The familiar Notification area is displayed in the bottom-right corner. You will see the Windows Start screen, File Explorer, and Internet Explorer icons. See Figure 1.3 to locate these desktop components.

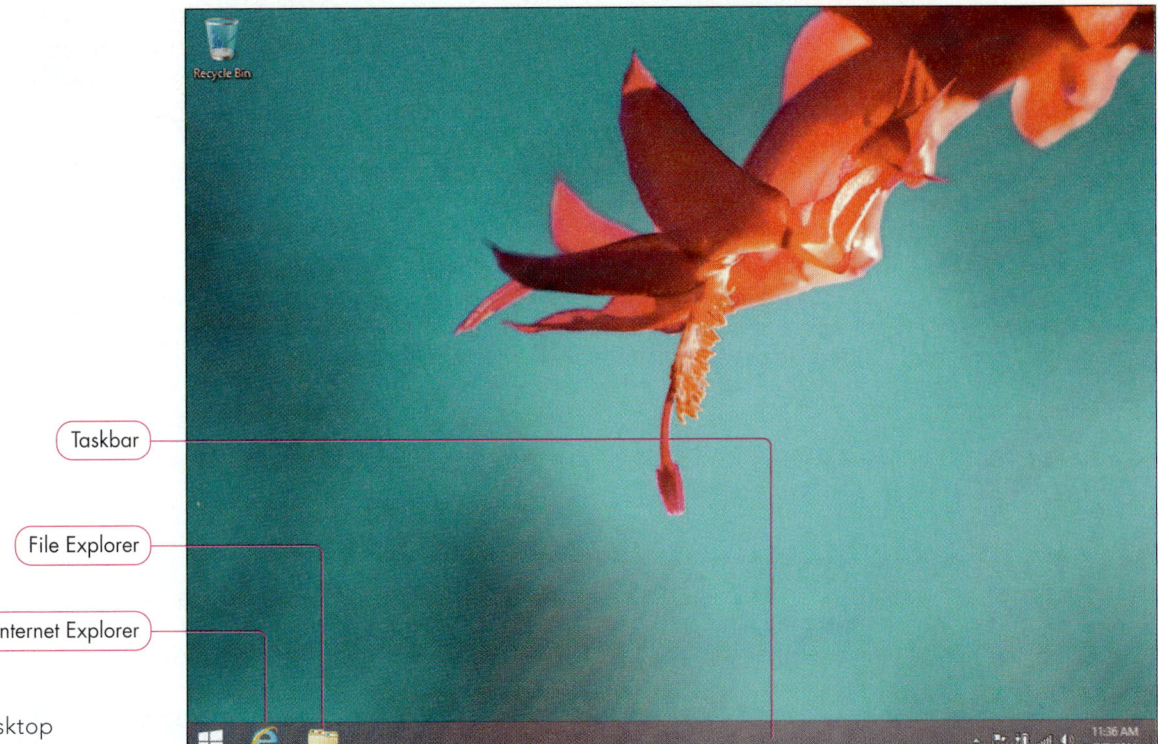

FIGURE 1.3 Desktop Components

You can add more toolbars, such as the Address bar, to the taskbar by right-clicking the taskbar, pointing to Toolbars, and then selecting Address. The Address bar can be used to locate Web sites using the URL or to perform a keyword search to locate Web sites about a specific topic. You can also add programs such as the ***Snipping Tool***. The Snipping Tool is a Windows 8.1.1 accessory program that allows you to capture, or ***snip***, a screen display so that you can save, annotate, or share it. You can remove all of the icons displayed on the taskbar by right-clicking the icon you want to remove and selecting *Unpin this program from taskbar*.

TIP Using the Snipping Tool

The Snipping Tool can be used to take all sizes and shapes of snips of the displayed screen. Options include Free-form Snip, Rectangle Snip, Window Snip, and Full-screen Snip. You can save your snip in several formats, such as PNG, GIF, JPEG, or Single file HTML. In addition, you can use a pen or highlighter to mark up your snips. This option is available after taking a snip and is located under the Tools menu in the Snipping Tool dialog box.

You can return to the Start screen by clicking the Start screen icon on the taskbar.

1. Logging in to Windows 8.1.1 with your Microsoft account provides access to Internet resources. What are some benefits of logging in this way? ***p. 2***
2. OneDrive allows you to collaborate with others. How might you use this service? ***p. 3***
3. What is the Start screen, and how is it different from the desktop? ***p. 3***
4. The desktop has been a feature of previous Windows operating systems. How is the Windows 8.1.1 desktop different from previous versions? ***p. 4***

Hands-On Exercises

1 Windows 8.1.1 Startup

The Spotted Begonia Art Gallery has just hired several new clerical assistants to help you develop promotional materials for the various activities coming up throughout the year. It will be necessary to have a central storage space where you can save the documents and presentations for retrieval from any location. You will also need to be able to collaborate with others on the documents by sharing them and adding comments. To begin, you will get a Microsoft account. You will access the desktop and pin a toolbar and a Windows 8.1.1 accessory program to the taskbar.

Skills covered: Log In with Your Microsoft Account • Identify the Start Screen Components and Interact with the Start Screen • Access the Desktop

STEP 1 » LOG IN WITH YOUR MICROSOFT ACCOUNT

You want to sign up for a Microsoft account so you can store documents and share them with others using the resources available with a Microsoft account, such as OneDrive. Refer to Figure 1.4 as you complete Step 1.

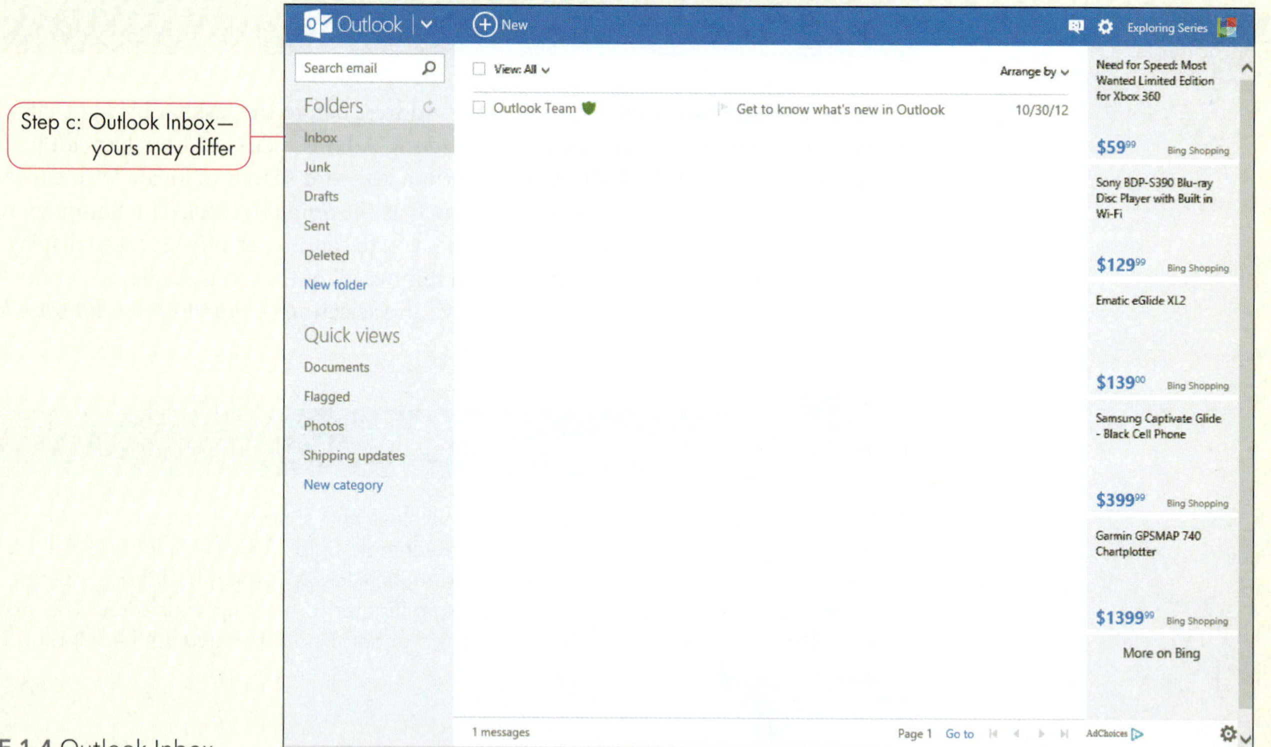

FIGURE 1.4 Outlook Inbox

a. Start your computer and enter your local username and password. On the Start screen, click the **Internet Explorer tile**. Click in the **Address bar** at the bottom of the screen. Type **live.com** and press **Enter**.

Internet Explorer displays, and you are taken to the Sign-up page for Outlook. This is where you can create a username and password for your Microsoft account.

> **TROUBLESHOOTING:** If you already have a Microsoft account, you can skip Step 1 and continue with Step 2. If someone else was already signed in at your computer, you can locate your username and click it to begin to log in.

b. Click the **Sign up now** link at the bottom of the screen. Fill in all text boxes and make all menu selections on the screen. Scroll down as needed. Type the **CAPTCHA code** carefully.

CAPTCHA is a scrambled code used with online forms to prevent mass sign-ups. It helps to ensure that a real person is requesting the account. You can choose not to accept e-mail with promotional offers by clicking the check box near the bottom of the screen to remove the check.

> **TROUBLESHOOTING:** You may want to write down your username and password so that you do not forget it the next time you want to log in with your Microsoft account. Keep this information in a safe and confidential location.

c. Click **I accept**. Your screen should display similarly to Figure 1.4.

Your Microsoft account is created, and you are taken to your Outlook Inbox.

d. Keep Internet Explorer open if you plan to continue using Outlook. Otherwise, sign out of Outlook and close Internet Explorer.

STEP 2 » IDENTIFY THE START SCREEN COMPONENTS AND INTERACT WITH THE START SCREEN

You decide to explore the Start screen components. Then you use the Desktop tile on the Start screen to access the desktop. Refer to Figure 1.5 as you complete Step 2.

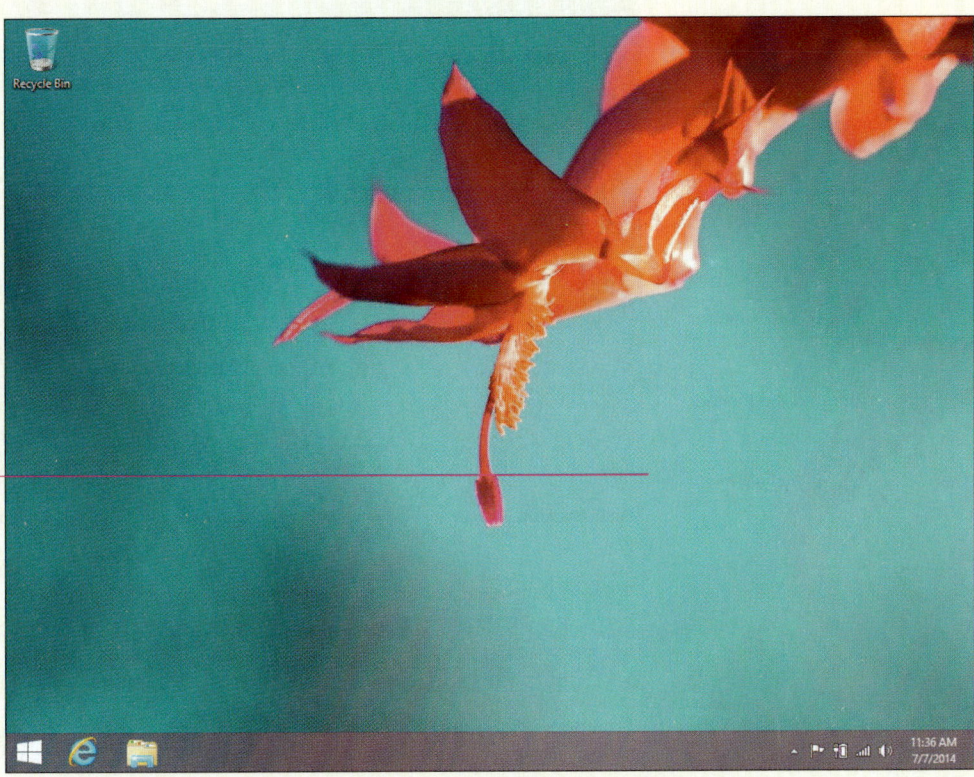

Step d: Display the Windows 8.1.1 desktop

FIGURE 1.5 Desktop

a. Point to the top-right corner to display the Charms. Click the **Start screen charm**.

Because you finished on the desktop after completing Step 1, clicking the Start screen charm takes you to the Start screen.

> **TROUBLESHOOTING:** If you skipped Step 1, log in to Windows with your username and password to display the Start screen.

b. Point to the bottom of the Start screen to display the horizontal scroll bar. Drag the scroll bar to the right to view all of the tiles available. Then drag the scrollbar back to the left to its original position.

Many components of the Start screen do not display until they are needed. This saves screen space on mobile devices. In this case, the horizontal scroll bar is hidden until needed.

c. Point to the bottom-right corner of the screen to display the Charms.

The Charms will display whenever you point to the top-right or bottom-right corners of the screen, regardless of the application you are using.

d. Locate and click the **Desktop tile**. See Figure 1.5.

STEP 3 ›› ACCESS THE DESKTOP

You would like to add some components to make the desktop easier to use. You customize the desktop by adding the Address toolbar and the Snipping Tool to the taskbar. Refer to Figure 1.6 as you complete Step 3.

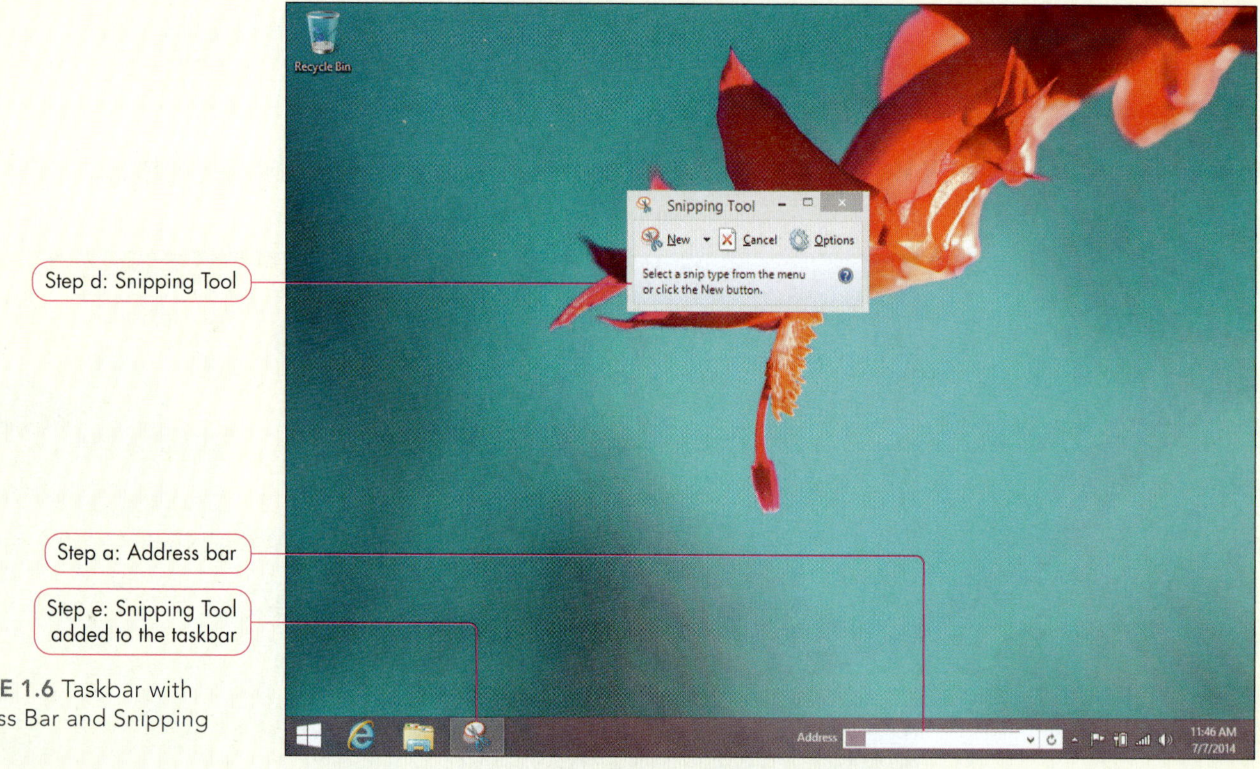

FIGURE 1.6 Taskbar with Address Bar and Snipping Tool

a. Locate and right-click the taskbar. Point to *Toolbars* and select **Address**.

The Address bar now displays on the right side of the taskbar.

b. Point to the top-right corner of the screen to display the Charms. Click the **Search charm**.

The Search pane displays on the right. The Search pane is organized into categories that you may want to search. For whatever category is selected, the relevant content is displayed.

TIP Viewing Dialog Box Components

In Windows 8.1.1, many dialog boxes have been changed to panes. This is in keeping with the sleek, clean look of Windows 8.1.1. Even though the look is different, the functionality remains the same.

c. Type **Sn** in the **Search box**. Below the search box, the results listed display everything that begins with Sn.

d. Click the **Snipping Tool app** in the results list.

   The Snipping Tool app displays on the desktop and the Snipping Tool icon displays on the taskbar.

e. Right-click the **Snipping Tool icon** on the taskbar. Click **Pin this program to taskbar**. See Figure 1.6.

   The Snipping Tool and the Address bar will now be part of your taskbar.

TROUBLESHOOTING: If you are in a lab and cannot keep these changes, you can remove the Snipping Tool icon from the taskbar. Right-click the icon and click *Unpin this program from taskbar*. You can remove the Address bar by right-clicking the taskbar, pointing to Toolbars, and then clicking Address to remove the check mark.

f. Click the **Snipping Tool icon**. Click the **New arrow** in the Snipping Tool on the desktop. Click **Full-screen Snip**.

   A snip of your desktop displays in the Snipping Tool program.

g. Click **File** and click **Save As**. Navigate to the location where you are saving your student files. Name your file **f01h1Desktop_LastFirst** using your own last name and first name. Check to see that *Portable Network Graphic file (PNG)* displays in the *Save as type* box. Click **Save**.

   You have created your first snip. Snips can be used to show what is on your screen. Notice the Snipping Tool app does not display in your snip. When you save files, use your last and first names. For example, as the Office Fundamentals author, I would name my document *f01h1Desktop_LawsonRebecca*.

TROUBLESHOOTING: If PNG does not display in the *Save as type* box, click the arrow on the right side of the box and select *Portable Network Graphic file (PNG)*.

h. Close the Snipping Tool. Submit the file based on your instructor's directions.

i. Shut down your computer if you are ready to stop working. Point to the top-right corner to display the Charms. Click the **Settings charm**, click the **Power icon**, and then click **Shut down**. Otherwise, leave your computer turned on for the next Hands-On Exercise.

Files and Folders

Most activities that you perform using a computer produce some type of output. That output could be games, music, or the display of digital photographs. Perhaps you use a computer at work to produce reports, financial worksheets, or schedules. All of those items are considered computer ***files***. Files include electronic data such as documents, databases, slide shows, and worksheets. Even digital photographs, music, videos, and Web pages are saved as files.

You use software to create and save files. For example, when you type a document on a computer, you first open a word processor such as Microsoft Word. In order to access files later, you must save them to a computer storage medium such as a hard drive or flash drive, or in the cloud at OneDrive. And just as you would probably organize a filing cabinet into a system of folders, you can organize storage media by ***folders*** that you name and into which you place data files. That way, you can easily retrieve the files later. Windows 8.1.1 provides tools that enable you to create folders and to save files in ways that make locating them simple.

In this section, you will learn to use File Explorer to manage folders and files.

Using File Explorer

File Explorer is an app that you can use to create and manage folders and files. The sole purpose of a computer folder is to provide a labeled storage location for related files so that you can easily organize and retrieve items. A folder structure can occur across several levels, so you can create folders within other folders—called ***subfolders***—arranged according to purpose. Windows 8.1.1 uses the concept of libraries, which are folders that gather files from different locations and display the files as if they were all saved in a single folder, regardless of where they are physically stored. Using File Explorer, you can manage folders, work with libraries, and view favorites (areas or folders that are frequently accessed).

Understand and Customize the Interface

You can access File Explorer in any of the following ways:

- Click the File Explorer icon from the taskbar on the desktop.
- Click File Explorer from the Start screen.
- Display the Charms (refer to Figure 1.1) and click the Search charm. Type F in the Search box and in the results list on the left, click File Explorer.

Figure 1.7 shows the File Explorer interface containing several areas. Some of those areas are described in Table 1.1.

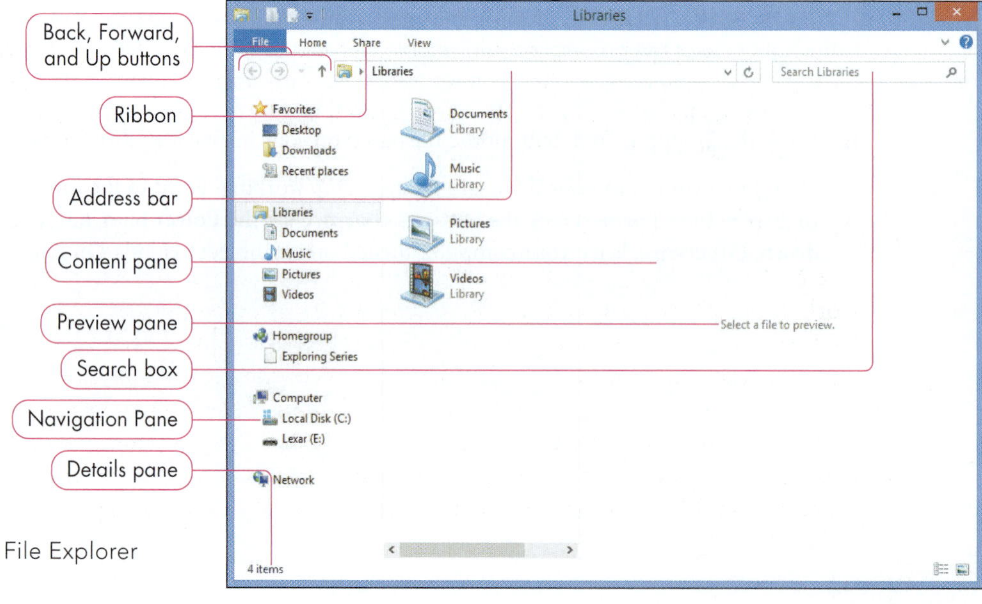

FIGURE 1.7 File Explorer Interface

TABLE 1.1 File Explorer Interface	
Navigation Pane	The Navigation Pane contains five areas: Favorites, Libraries, Homegroup, Computer, and Network. Click an item in the Navigation Pane to display contents and to manage files that are housed within a selected folder.
Back, Forward, and Up Buttons	Use these buttons to visit previously opened folders or libraries. Use the Up button to open the parent folder for the current location.
Ribbon	The Ribbon includes tabs and commands that are relevant to the currently selected item. If you are working with a music file, the Ribbon commands might include one for burning to a CD, whereas if you have selected a document, the Ribbon would enable you to open or share the file.
Address bar	The Address bar enables you to navigate to other folders or libraries.
Content pane	The Content pane shows the contents of the currently selected folder or library.
Search box	Find files and folders by typing descriptive text in the Search box. Windows immediately begins a search after you type the first character, further narrowing results as you type.
Details pane	The Details pane shows properties that are associated with a selected file. Common properties include information such as the author name and the date the file was last modified. This pane does not display by default but can display after clicking the View tab.
Preview pane	The Preview pane provides a snapshot of a selected file's contents. You can see file contents before actually opening the file. The Preview pane does not show the contents of a selected folder. This pane does not display by default but can display after clicking the View tab.

File Explorer has a Ribbon like all the Office applications. As you work with File Explorer, you might want to customize the view. The file and folder icons might be too small for ease of identification, or you might want additional details about displayed files and folders. Modifying the view is easy. To make icons larger or to provide additional detail, click the View tab (refer to Figure 1.7) and select from the views provided in the Layout group. If you want additional detail, such as file type and size, click Details. You can also change the size of icons by selecting Small, Medium, Large, or Extra Large icons. The List view shows the file names without added detail, whereas Tiles and Content views are useful to show file thumbnails (small pictures describing file contents) and varying levels of detail regarding file locations. To show or hide File Explorer panes, click the View tab and select the pane to hide or show in the Panes group. You can widen or narrow panes by dragging a border when the mouse changes to a double-headed arrow.

Work with Groups on the Navigation Pane

The ***Navigation Pane*** provides ready access to computer resources, folders, files, and networked peripherals such as printers. It is divided into five areas: Favorites, Libraries, Homegroup, Computer, and Network. Each of those components provides a unique way to organize contents. In Figure 1.8, the currently selected area is Computer.

Earlier, we used the analogy of computer folders to folders in a filing cabinet. Just as you would title folders in a filing cabinet according to their contents, computer folders are also titled according to content. Folders are physically located on storage media such as a hard drive or flash drive. You can also organize folders into ***libraries***, which are collections of files from different locations that are displayed as a single virtual folder. For example, the Pictures library includes files from the My Pictures folder and from the Public Pictures folder, both of which are physically housed on the hard drive. Although the library content comes from two separate folders, the contents are displayed as a single virtual folder.

Windows 8.1.1 includes several libraries that contain default folders or devices. For example, the Documents library includes the My Documents and Public Documents folders, but you can add subfolders if you wish so that they are also housed within the Documents library. To add a folder to a library, right-click the library, point to New, and then select Folder. You can name the folder at this point by typing the folder name. To remove a folder from the Documents library, open File Explorer, right-click the folder, and then select Delete.

The Computer area provides access to specific storage locations, such as a hard drive, CD/DVD drives, and removable media drives, including a flash drive. Files and folders housed on those storage media are accessible when you click Computer. For example, click drive C, shown under Computer in the Navigation Pane, to view its contents in the Content pane on the right. If you simply want to see the subfolders of the hard drive, click the arrow to the left of drive C to expand the view, showing all subfolders. The arrow is filled in and pointing down. Click the arrow again to collapse the view, removing subfolder detail. The arrow is open and pointing right. It is important to understand that clicking the arrow—as opposed to clicking the folder or area name—does not actually select an area or folder. It merely displays additional levels contained within the area. Clicking the folder or area, however, does select the item. Figure 1.8 illustrates the difference between clicking the folder or area name in the Navigation Pane and clicking the arrow to the left.

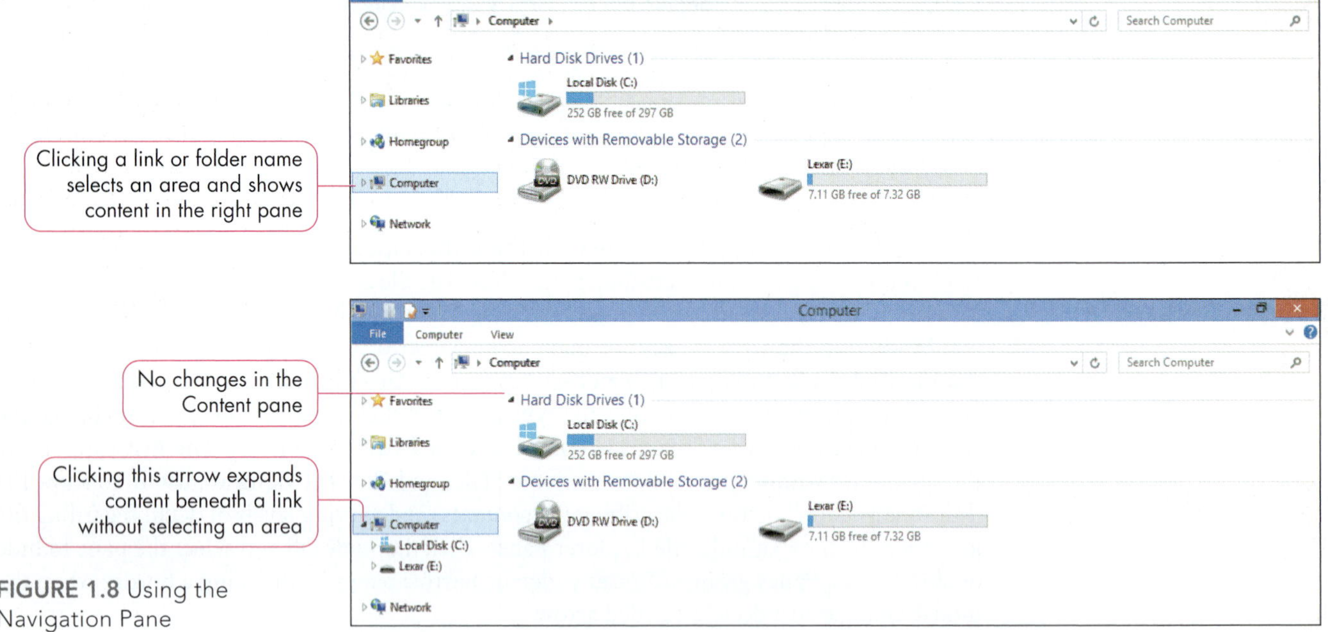

FIGURE 1.8 Using the Navigation Pane

To locate a folder using File Explorer:

1. Click the correct drive in the Navigation Pane (or double-click the drive in the Content pane).
2. Continue navigating through the folder structure until you find the folder that you want.
3. Click the folder in the Navigation Pane (or double-click the folder in the Content pane) to view its contents.

The Favorites area contains frequently accessed folders and recent searches. You can drag a folder, saved search, library, or disk drive to the Favorites area. To remove a favorite, simply right-click the favorite and select Remove. You cannot add files or Web sites as favorites.

Homegroup is a Windows 8.1.1 feature that enables you to share resources on a home network. You can easily share music, pictures, videos, and libraries with other people in your home through a homegroup. It is password protected, so you do not have to worry about privacy.

Windows 8.1.1 makes creating a home network easy, sharing access to the Internet and peripheral devices such as printers and scanners. The Network area provides quick access to those devices, enabling you to see the contents of network computers.

Working with Folders and Files

As you work with software to create a file, such as when you type a report using Microsoft Word, your primary concern will be saving the file so that you can retrieve it later if necessary. If you have created an appropriate and well-named folder structure, you can save the file in a location that is easy to find later.

Create a Folder

You can create a folder a couple of different ways. You can use File Explorer to create a folder structure, providing appropriate names and placing the folders in a well-organized hierarchy. You can also create a folder from within a software application at the time that you need it. Although it would be wonderful to always plan ahead, most often you will find the need for a folder at the same time that you have created a file. The two methods of creating a folder are described next.

STEP 1

Suppose you are beginning a new college semester and are taking four classes. To organize your assignments, you plan to create four folders on a flash drive, one for each class. After connecting the flash drive and closing any subsequent dialog box (unless the dialog box is warning of a problem with the drive), open File Explorer. Click Computer in the Navigation Pane. Click the removable (flash) drive in the Navigation Pane or double-click it in the Content pane. You can also create a folder on the hard drive in the same manner, by clicking drive C instead of the removable drive. Click the Home tab on the Ribbon. Click *New folder* in the New group. Type the new folder name, such as Biology, and press Enter. Repeat the process to create additional folders.

Undoubtedly, you will occasionally find that you have just created a file but have no appropriate folder in which to save the file. You might have just finished the slide show for your speech class but have forgotten first to create a speech folder for your assignments. Now what do you do? As you save the file, a process that is discussed later in this chapter, you can click Browse to bring up the Save As dialog box. Navigate to the drive where you want to store your file. Click *New folder* (see Figure 1.9), type the new folder name, and then double-click to save the name and open the new folder. After indicating the file name, click Save.

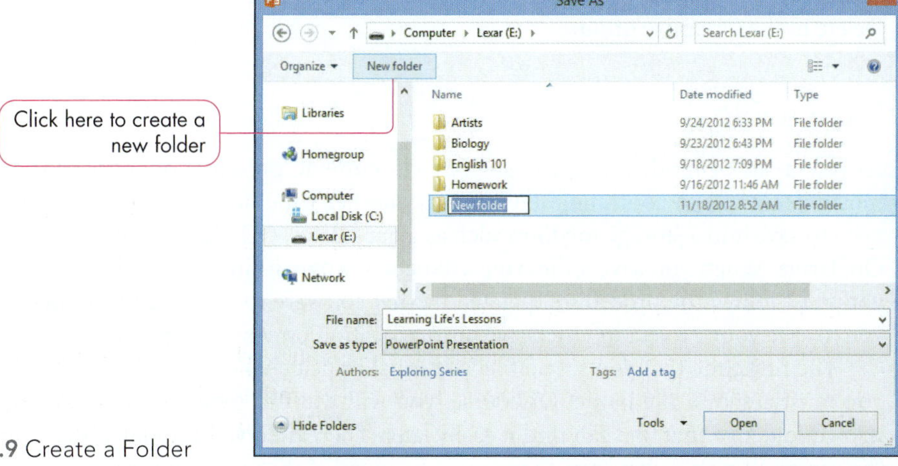

FIGURE 1.9 Create a Folder

OneDrive makes it easy to access your folders and files from any Internet-connected computer or mobile device. You can create new folders and organize existing folders just as you would when you use File Explorer. Other tasks that can be performed at OneDrive include opening, renaming, and deleting folders and files. To create a new folder at OneDrive, you can simply click the OneDrive tile on the Start screen. By default, you will see three items: Documents, Pictures, and Public Shared. You can right-click any of these three items to access icons for creating a new folder or to upload files. Once files and folders are added or created here, you can access them from any computer with Internet access at onedrive.live.com. Similarly, you can create folders or upload files and folders at OneDrive and then access them using the OneDrive tile on your Start screen.

Open, Rename, and Delete Folders and Files

You have learned that folders can be created in File Explorer but files are more commonly created in other ways, such as within a software package. File Explorer can create a new file, and you can use it to open, rename, and delete files just as you use it for folders.

Using the Navigation Pane, you can locate and select a folder containing a file that you want to open. For example, you might want to open the speech slide show so that you can practice before giving a presentation to the class. Open File Explorer and navigate to the speech folder. In your storage location, the file will display in the Content pane. Double-click the file. The program that is associated with the file will open the file. For example, if you have the PowerPoint program associated with that file type on your computer, then PowerPoint will open the file. To open a folder and display the contents, just click the folder in the Navigation Pane or double-click it in the Content pane.

STEP 3» At times, you may want to give a different name to a file or folder than the one that you originally gave it. Or perhaps you made a typographical mistake when you entered the name. In these situations, you should rename the file or folder. In File Explorer, move through the folder structure to find the folder or file. Right-click the name and select Rename. Type the new name and press Enter. You can also rename an item when you click the name twice—but much more slowly than a double-click. Type the new name and press Enter. Finally, you can click a file or folder once to select it, click the Home tab, and then select Rename in the Organize group. Type the new name and press Enter.

It is much easier to delete a folder or file than it is to recover it if you remove it by mistake. Therefore, be very careful when deleting items so that you are sure of your intentions before proceeding. When you delete a folder, all subfolders and all files within the folder are also removed. If you are certain you want to remove a folder or file, the process is simple. Right-click the item, click Delete, and then click Yes if asked to confirm removal to the Recycle Bin. Items are placed in the Recycle Bin only if you are deleting them from a hard drive. Files and folders deleted from a removable storage medium, such as a flash drive, are immediately and permanently deleted, with no easy method of retrieval. You can also delete an item (file or folder) when you click to select the item, click the Home tab, and then click Delete in the Organize group.

Save a File

STEP 2» As you create or modify a project such as a document, presentation, or worksheet, you will most likely want to continue the project at another time or keep it for later reference. You need to save it to a storage medium such as a hard drive, CD, flash drive, or in the cloud with OneDrive. When you save a file, you will be working within a software package. Therefore, you must follow the procedure dictated by that software to save the file. Office 2013 allows you to save your project to OneDrive or to a location on your computer.

The first time that you save a file, you must indicate where the file should be saved, and you must assign a file name. Of course, you will want to save the file in an appropriately named folder so that you can find it easily later. Thereafter, you can quickly save the file with the same settings, or you can change one or more of those settings, perhaps saving the file to a different storage device as a backup copy. Figure 1.10 shows a typical Save As pane for Office 2013 that enables you to select a location before saving the file.

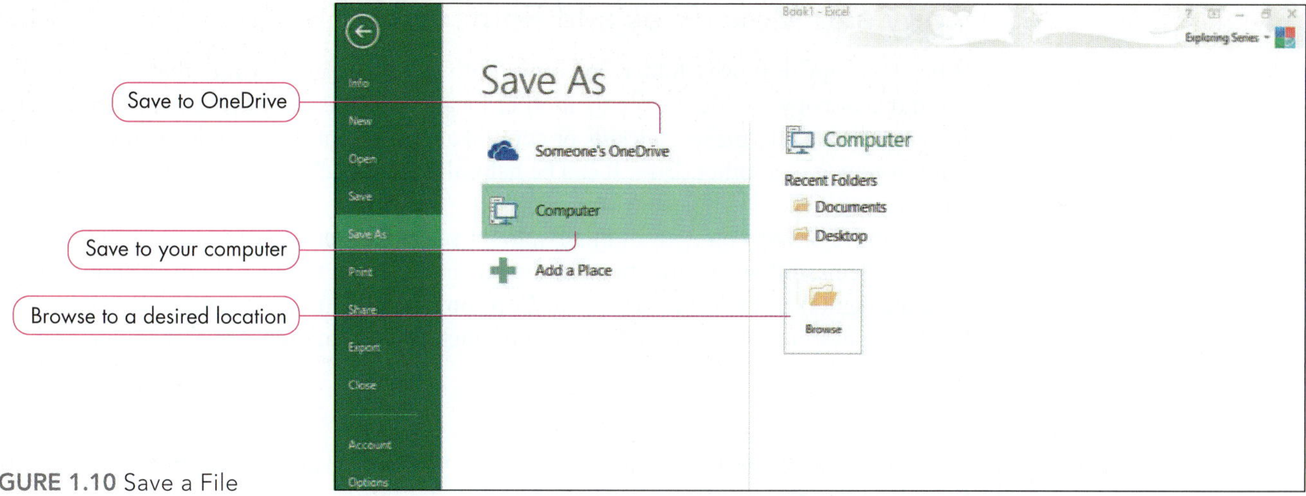

FIGURE 1.10 Save a File

Selecting, Copying, and Moving Multiple Files and Folders

You will want to select folders and files when you need to rename, delete, copy, or paste them, or open files and folders so that you can view the contents. Click a file or folder to *select* it; double-click a file or folder (in the Content pane) to *open* it. To apply an operation to several files at once, such as deleting or moving them, you will want to select all of them.

Select Multiple Files and Folders

You can select several files and folders, regardless of whether they are adjacent to each other in the file list. Suppose that your digital pictures are contained in the Pictures folder. You might want to delete some of the pictures because you want to clear up some hard drive space. To select pictures in the Pictures folder, open File Explorer and click the Pictures library. Locate the desired pictures in the Content pane. To select the adjacent pictures, select the first picture, press and hold Shift, and then click the last picture. All consecutive picture files will be highlighted, indicating that they are selected. At that point, you can delete, copy, or move the selected pictures at the same time.

If the files or folders to be selected are not adjacent, click the first item. Press and hold Ctrl while you click all desired files or folders, releasing Ctrl only when you have finished selecting the files or folders.

To select all items in a folder or disk drive, use File Explorer to navigate to the desired folder. Open the folder, press and hold Ctrl, and then press A on the keyboard. You can also click the Home tab, and in the Select group, click *Select all* to select all items.

TIP Using a Check Box to Select Items

In Windows 8.1.1, it is easy to make multiple selections, even if the items are not adjacent. Open File Explorer and select your drive or folder. Click the View tab and select Item check boxes in the Show/Hide group. As you move the mouse pointer along the left side of files and folders, a check box displays. Click in the check box to select the file. If you want to quickly select all items in the folder, click the check box that displays in the Name column heading.

Copy and Move Files and Folders

When you copy or move a folder, you move both the folder and any files that it contains. You can move or copy a folder or file to another location on the same drive or to another drive. If your purpose is to make a ***backup***, or copy, of an important file or folder, you will probably want to copy it to another drive. It can be helpful to have backup copies saved in the cloud at OneDrive as well.

STEP 4 »

To move or copy an item in File Explorer, select the item. If you want to copy or move multiple items, follow the directions in the previous section to select them all at once. Right-click the item(s) and select either Cut or Copy on the shortcut menu. In the Navigation Pane, locate the destination drive or folder, right-click the destination drive or folder, and then click Paste.

1. The File Explorer interface has several panes. Name them and identify their characteristics. ***p. 11***
2. After creating a file, such as a PowerPoint presentation, you want to save it. However, as you begin to save the file, you realize that you have not yet created a folder in which to place the file. Is it possible to create a folder as you are saving the file? If so, how? ***p. 13***
3. What should you consider when deleting files or folders from a removable storage medium such as a flash drive? ***p. 14***
4. Office 2013 enables you to save files to OneDrive or your computer. Why might it be helpful to save a file in both locations? ***p. 14***
5. You want to delete several files, but the files are not consecutively listed in File Explorer. How would you select and delete them? ***p. 15***

Hands-On Exercises

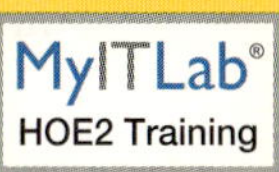

2 Files and Folders

You will soon begin to collect files from volunteers who are preparing promotional and record-keeping material for the Spotted Begonia Art Gallery. It is important that you save the files in appropriately named folders so that you can easily access them later. You can create folders on a hard drive, flash drive, or at OneDrive. You will select the drive on which you plan to save the various files. As you create a short document, you will save it in one of the folders. You will then make a backup copy of the folder structure, including all files, so that you do not run the risk of losing the material if the drive is damaged or misplaced.

Skills covered: Create Folders and Subfolders • Create and Save a File • Rename and Delete a Folder • Open and Copy a File

STEP 1 » CREATE FOLDERS AND SUBFOLDERS

You decide to create a folder titled *Artists* and then subdivide it into subfolders that will help categorize the artists' artwork promotional files as well as for general record keeping for the art gallery. Refer to Figure 1.11 as you complete Step 1.

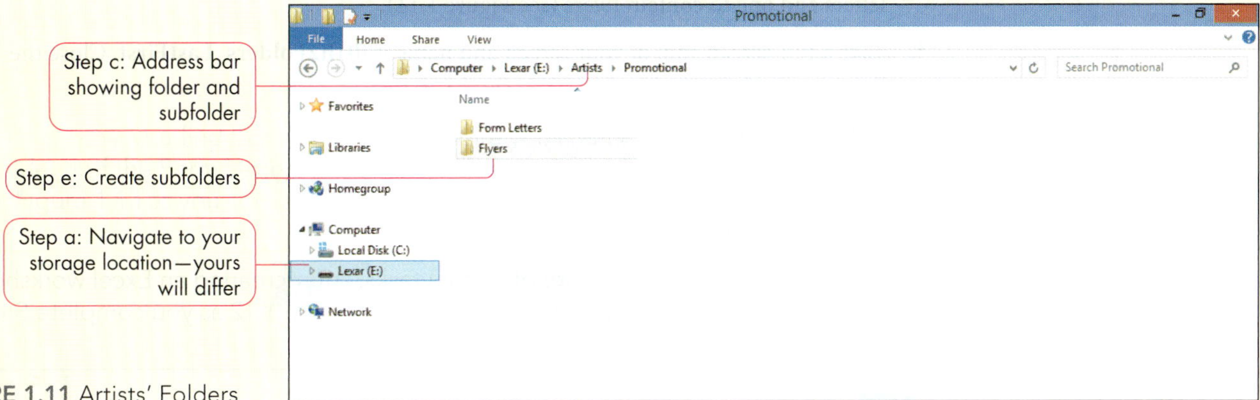

FIGURE 1.11 Artists' Folders

a. Navigate to the location where you are storing your files. If storing on your computer or a flash drive, navigate to the desktop. Click **File Explorer** on the taskbar and maximize the window. Click the **VIEW tab** and click to display the **Preview pane**, if necessary.

A removable drive is shown in Figure 1.11 and is titled *Lexar (E:)*, describing the drive manufacturer and the drive letter. Your storage area will be designated in a different manner, perhaps also identified by manufacturer (or perhaps you are saving your files on OneDrive). The storage area identification is likely to be different because the configuration of disk drives on your computer is unique.

> **TROUBLESHOOTING:** If you do not have a flash drive, you can use the hard drive. In the next step, simply click drive C in the Navigation Pane instead of the removable drive. You can also create and save folders and files at OneDrive.

b. Click the removable drive in the Navigation Pane (or click **drive C** if you are using the hard drive). Click the **HOME tab**, click **New folder** in the New group, type **Artists**, and then press **Enter**.

You create a folder where you can organize subfolders and files for the artists and their promotional materials and general record-keeping files.

d. Double-click the **Promotional Print folder**. Click **Flyers**. Press and hold **Shift** and click **Form Letters**. Both folders should be selected (highlighted). Right-click either folder and click **Delete**. If asked to confirm the deletion, click **Yes**. Click **Artists** in the Address bar.

Your screen should appear as shown in Figure 1.13. You decide that dividing the promotional material into flyers and form letters is not necessary, so you deleted both folders.

e. Take a full-screen snip of your screen and name it **f01h2Artists_LastFirst**. Close the Snipping Tool.

f. Leave File Explorer open for the next step.

STEP 4 » OPEN AND COPY A FILE

You hope to recruit more volunteers to work with the Spotted Begonia Art Gallery. The Volunteers worksheet will be a handy way to keep up with people and assignments, and as the list grows, knowing exactly where the file is saved will be important for easy access. You will modify the Volunteers worksheet and make a backup copy of the folder hierarchy. Refer to Figure 1.14 as you complete Step 4.

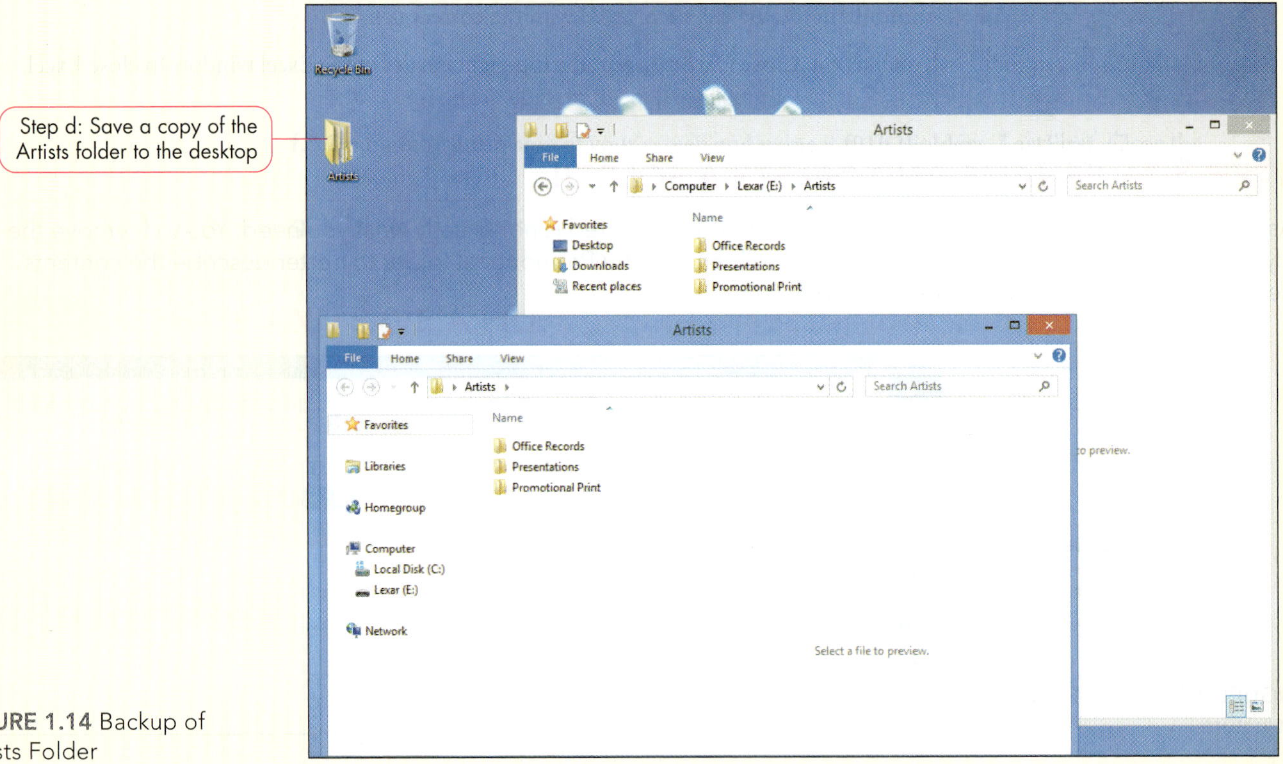

FIGURE 1.14 Backup of Artists Folder

a. Double-click the **Office Records folder**. Double-click *f01h2Volunteers_LastFirst*. Save the file with the new name **f01h2Stp4Volunteers_LastFirst** in the same location.

Because the file was created with Excel, that program opens, and the Volunteers worksheet is displayed.

b. Click **cell A11**, if necessary, and type **Office**. Press **Tab**, type **Adams**, and then press **Enter**. Click the **FILE tab** and click **Save**. The file is automatically saved in the same location with the same file name as before. Close Excel.

A neighbor, Sarah Adams, has volunteered to help in the office. You record that information on the worksheet and save the updated file in the Office Records folder.

c. Click the location where you save files in the Navigation pane in File Explorer so that the Artists folder displays in the Content pane. Right-click the **Artists folder** and click **Copy**.

d. Right-click **Desktop** in the Favorites group on the Navigation Pane and click **Paste**. Close File Explorer. If any other windows are open, close them also.

You made a copy of the Artists folder on the desktop.

e. Double-click the **Artists folder** on the desktop. Double-click the **Office Records folder**. Verify that the *f01h2Stp4Volunteers_LastFirst* worksheet displays in the folder. Take a full-screen snip of your screen and name it **f01h2Backup_LastFirst**. Close the Snipping Tool and close File Explorer.

f. Right-click the **Artists folder** on the desktop, select **Delete**, and then click **Yes** if asked to confirm the deletion.

You deleted the Artists folder from the desktop of the computer because you may be working in a computer lab and want to leave the computer as you found it. You may also want to empty the Recycle Bin.

g. Submit your files based on your instructor's directions.

Microsoft Office Software

Organizations around the world rely heavily on ***Microsoft Office*** software to produce documents, spreadsheets, presentations, and databases. Microsoft Office is a productivity software suite including a set of software applications, each one specializing in a particular type of output. You can use ***Word*** to produce all sorts of documents, including memos, newsletters, forms, tables, and brochures. ***Excel*** makes it easy to organize records, financial transactions, and business information in the form of worksheets. With ***PowerPoint***, you can create dynamic presentations to inform groups and persuade audiences. ***Access*** is relational database software that enables you to record and link data, query databases, and create forms and reports.

You will sometimes find that you need to use two or more Office applications to produce your intended output. You might, for example, find that a Word document you are preparing for your investment club should also include a summary of stock performance. You can use Excel to prepare the summary and then incorporate the worksheet in the Word document. Similarly, you can integrate Word tables and Excel charts into a PowerPoint presentation. The choice of which software applications to use really depends on what type of output you are producing. Table 1.2 describes the major tasks of these four primary applications in Microsoft Office.

TABLE 1.2 Microsoft Office Software

Office 2013 Product	Application Characteristics
Word 2013	Word processing software used with text to create, edit, and format documents such as letters, memos, reports, brochures, resumes, and flyers.
Excel 2013	Spreadsheet software used to store quantitative data and to perform accurate and rapid calculations with results ranging from simple budgets to financial analyses and statistical analyses.
PowerPoint 2013	Presentation graphics software used to create slide shows for presentation by a speaker, to be published as part of a Web site, or to run as a stand-alone application on a computer kiosk.
Access 2013	Relational database software used to store data and convert it into information. Database software is used primarily for decision making by businesses that compile data from multiple records stored in tables to produce informative reports.

As you become familiar with Microsoft Office, you will find that although each software application produces a specific type of output, all applications share common features. Such commonality gives a similar feel to each software application so that learning and working with Microsoft Office software products is easy. In this section, you will identify features common to Microsoft Office software, including such interface components as the Ribbon, the Backstage view, and the Quick Access Toolbar. You will also learn how to get help with an application.

Identifying Common Interface Components

As you work with Microsoft Office, you will find that each application shares a similar ***user interface***. The user interface is the screen display through which you communicate with the software. Word, Excel, PowerPoint, and Access share common interface elements, as shown in Figure 1.15. One of the feature options includes the availability of templates as well as new and improved themes when each application is opened. A ***template*** is a predesigned file that incorporates formatting elements, such as a theme and layouts, and may include content that can be modified. A ***theme*** is a collection of design choices that includes colors, fonts, and special effects used to give a consistent look to a document, workbook, or presentation. As you can imagine, becoming familiar with one application's interface makes it that much easier to work with other Office software.

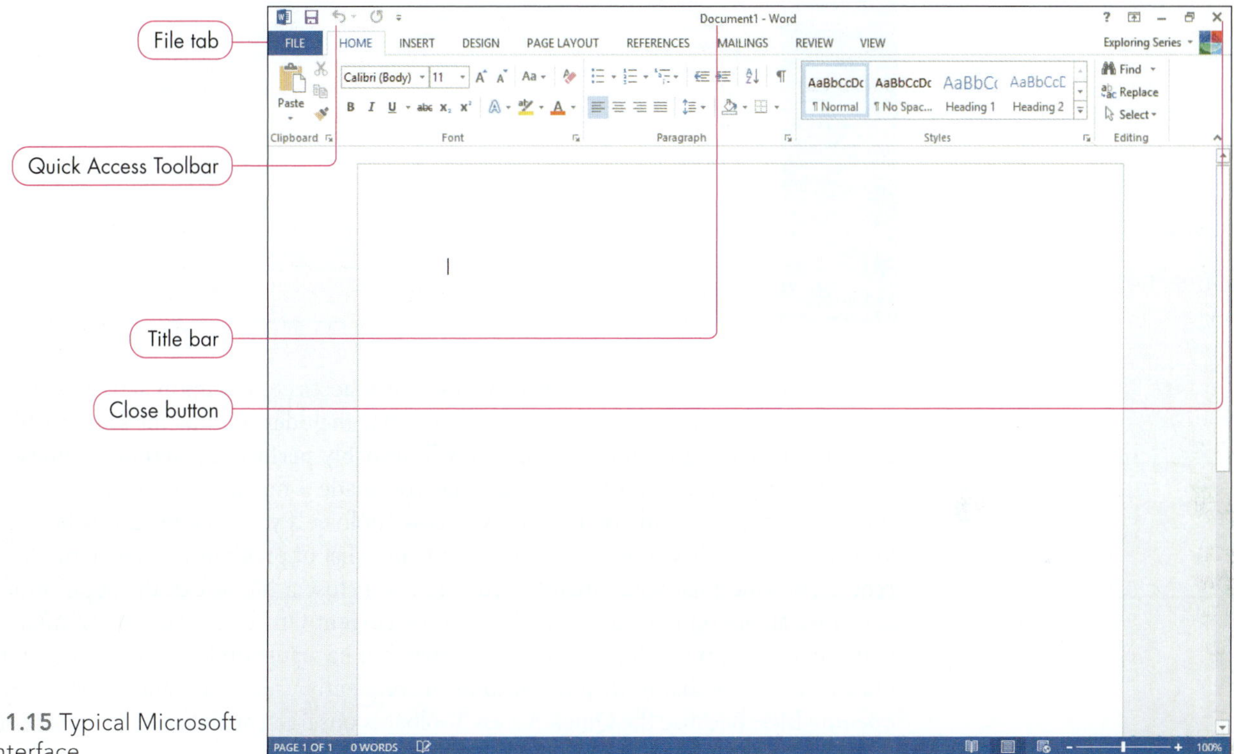

FIGURE 1.15 Typical Microsoft Office Interface

Use the Backstage View and the Quick Access Toolbar

The ***Backstage view*** is a component of Office 2013 that provides a concise collection of commands related to an open file. Using the Backstage view, you can find out information such as protection, permissions, versions, and properties. A file's properties include the author, file size, permissions, and date modified. You can create a new document or open, save, print, share, export, or close. The ***Quick Access Toolbar***, located at the top-left corner of any Office application window, provides fast access to commonly executed tasks such as saving a file and undoing recent actions. The ***title bar*** identifies the current file name and the application in which you are working. It also includes control buttons that enable you to minimize, maximize, restore down, or close the application window (see Figure 1.15).

You access the Backstage view by clicking the File tab. When you click the File tab, you will see the Backstage view (see Figure 1.16). Primarily focusing on file activities such as opening, closing, saving, printing, and beginning new files, the Backstage view also includes options for customizing program settings, signing in to your Office account, and exiting the program. It displays a file's properties, providing important information on file permission and sharing options. When you click the File tab, the Backstage view will occupy the entire application window, hiding the file with which you might be working. For example, suppose that as you are typing a report you need to check the document's properties. Click the File tab to display a Backstage view similar to that shown in Figure 1.16. You can return to the application—in this case, Word—in a couple of ways. Either click the Back arrow in the top-left corner or press Esc on the keyboard.

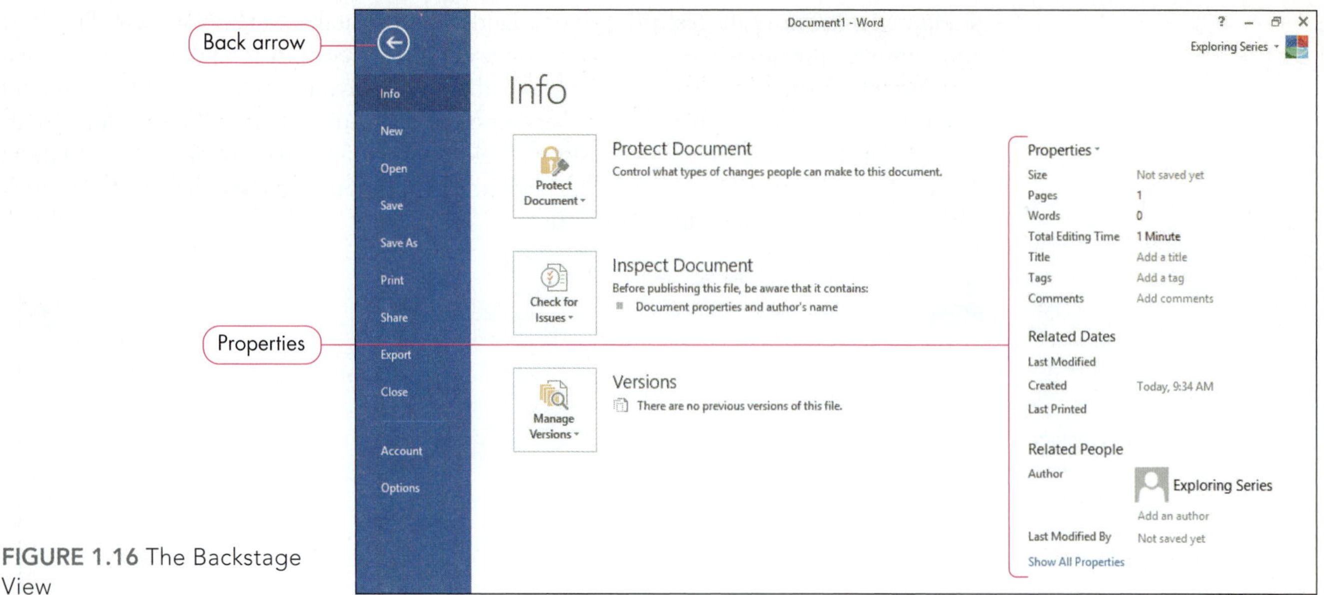

FIGURE 1.16 The Backstage View

STEP 4

The Quick Access Toolbar provides one-click access to common activities, as shown in Figure 1.17. By default, the Quick Access Toolbar includes buttons for saving a file and for undoing or redoing recent actions. You will probably perform an action countless times in an Office application and then realize that you made a mistake. You can recover from the mistake by clicking Undo on the Quick Access Toolbar. If you click the arrow beside Undo—known as the Undo arrow—you can select from a list of previous actions in order of occurrence. The Undo list is not maintained when you close a file or exit the application, so you can erase an action that took place during the current Office session only. Similar to Undo, you can also Redo (or Replace) an action that you have just undone. You can customize the Quick Access Toolbar to include buttons for frequently used commands such as printing or opening files. Because the Quick Access Toolbar is onscreen at all times, the most commonly accessed tasks are just a click away.

To customize the Quick Access Toolbar, click Customize Quick Access Toolbar (see Figure 1.17) and select from a list of commands. You can also click More Commands near the bottom of the menu options. If a command that you want to include on the toolbar is not on the list, you can right-click the command on the Ribbon and click *Add to Quick Access Toolbar*. Similarly, remove a command from the Quick Access Toolbar by right-clicking the icon on the Quick Access Toolbar and clicking *Remove from Quick Access Toolbar*. If you want to display the Quick Access Toolbar beneath the Ribbon, click Customize Quick Access Toolbar (see Figure 1.17) and click *Show Below the Ribbon*.

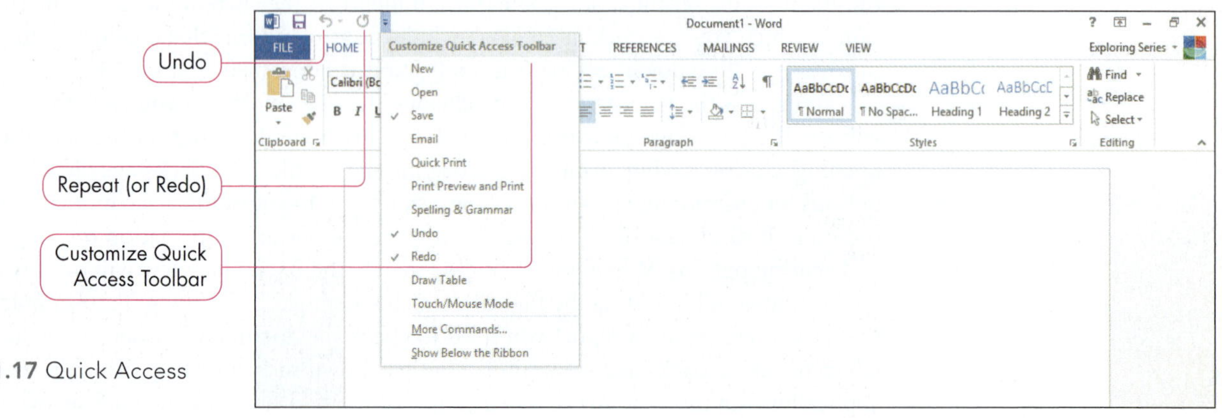

FIGURE 1.17 Quick Access Toolbar

Familiarize Yourself with the Ribbon

The ***Ribbon*** is the command center of Office applications. It is the long bar located just beneath the title bar, containing tabs, groups, and commands. Each ***tab*** is designed to appear much like a tab on a file folder, with the active tab highlighted. The File tab is always a darker shade than the other tabs and a different color depending on the application. Remember that clicking the File tab opens the Backstage view. Other tabs on the Ribbon enable you to modify a file. The active tab in Figure 1.18 is the Home tab.

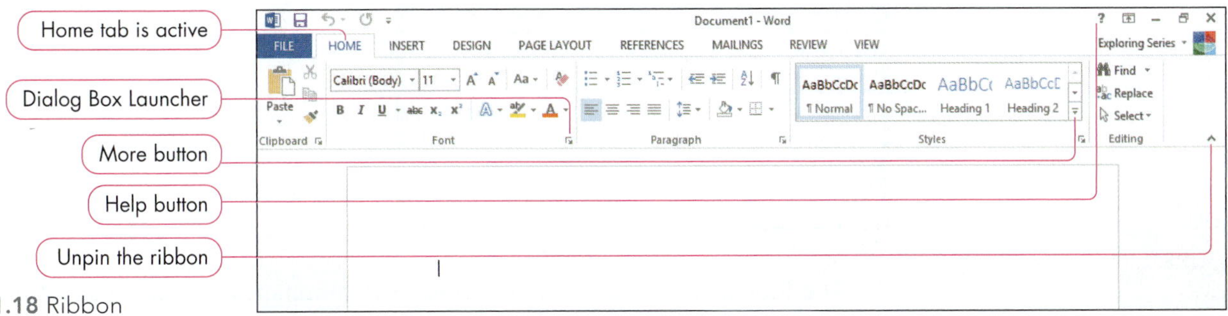

FIGURE 1.18 Ribbon

When you click a tab, the Ribbon displays several task-oriented ***groups***, with each group containing related ***commands***. A group is a subset of a tab that organizes similar tasks together. A command is a button or area within a group that you click to perform tasks. Microsoft Office is designed to provide the most functionality possible with the fewest clicks. For that reason, the Home tab, displayed when you first open an Office software application, contains groups and commands that are most commonly used. For example, because you will often want to change the way text is displayed, the Home tab in each Office application includes a Font group with activities related to modifying text. Similarly, other tabs contain groups of related actions, or commands, many of which are unique to the particular Office application.

Because Word, PowerPoint, Excel, and Access all share a similar Ribbon structure, you will be able to move at ease among those applications. Although the specific tabs, groups, and commands vary among the Office programs, the way in which you use the Ribbon and the descriptive nature of tab titles is the same regardless of which program you are working with. For example, if you want to insert a chart in Excel, a header in Word, or a shape in PowerPoint, you will click the Insert tab in any of those programs. The first thing that you should do as you begin to work with an Office application is to study the Ribbon. Take a look at all tabs and their contents. That way, you will have a good idea of where to find specific commands and how the Ribbon with which you are currently working differs from one that you might have used previously in another application.

If you are working with a large project, you might want to maximize your workspace by temporarily hiding the Ribbon. You can hide the Ribbon in several ways. Double-click the active tab to hide the Ribbon and double-click any tab to redisplay it. You can click *Unpin the ribbon* (see Figure 1.18), located at the right side of the Ribbon, and click any tab to redisplay the Ribbon.

The Ribbon provides quick access to common activities such as changing number or text formats or aligning data or text. Some actions, however, do not display on the Ribbon because they are not so common but are related to commands displayed on the Ribbon. For example, you might want to change the background of a PowerPoint slide to include a picture. In that case, you will need to work with a ***dialog box*** that provides access to more precise, but less frequently used, commands. Figure 1.19 shows the Font dialog box in Word, for example. Some commands display a dialog box when they are clicked. Other Ribbon groups include a ***Dialog Box Launcher*** that, when clicked, opens a corresponding dialog box (refer to Figure 1.18).

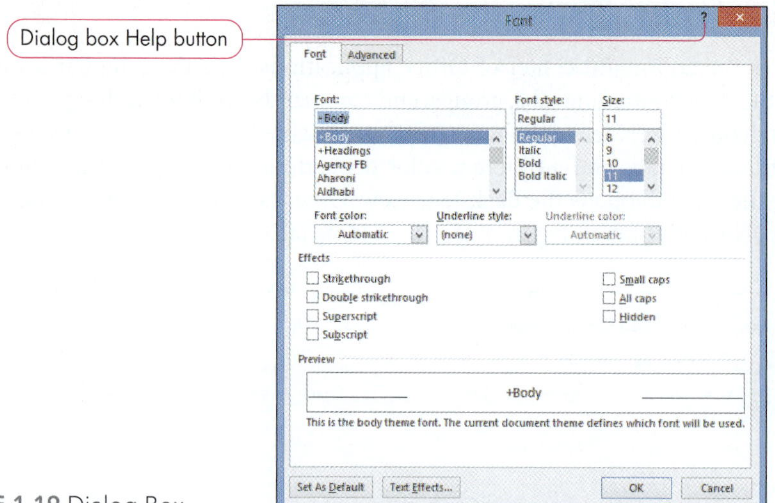

FIGURE 1.19 Dialog Box

The Ribbon contains many selections and commands, but some selections are too numerous to include in the Ribbon's limited space. For example, Word provides far more text styles than it can easily display at once, so additional styles are available in a ***gallery***. A gallery also provides a choice of Excel chart styles and PowerPoint transitions. Figure 1.20 shows an example of a PowerPoint Themes gallery. Most often, you can display a gallery of additional choices by clicking the More button (refer to Figure 1.18) that is found in some Ribbon selections.

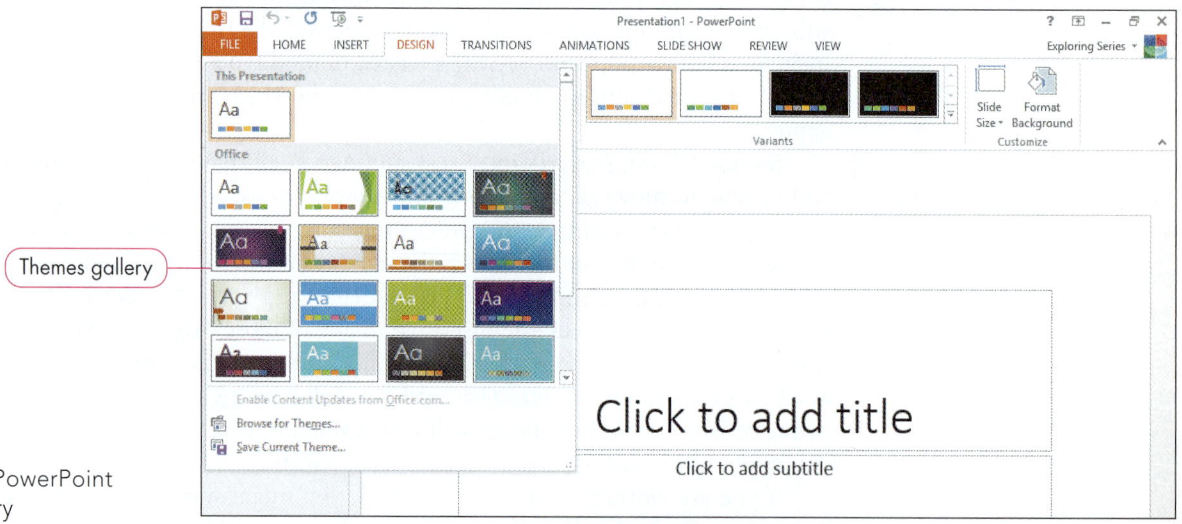

FIGURE 1.20 PowerPoint Themes Gallery

STEP 3

When editing a document, worksheet, or presentation, it is helpful to see the results of formatting changes before you make final selections. The feature that displays a preview of the results of a selection is called ***Live Preview***. You might, for example, be considering changing the font color of a selection in a document or worksheet. As you place the mouse pointer over a color selection in a Ribbon gallery or group, the selected text will temporarily display the color to which you are pointing. Similarly, you can get a preview of how color designs would display on PowerPoint slides by pointing to specific themes in the PowerPoint Themes group and noting the effect on a displayed slide. When you click the item, such as the font color, the selection is applied. Live Preview is available in various Ribbon selections among the Office applications.

Office applications also make it easy for you to work with objects such as pictures, ***clip art***, shapes, charts, and tables. Clip art is an electronic illustration that can be inserted into an Office project. When you include such objects in a project, they are considered separate components that you can manage independently. To work with an object, you must click to select it. When you select an object, the Ribbon is modified to include one or more ***contextual tabs*** that contain groups of commands related to the selected object. Figure 1.21 shows a contextual tab related to a selected SmartArt object in a Word document. When you click outside the selected object, the contextual tab disappears.

Contextual tab

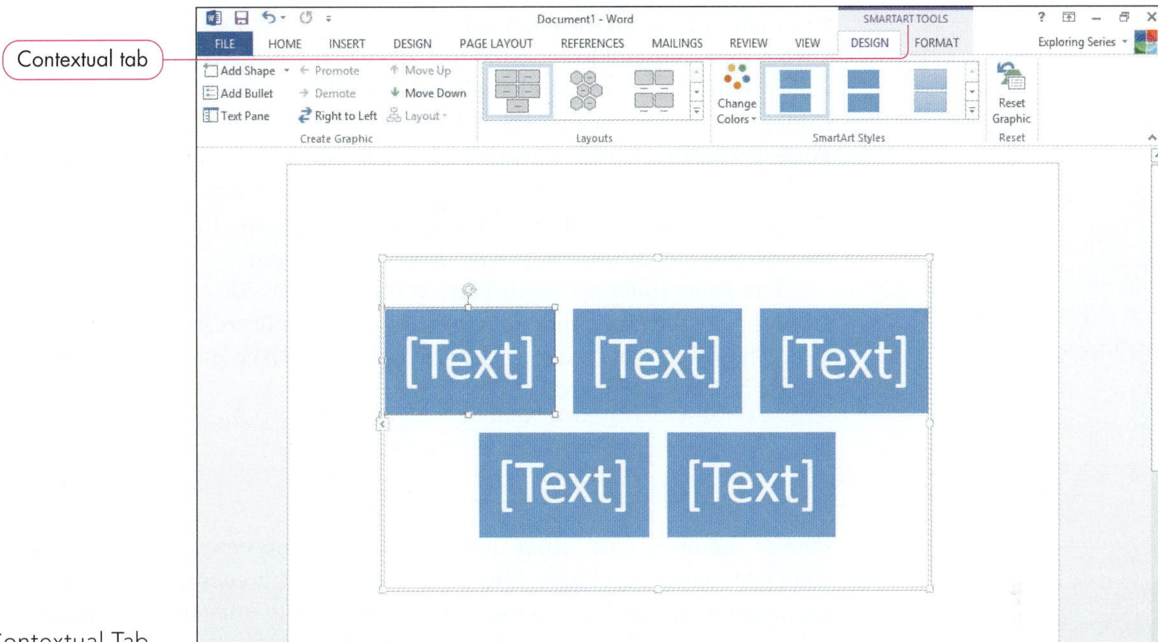

FIGURE 1.21 Contextual Tab

> **TIP Using Keyboard Shortcuts**
>
> You might find that you prefer to use keyboard shortcuts, which are keyboard equivalents for software commands, when they are available. Universal keyboard shortcuts include Ctrl+C (copy), Ctrl+X (cut), Ctrl+V (paste), and Ctrl+Z (undo). To move to the beginning of a Word document, to cell A1 in Excel, or to the first PowerPoint slide, press Ctrl+Home. To move to the end of those items, press Ctrl+End. Press Alt to display keyboard shortcuts, called a ***Key Tip***, for items on the Ribbon and Quick Access Toolbar. You can press the letter or number corresponding to Ribbon items to invoke the action from the keyboard. Press Alt again to remove the Key Tips.

Use the Status Bar

The ***status bar*** is located at the bottom of the program window and contains information relative to the open file. It also includes tools for changing the view of the file and for changing the zoom size of onscreen file contents. Contents of the status bar are unique to each specific application. When you work with Word, the status bar informs you of the number of pages and words in an open document. The Excel status bar displays summary information, such as average and sum, of selected cells. The PowerPoint status bar shows the slide number, total slides in the presentation, and the applied theme. It also provides access to notes and comments.

STEP 3»

Regardless of the application in which you are working, the status bar includes view buttons and a Zoom slider. You can also use the View tab on the Ribbon to change the current view or zoom level of an open file. The status bar's view buttons (see Figure 1.22) enable you to change the ***view*** of the open file. When creating a document, you might find it helpful to change the view. You might, for example, view a PowerPoint slide presentation with multiple slides displayed (Slide Sorter view) or with only one slide in large size (Normal view). In Word, you could view a document in Print Layout view (showing margins, headers, and footers), Web Layout view, or Read Mode.

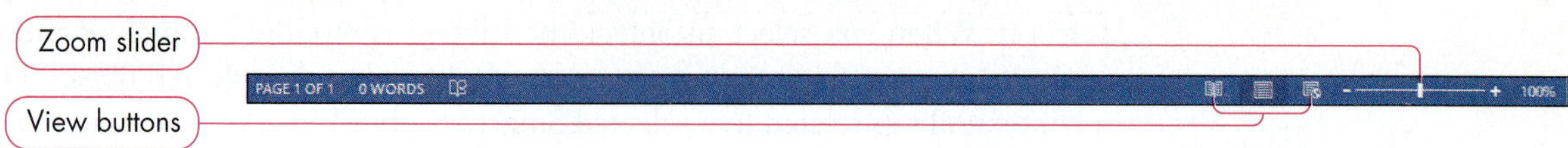

FIGURE 1.22 Word Status Bar

Additional views are available in the View tab. Word's Print Layout view is useful when you want to see both the document text and such features as margins and page breaks. Web Layout view is useful to see what the page would look like on the Internet. The Read Mode view provides a clean look that displays just the content without the Ribbon or margins. It is ideal for use on a tablet where the screen may be smaller than on a laptop or computer. PowerPoint, Excel, and Access also provide view options, although they are unique to the application. The most common view options are accessible from *View shortcuts* on the status bar of each application. As you learn more about Office applications, you will become aware of the views that are specific to each application.

STEP 1》

The ***Zoom slider*** always displays at the far right side of the status bar. You can drag the tab along the slider in either direction to increase or decrease the magnification of the file. Be aware, however, that changing the size of text onscreen does not change the font size when the file is printed or saved.

Getting Office Help

One of the most frustrating things about learning new software is determining how to complete a task. Thankfully, Microsoft includes comprehensive help in Office so that you are less likely to feel such frustration. As you work with any Office application, you can access help online as well as within the current software installation. Help is available through a short description that displays when you rest the mouse pointer on a command. Additionally, you can get help related to a currently open dialog box by clicking the question mark in the top-right corner of the dialog box, or when you click Help in the top-right corner of the application.

Use Office Help

STEP 2》

To access the comprehensive library of Office Help, click the Help button, displayed as a question mark on the far right side of the Ribbon (refer to Figure 1.18). The Help window provides assistance with the current application as well as a direct link to online resources and technical support. Figure 1.23 shows the Help window that displays when you click the Help button while in Excel. For general information on broad topics, click a link in the window. However, if you are having difficulty with a specific task, it might be easier to simply type the request in the Search online help box. Suppose you are seeking help with using the Goal Seek feature in Excel. Simply type *Goal Seek* or a phrase such as *find specific result by changing variables* in the Search box and press Enter (or click the magnifying glass on the right). Then select from displayed results for more information on the topic.

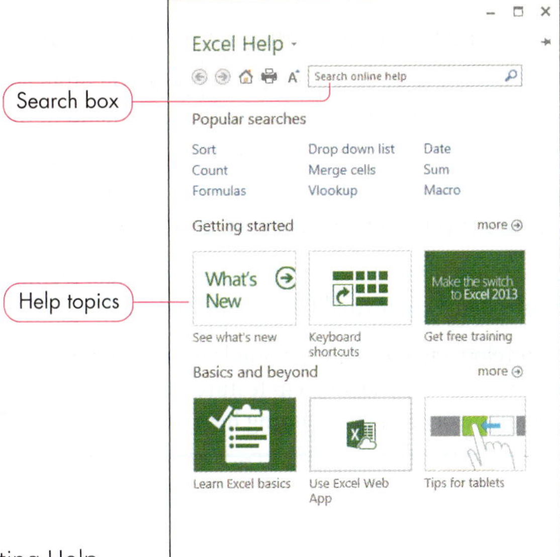

FIGURE 1.23 Getting Help

Use Enhanced ScreenTips

For quick summary information on the purpose of a command button, place the mouse pointer over the button. An ***Enhanced ScreenTip*** displays, giving the purpose of the command, short descriptive text, and a keyboard shortcut if applicable. Some ScreenTips include a suggestion for pressing F1 for additional help. The Enhanced ScreenTip in Figure 1.24 provides context-sensitive assistance.

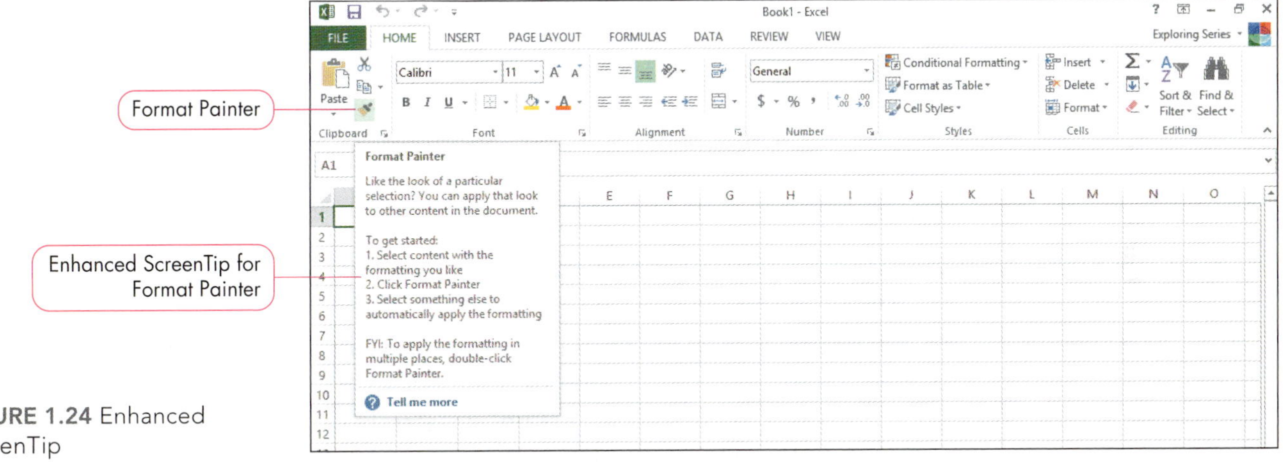

FIGURE 1.24 Enhanced ScreenTip

Get Help with Dialog Boxes

Getting help while you are working with a dialog box is easy. Simply click the Help button that displays as a question mark in the top-right corner of the dialog box (refer to Figure 1.19). The subsequent Help window will offer suggestions relevant to your task.

The Backstage View Tasks

When you work with Microsoft Office files, you will often want to open previously saved files, create new ones, print items, and save and close files. You will also find it necessary to indicate options, or preferences, for settings. For example, you might want a spelling check to occur automatically, or you might prefer to initiate a spelling check only occasionally. Because those tasks are applicable to each software application within the Office 2013 suite, they are accomplished through a common area in the Office interface—the Backstage view. Open the Backstage view by clicking the File tab. Figure 1.29 shows the area that displays when you click the File tab in PowerPoint. The Backstage view also enables you to exit the application and to identify file information, such as the author or date created.

In this section, you will explore the Backstage view, learning to create, open, close, and print files.

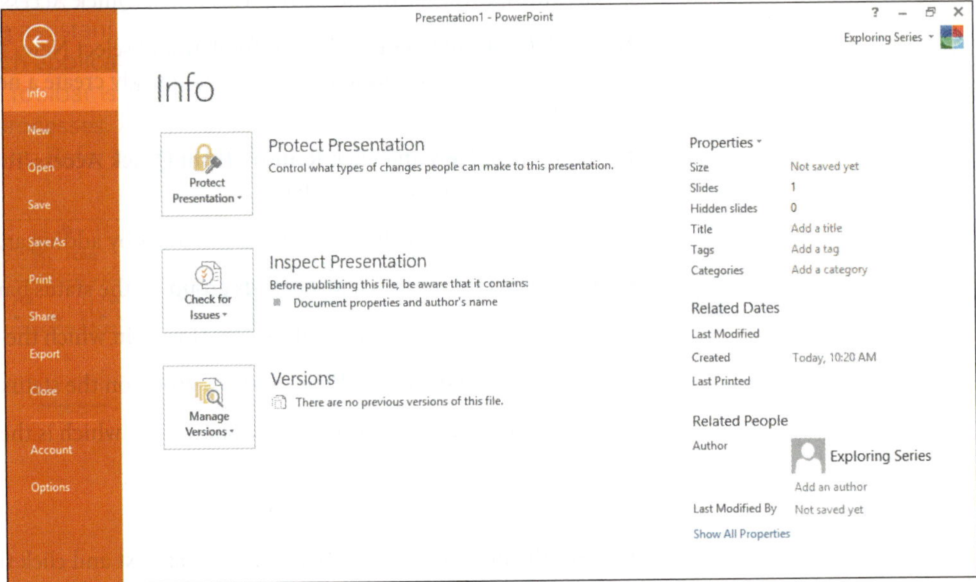

FIGURE 1.29 The Backstage View

Opening a File

When working with an Office application, you can begin by opening an existing file that has already been saved to a storage medium, or you can begin work on a new file. Both actions are available when you click the File tab. When you first open an application within the Office 2013 suite, you will need to decide which template you want to work with before you can begin working on a new file. You can also open a project that you previously saved to a disk.

Create a New File

After opening an Office application, such as Word, Excel, or PowerPoint, you will be presented with template choices. Click *Blank document* to start a new blank document. The word *document* is sometimes used generically to refer to any Office file, including a Word document, an Excel worksheet, or a PowerPoint presentation. Perhaps you are already working with a document in an Office application but want to create a new file. Simply click the File tab and click New. Click *Blank document* (or *Blank presentation* or *Blank workbook*, depending on the specific application).

Open a File Using the Open Dialog Box

STEP 1»

You may choose to open a previously saved file, such as when you work with the data files for this book or when you want to access any previously created file. You will work with the Open dialog box, as shown in Figure 1.30. The Open dialog box displays after you click Open from the File tab. You will click Computer and the folder or drive where your document is stored.

If it is not listed under Recent Folders, you can browse for it. Using the Navigation Pane, you will make your way to the file to be opened. Double-click the file or click the file name once and click Open. Most likely, the file will be located within a folder that is appropriately named to make it easy to find related files. Obviously, if you are not well acquainted with the file's location and file name, the process of opening a file could become quite cumbersome. However, if you have created a well-designed system of folders, as you learned to do in the "Files and Folders" section of this chapter, you will know exactly where to find the file.

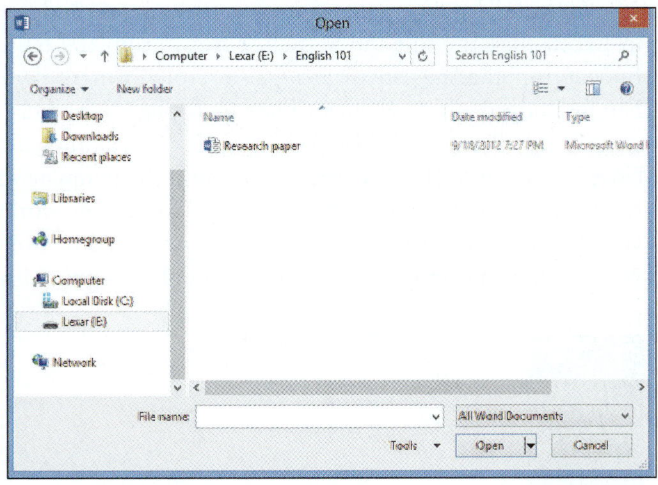

FIGURE 1.30 Open Dialog Box

Open a File Using the Recent Documents List

STEP 3»

You will often work with a file, save it, and then continue the project at a later time. Office simplifies the task of reopening the file by providing a Recent Documents list with links to your most recently opened files (see Figure 1.31). To access the list, click the File tab, click Open, and then select Recent Documents. Click any file listed in the Recent Documents list to open that document. The list constantly changes to reflect only the most recently opened files, so if it has been quite some time since you worked with a particular file, you might have to work with the Open dialog box instead of the Recent Documents list.

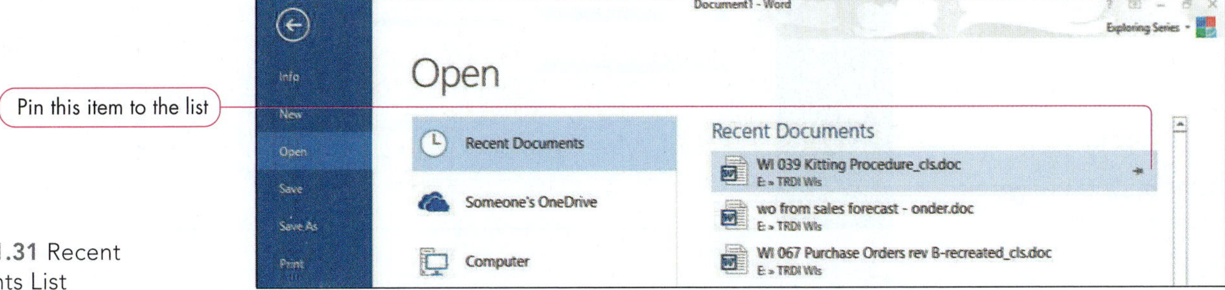

FIGURE 1.31 Recent Documents List

TIP Keeping Files on the Recent Documents List

The Recent Documents list displays a limited list of only the most recently opened files. You might, however, want to keep a particular file in the list regardless of how recently it was opened. In Figure 1.31, note the *Pin this item to the list* icon displays to the right of each file. Click the icon to pin the file to the list. At that point, you will always have access to the file by clicking the File tab and selecting the file from the Recent Documents list. The pushpin of the "permanent" file will change direction so that it appears to be inserted, indicating that it is a pinned item. If later you want to remove the file from the list, click the inserted pushpin, changing its direction and allowing the file to be bumped off the list when other, more recently opened, files take its place.

Open a File from the Templates List

You do not need to create a new file if you can access a predesigned file that meets your needs or one that you can modify fairly quickly to complete your project. Office provides templates, making them available when you click the File tab and New (see Figure 1.32). The Templates list is comprised of template groups available within the current Office installation on your computer. The Search box can be used to locate other templates that are available from Office.com. When you click one of the Suggested searches, you are presented with additional choices.

For example, you might want to prepare a home budget. After opening a blank worksheet in Excel, click the File tab and click New. From the template categories, you could click Budget from the *Suggested searches* list, scroll down until you find the right template, such as Family Budget, and then click Create to display the associated worksheet (or simply double-click Family Budget). If a Help window displays along with the worksheet template, click to close it or explore Help to learn more about the template. If you know only a little bit about Excel, you could then make a few changes so that the worksheet would accurately represent your family's financial situation. The budget would be prepared much more quickly than if you began the project with a blank workbook, designing it yourself.

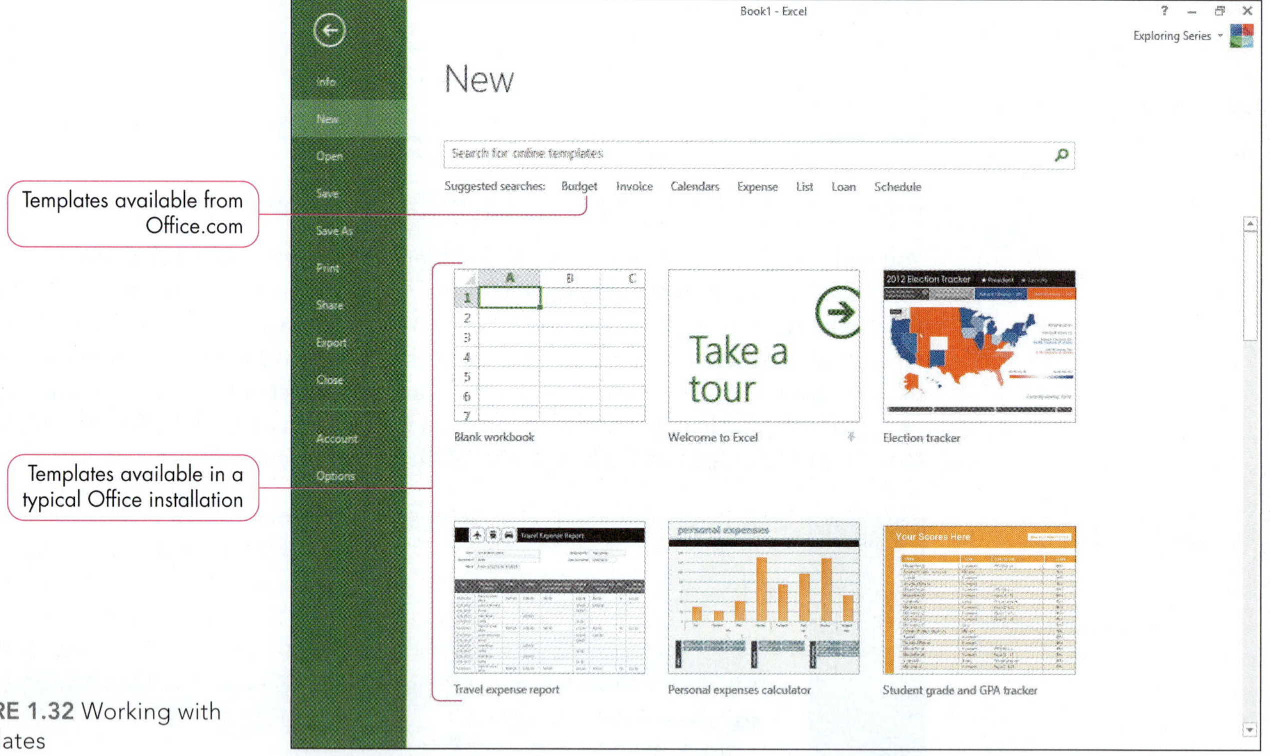

FIGURE 1.32 Working with Templates

Printing a File

There will be occasions when you will want to print an Office project. Before printing, you should preview the file to get an idea of how it will look when printed. That way, if there are obvious problems with the page setup, you can correct them before wasting paper on something that is not correct. When you are ready to print, you can select from various print options, including the number of copies and the specific pages to print. If you know that the page setup is correct and that there are no unique print settings to select, you can simply print the project without adjusting any print settings.

STEP 2

It is a good idea to take a look at how your document will appear before you print it. The Print Preview feature of Office enables you to do just that. In the Print pane, you will see all items, including any headers, footers, graphics, and special formatting. To view a project before printing, click the File tab and click Print. The subsequent Backstage view shows the file preview on the right, with print settings located in the center of the Backstage screen. Figure 1.33 shows a typical Backstage Print view.

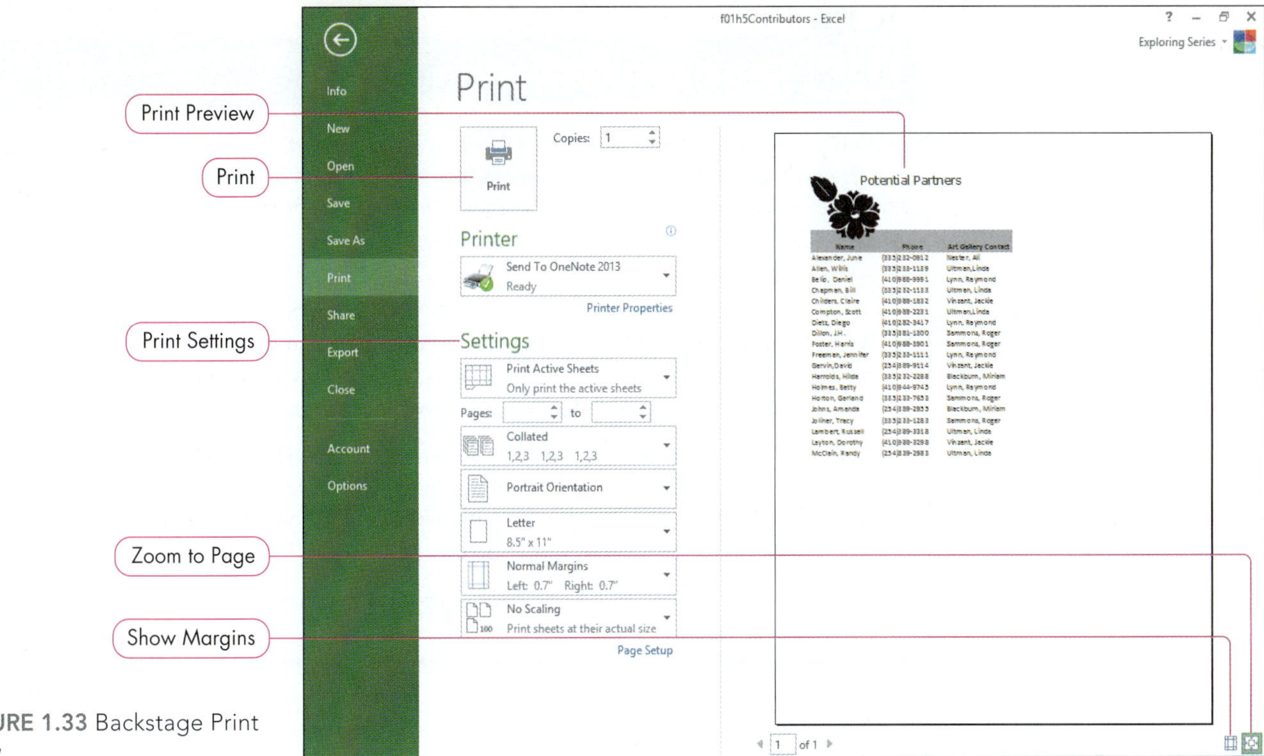

FIGURE 1.33 Backstage Print View

To show the margins of the document, click Show Margins (see Figure 1.33). To increase the size of the file preview, click *Zoom to Page* (see Figure 1.33). Both are found on the bottom-right corner of the preview. Remember that increasing the font size by adjusting the zoom applies to the current display only; it does not actually increase the font size when the document is printed or saved. To return the preview to its original view, click *Zoom to Page* once more.

Other options in the Backstage Print view vary depending on the application in which you are working. Regardless of the Office application, you will be able to access Settings options from the Backstage view, including page orientation (landscape or portrait), margins, and paper size. You will find a more detailed explanation of those settings in the "Page Layout Tab Tasks" section later in this chapter. To print a file, click Print (see Figure 1.33).

The Backstage Print view shown in Figure 1.33 is very similar across all Office applications. However, you will find slight variations specific to each application. For example, PowerPoint's Backstage Print view includes options for printing slides and handouts in various configurations and colors, whereas Excel's focuses on worksheet selections and Word's includes document options. Regardless of software, the manner of working with the Backstage view print options remains consistent.

Closing a File and Application

Although you can have several documents open at one time, limiting the number of open files is a good idea. Office applications have no problem keeping up with multiple open files, but you can easily become overwhelmed with them. When you are done with an open project, you will need to close it.

You can easily close any files that you no longer need. With the desired file on the screen, click the FILE tab and click the Close (X) button. Respond to any prompt that might display suggesting that you save the file. The application remains open, but the selected file is closed. To close the application, click the Close (X) button in the top-right corner.

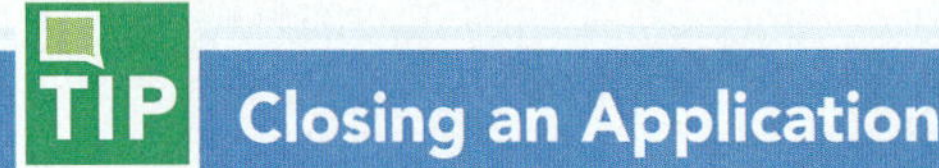

TIP Closing an Application

When you close an application, all open files within the application are also closed. You will be prompted to save any files before they are closed. A quick way to close an application is to click the X in the top-right corner of the application window.

Quick Concepts

1. You want to continue to work with a PowerPoint presentation that you worked with yesterday, but cannot remember where you saved the presentation on your hard drive. How can you open a file that you recently worked with? ***p. 37***
2. As part of your job search, you plan to develop a resume. However, you find it difficult to determine the right style for your resume, and wish you could begin with a predesigned document that you could modify. Is that possible with Word? If so, what steps would you take to locate a predesigned resume? ***p. 38***
3. Closing a file is not the same as closing an application, such as closing Excel. What is the difference? ***p. 39***

Hands-On Exercises

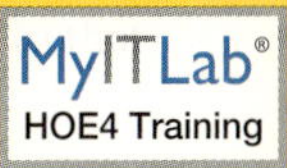

4 The Backstage View Tasks

Projects related to the Spotted Begonia Art Gallery's functions have begun to come in for your review and approval. You have received an informational flyer to be distributed to schools and supporting organizations around the city. It contains a new logo along with descriptive text. Another task on your agenda is to keep the project moving according to schedule. You will identify a calendar template to print and distribute. You will explore printing options, and you will save the flyer and the calendar as directed by your instructor.

Skills covered: Open and Save a File • Preview and Print a File • Open a File from the Recent Documents List and Open a Template

STEP 1 » OPEN AND SAVE A FILE

You have asked your staff to develop a flyer that can be used to promote the Spotted Begonia Art Gallery. You will open a Word document that may be used for the flyer, and you will save the document to a disk drive. Refer to Figure 1.34 as you complete Step 1.

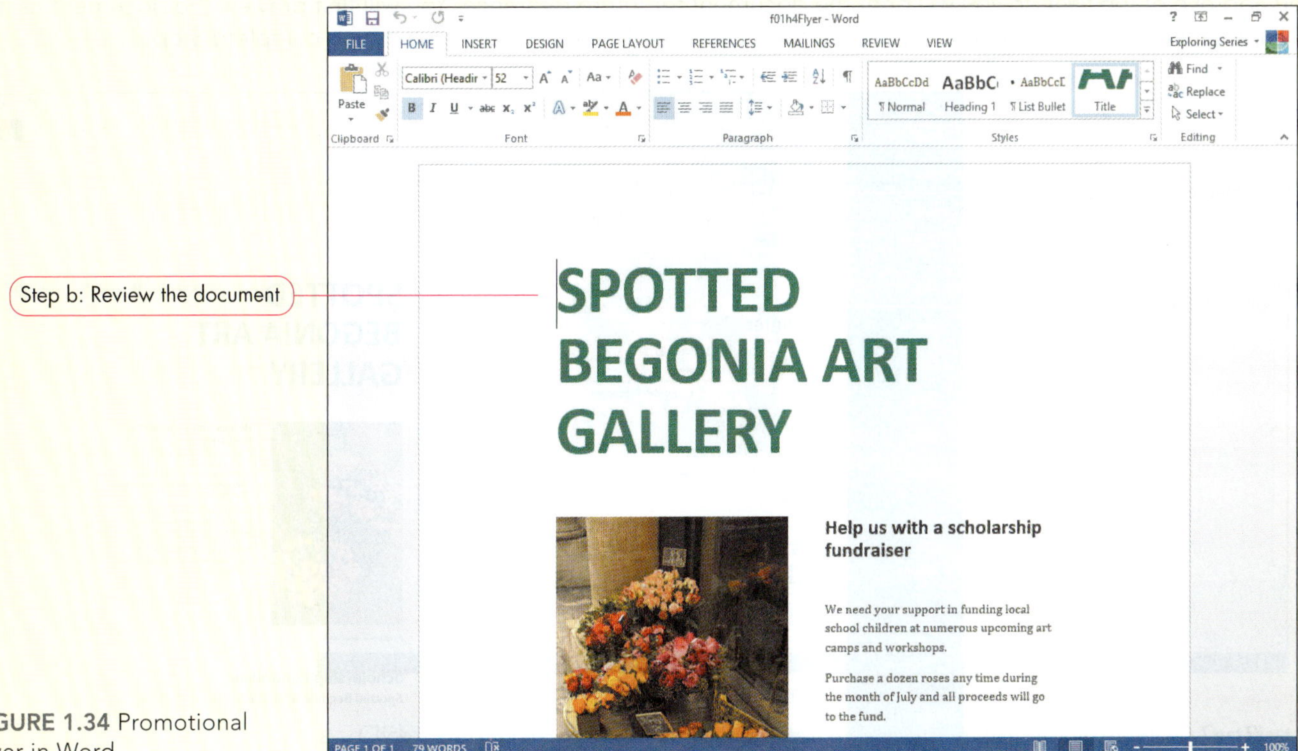

FIGURE 1.34 Promotional Flyer in Word

a. Navigate to the Start screen. Scroll across the tiles, if necessary, and click **Word 2013**. Click **Open Other Documents** at the bottom-left corner of the Word 2013 window.

   You have opened Microsoft Word because it is the program in which the promotional flyer is saved.

b. Click **Computer** and click **Browse**. Navigate to the location of your student files. Double-click *f01h4Flyer* to open the file shown in Figure 1.34. Familiarize yourself with the document. Then, if necessary, click **Read Mode** in the *View shortcuts* group on the Status bar to change to that view. Read through the document.

   The graphic and the flyer are submitted for your approval. A paragraph next to the graphic will serve as the launching point for an information blitz and the beginning of the fundraising drive.

d. Click the **FILE tab** and click **New**. Click **Calendar** from the list of the *Suggested searches* category just beneath the *Search online templates* box.

Office.com provides a wide range of calendar choices. You will select one that is appealing and that will help you keep projects on track.

e. Click a calendar of your choice from the gallery and click **Create**. Respond to and close any windows that may open.

The calendar that you selected opens in Word.

TROUBLESHOOTING: It is possible to select a template that is not certified by Microsoft. In that case, you might have to confirm your acceptance of settings before you click Download.

f. Click **Save** on the Quick Access Toolbar. If necessary, navigate to your Office Records subfolder (a subfolder of Artists) on the drive where you are saving your student files. Save the document as **f01h4Calendar_LastFirst**. Because this is the first time to save the calendar file, the Save button on the Quick Access Toolbar opens a dialog box in which you must indicate the location of the file and the file name.

g. Click **Save** and exit Word. Submit your files based on your instructor's directions.

Home Tab Tasks

You will find that you will repeat some tasks often, whether in Word, Excel, or PowerPoint. You will frequently want to change the format of numbers or words, selecting a different ***font*** or changing font size or color. A font is a complete set of characters, both upper- and lowercase letters, numbers, punctuation marks, and special symbols, with the same design including size, spacing, and shape. You might also need to change the alignment of text or worksheet cells. Undoubtedly, you will find a reason to copy or cut items and paste them elsewhere in the document, presentation, or worksheet. And you might want to modify file contents by finding and replacing text. All of those tasks, and more, are found on the Home tab of the Ribbon in Word, Excel, and PowerPoint. The Access interface is unique, sharing little with other Office applications, so this section will not address Access.

In this section, you will explore the Home tab, learning to format text, copy and paste items, and find and replace words or phrases. Figure 1.37 shows Home tab groups and tasks in the various applications. Note the differences and similarities between the groups.

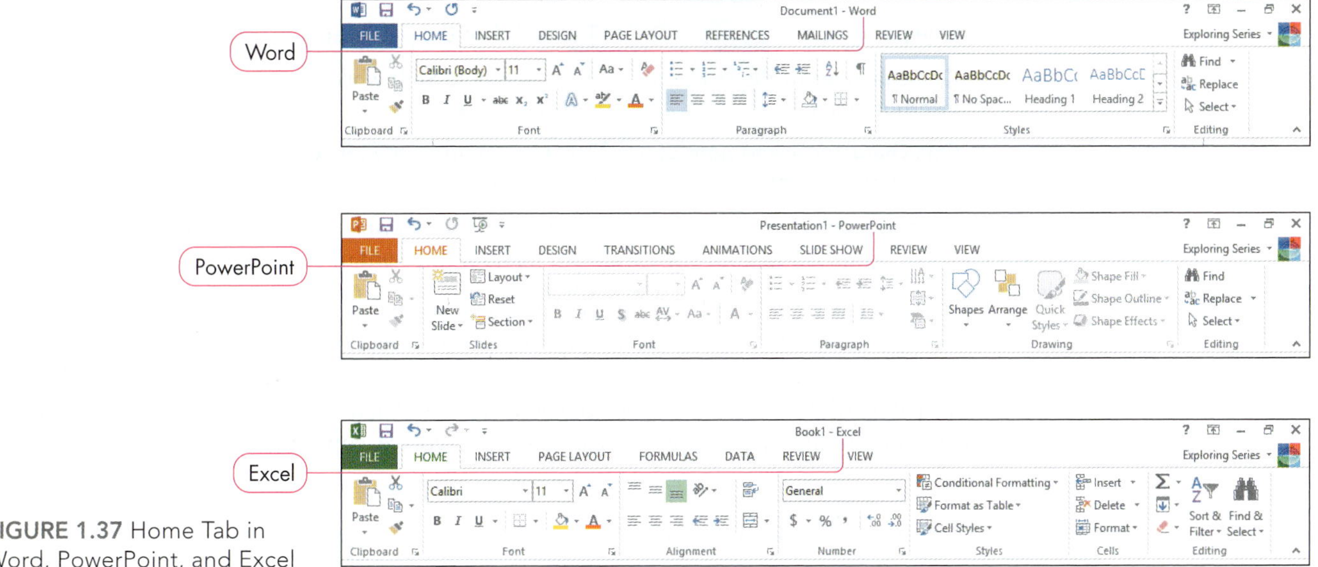

FIGURE 1.37 Home Tab in Word, PowerPoint, and Excel

Selecting and Editing Text

After creating a document, worksheet, or presentation, you will probably want to make some changes. You might prefer to center a title, or maybe you think that certain budget worksheet totals should be formatted as currency. You can change the font so that typed characters are larger or in a different style. You might even want to underline text to add emphasis. In all Office applications, the Home tab provides tools for selecting and editing text. You can also use the Mini toolbar for making quick changes to selected text.

Select Text to Edit

Before making any changes to existing text or numbers, you must first select the characters. A general rule that you should commit to memory is "Select, then do." A foolproof way to select text or numbers is to place the mouse pointer before the first character of the text you want to select, and then drag to highlight the intended selection. Before you drag, be sure that the mouse pointer takes on the shape of the letter *I*, called the *I-bar*. Although other methods for selecting exist, if you remember only one way, it should be the click-and-drag method. If your attempted selection falls short of highlighting the intended area, or perhaps highlights too much, simply click outside the selection and try again.

Apply Font Attributes

The way characters appear onscreen, including qualities such as size, spacing, and shape, is determined by the font. Each Office application has a default font, which is the font that will be in effect unless you change it. Other font attributes include boldfacing, italicizing, and font color, all of which can be applied to selected text. Some formatting changes, such as Bold and Italic, are called ***toggle*** commands. They act somewhat like light switches that you can turn on and off. For example, after having selected a word that you want to add bold to, click Bold in the Font group of the Home tab to turn the setting "on." If, at a later time, you want to remove bold from the word, select it again and click Bold. This time, the button turns "off" the bold formatting.

Change the Font

All applications within the Office suite provide a set of fonts from which you can choose. If you prefer a font other than the default, or if you want to apply a different font to a section of your project for added emphasis or interest, you can easily make the change by selecting a font from within the Font group on the Home tab. You can also change the font by selecting from the Mini toolbar, although that works only if you have first selected text.

Change the Font Size, Color, and Attributes

STEP 2

At times, you will want to make the font size larger or smaller, change the font color, underline selected text, or apply other font attributes. For example, if you are creating a handout for a special event, you may want to apply a different font to emphasize key information such as dates and times. Because such changes are commonplace, Office places those formatting commands in many convenient places within each Office application.

You can find the most common formatting commands in the Font group on the Home tab. As noted earlier, Word, Excel, and PowerPoint all share very similar Font groups that provide access to tasks related to changing the character font (refer to Figure 1.37). Remember that you can place the mouse pointer over any command icon to view a summary of the icon's purpose, so although the icons might at first appear cryptic, you can use the mouse pointer to quickly determine the purpose and applicability to your desired text change. You can also find a subset of those commands plus a few additional choices on the Mini toolbar.

If the font change that you plan to make is not included as a choice on either the Home tab or the Mini toolbar, you can probably find what you are looking for in the Font dialog box. Click the Dialog Box Launcher in the bottom-right corner of the Font group. Figure 1.40 shows a sample Font dialog box. Because the Font dialog box provides many formatting choices in one window, you can make several changes at once. Depending on the application, the contents of the Font dialog box vary slightly, but the purpose is consistent—providing access to choices related to modifying characters.

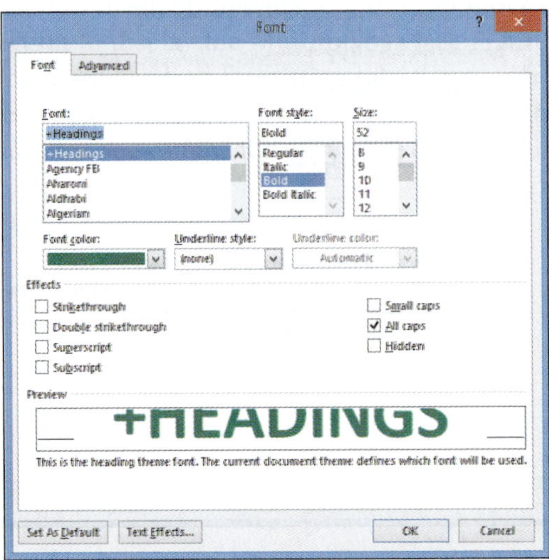

FIGURE 1.40 Font Dialog Box

Using the Clipboard Group Commands

On occasion, you will want to move or copy a selection from one area to another. Suppose that you have included text on a PowerPoint slide that you believe would be more appropriate on a different slide. Or perhaps an Excel formula should be copied from one cell to another because both cells should be totaled in the same manner. You can easily move the slide text or copy the Excel formula by using options found in the Clipboard group on the Home tab. The Office ***Clipboard*** is an area of memory reserved to temporarily hold selections that have been ***cut*** or ***copied*** and allows you to paste the selections. To cut means to remove a selection from the original location and place it in the Office Clipboard. To copy means to duplicate a selection from the original location and place a copy in the Office Clipboard. Although the Clipboard can hold up to 24 items at one time, the usual procedure is to ***paste*** the cut or copied selection to its final destination fairly quickly. To paste means to place a cut or copied selection into another location. When the computer is shut down or loses power, the contents of the Clipboard are erased, so it is important to finalize the paste procedure during the current session.

The Clipboard group enables you not only to copy and cut text and objects but also to copy formatting. Perhaps you have applied a font style to a major heading of a report and you realize that the same formatting should be applied to other headings. Especially if the heading includes multiple formatting features, you will save a great deal of time by copying the entire set of formatting options to the other headings. In so doing, you will ensure the consistency of formatting for all headings because they will appear exactly alike. Using the Clipboard group's ***Format Painter***, you can quickly and easily copy all formatting from one area to another in Word, PowerPoint, and Excel.

In Office, you can usually accomplish the same task in several ways. Although the Ribbon provides ample access to formatting and Clipboard commands (such as Format Painter, Cut, Copy, and Paste), you might find it convenient to access the same commands on a ***shortcut menu***. Right-click a selected item or text to open a shortcut menu such as the one shown in Figure 1.41. A shortcut menu is also called a *context menu* because the contents of the menu vary depending on the location at which you right-clicked.

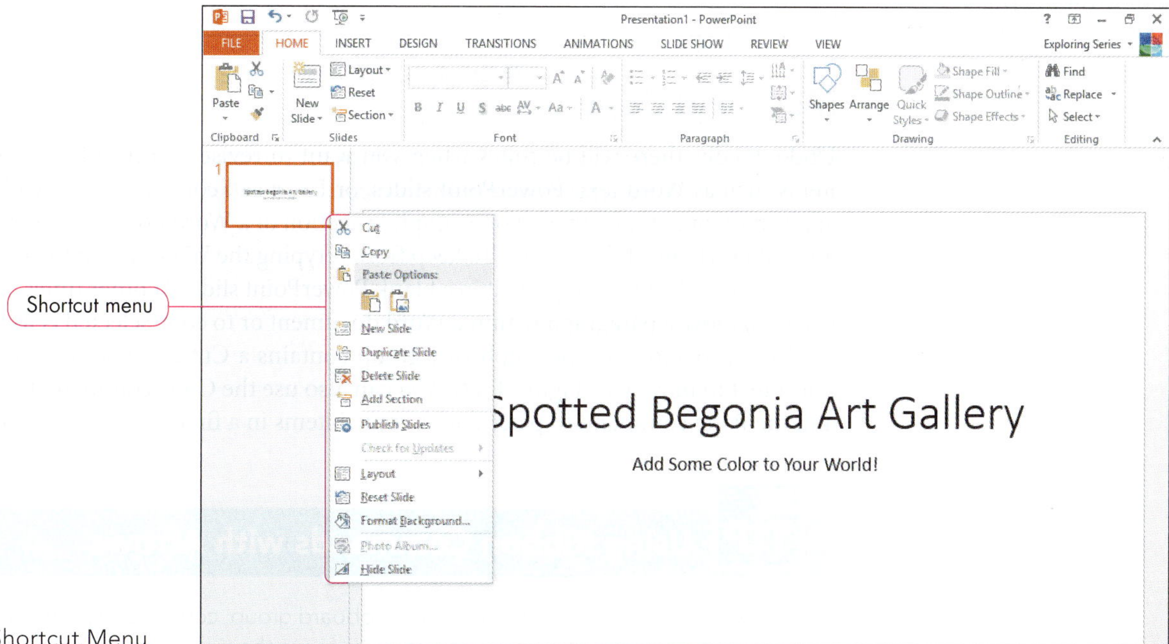

FIGURE 1.41 Shortcut Menu

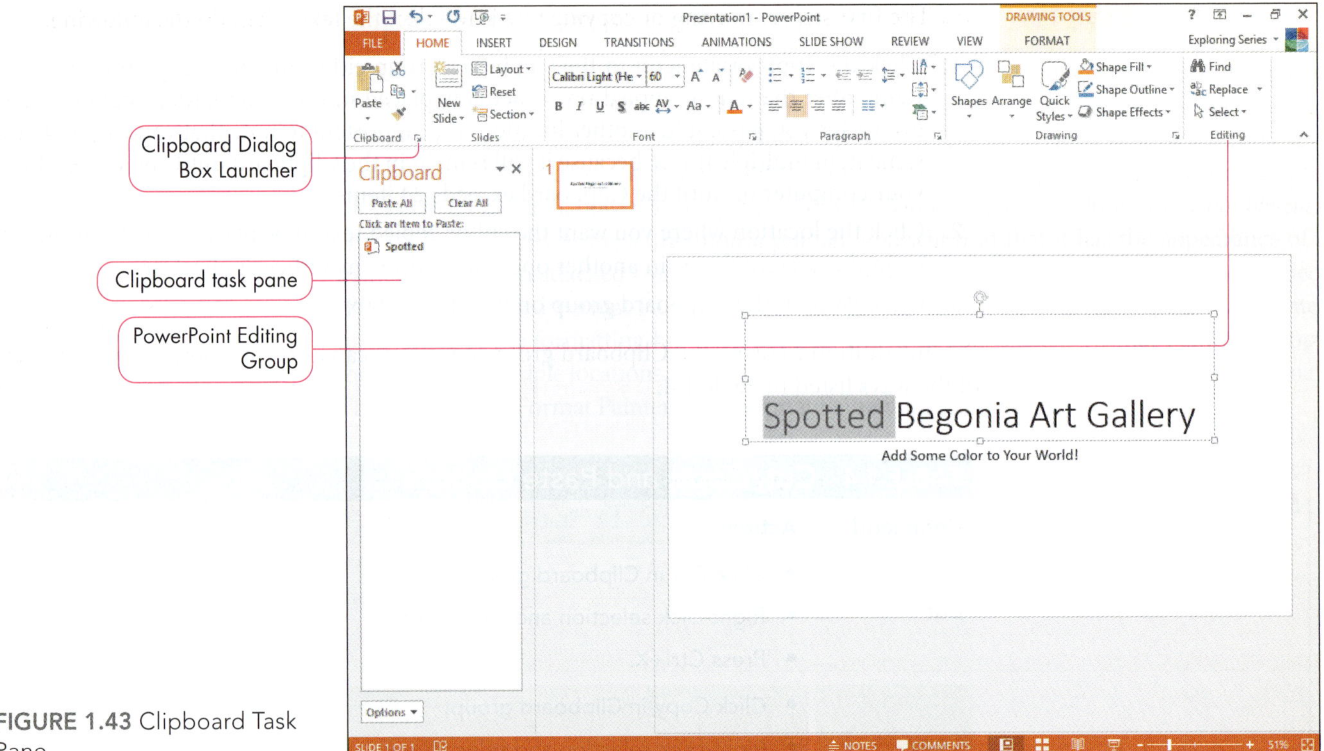

FIGURE 1.43 Clipboard Task Pane

Unless you specify otherwise when beginning a paste operation, the most recently added Clipboard item is pasted. You can, however, select an item from the Clipboard task pane to paste. Similarly, you can delete items from the Clipboard by making a selection in the Clipboard task pane. You can remove all items from the Clipboard by clicking Clear All. The Options button in the Clipboard task pane enables you to control when and where the Clipboard is displayed. Close the Clipboard task pane by clicking the Close (X) button in the top-right corner of the task pane or by clicking the arrow in the title bar of the Clipboard task pane and selecting Close.

Using the Editing Group Commands

The process of finding and replacing text is easily accomplished through options in the Editing group of the Home tab. The Editing group also enables you to select all contents of a project document, all text with similar formatting, or specific objects, such as pictures or charts. The Editing group is found at the far-right side of the Home tab in Excel, Word, and PowerPoint.

The Excel Editing group is unique in that it also includes options for sorting, filtering, and clearing cell contents; filling cells; and summarizing numeric data. Because those commands are relevant only to Excel, this chapter will not address them specifically.

Find and Replace Text

STEP 4»

Especially if you are working with a lengthy project, manually seeking a specific word or phrase can be time-consuming. Office enables you not only to ***find*** each occurrence of a series of characters, but also to ***replace*** what it finds with another series. You will at times find it necessary to locate each occurrence of a text item so that you can replace it with another or so that you can delete, move, or copy it. If you have consistently misspelled a person's name throughout a document, you can find the misspelling and replace it with the correct spelling in a matter of a few seconds, no matter how many times the misspelling occurs in the document. To begin the process of finding and replacing a specific item:

1. Click Replace in the Editing group on the HOME tab of Word or PowerPoint.
2. Or click Find & Select in the Editing group on the HOME tab of Excel. Then click Replace. The dialog box that displays enables you to indicate the word or phrase to find and replace.

The Advanced Find feature is one that you will use often as you work with documents in Word. It is beneficial to find each occurrence of a word you are searching for. But it is also very helpful to see all the occurrences of the word at once. Click Reading Highlight in the *Find and Replace* dialog box and select Highlight All to display each word highlighted, as shown in Figure 1.44. Click Reading Highlight again and select Clear Highlighting to remove the illumination.

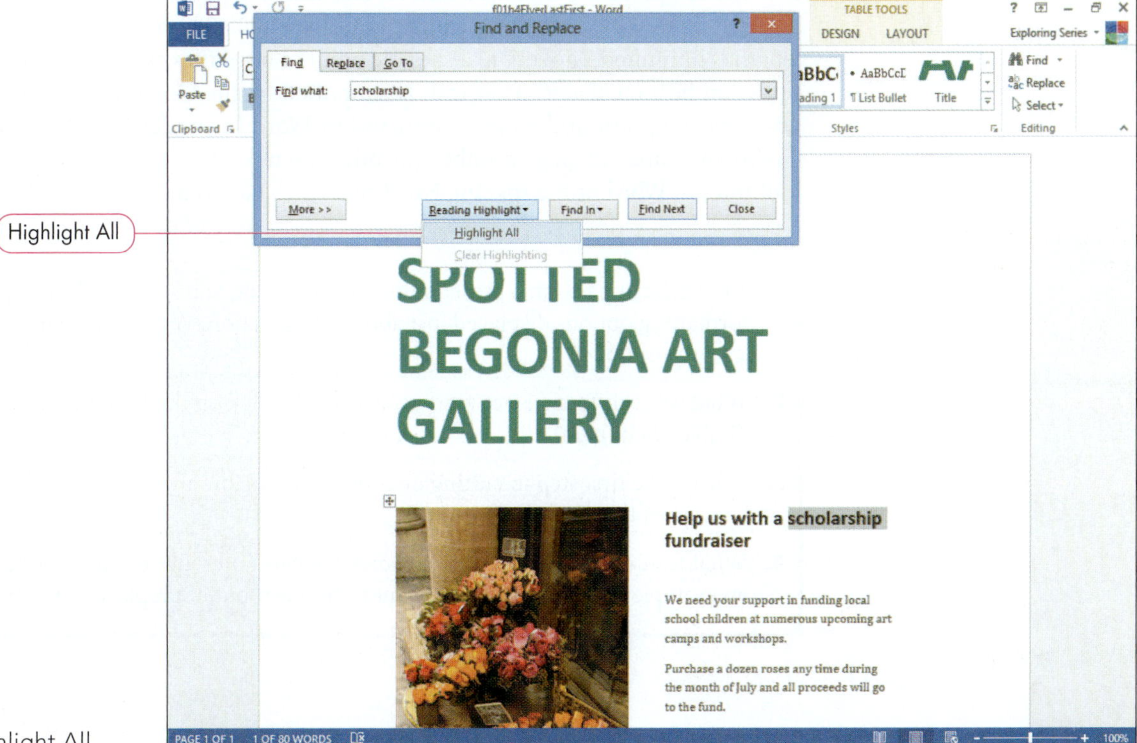

FIGURE 1.44 Highlight All

TIP Using a Shortcut to Find Items

Ctrl+F is a shortcut used to find items in a Word, Excel, or PowerPoint file. When you press Ctrl+F, the *Find and Replace* dialog box displays in Excel and PowerPoint. Pressing Ctrl+F in Word displays a feature—the Navigation Pane—at the left side of a Word document. When you type a search term in the Search Document area, Word finds and highlights all occurrences of the search term. The Navigation Pane also makes it easy to move to sections of a document based on levels of headings.

To find and replace selected text, type the text to locate in the *Find what* box and the replacement text in the *Replace with* box. You can narrow the search to require matching case or find whole words only. If you want to replace all occurrences of the text, click Replace All. If you want to replace only some occurrences, click Find Next repeatedly until you reach the occurrence that you want to replace. At that point, click Replace. When you are finished, click the Close button (or click Cancel).

Use Advanced Find and Replace Features

The *Find and Replace* feature enables you not only to find and replace text, but also to restrict and alter the format of the text at the same time. To establish the format criteria associated with either the *Find or Replace* portion of the operation:

1. Click the More button to expand the dialog box options. Click Format in the bottom-left corner of the dialog box.
2. Add formatting characteristics from the Font dialog box or Paragraph dialog box (as well as many other formatting features).

In addition to applying special formatting parameters on a *Find and Replace* operation, you can specify that you want to find or replace special characters. Click Special at the bottom of the *Find and Replace* dialog box to view the punctuation characters from which you can choose. For example, you might want to look for all instances in a document where an exclamation point is being used and replace it with a period.

An Excel worksheet can include more than 1,000,000 rows of data. A Word document's length is unlimited. Moving to a specific point in large files created in either of those applications can be a challenge. That task is simplified by the Go To option, found in the Editing group as an option of the Find command in Word (or under Find & Select in Excel). Click Go To and enter the page number (or other item, such as section, comment, bookmark, or footnote) in Word or the specific Excel cell. Click Go To in Word (or OK in Excel).

1. After selecting text in a presentation or document, you see a small transparent bar with formatting options displayed just above the selection. What is the bar called and what is its purpose? ***p. 46***
2. What is the difference between using a single-click on the Format Painter and using a double-click? ***p. 50***
3. What is the first step in cutting or copying text? How are cutting and copying related to the concept of the Clipboard? ***p. 51***
4. What feature can you use to very quickly locate and replace text in a document? Provide an example of when you might want to find text but not replace it. ***p. 52***

Hands-On Exercises

5 Home Tab Tasks

You have created a list of potential contributors to the Spotted Begonia Art Gallery. You have used Excel to record that list in worksheet format. Now you will review the worksheet and format its appearance to make it more attractive. You will also modify a promotional flyer. In working with those projects, you will put into practice the formatting, copying, moving, and editing information from the preceding section.

Skills covered: Move, Copy, and Paste Text • Select Text, Apply Font Attributes, and Use the Mini Toolbar • Use Format Painter and Work with the Mini Toolbar • Use the Font Dialog Box and Find and Replace Text

STEP 1 » MOVE, COPY, AND PASTE TEXT

Each contributor to the Spotted Begonia Art Gallery is assigned a contact person. You manage the worksheet that keeps track of those assignments, but the assignments sometimes change. You will copy and paste some worksheet selections to keep from having to retype data. You will also reposition a clip art image to improve the worksheet's appearance. Refer to Figure 1.45 as you complete Step 1.

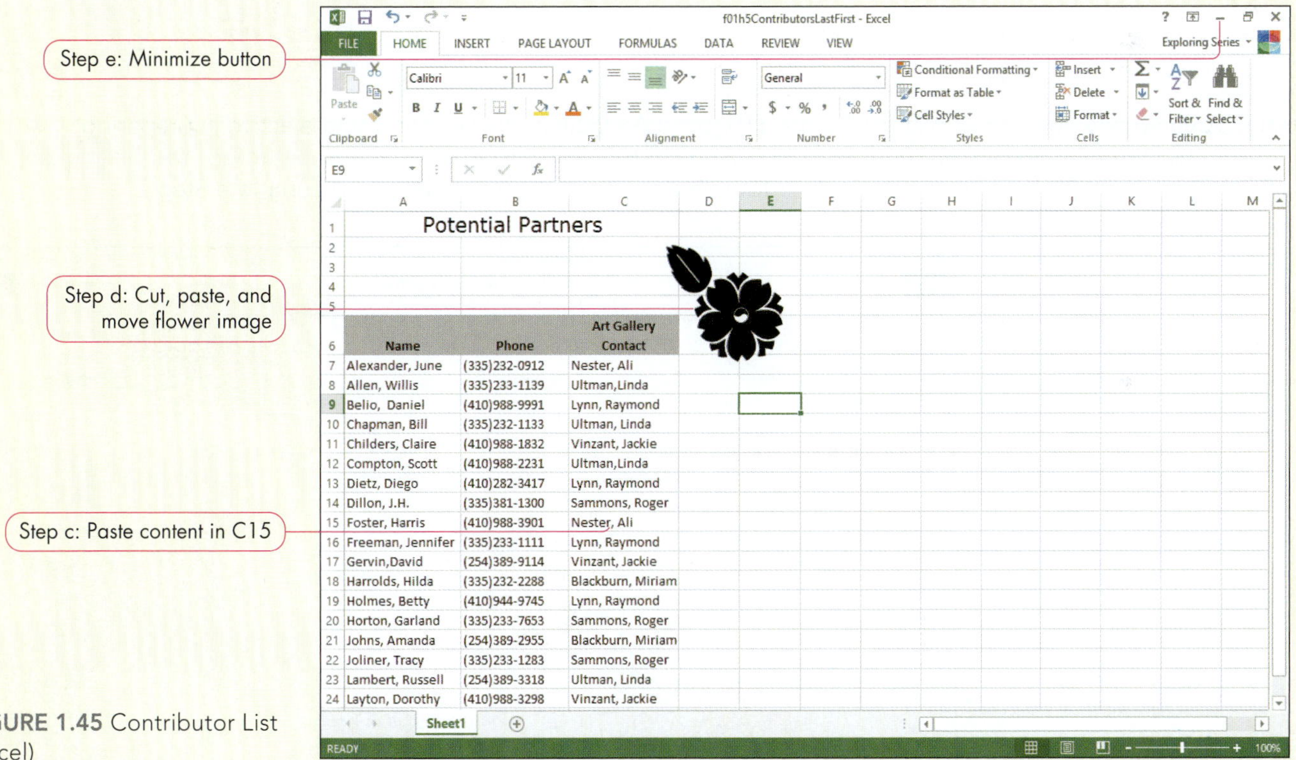

Name	Phone	Art Gallery Contact
Alexander, June	(335)232-0912	Nester, Ali
Allen, Willis	(335)233-1139	Ultman,Linda
Belio, Daniel	(410)988-9991	Lynn, Raymond
Chapman, Bill	(335)232-1133	Ultman, Linda
Childers, Claire	(410)988-1832	Vinzant, Jackie
Compton, Scott	(410)988-2231	Ultman,Linda
Dietz, Diego	(410)282-3417	Lynn, Raymond
Dillon, J.H.	(335)381-1300	Sammons, Roger
Foster, Harris	(410)988-3901	Nester, Ali
Freeman, Jennifer	(335)233-1111	Lynn, Raymond
Gervin,David	(254)389-9114	Vinzant, Jackie
Harrolds, Hilda	(335)232-2288	Blackburn, Miriam
Holmes, Betty	(410)944-9745	Lynn, Raymond
Horton, Garland	(335)233-7653	Sammons, Roger
Johns, Amanda	(254)389-2955	Blackburn, Miriam
Joliner, Tracy	(335)233-1283	Sammons, Roger
Lambert, Russell	(254)389-3318	Ultman, Linda
Layton, Dorothy	(410)988-3298	Vinzant, Jackie

FIGURE 1.45 Contributor List (Excel)

a. Navigate to the Start screen. Scroll across the tiles, if necessary, and click **Excel 2013**. Click **Open Other Workbooks**.

You have opened Microsoft Excel because it is the program in which the contributors list is saved.

b. Open the student data file *f01h5Contributors*. Save the file as **f01h5Contributors_LastFirst** in the Office Records folder (a subfolder of Artists) you created.

The potential contributors list shown in Figure 1.45 is displayed.

c. Click **cell C7** to select the cell that contains *Nester, Ali*, and click **Copy** in the Clipboard group on the HOME tab. Click **cell C15** to select the cell that contains *Sammons, Roger*, click **Paste** in the Clipboard group, and then press **Esc** to remove the selection from *Nester, Ali*.

   Ali Nester has been assigned as the Spotted Begonia Art Gallery contact for Harris Foster, replacing Roger Sammons. You make that replacement on the worksheet by copying and pasting Ali Nester's name in the appropriate worksheet cell.

d. Click the picture of the begonia. A box displays around the image, indicating that it is selected. Click **Cut** in the Clipboard group, click **cell D2**, and then click **Paste**. Drag the picture to resize and position it as needed (see Figure 1.45) so that it does not block any information in the list. Click anywhere outside the begonia picture to deselect it.

   You decide that the picture of the begonia will look better if it is placed on the right side of the worksheet instead of the left. You move the picture by cutting and pasting the object.

TROUBLESHOOTING: A Paste Options icon might display in the worksheet after you have moved the begonia picture. It offers additional options related to the paste procedure. You do not need to change any options, so ignore the button.

e. Click **Save** on the Quick Access Toolbar. Click **Minimize** to minimize the worksheet without closing it.

STEP 2 » SELECT TEXT, APPLY FONT ATTRIBUTES, AND USE THE MINI TOOLBAR

As the opening of a new showing at the Spotted Begonia Art Gallery draws near, you are active in preparing promotional materials. You are currently working on an informational flyer that is almost set to go. You will make a few improvements before approving the flyer for release. Refer to Figure 1.46 as you complete Step 2.

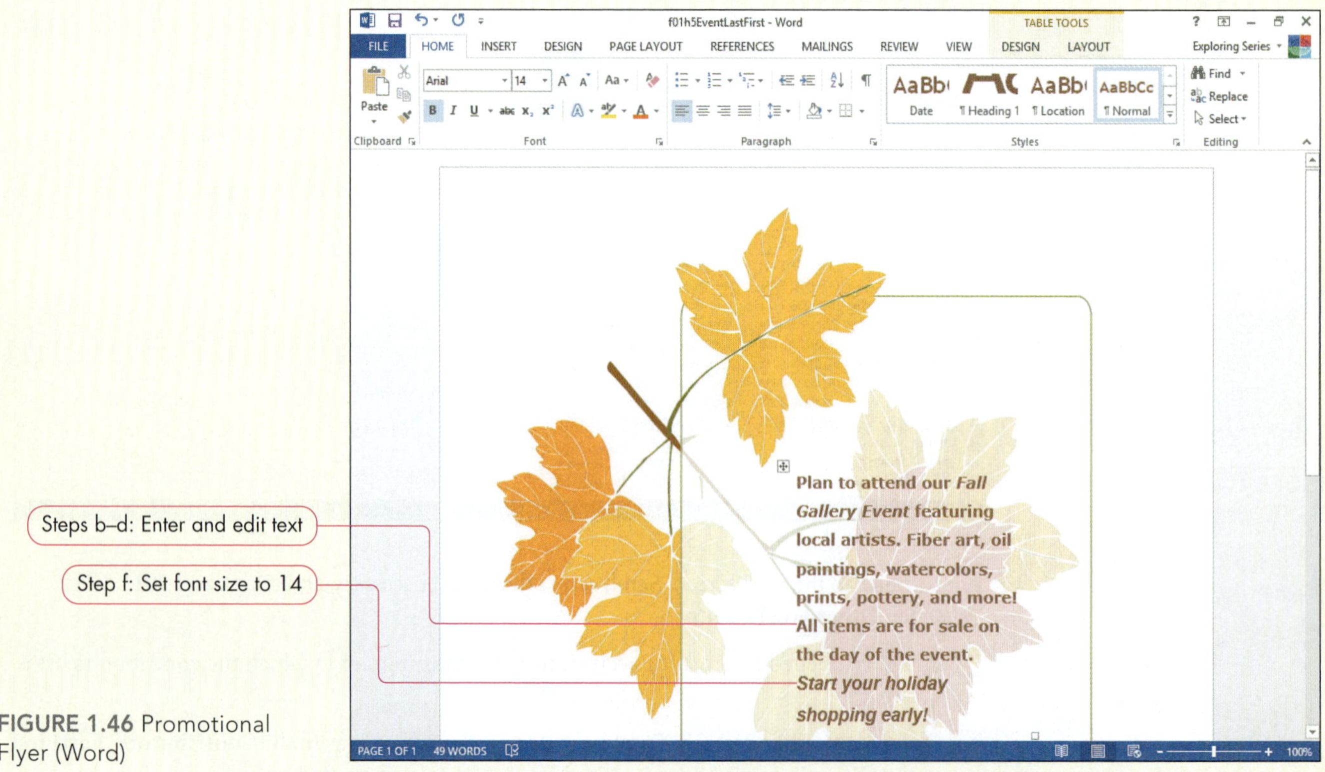

FIGURE 1.46 Promotional Flyer (Word)

a. Navigate to the Start screen. Scroll across the tiles, if necessary, and click **Word 2013**. Click **Open Other Documents**. Open *f01h5Event* and save the document as **f01h5Event_LastFirst** in the Promotional Print folder (a subfolder of Artists) you created.

   You plan to modify the promotional flyer slightly to include additional information about the Spotted Begonia Art Gallery.

> **TROUBLESHOOTING:** If you make any major mistakes in this exercise, you can close the file without saving it, open *f01h5Event* again, and then start this exercise over.

b. Click after the exclamation mark after the word *more* at the end of the first paragraph. Press **Enter** and type the following text. As you type, do not press Enter at the end of each line. Word will automatically wrap the lines of text.

   All items are for sale on the day of the event. Start your holiday shopping early! You'll find gifts for everyone on your list.

> **TROUBLESHOOTING:** If you make any mistakes while typing, press Backspace and correct them.

c. Select the sentence beginning with *You'll find gifts*. Press **Delete**.

   When you press Delete, selected text (or characters to the right of the insertion point) is removed. Deleted text is not placed in the Clipboard.

d. Select the words *Start your holiday shopping early!* Click **Italic** in the Font group on the HOME tab and click anywhere outside the selection to see the result.

e. Select both paragraphs but not the final italicized line. While still within the selection, move the mouse pointer slightly to display the Mini toolbar, click the **Font arrow** on the Mini toolbar, and then scroll to select **Verdana**.

> **TROUBLESHOOTING:** If you do not see the Mini toolbar, you might have moved too far away from the selection. In that case, click outside the selection and drag to select it once more. Without leaving the selection, move the mouse pointer slightly to display the Mini toolbar.

   You have changed the font of the two paragraphs.

f. Click after the period following the word *event* before the last sentence in the second paragraph. Press **Enter** and press **Delete** to remove the extra space before the first letter, if necessary. Drag to select the new line, click **Font Size arrow** in the Font group, and then select **14**. Click anywhere outside the selected area. Your document should appear as shown in Figure 1.46.

   You have increased font size to draw attention to the text.

g. Save the document and keep open for Step 3.

STEP 3 » USE FORMAT PAINTER AND WORK WITH THE MINI TOOLBAR

You are on a short timeline for finalizing the promotional flyer, so you will use a few shortcuts to avoid retyping and reformatting more than is necessary. You know that you can easily copy formatting from one area to another using Format Painter. The Mini toolbar can also help you make changes quickly. Refer to Figure 1.47 as you complete Step 3.

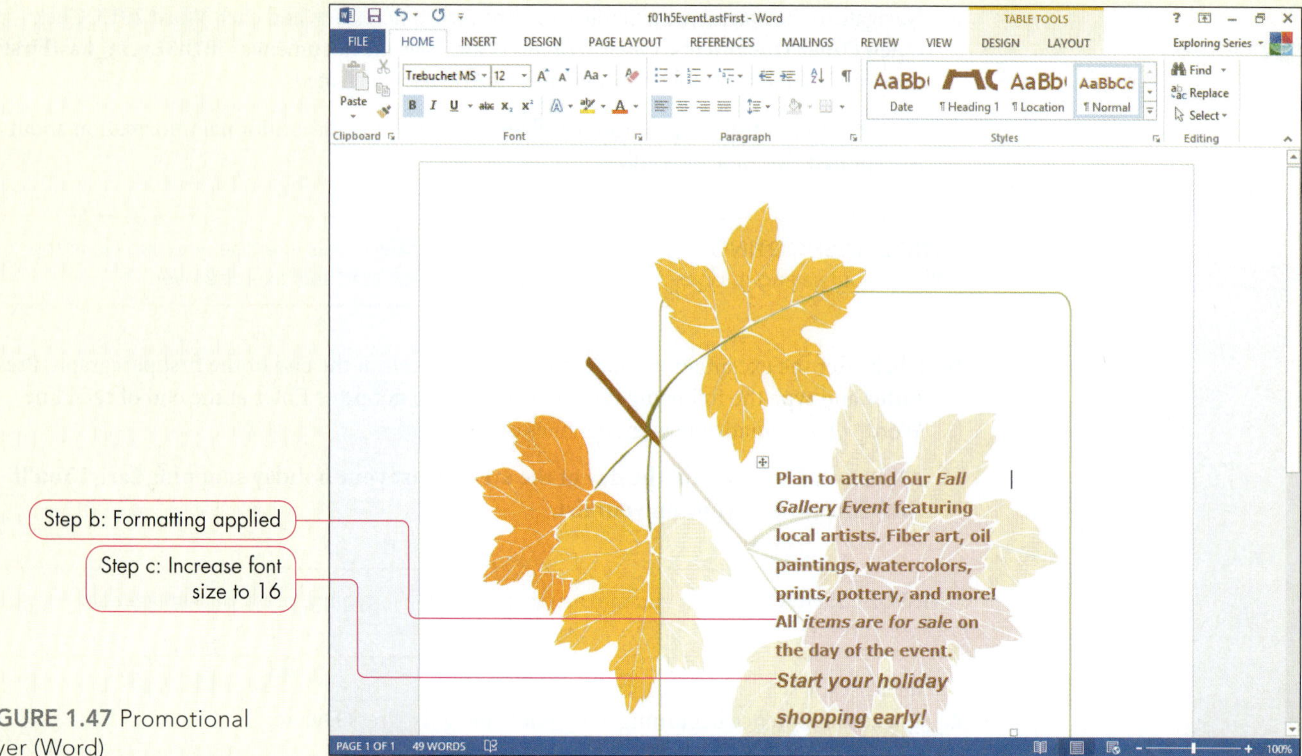

FIGURE 1.47 Promotional Flyer (Word)

a. Select the words *Fall Gallery Event* in the first paragraph and click **Format Painter** in the Clipboard group.

b. Select the words *items are for sale* in the sixth line. Click anywhere outside the selection to deselect the phrase.

The format of the area that you first selected (*Fall Gallery Event*) is applied to the line containing the phrase.

c. Select the text *Start your holiday shopping early!* in the Mini toolbar, click in the **Font Size box**, and then select **16** to increase the font size slightly. Click outside the selected area.

Figure 1.47 shows the final document as it should now appear.

d. Save the document as **f01h5Stp3Event_LastFirst** in the Promotional Print folder you created and close Word. Submit your file based on your instructor's directions.

The flyer will be saved with the same file name and in the same location as it was when you last saved the document in Step 2. As you close Word, the open document will also be closed.

STEP 4 » USE THE FONT DIALOG BOX AND FIND AND REPLACE TEXT

The contributors worksheet is almost complete. However, you first want to make a few more formatting changes to improve the worksheet's appearance. You will also quickly change an incorrect area code by using Excel's *Find and Replace* feature. Refer to Figure 1.48 as you complete Step 4.

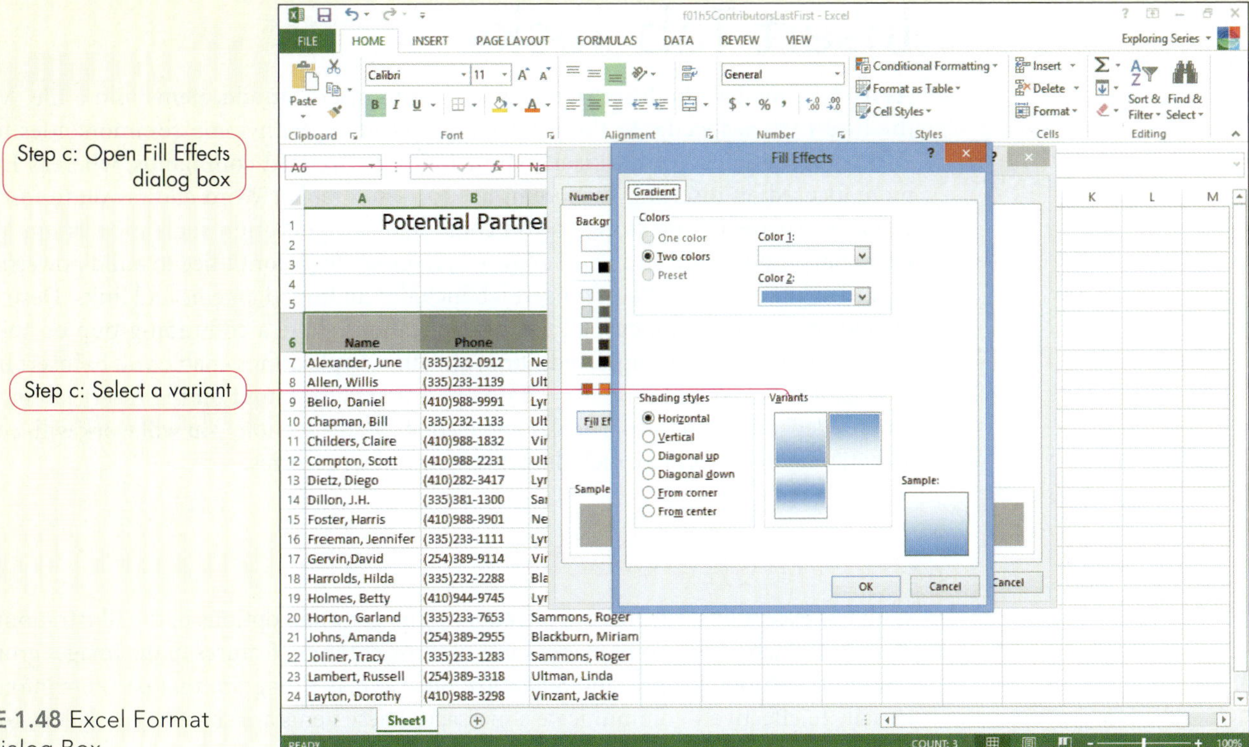

FIGURE 1.48 Excel Format Cells Dialog Box

a. Click the **Excel icon** on the taskbar to redisplay the contributors worksheet that you minimized in Step 1.

The Excel potential contributors list displays.

> **TROUBLESHOOTING:** If you closed Excel, you can find the correct worksheet in your Recent Documents list.

b. Drag to select **cells A6** through **C6**.

> **TROUBLESHOOTING:** Make sure the mouse pointer looks like a large white plus sign before dragging. It is normal for the first cell in the selected area to be a different shade. If you click and drag when the mouse pointer does not resemble a white plus sign, text may be moved or duplicated. In that case, click Undo on the Quick Access Toolbar.

c. Click the **Dialog Box Launcher** in the Font group to display the Format Cells dialog box. Click the **Fill tab** and click **Fill Effects**, as shown in Figure 1.48. Click any style in the *Variants* section, click **OK**, and then click **OK** once more to close the Format Cells dialog box. Click outside the selected area to see the final result.

The headings of the worksheet are shaded more attractively.

d. Click **Find & Select** in the Editing group and click **Replace**. Type **410** in the **Find what box**. Type **411** in the **Replace with box**, click **Replace All**, and then click **OK** when notified that Excel has made seven replacements. Click **Close** in the *Find and Replace* dialog box.

You discovered that you consistently typed an incorrect area code. You used Find and Replace to make the corrections quickly.

e. Save the workbook as **f01h5Stp4Contributors_LastFirst** in the Office Records folder you created. Exit Excel, if necessary. Submit your files based on your instructor's directions.

Insert Tab Tasks

As its title implies, the Insert tab enables you to insert, or add, items into a file. Much of the Insert tab is specific to the particular application, with some commonalities to other Office applications. Word's Insert tab includes text-related commands, whereas Excel's is more focused on inserting such items as charts and tables. Word allows you to insert apps from the Microsoft app store, so you could add an application such as Merriam-Webster Dictionary. Both Word and Excel allow you to insert Apps for Office to build powerful Web-backed solutions. PowerPoint's Insert tab includes multimedia items and links. Despite their obvious differences in focus, all Office applications share a common group on the Insert tab—the Illustrations group. In addition, all Office applications enable you to insert headers, footers, text boxes, and symbols. Those options are also found on the Insert tab in various groups, depending on the particular application. In this section, you will work with common activities on the Insert tab, including inserting online pictures.

Inserting Objects

With few exceptions, all Office applications share common options in the Illustrations group of the Insert tab. PowerPoint places some of those common features in the Images group. You can insert pictures, shapes, and ***SmartArt***. SmartArt is a diagram that presents information visually to effectively communicate a message. These items are considered objects, retaining their separate nature when they are inserted in files. That means that you can select them and manage them independently of the underlying document, worksheet, or presentation.

After an object has been inserted, you can click the object to select it or click anywhere outside the object to deselect it. When an object is selected, a border surrounds it with handles, or small dots, appearing at each corner and in the middle of each side. Figure 1.49 shows a selected object, surrounded by handles. Unless an object is selected, you cannot change or modify it. When an object is selected, the Ribbon expands to include one or more contextual tabs. Items on the contextual tabs relate to the selected object, enabling you to modify and manage it.

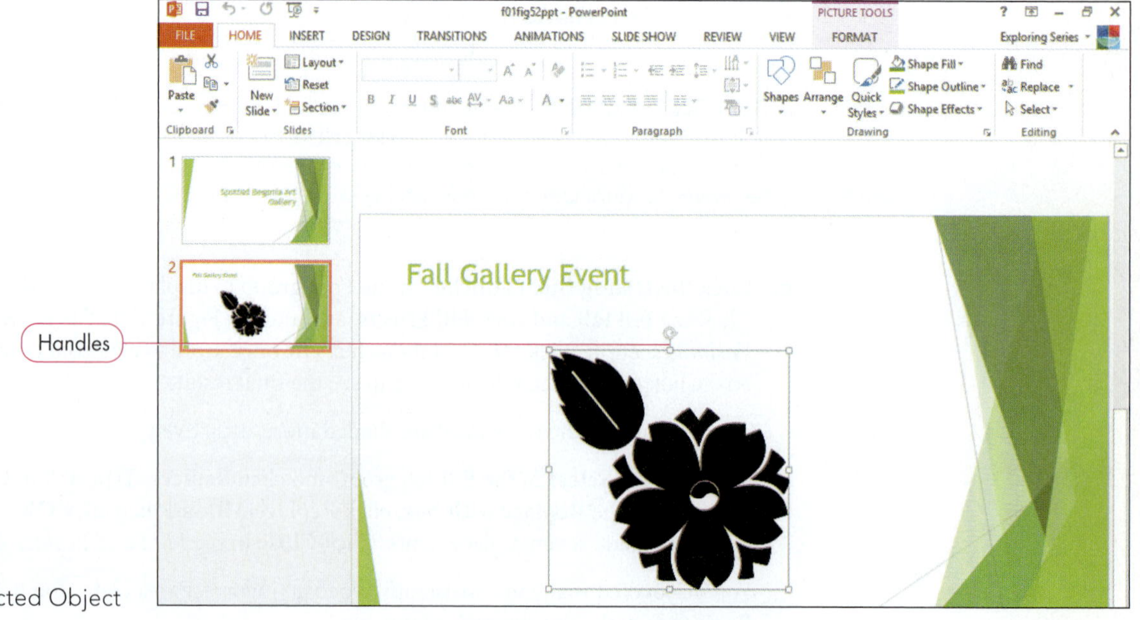

FIGURE 1.49 Selected Object

You can resize and move a selected object. Place the mouse pointer on any handle and drag (when the mouse pointer looks like a two-headed arrow) to resize the object. Be careful! If you drag a side handle, the object is likely to be skewed, possibly resulting in a poor image. Instead, drag a corner handle to proportionally resize the image. To move an object, drag the object when the mouse pointer looks like a four-headed arrow.

Insert Pictures

STEP 2»

Documents, worksheets, and presentations can include much more than just words and numbers. You can easily add energy and additional description to the project by including pictures and other graphic elements. Although a ***picture*** is usually just that—a digital photo—it is actually defined as a graphic element retrieved from storage media such as a hard drive or a CD. A picture could actually be a clip art item that you saved from the Internet onto your hard drive.

The process of inserting a picture is simple.

1. Click in the project where you want the picture to be placed. Make sure you know where the picture that you plan to use is stored.
2. Click the INSERT tab.
3. Click Pictures in the Illustrations group (or Images group in PowerPoint). The Insert Picture dialog box is shown in Figure 1.50. You can also use Online Pictures to search for and insert pictures.
4. Navigate to where your picture is saved and click Insert (or simply double-click the picture).

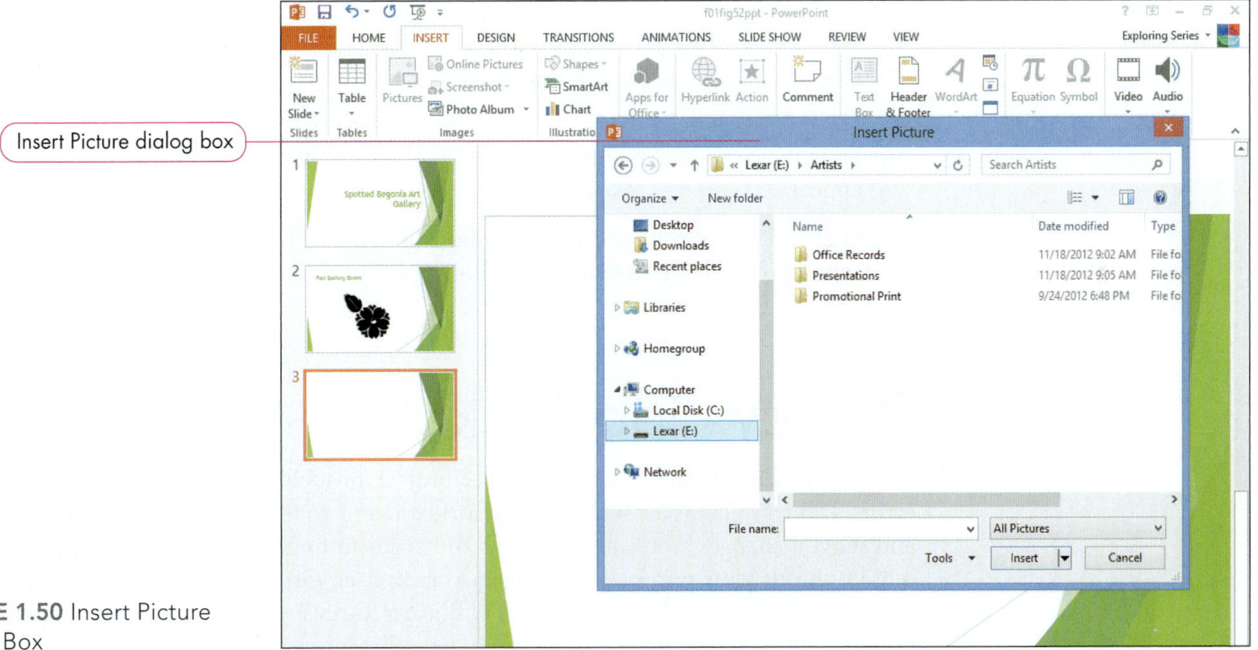

FIGURE 1.50 Insert Picture Dialog Box

In addition, on some slide layouts, PowerPoint displays Pictures and Online Pictures buttons that you can click to search for and select a picture for the slide.

Insert and Modify SmartArt

The SmartArt feature enables you to create a diagram and to enter text to provide a visual representation of data. To create a SmartArt diagram, choose a diagram type that fits the purpose: List, Process, Cycle, Hierarchy, Relationships, Matrix, Pyramid, and Picture. You can get additional SmartArt diagrams at Office.com. To insert a SmartArt object, do the following:

1. Click the INSERT tab.
2. Click SmartArt in the Illustrations group to display the Choose a SmartArt Graphic dialog box.
3. Click the type of SmartArt diagram you want in the left pane of the dialog box.
4. Click the SmartArt subtype from the center pane.
5. Preview the selected SmartArt and subtype in the right pane and click OK.

Once you select the SmartArt diagram type and the subtype, a Text pane opens in which you can enter text. The text you enter displays within the selected object. If the SmartArt diagram contains more objects than you need, click the object and press Delete.

The SmartArt Tools Design tab enables you to customize the design of a SmartArt diagram. You can modify the diagram by changing its layout, colors, and style. The layout controls the construction of the diagram. The style controls the visual effects, such as embossing and rounded corners of the diagram. The SmartArt Tools Format tab controls the shape fill color, border, and size options.

Insert and Format Shapes

You can insert a shape to add a visual effect to a worksheet. You can insert various types of lines, rectangles, basic shapes (such as an oval, a pie shape, or a smiley face), block arrows, equation shapes, flowchart shapes, stars and banners, and callouts. You can insert shapes, such as a callout, to draw attention to particular worksheet data. To insert a shape, do the following:

1. Click the INSERT tab.
2. Click Shapes in the Illustrations group.
3. Select the shape you want to insert from the Shapes gallery.
4. Drag the cross-hair pointer to create the shape in the worksheet where you want it to appear.

After you insert the shape, the Drawing Tools Format tab displays so that you can change the shape, apply a shape style with fill color, and adjust the size.

Review Tab Tasks

As a final touch, you should always check a project for spelling, grammatical, and word usage errors. If the project is a collaborative effort, you and your colleagues might add comments and suggest changes. You can even use a thesaurus to find synonyms for words that are not quite right for your purpose. The Review tab in each Office application provides all these options and more. In this section, you will learn to review a file, checking for spelling and grammatical errors. You will also learn to use a thesaurus to identify synonyms.

Reviewing a File

As you create or edit a file, you will want to make sure no spelling or grammatical errors exist. You will also be concerned with wording, being sure to select words and phrases that best represent the purpose of the document, worksheet, or presentation. On occasion, you might even find yourself at a loss for an appropriate word. Not to worry. Word, Excel, and PowerPoint all provide standard tools for proofreading, including a spelling and grammar checker and a thesaurus.

Check Spelling and Grammar

STEP 1

In general, all Office applications check your spelling and grammar as you type. If a word is unrecognized, it is flagged as misspelled or grammatically incorrect. Misspellings are identified with a red wavy underline, grammatical problems are underlined in green, and word usage errors (such as using *bear* instead of *bare*) have a blue underline. If the word or phrase is truly in error—that is, it is not a person's name or an unusual term that is not in the application's dictionary—you can correct it manually, or you can let the software correct it for you. If you right-click a word or phrase that is identified as a mistake, you will see a shortcut menu similar to that shown in Figure 1.51. If the application's dictionary can make a suggestion as to the correct spelling, you can click to accept the suggestion and make the change. If a grammatical rule is violated, you will have an opportunity to select a correction. However, if the text is actually correct, you can click Ignore or Ignore All (to bypass all occurrences of the flagged error in the current document). Click *Add to Dictionary* if you want the word to be considered correct whenever it appears in all documents. Similar selections on a shortcut menu enable you to ignore grammatical mistakes if they are not errors.

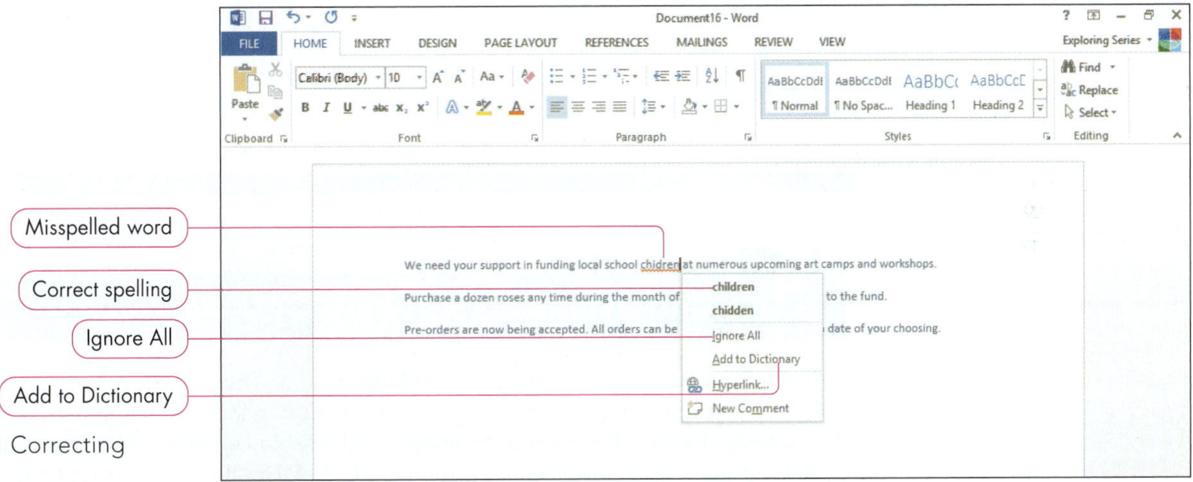

FIGURE 1.51 Correcting Misspelling

You might prefer the convenience of addressing possible misspellings and grammatical errors without having to examine each underlined word or phrase. To do so, click Spelling & Grammar in the Proofing group on the Review tab. Beginning at the top of the document, each identified error is highlighted in a pane similar to Figure 1.52. You can then choose how to address the problem by making a selection from the options in the pane.

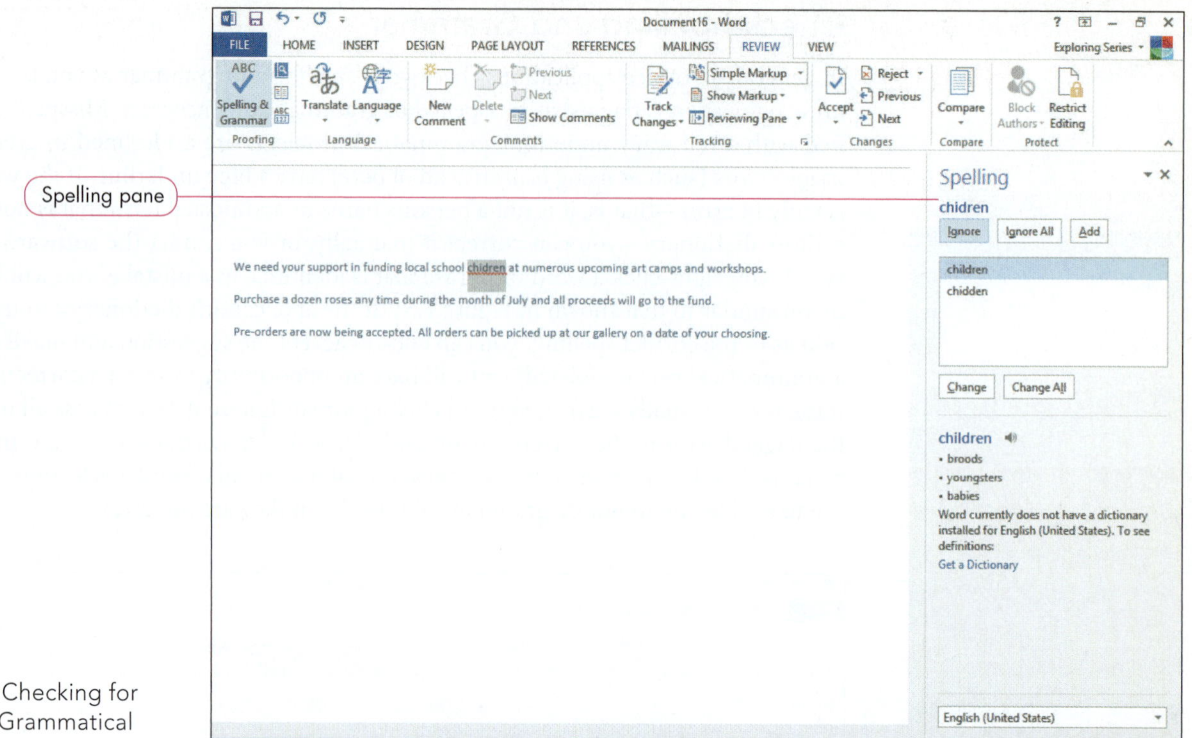

FIGURE 1.52 Checking for Spelling and Grammatical Errors

TIP Understanding Software Options

Many Office settings are considered ***default*** options. Thus, unless you specify otherwise, the default options are in effect. One such default option is the automatic spelling and grammar checker. If you prefer to enable and disable certain options or change default settings in an Office application, you can click the FILE tab and select Options. From that point, you can work through a series of categories, selecting or deselecting options at will. For example, if you want to change how the application corrects and formats text, you can select or deselect settings in the Proofing group.

Use the Thesaurus

As you write, there will be times when you are at a loss for an appropriate word. Perhaps you feel that you are overusing a word and want to find a suitable substitute. The Thesaurus is the Office tool to use in such a situation. Located in the Proofing group on the Review tab, Thesaurus enables you to search for synonyms, or words with similar meanings. Select a word and click Thesaurus in the Proofing group on the Review tab. A task pane displays on the right side of the screen, and synonyms are listed similar to those shown in Figure 1.53. You can also use the Thesaurus before typing a word to find substitutes. Simply click Thesaurus and type the word for which you are seeking a synonym in the Search box. Press Enter or click the magnifying glass to the right of the Search box for some suggestions. Finally, you can also identify synonyms when you right-click a word and point to Synonyms (if any are available). Click any word from the options offered to place it in the document.

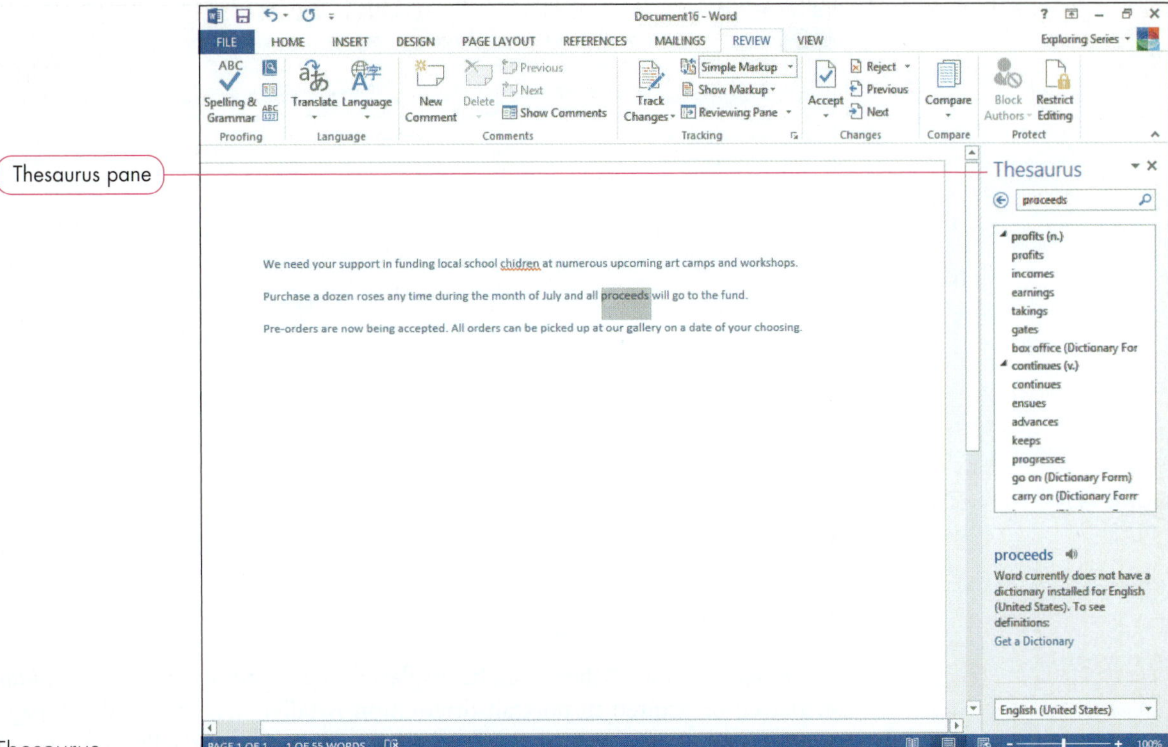

FIGURE 1.53 Thesaurus

Page Layout Tab Tasks

When you prepare a document or worksheet, you are concerned with the way the project appears onscreen and possibly in print. Unlike Word and Excel, a PowerPoint presentation is usually designed as a slide show, so it is not nearly as critical to concern yourself with page layout settings. The Page Layout tab in Word and Excel provides access to a full range of options such as margin settings and page orientation. In this section, you will identify page layout settings that are common to Office applications.

Because a document is most often designed to be printed, you will want to make sure it looks its best in printed form. That means that you will need to know how to adjust margins and how to change the page orientation. Perhaps the document or spreadsheet should be centered on the page vertically or the text should be aligned in columns. By adjusting page settings, you can do all these things and more. You will find the most common page settings, such as margins and page orientation, in the Page Setup group on the Page Layout tab. For less common settings, such as determining whether headers should print on odd or even pages, you can use the Page Setup dialog box.

Changing Margins

A ***margin*** is the area of blank space that displays to the left, right, top, and bottom of a document or worksheet. Margins are evident only if you are in Print Layout or Page Layout view or if you are in the Backstage view, previewing a document to print. To set or change margins, click the Page Layout tab. As shown in Figure 1.54, the Page Setup group enables you to change such items as margins and orientation. To change margins:

1. Click Margins in the Page Setup group on the PAGE LAYOUT tab.
2. If the margins that you intend to use are included in any of the preset margin options, click a selection. Otherwise, click Custom Margins to display the Page Setup dialog box in which you can create custom margin settings.
3. Click OK to accept the settings and close the dialog box.

You can also change margins when you click Print on the File tab.

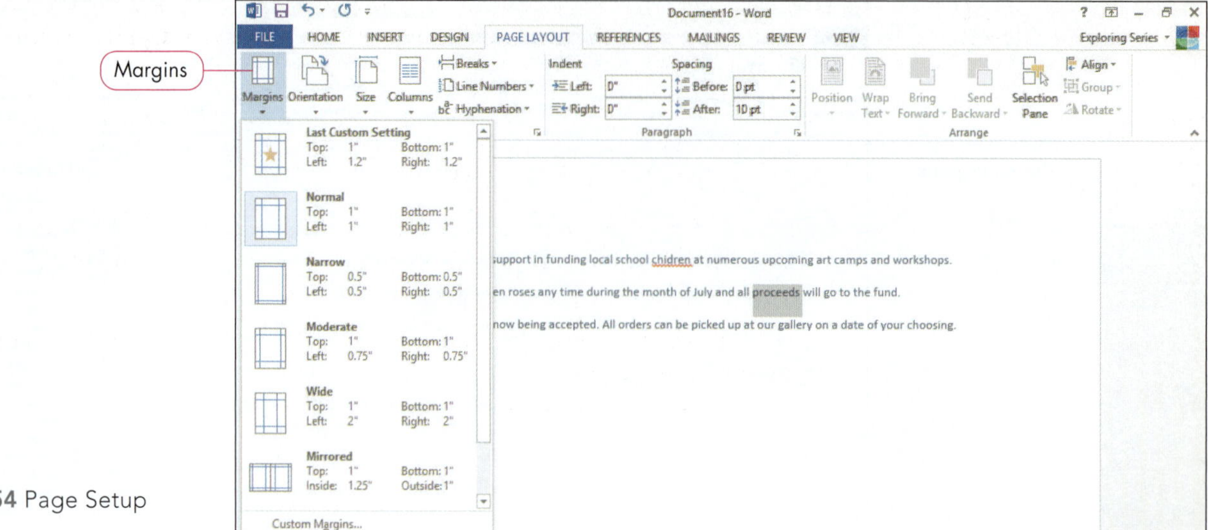

FIGURE 1.54 Page Setup Group

Changing Page Orientation

STEP 3

Documents and worksheets can be displayed in ***portrait*** orientation or in ***landscape***. A page displayed or printed in portrait orientation is taller than it is wide. A page in landscape orientation is wider than it is tall. Word documents are usually more attractive displayed in portrait orientation, whereas Excel worksheets are often more suitable in landscape. To select page orientation, click Orientation in the Page Setup group on the Page Layout tab (see Figure 1.55). Orientation is also an option in the Print area of the Backstage view.

Using the Page Setup Dialog Box

The Page Setup group contains the most commonly used page options in the particular Office application. Some are unique to Excel, and others are more applicable to Word. Other less common settings are available in the Page Setup dialog box only, displayed when you click the Page Setup Dialog Box Launcher. The subsequent dialog box includes options for customizing margins, selecting page orientation, centering vertically, printing gridlines, and creating headers and footers, although some of those options are available only when working with Word; others are unique to Excel. Figure 1.55 shows both the Excel and Word Page Setup dialog boxes.

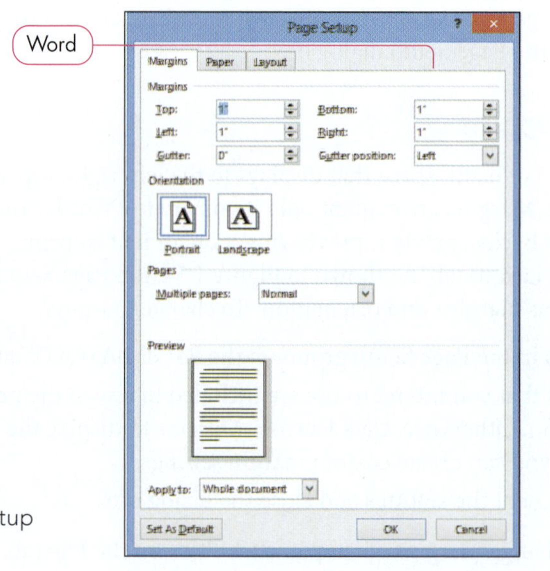

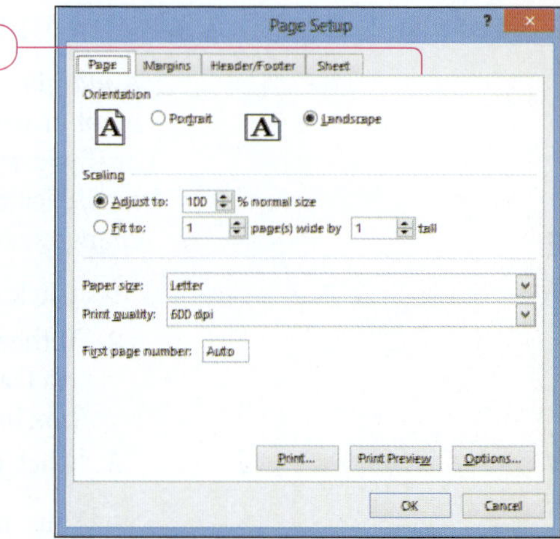

FIGURE 1.55 Page Setup Dialog Boxes

1. Give two ways to resize an object, such as a picture, that has been inserted in a document. ***p. 61***
2. Often, an Office application will identify a word as misspelled that is not actually misspelled. How can that happen? If a word is flagged as misspelled, how can you correct it (or ignore it if it is not actually an error)? ***p. 63***
3. Give two ways to change a document from a portrait orientation to landscape. Identify at least one document type that you think would be better suited for landscape orientation rather than portrait. ***p. 66***
4. What dialog box includes options for selecting margins, centering vertically, and changing page orientation? ***p. 66***

Hands-On Exercises

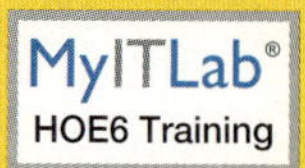

6 Insert Tab Tasks, Page Layout Tab Tasks, and Review Tab Tasks

A series of enrichment programs at the Spotted Begonia Art Gallery is nearing kickoff. You are helping plan a ceremony to commemorate the occasion. To encourage interest and participation, you will edit a PowerPoint presentation that is to be shown to civic groups, the local retiree association, and to city and county leaders to solicit additional funding. You know that pictures add energy to a presentation when used appropriately, so you will check for those elements, adding whatever is necessary. A major concern is making sure the presentation is error free and that it is available in print so that meeting participants can review it later. As a reminder, you also plan to have available a handout giving the time and date of the dedication ceremony. You will use the Insert tab to work with illustrations and the Review tab to check for errors, and you will use Word to generate an attractive handout as a reminder of the date.

Skills covered: Check Spelling and Use the Thesaurus • Insert Pictures • Change Margins and Page Orientation

STEP 1 » CHECK SPELLING AND USE THE THESAURUS

As you check the PowerPoint presentation that will be shown to local groups, you make sure no misspellings or grammatical mistakes exist. You also use the Thesaurus to find a suitable substitution for a word you feel should be replaced. Refer to Figure 1.56 as you complete Step 1.

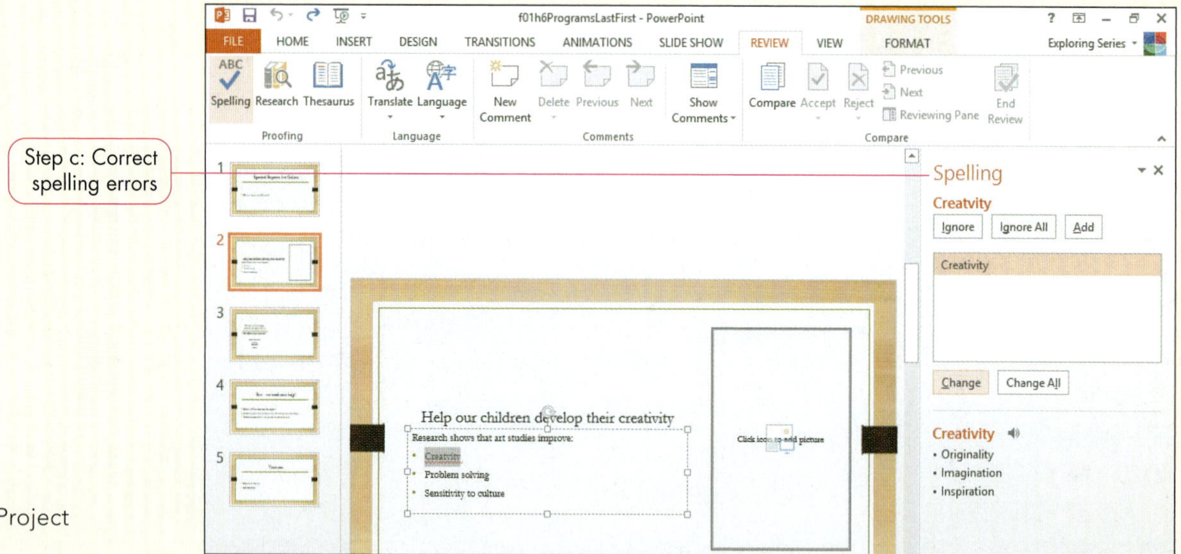

FIGURE 1.56 Project Presentation

a. Navigate to the Start screen. Scroll across the tiles, if necessary, and click **PowerPoint 2013**. Click **Open Other Presentations**. Open *f01h6Programs* and save the document as **f01h6Programs_LastFirst** in the Promotional Print folder (a subfolder of Artists) you created.

   The PowerPoint presentation opens, with Slide 1 shown in Normal view.

b. Click the **SLIDE SHOW tab** and click **From Beginning** in the Start Slide Show group to view the presentation. Click to advance from one slide to another. After the last slide, click to return to Normal view.

c. Click the **REVIEW tab** and click **Spelling** in the Proofing group. Correct any words that are misspelled by clicking the correction and clicking Change or Ignore in the Spelling pane. Click **Change** to accept *Creativity* on Slide 2, click **workshops** and click **Change** on Slide 3, and click **Change** to accept *Thank* for Slide 5. Refer to Figure 1.56. Click **OK** when the spell check is complete and close the pane.

d. Click **Slide 2** in the Slides pane on the left. Double-click the bulleted word *Creativity*, click **Thesaurus** in the Proofing group, point to *Imagination* in the Thesaurus pane, click the arrow to the right of the word, and then select **Insert**.

The word *Creativity* is replaced with the word *Imagination*.

e. Click the **Close (X) button** in the top-right corner of the Thesaurus pane.

f. Save the presentation.

STEP 2 » INSERT PICTURES

Although the presentation provides the necessary information and encourages viewers to become active participants in the enrichment programs, you believe that pictures might make it a little more exciting. Where appropriate, you will include a picture. Refer to Figure 1.57 as you complete Step 2.

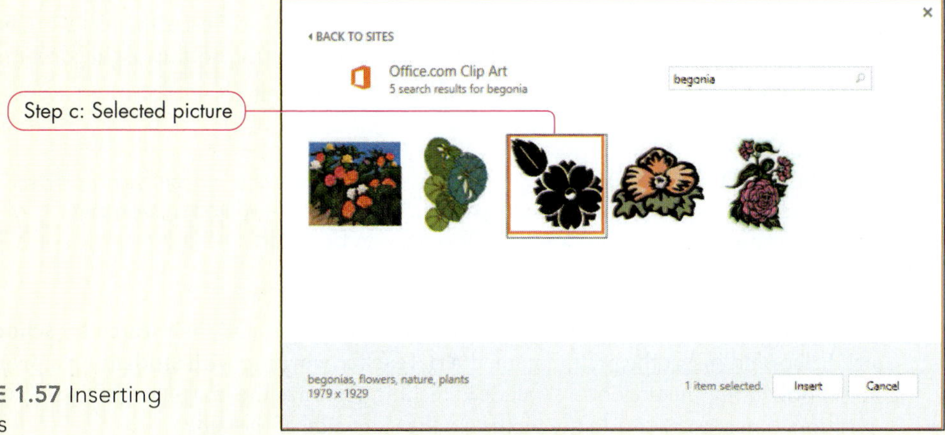

FIGURE 1.57 Inserting Pictures

a. Click **Slide 2** in the Slides pane on the left, if necessary. Click the **INSERT tab** and click **Online Pictures** in the Images group.

The Insert Pictures pane displays on the screen.

> **TROUBLESHOOTING:** You can add your own pictures to slides using the Pictures command. Or you can copy and paste images directly from a Web page.

b. Type **begonia** in the **Office.com Clip Art search box** and press **Enter**.

You will identify pictures that may be displayed on Slide 2.

c. Click to select the black flower shown in Figure 1.57 or use a similar image. Click **Insert**.

The picture may not be placed as you would like, but you will move and resize it in the next substep as necessary. Also, notice that the picture is selected, as indicated by the box and handles surrounding it.

> **TROUBLESHOOTING:** It is very easy to make the mistake of inserting duplicate pictures on a slide, perhaps because you clicked the image more than once in the task pane. If that should happen, you can remove any unwanted picture by clicking to select it and pressing Delete.

d. Click a corner handle—the small square on the border of the picture. Make sure the mouse pointer appears as a double-headed arrow. Drag to resize the image so that it fits well on the slide. Click in the center of the picture. The mouse pointer should appear as a four-headed arrow. Drag the picture slightly to the right corner of the slide. Make sure the picture is still selected (it should be surrounded by a box and handles). If it is not selected, click to select it.

> **TROUBLESHOOTING:** You may not need to perform this substep if the picture came in as desired. Proceed to the next substep if this occurs.

e. Click **Slide 5** in the Slides pane on the left. Click the **INSERT tab** and select **Online Pictures**. Type **happy art** in the **Office.com Clip Art search box** and press **Enter**. Click the **Three handprints picture** and click **Insert**.

   A picture is placed on the final slide.

f. Click to select the picture, if necessary. Drag a corner handle to resize the picture. Click the center of the picture and drag the picture to reposition it in the bottom-right corner of the slide, as shown in Figure 1.57.

> **TROUBLESHOOTING:** You can only move the picture when the mouse pointer looks like a four-headed arrow. If instead you drag a handle, the picture will be resized instead of moved. Click Undo on the Quick Access Toolbar and begin again.

g. Click **Slide 3**. Click the **INSERT tab**, click **Online Pictures**, and then search for **school art**. Select and insert the picture named **Art Teacher working with student on a project in school**. Using the previously practiced technique, resize the image height to **3.9"** and position as necessary to add the picture to the right side of the slide.

h. Save the presentation and exit PowerPoint. Submit your file based on your instructor's directions.

STEP 3 » CHANGE MARGINS AND PAGE ORIENTATION

You are ready to finalize the flyer promoting the workshops, but before printing it you want to see how it will look. You wonder if it would be better in landscape or portrait orientation, so you will try both. After adjusting the margins, you are ready to save the flyer for later printing and distribution. Refer to Figure 1.58 as you complete Step 3.

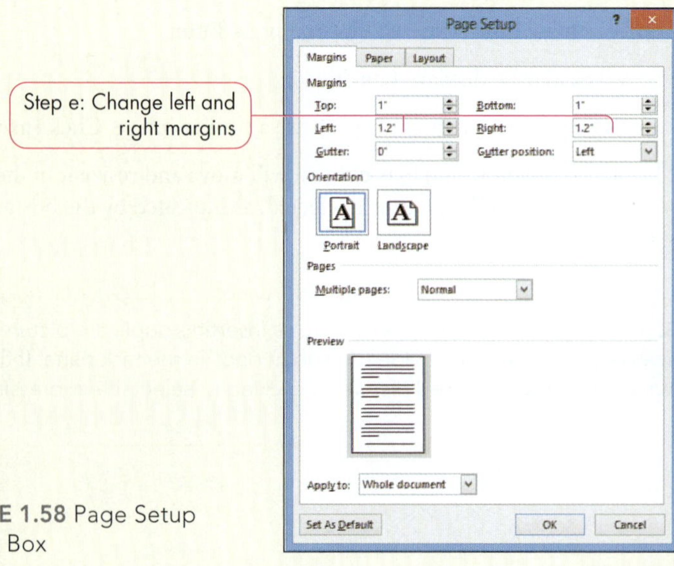

FIGURE 1.58 Page Setup Dialog Box

a. Navigate to the Start screen. Scroll across the tiles, if necessary, and click **Word 2013**. Click **Open Other Documents**. Open *f01h6Handout* and save the document as **f01h6Handout_LastFirst** in the Promotional Print folder (a subfolder of Artists) you created.

b. Click the **PAGE LAYOUT tab**, click **Orientation** in the Page Setup group, and then select **Landscape** to view the flyer in landscape orientation.

   You want to see how the handout will look in landscape orientation.

c. Click the **FILE tab**, click **Print**, and then click **Next Page** and click **Previous Page** (right- and left-pointing arrows at the bottom center of the preview page).

   The second page of the handout shows only the last two bullets and the contact information. You can see that the two-page layout is not an attractive option.

d. Click the **Back arrow** in the top-left corner. Click **Undo** on the Quick Access Toolbar. Click the **FILE tab** and click **Print**.

   The document fits on one page. Portrait orientation is a much better choice for the handout.

e. Click the **Back arrow** in the top-left corner. Click the **PAGE LAYOUT tab** if necessary, click **Margins** in the Page Setup group, and then select **Custom Margins**. Click the **spin arrow** beside the left margin box to increase the margin to **1.2**. Similarly, change the right margin to **1.2**. Refer to Figure 1.58. Click **OK**.

f. Save the document and exit Word. Submit your file based on your instructor's directions.

Chapter Objectives Review

After reading this chapter, you have accomplished the following objectives:

1. **Log in with your Microsoft account.**
   - Your Microsoft account connects you to all of Microsoft's Internet-based resources.
2. **Identify the Start screen components.**
   - The Start screen has a sleek, clean interface that is made up of tiles and Charms.
3. **Interact with the Start screen.**
   - Customize the Start screen to access programs and apps.
4. **Access the desktop.**
   - Simplified to accommodate mobile devices, laptops, and desktops.
5. **Use File Explorer.**
   - Understand and customize the interface: Change the view to provide as little or as much detail as you need.
   - Work with groups on the Navigation Pane: Provides access to all resources, folders, and files.
6. **Work with folders and files.**
   - Create a folder: A well-named folder structure can be created in File Explorer or within a program as you save a file.
   - Open, rename, and delete folders and files: File Explorer can be used to perform these tasks.
   - Save a file: When saving a file for the first time, you need to indicate the location and the name of the file.
7. **Select, copy, and move multiple files and folders.**
   - Select multiple files and folders: Folders and files can be selected as a group.
   - Copy and move files and folders: Folders and the files within them can be easily moved to the same or a different drive.
8. **Identify common interface components.**
   - Use the Backstage view and the Quick Access Toolbar: The Backstage view can perform several commands.
   - Familiarize yourself with the Ribbon: Provides access to common tasks.
   - Use the status bar: The status bar provides information relative to the open file and quick access to View and Zoom level options.
9. **Get Office Help.**
   - Use Office Help: The Help button links to online resources and technical support.
   - Use Enhanced ScreenTips: Provides the purpose of a command button as you point to it.
   - Get help with dialog boxes: Use the Help button in the top-right corner of a dialog box to get help relevant to the task.
10. **Open a file.**
    - Create a new file: A document can be created as a blank document or with a template.
    - Open a file using the Open dialog box: Previously saved files can be located and opened using a dialog box.
    - Open a file using the Recent Documents list: Documents that you have worked with recently display here.
    - Open a file from the Templates list: Templates are a convenient way to save time when designing a document.
11. **Print a file.**
    - Check and change orientation or perform other commands related to the look of your file before printing.
12. **Close a file and application.**
    - Close files you are not working on to avoid becoming overwhelmed.
13. **Select and edit text.**
    - Select text to edit: Commit to memory: "Select, then do."
    - Use the Mini toolbar: Provides instant access to common formatting commands after text is selected.
    - Apply font attributes: These can be applied to selected text with toggle commands.
    - Change the font: Choose from a set of fonts found within a Office applications.
    - Change the font size, color, and attributes: These command are located in the Font group on the Ribbon.
14. **Use the Clipboard group commands.**
    - Copy formats with the Format Painter: Copy formatting features from one section of text to another.
    - Move and copy text: Text can be selected, copied, and mov between applications or within the same application.
    - Use the Office Clipboard: This pane stores up to 24 cut or copied selections for use later on in your computing sessio
15. **Use the Editing group commands.**
    - Find and replace text: Finds each occurrence of a series of characters and replaces them with another series.
    - Use advanced find and replace feature: Change the format every occurrence of a series of characters.
16. **Insert objects.**
    - Insert pictures: You can insert pictures from a CD or other media, or from an online resource such as Office.com.
    - Insert and modify SmartArt: Create a diagram and to enter text to provide a visual of data.
    - Insert and format shapes: You can insert various types of lines and basic shapes.
17. **Review a file.**
    - Check spelling and grammar: All Office applications che and mark these error types as you type for later correctio
    - Use the Thesaurus: Enables you to search for synonyms.
18. **Use the Page Setup dialog box.**
    - Change margins: You can control the amount of blank spac that surrounds the text in your document.
    - Change margins and page orientations, and create heade and footers.

Key Terms Matching

Match the key terms with their definitions. Write the key term letter by the appropriate numbered definition.

a. Backstage view
b. Charms
c. Cloud storage
d. Find
e. Font
f. Format Painter
g. Group
h. Mini toolbar
i. Navigation Pane
j. Operating system
k. Quick Access Toolbar
l. Ribbon
m. OneDrive
n. Snip
o. Snipping Tool
p. Start screen
q. Subfolder
r. Tile
s. Windows 8.1.1
t. Windows 8.1.1 app

1. ______ A tool that copies all formatting from one area to another. **p. 49**

2. ______ Software that directs computer activities such as checking all components, managing system resources, and communicating with application software. **p. 2**

3. ______ A task-oriented section of the Ribbon that contains related commands. **p. 25**

4. ______ An app used to store, access, and share files and folders. **p. 2**

5. ______ Any of the several colorful block images found on the Start screen that when clicked takes you to a program, file, folder, or other Windows 8.1.1 app. **p. 3**

6. ______ A component of Office 2013 that provides a concise collection of commands related to an open file. **p. 23**

7. ______ A tool that displays near selected text that contains formatting commands. **p. 46**

8. ______ A level of folder structure indicated as a folder within another folder. **p. 10**

9. ______ An application specifically designed to run in the Start screen interface of Windows 8.1.1. **p. 3**

10. ______ A command used to locate each occurrence of a series of characters. **p. 52**

11. ______ A Windows 8.1.1 accessory program that allows you to capture a screen display so that you can save, annotate, or share it. **p. 5**

12. ______ What you see after starting your Windows 8.1.1 computer and entering your username and password. **p. 2**

13. ______ Provides handy access to commonly executed tasks such as saving a file and undoing recent actions. **p. 23**

14. ______ A Microsoft operating system released in 2012 that is available on laptops, desktops, and tablet computers. **p. 2**

15. ______ A component made up of five icons that provide similar functionality to the Start button found in previous versions of Windows. **p. 3**

16. ______ The captured screen display created by the Snipping Tool. **p. 5**

17. ______ The long bar located just beneath the title bar containing tabs, groups, and commands. **p. 25**

18. ______ Provides access to computer resources, folders, files, and networked peripherals. **p. 11**

19. ______ A technology used to store files and to work with programs that are stored in a central location on the Internet. **p. 2**

20. ______ A character design or the way characters display onscreen. **p. 45**

Multiple Choice

1. The Recent Documents list shows documents that have been previously:
   (a) Printed.
   (b) Opened.
   (c) Saved in an earlier software version.
   (d) Deleted.

2. Which of the following File Explorer features collects related data from folders and gives them a single name?
   (a) Network
   (b) Favorites
   (c) Libraries
   (d) Computer

3. When you want to copy the format of a selection but not the content, you should:
   (a) Double-click Copy in the Clipboard group.
   (b) Right-click the selection and click Copy.
   (c) Click Copy Format in the Clipboard group.
   (d) Click Format Painter in the Clipboard group.

4. Which of the following is *not* a benefit of using OneDrive?
   (a) Save your folders and files in the cloud.
   (b) Share your files and folders with others.
   (c) Hold video conferences with others.
   (d) Simultaneously work on the same document with others.

5. What does a red wavy underline in a document, spreadsheet, or presentation mean?
   (a) A word is misspelled or not recognized by the Office dictionary
   (b) A grammatical mistake exists
   (c) An apparent word usage mistake exists
   (d) A word has been replaced with a synonym

6. When you close a file:
   (a) You are prompted to save the file (unless you have made no changes since last saving it).
   (b) The application (Word, Excel, or PowerPoint) is also closed.
   (c) You must first save the file.
   (d) You must change the file name.

7. Live Preview:
   (a) Opens a predesigned document or spreadsheet that is relevant to your task.
   (b) Provides a preview of the results of a choice you are considering before you make a final selection.
   (c) Provides a preview of an upcoming Office version.
   (d) Enlarges the font onscreen.

8. You can get help when working with an Office application in which one of the following areas?
   (a) Help button
   (b) Status bar
   (c) The Backstage view
   (d) Quick Access Toolbar

9. The *Find and Replace* feature enables you to do which of the following?
   (a) Find all instances of misspelling and automatically correct (or replace) them
   (b) Find any grammatical errors and automatically correct (or replace) them
   (c) Find any specified font settings and replace them with another selection
   (d) Find any character string and replace it with another

10. A document or worksheet printed in landscape orientation is:
    (a) Taller than it is wide.
    (b) Wider than it is tall.
    (c) A document with 2" left and right margins.
    (d) A document with 2" top and bottom margins.

Practice Exercises

1 Designing Web Pages

You have been asked to make a presentation to the local business association. With the mayor's renewed emphasis on growing the local economy, many businesses are interested in establishing a Web presence. The business owners would like to know a little bit more about how Web pages are designed. In preparation for the presentation, you need to proofread and edit your PowerPoint file. This exercise follows the same set of skills as used in Hands-On Exercises 1–6 in the chapter. Refer to Figure 1.59 as you complete this exercise.

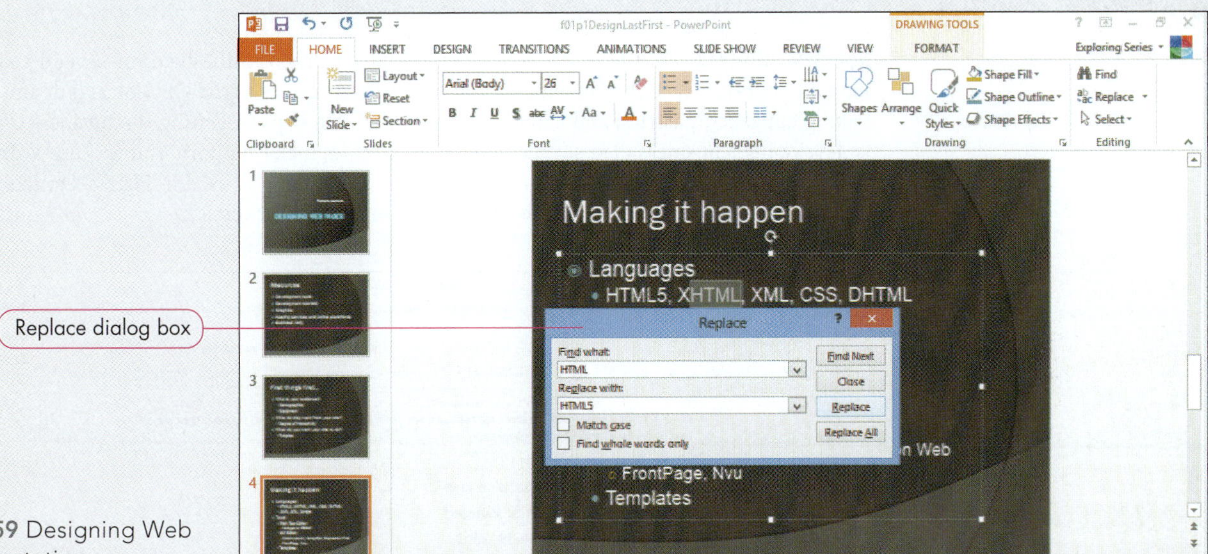

FIGURE 1.59 Designing Web Pages Presentation

a. Click **File Explorer** on the taskbar and select the location where you save your files. Click the **HOME tab** and click **New folder** in the New group. Type **Designing Web Pages** and press **Enter**. Take a snip, name it **f01p1DesignSnip_LastFirst**, and then save it in the Designing Web Pages folder. Close File Explorer.
b. Point to the bottom-right corner of your screen to display the Charms and click the **Start charm**. Scroll if necessary and click **PowerPoint 2013** to start PowerPoint. Open *f01p1Design* and save it as **f01p1Design_LastFirst** in the Designing Web Pages folder. In Slide 1, drag to select the text *Firstname Lastname* and type your own first and last names. Click an empty area of the slide to cancel the selection.
c. Click the **REVIEW tab** and click **Spelling** in the Proofing group. In the Spelling pane, click **Change** or **Ignore** to make or not make a change as needed. Most identified misspellings should be changed. The words *KompoZer* and *Nvu* are not misspelled, so you should ignore them when they are flagged. Click **OK** to end the spell check.
d. Click the **SLIDE SHOW tab**. Click **From Beginning** in the Start Slide Show group. Click each slide to view the show and press **Esc** on the last slide.
e. Click **Slide 2** in the Slides pane on the left. Drag to select the *Other tools* text and press **Backspace** on the keyboard to delete the text.
f. Click **Slide 4** in the Slides pane. Click the **HOME tab** and click **Replace** in the Editing group. Type **HTML** in the **Find what box** and **HTML5** in the **Replace with box**. Click **Find Next**. Read the slide and click **Replace** to change the first instance of *HTML*. Refer to Figure 1.59. Click **Close**.
g. Click **Replace** in the Editing group. Type **CSS** in the **Find what box** and **CSS5** in the **Replace with box**. Click **Replace All** and click **OK**. Click **Close**.
h. Drag to select the *FrontPage, Nvu* text and press **Backspace** on the keyboard to delete the text.
i. Press **Ctrl+End** to place the insertion point at the end of *Templates* and press **Enter**. Type **Database Connectivity** to create a new bulleted item.

j. Click the **FILE tab** and click **Print**. Click the **Full Page Slides arrow** and click **6 Slides Horizontal** to see a preview of all of the slides as a handout. Click the **Back arrow** and click the **HOME tab**.

k. Click **Slide 1** in the Slides pane to move to the beginning of the presentation.

l. Drag the **Zoom slider** on the status bar to the right to **130%** to magnify the text. Then use the **Zoom Slider** to return to **60%**.

m. Save and close the file. Submit your files based on your instructor's directions.

2 Upscale Bakery

You have always been interested in baking and have worked in the field for several years. You now have an opportunity to devote yourself full time to your career as the CEO of a company dedicated to baking cupcakes, pastries, and catering. One of the first steps in getting the business off the ground is developing a business plan so that you can request financial support. You will use Word to develop your business plan. This exercise follows the same set of skills as used in Hands-On Exercises 1, 3, 4, and 5 in the chapter. Refer to Figure 1.60 as you complete this exercise.

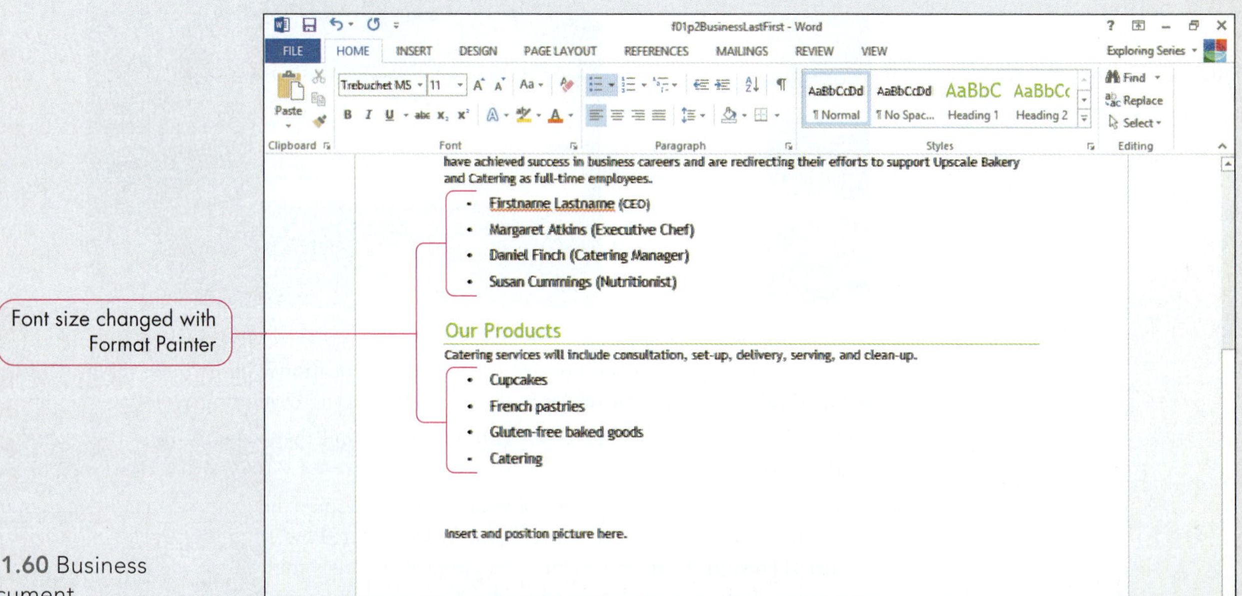

FIGURE 1.60 Business Plan Document

a. Click **File Explorer** on the taskbar and select the location where you save your files. Click the **HOME tab** and click **New folder** in the New group. Type **Business Plan** and press **Enter**.

   Take a snip, name it **f01p2BusinessSnip_LastFirst**, and save it in the Business Plan folder. Close File Explorer.

b. Point to the bottom-right corner of your screen to display the Charms and click the **Start charm**. Scroll if necessary and click **Word 2013** to start Word. Open *f01p2Business* and save it as **f01p2Business_LastFirst** in the Business Plan folder.

c. Click the **REVIEW tab** and click **Spelling & Grammar** in the Proofing group. Click **Change** for all suggestions.

d. Drag the paragraphs beginning with *Our Staff* and ending with *(Nutritionist)*. Click the **HOME tab** and click **Cut** in the Clipboard group. Click to the left of *Our Products* and click **Paste**.

e. Select the text *Your name* in the first bullet and replace it with your first and last names. Select that entire bullet and use the Mini toolbar to use Live Preview to see some other Font sizes. Then click **11** to increase the size.

f. Double-click the **Format Painter** in the Clipboard group on the HOME tab. Drag the Format Painter to change the other *Our Staff* bullets to **11**. Drag all four *Our Products* bullets. Click the **Format Painter button** to toggle it off and click outside of the text to deselect it. Refer to Figure 1.60.

g. Select the last line in the document, which says *Insert and position picture here.*, and press **Delete**. Click the **INSERT tab** and click **Online Pictures** in the Illustrations group.
- Click in the **Office.com Clip Art search box**, type **Cupcakes**, and then press **Enter**.
- Select **Cupcake with a single birthday candle** or select any image and click **Insert**. Do not deselect the image.
- Click the **PICTURE TOOLS FORMAT tab**, if necessary, click the **More button** in the Picture Styles group, and then click the **Soft Edge Rectangle** (sixth from the left on the top row).
- Click outside the picture.

h. Click the **FILE tab** and click **Print**. Change *Normal Margins* to **Moderate Margins**. Click the **Back arrow**.

i. Click the picture and click **Center** in the Paragraph group on the HOME tab.

j. Save and close the file. Submit your files based on your instructor's directions.

3 Best Friends Pet Care

You and a friend are starting a pet sitting service and have a few clients already. Billing will be a large part of your record keeping, so you are planning ahead by developing a series of folders to maintain those records. This exercise follows the same set of skills as used in Hands-On Exercises 1, 2, and 5 in the chapter. Refer to Figure 1.61 as you complete this exercise.

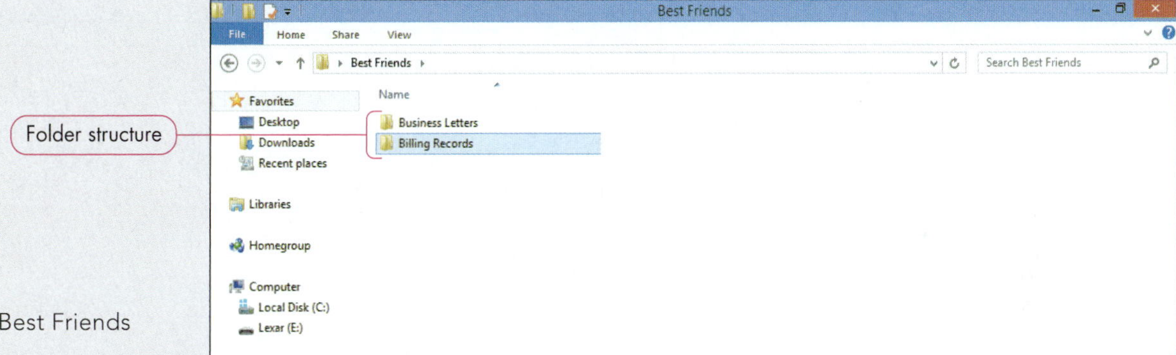

FIGURE 1.61 Best Friends Pet Care

a. Click **File Explorer** on the taskbar and select the location where you save your files. Click the **Home tab** and click **New folder** in the New group. Type **Best Friends** and press **Enter**.

b. Double-click **Best Friends** in the Content pane to open the folder. Create new subfolders as follows:
- Click the **Home tab** and click **New folder** in the New group. Type **Business Letters** and press **Enter**.
- Click the **Home tab** and click **New folder** in the New group. Type **Billing Records** and press **Enter**. Compare your results to Figure 1.61. Take a snip and name it **f01p3FriendsSnip_LastFirst**. Save it in the Billing Records subfolder of the Best Friends folder. Close File Explorer.

c. Navigate to the Start screen and click on **Word 2013**. Click **Open Other Documents** and open *f01p3Friends*. Save it as **f01p3Friends_LastFirst** in the Business Letters subfolder of the Best Friends folder.

d. Use *Find and Replace* to replace the text *Your Name* with your name by doing the following:
- Click **Replace** in the Editing group on the HOME tab.
- Type **Your name** in the **Find what box**. Type your first and last names in the **Replace with box**.
- Click **Replace** and click **OK**. Close the *Find and Replace* dialog box. Close, save changes to the document, and exit Word.

e. Click **File Explorer** on the taskbar so that you can rename one of your folders:
   - Click **Computer** in the Navigation Pane.
   - In the Content pane, navigate to the drive where you earlier created the Best Friends folder. Double-click the **Best Friends folder**.
   - Right-click **Billing Records**, click **Rename**, type **Accounting Records**, and then press **Enter**.

f. Take a snip and name it **f01p3FolderSnip_LastFirst**. Save it in the Business Letters subfolder of the Best Friends folder. Submit your files based on your instructor's directions.

Mid-Level Exercises

1 Reference Letter

You are an instructor at a local community college. A student has asked you to provide her with a letter of reference for a job application. You have used Word to prepare the letter, but now you need to make a few changes before it is finalized.

a. Open File Explorer. Create a new folder named **References** in the location where you are saving your student files. Take a snip, name it **f01m1ReferencesSnip_LastFirst**, and save it in the References folder. Close File Explorer.

b. Start Word. Open *f01m1Letter* and save it in the References folder as **f01m1Letter_LastFirst**.

c. Select the date and point to several font sizes in the Mini toolbar. Use the Live Preview to compare them. Click **11**.

d. Double-click the date and use the **Format Painter** to change the rest of the letter to font size 11.

e. Apply bold to the student's name, *Stacy VanPatten*, in the first sentence.

f. Correct all errors using Spelling & Grammar. Her last name is spelled correctly. Use the Thesaurus to find a synonym for *intelligent* and replace wih **gifted**. Change the *an* to *a* just before the new word. Replace each occurrence of *Stacy* with **Stacey**.

g. Move the last paragraph—beginning with *In my opinion*—to position it before the second paragraph—beginning with *Stacey is a gifted*.

h. Move the insertion point to the beginning of the document.

i. Change the margins to **Narrow**.

j. Preview the document as it will appear when printed.

k. Save and close the file. Submit your files based on your instructor's directions.

2 Medical Monitoring

You are enrolled in a Health Informatics program of study in which you learn to manage databases related to health fields. For a class project, your instructor requires that you monitor your blood pressure, recording your findings in an Excel worksheet. You have recorded the week's data and will now make a few changes before printing the worksheet for submission.

a. Open File Explorer. Create a new folder named **Medical** in the location where you are saving your student files. Take a snip, name it **f01m2MedicalSnip_LastFirst**, and save it in the Medical folder. Close File Explorer.

b. Start Excel. Open *f01m2Tracker* and save it as **f01m2Tracker_LastFirst** in the Medical folder.

c. Preview the worksheet as it will appear when printed. Change the orientation of the worksheet to **Landscape**. Preview the worksheet again.

d. Click in the cell to the right of *Name* and type your first and last names. Press **Enter**.

e. Change the font of the text in **cell C1** to **Verdana**. Use Live Preview to try some font sizes. Change the font size to **20**.

f. Check the spelling for the worksheet.

g. Get help on showing decimal places. You want to increase the decimal places for the values in **cells E22**, **F22**, and **G22** so that each value shows two places to the right of the decimal. Use Excel Help to learn how to do that. You might use *Increase Decimals* as a Search term. When you find the answer, select the three cells and increase the decimal places to **2**.

h. Click **cell A1** and insert a picture of your choice related to blood pressure. Be sure the image includes content from Office.com. Resize and position the picture so that it displays in an attractive manner. Format the picture with **Soft Edges** set to **4 pt**. Change the margins to **Wide**.

i. Open the Backstage view and adjust print settings to print two copies. You will not actually print two copies unless directed by your instructor.

j. Save and close the file. Submit your files based on your instructor's directions.

3 Today's Musical Artists

With a few of your classmates, you will use PowerPoint to create a single presentation on your favorite musical artists. Each student must create at least one slide and then all of the slides will be added to the presentation. Because everyone's schedule is varied, you should use either your Outlook account or OneDrive to pass the presentation file among the group.

a. Open File Explorer. Create a new folder named **Musical** in the location where you are saving your student files. Take a snip, name it **f01m3MusicalSnip_LastFirst**, and then save it in the Musical folder. Close File Explorer.

b. Start PowerPoint. Create a new presentation and save it as **f01m3Music_GroupName** in the Musical folder.

c. Add one slide that contains the name of the artist, the genre, and two or three interesting facts about the artist.

d. Insert a picture of the artist or clip art that represents the artist.

e. Put your name on the slide that you created. Save the presentation.

f. Pass the presentation to the next student so that he or she can perform the same tasks and save the presentation before passing it on to the next student. Continue until all group members have created a slide in the presentation.

g. Save and close the file. Submit your file based on your instructor's directions.

Beyond the Classroom

Fitness Planner

You will use Microsoft Excel to develop a fitness planner. Open *f01b2Exercise* and save it as **f01b2Exercise_LastFirst**. Because the fitness planner is a template, the exercise categories are listed, but without actual data. You will personalize the planner. Change the orientation to **Landscape**. Move the contents of **cell A2** (*Exercise Planner*) to **cell A1**. Click **cell A8** and use the Format Painter to copy the format of that selection to **cells A5** and **A6**. Increase the font size of **cell A1** to **26**. Use Excel Help to learn how to insert a header and put your name in the header. Begin the fitness planner, entering at least one activity in each category (warm-up, aerobics, strength, and cool-down). Submit as directed by your instructor.

Household Records

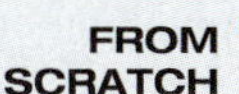

Use Microsoft Excel to create a detailed record of your household appliances and other items of value that are in your home. In case of burglary or disaster, an insurance claim is expedited if you are able to itemize what was lost along with identifying information such as serial numbers. You will then make a copy of the record on another storage device for safekeeping outside your home (in case your home is destroyed by a fire or weather-related catastrophe). Connect a flash drive to your computer and then use File Explorer to create a folder on the hard drive titled **Home Records**. Design a worksheet listing at least five fictional appliances and electronic equipment along with the serial number of each. Save the workbook as **f01b3Household_LastFirst** in the Home Records folder. Close the workbook and exit Excel. Use File Explorer to copy the Home Records folder from the hard drive to your flash drive. Use the Snipping Tool to create a full-screen snip of the screen display. Save it as **f01b3Disaster_LastFirst** in the Home Records folder. Close all open windows and submit as directed by your instructor.

Meetings

SOFT SKILLS CASE

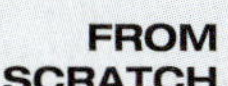

After watching the Meetings video, you will use File Explorer to create a series of folders and subfolders to organize meetings by date. Each folder should be named by month, day, and year. Three subfolders should be created for each meeting. The subfolders should be named **Agenda**, **Handouts**, and **Meeting Notes**. Use the Snipping Tool to create a full-screen snip of the screen display. Save it as **f01b4Meetings_LastFirs**t. Submit as directed by your instructor.

Capstone Exercise

You are a member of the Student Government Association (SGA) at your college. As a community project, the SGA is sponsoring a Stop Smoking drive designed to provide information on the health risks posed by smoking cigarettes and to offer solutions to those who want to quit. The SGA has partnered with the local branch of the American Cancer Society as well as the outreach program of the local hospital to sponsor free educational awareness seminars. As the secretary for the SGA, you will help prepare a PowerPoint presentation that will be displayed on plasma screens around campus and used in student seminars. You will use Microsoft Office to help with those tasks.

Manage Files and Folders

You will open, review, and save an Excel worksheet providing data on the personal monetary cost of smoking cigarettes over a period of years.

a. Create a folder called **SGA Drive**.

b. Start Excel. Open *f01c1Cost* from the student data files and save it in the SGA Drive folder as **f01c1Cost_LastFirst**.

c. Click **cell A10** and type your first and last names. Press **Enter**.

Modify the Font

To highlight some key figures on the worksheet, you will format those cells with additional font attributes.

a. Draw attention to the high cost of smoking for 10, 20, and 30 years by changing the font color in **cells G3 through I4** to **Red**.

b. Italicize the Annual Cost cells (**F3** and **F4**).

c. Click **Undo** on the Quick Access Toolbar to remove the italics. Click **Redo** to return the text to italics.

Insert a Picture

You will add a picture to the worksheet and then resize it and position it.

a. Click **cell G7** and insert an online picture appropriate for the topic of smoking.

b. Resize the picture and reposition it near cell B7.

c. Click outside the picture to deselect it.

Preview Print, Change Page Layout, and Print

To get an idea of how the worksheet will look when printed, you will preview the worksheet. Then you will change the orientation and margins before printing it.

a. Preview the document as it will appear when printed.

b. Change the page orientation to **Landscape**. Click the **PAGE LAYOUT tab** and change the margins to **Narrow**.

c. Preview the document as it will appear when printed.

d. Adjust the print settings to print two copies. You will not actually print two copies unless directed by your instructor.

e. Save and close the file.

Find and Replace

You have developed a PowerPoint presentation that you will use to present to student groups and for display on plasma screens across campus. The presentation is designed to increase awareness of the health problems associated with smoking. The PowerPoint presentation has come back from the reviewers with only one comment: A reviewer suggested that you spell out Centers for Disease Control and Prevention, instead of abbreviating it. You do not remember exactly which slide or slides the abbreviation might have been on, so you use *Find and Replace* to make the change quickly.

a. Start PowerPoint. Open *f01c1Quit* and save it in the SGA Drive folder as **f01c1Quit_LastFirst**.

b. Replace all occurrences of *CDC* with **Centers for Disease Control and Prevention**.

Cut and Paste and Insert a Text Box

The Mark Twain quote on Slide 1 might be more effective on the last slide in the presentation, so you will cut and paste it there in a text box.

a. On Slide 1, select the entire Mark Twain quote by clicking on the placeholder border. When the border is solid, the entire placeholder and its contents are selected.

b. On Slide 22, paste the quote, reposition it more attractively, and then format it in a larger font size.

Check Spelling and Change View

Before you call the presentation complete, you will spell check it and view it as a slide show.

a. Check spelling. The word *hairlike* is not misspelled, so it should not be corrected.

b. View the slide show and take the smoking quiz. Click after the last slide to return to the presentation.

c. Save and close the presentation. Exit PowerPoint. Submit both files included in this project as directed by your instructor.

Excel

Introduction to Excel

CHAPTER 1

What Is a Spreadsheet?

Yuri Arcurs/Shutterstock

OBJECTIVES

AFTER YOU READ THIS CHAPTER, YOU WILL BE ABLE TO:

CASE STUDY | OK Office Systems

You are an assistant manager at OK Office Systems (OKOS) in Oklahoma City. OKOS sells a wide range of computer systems, peripherals, and furniture for small- and medium-sized organizations in the metropolitan area. To compete against large, global, big-box office supply stores, OKOS provides competitive pricing by ordering directly from local manufacturers rather than dealing with distributors.

Alesha Bennett, the general manager, asked you to calculate the retail price, sale price, and profit analysis for selected items on sale this month. Using markup rates provided by Alesha, you need to calculate the retail price, the amount OKOS charges its customers for the products. For the sale, Alesha wants to give customers between a 10% and 30% discount on select items. You need to use those discount rates to calculate the sale prices. Finally, you will calculate the profit margin to determine the percentage of the final sale price over the cost.

After you create the initial pricing spreadsheet, you will be able to change values and see that the formulas update the results automatically. In addition, you will be able to insert data for additional sale items or delete an item based on the manager's decision.

Although your experience with Microsoft Office Excel 2013 may be limited, you are excited to apply your knowledge and skills to your newly assigned responsibility. In the Hands-On Exercises for this chapter, you will create and format the analytical spreadsheet to practice the skills you learn.

Introduction to Spreadsheets

Organizing, calculating, and evaluating quantitative data are important skills needed today for personal and managerial decision making. You track expenses for your household budget, maintain a savings plan, and determine what amount you can afford for a house or car payment. Retail managers create and analyze their organizations' annual budgets, sales projections, and inventory records. Charitable organizations track the donations they receive, the distribution of those donations, and overhead expenditures.

You can use a spreadsheet to maintain data and perform calculations. A ***spreadsheet*** is an electronic file that contains a grid of columns and rows used to organize related data and to display results of calculations, enabling interpretation of quantitative data for decision making.

Performing calculations using a calculator and entering the results into a ledger can lead to inaccurate values. If an input value is incorrect or needs to be updated, you have to recalculate the results manually, which is time-consuming and can lead to inaccuracies. A spreadsheet makes data entry changes easy. If the formulas are correctly constructed, the results recalculate automatically and accurately, saving time and reducing room for error.

In this section, you will learn how to design spreadsheets. In addition, you will explore the Excel window and learn the name of each window element. Then, you will enter text, values, and dates in a spreadsheet.

Exploring the Excel Window

In Excel, a ***worksheet*** is a single spreadsheet that typically contains descriptive labels, numeric values, formulas, functions, and graphical representations of data. A ***workbook*** is a collection of one or more related worksheets contained within a single file. By default, new workbooks contain one worksheet. Storing multiple worksheets within one workbook helps organize related data together in one file and enables you to perform calculations among the worksheets within the workbook. For example, you can create a budget workbook of 13 worksheets, one for each month to store your personal income and expenses and a final worksheet to calculate totals across the entire year.

Excel contains the standard interface of Microsoft Office applications:

- **Quick Access Toolbar:** Save, Undo, and Redo/Repeat commands
- **Title bar:** File name (such as Book1) and software name (such as Excel)
- **Control buttons:** Microsoft Excel Help, Full Screen Mode, Minimize, Restore Down, and Close
- **Ribbon:** Commands (such as Align Left) organized within groups (such as Alignment) on various tabs (such as Home)
- **Scroll bars:** Tools to scroll vertically and horizontally through a worksheet

Identify Excel Window Elements

Figure 1.1 identifies elements specific to the Excel window, and Table 1.1 lists and describes the Excel window elements.

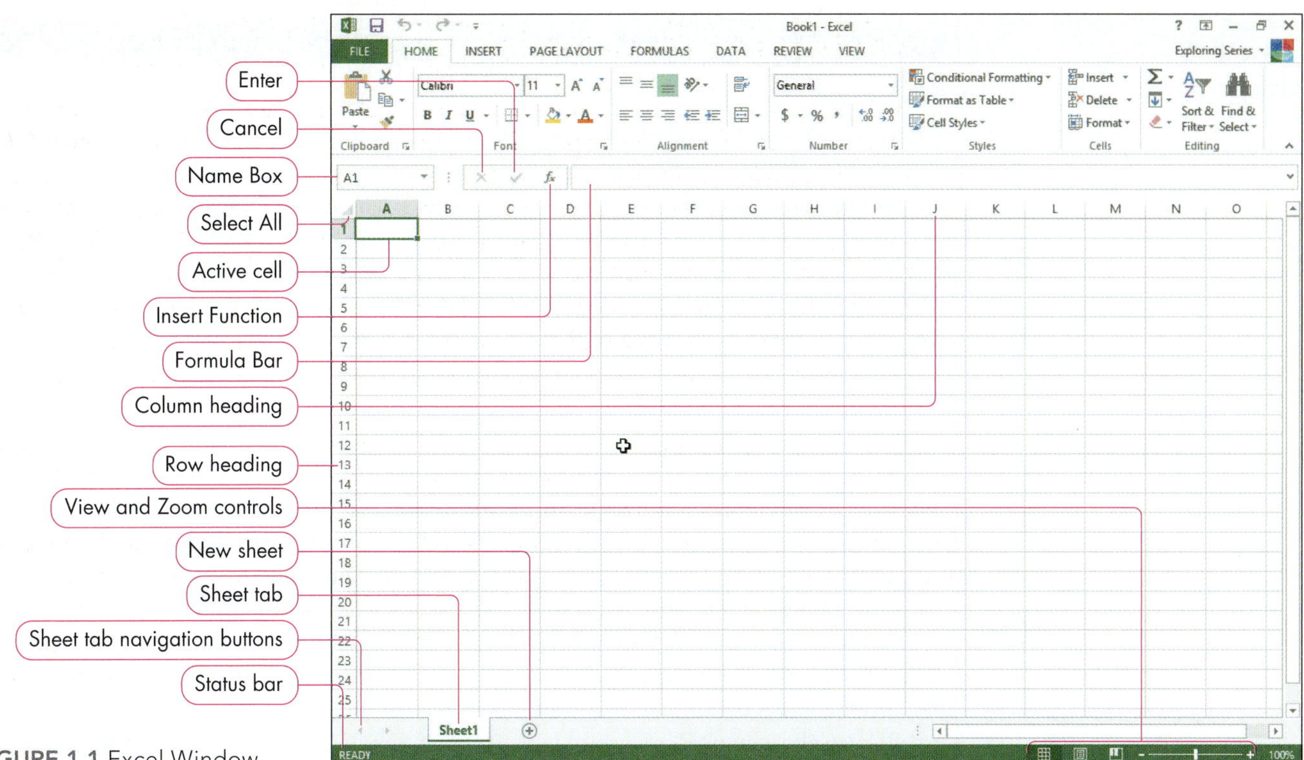

FIGURE 1.1 Excel Window

TABLE 1.1 Excel Elements

Element	Description
Name Box	The ***Name Box*** is an identifier that displays the address of the current cell in the worksheet. Use the Name Box to go to a cell, assign a name to one or more cells, or select a function.
Cancel	When you enter or edit data, click Cancel to cancel the data entry or edit and revert back to the previous data in the cell, if any. The Cancel icon changes from gray to red when you position the mouse pointer over it.
Enter	When you enter or edit data, click Enter to accept data typed in the active cell and keep the current cell active. The Enter icon changes from gray to blue when you position the mouse pointer over it.
Insert Function	Click to display the Insert Function dialog box to search for and select a function to insert into the active cell. The Insert Function icon changes from gray to green when you position the mouse pointer over it.
Formula Bar	The ***Formula Bar*** shows the contents of the active cell. You can enter or edit cell contents here or directly in the active cell. Drag the bottom border of the Formula Bar down to increase the height of the Formula Bar to display large amounts of data or a long formula contained in the active cell.
Select All	The triangle at the intersection of the row and column headings in the top-left corner of the worksheet. Click it to select everything contained in the active worksheet.
Column headings	The letters above the columns, such as A, B, C, and so on.
Row headings	The numbers to the left of the rows, such as 1, 2, 3, and so on.
Active cell	The active cell is the current cell, which is indicated by a dark green border.
Sheet tab	A ***sheet tab*** shows the name of a worksheet contained in the workbook. When you create a new Excel workbook, the default worksheet is named Sheet1.
New sheet	Inserts a new worksheet to the right of the current worksheet.
Sheet tab navigation buttons	If your workbook contains several worksheets, Excel may not show all the sheet tabs at the same time. Use the buttons to display the first, previous, next, or last worksheet.

TABLE 1.1 Excel Elements *(continued)*

Element	Description
Status bar	Displays information about a selected command or operation in progress. For example, it displays *Select destination and press ENTER or choose Paste* after you use the Copy command.
View controls	Click a view control to display the worksheet in Normal, Page Layout, or Page Break Preview. Normal view displays the worksheet without showing margins, headers, footers, and page breaks. Page Layout view shows the margins, header and footer area, and a ruler. Page Break Preview indicates where the worksheet will be divided into pages.
Zoom control	Drag the zoom control to increase the size of the worksheet onscreen to see more or less of the worksheet data.

Identify Columns, Rows, and Cells

A worksheet contains columns and rows, with each column and row assigned a heading. Columns are assigned alphabetical headings from columns A to Z, continuing from AA to AZ, and then from BA to BZ until XFD, which is the last of the possible 16,384 columns. Rows have numeric headings ranging from 1 to 1,048,576.

The intersection of a column and row is a ***cell***; a total of more than 17 billion cells are available in a worksheet. Each cell has a unique ***cell address***, identified by first its column letter and then its row number. For example, the cell at the intersection of column A and row 9 is cell A9. Cell references are useful when referencing data in formulas, or in navigation.

Navigate In and Among Worksheets

The ***active cell*** is the current cell. Excel displays a dark green border around the active cell in the worksheet, and the cell address of the active cell appears in the Name Box. The contents of the active cell, or the formula used to calculate the results of the active cell, appear in the Formula Bar. You can change the active cell by using the mouse to click in a different cell. If you work in a large worksheet, use the vertical and horizontal scroll bars to display another area of the worksheet and click in the desired cell to make it the active cell.

To navigate to a new cell, click it or use the arrow keys on the keyboard. When you press Enter, the next cell down in the same column becomes the active cell. Table 1.2 lists the keyboard navigation methods. The Go To command is helpful for navigating to a cell that is not visible onscreen.

TABLE 1.2 Keystrokes and Actions

Keystroke	Used to
↑	Move up one cell in the same column.
↓	Move down one cell in the same column.
←	Move left one cell in the same row.
→	Move right one cell in the same row.
Tab	Move right one cell in the same row.
Page Up	Move the active cell up one screen.
Page Down	Move the active cell down one screen.
Home	Move the active cell to column A of the current row.
Ctrl+Home	Make cell A1 the active cell.
Ctrl+End	Make the rightmost, lowermost active corner of the worksheet—the intersection of the last column and row that contains data—the active cell. Does not move to cell XFD1048576 unless that cell contains data.
F5 or Ctrl+G	Display the Go To dialog box to enter any cell address.

To display the contents of another worksheet within the workbook, click the sheet tab at the bottom-left corner of the workbook window. The active sheet tab has a white background color. After you click a sheet tab, you can then navigate within that worksheet.

Entering and Editing Cell Data

You should plan the structure before you start entering data into a worksheet. Using the OKOS case presented at the beginning of the chapter as an example, use the following steps to plan the worksheet design, enter and format data, and complete the workbook:

Plan the Worksheet Design

1. **State the purpose of the worksheet.** The purpose of the OKOS worksheet is to store data about products on sale and to calculate important details, such as the retail price based on markup, the sales price based on a discount rate, and the profit margin.
2. **Decide what input values are needed.** Input values are the initial values, such as variables and assumptions. You may change these values to see what type of effects different values have on the end results. For the OKOS worksheet, the input values include the costs OKOS pays the manufacturers, the markup rates, and the proposed discount rates for the sale. In some worksheets, you can create an ***input area***, a specific region in the worksheet to store and change the variables used in calculations. For example, if you applied the same Markup Rate and same Percent Off for all products, it would be easier to create an input area at the top of the worksheet to change the values in one location rather than in several locations.
3. **Decide what outputs are needed to achieve the purpose of the worksheet.** Outputs are the results you need to calculate. For the OKOS worksheet, the outputs include columns to calculate the retail price (i.e., the selling price to your customers), the sale price, and the profit margin. In some worksheets, you can create an ***output area***, the region in the worksheet to contain formulas dependent on the values in the input area.

Enter and Format the Data

4. **Enter the labels, values, and formulas in Excel.** Use the design plan (steps 2–3) as you enter labels, input values, and formulas to calculate the output. In the OKOS worksheet, descriptive labels (the product names) appear in the first column to indicate that the values on a specific row pertain to a specific product. Descriptive labels appear at the top of each column, such as Cost and Retail Price, to describe the values in the respective column. Change the input values to test that your formulas produce correct results. If necessary, correct any errors in the formulas to produce correct results. For the OKOS worksheet, change some of the original costs and markup rates to ensure the calculated retail price, selling price, and profit margin percentage results update correctly.
5. **Format the numerical values in the worksheet.** Align decimal points in columns of numbers and add number formats and styles. In the OKOS worksheet, use Accounting Number Format and the Percent Style to format the numerical data. Adjust the number of decimal places as needed.
6. **Format the descriptive titles and labels so that they stand out.** Add bold and color to headings so that they stand out and are attractive. Apply other formatting to headings and descriptive labels. In the OKOS worksheet, you will center the main title over all the columns, bold and center column labels over the columns, and apply other formatting to the headings. Figure 1.2 shows the completed OKOS worksheet.

Complete the Workbook

7. **Document the workbook as thoroughly as possible.** Include the current date, your name as the workbook author, assumptions, and purpose of the workbook. You can provide this documentation in a separate worksheet within the workbook. You can also add some documentation in the *Properties* section when you click the File tab.
8. **Save and share the completed workbook.** Preview and prepare printouts for distribution in meetings, send an electronic copy of the workbook to those who need it, or upload the workbook on a shared network drive or in the cloud.

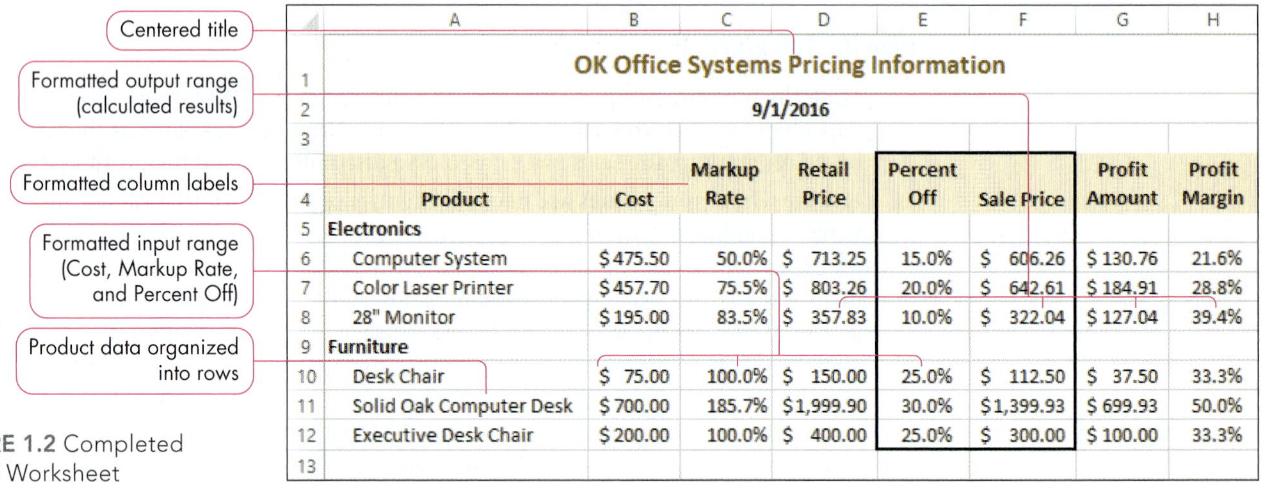

Centered title
Formatted output range (calculated results)
Formatted column labels
Formatted input range (Cost, Markup Rate, and Percent Off)
Product data organized into rows

	A	B	C	D	E	F	G	H
1	OK Office Systems Pricing Information							
2	9/1/2016							
3								
4	Product	Cost	Markup Rate	Retail Price	Percent Off	Sale Price	Profit Amount	Profit Margin
5	Electronics							
6	Computer System	$ 475.50	50.0%	$ 713.25	15.0%	$ 606.26	$ 130.76	21.6%
7	Color Laser Printer	$ 457.70	75.5%	$ 803.26	20.0%	$ 642.61	$ 184.91	28.8%
8	28" Monitor	$ 195.00	83.5%	$ 357.83	10.0%	$ 322.04	$ 127.04	39.4%
9	Furniture							
10	Desk Chair	$ 75.00	100.0%	$ 150.00	25.0%	$ 112.50	$ 37.50	33.3%
11	Solid Oak Computer Desk	$ 700.00	185.7%	$1,999.90	30.0%	$1,399.93	$ 699.93	50.0%
12	Executive Desk Chair	$ 200.00	100.0%	$ 400.00	25.0%	$ 300.00	$ 100.00	33.3%
13								

FIGURE 1.2 Completed OKOS Worksheet

Enter Text

Text is any combination of letters, numbers, symbols, and spaces not used in calculations. Excel treats phone numbers, such as 555-1234, and Social Security numbers, such as 123-45-6789, as text entries. You enter text for a worksheet title to describe the contents of the worksheet, as row and column labels to describe data, and as cell data. In Figure 1.2, the cells in column A, row 1, and row 4 contain text, such as *Product*. Text aligns at the left cell margin by default. To enter text in a cell, do the following:

STEP 1 »

1. Make sure the cell is active where you want to enter text.
2. Type the text.
3. Do one of the following to make another cell the active cell after entering data:
   - Press Enter on the keyboard.
   - Press an arrow key on the keyboard.
   - Press Tab on the keyboard.

   Do one of the following to keep the current cell the active cell after entering data:
   - Press Ctrl+Enter.
   - Click Enter (the check mark between the Name Box and the Formula Bar).

As soon as you begin typing a label into a cell, the ***AutoComplete*** feature searches for and automatically displays any other label in that column that matches the letters you typed. For example, *Computer System* is typed in cell A6 in Figure 1.2. When you start to type *Co* in cell A7, AutoComplete displays *Computer System* because a text entry previously typed starts with *Co*. Press Enter to accept the repeated label, or continue typing to enter a different label, such as *Color Laser Printer*.

TIP **Line Break in a Cell**

If a long text label does not fit well in a cell, you can insert a line break to display the text label on multiple lines within the cell. To insert a line break while you are typing a label, press Alt+Enter where you want to start the next line of text within the cell.

Enter Values

STEP 2

Values are numbers that represent a quantity or a measurable amount. Excel usually distinguishes between text and value data based on what you enter. The primary difference between text and value entries is that value entries can be the basis of calculations, whereas text cannot. In Figure 1.2, the data below the *Cost*, *Markup Rates*, and *Percent Off* labels are values. Values align at the right cell margin by default. After entering values, you can align decimal places and apply formatting by adding characters, such as $ or %.

Enter Dates

STEP 3

You can enter dates and times in a variety of formats in cells, such as 9/1/2016; 9/1/16; September 1, 2016; or 1-Sep-16. You can also enter times, such as 1:30 PM or 13:30. You should enter a static date to document when you create or modify a workbook or to document the specific point in time when the data were accurate, such as on a balance sheet or income statement. Later, you will learn how to use formulas to enter dates that update to the current date. In Figure 1.2, cell A2 contains a date. Dates are values, so they align at the right cell margin. However, the date in Figure 1.2 has been centered by the user.

Excel displays dates differently from the way it stores dates. For example, the displayed date 9/1/2016 represents the first day in September in the year 2016. Excel stores dates as serial numbers starting at 1 with January 1, 1900, so 9/1/2016 is stored as 42614 so that you can create formulas, such as to calculate how many days exist between two dates.

Enter Formulas

Formulas combine cell references, arithmetic operations, values, and/or functions used in a calculation. You must start the formula with an equal sign (=). In Figure 1.3, the data below the *Retail Price*, *Sale Price*, *Profit Amount*, and *Profit Margin* labels contain formulas. When a cell containing a formula is the active cell, the formula displays in the Formula Bar, and the result of the formula displays in the cell.

Edit and Clear Cell Contents

You can edit a cell's contents by doing one of the following:

- Click the cell, click in the Formula Bar, make the changes, and then click Enter (the check mark between the Name Box and the Formula Bar) to keep the cell the active cell.
- Double-click the cell, make changes in the cell, and then press Enter.
- Click the cell, press F2, make changes in the cell, and then press Enter.

You can clear a cell's contents by doing one of the following:

- Click the cell and press Delete.
- Click the cell, click Clear in the Editing group on the HOME tab, and then select Clear Contents.

f. Type the following text in the respective cells, pressing **Tab** after typing each of the first four column labels and pressing **Enter** after the last column label:

- **Markup Rate** in **cell C4**
- **Retail Price** in **cell D4**
- **Percent Off** in **cell E4**
- **Sale Price** in **cell F4**
- **Profit Margin** in **cell G4**

The text looks cut off when you enter data in the cell to the right. Do not worry about this now. You will adjust column widths and formatting later in this chapter.

TROUBLESHOOTING: If you notice a typographical error, click in the cell containing the error and retype the label. Or press F2 to edit the cell contents, move the insertion point using the arrow keys, press Backspace or Delete to delete the incorrect characters, type the correct characters, and then press Enter. If you type a label in an incorrect cell, click the cell and press Delete.

g. Save the changes you made to the workbook.

You should develop a habit of saving periodically. That way if your system unexpectedly shuts down, you will not lose everything you worked on.

STEP 2 » ENTER VALUES

Now that you have entered the descriptive labels, you need to enter the cost, markup rate, and percent off for each product. Refer to Figure 1.4 as you complete Step 2.

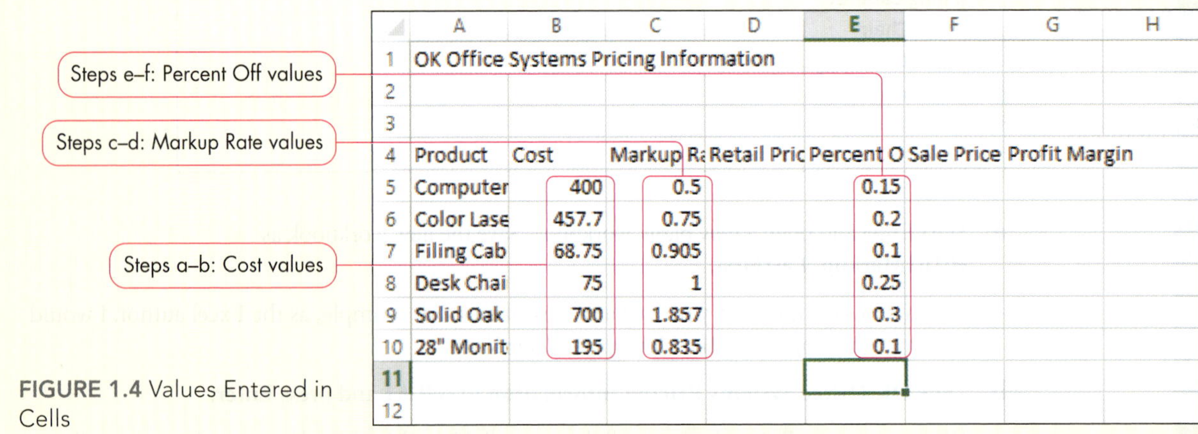

	A	B	C	D	E	F	G	H
1	OK Office Systems Pricing Information							
2								
3								
4	Product	Cost	Markup Ra	Retail Pric	Percent O	Sale Price	Profit Margin	
5	Computer	400	0.5		0.15			
6	Color Lase	457.7	0.75		0.2			
7	Filing Cab	68.75	0.905		0.1			
8	Desk Chai	75	1		0.25			
9	Solid Oak	700	1.857		0.3			
10	28" Monit	195	0.835		0.1			
11								
12								

FIGURE 1.4 Values Entered in Cells

a. Click **cell B5**, type **400**, and then press **Enter**.

b. Type the remaining costs in **cells B6** through **B10** shown in Figure 1.4.

Numeric Keypad

To improve your productivity, use the number keypad (if available) on the right side of your keyboard. It is much faster to type values and press Enter on the number keypad rather than using the numbers on the keyboard. Make sure Num Lock is active before using the number keypad to enter values.

c. Click **cell C5**, type **0.5**, and then press **Enter**.

You entered the markup rate as a decimal instead of a percentage. You will apply Percent Style later, but now you can concentrate on data entry. When you enter decimal values less than zero, you can type the period and value without typing the zero first, such as .5. Excel will automatically add the zero. You can also enter percentages as 50%, but the approach this textbook takes is to enter raw data without typing formatting such as % and to use number formatting options through Excel to display formatting symbols.

d. Type the remaining markup rates in **cells C6** through **C10** as shown in Figure 1.4.

e. Click **cell E5**, type **0.15**, and then press **Enter**.

You entered the Percent Off or markdown sale value as a decimal.

f. Type the remaining Percent Off values in **cells E6** through **E10** as shown in Figure 1.4 and save the workbook.

STEP 3 » ENTER A DATE AND CLEAR CELL CONTENTS

As you review the worksheet, you realize you need to provide a date to indicate when the sale starts. Refer to Figure 1.5 as you complete Step 3.

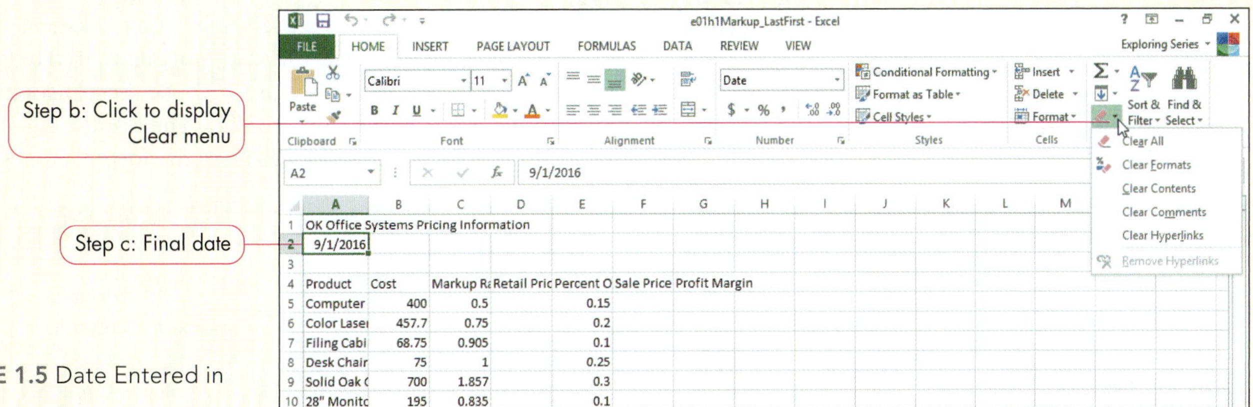

FIGURE 1.5 Date Entered in a Cell

a. Click **cell A2**, type **9/1**, and then press **Enter**.

The date aligns on the right cell margin by default. Excel displays *1-Sep* instead of *9/1*.

b. Click **cell A2**, click **Clear** in the Editing group on the HOME tab, and then select **Clear All**.

The Clear All command clears both cell contents and formatting in the selected cell(s).

c. Type **9/1/2016** in **cell A2** and press **Enter**.

TROUBLESHOOTING: If you did not use Clear All and typed 9/1/2016 in cell A2, Excel would have retained the previous date format and displayed 1-Sep again.

d. Save the workbook. Keep the workbook open if you plan to continue with the next Hands-On Exercise. If not, close the workbook and exit Excel.

Mathematics and Formulas

Formulas transform static numbers into meaningful results that can update as values change. For example, a payroll manager can build formulas to calculate the gross pay, deductions, and net pay for an organization's employees, or a doctoral student can create formulas to perform various statistical calculations to interpret his or her research data.

You can use formulas to help you analyze how results will change as the input data change. You can change the value of your assumptions or inputs and explore the results quickly and accurately. For example, if the interest rate changes from 4% to 5%, how would that affect your monthly payment? Analyzing different input values in Excel is easy after you build formulas. Simply change an input value and observe the change in the formula results.

In this section, you will learn how to use mathematical operations in Excel formulas. You will refresh your memory of mathematical order of precedence and how to construct formulas using cell addresses so that when the value of an input cell changes, the result of the formula changes without you having to modify the formula.

Creating Formulas

Start a formula by typing the equal sign (=), followed by the arithmetic expression. Do not include a space before or after the arithmetic operator. Figure 1.6 shows a worksheet containing data and results of formulas. The figure also displays the actual formulas used to generate the calculated results. For example, cell B6 contains the formula =B2+B3. Excel uses the value stored in cell B2 (10) and adds it to the value stored in cell B3 (2). The result—12—appears in cell B6 instead of the actual formula. The Formula Bar displays the formula entered into the active cell.

	A	B	C	D	E	F
1	**Description**	**Values**		**Description**	**Results**	**Formulas in Column E**
2	First input value	10		Sum of 10 and 2	12	=B2+B3
3	Second input value	2		Difference between 10 and 2	8	=B2-B3
4				Product of 10 and 2	20	=B2*B3
5				Results of dividing 10 by 2	5	=B2/B3
6				Results of 10 to the 2nd power	100	=B2^B3

FIGURE 1.6 Formula Results

TROUBLESHOOTING: If you type B2+B3 without the equal sign, Excel does not recognize that you entered a formula and stores the data as text.

Use Cell References in Formulas

STEP 1»
STEP 2»
STEP 3»

You should use cell references instead of values in formulas where possible. You may include values in an input area—such as dates, salary, or costs—that you will need to reference in formulas. Referencing these cells in your formulas, instead of typing the value of the cell to which you are referring, keeps your formulas accurate if the values change.

When you create a formula, you can type the cell references in uppercase, such as =B2+B3, or lowercase, such as =b2+b3. Excel changes cell references to uppercase.

In Figure 1.6, cell B2 contains 10, and cell B3 contains 2. Cell E2 contains =B2+B3 but shows the result, 12. If you change the value of cell B3 to 5, cell E2 displays the new result, which is 15. However, if you had typed actual values in the formula, =10+2, you would have to edit the formula each time an input value changes. This would be problematic, as you might forget to edit the formula or you might have a typographical error if you edit the formula. Always design worksheets in such a way as to be able to change input values without having to modify your formulas if an input value changes later.

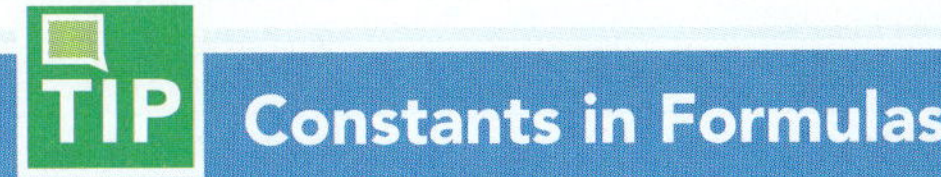

TIP Constants in Formulas

Use cell references instead of actual values in formulas, unless the value is a constant. For example, assume that 25% is stored in cell D10. To calculate the reciprocal of 25%, type =1-D10. The constant, 1, represents 100%, a value that never changes, although the percentage in cell D10 might change. In this situation, 100% – 25% is 75%.

Apply the Order of Precedence

The ***order of precedence*** (also called order of operations) is a rule that controls the sequence in which arithmetic operations are performed, which affects the results of the calculation. Excel performs mathematical calculations left to right in this order: **P**ercent, **E**xponentiation, **M**ultiplication or **D**ivision, and finally **A**ddition or **S**ubtraction. Some people remember the order of precedence with the phrase ***P****lease* ***E****xcuse* ***M****y* ***D****ear* ***A****unt* ***S****ally*.

Table 1.3 lists the complete order of precedence. This chapter focuses on orders 4, 5, and 6.

TABLE 1.3 Order of Precedence

Order	Description	Symbols
1	Reference Operators	colon (:), space, and comma (,)
2	Negation	-
3	Percent	%
4	Exponentiation	^
5	Multiplication and Division	* and / (respectively)
6	Addition and Subtraction	+ and – (respectively)
7	Concatenation	ampersand symbol (&) to connect two text strings
8	Comparison	Equal sign (=), greater than (>), and less than (<)

TIP Parentheses in Formulas

You can change the order of operations by using parentheses. For example, to add the values in cells A1 and A2 and multiply that result by the value in cell A3, enclose parentheses around the addition operation: =(A1+A2)*A3. Without parentheses, multiplication has a higher order of precedence than addition and will be calculated first.

Figure 1.7 shows formulas, the sequence in which calculations occur, calculations, the description, and the results of each order of precedence. The highlighted results are the final formula results. This figure illustrates the importance of symbols and use of parentheses.

	A	B	C	D	E	F
1	Input		Formula	Sequence	Description	Result
2	2		=A2+A3*A4+A5	1	3 (cell A3) * 4 (cell A4)	12
3	3			2	2 (cell A2) + 12 (order 1)	14
4	4			3	14 (order 2) + 5 (cell A5)	19
5	5					
6			=(A2+A3)*(A4+A5)	1	2 (cell A2) + 3 (cell A3)	5
7				2	4 (cell A4) + 5 (cell A5)	9
8				3	5 (order 1) * 9 (order 2)	45
9						
10			=A2/A3+A4*A5	1	2 (cell A2) / 3 (cell A3)	0.666667
11				2	4 (cell A4) * 5 (cell A5)	20
12				3	0.666667 (order 1) + 20 (order 2)	20.66667
13						
14			=A2/(A3+A4)*A5	1	3 (cell A3) + 4 (cell A4)	7
15				2	2 (cell A2) / 7 (order 1)	0.285714
16				3	0.285714 (order 2) * 5 (cell A5)	1.428571
17						
18			=A2^2+A3*A4%	1	4 (cell A4) is converted to percentage	0.04
19				2	2 (cell A2) to the power of 2	4
20				3	3 (cell A3) * 0.04 (order 1)	0.12
21				4	4 (order 2) + 0.12 (order 3)	4.12

FIGURE 1.7 Formula Results Based on Order of Precedence

Use Semi-Selection to Create a Formula

To decrease typing time and ensure accuracy, you can use ***semi-selection***, a process of selecting a cell or range of cells for entering cell references as you create formulas. Semi-selection is often called ***pointing*** because you use the mouse pointer to select cells as you build the formula. To use the semi-selection technique to create a formula, do the following:

1. Click the cell where you want to create the formula.
2. Type an equal sign (=) to start a formula.
3. Click the cell or drag to select the cell range that contains the value(s) to use in the formula. A moving marquee appears around the cell or range you select, and Excel displays the cell or range reference in the formula.
4. Type a mathematical operator.
5. Continue clicking cells, selecting ranges, and typing operators to finish the formula. Use the scroll bars if the cell is in a remote location in the worksheet, or click a worksheet tab to see a cell in another worksheet.
6. Press Enter to complete the formula.

Using Auto Fill

Auto Fill enables you to copy the contents of a cell or a range of cells by dragging the ***fill handle*** (a small green square appearing in the bottom-right corner of the active cell) over an adjacent cell or range of cells. To use Auto Fill, do the following:

1. Click the cell with the content you want to copy to make it the active cell.
2. Point to the fill handle in the bottom-right corner of the cell until the mouse pointer changes to the fill pointer (a thin black plus sign).
3. Drag the fill handle to repeat the content in other cells.

Copy Formulas with Auto Fill

STEP 4»

After you enter a formula in a cell, you can duplicate the formula without retyping it by using the fill handle to copy the formula in the active cell down a column or across a row, depending on how the data are organized. Excel adapts each copied formula based on the type of cell references in the original formula.

Complete Sequences with Auto Fill

You can also use Auto Fill to complete a sequence. For example, if you enter January in a cell, you can use Auto Fill to enter the rest of the months in adjacent cells. Other sequences you can complete are quarters (Qtr 1, etc.), weekdays, and weekday abbreviations, by typing the first item and using Auto Fill to complete the other entries. For numeric sequences, however, you must specify the first two values in sequence. For example, if you want to fill in 5, 10, 15, and so on, you must enter 5 and 10 in two adjacent cells, select the two cells, and then use Auto Fill so that Excel knows to increment by 5. Figure 1.8 shows the results of filling in months, abbreviated months, quarters, weekdays, abbreviated weekdays, and increments of 5.

	A	B	C	D	E	F	G	H	I
1	January	Jan	Qtr 1	Monday	Mon	5			
2	February	Feb	Qtr 2	Tuesday	Tue	10			
3	March	Mar	Qtr 3	Wednesday	Wed	15			
4	April	Apr	Qtr 4	Thursday	Thu	20			
5	May	May		Friday	Fri	25			
6	June	Jun		Saturday	Sat	30			
7	July	Jul		Sunday	Sun	35			
8	August	Aug							
9	September	Sep							
10	October	Oct							
11	November	Nov							
12	December	Dec							
13									
14									
15									

FIGURE 1.8 Auto Fill Examples

Immediately after you use Auto Fill, Excel displays the Auto Fill Options button in the bottom-right corner of the filled data (see Figure 1.8). Click Auto Fill Options to display five fill options: Copy Cells, Fill Series, Fill Formatting Only, Fill Without Formatting, or Flash Fill.

TIP Double-Clicking the Fill Handle

You can double-click the fill handle to quickly copy a formula down a column. Excel will copy the formula in the active cell for each row of data to calculate in your worksheet.

Displaying Cell Formulas

Excel shows the result of the formula in the cell (see the top half of Figure 1.9); however, you might want to display the formulas instead of the calculated results in the cells (see the bottom half of Figure 1.9). To display cell formulas, do one of the following:

STEP 5»

- Press Ctrl and the grave accent (`) key, sometimes referred to as the tilde key, in the top-left corner of the keyboard, below the Esc key.
- Click Show Formulas in the Formula Auditing group on the FORMULAS tab.

To hide the formulas and display the formula results again, repeat the preceding process.

Workbook and Worksheet Management

When you start a new blank workbook in Excel, the workbook contains one worksheet named Sheet1. However, you can add additional worksheets. The text, values, dates, and formulas you enter into the individual sheets are saved under one workbook file name. Having multiple worksheets in one workbook is helpful to keep related items together. For example, you might want one worksheet for each month to track your monthly income and expenses for one year. When tax time comes around, you have all your data stored in one workbook file.

Although you should plan the worksheet and workbook before you start entering data, you might need to add, delete, or rename worksheets. Furthermore, within a worksheet you may want to insert a new row to accommodate new data, delete a column that you no longer need, or adjust the size of columns and rows.

In this section, you will learn how to manage workbooks by renaming, inserting, and deleting worksheets. You will also learn how to make changes to worksheet columns and rows, such as inserting, deleting, and adjusting sizes.

Managing Worksheets

Creating a multiple-worksheet workbook takes some planning and maintenance. Worksheet tab names should reflect the contents of the respective worksheets. In addition, you can insert, copy, move, and delete worksheets within the workbook. You can even apply background color to the worksheet tabs so that they stand out onscreen. Figure 1.16 shows a workbook in which the sheet tabs have been renamed, colors have been applied to worksheet tabs, and a worksheet tab has been right-clicked so that the shortcut menu appears.

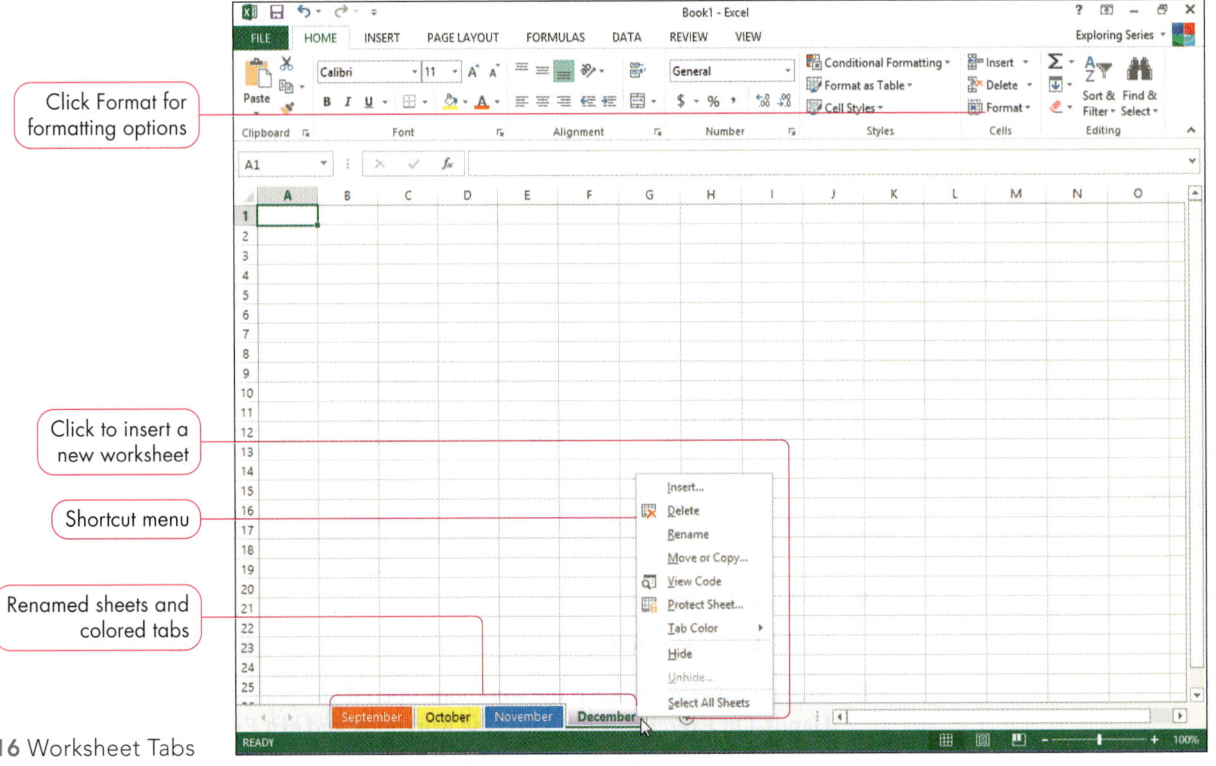

FIGURE 1.16 Worksheet Tabs

Rename a Worksheet

STEP 1

The default worksheet name Sheet1 does not describe the contents of the worksheet. You should rename worksheet tabs to reflect the sheet contents. For example, if your budget workbook contains monthly worksheets, name the worksheets September, October, etc. Although you can have spaces in worksheet names, keep worksheet names relatively short. The longer the worksheet names, the fewer sheet tabs you will see at the bottom of the workbook window without scrolling.

To rename a worksheet, do one of the following:

- Double-click a sheet tab, type the new name, and then press Enter.
- Click the sheet tab for the sheet you want to rename, click Format in the Cells group on the HOME tab (refer to Figure 1.16), select Rename Sheet (see Figure 1.17), type the new sheet name, and then press Enter.
- Right-click the sheet tab, select Rename from the shortcut menu (see Figure 1.16), type the new sheet name, and then press Enter.

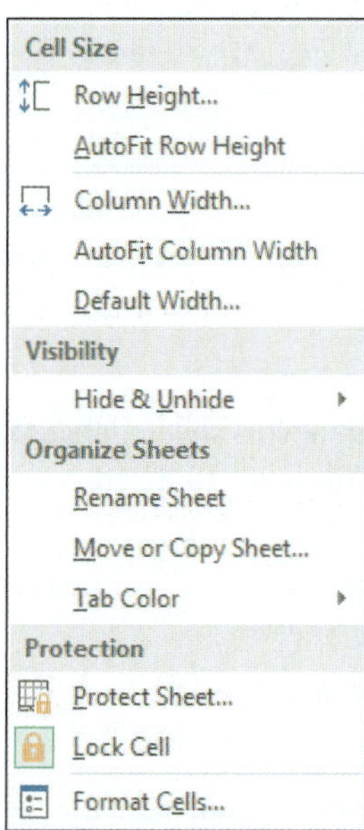

FIGURE 1.17 Format Menu

Change Worksheet Tab Color

STEP 1

The active worksheet tab is white with a green bottom border. When you use multiple worksheets, you might want to apply a different color to each worksheet tab to make the tab stand out or to emphasize the difference between sheets. For example, you might apply red to the September tab, green to the October tab, dark blue to the November tab, and purple to the December tab.

To change the color of a worksheet tab, do one of the following:

- Click the sheet tab for the sheet you want to rename, click Format in the Cells group on the HOME tab (refer to Figure 1.16), point to Tab Color (refer to Figure 1.17), and then click a color on the Tab Color palette.
- Right-click the sheet tab, point to Tab Color on the shortcut menu (refer to Figure 1.16), and then click a color on the Tab Color palette.

Insert and Delete a Worksheet

STEP 2》 Sometimes you need more than one worksheet in the workbook. For example, you might create a workbook that contains 12 worksheets—a worksheet for each month of the year. To insert a new worksheet, do one of the following:

- Click *New sheet* to the right of the last worksheet tab.
- Click the Insert arrow—either to the right or below Insert—in the Cells group on the HOME tab and select Insert Sheet.
- Right-click any sheet tab, select Insert from the shortcut menu (refer to Figure 1.16), click Worksheet in the Insert dialog box, and then click OK.
- Press Shift+F11.

TIP Ribbon Commands with Arrows

Some commands, such as Insert in the Cells group, contain two parts: the main command and an arrow. The arrow may be below or to the right of the command, depending on the command, window size, or screen resolution. Instructions in the Exploring Series use the command name to instruct you to click the main command to perform the default action, such as *Click Insert in the Cells group* or *Click Delete in the Cells group*. Instructions include the word arrow when you need to select an additional option, such as *Click the Insert arrow in the Cells group* or *Click the Delete arrow in the Cells group*.

If you no longer need the data in a worksheet, delete the worksheet. Doing so will eliminate extra data in a file and reduce file size. To delete a worksheet in a workbook, do one of the following:

- Click the Delete arrow—either to the right or below Delete—in the Cells group on the HOME tab and select Delete Sheet.
- Right-click any sheet tab and select Delete from the shortcut menu (refer to Figure 1.16).

If the sheet you are trying to delete contains data, Excel will display a warning: *You can't undo deleting sheets, and you might be removing some data. If you don't need it, click Delete.* If you try to delete a blank worksheet, Excel will not display a warning; it will immediately delete the sheet.

Move or Copy a Worksheet

After inserting and deleting worksheets, you can arrange the worksheet tabs in a different sequence, especially if the newly inserted worksheets do not fall within a logical sequence. To move a worksheet, do one of the following:

- Drag a worksheet tab to the desired location. As you drag a sheet tab, the pointer resembles a piece of paper. A down-pointing triangle appears between sheet tabs to indicate where the sheet will be placed when you release the mouse button.
- Click Format in the Cells group on the HOME tab (refer to Figure 1.16) and select *Move or Copy Sheet*, or right-click the sheet tab you want to move and select *Move or Copy* to display the *Move or Copy* dialog box (see Figure 1.18). You can move the worksheet within the current workbook, or you can move the worksheet to a different workbook. In the *Before sheet* list, select the worksheet you want to come after the moved worksheet and click OK. For example, you have just created a new worksheet named August and you want it to come before the September worksheet. You would select September in the *Before sheet* list.

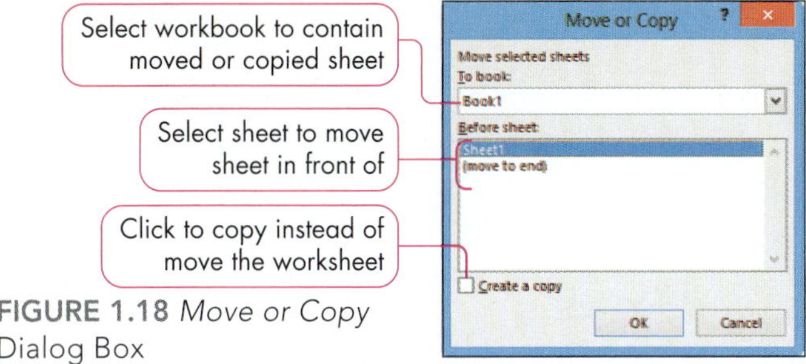

FIGURE 1.18 *Move or Copy* Dialog Box

After creating a worksheet, you may want to copy it to use as a template or starting point for similar data. For example, if you create a worksheet for your September budget, you can copy the worksheet and then easily edit the data on the copied worksheet to enter data for your October budget. Copying the entire worksheet would save you a lot of valuable time in entering and formatting the new worksheet. The process for copying a worksheet is similar to moving a sheet. To copy a worksheet, press and hold Ctrl as you drag the worksheet tab. Alternatively, display the *Move or Copy* dialog box, select the *To book* and *Before sheet* options (refer to Figure 1.18), click the *Create a copy* check box, and then click OK.

Managing Columns and Rows

As you enter and edit worksheet data, you can adjust the row and column structure. You can add rows and columns to add new data, or you can delete data you no longer need. Adjusting the height and width of rows and columns, respectively, can present the data better.

Insert Cells, Columns, and Rows

STEP 3» After you construct a worksheet, you might need to insert cells, columns, or rows to accommodate new data. For example, you might need to insert a new column to perform calculations or a new row to list a new product. When you insert cells, rows, and columns, cell addresses in formulas adjust automatically.

To insert a new column or row, do one of the following:

- Click in the column or row for which you want to insert a new column to the left or a new row above, respectively. Click the Insert arrow in the Cells group on the HOME tab and select Insert Sheet Columns or Insert Sheet Rows.
- Right-click the column (letter) or row (number) heading for which you want to insert a new column to the left or a new row above, respectively, and select Insert from the shortcut menu.

Excel inserts new columns to the left of the current column and new rows above the active row. If the current column is column C and you insert a new column, the new column becomes column C, and the original column C data are now in column D. Likewise, if the current row is 5 and you insert a new row, the new row is row 5, and the original row 5 data are now in row 6.

Inserting a cell is helpful when you realize that you left out an entry in one column after you have entered columns of data. Instead of inserting a new row for all columns, you just want to move the existing content down in one column to enter the missing value. You can insert a single cell in a particular row or column. To insert a cell, click in the cell where you want the new cell, click the Insert arrow in the Cells group on the Home tab, and then select Insert Cells. Select an option from the Insert dialog box (see Figure 1.19) to position the new cell and click OK. Alternatively, click Insert in the Cells group. The default action of clicking Insert is to insert a cell at the current location, which moves existing data down in that column only.

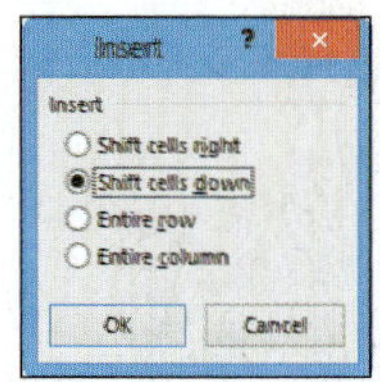

FIGURE 1.19 Insert Dialog Box

Delete Cells, Columns, and Rows

STEP 4

If you no longer need a cell, column, or row, you can delete it. In these situations, you are deleting the entire cell, column, or row, not just the contents of the cell to leave empty cells. As with inserting new cells, any affected formulas adjust the cell references automatically. To delete a column or row, do one of the following:

- Click the column or row heading for the column or row you want to delete. Click Delete in the Cells group on the HOME tab.
- Click in any cell within the column or row you want to delete. Click the Delete arrow in the Cells group on the HOME tab and select Delete Sheet Columns or Delete Sheet Rows, respectively.
- Right-click the column letter or row number for the column or row you want to delete and select Delete from the shortcut menu.

To delete a cell or cells, select the cell(s), click the Delete arrow in the Cells group, and then select Delete Cells to display the Delete dialog box (see Figure 1.20). Click the appropriate option to shift cells left or up and click OK. Alternatively, click Delete in the Cells group. The default action of clicking Delete is to delete the active cell, which moves existing data up in that column only.

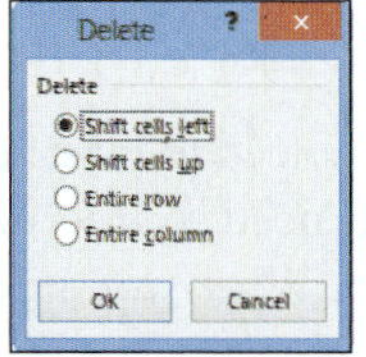

FIGURE 1.20 Delete Dialog Box

Adjust Column Width

STEP 5

After you enter data in a column, you often need to adjust the ***column width***—the number of characters that can fit horizontally using the default font or the number of horizontal pixels—to show the contents of cells. For example, in the worksheet you created in Hands-On Exercises 1 and 2, the labels in column A displayed into column B when those adjacent cells were empty. However, after you typed values in column B, the labels in column A appeared cut off. You will need to widen column A to show the full name of all of your products.

Pound Signs Displayed

Numbers appear as a series of pound signs (######) when the cell is too narrow to display the complete value, and text appears to be truncated.

To widen a column to accommodate the longest label or value in a column, do one of the following:

- Position the pointer on the vertical border between the current column heading and the next column heading. When the pointer displays as a two-headed arrow, double-click the border. For example, if column B is too narrow to display the content in that column, double-click the border between the column B and C headings.
- Click Format in the Cells group on the HOME tab (refer to Figure 1.16) and select AutoFit Column Width (refer to Figure 1.17).

To widen a column to an exact width, do one of the following:

- Drag the vertical border to the left to decrease the column width or to the right to increase the column width. As you drag the vertical border, Excel displays a ScreenTip specifying the width (see Figure 1.21) from 0 to 255 characters and in pixels.
- Click Format in the Cells group on the HOME tab (refer to Figure 1.16), select Column Width (refer to Figure 1.17), type a value in the Column width box in the Column Width dialog box, and then click OK.

ScreenTip displaying column width

Mouse pointer as you drag the border between column headings

Current column width

Column width when you release the mouse button

D14 | Width: 10.57 (79 pixels)

	A	B	C	D	E	F	G	H
1	OK Office Systems Pricing Information							
2	9/1/2016							
3								
4	Product	Cost	Markup Ra	Retail Pric	Percent O	Sale Price	Profit Margin	
5	Computer	475.5	0.5	713.25	0.15	606.263	0.275	
6	Color Lase	457.7	0.755	803.264	0.2	642.611	0.404	
7	Filing Cabi	68.75	0.905	130.969	0.05	124.42	0.80975	
8	Desk Chai	75	1	150	0.25	112.5	0.5	
9	Solid Oak	700	1.857	1999.9	0.3	1399.93	0.9999	
10	28" Monit	195	0.835	357.825	0.1	322.043	0.6515	

FIGURE 1.21 Changing Column Width

Adjust Row Height

When you increase the font size of cell contents, Excel automatically increases the ***row height***—the vertical measurement of the row. However, if you insert a line break or wrap text to create multiple lines of text in a cell, Excel might not increase the row height. You can adjust the row height in a way similar to how you change column width by double-clicking the border between row numbers or by selecting Row Height or AutoFit Row Height from the Format menu (refer to Figure 1.17). In Excel, row height is a value between 0 and 409 based on point size (abbreviated as pt) and pixels. Whether you are measuring font sizes or row heights, one point size is equal to 1/72 of an inch. Your row height should be taller than your font size. For example, with an 11-pt font size, the default row height is 15.

Multiple Column Widths and Row Heights

You can set the size for more than one column or row at a time to make the selected columns or rows the same size. Drag across the column or row headings for the area you want to format, and then set the size using any method.

Hide and Unhide Columns and Rows

STEP 6

If your worksheet contains confidential information, you might need to hide some columns and/or rows before you print a copy for public distribution. However, the column or row is not deleted. If you hide column B, you will see columns A and C side by side. If you hide row 3, you will see rows 2 and 4 together. Figure 1.22 shows that column B and row 3 are hidden. Excel displays a double line between ***column headings*** (such as between A and C), indicating one or more columns are hidden, and a double line between row headings (such as between 2 and 4), indicating one or more rows are hidden.

Double vertical line indicates hidden column

Double horizontal line indicates hidden row

	A	C	D
1			
2			
4			
5			

FIGURE 1.22 Hidden Column and Row

To hide a column or row, do one of the following:

- Click in the column or row you want to hide, click Format in the Cells group on the HOME tab (refer to Figure 1.16), point to Hide & Unhide (refer to Figure 1.17), and then select Hide Columns or Hide Rows, depending on what you want to hide.
- Right-click the column or row heading(s) you want to hide and select Hide.

You can hide multiple columns and rows at the same time. To select adjacent columns (such as columns B through E) or adjacent rows (such as rows 2 through 4), drag across the adjacent column or row headings. To hide nonadjacent columns or rows, press and hold Ctrl while you click the desired column or row headings. After selecting multiple columns or rows, use any acceptable method to hide the selected columns or rows.

To unhide a column or row, select the columns or rows on both sides of the hidden column or row. For example, if column B is hidden, drag across column letters A and C. Then do one of the following:

- Click Format in the Cells group on the HOME tab (refer to Figure 1.16), point to Hide & Unhide (refer to Figure 1.17), and then select Unhide Columns or Unhide Rows, depending on what you want to display again.
- Right-click the column(s) or row(s) you want to hide and select Unhide.

Unhiding Column A, Row 1, and All Hidden Rows/Columns

Unhiding column A or row 1 is different because you cannot select the row or column on either side. To unhide column A or row 1, type A1 in the Name Box and press Enter. Click Format in the Cells group on the Home tab, point to Hide & Unhide, and then select Unhide Columns or Unhide Rows to display column A or row 1, respectively. If you want to unhide all columns and rows, click Select All and use the Hide & Unhide submenu.

Quick Concepts

1. What is the benefit of renaming a worksheet? ***p. 105***
2. What are two ways to insert a new row in a worksheet? ***p. 107***
3. How can you delete cell B5 without deleting the entire row or column? ***p. 108***
4. When should you adjust column widths instead of using the default width? ***p. 108***

Hands-On Exercises

3 Workbook and Worksheet Management

After reviewing the OKOS worksheet, you decide to rename the worksheet, change the worksheet tab color, insert a worksheet, and delete an empty worksheet. In addition, you need to insert a column to calculate the amount of markup and delete a row containing data you no longer need. You also need to adjust column widths to display the labels in the columns.

Skills covered: Rename a Worksheet and Select a Tab Color • Insert, Move, and Delete a Worksheet • Insert a Column and Rows • Delete a Row • Adjust Column Width and Row Height • Hide and Unhide Columns

STEP 1 » RENAME A WORKSHEET AND SELECT A TAB COLOR

You want to rename Sheet1 to describe the worksheet contents and add a color to the sheet tab. Refer to Figure 1.23 as you complete Step 1.

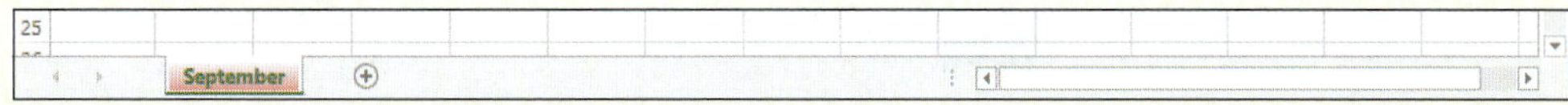

FIGURE 1.23 Renamed Worksheet with Tab Color

a. Open *e01h2Markup_LastFirst* if you closed it at the end of Hands-On Exercise 2 and save it as **e01h3Markup_LastFirst**, changing *h2* to *h3*.

b. Double-click the **Sheet1 sheet tab**, type **September**, and then press **Enter**.

   You renamed Sheet1 September.

c. Right-click the **September sheet tab**, point to *Tab Color*, and then click **Red** in the *Standard Colors* section.

   The worksheet tab color is red.

d. Save the workbook.

STEP 2 » INSERT, MOVE, AND DELETE A WORKSHEET

Your supervisor asks you to add another worksheet to the workbook. She wants you to place it before the September worksheet so that she can add August data. After you do this, she calls you on the phone and tells you that she won't be adding the August data after all. Therefore, you will delete that worksheet. Refer to Figure 1.24 as you complete Step 2.

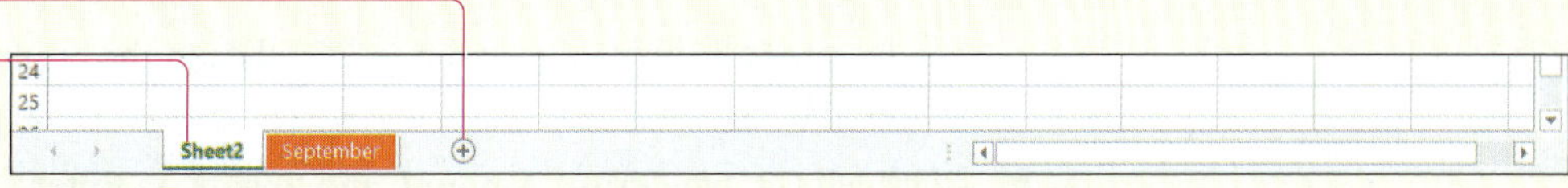

FIGURE 1.24 New Sheet Inserted

a. Click **New sheet**, the plus icon to the right of the September sheet tab.

   Excel adds a new worksheet named either Sheet1 or Sheet2 to the right of the previously active sheet.

b. Drag the **Sheet tab** to the left of the September sheet tab.

c. Click the **Sheet tab**, click the **Delete arrow** in the Cells group on the HOME tab, and then select **Delete Sheet**.

   You deleted the blank worksheet from the workbook.

TROUBLESHOOTING: Delete in the Cells group, like some other commands in Excel, contains two parts: the main command icon and an arrow. Click the main command icon when instructed to click Delete to perform the default action. Click the arrow when instructed to click the Delete arrow for additional command options.

TROUBLESHOOTING: Notice that Undo is unavailable on the Quick Access Toolbar. You cannot undo deleting a worksheet. It is deleted!

d. Save the workbook.

STEP 3 » INSERT A COLUMN AND ROWS

You decide that you need a column to display the amount of profit. Because profit is a dollar amount, you want to keep the profit column close to another column of dollar amounts. Therefore, you will insert the profit column before the profit margin (percentage) column. You also want to insert new rows for product information and category names. Refer to Figure 1.25 as you complete Step 3.

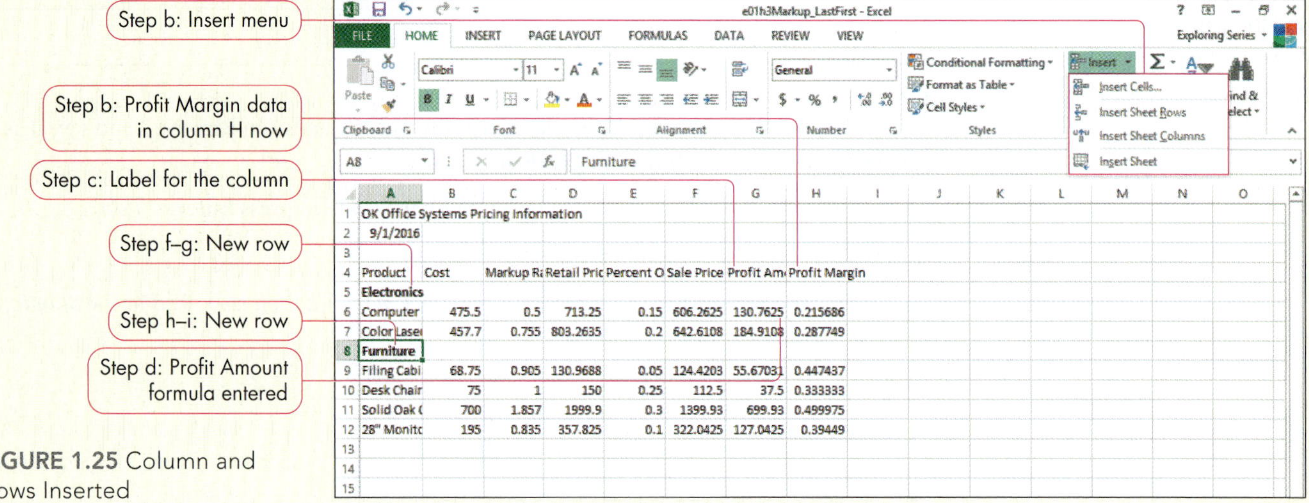

FIGURE 1.25 Column and Rows Inserted

a. Click **cell G5** (or any cell in column G), the column containing the Profit Margin.

You want to insert a column between the Sale Price and Profit Margin columns so that you can calculate the profit amount in dollars.

b. Click the **Insert arrow** in the Cells group and select **Insert Sheet Columns**.

You inserted a new, blank column G. The data in the original column G are now in column H.

c. Click **cell G4**, type **Profit Amount**, and then press **Enter**.

d. Make sure the active cell is **cell G5**. Type **=F5-B5** and click **Enter** (the check mark between the Name Box and the Formula Bar). Double-click the **cell G5 fill handle** to copy the formula down the column.

You calculated the profit amount by subtracting the original cost from the sale price. Although steps e and f below illustrate one way to insert a row, you can use other methods presented in this chapter.

e. Right-click the **row 5 heading**, the row containing the Computer System data.

Excel displays a shortcut menu consisting of commands you can perform.

f. Select **Insert** from the shortcut menu.

You inserted a new blank row 5, which is selected. The original rows of data move down a row each.

g. Click **cell A5**. Type **Electronics** and press **Ctrl+Enter**. Click **Bold** in the Font group on the HOME tab.

You typed and bolded the category name *Electronics* above the list of electronic products.

h. Right-click the **row 8 heading**, the row containing the Filing Cabinet data, and select **Insert** from the shortcut menu.

i. Click **cell A8**. Type **Furniture** and press **Ctrl+Enter**. Click **Bold** in the Font group on the HOME tab.

You typed and bolded the category name *Furniture* above the list of furniture products.

j. Save the workbook.

STEP 4 ›› DELETE A ROW

You just realized that you do not have enough filing cabinets in stock to offer on sale, so you need to delete the Filing Cabinet row. Refer to Figure 1.26 as you complete Step 4.

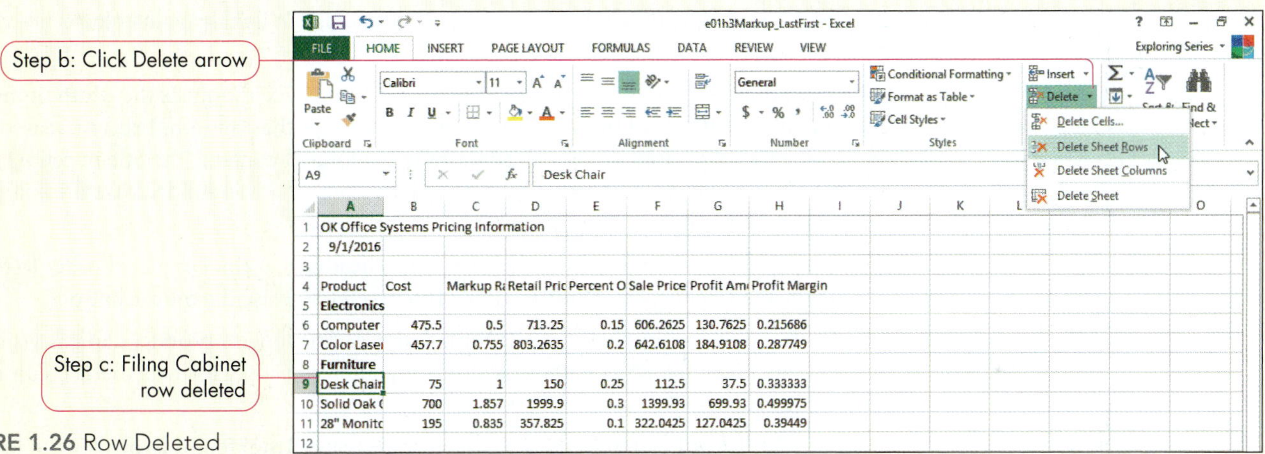

FIGURE 1.26 Row Deleted

a. Click **cell A9** (or any cell on row 9), the row that contains the Filing Cabinet data.

b. Click the **Delete arrow** in the Cells group.

c. Select **Delete Sheet Rows** and save the workbook.

The Filing Cabinet row is deleted and the remaining rows move up one row.

> **TROUBLESHOOTING:** If you accidentally delete the wrong row or accidentally select Delete Sheet Columns instead of Delete Sheet Rows, click Undo on the Quick Access Toolbar to restore the deleted row or column.

STEP 5 » ADJUST COLUMN WIDTH AND ROW HEIGHT

As you review your worksheet, you notice that the labels in column A appear cut off. You need to increase the width of that column to display the entire product names. In addition, you want to make row 1 taller. Refer to Figure 1.27 as you complete Step 5.

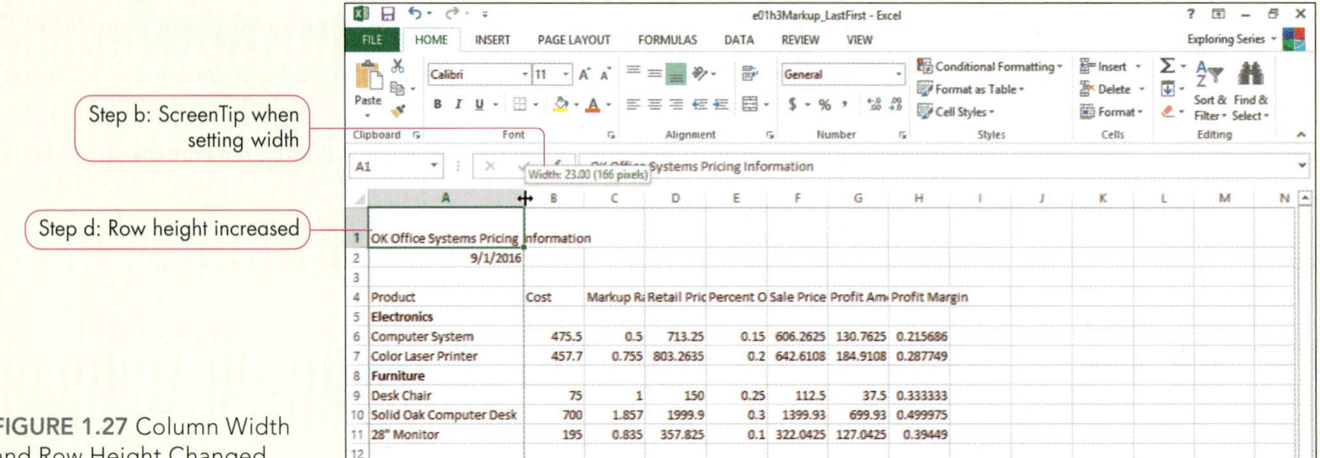

FIGURE 1.27 Column Width and Row Height Changed

a. Position the pointer between the column A and B headings. When the pointer looks like a double-headed arrow, double-click the border.

When you double-click the border between two columns, Excel adjusts the width of the column on the left side of the border to fit the contents of that column. Excel increased the width of column A based on the cell containing the longest content (the title in cell A1, which will eventually span over all columns). Therefore, you want to decrease the column to avoid so much empty space in column A.

b. Position the pointer between the column A and B headings again. Drag the border to the left until the ScreenTip displays **Width: 23.00 (166 pixels)**. Release the mouse button.

You decreased the column width to 23 for column A. The longest product name is visible. You will not adjust the other column widths until after you apply formats to the column headings in Hands-On Exercise 5.

c. Click **cell A1**. Click **Format** in the Cells group and select **Row Height** to display the Row Height dialog box.

d. Type **30** in the **Row height box** and click **OK**. Save the workbook.

You increased the height of the row that contains the worksheet title so that it is more prominent.

STEP 6 » HIDE AND UNHIDE COLUMNS

To focus on the dollar amounts, you decide to hide the markup rate, discount rate, and profit margin columns. Refer to Figure 1.28 as you complete Step 6.

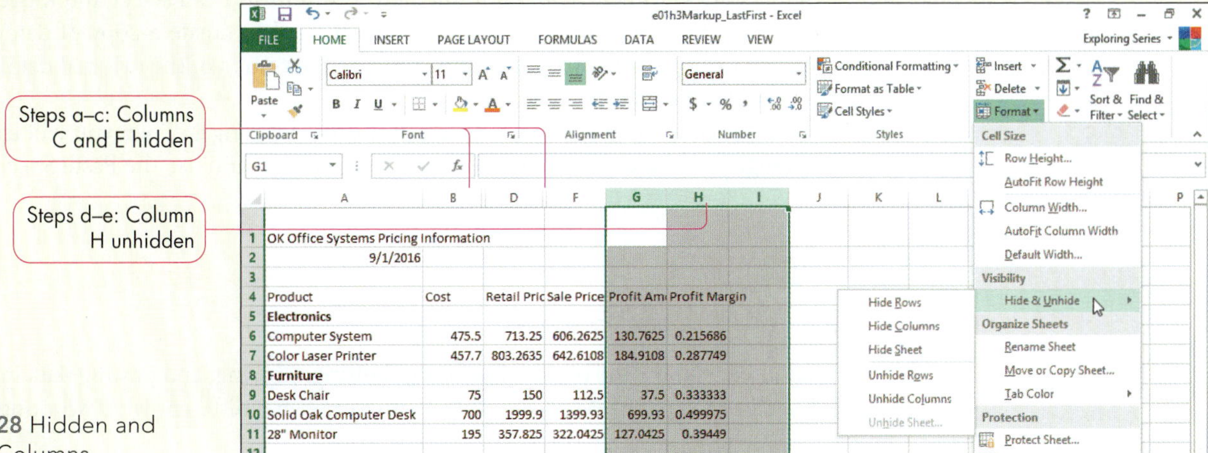

FIGURE 1.28 Hidden and Unhidden Columns

a. Click the **column C heading**, the column containing the Markup Rate values.

b. Press and hold **Ctrl** as you click the **column E heading** and the **column H heading**. Release Ctrl after selecting the headings.

Holding down Ctrl enables you to select nonadjacent ranges. You want to hide the rate columns temporarily.

c. Click **Format** in the Cells group, point to *Hide & Unhide*, and then select **Hide Columns**.

Excel hides the selected columns. You see a gap in column heading letters, indicating columns are hidden (refer to Figure 1.28).

d. Drag to select the **column G and I headings**.

You want to unhide column H, so you must select the columns on both sides of the hidden column.

e. Click **Format** in the Cells group, point to *Hide & Unhide*, and then select **Unhide Columns**.

Column H, which contains the Profit Margin values, is no longer hidden. You will keep the other columns hidden and save the workbook as evidence that you know how to hide columns. You will unhide the remaining columns in the next Hands-On Exercise.

f. Save the workbook. Keep the workbook open if you plan to continue with the next Hands-On Exercise. If not, close the workbook and exit Excel.

Clipboard Tasks

Although you plan worksheets before entering data, you might decide to move data to a different location in the same worksheet or even in a different worksheet. Instead of deleting the original data and then typing it in the new location, you can select and move data from one cell to another. In some instances, you might want to create a copy of data entered so that you can explore different values and compare the results of the original data set and the copied and edited data set.

In this section, you will learn how to select different ranges. Then you will learn how to move a range to another location, make a copy of a range, and use the Paste Special feature.

Selecting, Moving, Copying, and Pasting Data

You may already know the basics of selecting, cutting, copying, and pasting data in other programs, such as Microsoft Word. These tasks are somewhat different when working in Excel.

Select a Range

STEP 1 »

A ***range*** refers to a group of adjacent or contiguous cells. A range may be as small as a single cell or as large as the entire worksheet. It may consist of a row or part of a row, a column or part of a column, or multiple rows or columns, but will always be a rectangular shape, as you must select the same number of cells in each row or column for the entire range. A range is specified by indicating the top-left and bottom-right cells in the selection. For example, in Figure 1.29, the date is a single-cell range in cell A2, the Color Laser Printer data are stored in the range A6:G6, the cost values are stored in the range B5:B10, and the sales prices and profit margins are stored in range F5:G10. A ***nonadjacent range*** contains multiple ranges, such as C5:C10 and E5:E10. At times, you need to select nonadjacent ranges so that you can apply the same formatting at the same time, such as formatting the nonadjacent range C5:C10 and E5:E10 with Percent Style.

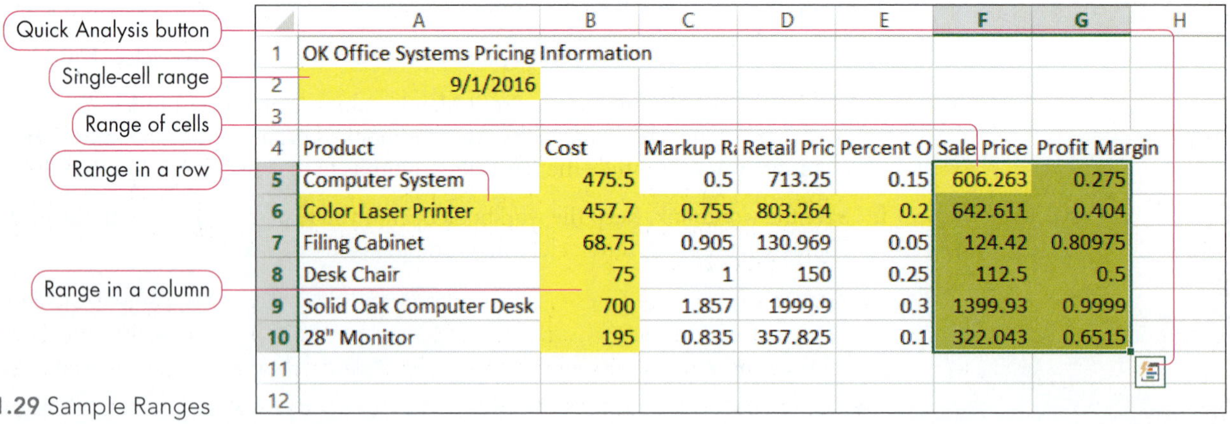

	A	B	C	D	E	F	G	H
1	OK Office Systems Pricing Information							
2	9/1/2016							
3								
4	Product	Cost	Markup Ra	Retail Pric	Percent O	Sale Price	Profit Margin	
5	Computer System	475.5	0.5	713.25	0.15	606.263	0.275	
6	Color Laser Printer	457.7	0.755	803.264	0.2	642.611	0.404	
7	Filing Cabinet	68.75	0.905	130.969	0.05	124.42	0.80975	
8	Desk Chair	75	1	150	0.25	112.5	0.5	
9	Solid Oak Computer Desk	700	1.857	1999.9	0.3	1399.93	0.9999	
10	28" Monitor	195	0.835	357.825	0.1	322.043	0.6515	
11								
12								

FIGURE 1.29 Sample Ranges

Table 1.4 lists methods you can use to select ranges, including nonadjacent ranges.

TABLE 1.4 Selecting Ranges	
To Select:	**Do This:**
A range	Drag until you select the entire range. Alternatively, click the first cell in the range, press and hold Shift, and then click the last cell in the range.
An entire column	Click the column heading.
An entire row	Click the row heading.
Current range containing data	Click in the range of data and press Ctrl+A.
All cells in a worksheet	Click Select All or press Ctrl+A twice.
Nonadjacent range	Select the first range, press and hold Ctrl, and then select additional range(s).

A green border appears around a selected range, and the Quick Analysis button displays in the bottom-right corner of the selected range. Any command you execute will affect the entire range. The range remains selected until you select another range or click in any cell in the worksheet.

Name Box

You can use the Name Box to select a range by clicking in the Name Box, typing a range address such as B15:D25, and then pressing Enter.

Move a Range to Another Location

STEP 1» You can move cell contents from one range to another. For example, you might need to move an input area from the right side of the worksheet to above the output range. When you move a range containing text and values, the text and values do not change. However, any formulas that refer to cells in that range will update to reflect the new cell addresses. To move a range, do the following:

1. Select the range.
2. Use the Cut command to copy the range to the Clipboard. Unlike cutting data in other Microsoft Office applications, the data you cut in Excel remain in their locations until you paste them elsewhere. After you click Cut, a moving dashed green border surrounds the selected range and the status bar displays *Select destination and press ENTER or choose Paste.*
3. Make sure the destination range—the range where you want to move the data—is the same size or greater than the size of the cut range. If any cells within the destination range contain data, Excel overwrites that data when you use the Paste command.
4. Click in the top-left corner of the destination range, and then use the Paste command to insert the data contained in the selected range and remove that data from the original range.

Copy and Paste a Range

STEP 2» You may need to copy cell contents from one range to another. For example, you might copy your January budget to another worksheet to use as a model for creating your February budget. When you copy a range, the original data remain in their original locations. Cell references in copied formulas adjust based on their relative locations to the original data. To copy a range, do the following:

1. Select the range.
2. Use the Copy command to copy the contents of the selected range to the Clipboard. After you click Copy, a moving dashed green border surrounds the selected range and the status bar displays *Select destination and press ENTER or choose Paste.*
3. Make sure the destination range—the range where you want to copy the data—is the same size or greater than the size of the copied range. If any cells within the destination range contain data, Excel overwrites that data when you use the Paste command.
4. Click in the top-left corner of the destination range where you want the duplicate data, and then use the Paste command. The original range still has the moving dashed green border, and the pasted copied range is selected with a solid green border. Figure 1.30 shows a selected range and a copy of the range.
5. Press Esc to turn off the moving dashed border around the originally selected range.

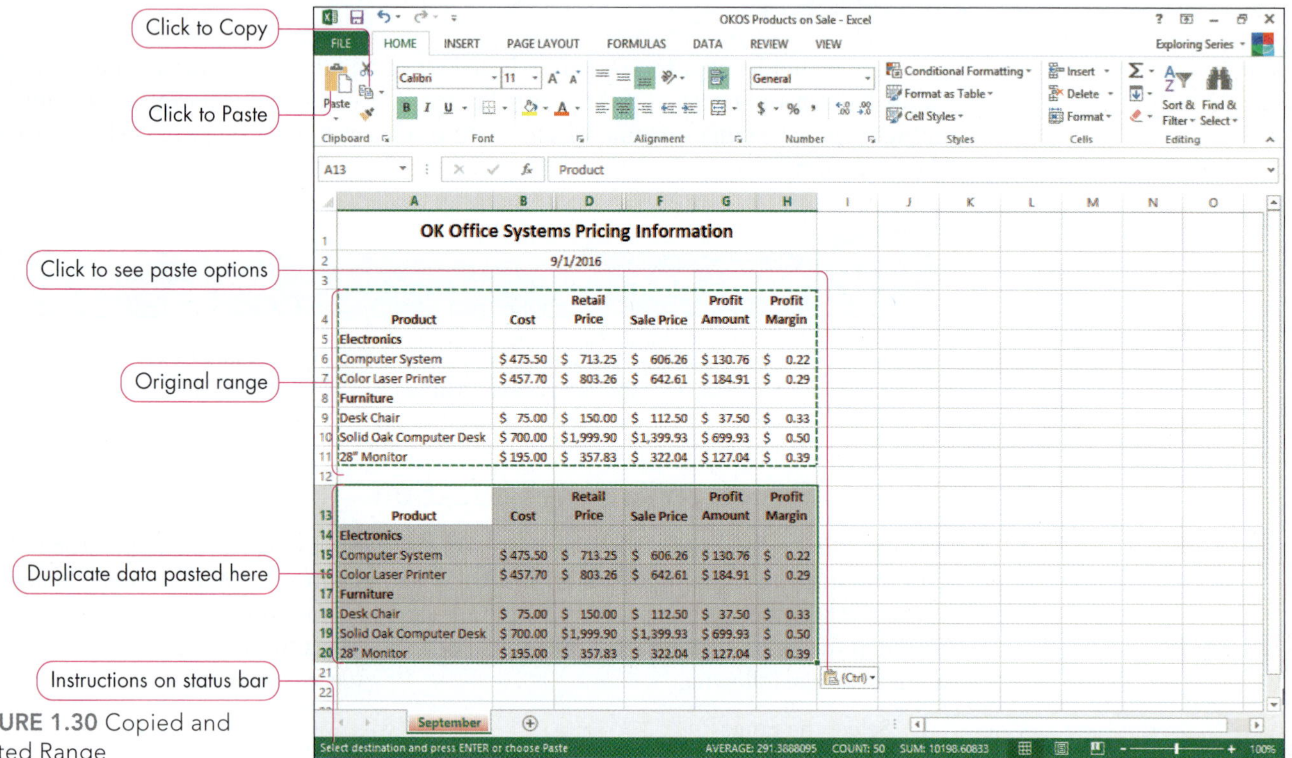

FIGURE 1.30 Copied and Pasted Range

Copy as Picture

Instead of clicking Copy, if you click the Copy arrow in the Clipboard group, you can select Copy (the default option) or Copy as Picture. When you select Copy as Picture, you copy an image of the selected data. You can then paste the image elsewhere in the workbook or in a Word document or PowerPoint presentation. However, when you copy the data as an image, you cannot edit individual cell data after you paste the image.

Use Paste Options and Paste Special

STEP 3

Sometimes you might want to paste data in a different format than they are in the Clipboard. For example, you might want to copy a range containing formulas and cell references, and paste the range as values in another workbook that does not have the referenced cells. If you want to copy data from Excel and paste them into a Word document, you can paste the Excel data as a worksheet object, as unformatted text, or in another format. To paste data from the Clipboard into a different format, click the Paste arrow in the Clipboard group, and hover over a command to see a ScreenTip and a preview of how the pasted data will look. In Figure 1.31, the preview shows that a particular paste option will maintain formulas and number formatting; however, it will not maintain the text formatting, such as font color and centered text. After previewing different paste options, click the one you want in order to apply it.

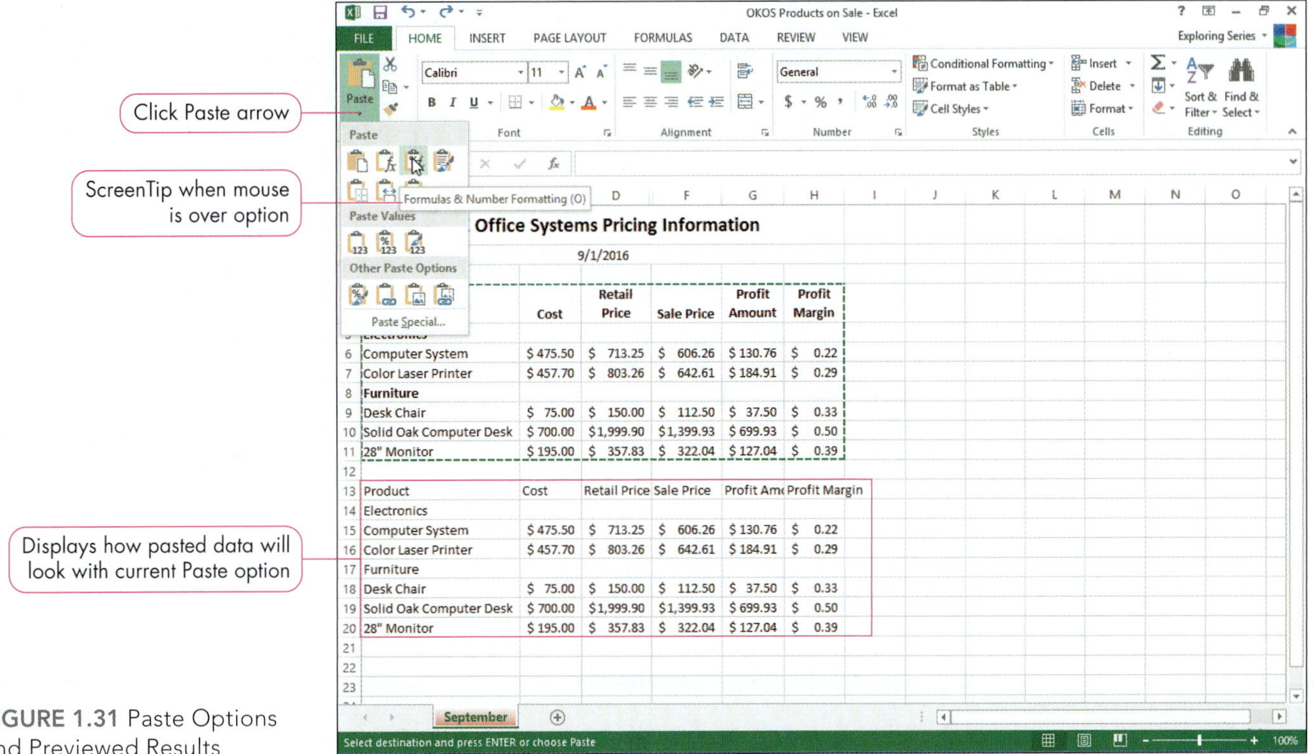

FIGURE 1.31 Paste Options and Previewed Results

For more specific paste options, click the Paste arrow, and then select Paste Special to display the Paste Special dialog box (see Figure 1.32). This dialog box contains more options than the Paste menu. Click the desired option and click OK.

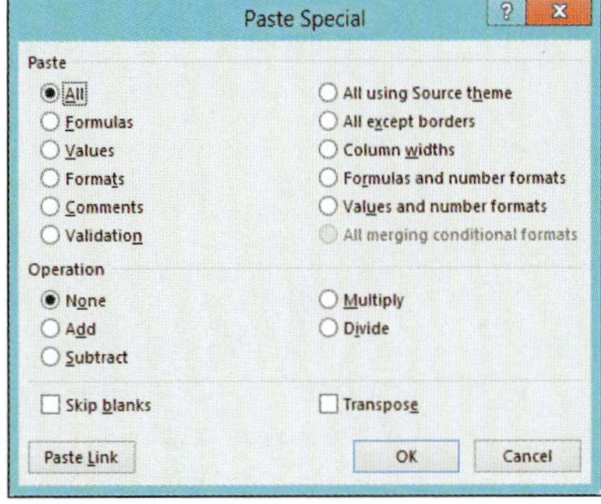

FIGURE 1.32 Paste Special Dialog Box

Paste Options Button

When you copy or paste data, Excel displays the ***Paste Options button*** in the bottom-right corner of the pasted data (refer to Figure 1.30). Click Paste Options to see different results for the pasted data.

Transposing Columns and Rows

After entering data into a worksheet, you might want to transpose the columns and rows so that the data in the first column appear as column labels across the first row, or the column labels in the first row appear in the first column. To transpose worksheet data, select and copy the original range, click the top-left corner of the destination range, click the Paste arrow, and then click Transpose.

Copy Excel Data to Other Programs

You can copy Excel data and use it in other applications, such as in a Word document or in a PowerPoint slide show. For example, you might perform statistical analyses in Excel, copy the data into a research paper in Word or create a budget in Excel, and then copy the data into a PowerPoint slide show for a meeting.

After selecting and copying a range in Excel, you must decide how you want the data to appear in the destination application. Click the Paste arrow in the destination application, such as Word, to see a gallery of options or to select the Paste Special option.

Quick Concepts

1. When you move or copy a worksheet, what are some of the decisions you must make? ***pp. 116–120***
2. How can you select nonadjacent ranges, such as B5:B10 and F5:F10? Why would you select nonadjacent ranges? ***pp. 116–117***
3. Why would you use the Paste Special options in Excel? ***p. 118***

Hands-On Exercises

4 Clipboard Tasks

You realize the 28" Monitor data is in the Furniture category instead of the Electronics category. You need to move the product to its appropriate location. In addition, your supervisor will ask you to enter data for a new product. Because it is almost identical to an existing product, you can copy the original data and edit the copied data to save time. You also want to experiment with the Paste Special option to see the results of using it in the OKOS workbook.

Skills covered: Select a Range and Move a Row to a New Location • Copy and Paste a Range • Use Paste Special

STEP 1 »» SELECT A RANGE AND MOVE A ROW TO A NEW LOCATION

You want to move the 28" Monitor product to be immediately after the Color Laser Printer product. Before moving the 28" Monitor row, you need to insert a blank row between the Color Laser Printer and Furniture rows. Refer to Figure 1.33 as you complete Step 1.

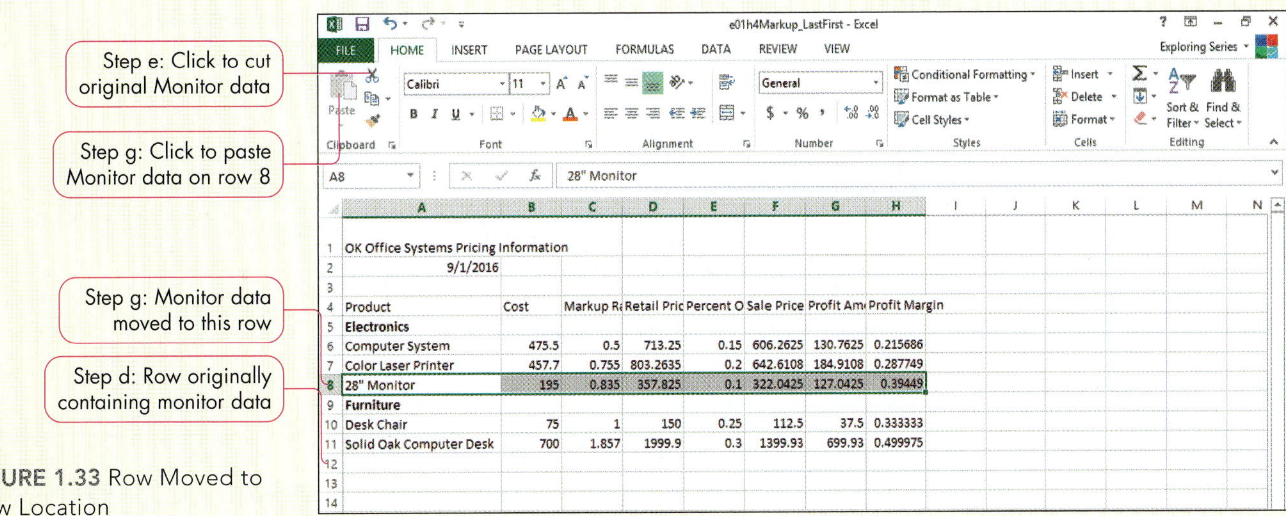

FIGURE 1.33 Row Moved to New Location

a. Open *e01h3Markup_LastFirst* if you closed it at the end of Hands-On Exercise 3 and save it as **e01h4Markup_LastFirst**, changing *h3* to *h4*.

b. Select the **column B, D, and F headings**. Unhide columns C and E as you learned in Hands-On Exercise 3.

   You kept those columns hidden when you saved the *e01h3Markup_LastFirst* workbook to preserve evidence that you know how to hide columns. Now you need the columns visible to continue.

c. Right-click the **row 8 heading** and select **Insert** from the menu.

   You need to insert a blank row so that you can move the *28" Computer Monitor* data to be between the *Color Laser Printer* and *Furniture* rows.

d. Select the **range A12:H12**.

   You selected the range of cells containing the 28" Monitor data.

e. Click **Cut** in the Clipboard group.

   A moving dashed green border outlines the selected range. The status bar displays the message *Select destination and press ENTER or choose Paste.*

f. Click **cell A8**, the new blank row you inserted in step c.

This is the first cell in the destination range.

g. Click **Paste** in the Clipboard group and save the workbook.

The 28" Monitor data are now located on row 8.

> **TROUBLESHOOTING:** If you cut and paste a row without inserting a new row first, Excel will overwrite the original row of data, which is why you inserted a new row in step c. If you forgot to do step c, click Undo until the 28" Monitor data is back in its original location and start with step c again.

STEP 2 » COPY AND PASTE A RANGE

Alesha told you that a new chair is on its way. She asked you to enter the data for the Executive Desk Chair. Because most of the data is the same as the Desk Chair data, you will copy the original Desk Chair data, edit the product name, and then change the cost to reflect the cost of the second chair. Refer to Figure 1.34 as you complete Step 2.

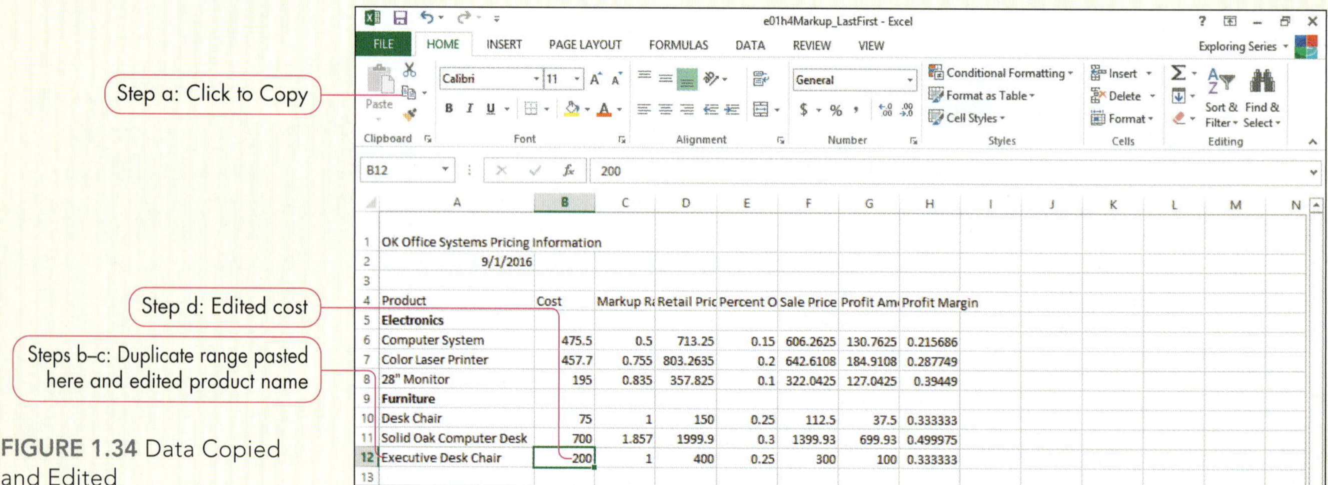

FIGURE 1.34 Data Copied and Edited

a. Select the **range A10:H10**, the row containing the Desk Chair product data, and click **Copy** in the Clipboard group.

b. Click **cell A12**, the location for the duplicate data, and click **Paste** in the Clipboard group. Press **Esc**.

The pasted range is selected in row 12.

c. Click **cell A12**, press **F2** to activate Edit Mode, press **Home**, type **Executive**, press **Spacebar**, and then press **Enter**.

You edited the product name.

d. Change the value in **cell B12** to **200**. Save the workbook.

The formulas calculate the results based on the new cost of 200 for the Executive Desk Chair.

STEP 3 ›› USE PASTE SPECIAL

During your lunch break, you want to experiment with some of the Paste Special options. Particularly, you are interested in pasting Formulas and Value & Source Formatting. First, you will bold the title and apply a font color to help you test these Paste Special options. Refer to Figure 1.35 as you complete Step 3.

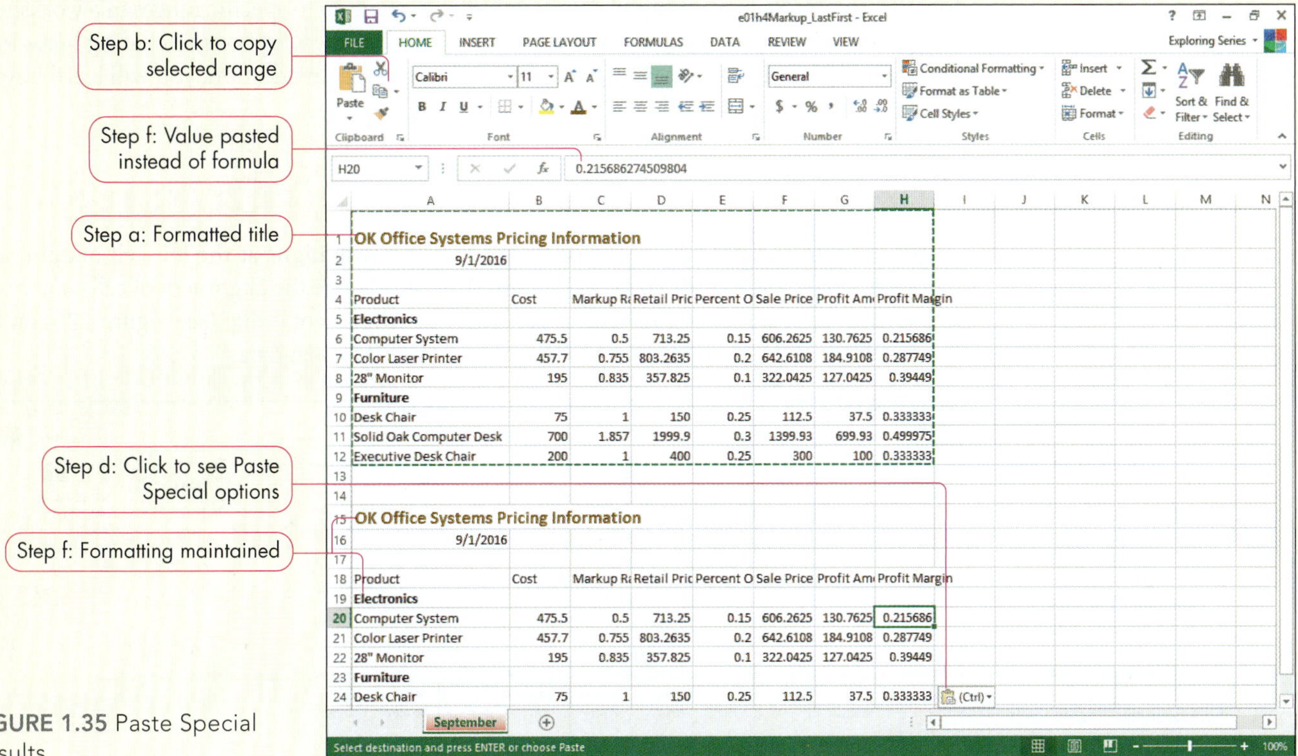

FIGURE 1.35 Paste Special Results

a. Click **cell A1**. Apply these font formats to the title: **14 pt**, **Bold**, and **Gold, Accent 4, Darker 50% font color** in the Font group on the HOME tab.

   You need to format text to see the effects of using different Paste Special options.

b. Select the **range A1:H12** and click **Copy** in the Clipboard group.

c. Click **cell A15**, the top-left corner of the destination range.

d. Click the **Paste arrow** in the Clipboard group and position the mouse pointer over *Formulas*.

   Without clicking the command, Excel shows you a preview of what that option would do. The pasted copy would not contain the font formatting you applied to the title or the bold on the two category names. In addition, the pasted date would appear as a serial number. The formulas would be maintained.

e. Position the mouse pointer over *Values & Source Formatting*.

   This option would preserve the formatting, but it would convert the formulas into the current value results.

f. Click **Values & Source Formatting**, click **cell H6** to see a formula, and then click **cell H20**. Press **Esc** to turn off the border.

   Cell H6 contains a formula, but in the pasted version, the equivalent cell H20 has converted the formula result into an actual value. If you were to change the original cost on row 20, the contents of cell H20 would not change. In a working environment, this is useful only if you want to capture the exact value in a point in time before making changes to the original data.

g. Save the workbook. Keep the workbook open if you plan to continue with the next Hands-On Exercise. If not, close the workbook and exit Excel.

Formatting

After entering data and formulas, you should format the worksheet. A professionally formatted worksheet—through adding appropriate symbols, aligning decimals, and using fonts and colors to make data stand out—makes finding and analyzing data easy. You apply different formats to accentuate meaningful details or to draw attention to specific ranges in a worksheet.

In this section, you will learn to apply different alignment options, including horizontal and vertical alignment, text wrapping, and indent options. In addition, you will learn how to format different types of values.

Applying Alignment and Font Options

Alignment refers to how data are positioned in cells. Text aligns at the left cell margin, and dates and values align at the right cell margin. You can change the alignment of cell contents to improve the appearance of data within the cells. The Alignment group (see Figure 1.36) on the Home tab contains several features to help you align and format data.

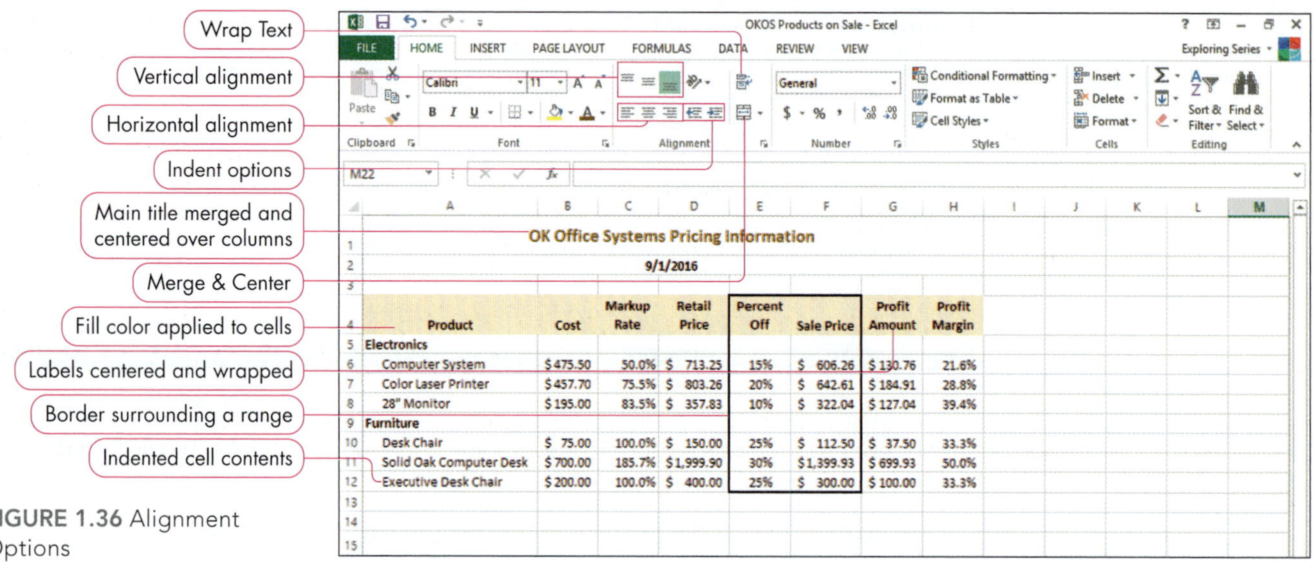

FIGURE 1.36 Alignment Options

TIP Alignment Options

The Format Cells dialog box contains additional alignment options. To open the Format Cells dialog box, click the Dialog Box Launcher in the Alignment group on the Home tab. The Alignment tab in the dialog box contains the options for aligning data.

Merge and Center Labels

You may want to place a title at the top of a worksheet and center it over the columns of data in the worksheet. You can center main titles over all columns in the worksheet, and you can center category titles over groups of related columns. To create a title, enter the text in the far left cell of the range. Select the range of cells across which you want to center the title and click Merge & Center in the Alignment group on the Home tab. Only data in the far left cell (or top right cell) are merged. Any other data in the merged cells are deleted. Excel merges the selected cells together into one cell, and the merged cell address is that of the original cell on the left. The data are centered between the left and right sides of the merged cell.

If you merge too many cells and want to split the merged cell back into its original multiple cells, click the merged cell and click Merge & Center. Unmerging places the data in the top-left cell.

For additional options, click the Merge & Center arrow. Table 1.5 lists the four merge options.

TABLE 1.5 Merge Options

Option	Results
Merge & Center	Merges selected cells and centers data into one cell.
Merge Across	Merges the selected cells but keeps text left aligned or values right aligned.
Merge Cells	Enables you to merge a range of cells on multiple rows as well as in multiple columns.
Unmerge Cells	Separates a merged cell into multiple cells again.

Change Horizontal and Vertical Cell Alignment

STEP 2»

Horizontal alignment specifies the position of data between the left and right cell margins, and ***vertical alignment*** specifies the position of data between the top and bottom cell margins. Bottom Align is the default vertical alignment (as indicated by the light green background), and Align Left is the default horizontal alignment for text. In Figure 1.36, the labels on row 4 have Center horizontal alignment and the title in row 1 has Middle Align vertical alignment.

If you increase row height, you might need to change the vertical alignment to position data better in conjunction with data in adjacent cells. To change alignments, click the desired alignment setting(s) in the Alignment group on the Home tab.

Rotate Cell Data

People sometimes rotate headings in cells. You can rotate data in a cell by clicking Orientation in the Alignment group and selecting an option, such as Angle Clockwise.

Wrap Text

STEP 2»

Sometimes you have to maintain specific column widths, but the data do not fit entirely. You can use ***wrap text*** to make data appear on multiple lines by adjusting the row height to fit the cell contents within the column width. When you click Wrap Text in the Alignment group, Excel wraps the text on two or more lines within the cell. This alignment option is helpful when the column headings are wider than the values contained in the column. In Figure 1.36, the *Markup Rate* and *Percent Off* labels on row 4 are examples of wrapped text.

Increase and Decrease Indent

STEP 3»

To offset labels, you can indent text within a cell. ***Indenting*** helps others see the hierarchical structure of data. Accountants often indent the word *Totals* in financial statements so that it stands out from a list of items above the total row. To indent the contents of a cell, click Increase Indent in the Alignment group on the Home tab. The more you click Increase Indent, the more text is indented in the cell. To decrease the indent, click Decrease Indent in the Alignment group. In Figure 1.36, *Computer System* and *Desk Chair* are indented.

TIP Indenting Values

Values right align by default. You should align the decimal places in a column of values. If the column label is wide, the values below it appear too far on the right. To preserve the values aligning at the decimal places, use the Align Right horizontal alignment and click Increase Indent to shift the values over to the left a little for better placement.

Apply Borders and Fill Color

STEP 4》 You can apply a border or fill color to accentuate data in a worksheet. A ***border*** is a line that surrounds a cell or a range of cells. You can use borders to offset some data from the rest of the worksheet data. To apply a border, select the cell or range that you want to have a border, click the Borders arrow in the Font group, and then select the desired border type. In Figure 1.36, a border surrounds the range E4:F12. To remove a border, select No Border from the Borders menu.

To add some color to your worksheet to add emphasis to data or headers, you can apply a fill color. ***Fill color*** is a background color that displays behind the data. You should choose a fill color that contrasts with the font color. For example, if the font color is Black, you might want to choose Yellow fill color. If the font color is White, you might want to apply Blue or Dark Blue fill color. To apply a fill color, select the cell or range that you want to have a fill color, click the Fill Color arrow on the Home tab, and then select the color choice from the Fill Color palette. In Figure 1.36, the column labels in row 4 contain the Gold, Accent 4, Lighter 80% fill color. If you want to remove a fill color, select No Fill from the bottom of the palette.

For additional border and fill color options, click the Dialog Box Launcher in the Font group to display the Format Cells dialog box. Click the Border tab to select border options, including the border line style and color. Click the Fill tab to set the background color, fill effects, and patterns.

Applying Number Formats

Values have no special formatting when you enter data. You should apply ***number formats*** based on the type of values in a cell, such as applying either the Accounting or Currency number format to monetary values. Changing the number format changes the way the number displays in a cell, but the format does not change the number's value. If, for example, you enter 123.456 into a cell and format the cell with the Currency number type, the value shows as $123.46 onscreen, but the actual value 123.456 is used for calculations. When you apply a number format, you can specify the number of decimal places to display onscreen.

Apply a Number Format

STEP 5》 The default number format is General, which displays values as you originally enter them. General does not align decimal points in a column or include symbols, such as dollar signs, percent signs, or commas. Table 1.6 lists and describes the primary number formats in Excel.

TABLE 1.6 Number Formats

Format Style	Display
General	A number as it was originally entered. Numbers are shown as integers (e.g., 12345), decimal fractions (e.g., 1234.5), or in scientific notation (e.g., 1.23E+10) if the number exceeds 11 digits.
Number	A number with or without the 1,000 separator (e.g., a comma) and with any number of decimal places. Negative numbers can be displayed with parentheses and/or red.
Currency	A number with the 1,000 separator and an optional dollar sign (which is placed immediately to the left of the number). Negative values are preceded by a minus sign or are displayed with parentheses or in red. Two decimal places display by default.
Accounting Number Format	A number with the 1,000 separator, an optional dollar sign (at the left border of the cell, vertically aligned within a column), negative values in parentheses, and zero values as hyphens. Two decimal places display by default. Changes alignment slightly within the cell.
Comma	A number with the 1,000 separator. Used in conjunction with Accounting Number Style to align commas and decimal places.
Date	The date in different ways, such as Long Date (March 14, 2016) or Short Date (3/14/16 or 14-Mar-16).
Time	The time in different formats, such as 10:50 PM or 22:50.
Percent Style	The value as it would be multiplied by 100 (for display purpose), with the percent sign. The default number of decimal places is zero if you click Percent Style in the Number group or two decimal places if you use the Format Cells dialog box. However, you should typically increase the number of decimal points to show greater accuracy.
Fraction	A number as a fraction; use when no exact decimal equivalent exists. A fraction is entered into a cell as a formula such as =1/3. If the cell is not formatted as a fraction, the formula results display.
Scientific	A number as a decimal fraction followed by a whole number exponent of 10; for example, the number 12345 would appear as 1.23E+04. The exponent, +04 in the example, is the number of places the decimal point is moved to the left (or right if the exponent is negative). Very small numbers have negative exponents.
Text	The data left aligned; is useful for numerical values that have leading zeros and should be treated as text, such as postal codes or phone numbers. Apply Text format before typing a leading zero so that the zero displays in the cell.
Special	A number with editing characters, such as hyphens in a Social Security number.
Custom	Predefined customized number formats or special symbols to create your own customized number format.

The Number group on the Home tab contains commands for applying ***Accounting Number Format***, ***Percent Style***, and ***Comma Style*** numbering formats. You can click the Accounting Number Format arrow and select other denominations, such as English pounds or euros. For other number formats, click the Number Format arrow and select the numbering format you want to use. For more specific numbering formats than those provided, select More Number Formats from the Number Format menu or click the Number Dialog Box Launcher to open the Format Cells dialog box with the Number tab options readily available. Figure 1.37 shows different number formats applied to values.

	A	B
1	General	1234.567
2	Number	1234.57
3	Currency	$1,234.57
4	Accounting	$ 1,234.57
5	Comma	1,234.57
6	Percent	12%
7	Short Date	3/1/2016
8	Long Date	Tuesday, March 1, 2016

FIGURE 1.37 Number Formats

Increase and Decrease Decimal Places

After applying a number format, you may need to adjust the number of decimal places that display. For example, if you have an entire column of monetary values formatted in Accounting Number Format, Excel displays two decimal places by default. If the entire column of values contains whole dollar values and no cents, displaying *.00* down the column looks cluttered. You can decrease the number of decimal places to show whole numbers only.

To change the number of decimal places displayed, click Increase Decimal in the Number group on the Home tab to display more decimal places for greater precision or Decrease Decimal to display fewer or no decimal places.

1. What is the importance of formatting a worksheet? ***p. 124***
2. Describe five alignment and font formatting techniques used to format labels that are discussed in this section. ***pp. 124–126***
3. What are the main differences between Accounting Number Format and Currency format? Which format has its own command on the Ribbon? ***p. 127***

Hands-On Exercises

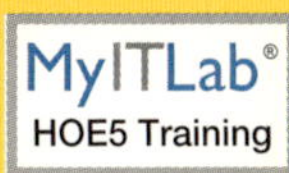

5 Formatting

In the first four Hands-On Exercises, you entered data about products on sale, created formulas to calculate markup and profit, and inserted new rows and columns to accommodate the labels *Electronics* and *Furniture* to identify the specific products. You are ready to format the worksheet. Specifically, you need to center the title, align text, format values, and then apply other formatting to enhance the readability of the worksheet.

Skills covered: Merge and Center the Title • Align Text Horizontally and Vertically and Wrap Text • Increase Indent • Apply Borders and Fill Color • Apply Number Formats and Increase and Decrease Decimal Places

STEP 1 » MERGE AND CENTER THE TITLE

To make the title stand out, you want to center it over all the data columns. You will use the Merge & Center command to merge cells and center the title at the same time. Refer to Figure 1.38 as you complete Step 1.

Step e: Date merged, centered, and bold A2:H2

	A	B	C	D	E	F	G	H
1	OK Office Systems Pricing Information							
2	9/1/2016							
3								
4	Product	Cost	Markup Ra	Retail Pric	Percent O	Sale Price	Profit Am	Profit Margin
5	**Electronics**							
6	Computer System	475.5	0.5	713.25	0.15	606.2625	130.7625	0.215686
7	Color Laser Printer	457.7	0.755	803.2635	0.2	642.6108	184.9108	0.287749
8	28" Monitor	195	0.835	357.825	0.1	322.0425	127.0425	0.39449
9	**Furniture**							
10	Desk Chair	75	1	150	0.25	112.5	37.5	0.333333
11	Solid Oak Computer Desk	700	1.857	1999.9	0.3	1399.93	699.93	0.499975
12	Executive Desk Chair	200	1	400	0.25	300	100	0.333333
13								

FIGURE 1.38 Title and Date Merged and Centered

a. Open *e01h4Markup_LastFirst* if you closed it at the end of Hands-On Exercise 4 and save it as **e01h5Markup_LastFirst**, changing *h4* to *h5*.

b. Select the **range A15:H26** and press **Delete**.

You maintained a copy of your Paste Special results in the *e01h4Markup_LastFirst* workbook, but you do not need it to continue.

c. Select the **range A1:H1**.

You want to center the title over all columns of data.

d. Click **Merge & Center** in the Alignment group.

Excel merges cells in the range A1:H1 into one cell and centers the title horizontally within the merged cell, which is cell A1.

> **TROUBLESHOOTING:** If you merge too many or not enough cells, you can unmerge the cells and start again. To unmerge cells, click in the merged cell. The Merge & Center command is shaded in green when the active cell is merged. Click Merge & Center to unmerge the cell. Then select the correct range to merge and use Merge & Center again.

c. Select the **range E4:F12**, click the **Border arrow** in the Font group, and then select **Thick Box Border**.

You applied a border around the selected cells.

d. Click in an empty cell below the columns of data to deselect the cells. Save the workbook.

STEP 5 » APPLY NUMBER FORMATS AND INCREASE AND DECREASE DECIMAL PLACES

You need to format the values to increase readability and look more professional. You will apply number formats and adjust the number of decimal points displayed. Refer to Figure 1.42 as you complete Step 5.

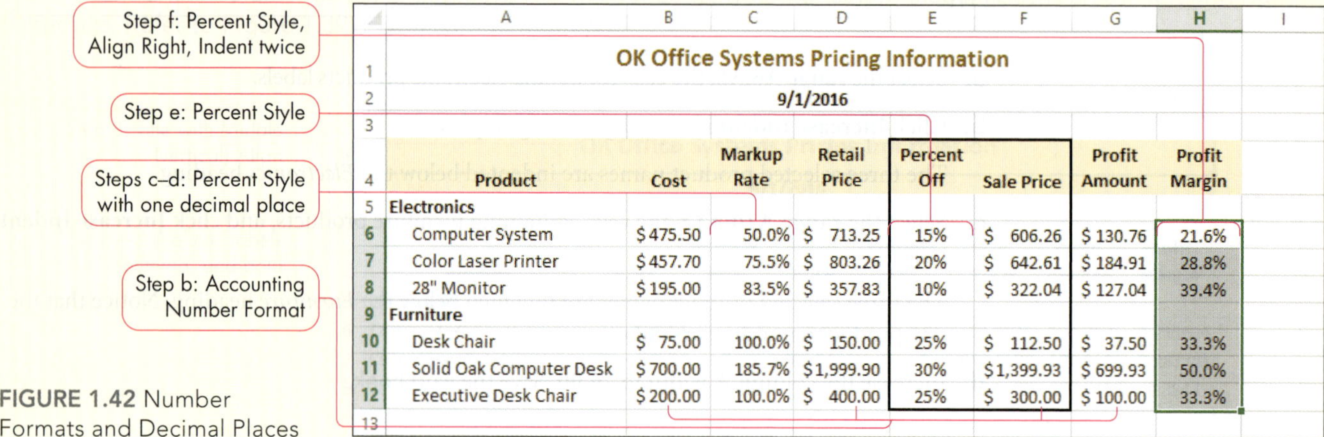

FIGURE 1.42 Number Formats and Decimal Places

a. Select the **range B6:B12.** Press and hold **Ctrl** as you select the **ranges D6:D12** and **F6:G12.**

Because you want to format nonadjacent ranges with the same formats, you hold down Ctrl.

b. Click **Accounting Number Format** in the Number group. If some cells contain pound signs, increase the column widths as needed.

You formatted the selected nonadjacent ranges with the Accounting Number Format. The dollar signs align on the left cell margins and the decimals align.

c. Select the **range C6:C12** and click **Percent Style** in the Number group.

You formatted the values in the selected ranges with Percent Style, showing whole numbers only.

d. Click **Increase Decimal** in the Number group.

You increased the decimal to show one decimal place to avoid misleading your readers by displaying the values as whole percentages.

e. Apply **Percent Style** to the **range E6:E12.**

f. Select the **range H6:H12**, apply **Percent Style**, and then click **Increase Decimal.**

g. Select the **range E6:E12**, click **Align Right**, and then click **Increase Indent** twice. Select the **range H6:H12**, click **Align Right**, and then click **Increase Indent**.

With values, you want to keep the decimal points aligned, but you can then use Increase Indent to adjust the indent so that the values appear more centered below the column labels.

h. Save the workbook. Keep the workbook open if you plan to continue with the next Hands-On Exercise. If not, close the workbook and exit Excel.

Page Setup and Printing

Although you might distribute workbooks electronically as e-mail attachments or you might upload workbooks to a corporate server, you should prepare the worksheets in the workbook for printing. You should prepare worksheets in case you need to print them or in case others who receive an electronic copy of your workbook need to print the worksheets. The Page Layout tab provides options for controlling the printed worksheet (see Figure 1.43).

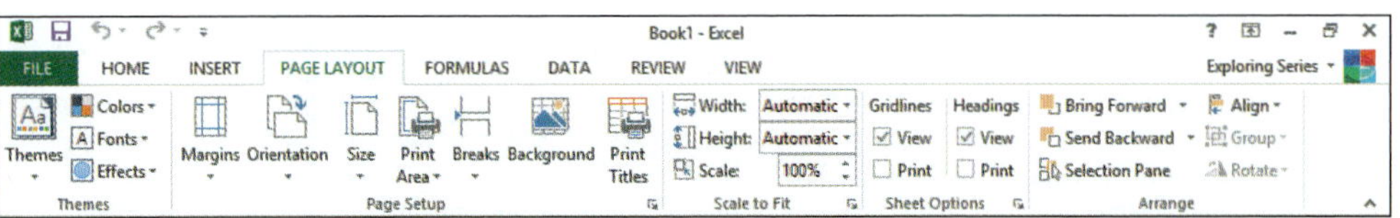

FIGURE 1.43 Page Layout Tab

In this section, you will select options on the Page Layout tab. Specifically, you will use the Page Setup, Scale to Fit, and Sheet Options groups. After selecting page setup options, you are ready to print your worksheet.

Selecting Page Setup Options

The Page Setup group on the Page Layout tab contains options to set the margins, select orientation, specify page size, select the print area, and apply other options. The *Scale to Fit* group contains options for adjusting the scaling of the spreadsheet on the printed page. When possible, use the commands in these groups to apply page settings. Table 1.7 lists and describes the commands in the Page Setup group.

TABLE 1.7 Page Setup Commands

Command	Description
Margins	Displays a menu to select predefined margin settings. The default margins are 0.75" top and bottom and 0.7" left and right. You will often change these margin settings to balance the worksheet data better on the printed page. If you need different margins, select Custom Margins.
Orientation	Displays orientation options. The default page orientation is portrait, which is appropriate for worksheets that contain more rows than columns. Select landscape orientation when worksheets contain more columns than can fit in portrait orientation. For example, the OKOS worksheet might appear better balanced in landscape orientation because it has eight columns.
Size	Displays a list of standard paper sizes. The default size is 8 1/2" by 11". If you have a different paper size, such as legal paper, select it from the list.
Print Area	Displays a list to set or clear the print area. When you have very large worksheets, you might want to print only a portion of that worksheet. To do so, select the range you want to print, click Print Area in the Page Setup group, and then select Set Print Area. When you use the Print commands, only the range you specified will be printed. To clear the print area, click Print Area and select Clear Print Area.
Breaks	Displays a list to insert or remove page breaks.
Background	Enables you to select an image to appear as the background behind the worksheet data when viewed onscreen (backgrounds do not appear when the worksheet is printed).
Print Titles	Enables you to select column headings and row labels to repeat on multiple-page printouts.

Specify Page Options

STEP 1

To apply several page setup options at once or to access options not found on the Ribbon, click the Page Setup Dialog Box Launcher. The Page Setup dialog box organizes options into four tabs: Page, Margins, Header/Footer, and Sheet. All tabs contain Print and Print Preview buttons. Figure 1.44 shows the Page tab.

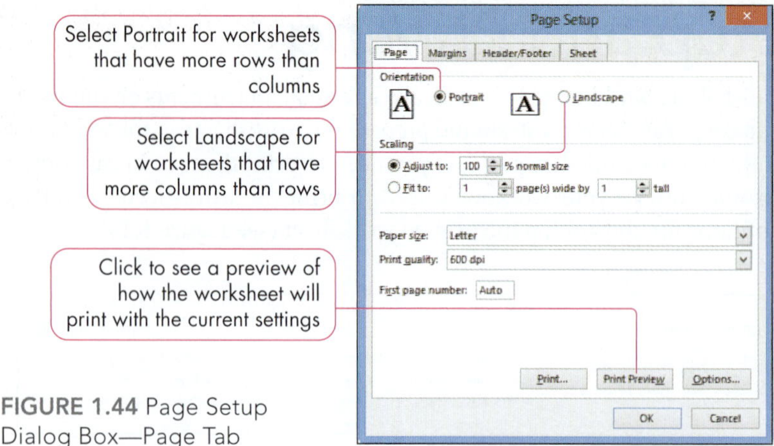

FIGURE 1.44 Page Setup Dialog Box—Page Tab

The Page tab contains options to select the orientation and paper size. In addition, it contains scaling options that are similar to the options in the *Scale to Fit* group on the Page Layout tab. You use scaling options to increase or decrease the size of characters on a printed page, similar to using a zoom setting on a photocopy machine. You can also use the *Fit to* option to force the data to print on a specified number of pages.

Set Margins Options

STEP 2» The Margins tab (see Figure 1.45) contains options for setting the specific margins. In addition, it contains options to center the worksheet data horizontally or vertically on the page. To balance worksheet data equally between the left and right margins, Excel users often center the page horizontally.

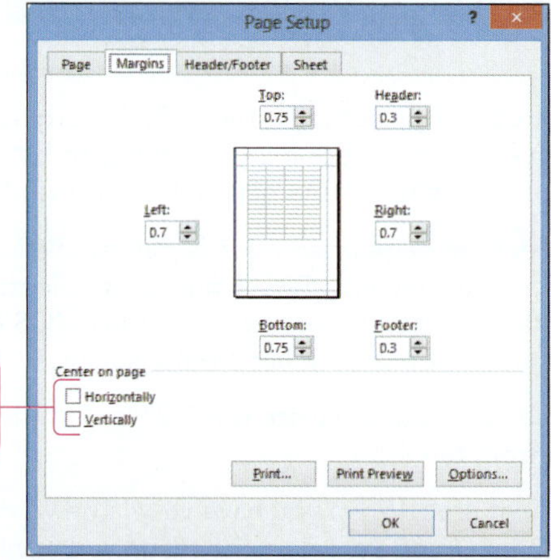

FIGURE 1.45 Page Setup Dialog Box—Margins Tab

Create Headers and Footers

STEP 3» The Header/Footer tab (see Figure 1.46) lets you create a header and/or footer that appears at the top and/or bottom of every printed page. Click the arrows to choose from several preformatted entries, or alternatively, you can click Custom Header or Custom Footer, insert text and other objects, and then click the appropriate formatting button to customize your headers and footers. You can use headers and footers to provide additional information about the worksheet. You can include your name, the date the worksheet was prepared, and page numbers, for example.

You can create different headers or footers on different pages, such as one header with the file name on odd-numbered pages and a header containing the date on even-numbered pages. Click the *Different odd and even pages* check box in the Page Setup dialog box (see Figure 1.46).

You might want the first page to have a different header or footer from the rest of the printed pages, or you might not want a header or footer to show up on the first page but want the header or footer to display on the remaining pages. Click the *Different first page* check box in the Page Setup dialog box to specify a different first page header or footer (see Figure 1.46).

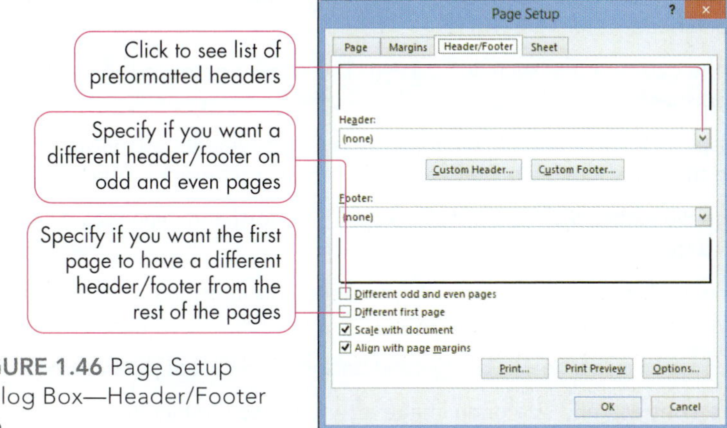

FIGURE 1.46 Page Setup Dialog Box—Header/Footer Tab

Instead of creating headers and footers using the Page Setup dialog box, you can click the Insert tab and click Header & Footer in the Text group. Excel displays the worksheet in ***Page Layout view*** with the insertion point in the center area of the header. You can click inside the left, center, or right section of a header or footer. When you do, Excel displays the Header & Footer Tools Design contextual tab (see Figure 1.47). You can enter text or insert data from the Header & Footer Elements group on the tab. Table 1.8 lists and describes the options in the Header & Footer Elements group. To get back to ***Normal view***, click any cell in the worksheet and click Normal in the Workbook Views group on the View tab.

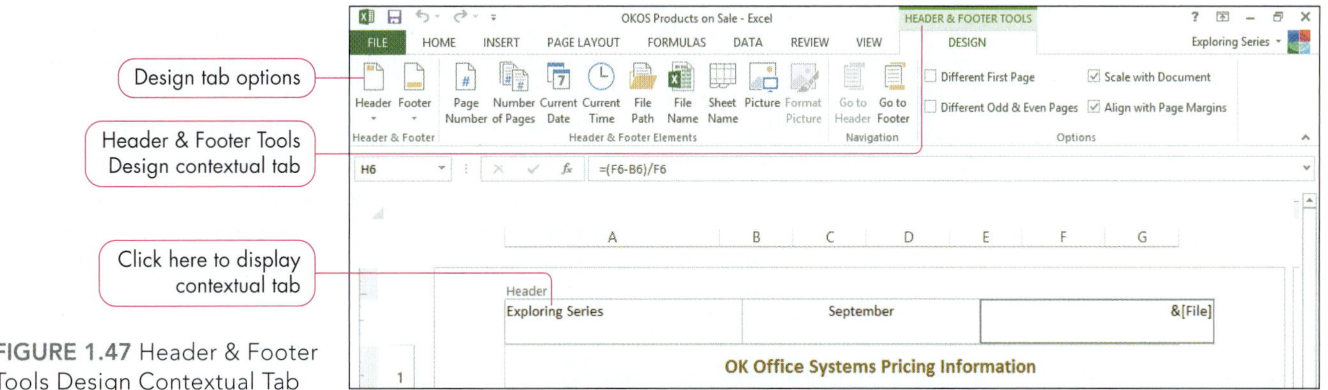

FIGURE 1.47 Header & Footer Tools Design Contextual Tab

TABLE 1.8 Header & Footer Elements Options	
Option Name	**Result**
Page Number	Inserts the code &[Page] to display the current page number.
Number of Pages	Inserts the code &[Pages] to display the total number of pages that will print.
Current Date	Inserts the code &[Date] to display the current date, such as 5/19/2016. The date updates to the current date when you open or print the worksheet.
Current Time	Inserts the code &[Time] to display the current time, such as 5:15 PM. The time updates to the current time when you open or print the worksheet.
File Path	Inserts the code &[Path]&[File] to display the path and file name, such as C:\Documents\e01h4Markup. This information changes if you save the workbook with a different name or in a different location.
File Name	Inserts the code &[File] to display the file name, such as e01h4Markup. This information changes if you save the workbook with a different name.
Sheet Name	Inserts the code &[Tab] to display the worksheet name, such as September. This information changes if you rename the worksheet.
Picture	Inserts the code &[Picture] to display and print an image as a background behind the data, not just the worksheet.
Format Picture	Enables you to adjust the brightness, contrast, and size of an image after you use the Picture option.

View Tab

If you click the View tab and click Page Layout, Excel displays an area *Click to add header* at the top of the worksheet.

Select Sheet Options

STEP 5» The Sheet tab (see Figure 1.48) contains options for setting the print area, print titles, print options, and page order. Some of these options are also located in the Sheet Options group on the Page Layout tab on the Ribbon. By default, Excel displays gridlines onscreen to show you each cell's margins, but the gridlines do not print unless you specifically select the Gridlines check box in the Page Setup dialog box or the Print Gridlines check box in the Sheet Options group on the Page Layout tab. In addition, Excel displays row (1, 2, 3, etc.) and column (A, B, C, etc.) headings onscreen. However, these headings do not print unless you click the *Row and column headings* check box in the Page Setup dialog box or click the Print Headings check box in the Sheet Options group on the Page Layout tab.

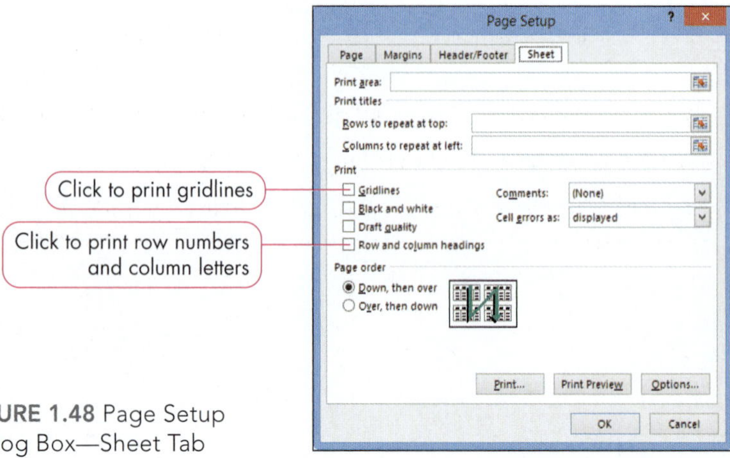

FIGURE 1.48 Page Setup Dialog Box—Sheet Tab

TIP Printing Gridlines and Headings

For most worksheets, you do not need to print gridlines and row/column headings. However, when you want to display and print cell formulas instead of formula results, you might want to print the gridlines and row/column headings. Doing so will help you analyze your formulas. The gridlines help you see the cell boundaries, and the headings help you identify what data are in each cell. At times, you might want to display gridlines to separate data on a regular printout to increase readability.

Previewing and Printing a Worksheet

Before printing a worksheet, you should click the File tab and select Print. The Microsoft Office Backstage view displays print options and displays the worksheet in print preview mode. This mode helps you see in advance if the data are balanced on the page or if data will print on multiple pages.

You can specify the number of copies to print and which printer to use to print the worksheet. The first option in the Settings area enables you to specify what to print. The default option is Print Active Sheets. You can choose other options, such as Print Entire Workbook or Print Selection. You can also specify which pages to print. If you are connected to a printer capable of duplex printing, you can print on only one side or print on both sides. You can also collate, change the orientation, specify the paper size, adjust the margins, and adjust the scaling.

The bottom of the Print window indicates how many pages will print. If you do not like how the worksheet will print, click the Page Layout tab so that you can adjust margins, scaling, column widths, and so on until the worksheet data appear the way you want them to print.

TIP Printing Multiple Worksheets

To print more than one worksheet at a time, select the sheets you want to print. To select adjacent sheets, click the first sheet tab, press and hold Shift, and then click the last sheet tab. To select nonadjacent sheets, press and hold Ctrl as you click each sheet tab. When you display the Print options in the Microsoft Office Backstage view, Print Active Sheets is one of the default settings. If you want to print all of the worksheets within the workbook, change the setting to Print Entire Workbook.

1. What helps determine whether you use portrait or landscape orientation for a worksheet? **p. 133**
2. Why would you select a *Center on page* option if you have already set the margins? **p. 134**
3. List at least five elements you can insert in a header or footer. **p. 136**
4. Why would you want to print gridlines and row and column headings? **p. 136**

Sunday	Monday	Tuesday	Wednesday	Thursday	Friday	Saturday
1	2	3	4	5	6	7
8	9	10	11	12	13	14
15	16	17	18	19	20	21
22	23	24	25	26	27	28
29	30	31				

May 2016

FIGURE 1.53 May 2016 Calendar

a. Click the **FILE tab**, select **New**, and then click **Blank workbook**. Save the workbook as **e01p2May2016_LastFirst**.

b. Type **'May 2016** in **cell A1** and click **Enter** on the left side of the Formula Bar.

> **TROUBLESHOOTING:** If you do not type the apostrophe before *May 2016*, the cell will display *May-16* instead of *May 2016*.

c. Format the title:
- Select the **range A1:G1** and click **Merge & Center** in the Alignment group.
- Apply **48 pt font size**.
- Click the **Fill Color arrow** and click **Green, Accent 6, Lighter 40%** in the *Theme Colors* section of the color palette.

d. Complete the days of the week:
- Type **Sunday** in **cell A2** and click **Enter** on the left side of the Formula Bar.
- Drag the **cell A2 fill handle** across the row through **cell G2** to use Auto Fill to complete the rest of the weekdays.
- Click the **Fill Color arrow** and select **Green, Accent 6, Lighter 60%**. Click the **Font Color arrow** and click **Green, Accent 6, Darker 50%**. Apply bold and **14 pt font size**. Click **Middle Align** and click **Center** in the Alignment group.

e. Complete the days of the month:
- Type **1** in **cell A3** and press **Ctrl+Enter**. Drag the **cell A3 fill handle** across the row through **cell G3**. Click **Auto Fill Options** in the bottom-right corner of the filled data and select **Fill Series**.
- Type **=A3+7** in **cell A4** and press **Ctrl+Enter**. Usually you avoid numbers in formulas, but the number of days in a week is always 7. Drag the **cell A4 fill handle** down through **cell A7** to get the date for each Sunday in May.
- Keep the **range A4:A7** selected and drag the fill handle across through **cell G7**. Select the **range D7:G7** and press **Delete** to delete the extra days.

f. Format the columns and rows:
- Select **columns A:G**. Click **Format** in the Cells group, select **Column Width**, type **16** in the **Column width box**, and then click **OK**.
- Select **row 2**. Click **Format** in the Cells group, select **Row Height**, type **54**, and then click **OK**.

Excel

Formul
Functi

Yuri Arcurs/Shutterstock

Performing Quant

OBJECTIVES

1. Use relative, absolute, formulas p. 158
2. Correct circular referer
3. Insert a function p. 16
4. Insert basic math and
5. Use date functions p.

CASE STUD

You are an assistant t Company. Erica spen clients, and preparin analyze mortgage da

Today, Erica prov down payment, mort perform some basic c tem to verify if it is ca financed, the periodi of the house cost tha calculate totals, avera

Furthermore, you up interest rates fro how much (if any) th

4 Problem-Solving v

OLLABORATION CASE

Mid-Level

1 Restaurant Recei

FROM SCRATCH 

FIGURE 1.55 Matt's Sports Grill Receipt

DISCOVER 

- Select **rows 3:7**. Set an **80 row height**.
- Select the **range A2:G7**. Click the **Borders arrow** in the Font group and select **All Borders**.
- Select the **range A3:G7**. Click **Top Align** and **Align Left** in the Alignment group. Click **Increase Indent**. Bold the numbers and apply **12 pt font size**.

g. Double-click the **Sheet1 tab**, type **May**, and then press **Enter**.

h. Deselect the range and click the **PAGE LAYOUT tab**. Click **Orientation** in the Page Setup group and select **Landscape**.

i. Click the **INSERT tab** and click **Header & Footer** in the Text group. Click in the left side of the header and type your name. Click in the center of the header and click **Sheet Name** in the Header & Footer Elements group on the DESIGN tab. Click in the right side of the header and click **File Name** in the Header & Footer Elements group on the DESIGN tab. Click in any cell in the workbook and click **Normal** on the status bar.

j. Save and close the file, and submit based on your instructor's directions.

3 Downtown Theatre

You are the assistant manager at Downtown Theatre, where touring Broadway plays and musicals are performed. You need to complete a spreadsheet to help you analyze ticket sales by seating chart for each performance. The spreadsheet will identify the seating sections, total seats in each section, and the number of seats sold for a performance. You will then calculate the percentage of seats sold and unsold. This exercise follows the same set of skills as used in Hands-On Exercises 1–6 in the chapter. Refer to Figure 1.54 as you complete this exercise.

	A	B	C	D	E
1	Downtown Theatre				
2	Ticket Sales by Seating Section				
3	3/31/2016				
4					
5	Section	Available Seats	Seats Sold	Percentage Sold	Percentage Unsold
6	Box Seats	25	12	48.0%	52.0%
7	Front Floor	120	114	95.0%	5.0%
8	Back Floor	132	108	81.8%	18.2%
9	Tier 1	40	40	100.0%	0.0%
10	Mezzanine	144	138	95.8%	4.2%
11	Balcony	106	84	79.2%	20.8%

FIGURE 1.54 Theatre Seating Data

a. Open *e01p3TicketSales* and save it as **e01p3TicketSales_LastFirst**.

b. Double-click the **Sheet1 tab**, type **Seating**, and then press **Enter**.

c. Type **3/31/2016** in **cell A3** and press **Enter**.

d. Adjust alignments and font attributes by doing the following from the Alignment and Font groups on the HOME tab:
- Select the **range A1:E1**, click **Merge & Center**, click **Bold**, click the **Font Size arrow**, and then select **16**.
- Use the Merge & Center command to merge the **range A2:E2** and center the subtitle.
- Use the Merge & Center command to merge the **range A3:E3** and center the date.
- Select the **range A5:E5**, click **Wrap Text**, click **Center**, and then click **Bold** to format the column labels.

e. Right-click the **row 9 heading** and select **Insert** from the shortcut menu to insert a new row. Type the following data in the new row: **Back Floor**, **132**, **108**.

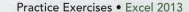

Formula Basics

When you increase your understanding of formulas, you can build robust workbooks that perform a variety of calculations for quantitative analysis. Your ability to build sophisticated workbooks and to interpret the results increases your value to any organization. By now, you should be able to build simple formulas using cell references and mathematical operators and using the order of precedence to control the sequence of calculations in formulas.

In this section, you will create formulas in which cell addresses change or remain fixed when you copy them. Finally, you will learn how to identify and prevent circular references in formulas.

Using Relative, Absolute, and Mixed Cell References in Formulas

When you copy a formula, Excel either adjusts or preserves the cell references in the copied formulas based on how the cell references appear in the original formula. Excel uses three different ways to reference a cell in a formula: relative, absolute, and mixed. When you create a formula that you will copy to other cells, ask yourself the following question:

> Do the cell references need to adjust for the copied formulas, or should the cell references always refer to the same cell location, regardless of where the copied formula is located?

Use a Relative Cell Reference

STEP 1

A ***relative cell reference*** indicates a cell's relative location, such as five rows up and one column to the left, from the cell containing the formula. When you copy a formula containing a relative cell reference, the cell references in the copied formula change relative to the position of the copied formula. Regardless of where you copy the formula, the cell references in the copied formula maintain the same relative distance from the cell containing the copied formula, as the cell references the relative location to the original formula cell.

In Figure 2.1, the formulas in column F contain relative cell references. When you copy the original formula =D2-E2 from cell F2 down to cell F3, the copied formula changes to =D3-E3. Because you copy the formula *down* the column to cell F3, the column letters in the formula stay the same, but the row numbers change to reflect the row to which you copied the formula. Using relative cell addresses to calculate the amount financed ensures that each borrower's down payment is subtracted from his or her respective house cost.

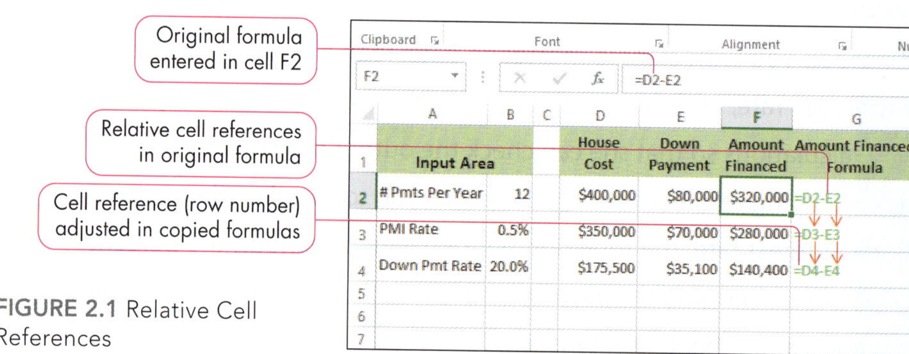

FIGURE 2.1 Relative Cell References

Use an Absolute Cell Reference

STEP 2

An ***absolute cell reference*** provides a permanent reference to a specific cell. When you copy a formula containing an absolute cell reference, the cell reference in the copied formula does not change, regardless of where you copy the formula. An absolute cell reference appears with a dollar sign before both the column letter and row number, such as $B$4.

In Figure 2.2, each down payment is calculated by multiplying the respective house cost by the down payment rate (20%). Cell E2 contains =D2*$B$4 ($400,000*20.0%) to calculate the first borrower's down payment ($80,000). When you copy the formula down to the next row, the copied formula in cell E3 is =D3*$B$4. The relative cell reference D2 changes to D3 (for the next house cost) and the absolute cell reference $B$4 remains the same to refer to the 20.0% down payment rate. This formula ensures that the cell reference to the house cost changes for each row but that the house cost is always multiplied by the rate in cell B4.

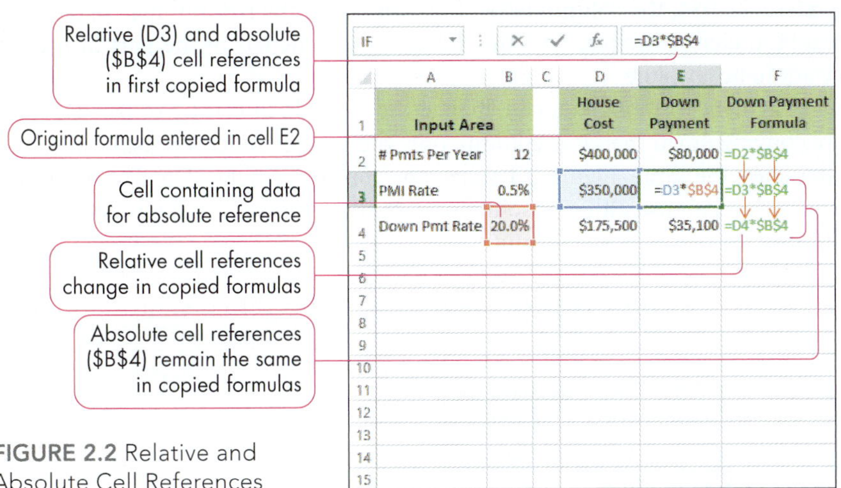

FIGURE 2.2 Relative and Absolute Cell References

Input Area and Absolute Cell References

Figure 2.2 illustrates an input area, a range in a worksheet that contains values that you can change. You build formulas using absolute references to the cells in the input area. By using cell references from an input area, you can change the value in the input area and the formulas that refer to those cells will update automatically. If an input value changes (e.g., the down payment rate changes from 20% to 25%), enter the new input value in only one cell (e.g., B4), and Excel recalculates the amount of down payment for all the formulas.

Figure 2.3 shows what happens if the down payment formula used a relative reference to cell B4. If the original formula in cell E2 is =D2*B4, the copied formula becomes =D3*B5 in cell E3. The relative cell reference to B4 changes to B5 when you copy the formula down. Because cell B5 is empty, the $350,000 house cost in cell D3 is multiplied by 0, giving a $0 down payment, which is not a valid down payment amount.

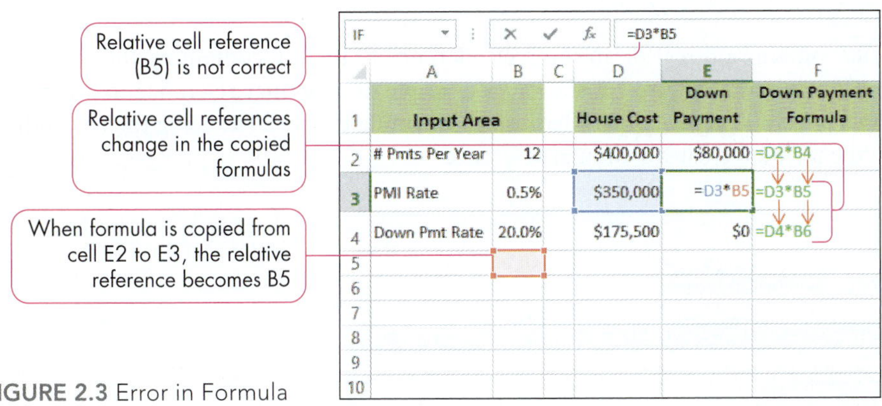

FIGURE 2.3 Error in Formula

Use a Mixed Cell Reference

STEP 3

A ***mixed cell reference*** combines an absolute cell reference with a relative cell reference. When you copy a formula containing a mixed cell reference, either the column letter or the row number that has the absolute reference remains fixed while the other part of the cell reference that is relative changes in the copied formula. $B4 and B$4 are examples of mixed cell references. In the reference $B4, the column B is absolute, and the row number is relative; when you copy the formula, the column letter, B, does not change, but the row number will change. In the reference B$4, the column letter, B, changes, but the row number, 4, does not change. To create a mixed reference, type the dollar sign to the left of the part of the cell reference you want to be absolute.

In the down payment formula, you can change the formula in cell E2 to be =D2*B$4. Because you are copying down the same column, only the row reference 4 must be absolute; the column letter stays the same. Figure 2.4 shows the copied formula =D3*B$4 in cell E3. In situations where you can use either absolute or mixed references, consider using mixed references to shorten the length of the formula.

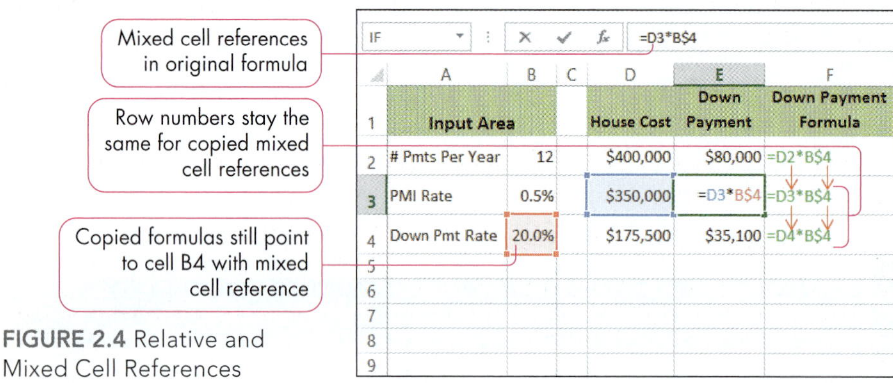

FIGURE 2.4 Relative and Mixed Cell References

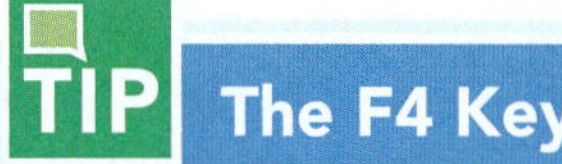

The F4 Key

The F4 key toggles through relative, absolute, and mixed references. Click a cell reference within a formula on the Formula Bar and press F4 to change it. For example, click in B4 in the formula =D2*B4. Press F4 and the relative cell reference (B4) changes to an absolute cell reference ($B$4). Press F4 again and $B$4 becomes a mixed reference (B$4); press F4 again and it becomes another mixed reference ($B4). Press F4 a fourth time and the cell reference returns to the original relative reference (B4).

Correcting Circular References

If a formula contains a direct or an indirect reference to the cell containing the formula, a ***circular reference*** exists. Figure 2.5 shows an example of a circular reference in a formula. The formula in cell E2 is =E2*$B$4. Because the formula is in cell E2, using the cell address E2 within the formula creates a circular reference.

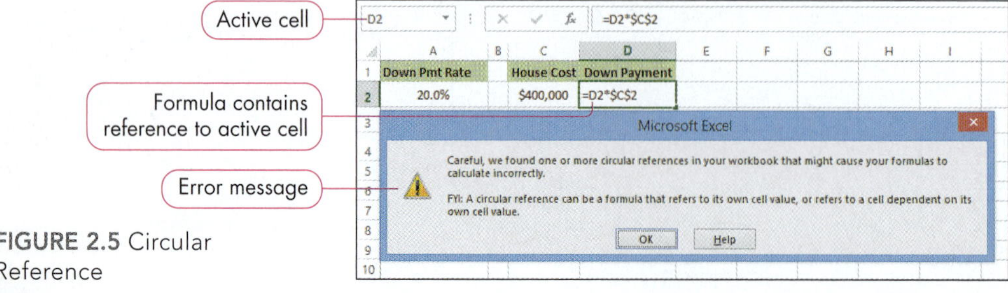

FIGURE 2.5 Circular Reference

Circular references usually cause inaccurate results. Excel displays a warning message when you enter a formula containing a circular reference or when you open an Excel workbook that contains an existing circular reference. Click Help to display the *Find and fix a circular reference* Help topic or click OK to accept the circular reference. Until you resolve a circular reference, the status bar indicates the location of a circular reference, such as CIRCULAR REFERENCES: E2.

TIP Green Triangles

Excel displays a green triangle in the top-left corner of a cell if it detects a potential error in a formula. Click the cell to see the Trace Error button (yellow diamond with exclamation mark). When you click Trace Error, Excel displays information about the potential error and how to correct it. In some cases, Excel may anticipate an inconsistent formula or the omission of adjacent cells in a formula. For example, if a column contains values for the year 2016, the error message indicates that you did not include the year itself. However, the year 2016 is merely a label and should not be included; therefore, you would ignore that error message.

1. What happens when you copy a formula containing a relative cell reference one column to the right? ***p. 158***
2. Why would you use an absolute reference in a formula? ***p. 158***
3. What is a circular reference? Provide an example. ***p. 160***

Hands-On Exercises

1 Formula Basics

Erica prepared a workbook containing data for five mortgages financed with the Townsend Mortgage Company. The data include house cost, down payment, mortgage rate, number of years to pay off the mortgage, and the financing date for each mortgage.

Skills covered: Use a Relative Cell Reference in a Formula • Use an Absolute Cell Reference in a Formula • Use a Mixed Cell Reference in a Formula • Correct a Circular Reference

STEP 1 » USE A RELATIVE CELL REFERENCE IN A FORMULA

You need to calculate the amount financed by each borrower by creating a formula with relative cell references that calculates the difference between the house cost and the down payment. After verifying the results of the amount financed by the first borrower, you will copy the formula down the Amount Financed column to calculate the other borrowers' amounts financed. Refer to Figure 2.6 as you complete Step 1.

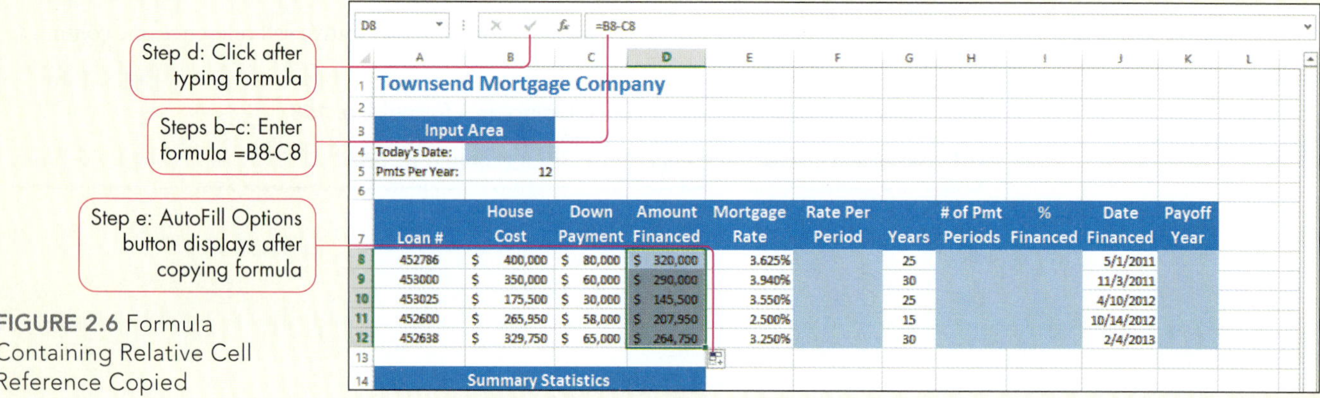

FIGURE 2.6 Formula Containing Relative Cell Reference Copied

a. Open *e02h1Loans* and save it as **e02h1Loans_LastFirst**.

> **TROUBLESHOOTING:** If you make any major mistakes in this exercise, you can close the file, open *e02h1Loans* again, and then start this exercise over.

The workbook contains two worksheets: Details (for Hands-On Exercises 1 and 2) and Payment Info (for Hands-On Exercises 3 and 4). You will enter formulas in the shaded cells.

b. Click **cell D8** in the Details sheet. Type = and click **cell B8**, the cell containing the first borrower's house cost.

c. Type - and click **cell C8**, the cell containing the down payment by the first borrower.

d. Click **Enter** (the check mark between the Name Box and Formula Bar) to complete the formula.

   The first borrower financed (i.e., borrowed) $320,000, the difference between the cost ($400,000) and the down payment ($80,000).

e. Double-click the **cell D8 fill handle**.

   You copied the formula down the Amount Financed column for each mortgage row.

TIP Auto Fill Options

The Auto Fill Options button appears in the bottom-right corner of the copied formulas. If you click it, you can see that the default is Copy Cells. If you want to copy only formatting, click Fill Formatting Only. If you want to copy data only, click Fill Without Formatting.

f. Click **cell D9** and view the formula in the Formula Bar.

The formula in cell D8 is =B8-C8. The formula pasted in cell D9 is =B9-C9. Because the original formula contained relative cell references, when you copy the formula down to the next row, the row numbers for the cell references change. Each result represents the amount financed for that particular borrower.

g. Press [↓] and look at the cell references in the Formula Bar to see how the references change for each formula you copied. Save the workbook with the new formula you created.

STEP 2 » USE AN ABSOLUTE CELL REFERENCE IN A FORMULA

Column E contains the annual percentage rate (APR) for each mortgage. Because the borrowers will make monthly payments, you need to calculate the monthly interest rate by dividing the APR by 12 (the number of payments in one year) for each borrower. Refer to Figure 2.7 as you complete Step 2.

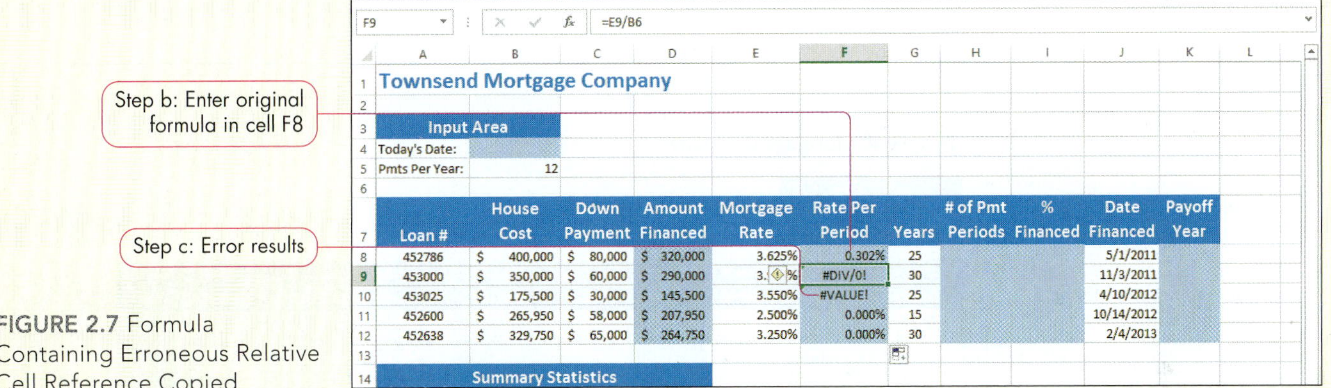

FIGURE 2.7 Formula Containing Erroneous Relative Cell Reference Copied

a. Click **cell F8**.

You need to create a formula to calculate the monthly interest rate for the first borrower.

b. Type **=E8/B5** and click **Enter** (the checkmark between the Name Box and the Formula Bar).

Typically, you should avoid typing values directly in formulas. Although the number of months in one year is always 12, use a reference to cell B5, where the number of payments per year is placed in the input area, so that the company can change the payment period to bimonthly (24 payments per year) or quarterly (four payments per year) without adjusting the formula.

c. Double-click the **cell F8 fill handle**, click **cell F9**, and then view the results (see Figure 2.7).

An error icon displays to the left of cell F9, cell F9 displays #DIV/0!, and cell F10 displays #VALUE!. The original formula was =E8/B5. Because you copied the formula =E8/B5 down the column, the first copied formula is =E9/B6, and the second copied formula is =E10/B7. Although you want the mortgage rate cell reference (E8) to change (E9, E10, etc.) from row to row, you do not want the divisor (cell B5) to change. You need all formulas to divide by the value stored in cell B5, so you will edit the formula to make B5 an absolute reference.

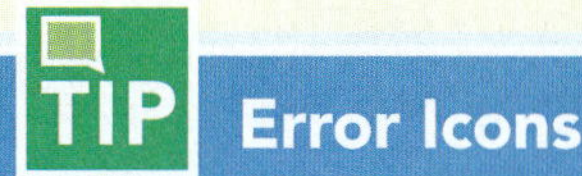

Error Icons

You can position the mouse pointer over the error icon to see a tip indicating what is wrong, such as *The formula or function used is dividing by zero or empty cells.* You can click the icon to see a menu of options to learn more about the error and how to correct it.

d. Click **Undo** in the Quick Access Toolbar to undo the Auto Fill process. Click within or to the right of **B5** in the Formula Bar.

e. Press **F4** and click **Enter** (the checkmark between the Name Box and the Formula Bar).

Excel changes the cell reference from B5 to $B$5, making it an absolute cell reference.

f. Copy the formula down the Rate Per Period column. Click **cell F9** and view the formula in the Formula Bar. Save the workbook.

The formula in cell F9 is =E9/$B$5. The reference to E9 is relative and the reference to B5 is absolute.

STEP 3 » USE A MIXED CELL REFERENCE IN A FORMULA

The next formula you create will calculate the total number of payment periods for each loan. Refer to Figure 2.8 as you complete Step 3.

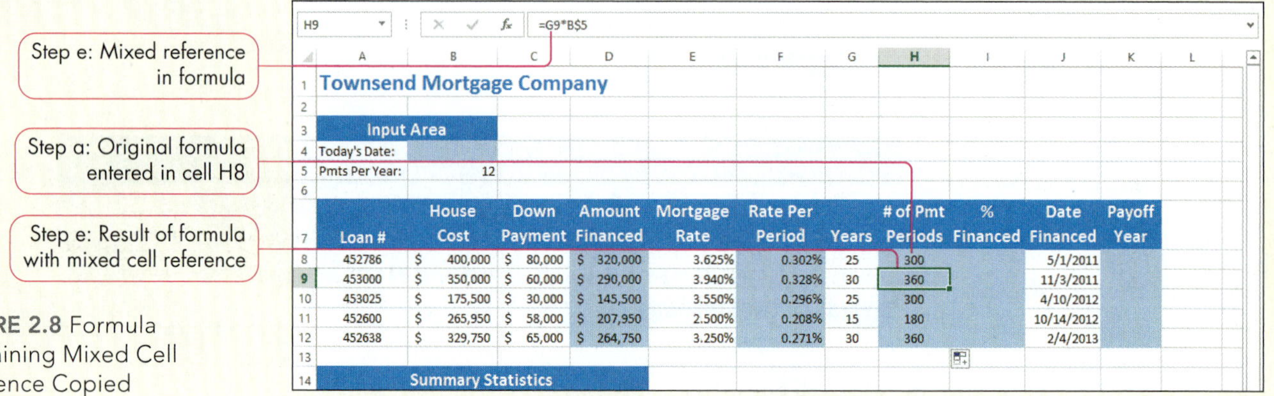

	A	B	C	D	E	F	G	H	I	J	K
1	Townsend Mortgage Company										
2											
3	Input Area										
4	Today's Date:										
5	Pmts Per Year:	12									
6											
7	Loan #	House Cost	Down Payment	Amount Financed	Mortgage Rate	Rate Per Period	Years	# of Pmt Periods	% Financed	Date Financed	Payoff Year
8	452786	$ 400,000	$ 80,000	$ 320,000	3.625%	0.302%	25	300		5/1/2011	
9	453000	$ 350,000	$ 60,000	$ 290,000	3.940%	0.328%	30	360		11/3/2011	
10	453025	$ 175,500	$ 30,000	$ 145,500	3.550%	0.296%	25	300		4/10/2012	
11	452600	$ 265,950	$ 58,000	$ 207,950	2.500%	0.208%	15	180		10/14/2012	
12	452638	$ 329,750	$ 65,000	$ 264,750	3.250%	0.271%	30	360		2/4/2013	
13											
14	Summary Statistics										

FIGURE 2.8 Formula Containing Mixed Cell Reference Copied

a. Click **cell H8** and type **=G8*B5**.

You need to multiply the number of years (25) by the number of payment periods in one year (12) using cell references.

b. Press **F4** to make the B5 cell reference absolute and click **Enter** (the checkmark between the Name Box and Formula Bar).

You want B5 to be absolute so that the cell reference remains B5 when you copy the formula. The product of 25 years and 12 months is 300 months or payment periods.

c. Copy the formula down the # of Pmt Periods column.

The first copied formula is =G9*$B$5, and the result is 360. You want to see what happens if you change the absolute reference to a mixed reference and copy the formula again. Because you are copying down a column, the column letter B can be relative because it will not change either way, but the row number 5 must be absolute.

d. Click **Undo** on the Quick Access Toolbar to undo the copied formulas.

Cell H8 is the active cell.

e. Click within the **$B$5 cell reference** in the Formula Bar. Press **F4** to change the cell reference to a mixed cell reference: B$5. Press **Ctrl+Enter** and copy the formula down the # of Pmt Periods column. Click **cell H9**. Save the workbook.

The first copied formula is =G9*B$5 and the result is still 360. In this situation, using either an absolute reference or a mixed reference provides the same results.

STEP 4 » CORRECT A CIRCULAR REFERENCE

Erica wants to know what percentage of the house cost each borrower will finance. As you create the formula, you enter a circular reference. After studying the results, you correct the circular error and plan future formulas that avoid this problem. Refer to Figure 2.9 as you complete Step 4.

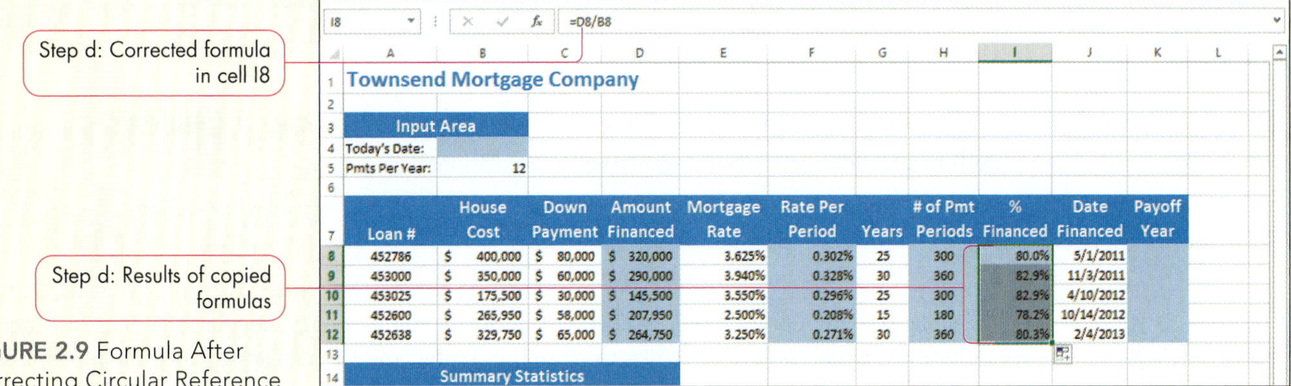

FIGURE 2.9 Formula After Correcting Circular Reference

a. Click **cell I8**, type **=I8/B8**, and then press **Enter**.

The Circular Reference Warning message box displays.

> **TROUBLESHOOTING:** If the message box does not display, close the workbook and exit Excel. Start Excel, open the workbook again, and then repeat Step 4a. Sometimes the message box appears only once while Excel is running. If you had previously experimented with a circular reference during a work session, the message box might not display. However, exiting Excel and opening it again will enable the message box to display.

b. Read the description of the error and click **Help**.

The Excel Help window opens, displaying information about circular references.

c. Read the circular reference information, close the Excel Help window, and then click **OK** in the message box.

The left side of the status bar displays *CIRCULAR REFERENCES: I8.*

Because the formula is stored in cell I8, the formula cannot refer to the cell itself. You need to divide the value in the Amount Financed column by the value in the House Cost column.

d. Click **cell I8** and edit the formula to be **=D8/B8**. Copy the formula down the % Financed column.

The first borrower financed 80% of the cost of the house: $320,000 financed divided by $400,000 cost.

e. Save the workbook. Keep the workbook open if you plan to continue with the next Hands-On Exercise. If not, close the workbook and exit Excel.

Function Basics

An Excel ***function*** is a predefined computation that simplifies creating a formula that performs a complex calculation. Excel contains more than 400 functions, which are organized into 14 categories. Table 2.1 lists and describes the primary function categories used in this chapter.

TABLE 2.1 Function Categories and Descriptions

Category	Description
Date & Time	Provides methods for manipulating date and time values.
Financial	Performs financial calculations, such as payments, rates, present value, and future value.
Logical	Performs logical tests and returns the value of the tests. Includes logical operators for combined tests, such as AND, OR, and NOT.
Lookup & Reference	Looks up values, creates links to cells, or provides references to cells in a worksheet.
Math & Trig	Performs standard math and trigonometry calculations.
Statistical	Performs common statistical calculations, such as averages and standard deviations.

When using functions, you must adhere to correct ***syntax***, the rules that dictate the structure and components required to perform the necessary calculations. Start a function with an equal sign, followed by the function name, and then its arguments in parentheses.

- The function name describes the purpose of the function. For example, the function name SUM indicates that the function sums, or adds, values.
- A function's ***arguments*** specify the inputs—such as cells, values, or arithmetic expressions—that are required to complete the operation. In some cases, a function requires multiple arguments separated by commas.

In this section, you will learn how to insert common functions using the keyboard and the Insert Function and Function Arguments dialog boxes.

Inserting a Function

To insert a function by typing, first type an equal sign, and then begin typing the function name. ***Formula AutoComplete*** displays a list of functions and defined names that match letters as you type a formula. For example, if you type =SU, Formula AutoComplete displays a list of functions and names that start with *SU* (see Figure 2.10). You can double-click the function name from the list or continue typing the function name. You can even scroll through the list to see the ScreenTip describing the function.

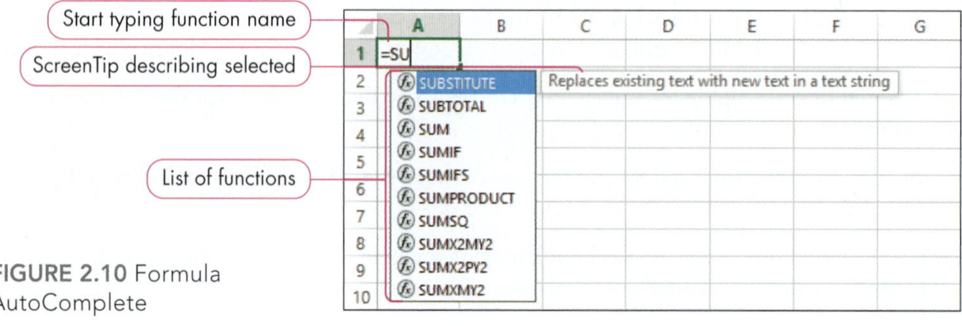

FIGURE 2.10 Formula AutoComplete

After you type the function name and opening parenthesis, Excel displays the ***function ScreenTip***, a small pop-up description that displays the function's arguments. The argument you are currently entering is bold in the function ScreenTip (see Figure 2.11). Square brackets indicate optional arguments. For example, the SUM function requires the number1 argument, but the number2 argument is optional. Click the argument name in the function ScreenTip to select the actual argument in the formula you are creating if you want to make changes to the argument.

	A	B	C	D	E	F	G
1	=SUM(						
2	SUM(**number1**, [number2], ...)						
3							

FIGURE 2.11 Function ScreenTip

You can also use the Insert Function dialog box to search for a function, select a function category, and select a function from the list (see Figure 2.12). The dialog box is helpful if you want to browse a list of functions, especially if you are not sure of the function you need and want to see descriptions.

To display the Insert Function dialog box, click Insert Function *fx* (located between the Name Box and the Formula Bar) or click Insert Function in the Function Library group on the Formulas tab. From within the dialog box, select a function category, such as Most Recently Used, and select a function to display the syntax and a brief description of that function. Click *Help on this function* to display details about the selected function.

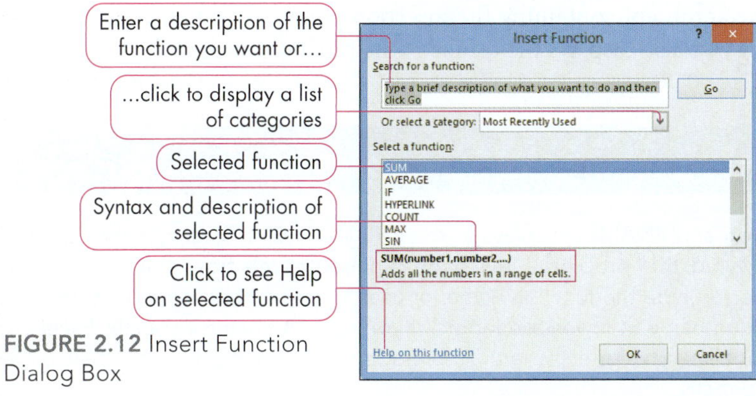

FIGURE 2.12 Insert Function Dialog Box

When you find the function you want, click OK. The Function Arguments dialog box opens so that you can enter the arguments for that specific function (see Figure 2.13). The following list explains the arguments in the Function Arguments dialog box:

- Argument names in **bold** (such as Number1 in the SUM function) are required.
- Argument names that are not bold (such as Number2 in the SUM function) are optional. The function can operate without the optional argument, which is used when you need additional specifications to calculate a result.

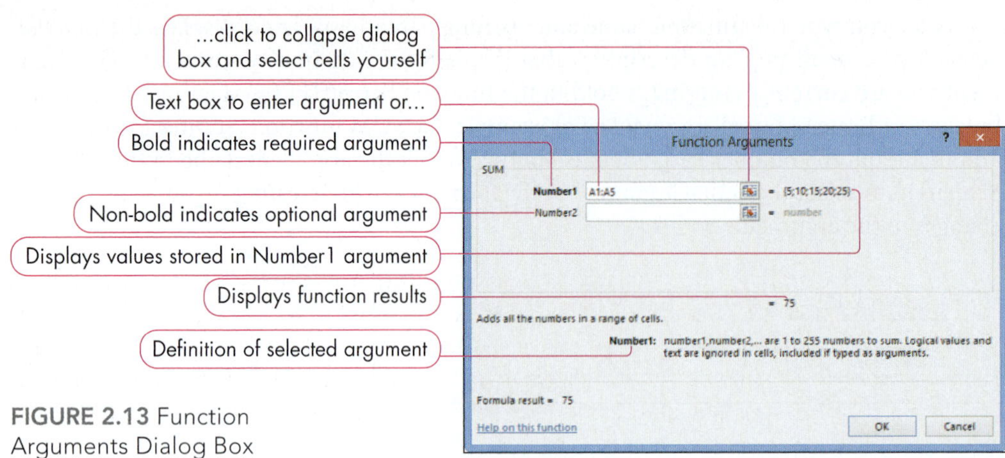

FIGURE 2.13 Function Arguments Dialog Box

Type the cell references in the argument boxes or click a collapse button to the right side of an argument box to collapse the dialog box and select the cell or range of cells in the worksheet to designate as that argument. If you click the collapse button to select a range, you need to click the expand button to expand the dialog box again. The value, or results, of a formula contained in the argument cell displays on the right side of the argument box (such as 5; 10; 15; 20; 25—the values stored in the range A1:A5 used for the Number1 argument). If the argument is not valid, Excel displays an error description on the right side of the argument box.

The bottom of the Function Arguments dialog box displays a description of the function and a description of the argument containing the insertion point. As you enter arguments, the bottom of the dialog box also displays the results of the function, such as 75.

TIP #Name?

If you enter a function and #NAME? displays in the cell, you might have mistyped the function name. To avoid this problem, select the function name from the Formula AutoComplete list as you type the function name, or use the Insert Function dialog box. You can type a function name in lowercase letters. If you type the name correctly, Excel converts the name to all capital letters when you press Enter, indicating that you spelled the function name correctly.

Inserting Basic Math and Statistics Functions

Excel includes commonly used math and statistical functions that you can use for a variety of calculations. For example, you can insert functions to calculate the total amount you spend on dining out in a month, the average amount you spend per month downloading music from iTunes®, your highest electric bill, and your lowest time to run a mile this week.

Calculate a Total with the SUM Function

STEP 1»

The ***SUM function*** totals values in two or more cells and displays the result in the cell containing the function. This function is more efficient to create when you need to add the values contained in three or more cells. For example, to add the contents of cells A2 through A14, you could enter =A2+A3+A4+A5+A6+A7+A8+A9+A10+A11+A12+A13+A14, which is time-consuming and increases the probability of entering an inaccurate cell reference, such as entering a cell reference twice or accidentally leaving out a cell reference. Instead, you should use the SUM function, =SUM(A2:A14).

=SUM(number 1, [number 2],...)

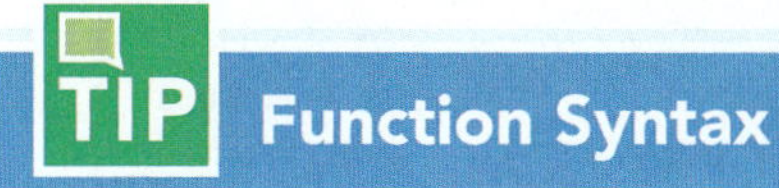

Function Syntax

In this book, the function syntax lines are highlighted. Brackets [ ] indicate optional arguments; however, do not actually type the brackets when you enter the argument.

The SUM function contains one required argument (Number1) that represents a range of cells to add. The range, such as A2:A14, specifies the first and last cells containing values to SUM. Excel will sum all cells within that range. The Number2 optional argument is used when you want to sum values stored in nonadjacent cells or ranges, such as =SUM(A2:A14,F2:F14). The ellipsis in the function syntax indicates you can add as many additional ranges as desired, separated by commas.

Avoiding Functions for Basic Formulas

Do not use a function for a basic mathematical expression. For example, although =SUM(B4/C4) produces the same result as =B4/C4, the SUM function is not needed to perform the basic arithmetic division. Furthermore, someone taking a quick look at that formula might assume it performs addition instead of division. Use the most appropriate, clear-cut formula, =B4/C4.

To insert the SUM function (for example, to sum the values in the range A2:A14), do one of the following:

- Type =SUM(A2:A14) and press Enter.
- Type =SUM(and drag to select the range A2:A14 with the mouse. Type the ending #) and press Enter.
- Click in cell A15, click Sum in the Editing group on the HOME tab, press Enter to select the suggested range or type (or drag to select) A2:A14, and then press Enter.
- Click in cell A15, click Sum in the Function Library group on the FORMULAS tab, press Enter to select the suggested range or type A2:A14, and then press Enter.

Figure 2.14 shows the result of using the SUM function in cell D2 to total scores (898).

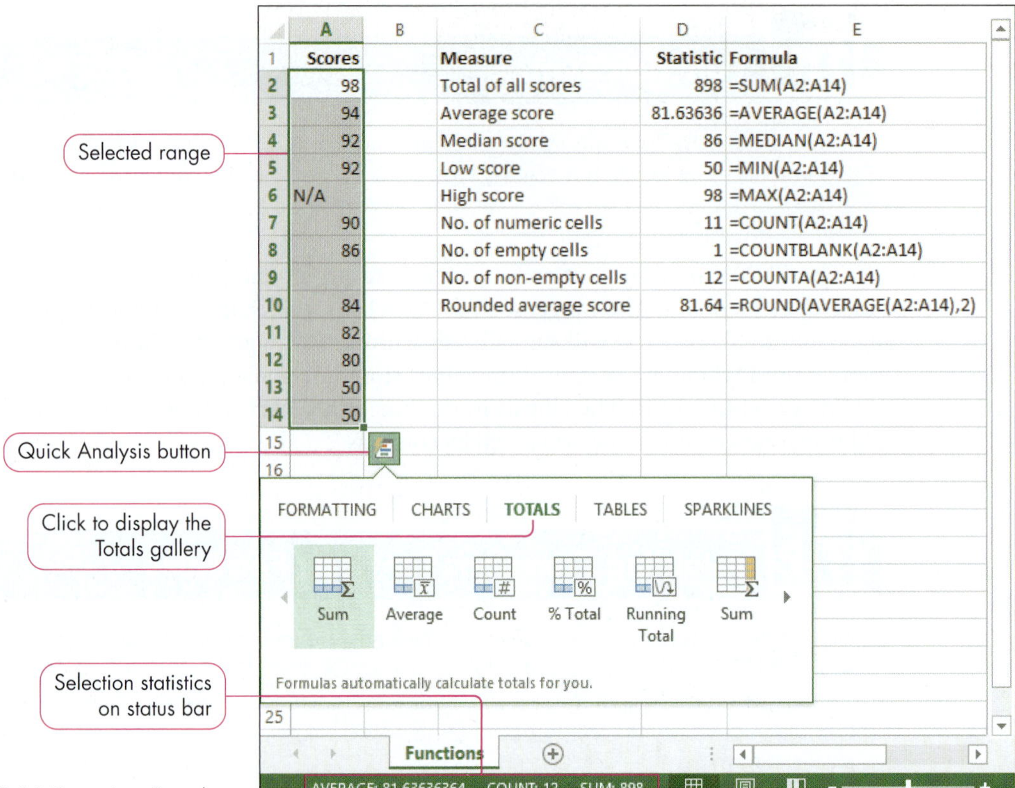

FIGURE 2.14 Function Results

TIP Sum Arrow

If you click Sum, Excel inserts the SUM function. However, if you click the Sum arrow in the Editing group on the Home tab or in the Function Library group on the Formulas tab, Excel displays a list of basic functions to select: Sum, Average, Count Numbers, Max, and Min. If you want to insert another function, select More Functions from the list.

Find Central Tendency with AVERAGE and MEDIAN

STEP 2》 People often describe data based on central tendency, which means that values tend to cluster around a central value. Excel provides two functions to calculate central tendency: AVERAGE and MEDIAN. The ***AVERAGE function*** calculates the arithmetic mean, or average, for the values in a range of cells. You can use this function to calculate the class average on a biology test or the average number of points scored per game by a basketball player. In Figure 2.14, =AVERAGE(A2:A14) in cell D3 returns 81.63636 as the average test score. The AVERAGE function ignores empty cells and cells containing N/A or text.

=AVERAGE(number 1,[number2],...)

STEP 3》 The ***MEDIAN function*** finds the midpoint value, which is the value that one half of the data set is above or below. The median is particularly useful because extreme values often influence arithmetic mean calculated by the AVERAGE function. In Figure 2.14, the two extreme test scores of 50 distort the average. The rest of the test scores range from 80 to 98. Cell D4 contains =MEDIAN(A2:A14). The median for test scores is 86, which indicates that half the test scores are above 86 and half the test scores are below 86. This statistic is more reflective of the data set than the average is. The MEDIAN function ignores empty cells and cells containing N/A or text.

=MEDIAN(number 1,[number 2],...)

Identify Low and High Values with MIN and MAX

STEP 4 The ***MIN function*** analyzes an argument list to determine the lowest value, such as the lowest score on a test. Manually inspecting a range of values to identify the lowest value is inefficient, especially in large spreadsheets. If you change values in the range, the MIN function will identify the new lowest value and display it in the cell containing the MIN function. In Figure 2.14, =MIN(A2:A14) in cell D5 identifies that 50 is the lowest test score.

=MIN(number 1,[number 2],...)

The ***MAX function*** analyzes an argument list to determine the highest value, such as the highest score on a test. Like the MIN function, when the values in the range change, the MAX function will display the new highest value within the range of cells. In Figure 2.14, =MAX(A2:A14) in cell D6 identifies 98 as the highest test score.

=MAX(number 1,[number 2],...)

TIP Nonadjacent Ranges

You can use multiple ranges as arguments, such as finding the largest number within two nonadjacent (nonconsecutive) ranges. For example, you can find the highest test score where some scores are stored in cells A2:A14 and others are stored in cells K2:K14. Separate each range with a comma in the argument list, so that the formula is =MAX(A2:A14,K2:K14).

Identify the Total Number with COUNT Functions

Excel provides three basic count functions—COUNT, COUNTBLANK and COUNTA—to count the cells in a range that meet a particular criterion. The ***COUNT function*** tallies the number of cells in a range that contain values you can use in calculations, such as numerical and date data, but excludes blank cells or text entries from the tally. In Figure 2.14, the selected range spans 13 cells; however, =COUNT(A2:A14) in cell D7 returns 11, the number of cells that contain numerical data. It does not count the cell containing the text *N/A* or the blank cell.

The ***COUNTBLANK function*** tallies the number of cells in a range that are blank. In Figure 2.14, =COUNTBLANK(A2:A14) in cell D8 identifies that one cell in the range A2:A14 is blank. The ***COUNTA function*** tallies the number of cells in a range that are not blank, that is, cells that contain data, whether a value, text, or a formula. In Figure 2.14, =COUNTA(A2:A14) in cell D9 returns 12, indicating the range A2:A14 contains 12 cells that contain some form of data. It does not count the blank cell.

=COUNT(number 1,[number 2],...)
=COUNTBLANK(number 1,[number 2],...)
=COUNTA(number 1,[number 2],...)

TIP Status Bar Statistics: Average, Count, and Sum

When you select a range of cells containing values, by default Excel displays the average, count, and sum of those values on the status bar (see Figure 2.14). You can customize the status bar to show other selection statistics, such as the minimum and maximum values for a selected range. To display or hide particular selection statistics, right-click the status bar and select the statistic.

Perform Calculations with Quick Analysis Tools

Excel 2013 contains a new feature called ***Quick Analysis***, which is a set of analytical tools you can use to apply formatting, create charts or tables, and insert basic functions. When you select a range of data, the Quick Analysis button displays in the bottom-right corner of the selected range. Click the Quick Analysis button to display the Quick Analysis gallery and select the analytical tool to meet your needs.

Figure 2.14 shows the TOTALS options so that you can sum, average, or count the values in the selected range. Select % Total to display the percentage of the grand total of two or more columns. Select Running Total to provide a cumulative total at the bottom of multiple columns.

Use Other Math and Statistical Functions

In addition to the functions you have learned in this chapter, Excel provides more than 100 other math and statistical functions. Table 2.2 lists and describes some of these functions that you might find helpful in your business, education, and general statistics courses.

TABLE 2.2 Math and Statistical Functions

Function Syntax	Description
=ABS(number)	Displays the absolute (i.e., positive) value of a number.
=FREQUENCY(data_array,bins_array)	Counts how often values appear in a given range.
=INT(number)	Rounds a value number down to the nearest whole number.
=MODE.SNGL(number1,[number2],...)	Displays the most frequently occurring value in a list.
=RANK.AVG(number,ref,[order])	Identifies a value's rank within a list of values; returns an average rank for identical values.
=RANK.EQ(number,ref,[order])	Identifies a value's rank within a list of values; the top rank is identified for all identical values.
=ROUND(number,num_digits)	Rounds a value to a specific number of digits. Rounds numbers of 5 and greater up and those less than 5 down.

Round Versus Decrease Decimal Points

When you click Decrease Decimal in the Number group to display fewer or no digits after a decimal point, Excel still stores the original value's decimal places so that those digits can be used in calculations. The ROUND function changes the stored value to its rounded state.

Nest Functions as Arguments

A ***nested function*** occurs when one function is embedded as an argument within another function. Each function has its own set of arguments that must be included. For example, cell D10 in Figure 2.14 contains =ROUND(AVERAGE(A2:A14),2). The ROUND function requires two arguments: number and num_digits.

The AVERAGE function is nested in the *number* argument of the ROUND function. AVERAGE(A2:A14) returns 81.63636. That value is then rounded to two decimal places, indicated by 2 in the *num_digits* argument. The result is 81.64. If you change the second argument from 2 to 0, such as =ROUND(AVERAGE(A2:A14),0), the result would be 82.

Using Date Functions

Because Excel treats dates as serial numbers, you can perform calculations using dates. For example, assume today is January 1, 2016, and you graduate on May 6, 2016. To determine how many days until graduation, subtract today's date from the graduation date. Excel uses the serial numbers for these dates (42370 and 42494) to calculate the difference of 126 days.

Insert the TODAY Function

STEP 5»

The ***TODAY function*** displays the current date, such as 6/14/2016, in a cell. Excel updates the function results when you open or print the workbook. The TODAY() function does not require arguments, but you must include the parentheses. If you omit the parentheses, Excel displays #NAME? in the cell with a green triangle in the top-left corner of the cell. When you click the cell, an error icon appears that you can click for more information.

=TODAY()

Insert the NOW Function

The ***NOW function*** uses the computer's clock to display the date and military time, such as 6/14/2016 15:30, that you last opened the workbook. (Military time expresses time on a 24-hour period where 1:00 is 1 a.m. and 13:00 is 1 p.m.) The date and time will change every time the workbook is opened. Like the TODAY function, the NOW function does not require arguments, but you must include the parentheses. Omitting the parentheses creates a #NAME? error.

=NOW()

Update the Date and Time

Both the TODAY and NOW functions display the date/time the workbook was last opened or last calculated. These functions do not continuously update the date and time while the workbook is open. To update the date and time, press F9 or click the Formulas tab and click *Calculate now* in the Calculation group.

Use Other Date & Time Functions

Excel contains a variety of other date functions. You can use these functions to calculate when employees are eligible for certain benefits, what the date is six months from now, or what day of the week a particular date falls on. Table 2.3 describes and Figure 2.15 shows examples of some date functions.

TABLE 2.3 Date Functions

Function Syntax	Description
=DATE(year,month,day)	Returns the serial number for a date.
=DAY(serial_number)	Displays the day (1–31) within a given month for a date or its serial number.
=EDATE(start_date,months)	Displays the serial number using the General format of a date a specified number of months in the future (using a positive value) or past (using a negative value). Displays the actual future or past date in Short Date format.
=EOMONTH(start_date,months)	Identifies the serial number of the last day of a month using General format or the exact last day of a month using Short Date format for a specified number of months from a date's serial number.
=MONTH(serial_number)	Returns the month (1–12) for a serial number, where 1 is January and 12 is December.
=WEEKDAY(serial_number,[return_type])	Identifies the weekday (1–7) for a serial number, where 1 is Sunday and 7 is Saturday (the default with no second argument); can specify a second argument for different numbers assigned to weekdays (see Help).
=YEAR(serial_number)	Identifies the year for a serial number.
=YEARFRAC(start_date,end_date,[basis])	Calculates the fraction of a year between two dates based on the number of whole days.

	A	B	C	D	E	F
1	Inputs:	7	11	2016	10/17/2016	
2						
3	Description			Format	Result	Formula
4	Today's Date			Short Date	10/17/2016	=TODAY()
5	Today's Date			Other Date	October 17, 2016	=TODAY()
6	Today's Date and Military Time			Date/Time	10/17/2016 17:15	=NOW()
7	Serial # of Date			General	42562	=DATE(D1,B1,C1)
8	Serial # of Date			Short Date	7/11/2016	=DATE(D1,B1,C1)
9	Day within the Month			General	17	=DAY(E4) or =DAY(TODAY())
10	Serial # of Date 3 Months in Future			General	42752	=EDATE(E4,3)
11	Date 3 Months in Future			Short Date	1/17/2017	=EDATE(E4,3)
12	Date 3 Years in Future			Short Date	10/17/2019	=EDATE(E4,3*12)
13	Date 2 Months Ago			Short Date	8/17/2016	=EDATE(E4,-2)
14	Serial # of Date 6 Months in Future			General	42746	=EDATE(DATE(D1,B1,C1),6)
15	Serial # of Last Day in 6 Months			General	42855	=EOMONTH(E4,6) or =EOMONTH(TODAY())
16	Last Day of 6 Months in Future			Short Date	4/30/2017	=EOMONTH(E4,6) or =EOMONTH(TODAY())
17	Month Number (where 6=June)			General	10	=MONTH(E5) or =MONTH(TODAY())
18	Week day (1=Sunday; 7=Saturday)			General	2	=WEEKDAY(E4)
19	Week day (1=Monday; 7=Sunday)			General	1	=WEEKDAY(E4,2)
20	Year for a Serial Date			General	2016	=YEAR(E4) or =YEAR(TODAY())
21	Fraction of Year 7/11/2016-10/17/2016			General	0.266666667	=YEARFRAC(DATE(D1,B1,C1),E1)

FIGURE 2.15 Date Function Examples

You can nest a date function inside another date function, such as =DAY(TODAY()). This nested function TODAY() first identifies today's date, and from that date, the DAY function identifies the day of the month. In Figure 2.15, cell E21 contains =YEARFRAC(DATE(D1,B1,C1),E1). The DATE function is nested to combine values in three cells (D1, B1, and C1) to build a date (7/11/2016). Excel finds the number of days between that date and 10/17/2016, the date stored in cell E1. From there, the YEARFRAC function calculates the fraction of a year (26.667%) between those two dates. Had 7/11/2016 been stored as a date in a single cell, the formula would simplify to something like =YEARFRAC(D1,E1).

TIP Date Functions and Arithmetic Operations

You can combine date functions with arithmetic operations. For example, you sign a lease on June 14, 2016, for three years. The starting date is stored in cell E4. What date does your lease expire? Enter =EDATE(E4,3*12)-1 to calculate the expiration date. The first argument, E4, is the cell containing the start date, and the second argument, 3*12, equals three years containing 12 months each, or 36 months. (In an actual worksheet, you should store the value 36 in a cell instead of typing numbers in the argument.) That result is June 14, 2019, but the lease actually expires the day before. So you must then subtract 1 from the function result to calculate the June 13, 2019, date.

Quick Concepts

1. What visual features help guide you through typing a function directly in a cell? ***pp. 166–167***
2. What type of data do you enter in a Function Arguments dialog box, and what are four things the dialog box tells you? ***pp. 167–168***
3. What is the difference between the AVERAGE and MEDIAN functions? ***p. 170***
4. What is a nested function, and why would you create one? ***p. 172***
5. Provide three examples of using date functions to determine something specific. ***p. 173***

Hands-On Exercises

2 Function Basics

The Townsend Mortgage Company's worksheet contains an area in which you must enter summary statistics. In addition, you need to include today's date and identify the year in which each mortgage will be paid off.

Skills covered: Use the SUM Function • Use the AVERAGE Function • Use the MEDIAN Function • Use the MIN, MAX, and COUNT Functions • Use the TODAY and YEAR Functions

STEP 1 » USE THE SUM FUNCTION

The first summary statistic you need to calculate is the total value of the houses bought by the borrowers. You will use the SUM function. Refer to Figure 2.16 as you complete Step 1.

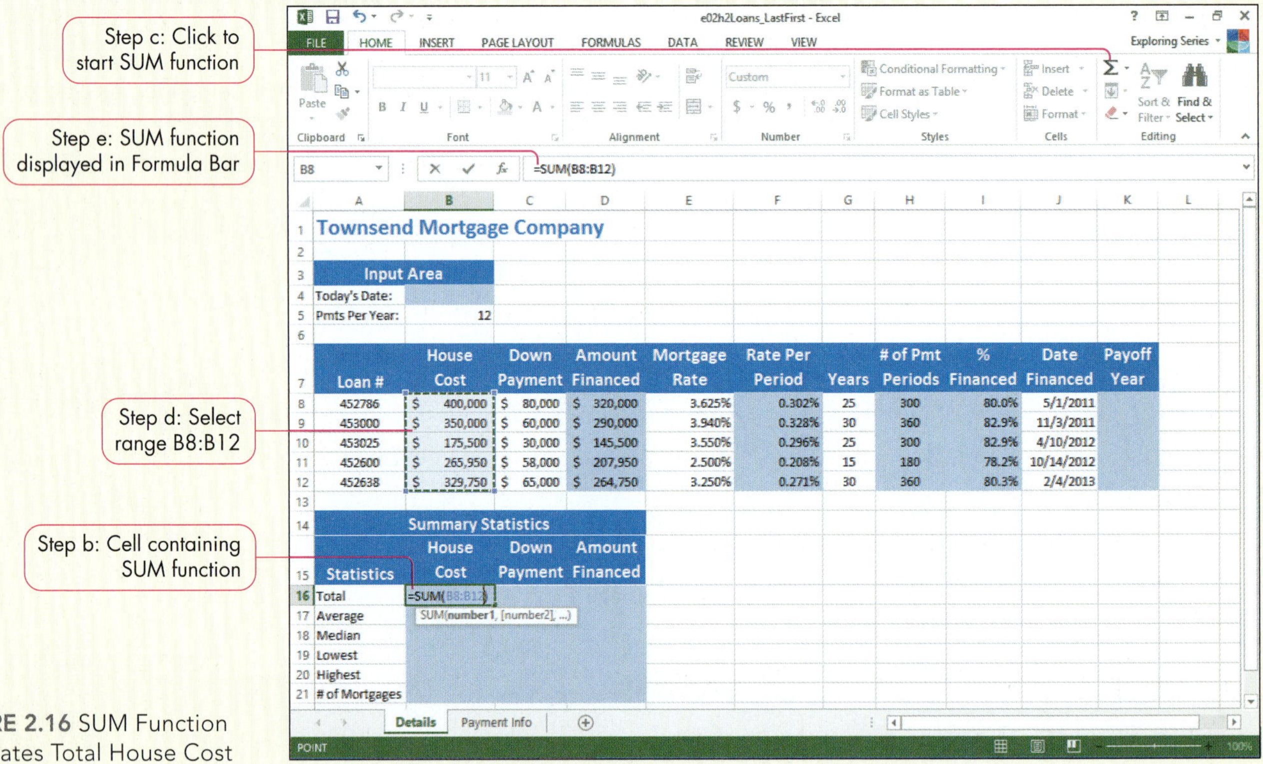

FIGURE 2.16 SUM Function Calculates Total House Cost

a. Open *e02h1Loans_LastFirst* if you closed it at the end of Hands-On Exercise 1 and save it as **e02h2Loans_LastFirst**, changing *h1* to *h2*.

b. Make sure the Details worksheet is active and click **cell B16**, the cell where you will enter a formula for the total house cost.

c. Click **Sum** in the Editing group on the HOME tab.

> **TROUBLESHOOTING:** Click the main part of the Sum command. If you click the Sum arrow, select Sum.

Excel anticipates the range of cells containing values you want to sum based on where you enter the formula—in this case, A8:D15. This is not the correct range, so you must enter the correct range.

d. Select the **range B8:B12**, the cells containing house costs.

As you use the semi-selection process, Excel enters the range in the SUM function.

> **TROUBLESHOOTING:** If you entered the function without changing the arguments, repeat steps b–d or edit the arguments in the Formula Bar by deleting the default range, typing B8:B12 between the parentheses and pressing Enter.

e. Click **Enter** (the checkmark between the Name Box and Formula Bar) and save the workbook.

Cell B16 contains the function = SUM(B8:B12), and the result is $1,521,200.

STEP 2 » USE THE AVERAGE FUNCTION

Before copying the functions to calculate the total down payments and amounts financed, you want to calculate the average house cost bought by the borrowers in your list. Refer to Figure 2.17 as you complete Step 2.

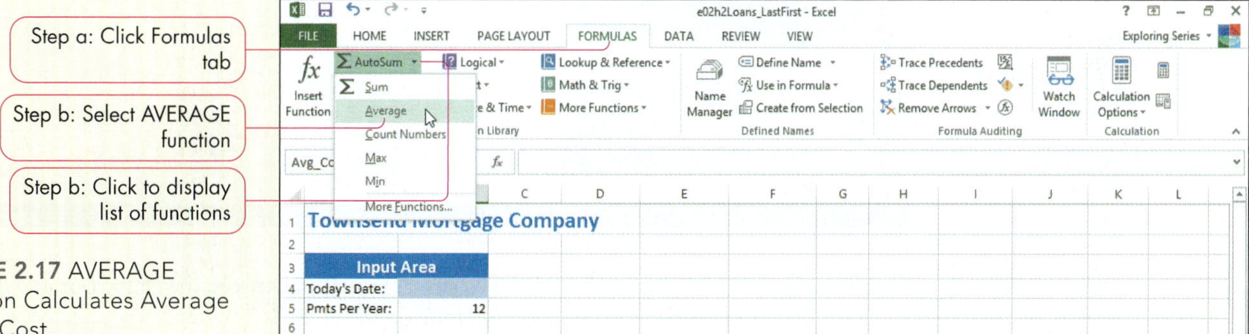

FIGURE 2.17 AVERAGE Function Calculates Average House Cost

a. Click the **FORMULAS tab** and click **cell B17**, the cell where you will display the average cost of the houses.

b. Click the **Sum arrow** in the Function Library group and select **Average**.

Excel selects cell B15, which is the total cost of the houses. You need to change the range.

> **TROUBLESHOOTING:** Sum, like some other commands in Excel, contains two parts: the main command icon and an arrow. Click the main command icon when instructed to click Sum to perform the default action. Click the arrow when instructed to click the Sum arrow for additional options. If you accidentally clicked Sum instead of the arrow, press Esc to cancel the SUM function from being completed and try step b again.

c. Select the **range B8:B12**, the cells containing the house costs.

The function is =AVERAGE(B8:B12).

d. Press **Enter**, make **cell B18** the active cell, and save the workbook.

The average house cost is $304,240.

STEP 3 » USE THE MEDIAN FUNCTION

You realize that extreme house costs may distort the average. Therefore, you decide to identify the median house cost to compare it to the average house cost. Refer to Figure 2.18 as you complete Step 3.

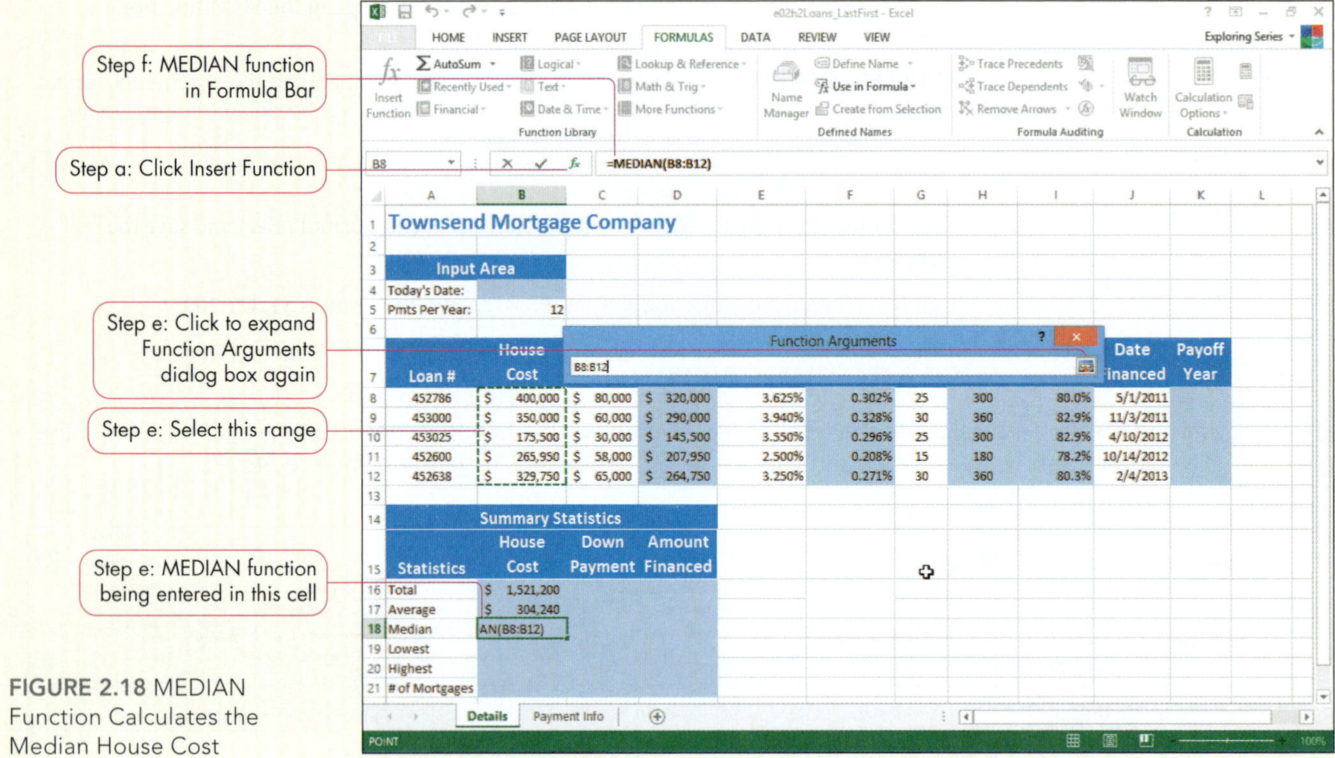

FIGURE 2.18 MEDIAN Function Calculates the Median House Cost

a. Make sure **cell B18** is the active cell. Click **Insert Function** between the Name Box and the Formula Bar, or in the Function Library group on the FORMULAS tab.

   The Insert Function dialog box opens. Use this dialog box to select the MEDIAN function since it is not available on the Ribbon.

b. Type **median** in the **Search for a function box** and click **Go**.

   Excel displays a list of functions in the *Select a function* list. The MEDIAN function is selected at the top of the list; the bottom of the dialog box displays the syntax and the description.

c. Read the MEDIAN function's description and click **OK**.

   The Function Arguments dialog box opens. It contains one required argument, Number1, representing a range of cells containing values. It has an optional argument, Number2, which you can use if you have nonadjacent ranges that contain values.

d. Click the **collapse button** to the right of the Number1 box.

   You collapsed the Function Arguments dialog box so that you can select the range.

e. Select the **range B8:B12** and click the **expand button** in the Function Arguments dialog box.

   The Function Arguments dialog box expands, displaying B8:B12 in the Number1 box.

f. Click **OK** to accept the function arguments and close the dialog box. Save the workbook.

   Half of the houses purchased cost more than the median, $329,750, and half of the houses cost less than this value. Notice the difference between the median and the average: The average is lower because it is affected by the lowest-priced house, $175,500.

STEP 4 ›› USE THE MIN, MAX, AND COUNT FUNCTIONS

Erica wants to know the least and most expensive houses so that she can analyze typical customers of the Townsend Mortgage Company. You will use the MIN and MAX functions to obtain these statistics. In addition, you will use the COUNT function to tally the number of mortgages in the sample. Refer to Figure 2.19 as you complete Step 4.

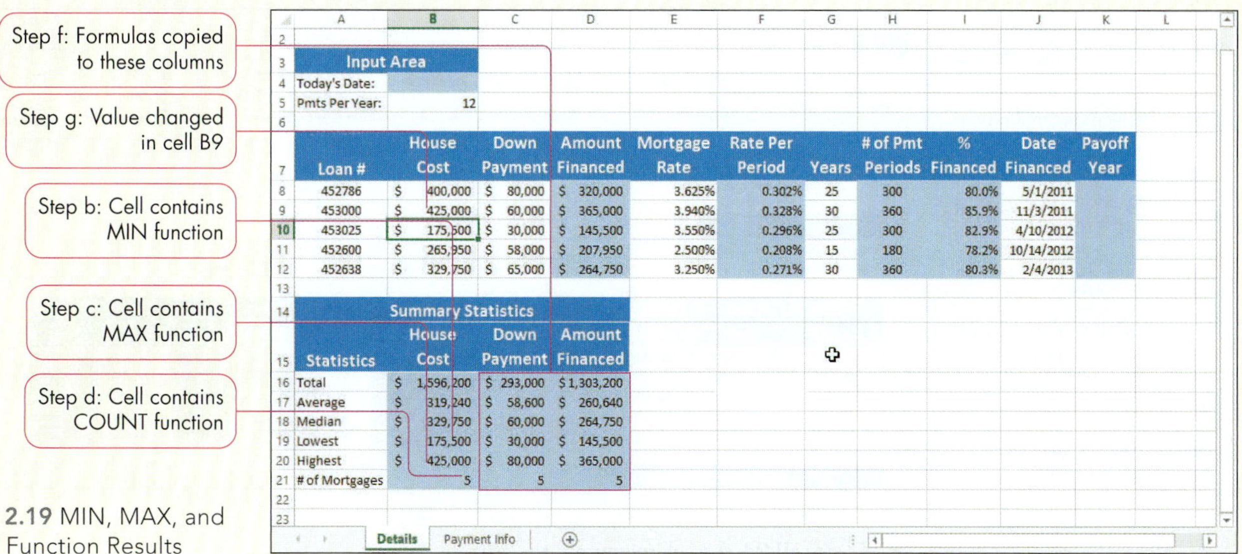

FIGURE 2.19 MIN, MAX, and COUNT Function Results

a. Click **cell B19**, the cell to display the cost of the lowest-costing house.

b. Click the **Sum arrow** in the Function Library group, select **Min**, select the **range B8:B12**, and then press **Enter**.

   The MIN function identifies that the lowest-costing house is $175,500.

c. Click **cell B20**, if necessary. Click the **Sum arrow** in the Function Library group, select **Max**, select the **range B8:B12**, and then press **Enter**.

   The MAX function identifies that the highest-costing house is $400,000.

d. Click **cell B21**, if necessary. Type **=COUNT(B8:B12)** and press **Enter**.

   As you type the letter *C*, Formula AutoComplete suggests functions starting with *C*. As you continue typing, the list of functions narrows. After you type the beginning parenthesis, Excel displays the function ScreenTip, indicating the arguments for the function. The range B8:B12 contains five cells.

e. Select the **range B16:B21**.

   You want to select the range of original statistics to copy the cells all at one time to the next two columns.

f. Drag the fill handle to the right by two columns to copy the functions. Click **cell D21**.

   Because you used relative cell references in the functions, the range changes from =COUNT(B8:B12) to =COUNT(D8:D12).

g. Change the value in **cell B9** to **425000**. Save the workbook.

   The results of several formulas and functions change, including the total, average, and max house costs.

STEP 5 » USE THE TODAY AND YEAR FUNCTIONS

You have two date functions (TODAY and YEAR) to enter to complete the first worksheet. The TODAY function will display today's date, and you will use the YEAR function in a formula to calculate the payoff year for each mortgage. Refer to Figure 2.20 as you complete Step 5.

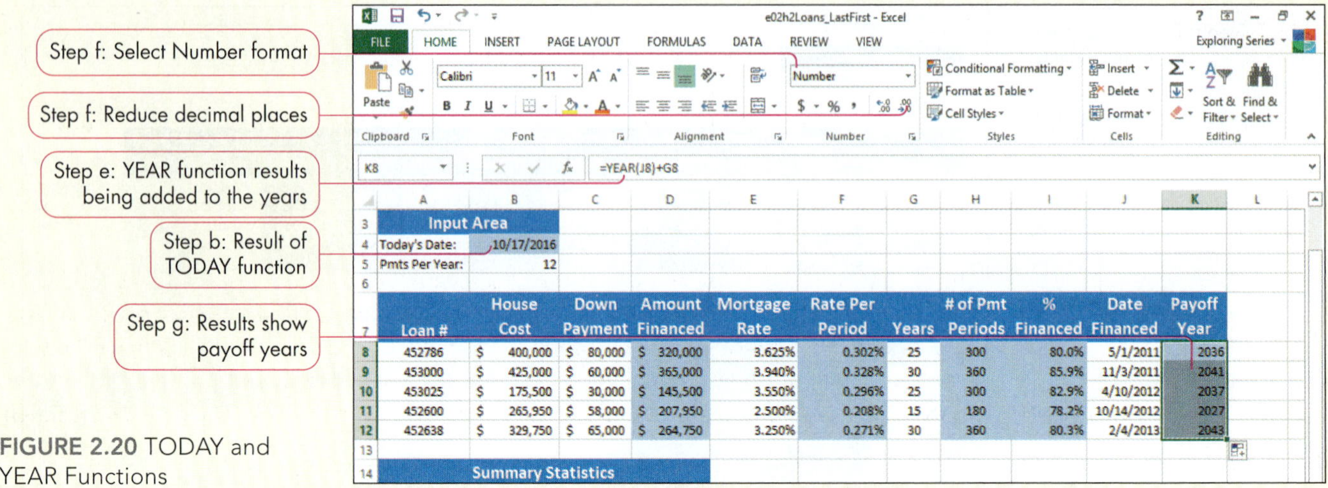

FIGURE 2.20 TODAY and YEAR Functions

a. Click **cell B4**, the cell to contain the current date.

b. Click **Date & Time** in the Function Library group, select **TODAY** to display the Function Arguments dialog box, and then click **OK** to close the dialog box.

   The Function Arguments dialog box opens, although no arguments are necessary for this function. Excel inserts the current date in Short Date format, such as 1/2/2016, based on the computer system's date.

c. Click **cell K8**, click **Date & Time** in the Function Library group, scroll through the list, and then select **YEAR**.

   The Function Arguments dialog box opens so that you can enter the argument, a serial number for a date.

d. Click **cell J8** to enter it in the **Serial_number box**. Click **OK**.

   The function returns 2011, the year the first mortgage was taken out. However, you want the year the mortgage will be paid off. The YEAR function returns the year from a date. You need to add the years to the result of the function to calculate the year that the borrower will pay off the mortgage.

e. Press **F2** to edit the formula stored in **cell K8**. With the insertion point on the right side of the closing parenthesis, type **+G8** and press **Ctrl+Enter**.

   Pressing Ctrl+Enter is the alternative to clicking Enter by the Formula Bar. It keeps the current cell as the active cell. The results show a date: 7/28/1905. You need to apply the Number format to display the year.

f. Click the **HOME tab**, click the **Number Format arrow** in the Number group, and then select **Number**. Decrease the number of decimal places to show the value as a whole number.

   You applied the Number format instead of the Comma format because although the Comma format is correct for quantities, such as 2,036 units, it is not appropriate for the year 2036.

g. Copy the formula down the Payoff Year column.

h. Save the workbook. Keep the workbook open if you plan to continue with the next Hands-On Exercise. If not, close the workbook and exit Excel.

Logical, Lookup, and Financial Functions

As you prepare complex spreadsheets using functions, you will frequently use three function categories: logical, lookup and reference, and finance. Logical functions test the logic of a situation and return a particular result. Lookup and reference functions are useful when you need to look up a value in a list to identify the applicable value. Financial functions are useful to anyone who plans to take out a loan or invest money.

In this section, you will learn how to use the logical, lookup, and financial functions.

Determining Results with the IF Function

STEP 3»

The most common logical function is the ***IF function***, which returns one value when a condition is met or is true and returns another value when the condition is not met or is false. For example, a company gives a $500 bonus to employees who sold *over* $10,000 in merchandise this week, but no bonus to employees who did not sell over $10,000 in merchandise. Figure 2.21 shows a worksheet containing the sales data for three representatives and their bonuses, if any.

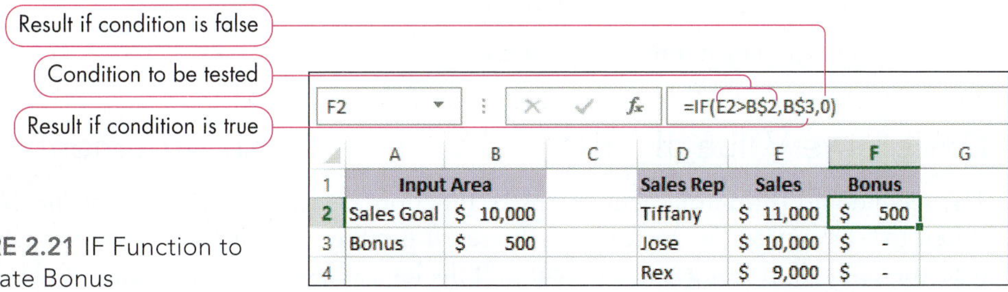

	A	B	C	D	E	F	G
1	Input Area			Sales Rep	Sales	Bonus	
2	Sales Goal	$ 10,000		Tiffany	$ 11,000	$ 500	
3	Bonus	$ 500		Jose	$ 10,000	$ -	
4				Rex	$ 9,000	$ -	

FIGURE 2.21 IF Function to Calculate Bonus

The IF function has three arguments: (1) a condition that is tested to determine if it is either true or false, (2) the resulting value if the condition is true, and (3) the resulting value if the condition is false.

=IF(logical_test,value_if_true,value_if_false)

You might find it helpful to create two flowcharts to illustrate an IF function. First, construct a flowchart that uses words and numbers to illustrate the condition and results. For example, the left flowchart in Figure 2.22 illustrates the condition to see if sales are greater than $10,000, and the $500 bonus if the condition is true or $0 if the condition is false. Then, create a second flowchart similar to the one on the right side of Figure 2.22 that replaces the words and values with actual cell references. Creating these flowcharts can help you construct the IF function that is used in cell F2 in Figure 2.21.

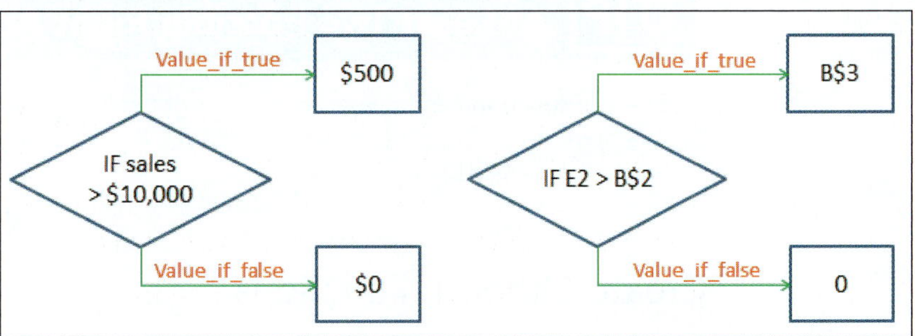

FIGURE 2.22 Flowcharts Illustrating IF Function

Design the Logical Test

The first argument for the IF function is the logical test. The ***logical test*** is a formula that contains either a value or an expression that evaluates to true or false. The logical expression is typically a binary expression, meaning that it requires a comparison between at least two variables, such as the values stored in cells E2 and B2. Table 2.4 lists and describes the logical operators to make the comparison in the logical test.

In Figure 2.21, cell F2 contains an IF function where the logical test is E2>B$2 to determine if Tiffany's sales in cell E2 are greater than the sales goal in cell B2. The reference to cell B2 can be mixed B$2 or absolute $B$2. Either way, copying the function down the column will compare each sales representative's sales with the $10,000 value in cell B2.

TABLE 2.4 Logical Operators

Operator	Description
=	Equal to
<>	Not equal to
<	Less than
>	Greater than
<=	Less than or equal to
>=	Greater than or equal to

Design the Value_If_True and Value_If_False Arguments

The second and third arguments of an IF function are value_if_true and value_if_false. When Excel evaluates the logical test, the result is either true or false. If the logical test is true, the value_if_true argument executes. If the logical test is false, the value_if_false argument executes. Only one of the last two arguments is executed; both arguments cannot be executed, because the logical test is either true or false but not both.

The value_if_true and value_if_false arguments can contain text, cell references, formulas, or constants (not recommended unless –1, 1, or 0). In Figure 2.21, cell F2 contains an IF function in which the value_if_true argument is B$3 and the value_if_false argument is 0. Because the logical test (E2>B$2) is true—that is, Tiffany's sales of $11,000 are greater than the $10,000 goal—the value_if_true argument is executed, and the result displays $500, the value that is stored in cell B3.

Jose's sales of $10,000 are not *greater than* $10,000, and Rex's sales of $9,000 are not *greater than* $10,000. Therefore, the value_if_false argument is executed and returns no bonus in cells F3 and F4.

At Least Two Possible Right Answers

Every IF function can have at least two right solutions to produce the same results. For example, if the logical test is E2<=B$2 for Figure 2.21, the value_if_true is 0, and the value_if_false is B$3.

Create Other IF Functions

Figure 2.23 illustrates several IF functions, how they are evaluated, and their results. The input area contains values that are used in the logical tests and results. You can create this worksheet with the input area and IF functions to develop your understanding of how IF functions work.

	A	B	C
1	**Input Values**		
2	$1,000		
3	$2,000		
4	10%		
5	5%		
6	$250		
7			
8	**IF Function**	**Evaluation**	**Result**
9	=IF(A2=A3,A4,A5)	$1,000 is equal to $2,000: FALSE	5%
10	=IF(A2<A3,A4,A5)	$1,000 is less than $2,000: TRUE	10%
11	=IF(A2<>A3,"Not Equal","Equal")	$1,000 and $2,000 are not equal: TRUE	Not Equal
12	=IF(A2>A3,(A2*A4),(A2*A5))	$1,000 is greater than $2,000: FALSE	$50
13	=IF(A2>A3,A2*A4,MAX(A2*A5,A6))	$1,000 is greater than $2,000: FALSE	$250
14	=IF(A2*A4=A3*A5,A6,0)	$100 (A2*A4) is equal to $100 (A3*A5): TRUE	$250

FIGURE 2.23 Sample IF Functions

- **Cell A9.** The logical test A2=A3 compares the values in cells A2 and A3 to see if they are equal. Because $1,000 is not equal to $2,000, the logical test is false. The value_if_false argument is executed, which displays 5%, the value stored in cell A5.
- **Cell A10.** The logical test A2<A3 determines if the value in cell A2 is less than the value in A3. Because $1,000 is less than $2,000, the logical test is true. The value_if_true argument is executed, which displays the value stored in cell A4, which is 10%.
- **Cell A11.** The logical test A2<>A3 determines if the values in cells A2 and A3 are not equal. Because $1,000 and $2,000 are not equal, the logical test is true. The value_if_true argument is executed, which displays the text *Not Equal*.
- **Cell A12.** The logical test A2>A3 is false. The value_if_false argument is executed, which multiplies the value in cell A2 ($1,000) by the value in cell A5 (5%) and displays $50. The parentheses in the value_if_true (A2*A4) and value_if_false (A2*A5) arguments are optional. They are not required but may help you read the function arguments better.
- **Cell A13.** The logical test A2>A3 is false. The value_if_false argument, which contains a nested MAX function, is executed. The MAX function, MAX(A2*A5,A6), multiplies the values in cells A2 ($1,000) and A5 (5%) and returns the higher of the product ($50) and the value stored in cell A6 ($250).
- **Cell A14.** The logical test A2*A4=A3*A5 is true. The contents of cell A2 ($1,000) are multiplied by the contents of cell A4 (10%) for a result of $100. That result is then compared to the result of A3*A5, which is also $100. Because the logical test is true, the function returns the value of cell A6 ($250).

TIP Using Text in Formulas

You can use text within a formula. For example, you can build a logical test comparing the contents of cell A1 to specific text, such as A1="Input Values". The IF function in cell A11 in Figure 2.23 uses "Not Equal" and "Equal" in the value_if_true and value_if_false arguments. When you use text in a formula or function, you must enclose the text in quotation marks. However, do not use quotation marks around formulas, cell references, or values.

TIP Nest Functions in IF Functions

You can nest functions in the logical test, value_if_true, and value_if_false arguments of the IF function. When you nest functions as arguments, make sure the nested function contains the required arguments for it to work and that you nest the function in the correct argument to calculate accurate results. For example, cell C13 in Figure 2.23 contains a nested MAX function in the value_if_false argument.

Using Lookup Functions

You can use lookup and reference functions to look up values to perform calculations or display results. For example, when you order merchandise on a Web site, the Web server looks up the shipping costs based on weight and distance, or at the end of a semester, your professor uses your average, such as 88%, to look up the letter grade to assign, such as B+.

Create the Lookup Table

A ***lookup table*** is a range containing a table of values or text that can be retrieved. The table should contain at least two rows and two columns, not including headings. Figure 2.24 illustrates a college directory with three "columns." The first column contains professors' names. You look up a professor's name in the first column to see his or her office (second "column") and phone extension (third "column").

Brazil, Estivan	GT 218b	7243
Fiedler, Zazilia	CS 417	7860
Lam, Kaitlyn	SC 124a	7031
Rodriquez, Lisa	GT 304	7592
Yeung, Bradon	CS 414	7314

FIGURE 2.24 College Directory Lookup Table Analogy

It is important to plan the table so that it conforms to the way in which Excel can utilize the data in it. Excel cannot interpret the structure of Table 2.5. To look up a value in a range (such as the range 80–89), you must arrange data from the lowest to the highest value and include only the lowest value in the range (such as 80) instead of the complete range. If the values you look up are *exact* values, you can arrange the first column in any logical order. The lowest value for a category or in a series is the ***breakpoint***. The first column contains the breakpoints—such as 60, 70, 80, and 90—or the lowest values to achieve a particular grade. The lookup table contains one or more additional columns of related data to retrieve. Table 2.6 shows how to construct the lookup table in Excel.

TABLE 2.5 Grading Scale

Range	Grade
90–100	A
80–89	B
70–79	C
60–69	D
Below 60	F

TABLE 2.6 Grades Lookup Table

Range	Grade
0	F
60	D
70	C
80	B
90	A

Understand the VLOOKUP Function Syntax

STEP 1»

The ***VLOOKUP function*** accepts a value, looks the value up in a vertical lookup table, and returns a result. Use VLOOKUP to search for exact matches or for the nearest value that is less than or equal to the search value, such as assigning a B grade for an 87% class average. The VLOOKUP function has the following three required arguments and one optional argument: (1) lookup_value, (2) table_array, (3) col_index_number, and (4) range_lookup.

```
=VLOOKUP(lookup_value,table_array,col_index_number,[range_lookup])
```

Figure 2.25 shows a partial grade book that contains a vertical lookup table, as well as the final scores and letter grades. The function in cell F3 is =VLOOKUP(E3,$A$3:$B$7,2).

Value (final score) to look up

Table array range

Use second column within the table to return letter grade

F3 | =VLOOKUP(E3,$A$3:$B$7,2)

	A	B	C	D	E	F	G
1	Grading Scale			Partial Gradebook			
2	Breakpoint	Grade		Names	Final Score	Letter Grade	
3	0	F		Abbott	85	B	
4	60	D		Carter	69	D	
5	70	C		Hon	90	A	
6	80	B		Jackson	74	C	
7	90	A		Miller	80	B	
8				Nelsen	78	C	

FIGURE 2.25 VLOOKUP Function for Grade Book

The ***lookup value*** is the cell reference of the cell that contains the value to look up. The lookup value for the first student is cell E3, which contains 85. The ***table array*** is the range that contains the lookup table: $A$3:$B$7. The table array range must be absolute and cannot include column labels for the lookup table. The ***column index number*** is the column number in the lookup table that contains the return values. In this example, the column index number is 2.

TIP Using Values in Formulas

You know to avoid using values in formulas because the input values in a worksheet cell might change. However, the value 2 is used in the col_index_number argument of the VLOOKUP function. The 2 refers to a particular column within the lookup table and is an acceptable use of a number within a formula.

Understand How Excel Processes the Lookup

Here is how the VLOOK function works:

1. The function identifies the value-stored cell used as the lookup value argument.
2. Excel searches the first column of the lookup table until it (a) finds an exact match (if possible) or (b) identifies the correct range if the lookup table contains breakpoints for range.
3. If Excel finds an exact match, it returns the value stored in the column designated by the column index number on that same row. If breakpoints are used and the lookup value is larger than the breakpoint, it looks to the next breakpoint to see if the lookup value is larger than that breakpoint also. When Excel detects that the lookup value is not greater than the next breakpoint, it stays on that row. It then uses the column index number to identify the column containing the value to return for the lookup value. Because Excel goes sequentially through the breakpoints, it is mandatory that the breakpoints are arranged from the lowest value to the highest value for ranges.

In Figure 2.25, the VLOOKUP function assigns letter grades based on final scores. Excel identifies the lookup value (85 in cell E3) and compares it to the values in the first column of the lookup table (range A3:B7). It tries to find an exact match of 85; however, the table contains breakpoints rather than every conceivable score. Because the lookup table is arranged from the lowest to the highest breakpoints, Excel detects that 85 is greater than the 80 breakpoint but is not greater than the 90 breakpoint. Therefore, it stays on the 80 row. Excel looks at the second column (column index number of 2) and returns the letter grade of B. The B grade is then stored in cell F3.

Use the Range_Lookup Argument

Instead of looking up values in a range, you can look up a value for an exact match using the optional range_lookup argument in the VLOOKUP function. By default, the range_lookup is set implicitly to TRUE, which is appropriate to look up values in a range. Omitting the optional argument or typing TRUE in it enables the VLOOKUP function to find the closest match in the table to the lookup value.

To look up an exact match, enter FALSE in the range_lookup argument. For example, if you are looking up product numbers, you must find an exact match to display the price. The function would look like this: =VLOOKUP(D15,$A$1:$B$50,2,FALSE). The function returns a value for the first lookup value that matches the first column of the lookup table. If no exact match is found, the function returns #N/A.

Nest Functions Inside the VLOOKUP Function

You can nest functions as arguments inside the VLOOKUP function. For example, Figure 2.26 illustrates shipping amounts that are based on weight and location (Boston or Chicago). In the VLOOKUP function in cell C3, the lookup_value argument looks up the weight of a package in cell A3. That weight (14 pounds) is looked up in the table_array argument, which is $E$3:$G$5. To determine which column of the lookup table to use, an IF function is nested as the column_index_number argument. The nested IF function compares the city stored in cell B3 to the text *Boston*. If cell B3 contains *Boston*, it returns 2 to use as the column_index_number to identify the shipping value for a package that is going to Boston. If cell B3 does not contain *Boston* (i.e., the only other city in this example is *Chicago*), the column_index_number is 3.

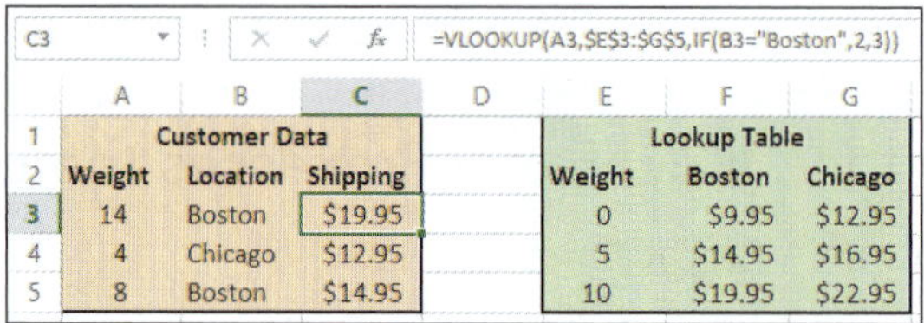

FIGURE 2.26 IF Function Nested in VLOOKUP Function

Use the HLOOKUP Function

You can design a lookup table horizontally where the first row contains the values for the basis of the lookup or the breakpoints, and additional rows contain data to be retrieved. With a horizontal lookup table, use the ***HLOOKUP function***. Table 2.7 shows how the grading scale would look as a horizontal lookup table.

TABLE 2.7 Horizontal Lookup Table

0	60	70	80	90
F	D	C	B	A

The syntax is almost the same as the syntax for the VLOOKUP function, except the third argument is row_index_number instead of col_index_number.

=HLOOKUP(lookup_value,table_array,row_index_number,[range_lookup])

Calculating Payments with the PMT Function

STEP 2» Excel contains several financial functions to help you perform calculations with monetary values. If you take out a loan to purchase a car, you need to know the monthly payment, which depends on the price of the car, the down payment, and the terms of the loan, in order to determine if you can afford the car. The decision is made easier by developing the worksheet in Figure 2.27 and by changing the various input values as indicated.

B9 | fx =PMT(B6,B8,-B3)

	A	B	C	D
1	Purchase Price	$25,999.00		
2	Down Payment	$ 5,000.00		
3	Amount to Finance	$20,999.00		
4	Payments per Year	12		
5	Interest Rate (APR)	3.500%		
6	Periodic Rate (Monthly)	0.292%		
7	Term (Years)	5		
8	No. of Payment Periods	60		
9	Monthly Payment	$ 382.01		
10				

FIGURE 2.27 Car Loan Worksheet

Creating a loan model helps you evaluate options. You realize that the purchase of a $25,999 car is prohibitive because the monthly payment is $382.01. Purchasing a less expensive car, coming up with a substantial down payment, taking out a longer-term loan, or finding a better interest rate can decrease your monthly payments.

The ***PMT function*** calculates payments for a loan with a fixed amount at a fixed periodic rate for a fixed time period. The PMT function uses three required arguments and up to two optional arguments: (1) rate, (2) nper, (3) pv, (4) fv, and (5) type.

=PMT(rate,nper,pv,[fv],[type])

The ***rate*** is the periodic interest rate, the interest rate per payment period. If the annual percentage rate (APR) is 12% and you make monthly payments, the periodic rate is 1% (12%/12 months). With the same APR and quarterly payments, the periodic rate is 3% (12%/4 quarters). Divide the APR by the number of payment periods in one year. However, instead of dividing the APR by 12 within the PMT function, calculate the periodic interest rate in cell B6 in Figure 2.27 and use that calculated rate in the PMT function.

The ***nper*** is the total number of payment periods. The term of a loan is usually stated in years; however, you make several payments per year. For monthly payments, you make 12 payments per year. To calculate the nper, multiply the number of years by the number of payments in one year. Instead of calculating the number of payment periods in the PMT function, calculate the number of payment periods in cell B8 and use that calculated value in the PMT function.

The ***pv*** is the present value of the loan. The result of the PMT function is a negative value because it represents your debt. However, you can display the result as a positive value by typing a minus sign in front of the present value cell reference in the PMT function.

1. Describe the three arguments for an IF function. ***pp. 181–182***
2. How should you structure a vertical lookup table if you need to look up values in a range? ***p. 186***
3. What are the first three arguments of a PMT function? Why would you have to divide by or multiply an argument by 12? ***p. 187***

Hands-On Exercises

3 Logical, Lookup, and Financial Functions

Erica wants you to complete another model that she might use for future mortgage data analysis. As you study the model, you realize you need to incorporate logical, lookup, and financial functions.

Skills covered: Use the VLOOKUP Function • Use the PMT Function • Use the IF Function

STEP 1 » USE THE VLOOKUP FUNCTION

Rates vary based on the number of years to pay off the loan. Erica created a lookup table for three common mortgage years, and she entered the current APR. The lookup table will provide efficiency later when the rates change. You will use the VLOOKUP function to display the correct rate for each customer based on the number of years of the respective loans. Refer to Figure 2.28 as you complete Step 1.

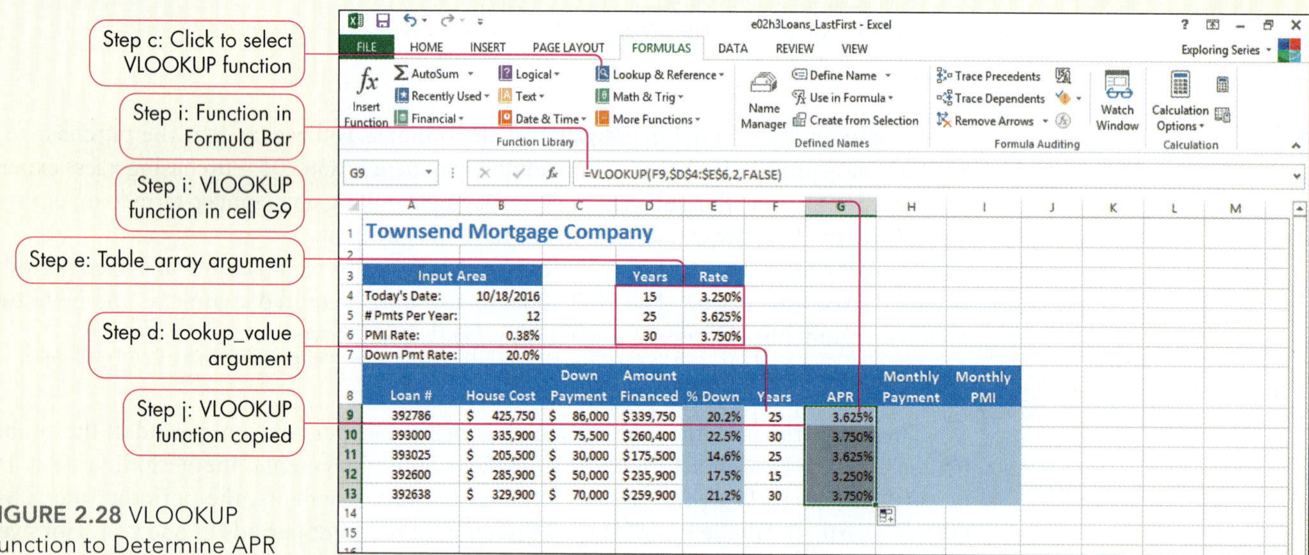

FIGURE 2.28 VLOOKUP Function to Determine APR

a. Open *e02h2Loans_LastFirst* if you closed it at the end of Hands-On Exercise 2 and save it as **e02h3Loans_LastFirst**, changing *h2* to *h3*.

b. Click the **Payment Info worksheet tab** to display the worksheet containing the data to complete. Click **cell G9**, the cell that will store the APR for the first customer.

c. Click the **FORMULAS tab**, click **Lookup & Reference** in the Function Library group, and then select **VLOOKUP**.

   The Function Arguments dialog box opens.

d. Click **F9** to enter F9 in the **Lookup_value box**.

   Cell F9 contains the value you need to look up from the table: 25 years.

> **TROUBLESHOOTING:** If you cannot see the cell you need to use in an argument, click the Function Arguments dialog box title bar and drag the dialog box on the screen until you can see and click the cell you need for the argument. Alternatively, you can click the collapse button to the right of the argument box to collapse the dialog box so that you can select the range. After selecting the range, click the expand button to expand the dialog box.

e. Press **Tab** and select the **range D4:E6** in the **Table_array box.**

This is the range that contains that data for the lookup table. The Years values in the table are arranged from lowest to highest. Do **not** select the column labels for the range.

Anticipate what will happen if you copy the formula down the column. What do you need to do to ensure that the cell references always point to the exact location of the table? If your answer is to make the table array cell references absolute, then you answered correctly.

f. Press **F4** to make the range references absolute.

The Table_array box now contains $D$4:$E$6.

g. Press **Tab** and type **2** in the **Col_index_num box.**

The second column of the lookup table contains the APRs that you want to return and display in the cells containing the formulas.

h. Press **Tab** and type **False** in the **Range_lookup box.**

You want the formula to display an error if an incorrect number of years has been entered. To ensure an exact match to look up in the table, you enter *False* in the optional argument.

i. Click **OK.**

The VLOOKUP function looks up the first person's years (25), finds an exact match in the first column of the lookup table, and then returns the corresponding APR, which is 3.625%.

j. Copy the formula down the column and save the workbook.

Spot check the results to make sure the function returned the correct APR based on the number of years.

STEP 2 » USE THE PMT FUNCTION

The worksheet now has all the necessary data for you to calculate the monthly payment for each loan: the APR, the number of years for the loan, the number of payment periods in one year, and the initial loan amount. You will use the PMT function to calculate the monthly payment, which includes paying back the principal amount with interest. This calculation does not include escrow amounts, such as property taxes or insurance. Refer to Figure 2.29 as you complete Step 2.

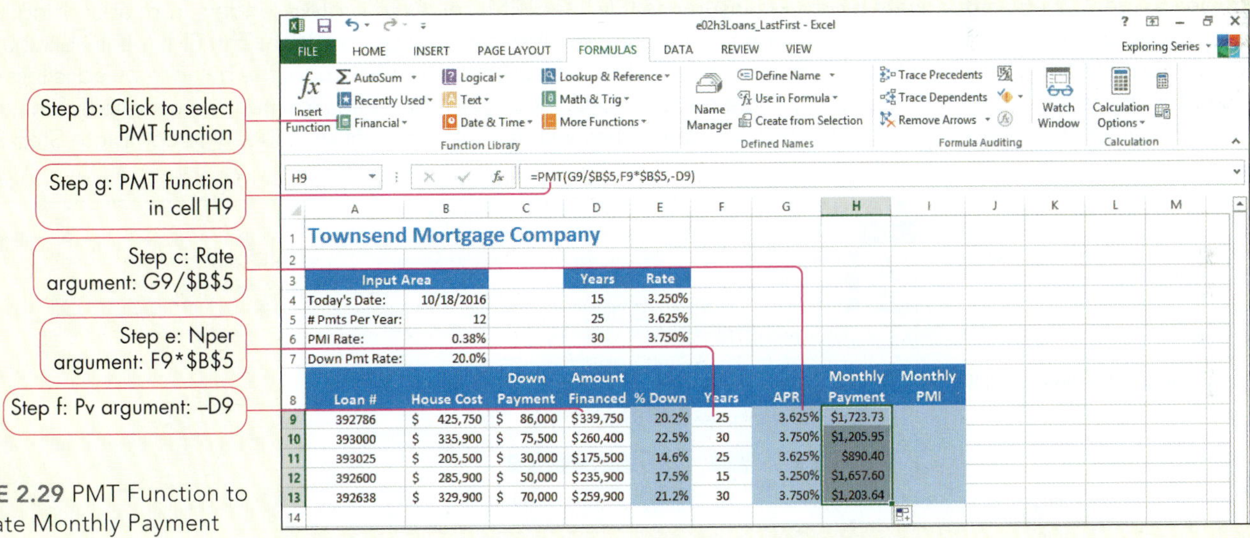

FIGURE 2.29 PMT Function to Calculate Monthly Payment

a. Click **cell H9**, the cell that will store the payment for the first customer.

b. Click **Financial** in the Function Library group, scroll through the list, and then select **PMT.**

TROUBLESHOOTING: Make sure you select PMT, not PPMT. The PPMT function calculates the principal portion of a particular monthly payment, not the total monthly payment itself.

The Function Arguments dialog box opens.

c. Type **G9/B5** in the **Rate box**.

Think about what will happen if you copy the formula. The argument will be G10/B6 for the next customer. Are those cell references correct? G10 does contain the APR for the next customer, but B6 does not contain the correct number of payments in one year. Therefore, you need to make B5 an absolute cell reference because the number of payments per year does not vary.

d. Press **F4** to make the reference to cell B5 absolute.

e. Press **Tab** and type **F9*$B$5** in the **Nper box**.

You calculate the nper by multiplying the number of years by the number of payments in one year. You must make B5 an absolute cell reference so that it does not change when you copy the formula down the column.

f. Press **Tab** and type **-D9** in the **Pv box**.

The bottom of the dialog box indicates that the monthly payment is 1723.73008 or $1,723.73.

TROUBLESHOOTING: If the payment displays as a negative value, you probably forgot to type the minus sign in front of the D9 reference in the Pv box. Edit the function and type the minus sign in the correct place.

g. Click **OK**. Copy the formula down the column and save the workbook.

STEP 3 » USE THE IF FUNCTION

Lenders often want borrowers to have a 20% down payment. If borrowers do not put in 20% of the cost of the house as a down payment, they pay a private mortgage insurance (PMI) fee. PMI serves to protect lenders from absorbing loss if the borrower defaults on the loan, and it enables borrowers with less cash to secure a loan. The PMI fee is about 0.38% of the amount financed. Some borrowers have to pay PMI for a few months or years until the balance owed is less than 80% of the appraised value. The worksheet contains the necessary values input area. You need to use the IF function to determine which borrowers must pay PMI and how much they will pay. Refer to Figure 2.30 as you complete Step 3.

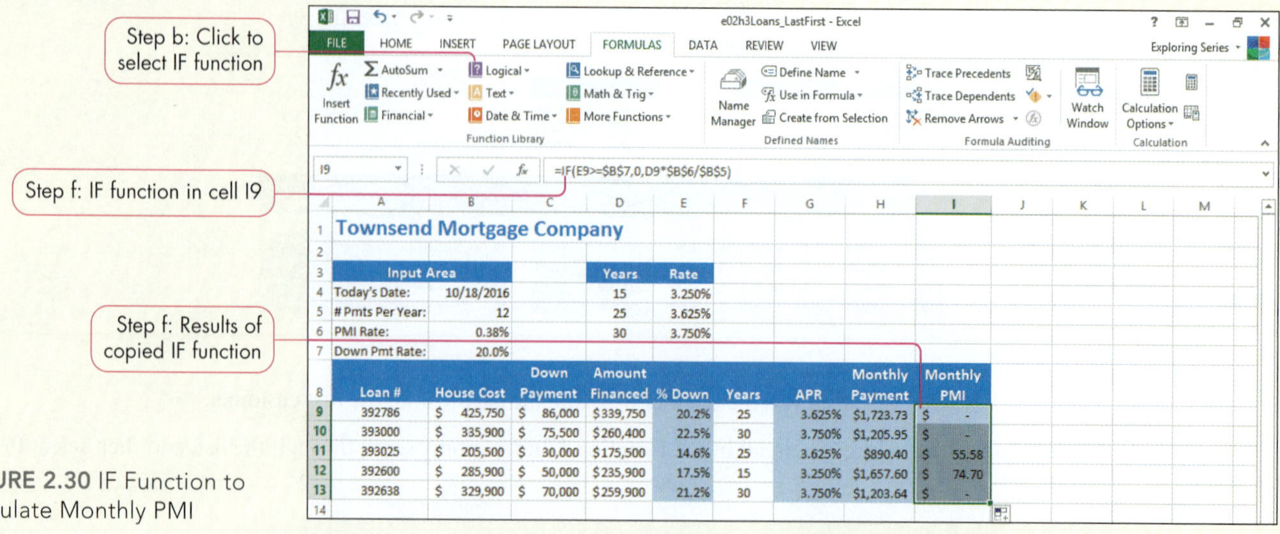

FIGURE 2.30 IF Function to Calculate Monthly PMI

a. Click **cell I9**, the cell that will store the PMI, if any, for the first customer.

b. Click **Logical** in the Function Library group and select **IF**.

The Function Arguments dialog box opens. You need to enter the three arguments.

c. Type **E9>=$B$7** in the **Logical_test box**.

The logical test compares the down payment percentage to see if the customer's down payment is at least 20%, the threshold stored in B7, of the amount financed. The customer's percentage cell reference needs to be relative so that it will change when you copy it down the column; however, cell B7 must be absolute because it contains the threshold value.

d. Press **Tab** and type **0** in the **Value_if_true box**.

If the customer makes a down payment that is at least 20% of the purchase price, the customer does not pay PMI. The first customer paid 20% of the purchase price, so he or she does not have to pay PMI.

e. Press **Tab** and type **D9*$B$6/$B$5** in the **Value_if_false box**.

If the logical test is false, the customer must pay PMI, which is calculated by dividing the yearly PMI (0.38%) by 12 and multiplying the result by the amount financed.

f. Click **OK** and copy the formula down the column.

The third and fourth customers must pay PMI because their respective down payments were less than 20% of the purchase price.

TROUBLESHOOTING: If the results are not as you expected, check the logical operators. People often mistype < and > or forget to type = for >= situations. Correct any errors in the original formula and copy the formula again.

g. Save the workbook. Keep the workbook open if you plan to continue with the next Hands-On Exercise. If not, close the workbook and exit Excel.

Range Names

To simplify entering ranges in formulas, you can use range names. A ***range name*** is a word or string of characters assigned to one or more cells. Think of range names in this way: Your college identifies you by your student ID; however, your professors call you by an easy-to-remember name, such as Micah or Vanessa. Similarly, instead of using cell addresses, you can use descriptive range names in formulas. Going back to the VLOOKUP example shown in Figure 2.25, you can assign the range name *Grades* to cells A3:B7 and modify the VLOOKUP function to be =VLOOKUP(E3,Grades,2), using the range name *Grades* in the formula. Another benefit of using range names is that they are absolute references, which helps ensure accuracy in your calculations.

In this section, you will work with range names. First, you will learn how to create and maintain range names. Then you will learn how to use a range name in a formula.

Creating and Maintaining Range Names

Each range name within a workbook must be unique. For example, you cannot assign the name *COST* to ranges on several worksheets or on the same sheet. After you create a range name, you might need to change its name or range. If you no longer need a range name, you can delete it. You can also insert in the workbook a list of range names and their respective cell ranges for reference.

Create a Range Name

STEP 1 »

A range name can contain up to 255 characters, but it must begin with a letter or an underscore. You can use a combination of upper- or lowercase letters, numbers, periods, and underscores throughout the range name. A range name cannot include spaces or special characters. You should create range names that describe the range of cells being named, but names cannot be identical to the cell contents. Keep the range names short to make them easier to use in formulas. Table 2.8 lists acceptable and unacceptable range names.

TABLE 2.8 Range Names

Name	Description
Grades	Acceptable range name
COL	Acceptable abbreviation for cost-of-living
Tax_Rate	Acceptable name with underscore
Commission Rate	Unacceptable name; cannot use spaces in names
Discount Rate %	Unacceptable name; cannot use special symbols and spaces
2016_Rate	Unacceptable name; cannot start with a number
Rate_2016	Acceptable name with underscore and numbers

To create a range name, select the range you want to name and do one of the following:

- Click in the Name Box, type the range name, and then press Enter.
- Click the FORMULAS tab, click Define Name in the Defined Names group to open the New Name dialog box (see Figure 2.31), type the range name in the Name Box, and then click OK.
- Click the FORMULAS tab, click Name Manager in the Defined Names group to open the Name Manager dialog box, click New, type the range name in the Name Box, click OK, and then click Close.

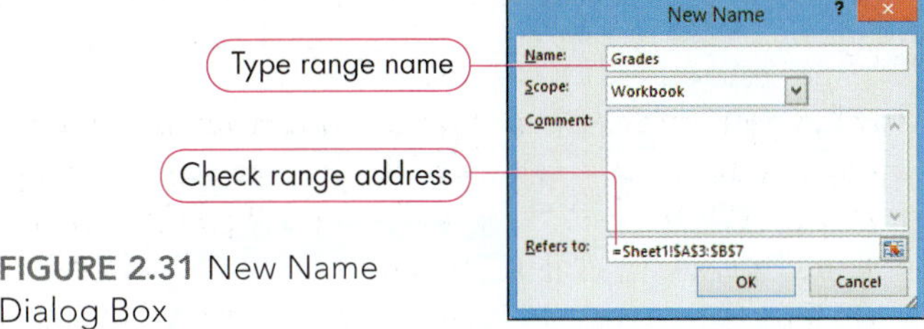

FIGURE 2.31 New Name Dialog Box

You can create several range names at the same time if your worksheet includes ranges with values and descriptive labels. To do this, select the range of cells containing the labels that you want to become names and the cells that contain the values to name, click *Create from Selection* in the Defined Named group on the Formulas tab, and then select an option in the *Create Names from Selection* dialog box (see Figure 2.32).

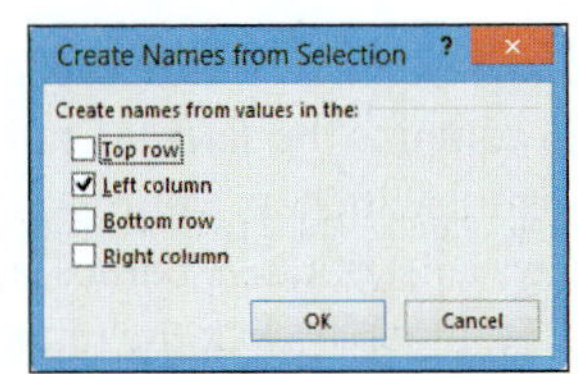

FIGURE 2.32 Create Names from Selection Dialog Box

Edit or Delete a Range Name

STEP 2»

Use the Name Manager dialog box to edit, delete, and create range names. To open the Name Manager dialog box shown in Figure 2.33, click Name Manager in the Defined Names group on the Formulas tab. To edit a range or range name, click the range name in the list and click Edit. In the Edit Name dialog box, make your edits and click OK.

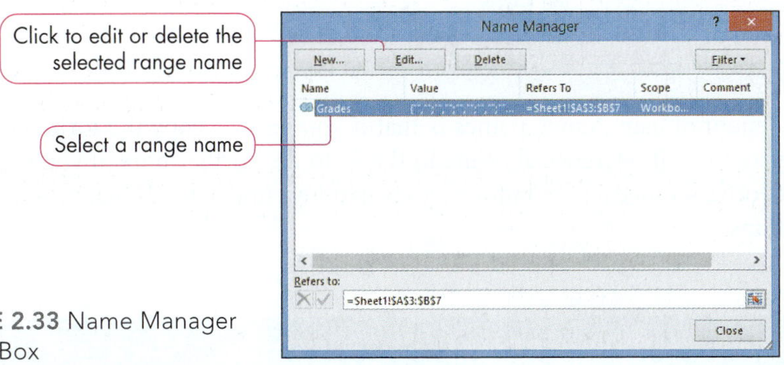

FIGURE 2.33 Name Manager Dialog Box

To delete a range name, open the Name Manager dialog box, select the name you want to delete, click Delete, and then click OK in the confirmation message box.

If you change a range name, any formulas that use the range name reflect the new name. For example, if a formula contains =cost*rate and you change the name rate to tax_rate, Excel updates the formula to be =cost*tax_rate. If you delete a range name and a formula depends on that range name, Excel displays #NAME?—indicating an Invalid Name Error.

Insert a Table of Range Names

STEP 4»

You can document a workbook by inserting a list of range names in a worksheet. To insert a list of range names, click *Use in Formula* in the Defined Names group on the Formulas tab and select Paste Names. The Paste Name dialog box opens (see Figure 2.34), listing all range names in the current workbook. Click Paste List to insert a list of range names in alphabetical order. The first column contains a list of range names, and the second column contains the worksheet names and range locations.

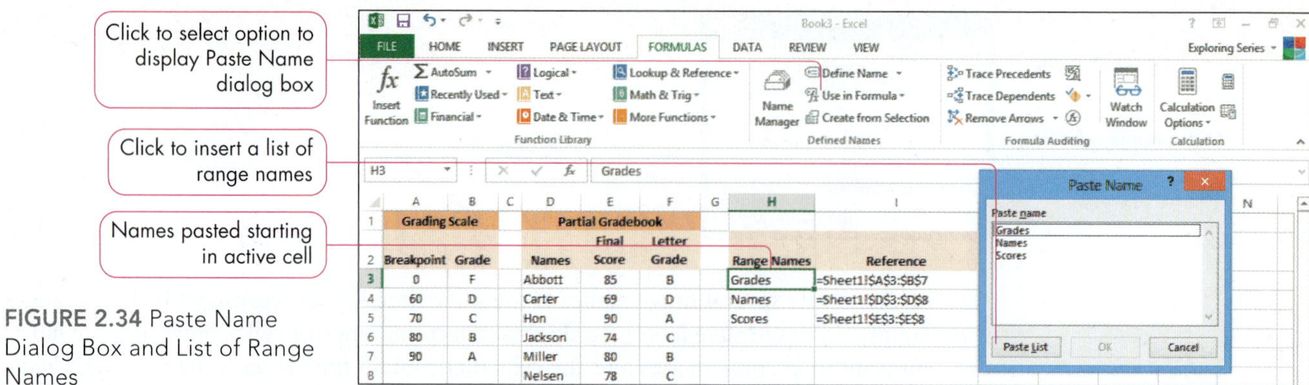

FIGURE 2.34 Paste Name Dialog Box and List of Range Names

Using Range Names in Formulas

STEP 3» You can use range names in formulas instead of cell references. For example, if cell C15 contains a purchase amount, and cell C5 contains the sales tax rate, instead of typing =C15*C5, you can type the range names in the formula, such as =purchase*tax_rate. When you type a formula, Formula AutoComplete displays a list of range names, as well as functions, that start with the letters as you type (see Figure 2.35). Double-click the range name to insert it in the formula.

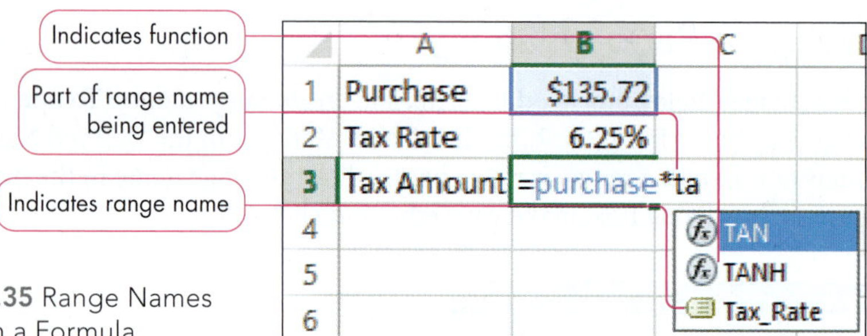

FIGURE 2.35 Range Names Inserted in a Formula

Another benefit of using range names is that if you have to copy the formula, you do not have to make the cell reference absolute in the formula. Furthermore, if you share your workbook with others, range names in formulas help others understand what values are used in the calculations.

TIP Go to a Range Name

Use the Go To dialog box to go to the top-left cell in a range specified by a range name.

Quick Concepts

1. What is a range name? ***p. 192***
2. List at least five guidelines and rules for naming a range. ***p. 192***
3. What is the purpose of inserting a list of range names in a worksheet? What is contained in the list, and how is it arranged? ***p. 194***

Hands-On Exercises

4 Range Names

You decide to simplify the VLOOKUP function by using a range name for the APR rates lookup table instead of the actual cell references. After creating a range name, you will modify some range names Erica created and create a list of range names.

Skills covered: Create a Range Name • Edit and Delete Range Names • Use a Range Name in a Formula • Insert a List of Range Names

STEP 1 » CREATE A RANGE NAME

You want to assign a range name to the lookup table of years and APRs. Refer to Figure 2.36 as you complete Step 1.

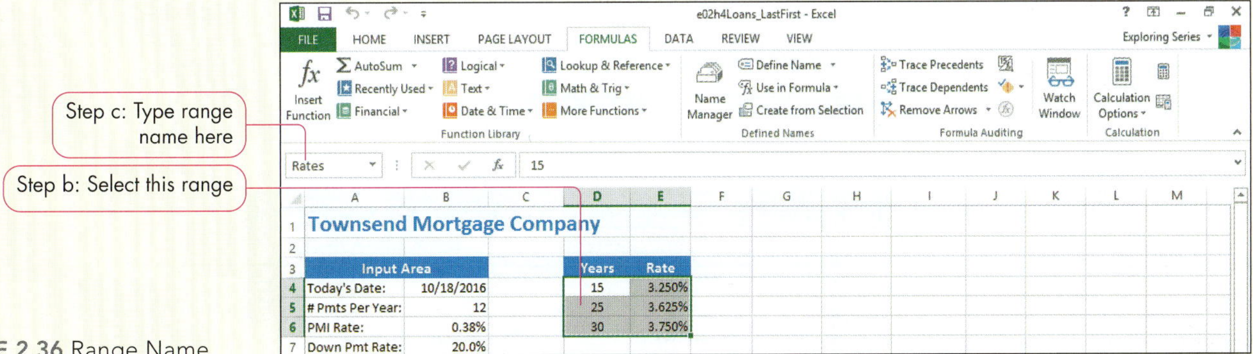

FIGURE 2.36 Range Name

a. Open *e02h3Loans_LastFirst* if you closed it at the end of Hands-On Exercise 3 and save it as **e02h4Loans_LastFirst**, changing *h3* to *h4*.

b. Make sure the **Payment Info worksheet tab** is active. Select **range D4:E6** (the lookup table).

c. Click in the **Name Box**, type **Rates**, and then press **Enter**. Save the workbook.

STEP 2 » EDIT AND DELETE RANGE NAMES

You noticed that Erica added some range names. You will use the Name Manager dialog box to view and make changes to the range names, such as reducing the length of two range names and deleting another range name. Refer to Figure 2.37 as you complete Step 2.

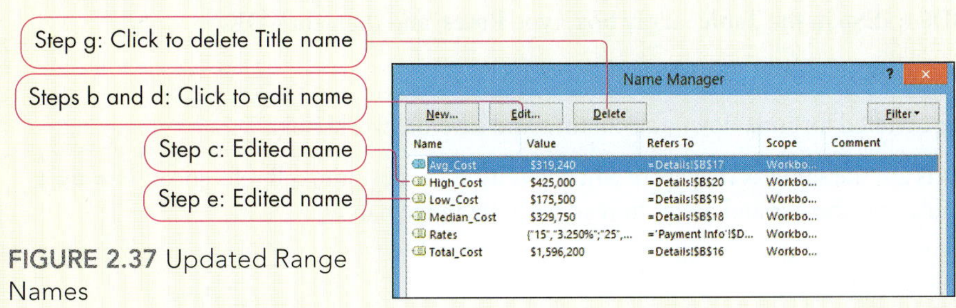

FIGURE 2.37 Updated Range Names

a. Click **Name Manager** in the Defined Names group on the FORMULAS tab.

The Name Manager dialog box opens.

b. Select **Highest_House…** and click **Edit** to open the Edit Name dialog box.

c. Type **High_Cost** in the **Name Box** and click **OK**.

d. Select **Lowest_House...** and click **Edit**.

e. Type **Low_Cost** in the **Name Box** and click **OK**.

f. Select **Title** in the Name Manager dialog box.

   This range name applies to a cell containing text, which does not need a name as it cannot be used in calculations. You decide to delete the range name.

g. Click **Delete**, read the warning message box, and then click **OK** to confirm the deletion of the Title range name.

h. Click **Close** and save the workbook.

STEP 3 » USE A RANGE NAME IN A FORMULA

You will modify the VLOOKUP function by replacing the existing Table_array argument with the range name. This will help Erica interpret the VLOOKUP function. Refer to Figure 2.38 as you complete Step 3.

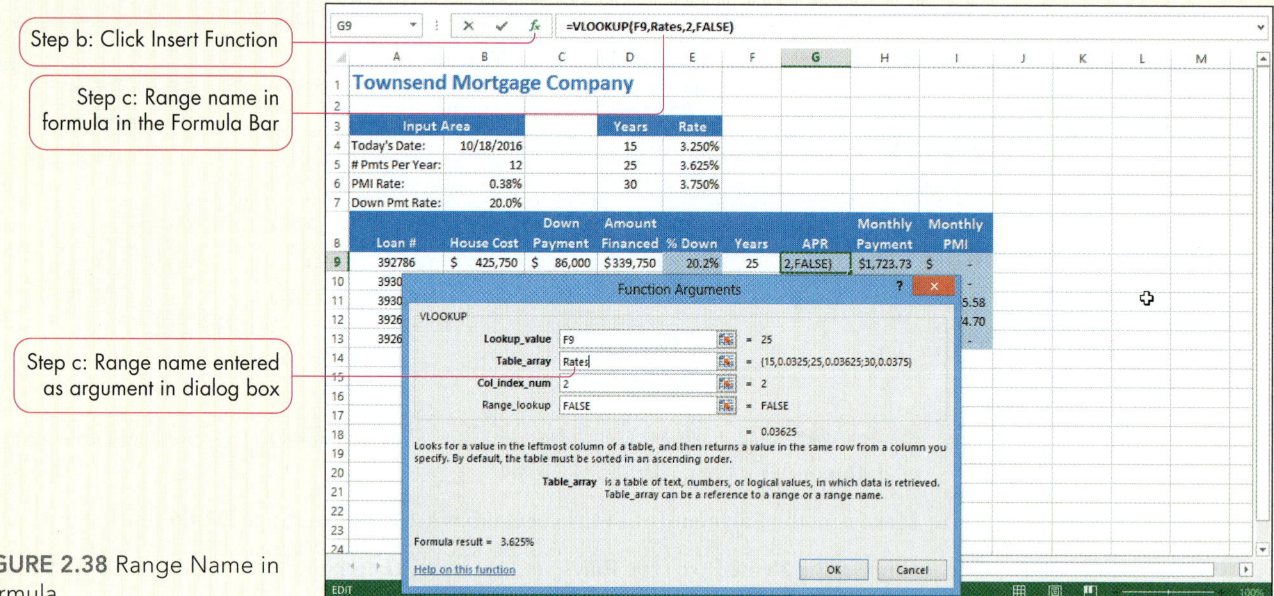

FIGURE 2.38 Range Name in Formula

a. Click **cell G9**, the cell containing the VLOOKUP function.

b. Click **Insert Function** between the Name Box and the Formula Bar to open the Function Arguments dialog box.

   The Table_array argument contains $D$4:$E$6, the absolute reference to the lookup table.

c. Select **$D$4:$E$6** in the **Table_array box**, type **Rates**, and then click **OK**.

   The new function is =VLOOKUP(F9,Rates,2,FALSE).

d. Copy the updated formula down the column and save the workbook.

   The results are the same as they were when you used the absolute cell references. However, the formulas are shorter and easier to read with the range names.

STEP 4 » INSERT A LIST OF RANGE NAMES

Before submitting the completed workbook to Erica, you want to create a documentation worksheet that lists all of the range names in the workbook. Refer to Figure 2.39 as you complete Step 4.

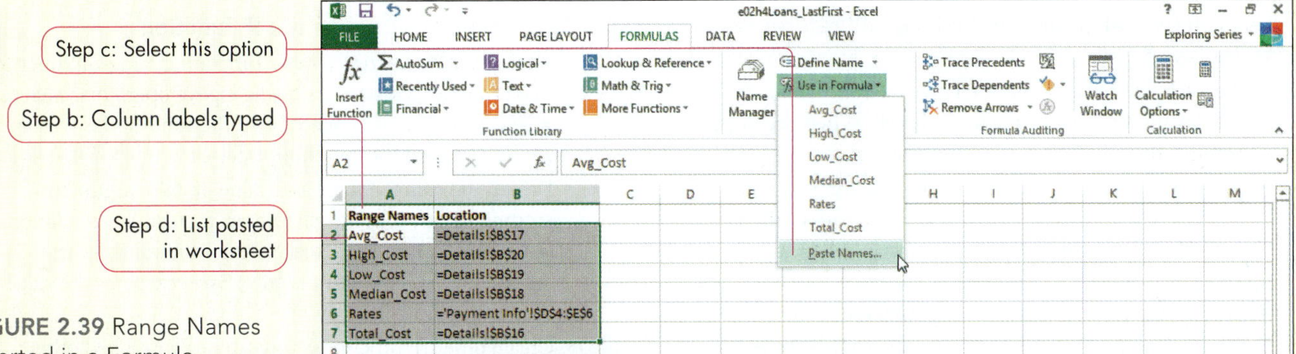

FIGURE 2.39 Range Names Inserted in a Formula

a. Click **New sheet** to the right of the worksheet tabs and double-click the default sheet name, **Sheet1**. Type **Range Names** and press **Enter**.

You inserted and renamed the new worksheet to reflect the data you will add to it.

b. Type **Range Names** in **cell A1** and type **Location** in **cell B1**. Bold these headings.

These column headings will display above the list of range names.

c. Click **cell A2**, click **Use in Formula** in the Defined Names group on the FORMULAS tab, and then select **Paste Names**.

The Paste Name dialog box opens, displaying all of the range names in the workbook.

d. Click **Paste List**.

Excel pastes an alphabetical list of range names starting in cell A2. The second column displays the locations of the range names.

e. Increase the widths of columns A and B to fit the data.

f. Save and close the workbook, and submit based on your instructor's directions.

List of Range Names

When you paste range names, the list will overwrite any existing data in a worksheet, so consider pasting the list in a separate worksheet. If you add, edit, or delete range names, the list does not update automatically. To keep the list current, you would need to paste the list again.

Chapter Objectives Review

After reading this chapter, you have accomplished the following objectives:

1. Use relative, absolute, and mixed cell references in formulas.

- Use a relative cell address: A relative reference indicates a cell's location relative to the formula cell. When you copy the formula, the relative cell reference changes.
- Use an absolute cell reference: An absolute reference is a permanent pointer to a particular cell, indicated with $ before the column letter and row number, such as $B$5. When you copy the formula, the absolute cell reference does not change.
- Use a mixed cell reference: A mixed reference contains part absolute and part relative reference, such as $B5 or B$5. Either the column or row reference changes, while the other remains constant when you copy the formula.

2. Correct circular references.

- A circular reference occurs when a formula refers to the cell containing the formula. The status bar indicates the location of a circular reference.

3. Insert a function.

- A function is a predefined formula that performs a calculation. It contains the function name and arguments. Formula AutoComplete, function ScreenTips, and the Insert Function dialog box help you select and create functions. The Function Arguments dialog box guides you through entering requirements for each argument.

4. Insert basic math and statistics functions.

- Calculate the total with the SUM function: The SUM function calculates the total of a range of values. The syntax is =SUM(number1,[number2],...).
- Find central tendency with AVERAGE and MEDIAN: The AVERAGE function calculates the arithmetic mean of values in a range. The MEDIAN function identifies the midpoint value in a set of values.
- Identify low and high values with MIN and MAX: The MIN function identifies the lowest value in a range, whereas the MAX function identifies the highest value in a range.
- Identify the total number with COUNT functions: The COUNT function tallies the number of cells in a range, whereas the COUNTBLANK function tallies the number of blank cells in a range.
- Use other math and statistical functions: Excel contains other math and statistical functions, such as MODE.
- Nest functions as arguments: You can nest one function inside another function's argument, such as nesting the AVERAGE function inside the ROUND function: =ROUND(AVERAGE(A2:A14),2).

5. Use date functions.

- Insert the TODAY function: The TODAY function displays the current date.
- Insert the NOW function: The NOW function displays the current date and time.
- Use other date functions: Excel contains a variety of date and time functions.

6. Determine results with the IF function.

- Design the logical test: The IF function is a logical function that evaluates a logical test using logical operators, such as <, >, and =, and returns one value if the condition is true and another value if the condition is false.
- Design the value_if_true and value_if_false arguments: The arguments can contain cell references, text, or calculations. If a logical test is true, Excel executes the value_if_true argument. If a logical test is false, Excel executes the value_if_false argument.
- Create other IF functions: You can nest or embed other functions inside one or more of the arguments of an IF function to create more complex formulas.

7. Use lookup functions.

- Create the lookup table: Design the lookup table using exact values or the breakpoints for ranges. If using breakpoints, the breakpoints must be in ascending order.
- Understand the VLOOKUP syntax: The VLOOKUP function contains the required arugments lookup_value, table_array, and col_index_num and one optional argument, range_lookup.
- Understand how Excel processes the lookup: The VLOOKUP function looks up a value for a particular record, compares it to a lookup table, and returns a result in another column of the lookup table.
- Use the range_lookup argument: If an exact match is required, the optional fourth argument should be FALSE; otherwise, the fourth argument can remain empty.
- Nest functions inside the VLOOKUP function: You can nest functions inside one or more arguments.
- Use the HLOOKUP function: The HLOOKUP function looks up values by row (horizontally) rather than by column (vertically).

8. Calculate payments with the PMT function.

- The PMT function calculates periodic payments for a loan with a fixed interest rate and a fixed term. The PMT function requires the periodic interest rate, the total number of payment periods, and the original value of the loan.

9. Create and maintain range names.

- Create a range name: A range name may contain letters, numbers, and underscores, but must start with either a letter or an underscore.
- Edit or delete a range name: Use the Name Manager dialog box to edit, create, or delete range names.
- Insert a table of range names: The first column contains an alphabetical list of range names, and the second column contains a list of their ranges.

10. Use range names in formulas.

- You can use range names in formulas to make the formulas easier to interpret by using a descriptive name for the value(s) contained in a cell or range.

Key Terms Matching

Match the key terms with their definitions. Write the key term letter by the appropriate numbered definition.

- **a.** Absolute cell reference
- **b.** Argument
- **c.** AVERAGE function
- **d.** Circular reference
- **e.** COUNT function
- **f.** IF function
- **g.** Logical test
- **h.** Lookup table
- **i.** MAX function
- **j.** MEDIAN function
- **k.** MIN function
- **l.** Mixed cell reference
- **m.** NOW function
- **n.** PMT function
- **o.** Range name
- **p.** Relative cell reference
- **q.** SUM function
- **r.** Syntax
- **s.** TODAY function
- **t.** VLOOKUP function

1. ______ A set of rules that governs the structure and components for properly entering a function. **p. 166**
2. ______ Displays the current date. **p. 166**
3. ______ Indicates a cell's specific location; the cell reference does not change when you copy the formula. **p. 158**
4. ______ Occurs when a formula directly or indirectly refers to itself. **p. 160**
5. ______ An input, such as a cell reference or value, needed to complete a function. **p. 166**
6. ______ Identifies the highest value in a range. **p. 171**
7. ______ Tallies the number of cells in a range that contain values. **p. 171**
8. ______ Looks up a value in a vertical lookup table and returns a related result from the lookup table. **p. 185**
9. ______ A range that contains data for the basis of the lookup and data to be retrieved. **p. 184**
10. ______ Calculates the arithmetic mean, or average, of values in a range. **p. 170**
11. ______ Identifies the midpoint value in a set of values. **p. 170**
12. ______ Displays the current date and time. **p. 173**
13. ______ Evaluates a condition and returns one value if the condition is true and a different value if the condition is false. **p. 181**
14. ______ Calculates the total of values contained in two or more cells. **p. 168**
15. ______ Calculates the periodic payment for a loan with a fixed interest rate and fixed term. **p. 187**
16. ______ Indicates a cell's location from the cell containing the formula; the cell reference changes when the formula is copied. **p. 158**
17. ______ Contains both an absolute and a relative cell reference in a formula; the absolute part does not change but the relative part does when you copy the formula. **p. 160**
18. ______ A word or string of characters that represents one or more cells. **p. 192**
19. ______ An expression that evaluates to true or false. **p. 182**
20. ______ Displays the lowest value in a range. **p. 171**

Multiple Choice

1. If cell D15 contains the formula =$C$5*D$15, what is the D15 in the formula?
   (a) Relative reference
   (b) Absolute reference
   (c) Circular reference
   (d) Range name

2. What function would most appropriately accomplish the same thing as =(B5+C5+D5+E5+F5)/5?
   (a) =SUM(B5:F5)/5
   (b) =AVERAGE(B5:F5)
   (c) =MEDIAN(B5:F5)
   (d) =COUNT(B5:F5)

3. When you start =AV, what displays a list of functions and defined names?
   (a) Function ScreenTip
   (b) Formula AutoComplete
   (c) Insert Function dialog box
   (d) Function Arguments dialog box

4. A formula containing the entry =$B3 is copied to a cell one column to the right and two rows down. How will the entry appear in its new location?
   (a) =$B3
   (b) =B3
   (c) =$C5
   (d) =$B5

5. Cell B10 contains a date, such as 1/1/2016. Which formula will determine how many days are between that date and the current date, given that the cell containing the formula is formatted with Number Format?
   (a) =TODAY()
   (b) =CURRENT()-B10
   (c) =TODAY()-B10
   (d) =TODAY()+NOW()

6. Given that cells A1, A2, and A3 contain values 2, 3, and 10, respectively, and B6, C6, and D6 contain values 10, 20, and 30, respectively, what value will be returned by the function =IF(B6>A3,C6*A1,D6*A2)?
   (a) 10
   (b) 40
   (c) 60
   (d) 90

7. Given the function =VLOOKUP(C6,$D$12:$F$18,3), the entries in:
   (a) Range D12:D18 are in ascending order.
   (b) Range D12:D18 are in descending order.
   (c) The third column of the lookup table must be text only.
   (d) Range D12:D18 contain multiple values in each cell.

8. The function =PMT(C5,C7,-C3) is stored in cell C15. What must be stored in cell C5?
   (a) APR
   (b) Periodic interest rate
   (c) Loan amount
   (d) Number of payment periods

9. Which of the following is *not* an appropriate use of the SUM function?
   (a) =SUM(B3:B45)
   (b) =SUM(F1:G10)
   (c) =SUM(A8:A15,D8:D15)
   (d) =SUM(D15-C15)

10. Which of the following is *not* an acceptable range name?
    (a) FICA
    (b) Test_Weight
    (c) Goal for 2016
    (d) Target_2015

Practice Exercises

1 Blue Canadian Skies Airlines

You are an analyst for Blue Canadian Skies Airlines, a regional airline headquartered in Victoria. Your assistant developed a template for you to store daily flight data about the number of passengers per flight. Each regional aircraft can hold up to 70 passengers. You need to calculate the occupancy rate (the percent of each flight that is occupied), daily statistics (such as total number of passengers, averages, least full flights, etc.), and weekly statistics per flight number. This exercise follows the same set of skills as used in Hands-On Exercises 1 and 2 in the chapter. Refer to Figure 2.40 as you complete this exercise.

Blue Canadian Skies Airlines

Aircraft Capacity: 70

Daily Flight Information

Flight Info		Sunday		Monday		Tuesday		Wednesday		Thursday		Friday		Saturday	
Flight #	Destination	# Pass	% Full	# Pass	% Full	# Pass	% Full	# Pass	% Full	# Pass	% Full	# Pass	% Full	# Pass	% Full
4520	YEG	60	85.7%	65	92.9%	55	78.6%	65	92.9%	62	88.6%	50	71.4%		
3240	YYC	35	50.0%	57	81.4%			60	85.7%			55	78.6%		
425	YDA	50	71.4%	70	100.0%	48	68.6%	66	94.3%	68	97.1%			55	78.6%
345	YMM	69	98.6%	70	100.0%	61	87.1%	66	94.3%	70	100.0%	68	97.1%	67	95.7%
3340	YWG	45	64.3%	61	87.1%	64	91.4%	45	64.3%	48	68.6%	66	94.3%		
418	YZF	65	92.9%	67	95.7%	58	82.9%	66	94.3%	55	78.6%	69	98.6%	66	94.3%
4526	YYZ	68	97.1%	70	100.0%	58	82.9%			63	90.0%	70	100.0%	68	97.1%
300	YXE	70	100.0%	70	100.0%			61	87.1%	70	100.0%	59	84.3%		
322	YOW	70	100.0%	60	85.7%	48	68.6%			65	92.9%	68	97.1%	69	98.6%
349	YMX	70	100.0%	64	91.4%	67	95.7%			66	94.3%	70	100.0%	55	78.6%
Daily Statistics															
Total # of Passengers		602		654		459		429		567		575		380	
Averages		60.2	86%	65.4	93%	57.375	82%	61.2857	88%	63	90%	63.8889	91%	63.3333	90%
Medians		66.5	95%	66	94%	58	83%	65	93%	65	93%	68	97%	66.5	95%
Least Full Flights		35	50%	57	81%	48	69%	45	64%	48	69%	50	71%	55	79%
Most Full Flights		70	100%	70	100%	67	96%	66	94%	70	100%	70	100%	69	99%
# of Flights per Day		10		10		8		7		9		9		6	

Stats

FIGURE 2.40 Blue Canadian Skies Airlines

a. Open *e02p1Flights* and save it as **e02p1Flights_LastFirst**.

b. Click **cell D6**, the cell to display the occupancy percent for Flight 4520 on Sunday, and do the following:
   - Type =**C6/$C$2** and click **Enter** (the checkmark between the Name Box and the Formula Bar). The occupancy rate of Flight 4520 is 85.7%.
   - Double-click the **cell D6 fill handle** to copy the formula down the column.

c. Click **cell D7**. When you copy a formula, Excel also copies the original cell's format. The cell containing the original formula did not have a bottom border, so when you copied the formula down the column, Excel formatted it to match the original cell with no border. To reapply the border, click **cell D15**, click the **Border arrow** in the Font group on the HOME tab, and then select **Bottom Border**.

d. Select the **range D6:D15**, click **Copy**, click **cell F6**, and then click **Paste**. The formula in cell F6 is =E6/$C$2. The first cell reference changes from C6 to E6, maintaining its relative location from the pasted formula. $C$2 remains absolute so that the number of passengers per flight is always divided by the value stored in cell C2. The copied range is still in the Clipboard. Paste the formula into the remaining % Full columns (columns H, J, L, N, and P). Press **Esc**.

e. Clean up the data by deleting *0.0%* in cells, such as H7. The 0.0% is misleading, as it implies the flight was empty; however, some flights do not operate on all days. Check your worksheet against the *Daily Flight Information* section in Figure 2.40.

f. Calculate the total number of passengers per day by doing the following:
   - Click **cell C18** and click **Sum** in the Editing group.
   - Select the **range C6:C15** and press **Enter**.

g. Calculate the average number of passengers per day by doing the following:
   - Click **cell C19**, click the **Sum arrow** in the Editing group, and then select **Average**.
   - Select the **range C6:C15** and click **Enter** (the checkmark between the Name Box and the Formula Bar).

h. Calculate the median number of passengers per day by doing the following:
   - Click **cell C20**.
   - Click **Insert Function**, type **median** in the **Search for a function box**, and then click **Go**.
   - Click **MEDIAN** in the **Select a function box** and click **OK**.
   - Select the **range C6:C15** to enter it in the **Number1 box** and click **OK**.

i. Calculate the least number of passengers on a daily flight by doing the following:
   - Click **cell C21**, click the **Sum arrow** in the Editing group, and then select **Min**.
   - Select the **range C6:C15** and press **Enter**.

j. Calculate the most passengers on a daily flight by doing the following:
   - Click **cell C22** if necessary, click the **Sum arrow** in the Editing group, and then select **Max**.
   - Select the **range C6:C15** and press **Enter**.

k. Calculate the number of flights for Sunday by doing the following:
   - Click **cell C23** if necessary, click the **Sum arrow** in the Editing group, and then select **Count Numbers**.
   - Select the **range C6:C15** and press **Enter**.

l. Calculate the average, median, least full, and most full percentages in **cells D19:D22**. Format the values with Percent Style with zero decimal places. Do not copy the formulas from column C to column D, as that will change the borders. Select **cells C18:D23**, copy the range, and then paste in these cells: **E18**, **G18**, **I18**, **K18**, **M18**, and **O18**. Press **Esc** after pasting.

m. Create a footer with your name on the left side, the sheet name code in the center, and the file name code on the right side.

n. Save and close the workbook, and submit based on your instructor's directions.

2 Steggel Consulting Firm Salaries

You work in the Human Resources Department at Steggell Consulting Firm. You are preparing a model to calculate bonuses based on performance ratings, where ratings between 1 and 1.9 do not receive bonuses, ratings between 2 and 2.9 earn $100 bonuses, ratings between 3 and 3.9 earn $250 bonuses, ratings between 4 and 4.9 earn $500 bonuses, and ratings of 5 or higher earn $1,000 bonuses. In addition, you need to calculate annual raises based on years employed. Employees who have worked five or more years earn a 3.25% raise; employees who have not worked at least five years earn a 2% raise. This exercise follows the same set of skills as used in Hands-On Exercises 1–4 in the chapter. Refer to Figure 2.41 as you complete this exercise.

a. Open *e02p2Salary* and save it as **e02p2Salary_LastFirst**.

b. Click **cell B4**, click the **FORMULAS tab**, click **Date & Time** in the Function Library group, select **TODAY**, and then click **OK** to enter today's date in the cell.

c. Enter a formula to calculate the number of years employed by doing the following:
   - Click **cell C11**, click **Date & Time** in the Function Library group, scroll through the list, and then select **YEARFRAC**.
   - Click **cell A11** to enter the cell reference in the **Start_date box**.
   - Press **Tab** and click **cell B4** to enter the cell reference in the **End_date box**.
   - Press **F4** to make **cell B4** absolute and click **OK**. (Although you could have used the formula =($B$4-A11)/365 to calculate the number of years, the YEARFRAC function provides better accuracy because it accounts for leap years and the divisor 365 does not. The completed function is =YEARFRAC(A11,$B$4).
   - Double-click the **cell C11 fill handle** to copy the YEARFRAC function down the Years Employed column. Your results will differ based on the date contained in cell B4.

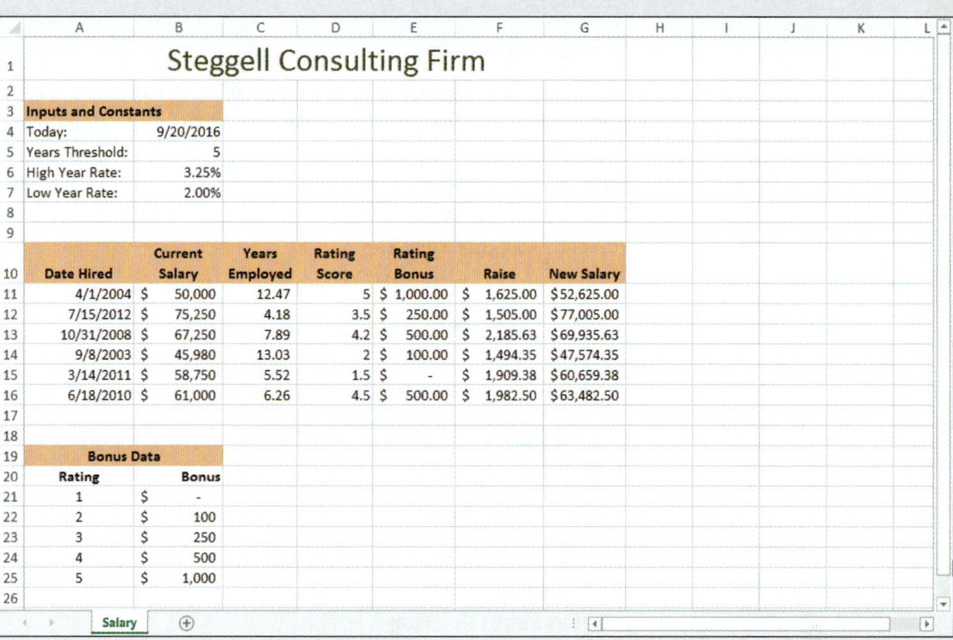

	A	B	C	D	E	F	G
1	Steggell Consulting Firm						
2							
3	Inputs and Constants						
4	Today:	9/20/2016					
5	Years Threshold:	5					
6	High Year Rate:	3.25%					
7	Low Year Rate:	2.00%					
8							
9							
10	Date Hired	Current Salary	Years Employed	Rating Score	Rating Bonus	Raise	New Salary
11	4/1/2004	$ 50,000	12.47	5	$ 1,000.00	$ 1,625.00	$52,625.00
12	7/15/2012	$ 75,250	4.18	3.5	$ 250.00	$ 1,505.00	$77,005.00
13	10/31/2008	$ 67,250	7.89	4.2	$ 500.00	$ 2,185.63	$69,935.63
14	9/8/2003	$ 45,980	13.03	2	$ 100.00	$ 1,494.35	$47,574.35
15	3/14/2011	$ 58,750	5.52	1.5	$ -	$ 1,909.38	$60,659.38
16	6/18/2010	$ 61,000	6.26	4.5	$ 500.00	$ 1,982.50	$63,482.50
17							
18							
19	Bonus Data						
20	Rating	Bonus					
21	1	$ -					
22	2	$ 100					
23	3	$ 250					
24	4	$ 500					
25	5	$ 1,000					
26							

Salary

FIGURE 2.41 Steggell Consulting Firm

d. Enter the breakpoint and bonus data for the lookup table by doing the following:
- Click **cell A21**, type **1**, and then press **Ctrl+Enter**.
- Click the **HOME tab**, click **Fill** in the Editing group, and then select **Series**. Click **Columns** in the *Series in* section, leave the **Step value** at **1**, type **5** in the **Stop value box**, and then click **OK**.
- Click **cell B21**. Enter **0**, **100**, **250**, **500**, and **1000** down the column. The cells have been formatted with Accounting Number Format with zero decimal places.
- Select **range A21:B25**, click in the **Name Box**, type **Bonus**, and then press **Enter**.

e. Enter the bonus based on rating by doing the following:
- Click **cell E11** and click the **FORMULAS tab**.
- Click **Lookup & Reference** in the Function Library group and select **VLOOKUP**.
- Type **D11** in the **Lookup_value box**, type **Bonus** in the **Table_array box**, type **2**, and then click **OK**. The completed function is =VLOOKUP(D11,Bonus,2).
- Double-click the **cell E11 fill handle** to copy the formula down the Rating Bonus column.

f. Enter the raise based on years employed by doing the following:
- Click **cell F11**, click **Logical** in the Function Library group, and then select **IF**.
- Type **C11>=$B$5** to compare the years employed to the absolute reference of the five-year threshold in the **Logical_test box**.
- Press **Tab** and type **B11*$B$6** to calculate a 3.25% raise for employees who worked five years or more in the **Value_if_true box**.
- Press **Tab** and type **cell B11*$B$7** to calculate a 2% raise for employees who worked less than five years in the Value_if_false box. Click **OK**. The completed function is =IF(C11>=$B$5,B11*$B$6,B11*$B$7).
- Double-click the **cell F11 fill handle** to copy the formula down the Raise column.

g. Click **cell G11**. Type **=B11+E11+F11** to add the current salary, the bonus, and the raise to calculate the new salary. Double-click the **cell G11 fill handle** to copy the formula down the column.

h. Create a footer with your name on the left side, the sheet name code in the center, and the file name code on the right side.

i. Save and close the workbook, and submit based on your instructor's directions.

3 New Car Loan

After obtaining a promotion at work, you want to buy a luxury car, such as a Lexus or Infinity. Before purchasing a car, you want to create a worksheet to estimate the monthly payment based on the purchase price (including accessories, taxes, and license plate), APR, down payment, and years. You will assign range names and use range names in the formulas to make them easier to analyze. This exercise follows the same set of skills as used in Hands-On Exercises 1–4 in the chapter. Refer to Figure 2.42 as you complete this exercise.

	A	B	C
1	Car Loan		
2			
3	**Inputs**		
4	Cost of Car*	45000	
5	Down Payment	10000	
6	APR	0.0399	
7	Years	5	
8	Payments Per Year	12	
9	*Includes taxes, etc.		
10			
11	**Outputs**		
12	Loan	=Cost-Down	
13	Monthly Payment	=PMT(APR/Months,Years*Months,-Loan)	
14	Total to Repay Loan	=Years*Months*Payment	
15	Total Interest Paid	=Repaid-Loan	
16			

FIGURE 2.42 Car Loan

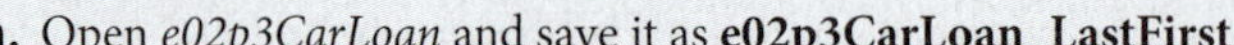

a. Open *e02p3CarLoan* and save it as **e02p3CarLoan_LastFirst**.

b. Name the input values by doing the following:

- Select the **range A4:B8**.
- Click the **FORMULAS tab** and click **Create from Selection** in the Defined Names group.
- Make sure *Left column* is selected and click **OK**.
- Click each input value cell in the **range B4:B8** and look at the newly created names in the Name Box.

c. Edit the range names by doing the following:

- Click **Name Manager** in the Defined Names group.
- Click **Cost_of_Car**, click **Edit**, type **Cost**, and then click **OK**.
- Change *Down_Payment* to **Down**.
- Change *Payments_Per_Year* to **Months**.
- Click **Close** to close the Name Manager.

d. Name the output values in the **range A12:B15** using the *Create from Selection* method you used in step b to assign names to the empty cells in the range B12:B15. However, you will use the range names as you build formulas in the next few steps. Edit the range names using the same approach you used in step c.

- Change *Monthly_Payment* to **Payment.**
- Change *Total_Interest_Paid* to **Interest**.
- Change *Total_to_Repay_Loan* to **Repaid**.
- Click **Close** to close the Name Manager.

e. Enter the formula to calculate the amount of the loan by doing the following:
   - Click **cell B12**. Type **=Cos** and double-click **Cost** from the Function AutoComplete list. If the list does not appear, type the entire name **Cost**.
   - Press - and type **do**, and then double-click **Down** from the Function AutoComplete list.
   - Press **Enter** to enter the formula =Cost-Down.

f. Calculate the monthly payment of principal and interest by doing the following:
   - Click the **FORMULAS tab**. Click **cell B13**. Click **Financial** in the Function Library group, scroll down, and then select **PMT**.
   - Type **APR/Months** in the **Rate box**.
   - Press **Tab** and type **Years*Months** in the **Nper box**.
   - Press **Tab**, type **-Loan** in the **Pv box**, and then click **OK**. The completed function is =PMT(APR/Months,Years*Months,-Loan).

g. Enter the total amount to repay loan formula by doing the following:
   - Click **cell B14**. Type = to start the formula.
   - Click **Use in Formula** in the Defined Names group and select **Years**.
   - Type *, click **Use in Formula** in the Defined Names group, and then select **Months**.
   - Type *, click **Use in Formula** in the Defined Names group, and then select **Payment**.
   - Press **Enter**. The completed formula is =Years*Months*Payment.

h. Use the skills from step g to enter the formula **=Repaid-Loan** in **cell B15**.

i. Select the **range B12:B15**, click the **HOME tab**, and then click **Accounting Number Format** in the Number group.

j. Select the option to center the worksheet data between the left and right margins in the Page Setup dialog box.

k. Create a footer with your name on the left side, the sheet name code in the center, and the file name code on the right side.

l. Right-click the **Car sheet tab**, select **Move or Copy** from the menu, click **(move to end)** in the *Before sheet* section, click the **Create a copy check box**, and then click **OK**. Rename the Car (2) sheet **Formulas**.

m. Make sure the Formulas sheet is active. Click the **FORMULAS tab** and click **Show Formulas** in the Formula Auditing group. Widen column B to display entire formulas.

n. Click the **PAGE LAYOUT tab** and click the **Gridlines Print check box** and the **Headings Print check box** in the Sheet Options group to select these two options.

o. Insert a new sheet, name it **Names**, type **Range Name** in **cell A1**, and then type **Location** in **cell B1**. Apply bold to these column labels. Click **cell A2**, click the **FORMULAS tab**, click **Use in Formula**, select **Paste Names**, and then click **Paste List** to paste an alphabetical list of range names in the worksheet. Adjust the column widths. Apply the same Page Setup settings and footer to the Formulas and Cars worksheets.

p. Save and close the workbook, and submit based on your instructor's directions.

Mid-Level Exercises

1 Metropolitan Zoo Gift Shop Weekly Payroll

ANALYSIS CASE 

As manager of the gift shop at the Metropolitan Zoo, you are responsible for managing the weekly payroll. Your assistant developed a partial worksheet, but you need to enter the formulas to calculate the regular pay, overtime pay, gross pay, taxable pay, withholding tax, FICA, and net pay. In addition, you want to total pay columns and calculate some basic statistics. As you construct formulas, make sure you use absolute and relative cell references correctly in formulas and avoid circular references.

a. Open the *e02m1Payroll* workbook and save it as **e02m1Payroll_LastFirst**.

b. Study the worksheet structure and read the business rules in the Notes section.

c. Use IF functions to calculate the regular pay and overtime pay based on a regular 40-hour workweek in **cells E5** and **F5**. Pay overtime only for overtime hours. Calculate the gross pay based on the regular and overtime pay. Abram's regular pay is $398. With 8 overtime hours, Abram's overtime pay is $119.40.

d. Create a formula in **cell H5** to calculate the taxable pay. Multiply the number of dependents by the deduction per dependent and subtract that from the gross pay. With two dependents, Abram's taxable pay is $417.40.

e. Use a VLOOKUP function in **cell I5** to identify and calculate the federal withholding tax. With a taxable pay of $417.40, Abram's tax rate is 25% and the withholding tax is $104.35. The VLOOKUP function returns the applicable tax rate, which you must then multiply by the taxable pay.

f. Calculate FICA in **cell J5** based on gross pay and the FICA rate and calculate the net pay in **Cell K5**.

g. Calculate the total regular pay, overtime pay, gross pay, taxable pay, withholding tax, FICA, and net pay on row 17.

h. Copy all formulas down their respective columns.

i. Apply **Accounting Number Format** to the **range C5:C16**. Apply **Accounting Number Format** to the first row of monetary data and to the total row. Apply **Comma Style** to the monetary values for the other employees. Underline the last employee's monetary values and use the Format Cells dialog box to apply **Double Accounting Underline** for the totals.

j. Insert appropriate functions to calculate the average, highest, and lowest values in the Summary Statistics area (the **range I21:K23**) of the worksheet.

k. At your instructor's discretion, use Help to learn about the FREQUENCY function. The Help feature contains sample data for you to copy and practice in a new worksheet to learn about this function. You can close the practice worksheet containing the Help data without saving it. You want to determine the number (frequency) of employees who worked less than 20 hours, between 20 and 29 hours, between 30 and 40 hours, and over 40 hours. **Cells J28:J31** list the ranges. You need to translate this range into correct values for the Bin column in **cells I28:I31** and enter the FREQUENCY function in **cells K28:K31**. The function should identify one employee who worked between 0 and 19 hours and six employees who worked more than 40 hours.

l. Apply other page setup formats as needed.

m. Insert a new sheet named **Overtime**. List the number of overtime hours for the week. Calculate the yearly gross amount spent on overtime assuming the same number of overtime hours per week. Add another row with only half the overtime hours (using a formula). What is your conclusion and recommendation on overtime? Format this worksheet.

n. Insert a footer with your name on the left side, the sheet name code in the center, and the file name code on the right side of both worksheets.

o. Save and close the workbook, and submit based on your instructor's directions.

2 Mortgage Calculator

As a financial consultant, you work with people who are planning to buy a new house. You want to create a worksheet containing variable data (the price of the house, down payment, date of the first payment, and borrower's credit rating) and constants (property tax rate, years, and number of payments in one year). Borrowers pay 0.5% private mortgage insurance (PMI) on the loan amount if they do not make at least a 20% down payment. A borrower's credit rating determines the required down payment percentage and APR. For example, a person with an excellent credit rating may make only a 5% down payment with a 3.25% APR loan. A person with a fair credit rating will make a 15% down payment and have a higher APR at 5.25%. Your worksheet needs to perform various calculations. The filled cells in column F indicate cells containing formulas, not values. Refer to Figure 2.43 as you complete this exercise.

	A	B	C	D	E	F
1	Mortgage Calculator					
2						
3	Inputs				Intermediate Calculations	
4	Negotiated Cost of House		$ 375,000.00		APR Based on Credit Rating	3.25%
5	Additional Down Payment		$ 5,000.00		Min Down Payment Required	$ 18,750.00
6	Date of First Payment		5/1/2016		Annual Property Tax	$ 2,812.50
7	Credit Rating		Excellent		Annual PMI	$ 1,756.25
8						
9	Constants				Outputs	
10	Property Tax Rate		0.75%		Total Down Payment	$ 23,750.00
11	Down Payment to Avoid PMI		20.00%		Amount of the Loan	$351,250.00
12	PMI Rate		0.50%		Monthly Payment (P&I)	$1,528.66
13	Term of Loan in Years		30		Monthly Property Tax	234.38
14	# of Payments Per Year		12		Monthly PMI	146.35
15					Total Monthly Payment	$ 1,909.39
16	Credit	Down Payment	APR		Date of Last Payment	4/1/2046
17	Excellent	5%	3.25%			
18	Good	10%	3.50%			
19	Fair	15%	4.25%			
20	Poor	20%	5.25%			
21						

FIGURE 2.43 Mortgage Data

a. Start a new Excel workbook, save it as **e02m2Loan_LastFirst**, rename Sheet1 **Payment**, add a new sheet, and then rename it **Range Names**.

b. Select the **Payment sheet**, type **Mortgage Calculator** in **cell A1**, and then merge and center the title on the first row in the **range A1:F1**. Apply bold, **18 pt size**, and **Gold, Accent 4, Darker 25% font color**.

c. Create and format the Inputs and Constants areas by doing the following:
   - Type the labels in the **range A3:A20**. For each label, such as *Negotiated Cost of House*, merge the cells, such as the **range A4:B4**, and apply **Align Text Left**. You will have to merge cells for nine labels.
   - Enter and format the *Inputs* and *Constants* values in column C.

d. Create the lookup table in the **range A16:C20** to use the credit ratings to identify the appropriate required percentage down payment and the respective APR by doing the following:
   - Type **Credit**, **Down Payment**, and **APR** in the **range A16:C16**.
   - Type the four credit ratings in the first column, the required down payment percentages in the second column, and the respective APRs in the third column.
   - Format the percentages, apply **Align Text Right**, and then indent the percentages in the cells as needed.

e. Assign range names to cells containing individual values in the Inputs and Constants sections. Do *not* use the *Create from Selection* feature because the labels are stored in merged cells. Assign a range name to the lookup table.

f. Type labels in the *Intermediate Calculations* and *Outputs* sections in column E and assign a range name to each cell in the **ranges F4:F7** and **F10:F12**. Widen column E as needed.

g. Enter formulas in the *Intermediate Calculations* and *Outputs* sections using range names to calculate the following:

- **APR** based on the borrower's credit rating by using a lookup function. Include the range_lookup argument to ensure an *exact match*. For example, a borrower who has an Excellent rating gets a 3.25% APR.

- **Minimum down payment required** amount by using a lookup function and calculation. Include the range_lookup argument to ensure an *exact match*. For example, a borrower who has an Excellent rating is required to pay a minimum of 5% down payment of the negotiated purchase price. Multiply the function results by the negotiated cost of the house. Hint: The calculation comes after the closing parenthesis.
- **Annual property tax** based on the negotiated cost of the house and the annual property tax rate.
- **Annual PMI**. If the borrower's total down payment (required and additional) is 20% or higher of the negotiated purchase price (multiply the cost by the PMI avoidance percentage), PMI is zero. If the total down payment is less than 20%, the borrower has to pay PMI based on multiplying the amount of the loan by the PMI rate.
- **Total down payment**, which is sum of the required minimum down payment (calculated previously) and any additional down payment entered in the Inputs section.
- **Amount of the loan**, which is the difference between the negotiated cost of the house and the total down payment.
- **Monthly payment** of principal and interest using the PMT function.
- **Monthly property tax**, the **monthly PMI**, and the **total monthly payment**.
- **Last payment date** using the EDATE function. The function's second argument must calculate the correct number of months based on the total length of the loan. For example, if the first payment date is 5/1/2016, the final payment date is 4/1/2046 for a 30-year loan. The last argument of the function must subtract 1 to ensure the last payment date is correct. If the last payment date calculated to 5/1/2046, you would be making an extra payment.

h. Format each section with fill color, bold, underline, number formats, borders, and column widths as shown in the figure.

i. Paste a list of range names in the Range Names worksheet. Insert a row above the list and type and format column labels above the two columns in the list of range names.

j. Center the worksheet data horizontally between the left and right margins.

k. Insert a footer with your name on the left side, the sheet name code in the center, and the file name code on the right side of both sheets.

l. Save and close the workbook, and submit based on your instructor's directions.

3 Professor's Grade Book

You are a teaching assistant for Dr. Denise Gerber, who teaches an introductory C# programming class at your college. One of your routine tasks is to enter assignment and test grades into the grade book. Now that the semester is almost over, you need to create formulas to calculate category averages, the overall weighted average, and the letter grade for each student. In addition, Dr. Gerber wants to see general statistics, such as average, median, low, and high for each graded assignment and test, as well as category averages and total averages. Furthermore, you need to create the grading scale on the documentation worksheet and use it to display the appropriate letter grade for each student.

a. Open *e02m3Grades* and save it as **e02m3Grades_LastFirst**.

b. Use breakpoints to enter the grading scale in the correct structure on the Documentation worksheet and name the grading scale range **Grades**. The grading scale is as follows:

95+	A
90–94.9	A–
87–89.9	B+
83–86.9	B
80–82.9	B–
77–79.9	C+
73–76.9	C
70–72.9	C–
67–69.9	D+
63–66.9	D
60–62.9	D–
0–59.9	F

c. Calculate the total lab points earned for the first student in **cell T8** in the Grades worksheet. The first student earned 93 lab points.

d. Calculate the average of the two midterm tests for the first student in **cell W8**. The student's midterm test average is 87.

e. Calculate the assignment average for the first student in **cell I8**. The formula should drop the lowest score before calculating the average. Hint: You need to use a combination of three functions: SUM, MIN, and COUNT. The argument for each function for the first student is B8:H8. Find the total points and subtract the lowest score. Then divide the remaining points by the number of assignments minus 1. The first student's assignment average is 94.2 after dropping the lowest assignment score.

f. Calculate the weighted total points based on the four category points (assignment average, lab points, midterm average, and final exam) and their respective weights (stored in the **range B40:B43**) in **cell Y8**. Use relative and absolute cell references as needed in the formula. The first student's total weighted score is 90.

g. Use a VLOOKUP function to calculate the letter grade equivalent in **cell Z8**. Use the range name in the function. The first student's letter grade is A–.

h. Copy the formulas down their respective columns for the other students.

i. Name the passing score threshold in **cell B5** with the range name **Passing**. Use an IF function to display a message in the last grade book column based on the student's semester performance. If a student earned a final score of 70 or higher, display *Enroll in CS 202*. Otherwise, display *RETAKE CS 101*. Remember to use quotation marks around the text arguments.

j. Calculate the average, median, low, and high scores for each assignment, lab, test, category average, and total score. Display individual averages with no decimal places; display category and final score averages with one decimal place. Display other statistics with no decimal places.

k. Insert a list of range names in the designated area in the Documentation worksheet. Complete the documentation by inserting your name, today's date, and a purpose statement in the designated areas.

l. At your instructor's discretion, add a column to display each student's rank in the class. Use Help to learn how to insert the RANK function.

m. Select page setup options as needed to print the Grades worksheet on one page.

n. Insert a footer with your name on the left side, the sheet name code in the center, and the file name code on the right side of each worksheet.

o. Save and close the workbook, and submit based on your instructor's directions.

Chart Creation Basics

The expression "a picture is worth a thousand words" means that a visual can be a more effective way to communicate or interpret data than words or numbers. Storing, organizing, and performing calculations on quantitative data are important, but you must also be able to analyze the data. A ***chart*** is a visual representation of numerical data that compares data and helps reveal trends or patterns to help people make informed decisions. An effective chart depicts data in a clear, easy-to-interpret manner and contains enough data to be useful without overwhelming your audience.

A chart may include several chart elements. The ***chart area*** contains the entire chart and all of its elements, including the plot area, titles, legend, and labels. The ***plot area*** is the region containing the graphical representation of the values in the data series. Two axes form a border around the plot area.

The ***X-axis*** is a horizontal border that provides a frame of reference for measuring data horizontally. The ***Y-axis*** is a vertical border that provides a frame of reference for measuring data vertically. Excel refers to the axes as the category axis and value axis. The ***category axis*** displays descriptive group names or labels (such as college names, cities, or equal amounts of time) to identify data. Categories are usually defined by column or row labels (such as job titles or years) in the worksheet. The ***value axis*** displays incremental numbers to identify the worksheet values (such as number of jobs or revenue) used to create the chart. A ***legend*** is a key that identifies the color, gradient, picture, texture, or pattern assigned to each data series in a chart. For example, blue might represent values for 2010, and orange might represent values for 2020.

In this section, you will select the data source, choose the best chart type to represent numerical data, and designate the chart's location.

Selecting the Data Source

Before creating a chart, organize the worksheet data so that the values in columns and rows are on the same value system (such as dollars or units), make sure labels are descriptive, and delete any blank rows or columns that exist in the primary data set. Look at the structure of the worksheet—the column labels, the row labels, the quantitative data, and the calculated values. Decide what you want to convey to your audience by answering these questions:

- Does the worksheet hold a single set of data, such as average snowfall at one ski resort, or multiple sets of data, such as average snowfall at several ski resorts?
- Do you want to depict data for one specific time period or over several time periods, such as several years or decades?

Identify the data range by selecting values and labels that you want to include in the chart. If the values and labels are not stored in adjacent cells, hold Ctrl while selecting the nonadjacent ranges. Do not select worksheet titles or subtitles; doing so would add unnecessary data to the chart.

Figure 3.1 shows a worksheet containing computer-related job titles, the number of jobs in 2010, the projected number of jobs by 2020, and other details. Row 3 contains labels merged and centered over individual column labels in row 5. Row 4 is blank and hidden. It is a good practice to insert a blank row between merged labels and individual column labels. Without the blank row, you would not be able to correctly sort data; the column headings would be sorted with the data.

Each cell containing a value is a ***data point***. For example, the value 110,800 is a data point for the number of Database Administrators in 2010. A group of related data points that display in row(s) or column(s) in the worksheet create a ***data series***. For example, the values 110,800 and 144,800 comprise the Database Administrators data series. Row and column labels (such as job titles, years, growth, etc.) are used to create ***category labels*** in charts.

	A	B	C	D	E	F
1	Computer-Related Jobs					
2						
3		# of Jobs		Job Growth		Median Pay
5		2010	2020 Est.	% Growth	# of New Jobs	2010
6	Database Administrators	110,800	144,800	31%	34,000	$ 73,490
7	Info Security Analysts	302,300	367,900	22%	65,600	$ 75,600
8	CIS Managers	307,900	363,700	18%	55,800	$ 115,780
9	Network/System Admins	347,200	443,800	28%	96,600	$ 69,160
10	Programmers	363,100	406,800	12%	43,700	$ 71,380
11	Software App Developers	520,800	664,500	28%	143,700	$ 90,530
12	Systems Analysts	544,400	664,800	22%	120,400	$ 77,740
14	Source: Bureau of Labor Statistics, U.S. Department of Labor, *Occupational Outlook Handbook, 2012-13 Edition*, on the Internet at http://www.bls.gov/					

FIGURE 3.1 Sample Data Set

TIP Avoid Using Data Aggregates and Individual Values

Make sure that each data series uses the same scale. For example, do not include data aggregates (such as totals or averages) with individual values. The data source used to create the chart in Figure 3.2 mixes individual number of jobs by title with the total number of jobs, which distorts the scale from the comparison of the number of jobs for each job title.

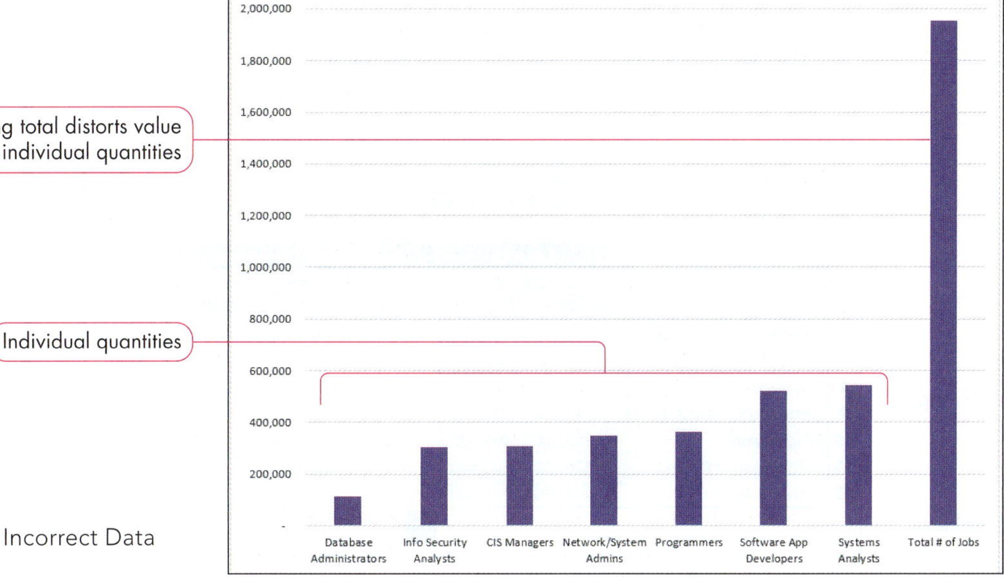

FIGURE 3.2 Incorrect Data Source

TIP Charts Update When Data Change

After you create a chart, you may need to change the worksheet data. When you change the worksheet data, Excel updates any charts that you created based on the data.

Choosing a Chart Type

When you select a range of cells and position the mouse pointer over that selected range, Excel displays the Quick Analysis button in the bottom-right corner of the selected area. The Excel 2013 Quick Analysis tool enables you to use analytical tools, such as charts, to quickly

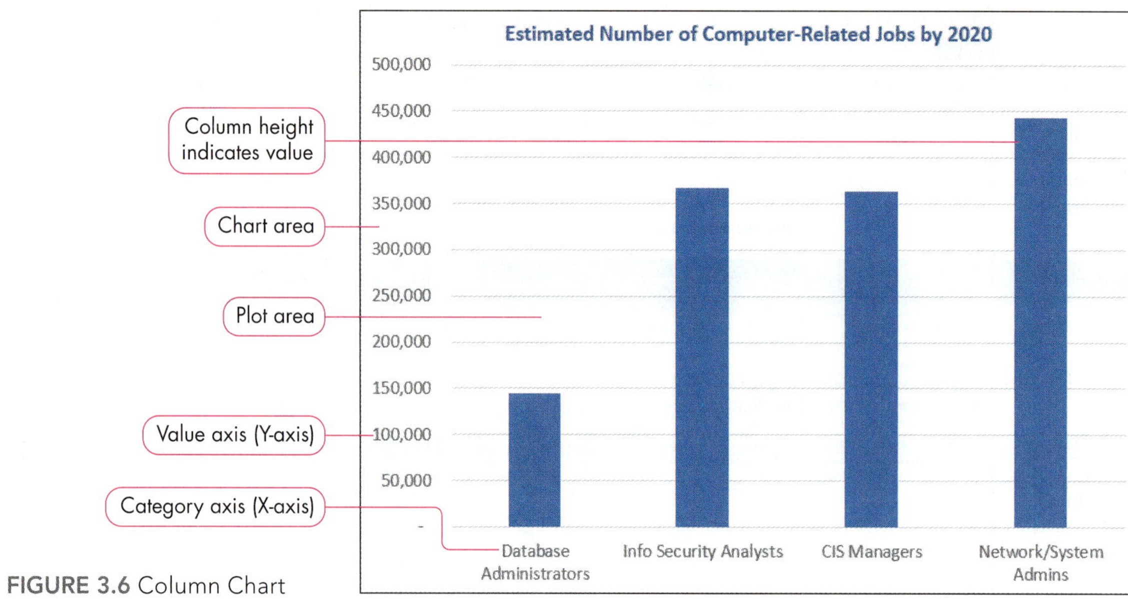

FIGURE 3.6 Column Chart

A ***clustered column chart*** compares groups—or clusters—of columns set side by side for easy comparison. The clustered column chart facilitates quick comparisons across data series, and it is effective for comparing several data points among categories. Figure 3.7 shows a clustered column chart created from the data in Figure 3.1. By default, the row labels appear on the category axis, and the yearly data series appear as columns with the value axis showing incremental numbers. Excel assigns a different color to each yearly data series and includes a legend so that you will know what color represents which data series. The 2010 data series is light blue, and the 2020 data series is dark blue. This chart makes it easy to compare the predicted job growth from 2010 to 2020 for each job title and then to compare the trends among job titles.

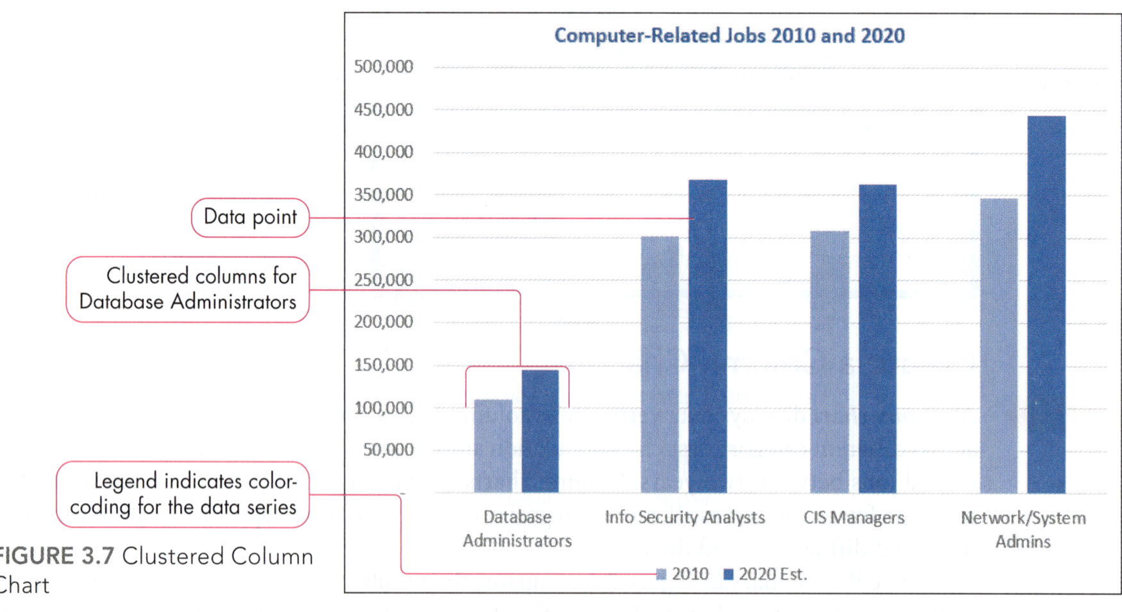

FIGURE 3.7 Clustered Column Chart

Figure 3.8 shows a clustered column chart in which the categories and data series are reversed. The years appear on the category axis, and the job titles appear as color-coded data series and in the legend. This chart gives a different perspective from that in Figure 3.7 in that it compares the number of jobs within a given year, such as 2010.

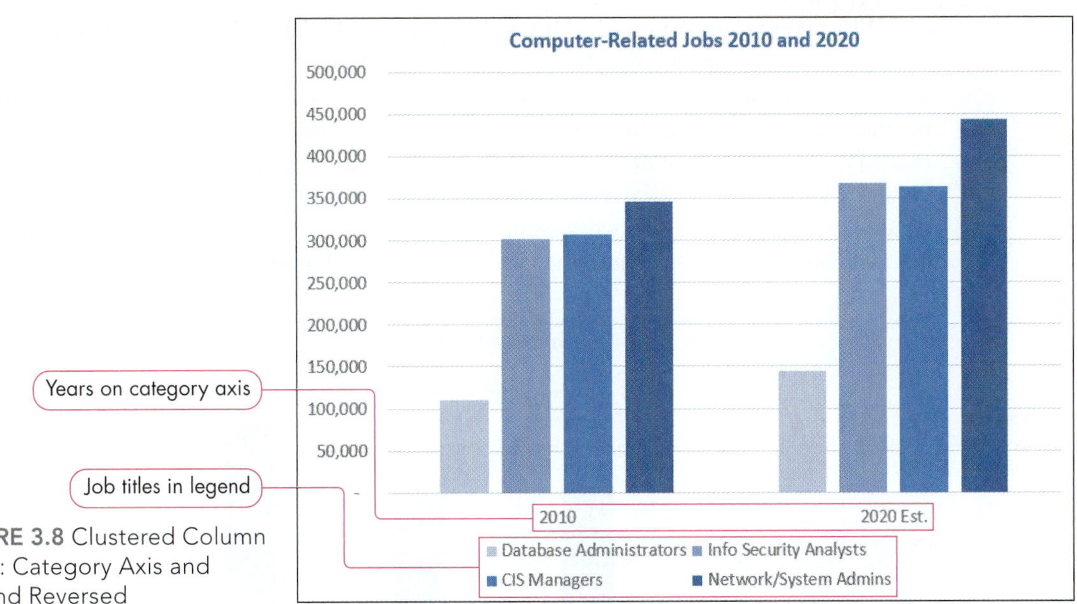

FIGURE 3.8 Clustered Column Chart: Category Axis and Legend Reversed

A ***stacked column chart*** shows the relationship of individual data points to the whole category. A stacked column chart displays only one column for each category. Each category within the stacked column is color-coded for one data series. Use the stacked column chart when you want to compare total values across categories, as well as to display the individual category values. Figure 3.9 shows a stacked column chart in which a single column represents each categorical year, and each column stacks color-coded data-point segments representing the different jobs. The stacked column chart enables you to compare the total number of computer-related jobs for each year. The height of each color-coded data point enables you to identify the relative contribution of each job to the total number of jobs for a particular year. A disadvantage of the stacked column chart is that the segments within each column do not start at the same point, making it more difficult to compare individual segment values across categories.

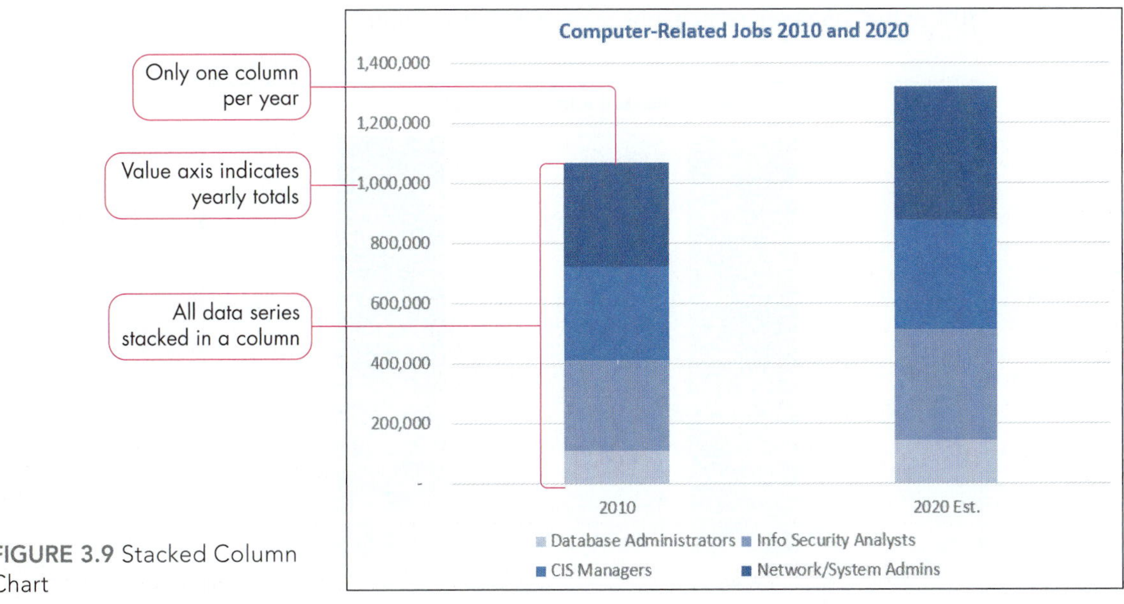

FIGURE 3.9 Stacked Column Chart

When you create a stacked column chart, make sure data are *additive*: each column represents a sum of the data for each segment. Figure 3.9 correctly uses years as the category axis and the jobs as data series. Within each year, Excel adds the number of jobs, and the columns display the total number of jobs. For example, the estimated total number of computer-related jobs in 2020 is about 1,300,000. Figure 3.10 shows an incorrectly constructed stacked column chart because the yearly number of jobs by job title is *not* additive. It is incorrect to state that about 800,000 Network/System Admin jobs exist. Be careful when constructing stacked column charts to ensure that they lead to logical interpretation of data.

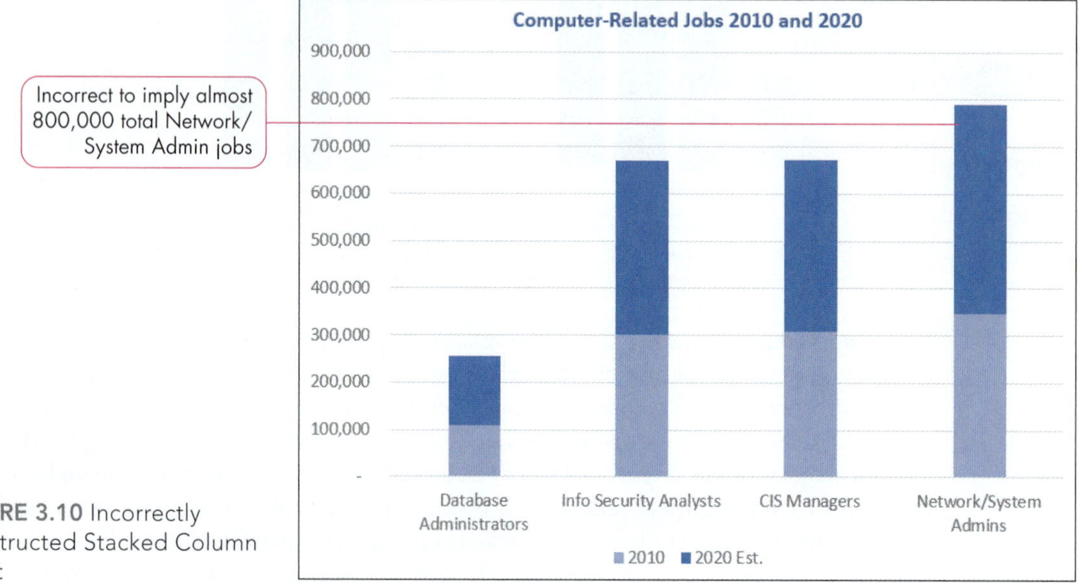

FIGURE 3.10 Incorrectly Constructed Stacked Column Chart

A ***100% stacked column chart*** converts individual data points into percentages of the total value. Each data series is a different color of the stack, representing a percentage. The total of each column is 100%. This type of chart depicts contributions to the whole. For example, the chart in Figure 3.11 illustrates that Network/System Admins account for over 30% of the computer-related jobs represented by the four job categories.

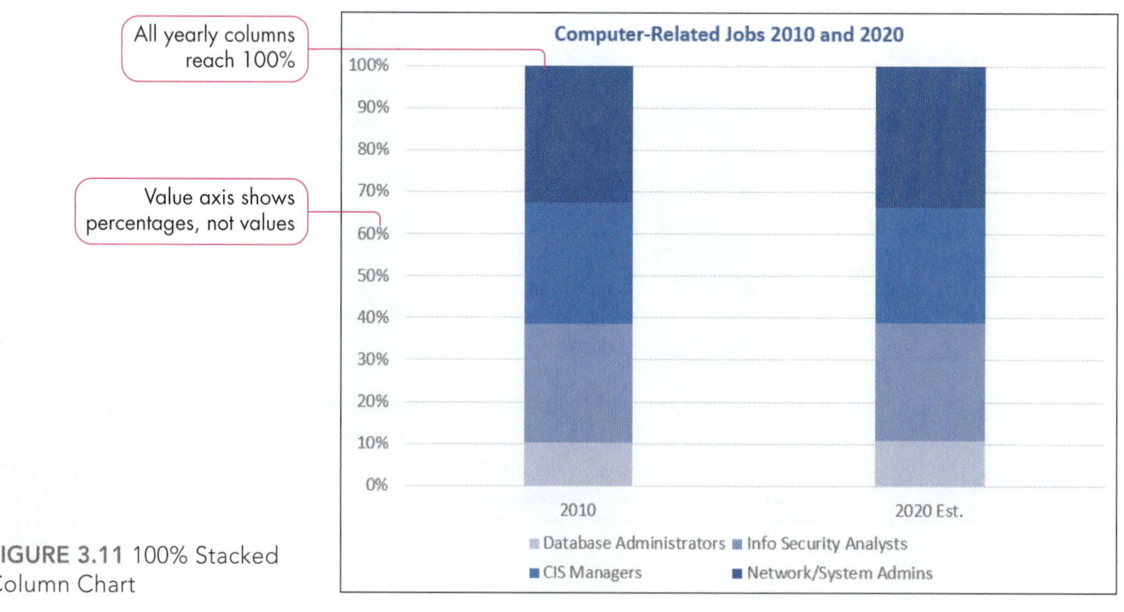

FIGURE 3.11 100% Stacked Column Chart

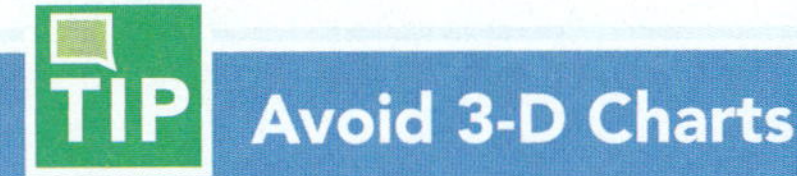

Avoid 3-D Charts

Avoid creating 3-D charts, because the third dimension is a superficial enhancement that usually distorts the charted data. For example, some columns appear taller or shorter than they actually are because of the angle of the 3-D effect, or some columns might be hidden by taller columns in front of them.

Create a Bar Chart

STEP 3» A ***bar chart*** compares values across categories using horizontal bars. The horizontal axis displays values, and the vertical axis displays categories (see Figure 3.12). Bar charts and column charts tell a similar story: they both compare categories of data. A bar chart is preferable when category names are long, such as *Database Administrators*. A bar chart enables category names to appear in an easy-to-read format, whereas a column chart might display category names at an awkward angle or in a smaller font size. The overall decision between a column and a bar chart may come down to the fact that different data may look better with one chart type than the other.

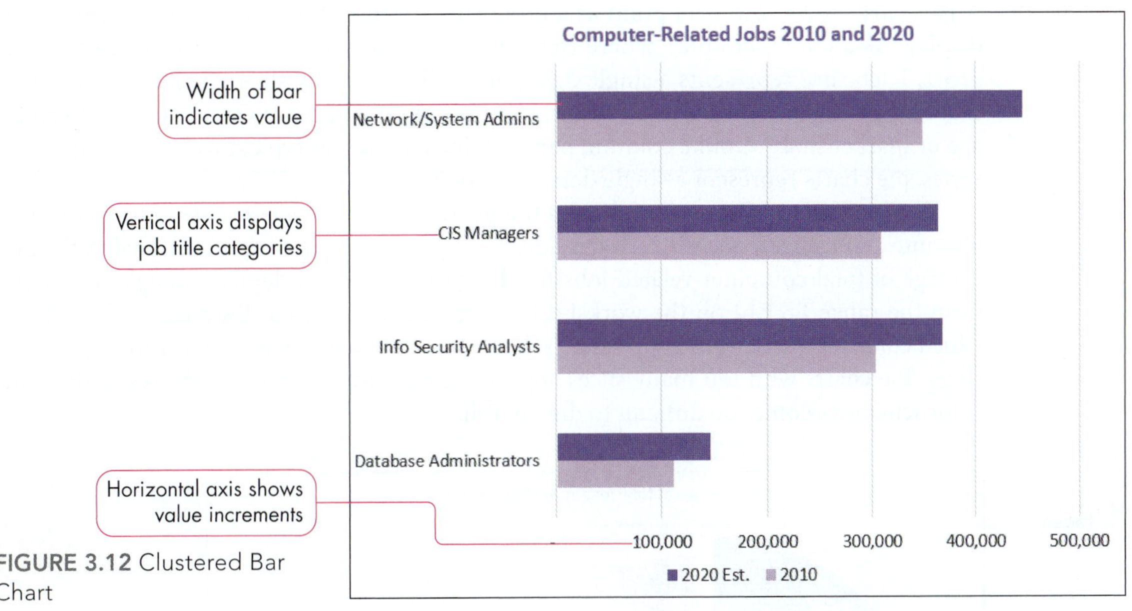

FIGURE 3.12 Clustered Bar Chart

Create a Line Chart

A ***line chart*** displays lines connecting data points to show trends over equal time periods. Excel displays each data series with a different line color. The category axis (X-axis) represents time, such as 10-year increments, whereas the value axis (Y-axis) represents the value, such as money or quantity. A line chart enables you to detect trends because the line continues to the next data point. To show each data point, choose the Line with Markers chart type. Figure 3.13 shows a line chart indicating the number of majors from 2005 to 2020 at five-year increments. The number of Arts majors remains relatively constant, but the number of Tech & Computing majors increases significantly over time, especially between the years 2010 and 2020.

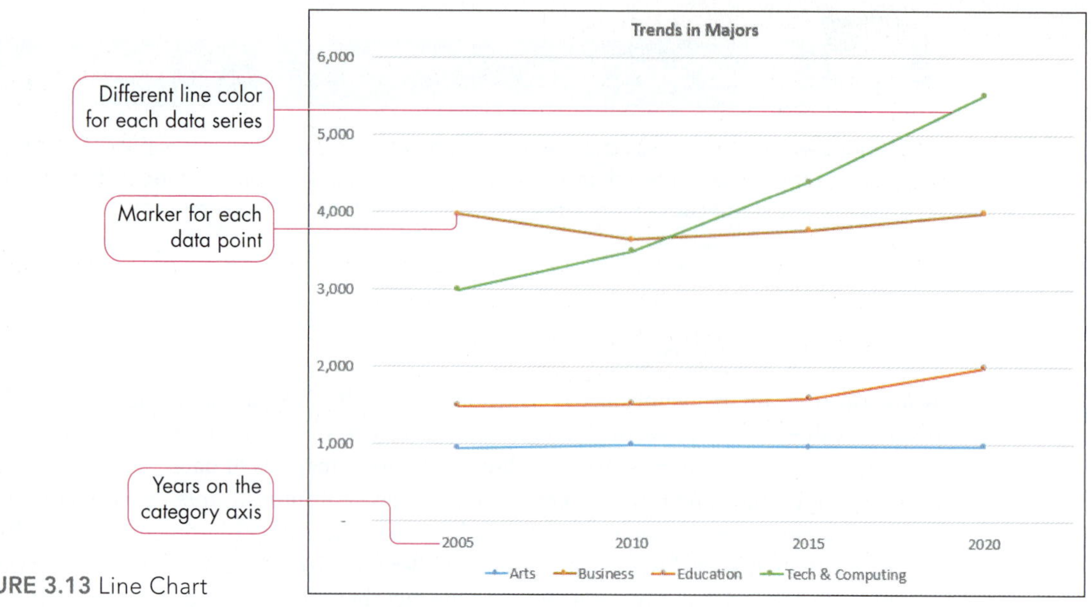

FIGURE 3.13 Line Chart

Create a Pie Chart

STEP 4

A ***pie chart*** shows each data point as a proportion to the whole data series. The pie chart displays as a circle, or "pie," where the entire pie represents the total value of the data series. Each slice represents a single data point. The larger the slice, the larger percentage that data point contributes to the whole. Use a pie chart when you want to convey percentage or market share. Unlike column, bar, and line charts that typically chart multiple data series, pie charts represent a single data series only.

The pie chart in Figure 3.14 divides the pie representing the estimated number of new jobs into seven slices, one for each job title. The size of each slice is proportional to the percentage of total computer-related jobs for that year. The chart depicts a single data series from the range E6:E12 on the worksheet in Figure 3.1. Excel creates a legend to indicate which color represents which pie slice. When you create a pie chart, limit it to about seven slices. Pie charts with too many slices appear too busy to interpret, or shades of the same color scheme become too difficult to distinguish.

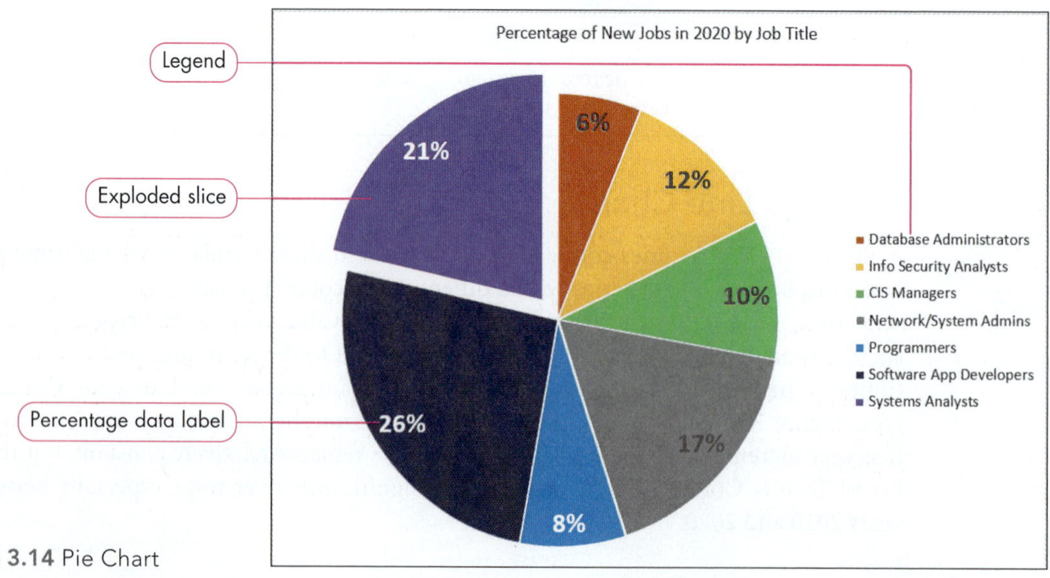

FIGURE 3.14 Pie Chart

The projected number of new Systems Analyst jobs is 33,900, which accounts for 21% of the new jobs. You can focus a person's attention on a particular slice by separating one or more slices from the rest of the chart in an ***exploded pie chart***, as shown in Figure 3.14.

Change the Chart Type

After you create a chart, you may decide that the data would be better represented by a different type of chart. For example, you might decide a bar chart would display the labels better than a column chart. When you select a chart, Chart Tools displays on the Ribbon with the Design and Format tabs. To change the type of an existing chart, do the following:

1. Select the chart and click the DESIGN tab.
2. Click Change Chart Type in the Type group to open the Change Chart Type dialog box, which is similar to the Insert Chart dialog box.
3. Click the ALL CHARTS tab within the dialog box.
4. Click a chart type on the left side of the dialog box.
5. Click a chart subtype on the right side of the dialog box and click OK.

Create Other Chart Types

Two other chart types that are used for specialized analysis are X Y (scatter) charts and stock charts.

An ***X Y (scatter) chart*** shows a relationship between two numerical variables using their X and Y coordinates. Excel plots one variable on the horizontal X-axis and the other variable on the vertical Y-axis. Scatter charts are often used to represent data in educational, scientific, and medical experiments. Figure 3.15 shows the relationship between the number of minutes students view a training video and their test scores.

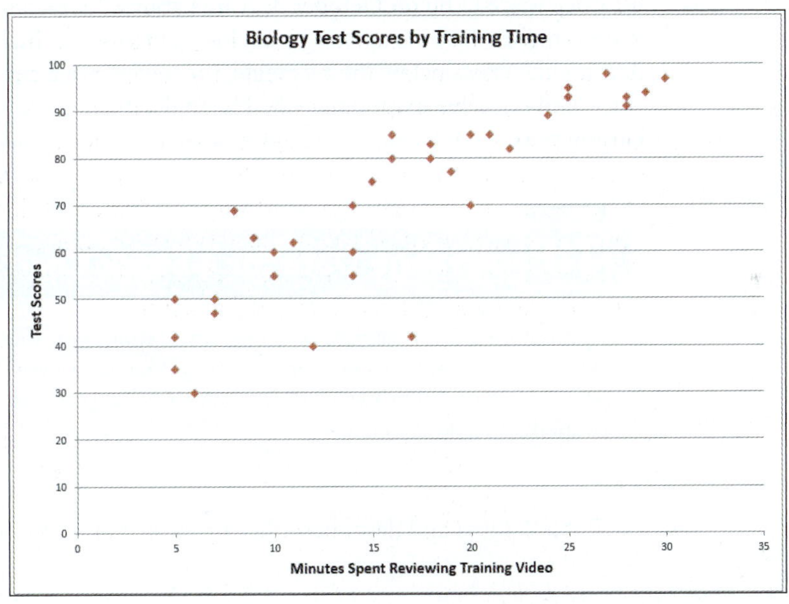

FIGURE 3.15 X Y (Scatter) Chart

A ***stock chart*** shows fluctuations in stock changes. You can select one of four stock subtypes: High-Low-Close, Open-High-Low-Close, Volume-High-Low-Close, and Volume-Open-High-Low-Close. The High-Low-Close stock chart marks a stock's trading range on a given day with a vertical line from the lowest to the highest stock prices. Rectangles mark the opening and closing prices. Figure 3.16 shows three days of stock prices for a particular company.

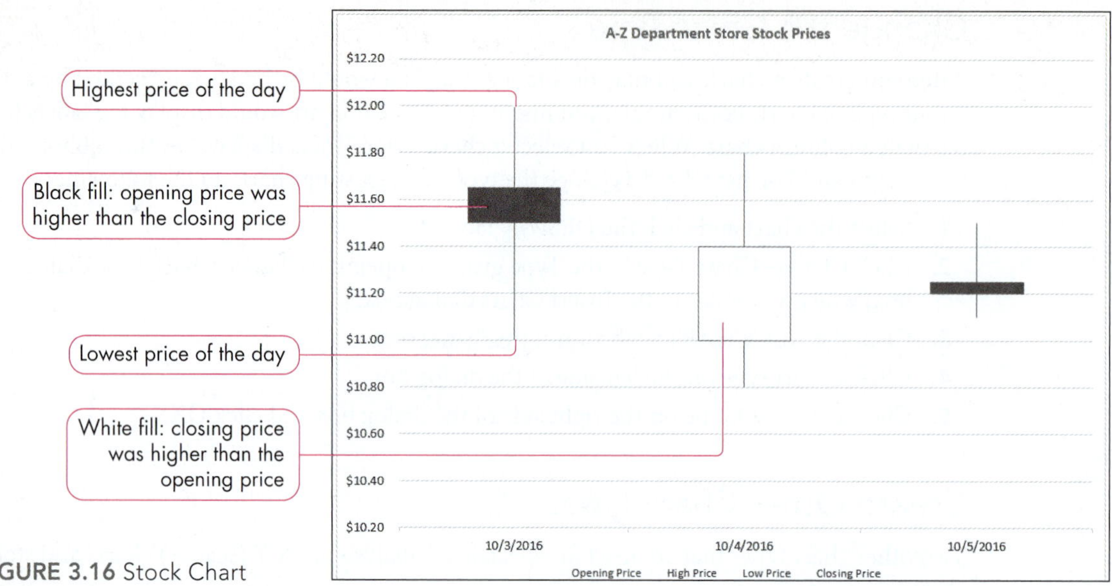

FIGURE 3.16 Stock Chart

The rectangle represents the difference in the opening and closing prices. If the rectangle has a white fill, the closing price is higher than the opening price. If the rectangle has a black fill, the opening price is higher than the closing price. In Figure 3.16, on October 3, the opening price was $11.65, and the closing price was $11.50. A line below the rectangle indicates that the lowest trading price is lower than the opening and closing prices. The lowest price was $11.00 on October 3. A line above the rectangle indicates the highest trading price is higher than the opening and closing prices. The highest price was $12.00 on October 3. If no line exists below the rectangle, the lowest price equals either the opening or closing price, and if no line exists above the rectangle, the highest price equals either the opening or closing price.

TIP Arrange Data for a Stock Chart

To create an Open-High-Low-Close stock chart, you must arrange data with Opening Price, High Price, Low Price, and Closing Price as column labels in that sequence. If you want to create other variations of stock charts, you must arrange data in a structured sequence required by Excel.

Table 3.2 lists and describes other types of charts you can create in Excel.

TABLE 3.2 Other Chart Types		
Chart	**Chart Type**	**Description**
	Area	Similar to a line chart in that it shows trends over time; however, the area chart displays colors between the lines to help illustrate the magnitude of changes.
	Surface	Represents numeric data and numeric categories. Takes on some of the same characteristics as a topographic map of hills and valleys.
	Doughnut	A derivative of a pie chart showing relationship of parts to a whole, but the doughnut chart can display more than one data series.
	Bubble	A derivative of a scatter chart in which both the horizontal and vertical axes are value axes. The third value determines the size of the bubble, where the larger the value, the larger the bubble. Do not select the column labels, as they might distort the data.
	Radar	Uses each category as a spoke radiating from the center point to the outer edges of the chart. Each spoke represents each data series, and lines connect the data points between spokes, similar to a spider web. You can create a radar chart to compare aggregate values for several data series.
	Combo	Combines two chart types (such as column and line) to plot different data types (such as values and percentages).

Moving, Sizing, and Printing a Chart

Excel inserts the chart as an embedded object in the current worksheet, often to the right side of, but sometimes on top of and covering up, the data area. After you insert a chart, you usually need to move it to a different location, adjust its size, and prepare to print it.

Move a Chart

To move the chart on the active worksheet, position the mouse pointer over the chart area. When you see the Chart Area ScreenTip and the mouse pointer includes the white arrowhead and a four-headed arrow, drag the chart to the desired location.

You can place the chart in a separate worksheet, called a ***chart sheet***. A chart sheet contains a single chart only; you cannot enter data and formulas on a chart sheet. If you leave the chart in the same worksheet, you can print the data and chart on the same page. If you want to print or view a full-sized chart, move the chart to its own chart sheet. To move a chart to another sheet or a chart sheet, do the following:

1. Select the chart.
2. Click the DESIGN tab and click Move Chart in the Location group to open the Move Chart dialog box (see Figure 3.17).
3. Select one of these options to indicate where you want to move the chart:
   - Click *New sheet* to move the chart to its own sheet.
   - Click *Object in*, click the *Object in* arrow, and select the worksheet to which you want to move the chart. The default chart sheet is Chart1, but you can rename it in the Move Chart dialog box or similarly to the way you rename other sheet tabs. Click OK.

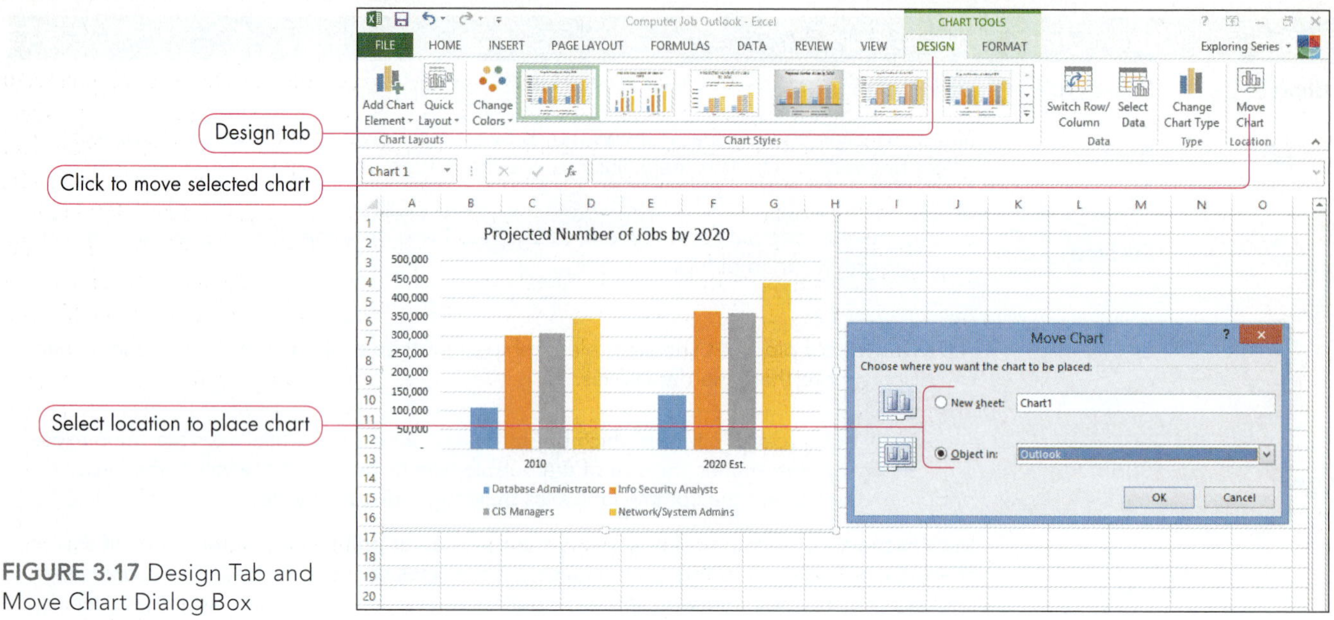

FIGURE 3.17 Design Tab and Move Chart Dialog Box

Size a Chart

If you keep a chart in a worksheet, you can size it to fit in a particular range or to ensure the chart elements are proportional. To change the chart size, do the following:

1. Select the chart.
2. Position the mouse pointer on the outer edge of the chart where you see eight small white-filled squares, called ***sizing handles***.
3. When the mouse pointer changes to a two-headed arrow, drag the border to adjust the chart's height or width. Drag a corner sizing handle to increase or decrease the height and width of the chart at the same time. Press and hold down Shift as you drag a corner sizing handle to change the height and width proportionately.

You can also change the chart size by clicking the Format tab and changing the height and width values in the Size group (see Figure 3.18).

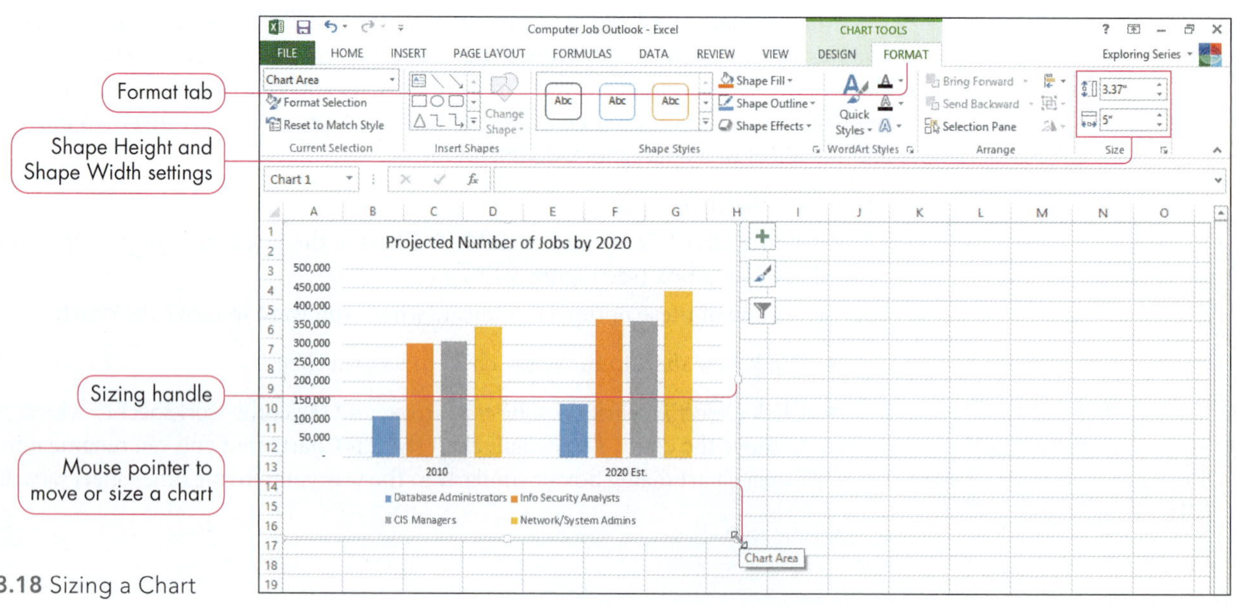

FIGURE 3.18 Sizing a Chart

Print a Chart

If you embedded a chart on the same sheet as the data source, you need to decide if you want to print the data only, the data *and* the chart, or the chart only. To print the data only, select the data, click the File tab, click Print, click the first arrow in the Settings section and select Print Selection, and then click Print. To print only the chart, select the chart, click the File tab, click Print, make sure the default setting is Print Selected Chart, and then click Print to print the chart as a full-page chart. If the data and chart are on the same worksheet, print the worksheet contents to print both, but do not select either the chart or the data before displaying the Print options. The preview shows you what will print. Make sure it displays what you want to print before clicking Print.

If you moved the chart to a chart sheet, the chart is the only item on that worksheet. When you display the print options, the default is Print Active Sheets, and the chart will print as a full-page chart.

1. Why should you not include aggregates, such as totals or averages, along with individual data series in a chart? ***p. 217***
2. What is the purpose of each of these chart types: (a) column, (b) bar, (c) line, and (d) pie? ***p. 218***
3. How can you use the Quick Analysis button to create a chart? ***p. 218***
4. After you create a chart, where is it located by default? What do you usually do to the chart immediately after creating it? ***p. 227***

Hands-On Exercises

1 Chart Creation Basics

Doug Demers, your assistant, gathered data about seven computer-related jobs from the *Occupational Outlook Handbook* online. He organized the data into a structured worksheet that contains the job titles, the number of jobs in 2010, the projected number of jobs by 2020, and other data. Now you are ready to transform the data into visually appealing charts.

Skills covered: Create a Clustered Column Chart • Create a Bar Chart • Change the Chart Position, Size, and Type • Create a Pie Chart

STEP 1 » CREATE A CLUSTERED COLUMN CHART

You want to compare the number of jobs in 2010 to the projected number of jobs in 2020 for all seven computer-related professions that Doug entered into the worksheet. You decide to create a clustered column chart to depict this data. After you create this chart, you will move it to its own chart sheet. Refer to Figure 3.19 as you complete Step 1.

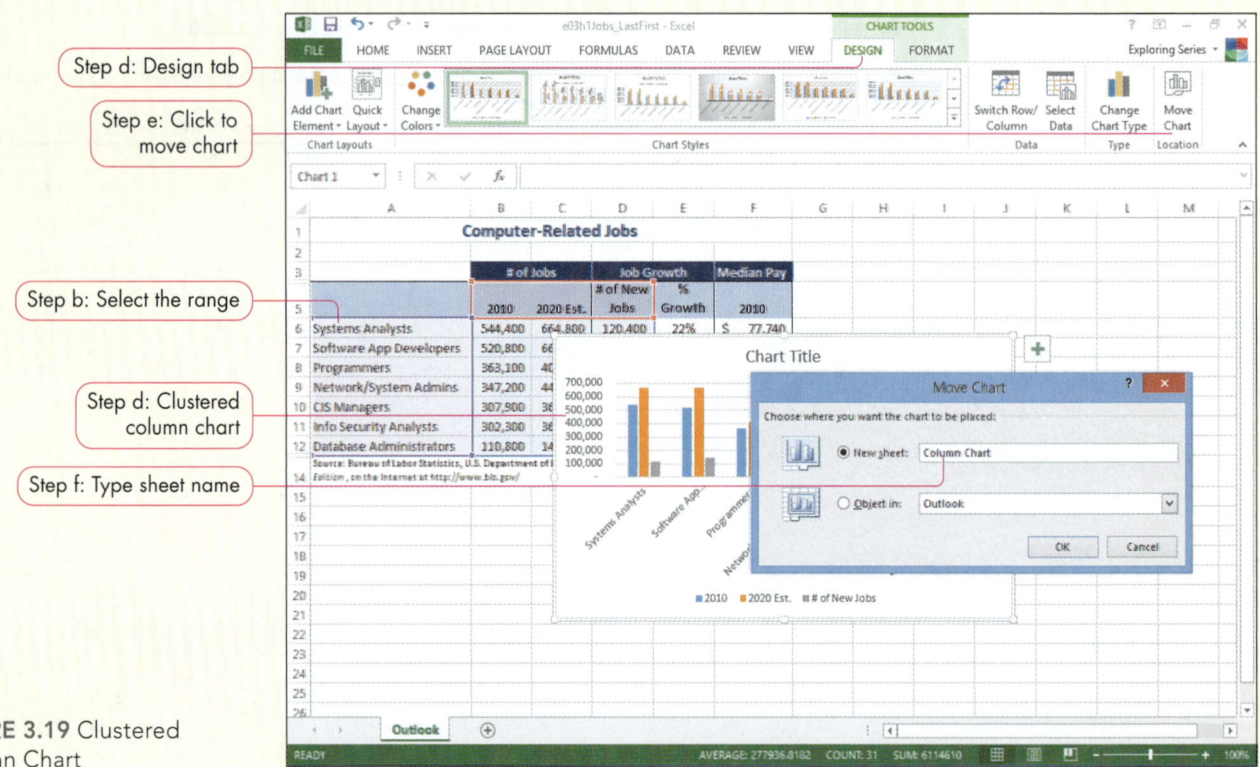

FIGURE 3.19 Clustered Column Chart

a. Open *e03h1Jobs* and save it as **e03h1Jobs_LastFirst**.

> **TROUBLESHOOTING:** If you make any major mistakes in this exercise, you can close the file, open *e03h1Jobs* again, and then start this exercise over.

b. Select the **range A5:D12**.

You selected the job titles, the number of jobs in 2010, the projected number of jobs in 2020, and the number of new jobs.

c. Click the **Quick Analysis button** at the bottom-right corner of the selected range and click **CHARTS**.

   The Quick Analysis gallery displays recommended charts based on the selected range.

d. Position the mouse pointer over *Clustered Column* to see a live preview of what the chart would look like and click **Clustered Column**.

   Excel inserts a clustered column chart based on the selected data.

   The DESIGN tab displays on the Ribbon.

e. Click **Move Chart** in the Location group to open the Move Chart dialog box.

f. Click **New sheet**, type **Column Chart**, and click **OK**. Save the workbook.

   Excel moves the clustered column chart to a new sheet called Column Chart. Later, you will modify the chart.

STEP 2 » CREATE A BAR CHART

You want to create a bar chart to depict the number of jobs in 2010 and the number of new jobs that will be created by 2020. Refer to Figure 3.20 as you complete Step 2.

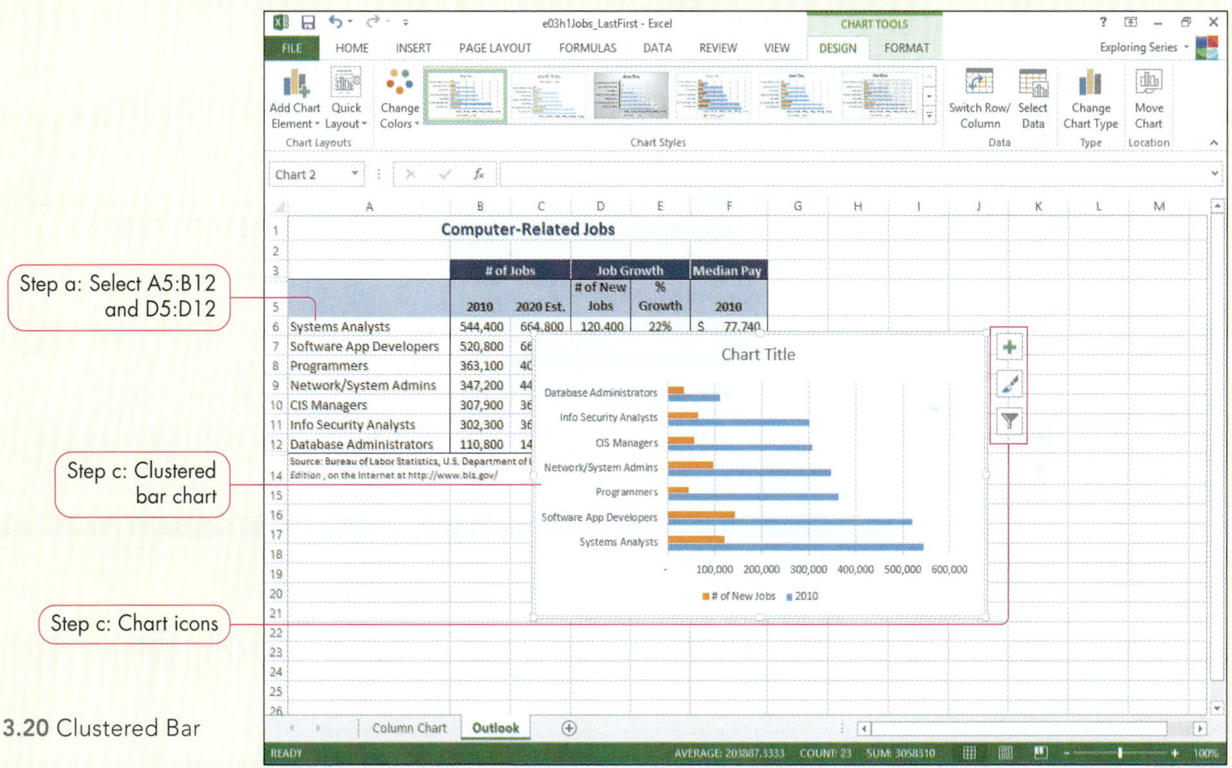

FIGURE 3.20 Clustered Bar Chart

a. Click the **Outlook sheet tab**, select the **range A5:B12**, press and hold **Ctrl**, and then select the range **D5:D12**.

   You selected the job title labels, the number of jobs in 2010, and the number of new jobs.

TIP Parallel Ranges

Nonadjacent ranges should be parallel so that the legend will correctly reflect the data series. This means that each range should contain the same number of related cells. For example, A5:A12, B5:B12, and D5:D12 are parallel ranges.

b. Click the **INSERT tab** and click **Insert Bar Chart** in the Charts group.

   A gallery containing thumbnails of different bar charts displays.

c. Click **Clustered Bar** in the 2-D Bar group. Save the workbook.

   Excel inserts the clustered bar chart in the worksheet. Three icons display to the right side of the selected chart: Chart Elements, Chart Styles, and Chart Filters.

STEP 3 ›› CHANGE THE CHART POSITION, SIZE, AND TYPE

Because the bar chart overlaps the data, you need to move it. You decide to position it below the job outlook data and adjust its size. Finally, you want to change the chart to a stacked bar chart to show the total jobs in 2020 based on the number of jobs in 2010 and the number of new jobs. Refer to Figure 3.21 as you complete Step 3.

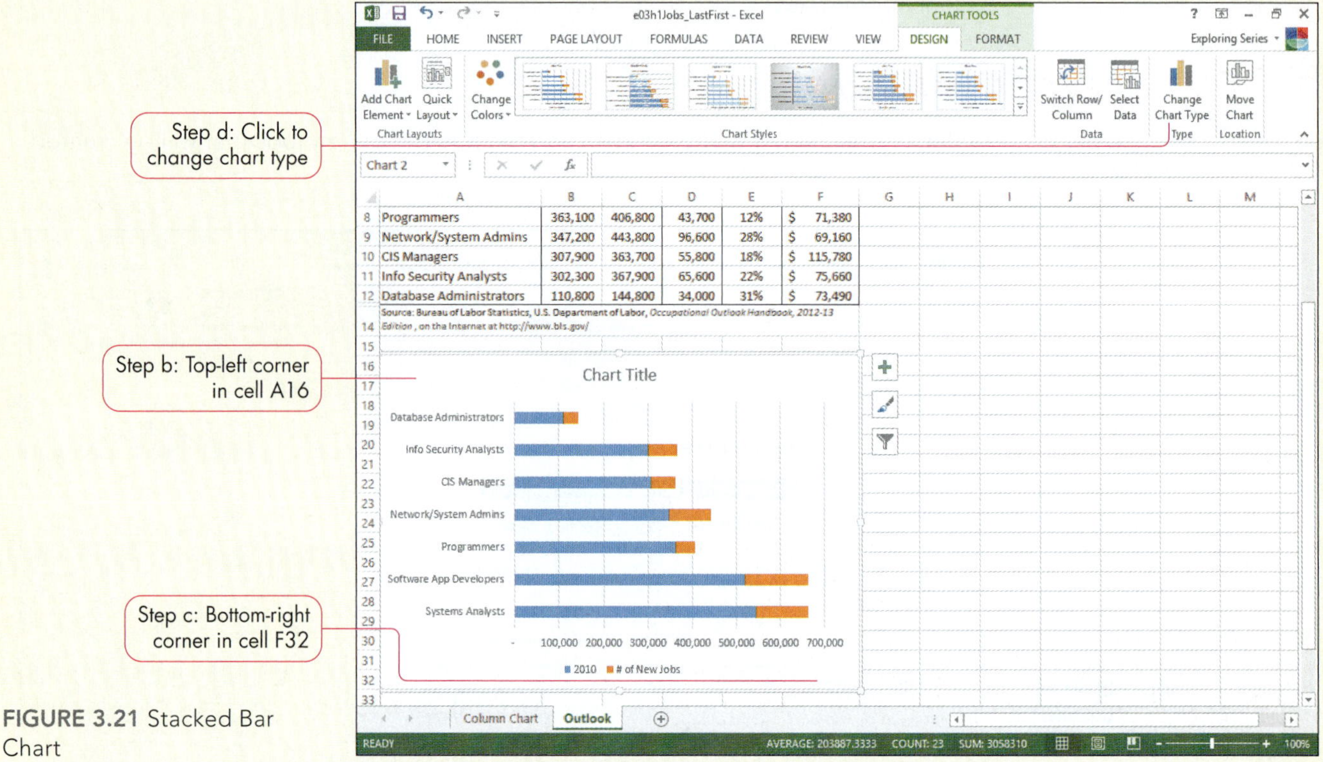

FIGURE 3.21 Stacked Bar Chart

a. Position the mouse pointer over the empty area of the chart area.

   The mouse pointer includes a four-headed arrow with the regular white arrowhead, and the Chart Area ScreenTip displays.

> **TROUBLESHOOTING:** Make sure you see the Chart Area ScreenTip as you perform step b. If you move the mouse pointer to another chart element—such as the legend—you will move or size that element instead of moving the entire chart.

b. Drag the chart so that the top-left corner of the chart appears in **cell A16**.

   You positioned the chart below the worksheet data.

c. Drag the bottom-right sizing handle through **cell F32**.

   You changed both the height and the width at the same time.

d. Click **Change Chart Type** in the Type group, click **Stacked Bar** in the top center of the dialog box, and then click **OK**. Save the workbook.

Excel stacks the 2010 number of new jobs data series into one column per job title. This chart tells the story of where the projected number of jobs in 2020 come from: the number of existing jobs in 2010 (blue) and the number of new jobs (orange).

STEP 4 » CREATE A PIE CHART

You decide to create a pie chart that depicts the percentage of new jobs by job title created out of the total number of new jobs created, which is 559,800. After creating the pie chart, you will move it to its own sheet. Finally, you want to draw attention to the job that has the largest slice by exploding it. Refer to Figure 3.22 as you complete Step 4.

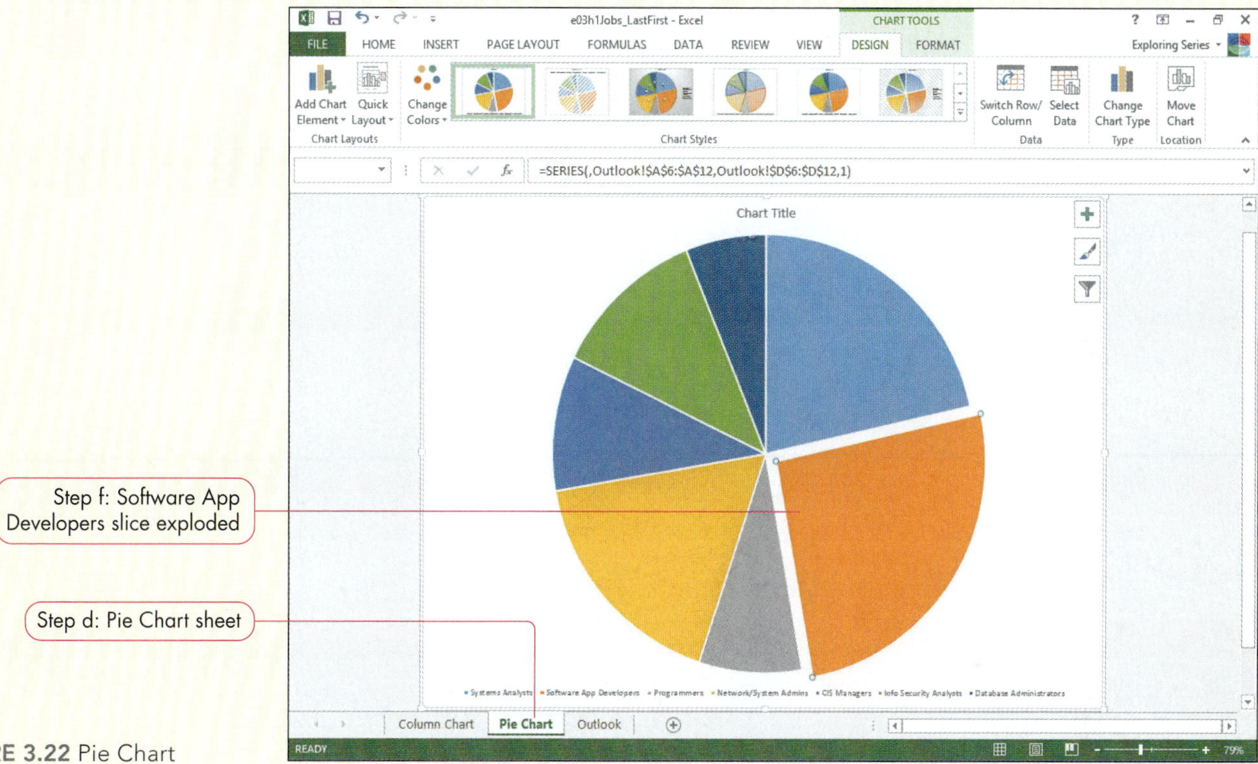

FIGURE 3.22 Pie Chart

a. Select the **range A6:A12** and press and hold **Ctrl** as you select the **range D6:D12**.

TROUBLESHOOTING: Do not select cells A5 and D5 this time because you are creating a pie chart. Doing so would add unnecessary data to the chart.

b. Click the **INSERT tab**, click **Insert Pie or Doughnut** in the Charts group, and then select **Pie** in the 2-D Pie group on the gallery.

The pie chart may overlap part of the worksheet data and the stacked bar chart.

c. Click **Move Chart** in the Location group on the DESIGN tab.

The Move Chart dialog box opens.

d. Click **New sheet**, type **Pie Chart**, and then click **OK**.

Excel creates a new sheet called Pie Chart. The pie chart is the only object on that sheet.

e. Click the **Software App Developers orange slice**, pause, and then click it again.

The first click selects all slices of the pie. The second click selects only the Software App Developers slice.

TROUBLESHOOTING: If you double-click the pie chart, the Format Data Series task pane opens on the right side of the chart. Click its Close button and click the orange slice one time.

f. Drag the **Software App Developers orange slice** away from the pie a little bit.

g. Save the workbook. Keep the workbook open if you plan to continue with the next Hands-On Exercise. If not, close the workbook and exit Excel.

Chart Elements

After you create a chart, you usually need to add components to describe the chart. Adding descriptive text for labels provides information for the reader to comprehend the chart. When you create a chart, one or more components may display by default. For example, when you created the charts in Hands-On Exercise 1, Excel displayed a placeholder for the chart title and displayed a legend so that you know which color represents which data series.

When you select a chart, Excel displays three icons to the right side the chart, the first of which is Chart Elements. In addition, the Design tab contains the Chart Layouts group so that you can add and customize chart elements.

In this section, you will learn how to add and format chart elements.

Adding Chart Elements

A ***chart element*** is a component that completes or helps clarify the chart. Some chart elements, such as chart titles, should be included in every chart. Other elements are optional. Table 3.3 describes the chart elements, and Figure 3.23 illustrates several chart elements.

TABLE 3.3 Chart Elements

Element	Description
Axes	Category axis labels, such as job titles, and the value axis quantities in increments in column, bar, and line charts. Axes display by default.
Axis titles	Labels that describe the category and value axes. You can display axis titles, such as *In Millions of Dollars* or *Top 7 Computer Job Titles*, to clarify the axes. Axis titles are not displayed by default.
Chart title	Label that describes the entire chart. It should reflect the purpose of the chart. For example, *Houses Sold* is too generic, but *Houses Sold in Seattle in 2016* indicates the what (Houses), the where (Seattle), and the when (2016). The default is *Chart Title*.
Data labels	Descriptive labels that show exact value or name of a data point. Data labels are not displayed by default.
Data table	A grid that contains the data source values and labels. If you embed a chart on the same worksheet as the data source, you might not need to include a data table. Only add a data table with a chart that is on a chart sheet.
Error bars	Visuals that indicate the standard error amount, a percentage, or a standard deviation for a data point or marker. Error bars are not displayed by default.
Gridlines	Horizontal or vertical lines that span across the chart to help people identify the values plotted by the visual elements, such as a column. Excel displays horizontal gridlines for column, line, scatter, stock, surface, and bubble charts and vertical gridlines for bar charts. Gridlines may display by default, depending on the chart type.
Legend	A key that identifies the color, gradient, picture, texture, or pattern assigned to each data series. The legend is displayed by default for particular charts.
Trendline	A line that depicts trends or helps forecast future data, such as estimating future sales or number of births in a region. You can add a trendline to column, bar, line, stock, scatter, and bubble charts. Excel will analyze the current trends to display a line indicating future values based on the current trend.

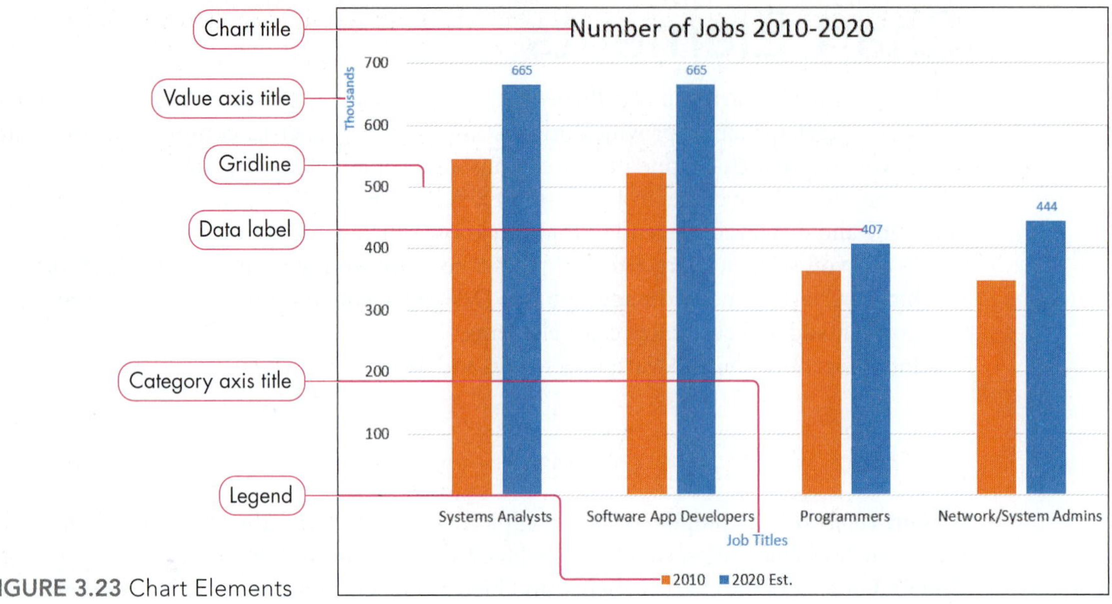

FIGURE 3.23 Chart Elements

To add a chart element, do the following:

1. Click the Chart Elements button to the right side of the chart (see Figure 3.24).
2. Click an empty check box to display an element, or position the mouse pointer on an element and click the triangle to select more specific chart elements. For example, if you click the triangle to the right of Axis Titles, you select on which axis to include a title.
3. If you selected a title, type the text for the title, and then press Enter.
4. Click the Chart Elements button again to close the menu.

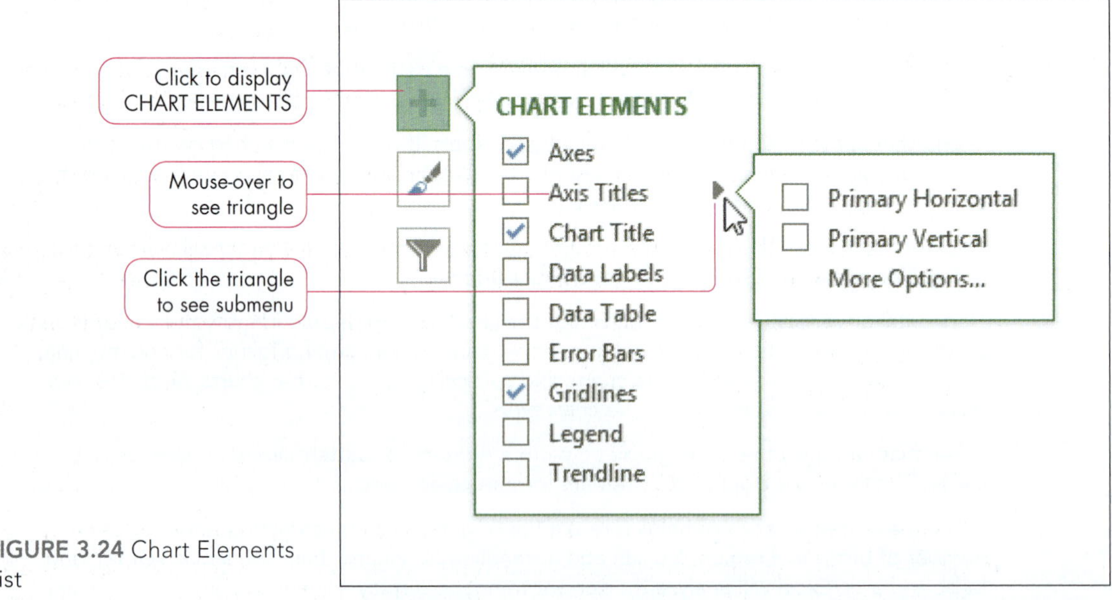

FIGURE 3.24 Chart Elements List

TIP Remove an Element

To remove an element, click Chart Elements and deselect a check box. Alternatively, click Add Chart Element in the Chart Layouts group on the Chart Tools Design tab, position the mouse pointer over the element name, and then select None.

To use the Design tab to add or remove a chart element, do the following:

1. Click the DESIGN tab.
2. Click Add Chart Element in the Chart Layouts group.
3. Point to an element and select from that element's submenu (see Figure 3.25).
4. If you selected a title, type the text for the title and press Enter.

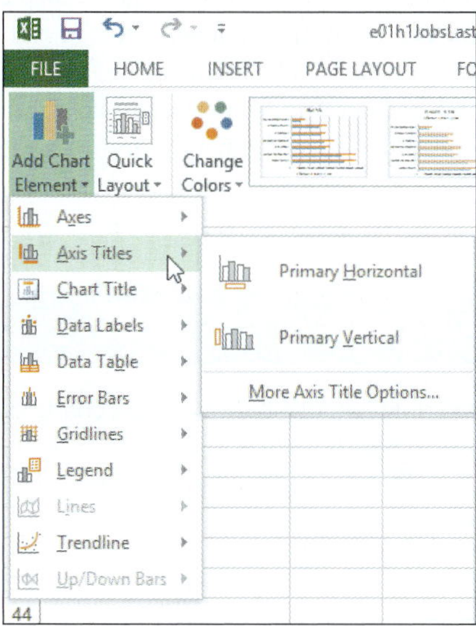

FIGURE 3.25 Chart Elements Menu and Submenu

Position the Chart Title

Excel includes the placeholder text *Chart Title* above the chart when you create a chart. You should replace that text with a descriptive title. To change the chart title text, click the Chart Title placeholder, type the text, and then press Enter. You can select the position of the title by doing the following:

1. Click the Chart Elements button to the right side of the chart.
2. Position the mouse pointer over Chart Title and click the triangle on the right side.
3. Select one of the options:
    - Above Chart: Centers the title above the plot area, decreasing the plot area size to make room for the chart title.
    - Centered Overlay: Centers the chart title horizontally without resizing the plot area; the title displays over the top of the plot area.
    - More Options: Opens the Format Chart Title task pane so that you can apply fill, border, and alignment settings.
4. Click the Chart Elements button to close the menu.

Include and Position Axis Titles

STEP 2»

Excel does not include axis titles by default; however, you can display titles. When you click Chart Elements and click the triangle on the right side of Axis Titles, you can select Primary Horizontal and Primary Vertical. The horizontal axis title displays below the category labels, and the rotated vertical axis title displays on the left side of the value axis. After including these titles, you can click the respective title, type the text for the title, and then press Enter.

Include and Position Data Labels

STEP 3»

Excel does not include data labels by default; however, you can display the exact values of the data points in the chart. When you click Chart Elements and click the triangle on the right side of Data Labels, you can select where the labels display.

By default, Excel adds data labels to all data series. If you want to display data labels for only one series, select the data labels for the other data series and press Delete. In Figure 3.23, data labels are included for the 2020 data series but not the 2010 data series.

Position the Legend

When you create a multiple series chart, the legend displays, providing a key to the color-coded data series. You can position the legend to the right, top, bottom, or left of the plot area. Choose the position based on how the legend's placement affects the chart. Make sure that the columns, bars, or lines appear proportionate and well balanced after you position the legend. You may need to adjust the height and/or width of the entire chart to achieve a balanced appearance.

TIP Quick Layout

Use Quick Layout to apply predefined layouts to a chart. Specifically, you can apply a layout to add several chart elements at one time. Click Quick Layout in the Chart Layouts group on the Design tab (see Figure 3.26) and select a layout. Each layout contains predefined chart elements and their positions.

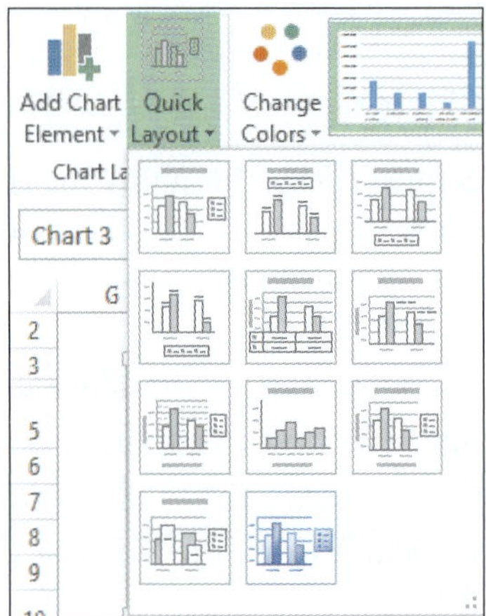

FIGURE 3.26 Quick Layout Gallery

Formatting Chart Elements

When you position the mouse pointer over the chart, Excel displays a ScreenTip with the name of that chart element. To select a chart element, click it when you see the ScreenTip, or click the Format tab, click the Chart Elements arrow in the Current Selection group, and then select the element from the list.

STEP 1 After you select a chart element, you can format it. For example, you might want to apply 18-pt font size to the chart title. In addition, you might want to change the fill color of a data series to red. You can apply these formats from the Home tab:

- Font for titles, axes, and labels
- Font Size for titles, axes, and labels
- Font Color for titles, axes, and labels
- Fill Color for column, bar, and line data series or background fill color behind titles and labels

Format the Chart Area, Plot Area, and Data Series

STEP 4» You can apply multiple settings, such as fill colors and borders, at once using a Format task pane. To display a chart element's task pane, double-click the chart element. Figure 3.27 displays the Format Chart Area, Format Plot Area, and Format Data Series task panes. All three task panes include the same fill and border elements. After you select a fill option, such as *Gradient fill*, the remaining options change in the task pane.

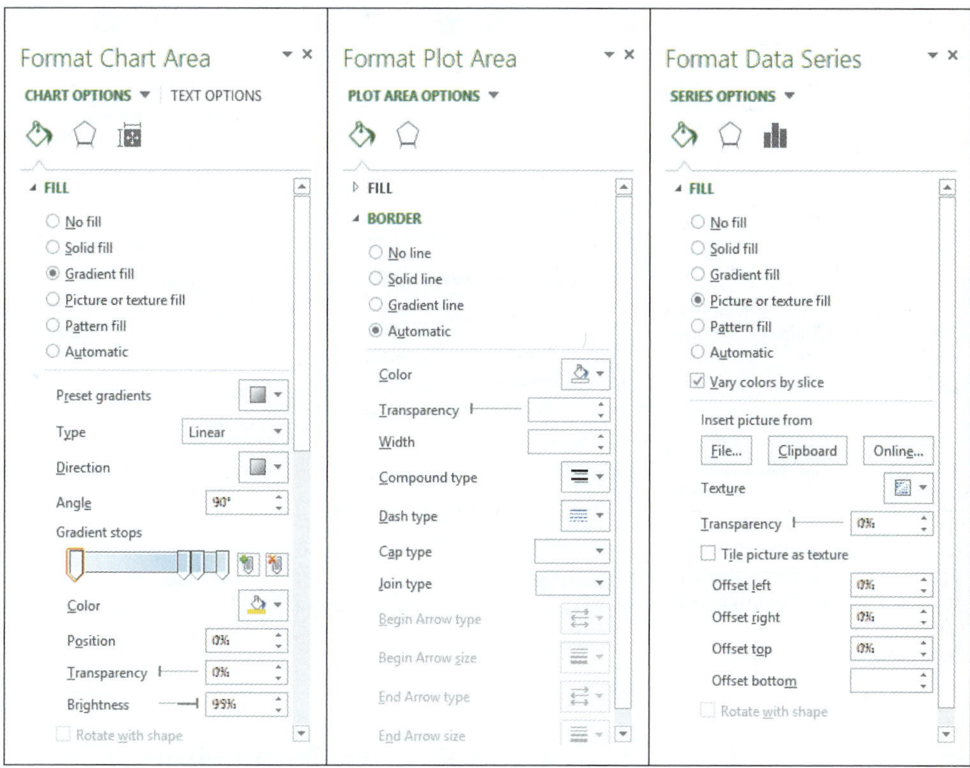

FIGURE 3.27 Format Task Panes

For less formal presentations, you might want to use images or a texture to fill the data series, chart area, or plot area instead of a solid fill color. To use an image or a texture, click the Fill & Line icon at the top of the task pane, click Fill, and then click *Picture or texture fill* in the Format Data Series task pane. Click File or Online in the *Insert picture from* section and insert an image file or search online to insert an image. The image is stretched by default, but you can select the Stack option to avoid distorting the image. To add a texture, click *Picture or texture fill*, click Texture, and then select a textured background from the gallery of textures. Generally, do not mix images and textures.

Format Axes

Based on the data source values and structure, Excel determines the starting, incremental, and stopping values that display on the value axis when you create the chart. You might want to adjust the value axis. For example, when working with large values such as 4,567,890, the value axis displays increments, such as 4,000,000 and 5,000,000. You can simplify the value axis by displaying values in millions, so that the values on the axis are 4 and 5 with the word *Millions* placed by the value axis to indicate the units. Figure 3.28 shows the Format Axis task pane. Diagonal black triangles, such as Axis Options, indicate all of a category's options are displayed (see the left task pane in Figure 3.28). Triangles with a white fill, such as Number, indicate the category options are not displayed (see the left task pane in Figure 3.28). You might need to scroll down and click a category name, such as Number, to see additional options. The task pane on the right side of Figure 3.28 shows the Number options after clicking the triangle.

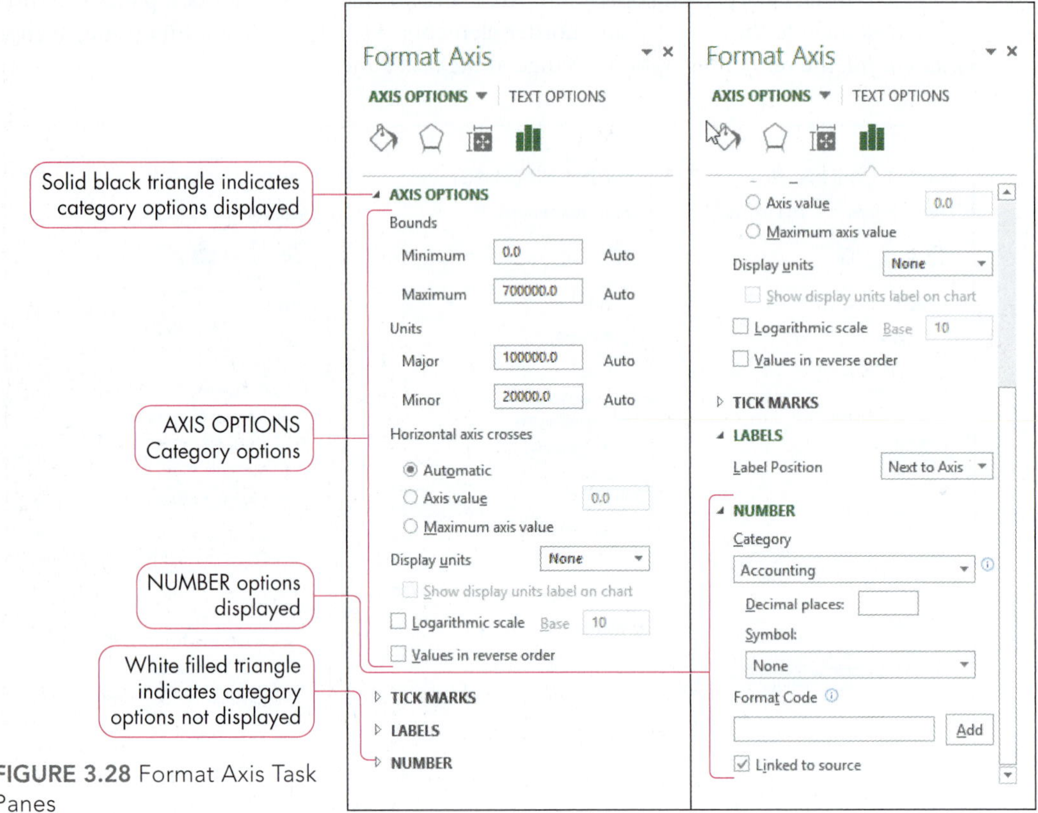

FIGURE 3.28 Format Axis Task Panes

Insert and Format Data Labels

When you select a data label, Excel selects all data labels in that data series. To format the labels, double-click a data label to open the Format Data Labels task pane (see Figure 3.29). The Format Data Labels task pane enables you to specify what to display as the label. The default setting for Label Contains options is Value, but you can display additional label contents, such as the Category Name. However, displaying too much label content can clutter the chart. You can also specify the Label Position, such as Center or Outside End. If the numeric data labels are not formatted, click Number and apply number formats.

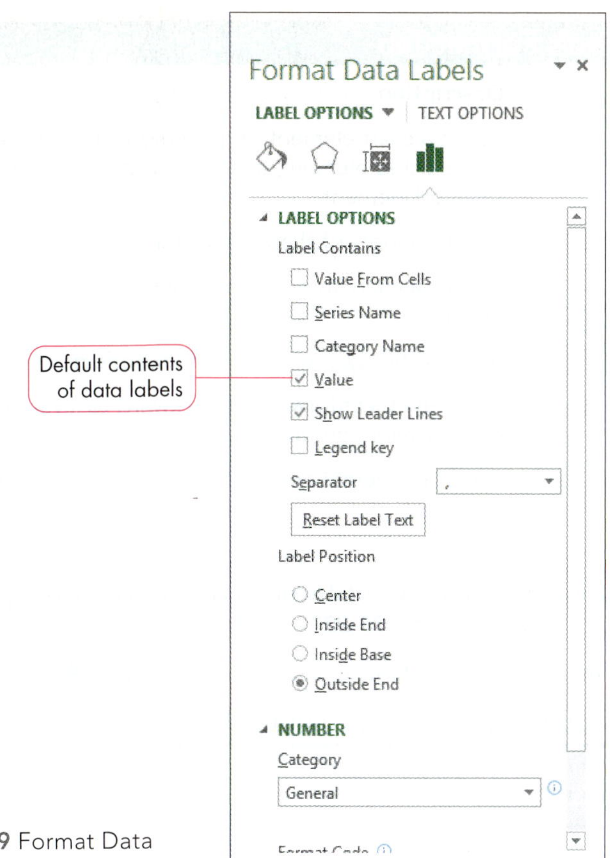

FIGURE 3.29 Format Data Labels Task Pane

> **TIP Pie Chart Data Labels**
>
> When you first create a pie chart, Excel generates a legend to identify the category labels for the different slice colors, but it does not display data labels. You can display Values, Percentages, and even Category Labels on or next to each slice. Pie charts often include percentage data labels. If you also include category labels, remove the legend to avoid duplicating elements.

Use the Chart Tools Format Tab

The Format tab contains options to select a chart element, insert shapes, apply shape styles, apply WordArt styles, arrange objects, and specify the size of an object. Table 3.4 lists and describes the groups on the Format tab.

You can change the color scheme by clicking the Chart Styles button on the right side of the chart and clicking Color or click Change Colors in the Chart Styles group on the Design tab. You can select from the Colorful and Monochromatic sections.

Modifying the Data Source

The data source is the range of worksheet cells that are used to construct a chart. Although you should select the data source carefully before creating a chart, you may decide to alter that data source after you create and format the chart. The Data group on the Design tab is useful for adjusting the data source.

Create Chart Filters

STEP 2»

A ***chart filter*** controls which data series and categories are visible in a chart. By default, all the data you selected to create the chart are used to construct the data series and categories. However, you can apply a chart filter to hide extraneous data. Click the Chart Filter button to the right side of the chart to display the options (see Figure 3.36). A check mark indicates the data series or category currently displayed in the chart. Click a check box to deselect or hide a data series or category.

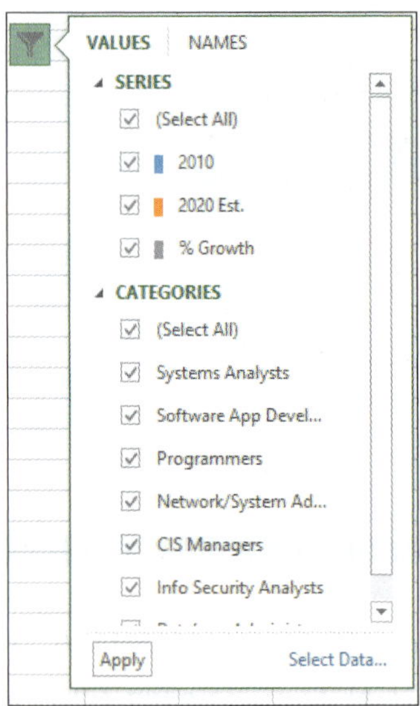

FIGURE 3.36 Chart Filter Options

You can click Select Data in the Data group on the Design tab to open the Select Data Source dialog box (see Figure 3.37). This dialog box is another way to filter which categories and data series are visible in your chart.

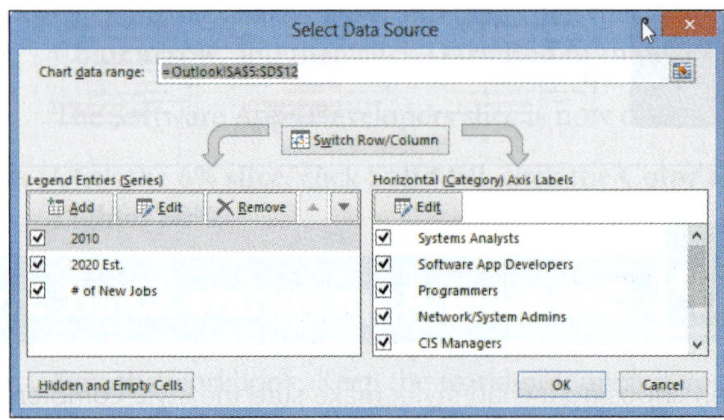

FIGURE 3.37 Select Data Source Dialog Box

Switch Row and Column Data

You can switch data used to create the horizontal axis and the legend. In Figure 3.38, the chart on the left uses the job titles to build the data series and legend, and the years display on the horizontal axis. The chart on the right shows the results after switching the data: the job titles build the horizontal axis, and the years build the data series and legend. To switch the data, click Switch Row/Column in the Data group on the Design tab.

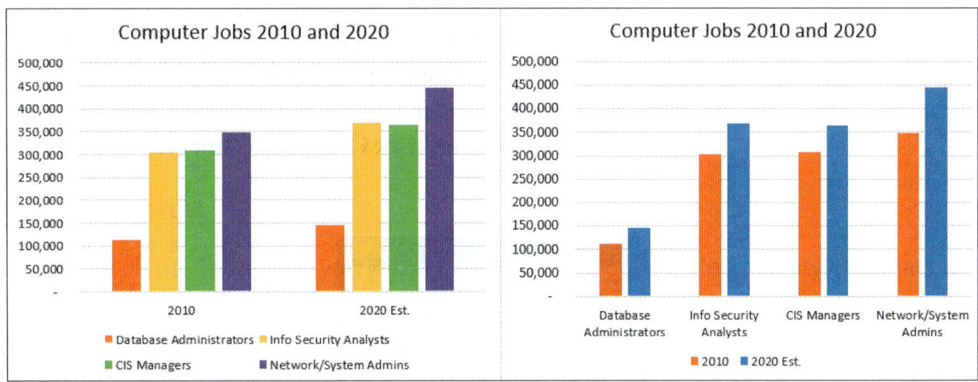

FIGURE 3.38 Original Chart and Chart with Reversed Rows/Columns

Creating and Customizing Sparklines

A ***sparkline*** is a small line, column, or win/loss chart contained in a single cell. The purpose of a sparkline is to present a condensed, simple, succinct visual illustration of data. Unlike a regular chart, a sparkline does not include a chart title or axis labels. Inserting sparklines next to data helps your audience understand data quickly without having to look at a full-scale chart.

Figure 3.39 shows three sample sparklines: line, column, and win/loss. The line sparkline shows trends over time, such as each student's trends in test scores. The column sparkline compares test averages. The win/loss sparkline depicts how many points a team won or lost each game.

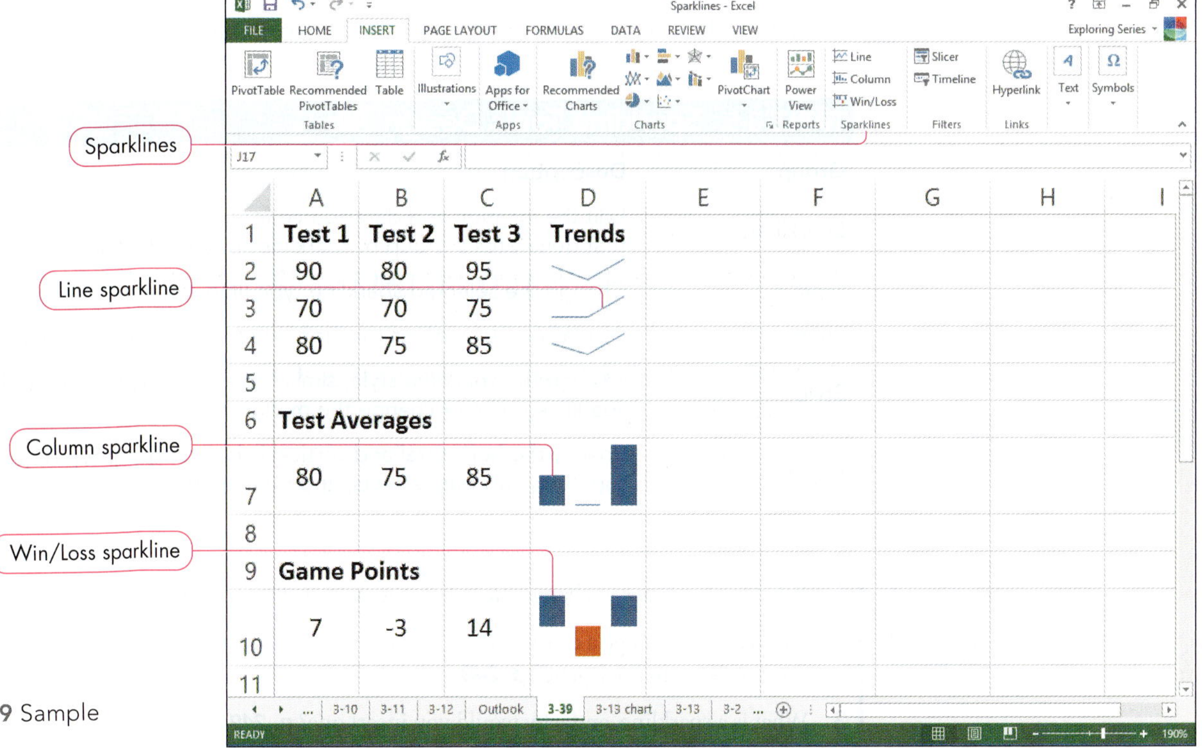

FIGURE 3.39 Sample Sparklines

Mid-Level Exercises

1 Airport Passenger Counts

As an analyst for the airline industry, you track the number of passengers at major U.S. airports. One worksheet you created lists the number of total yearly passengers at the top five airports for four years. To prepare for an upcoming meeting, you need to create a chart to compare the number of passengers for each airport. In addition, you want to insert sparklines to visually represent trends in passengers at each airport.

a. Open *e03m1Airports* and save it as **e03m1Airports_LastFirst**.

b. Create a clustered column chart for the **range A4:E9**. Position the chart to fit in the **range A15:F34**.

c. Customize the chart style by doing the following:
   - Apply **Style 8 chart style**.
   - Select **Color 6** in the *Monochromatic* section of the Change Colors gallery.
   - Change the fill color of the 2011 data series to **White, Background 1**.

d. Enter **Passengers by Top U.S. Airports** as the chart title.

e. Adjust the value axis by doing the following:
   - Change the display units to **Millions** for the value axis.
   - Edit the axis title to display **MILLIONS OF PASSENGERS**.

f. Display data labels above the columns for the 2011 data series only.

g. Insert Line sparklines in the **range F5:F9** to illustrate the data in the **range B5:E9**. This should insert a sparkline to represent yearly data for each airport.

h. Customize the sparklines by doing the following:
   - Show the high and low points in each sparkline.
   - Apply **Black, Text 1 color** to the high point marker in each sparkline.
   - Apply **Dark Red color** to the low point marker in each sparkline.

i. Merge cells in the **range A36:F41**, wrap text, and then apply **Top Align** and **Align Left** alignments.

j. Compose a paragraph that analyzes the trends depicted by the airport sparklines. Notice the overall trends in decreased and increased number of passengers and any unusal activity for an airport. Spell check the worksheet and correct any errors.

k. Insert a footer with your name on the left side, the sheet name code in the center, and the file name code on the right side on all worksheets.

l. Save and close the workbook, and submit based on your instructor's directions.

2 Grade Analysis

You are a teaching assistant for Dr. Monica Unice's introductory psychology class. You have maintained her grade book all semester, entering three test scores for each student and calculating the final average. Dr. Unice wants to see a chart that shows the percentage of students who earn each letter grade. You decide to create a pie chart. She wants to see if a correlation exists between attendance and students' final grades, so you will create a scatter chart.

a. Open *e03m2Psych* and save it as **e03m2Psych_LastFirst**.

b. Create a pie chart from the Final Grade Distribution data located below the student data and move the pie chart to its own sheet named **Grades Pie**.

c. Customize the pie chart with these specifications:
   - Style 7 chart style
   - Chart title: **PSY 2030 Final Grade Distribution - Fall 2016**
   - B grade slice exploded
   - Legend: none

d. Add centered data labels and customize the labels with these specifications:
   - Label captions: **Percentage** and **Category Name**; no values
   - 28-pt size; Black, Text 1 font color, and bold

e. Create a Scatter with only Markers chart using the attendance record and final averages from the Grades worksheet. Move the scatter chart to its own sheet named **Scatter Chart**.

f. Apply these label settings to the scatter chart:
   - Legend: none
   - Chart title: **Attendance-Final Average Relationship**
   - Primary horizontal axis title: **Percentage of Attendance**
   - Primary vertical axis title: **Student Final Averages**

g. Use Help to learn how to apply the following axis settings:
   - Vertical axis: 40 minimum bounds, 100 maximum bounds, 10 major units, and a number format with zero decimal places
   - Horizontal axis: 40 minimum bounds, automatic maximum bounds, automatic units

h. Apply **12 pt font size** to the vertical axis title, vertical axis, horizontal axis title, and horizontal axis.

i. Add the **Parchment texture fill** to the plot area and insert a linear trendline.

j. Insert a footer with your name on the left side, the sheet name code in the center, and the file name code on the right side for the two chart sheets.

k. Save and close the workbook, and submit based on your instructor's directions.

3 Box Office Movies

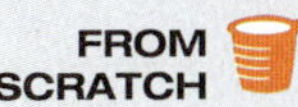

You and two of your friends like to follow the popularity of new movies at the theater. You will research current movies that have been showing for four weeks and decide which movies to report on. Work in teams of three for this activity. After obtaining the data, your team will create applicable charts to illustrate the revenue data. Team members will critique each other's charts.

a. Have all three team members log in to a chat client and engage in a dialogue about which movies are currently playing. Each member should research a different theater to see what is playing at that theater. Decide on six movies that have been in theaters for at least four weeks to research. Save a copy of your instant message dialogue and submit based on your instructor's directions.

b. Divide the six movies among the three team members. Each member should research the revenue reported for two movies for the past four weeks. Make sure your team members use the same source to find the data.

Student 1:

c. Create a new Excel workbook and enter appropriate column labels and the four-week data for all six movies. Name Sheet1 **Data**.

d. Format the data appropriately. Save the workbook as **e03t1CurrentMovies_GroupName**. Upload the workbook to a shared location, such as SkyDrive, and contact the next student.

Student 2:

e. Create a line chart to show the trends in revenue for the movies for the four-week period.

f. Add a chart title, format the axes appropriately, select a chart style, and then apply other formatting.

g. Move the chart to its own sheet named **Trends**. Save the workbook, upload it to the shared location, and then contact the next student.

Student 3:

h. Add a column to the right of the four-week data and total each movie's four-week revenue.

i. Create a pie chart depicting each movie's percentage of the total revenue for your selected movies.

j. Add a chart title, explode one pie slice, add data labels showing percentages and movie names, and then apply other formatting.

k. Move the chart to its own sheet named **Revenue Chart**. Save the workbook, upload it to the shared location, and then contact the first student.

Student 1:

l. Critique the charts. Insert a new worksheet named **Chart Critique** that provides an organized critique of each chart. Type notes that list each team member's name and specify what each student's role was in completing this exercise.

m. Save the workbook, upload it to the shared location, and then contact the second student.

Student 2:

n. Read the critique of the line chart and make any appropriate changes for the line chart. On the critique worksheet, provide a response to each critique and why you made or did not make the suggested change.

o. Save the workbook, upload it to the shared location, and then contact the third student.

Student 3:

p. Read the critique of the pie chart and make any appropriate changes for the pie chart. On the critique worksheet, provide a response to each critique and why you made or did not make the suggested change.

q. Save and close the workbook. Submit based on your instructor's directions.

Beyond the Classroom

Historical Stock Prices

You are interested in investing in the stock market. First, you need to research the historical prices for a particular stock. Launch a Web browser, go to money.msn.com/investing/, type a company name, such as Apple, and then select the company name from a list of suggested companies. Click the **Historical Prices link**. Copy the stock data (date, high, low, open, close, volume) for a six-month period and paste it in a new workbook, adjusting the column widths to fit the data. Save the workbook as **e03b2StockData_LastFirst**. Rename Sheet1 **Data**. Display data for only the first date listed for each month; delete rows containing data for other dates. Sort the list from the oldest date to the newest date. Use Help if needed to learn how to sort data and how to create a Volume-Open-High-Low-Close chart. Then rearrange the data columns in the correct sequence. Format the data and column labels. Insert a row to enter the company name and insert another row to list the company's stock symbol, such as AAPL. Copy the URL from the Web browser and paste it as a source below the list of data and the date you obtained the data. Merge the cells containing the company name and stock symbol through the last column of data and word-wrap the URL.

Create a Volume-Open-High-Low-Close chart on a new chart sheet named **Chart**. Type an appropriate chart title. Set the primary vertical axis (left side) unit measurement to millions and include an axis title **Volume in Millions**. Include a secondary vertical axis (right side) title **Stock Prices**. Apply **Currency number style** with 0 decimal places for the secondary axis values. Apply **11-pt size** to the vertical axes and category axis. Use Help to research how to insert text boxes. Insert a text box that describes the stock chart: white fill rectangles indicate the closing price was higher than the opening price; black fill rectangles indicate the closing price was lower than the opening price; etc. Create a footer with your name, the sheet name code, and the file name code on both worksheets. Save and close the workbook, and submit based on your instructor's directions.

Harper County Houses Sold

You want to analyze the number of houses sold by type (e.g., rambler, two story, etc.) in each quarter during 2012. Your intern created an initial chart, but it contains a lot of problems. Open *e03b3Houses* and save it as **e03b3Houses_LastFirst**. Identify the errors and poor design for the chart. Below the chart, list the errors and your corrections in a two-column format. Then correct problems in the chart. Create a footer with your name, the sheet name code, and the file name code. Adjust the margins and scaling to print the worksheet data, including the error list, and the chart on one page. Save and close the workbook, and submit based on your instructor's directions.

Time Management

FROM SCRATCH

After reviewing the video on time-management skills, start a new workbook and save it as **e03b4Time_LastFirst**. List the major activities you do each week (e.g., sleeping, attending classes, eating, etc.) in the first column. In the second column, enter the number of hours per week you spend on each task. For example, if you sleep 8 hours each night, enter 56 (8 hours × 7 nights). Insert the SUM function to total the hours. The total hours per week is 168, so the total time of all activities should be 168. Adjust any values until the total is correct. Create a pie chart based on this data, include and format percentage data labels, and include an appropriate chart title. Below the data and chart, type a recommendation for yourself to improve your time-management skills. Create a footer with your name, the sheet name code, and the file name code. Save and close the workbook, and submit based on your instructor's directions.

Capstone Exercise

You are an assistant manager at Premiere Movie Source, an online company that enables customers to download movies for a fee. You need to track movie download sales by genre. You gathered the data for November 2016 and organized it in an Excel workbook. You are ready to create charts to help represent the data so that you can make a presentation to your manager later this week.

Set Chart Filters, Position, and Size

You created a clustered column chart, but you selected too many cells for the data source. You need to open the workbook and set chart filters to exclude extraneous data sources. In addition, you want to position and size the chart below the data.

a. Open the *e03c1Movies* workbook and save it as **e03c1Movies_LastFirst**.

b. Set chart filters to remove the Category Totals and the Weekly Totals.

c. Position and size the chart to fill the **range A18:K37**.

d. Change the row and column orientation so that the weeks appear in the category axis and the genres appear in the legend.

Add Chart Labels

You need to enter text for the chart title and add a value axis title. In addition, you want to position the legend on the right side because it is easier to read a vertical, alphabetical list rather than a horizontal list of genres.

a. Enter the text **November 2016 Downloads by Genre** as the chart title, bold the title, and then apply **Black, Text 1 font color**.

b. Add a value axis title: **Number of Downloads**. Apply **Black, Text 1 font color**.

c. Move the legend to the right side of the chart.

Format Chart Elements

You are ready to apply the finishing touches to the clustered column chart. You will format the category axis by adjusting the font size and applying a darker font color. You will add and adjust data labels to the Drama data series to emphasize this series.

a. Format the category axis with **11-pt size** and **Black, Text 1 font color**.

b. Select the **Drama data series** and add data labels in the Outside End position.

c. Add a **Gradient fill** to the data labels.

Insert and Format Sparklines

You want to show weekly trends for each genre by inserting sparklines in the column to the right of Category Totals.

a. Click **cell G5** and insert Line Sparklines for the weekly data for each category and the weekly totals, but do not include the category totals for the data range. The location range should be **G5:G15**.

b. Apply the **Sparkline Style Accent 3 (no dark or light) sparkline style**.

c. Show the high point and markers.

d. Change the high point marker color to **Red**.

Create a Stacked Bar Chart

You want to create a bar chart to show how the weekly totals contribute to the month totals by genre.

a. Select the **range A4:E14**. Create a clustered bar chart.

b. Move the chart to its own sheet named **Bar Chart**.

c. Change the chart type to a stacked bar chart.

d. Add a chart title above the chart and enter **November 2016 Weekly Downloads**.

Format the Bar Chart

You want to enhance the appearance of the chart by applying a chart style and adjusting the axis values.

a. Apply bold and **Blue, Accent 5 font color** to the chart title.

b. Apply **11-pt font size** to the category axis, value axis, and the legend.

c. Use the AXIS OPTIONS to display the value axis in units of **Thousands**, set the Major Units to **500**, and apply the **Number format** with 1 decimal place.

d. Use the AXIS OPTIONS to format the category axis so that the category labels are in reverse order.

Finalizing the Charts

You want to prepare the workbook in case someone wants to print the data and charts. To ensure the worksheet data and chart print on the same page, you need to adjust the page setup options.

a. Create a footer on each worksheet with your name, the sheet name code, and the file name code.

b. Apply **landscape orientation** for the Data worksheet.

c. Set **0.2"** left, right, top, and bottom margins for the original worksheet.

d. Change the scaling so that the worksheet fits on only one page.

e. Save and close the workbook, and submit based on your instructor's directions.

Excel

Datasets and Tables

CHAPTER 4

Managing Large Volumes of Data

Yuri Arcurs/Shutterstock

OBJECTIVES AFTER YOU READ THIS CHAPTER, YOU WILL BE ABLE TO:

CASE STUDY | Reid Furniture Store

Vicki Reid owns Reid Furniture Store in Portland, Oregon. She divided her store into four departments: Living Room, Bedroom, Dining Room, and Appliances. All merchandise is categorized into one of these four departments for inventory records and sales. Vicki has four sales representatives: Chantalle Desmarais, Jade Gallagher, Sebastian Gruenewald, and Ambrose Sardelis. The sales system tracks which sales representative processed each transaction.

The business has grown rapidly, and Vicki hired you to analyze the sales data in order to increase future profits. For example, which department generates the most sales? Who is the leading salesperson? Do most customers purchase or finance? Are sales promotions necessary to promote business, or will customers pay the full price?

You downloaded March 2016 data from the sales system into an Excel workbook. To avoid extraneous data that is not needed in the analysis, you did not include customer names, accounts, or specific product numbers. The downloaded file contains transaction numbers, dates, sales representative names, departments, general merchandise description, total price, payment type, transaction type, and the total price.

Large Datasets

So far you have worked with worksheets that contain small datasets, a collection of structured, related data in a limited number of columns and rows. In reality, you will probably work with large datasets consisting of hundreds or thousands of rows and columns of data. When you work with small datasets, you can usually view most or all of the data without scrolling. When you work with large datasets, you probably will not be able to see the entire dataset onscreen even on a large, widescreen monitor set at high resolution. You might want to keep the column and row labels always in view, even as you scroll throughout the dataset. Figure 4.1 shows the Reid Furniture Store's March 2016 sales transactions. Because it contains a lot of transactions, the entire dataset is not visible. You could decrease the zoom level to display more transactions; however, doing so decreases the text size onscreen, making it hard to read the data.

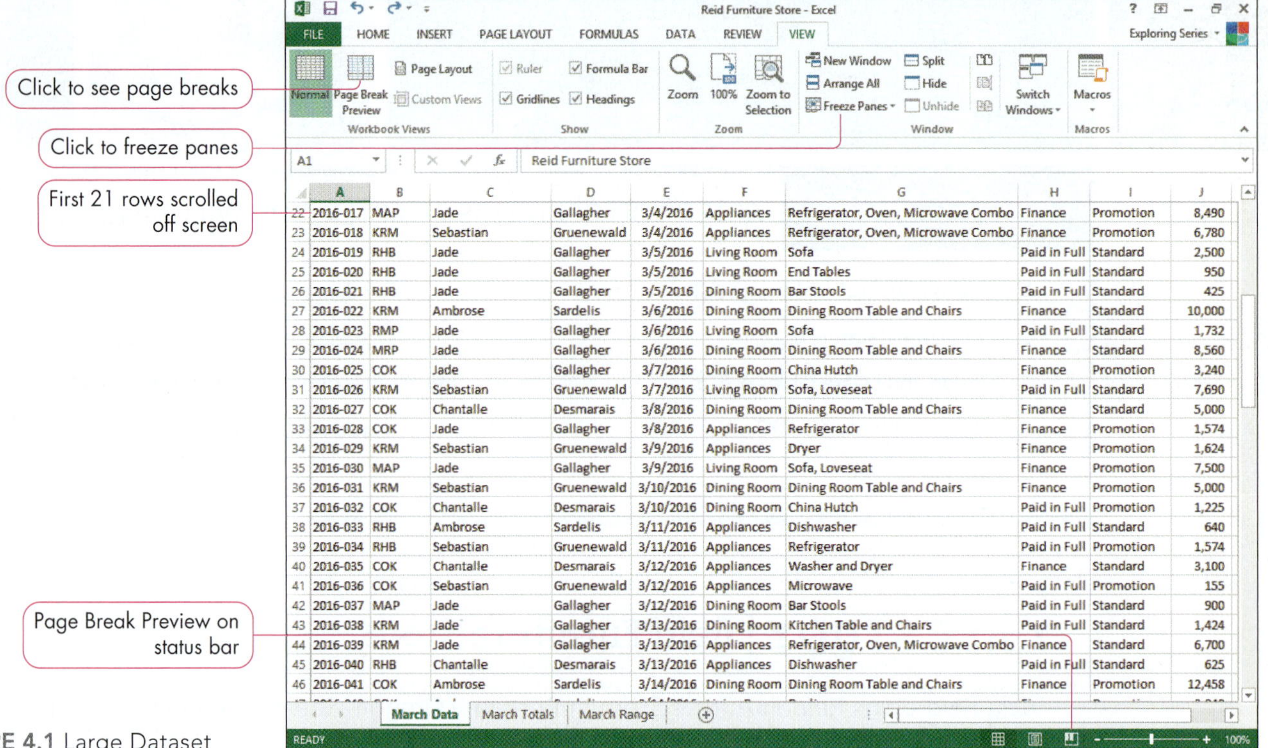

FIGURE 4.1 Large Dataset

As you work with larger datasets, realize that the data will not always fit on one page. You will need to preview the automatic page breaks and probably insert some manual page breaks in more desirable locations, or you might want to print only a selected range within the large dataset to distribute to others.

In this section, you will learn how to keep labels onscreen as you scroll through a large dataset. In addition, you will learn how to manage page breaks, print only a range instead of an entire worksheet, and print column labels at the top of each page of a large dataset.

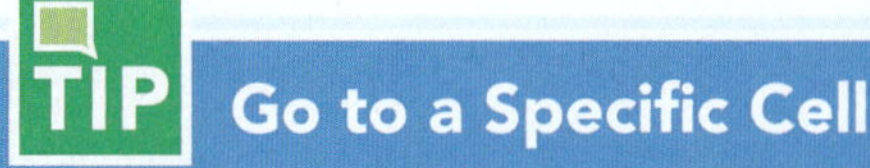

TIP Go to a Specific Cell

You can navigate through a large worksheet by using the Go To command. Click Find & Select in the Editing group on the Home tab and select Go To (or press F5 or Ctrl+G) to display the Go To dialog box, enter the cell address in the Reference box, and then press Enter to go to the cell.

You can also click in the Name Box, type the cell reference, and then press Enter to go to a specific cell.

Freezing Rows and Columns

When you scroll to parts of a dataset not initially visible, some rows and columns disappear from view. When the row and column labels scroll off the screen, you may not remember what each column represents. You can keep labels onscreen by freezing them. ***Freezing*** is the process of keeping rows and/or columns visible onscreen at all times even when you scroll through a large dataset. Table 4.1 describes the three freeze options.

TABLE 4.1 Freeze Options

Option	Description
Freeze Panes	Keeps both rows and columns above and to the left of the active cell visible as you scroll through a worksheet.
Freeze Top Row	Keeps only the top row visible as you scroll through a worksheet.
Freeze First Column	Keeps only the first column visible as you scroll through a worksheet.

STEP 1 »

To freeze labels, click the View tab, click Freeze Panes in the Window group, and then select a freeze option. To freeze one or more rows and columns, use the Freeze Panes option. Before selecting this option, make the active cell one row below and one column to the right of the rows and columns you want to freeze. For example, to freeze the first five rows and the first column, make cell B6 the active cell before clicking the Freeze Panes option. As Figure 4.2 shows, Excel displays a horizontal line below the last frozen row (row 5) and a vertical line to the right of the last frozen column (column A). Unfrozen rows (such as rows 6–14) and unfrozen columns (such as columns B and C) are no longer visible as you scroll down and to the right, respectively.

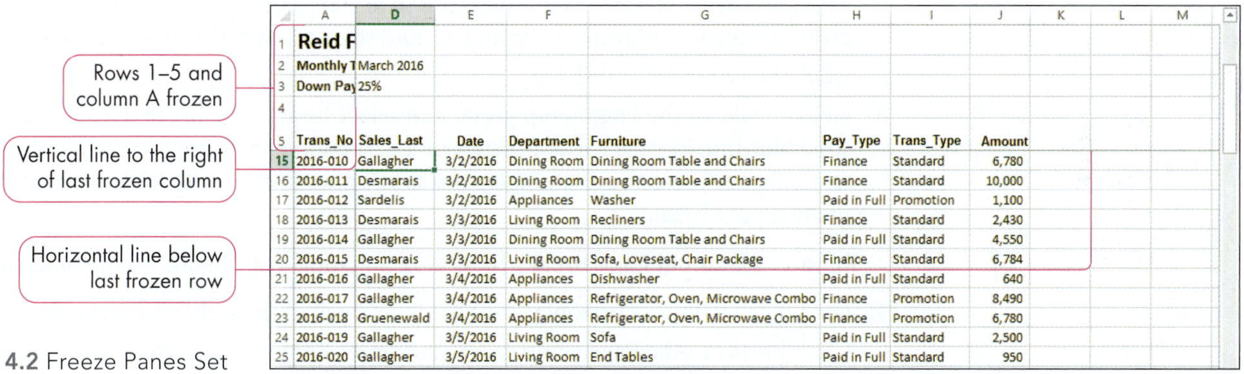

Rows 1–5 and column A frozen

Vertical line to the right of last frozen column

Horizontal line below last frozen row

	A	D	E	F	G	H	I	J	K	L	M
1	Reid F										
2	Monthly T	March 2016									
3	Down Pa	25%									
4											
5	Trans_No	Sales_Last	Date	Department	Furniture	Pay_Type	Trans_Type	Amount			
15	2016-010	Gallagher	3/2/2016	Dining Room	Dining Room Table and Chairs	Finance	Standard	6,780			
16	2016-011	Desmarais	3/2/2016	Dining Room	Dining Room Table and Chairs	Finance	Standard	10,000			
17	2016-012	Sardelis	3/2/2016	Appliances	Washer	Paid in Full	Promotion	1,100			
18	2016-013	Desmarais	3/3/2016	Living Room	Recliners	Finance	Standard	2,430			
19	2016-014	Gallagher	3/3/2016	Dining Room	Dining Room Table and Chairs	Paid in Full	Standard	4,550			
20	2016-015	Desmarais	3/3/2016	Living Room	Sofa, Loveseat, Chair Package	Finance	Standard	6,784			
21	2016-016	Gallagher	3/4/2016	Appliances	Dishwasher	Paid in Full	Standard	640			
22	2016-017	Gallagher	3/4/2016	Appliances	Refrigerator, Oven, Microwave Combo	Finance	Promotion	8,490			
23	2016-018	Gruenewald	3/4/2016	Appliances	Refrigerator, Oven, Microwave Combo	Finance	Promotion	6,780			
24	2016-019	Gallagher	3/5/2016	Living Room	Sofa	Paid in Full	Standard	2,500			
25	2016-020	Gallagher	3/5/2016	Living Room	End Tables	Paid in Full	Standard	950			

FIGURE 4.2 Freeze Panes Set

To unlock the rows and columns from remaining onscreen as you scroll, click Freeze Panes in the Window group and select Unfreeze Panes, which only appears on the menu when you have frozen rows and/or columns. After you unfreeze the panes, the Freeze Panes option appears instead of Unfreeze Panes on the menu again.

When you freeze panes and press Ctrl+Home, the first unfrozen cell is the active cell instead of cell A1. For example, with column A and rows 1 through 5 frozen in Figure 4.2, pressing Ctrl+Home makes cell B6 the active cell. If you need to edit a cell in the frozen area, click the particular cell to make it active and edit the data.

Printing Large Datasets

For a large dataset, some columns and rows may print on several pages. Analyzing the data on individual printed pages is difficult when each page does not contain column and row labels. To prevent wasting paper, always use Print Preview. Doing so enables you to adjust page settings until you are satisfied with how the data will print.

The Page Layout tab (see Figure 4.3) contains options to help you prepare large datasets to print. Previously, you changed the page orientation, set different margins, and adjusted the scaling. In addition, you can manage page breaks, set the print area, and print titles.

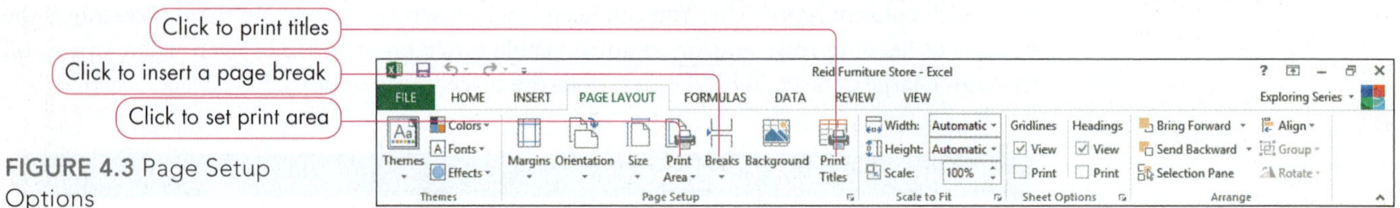

FIGURE 4.3 Page Setup Options

Display and Change Page Breaks

Based on the paper size, orientation, margins, and other settings, Excel identifies how much data can print on a page. Then it displays a ***page break***, indicating where data will start on another printed page. To identify where these automatic page breaks will occur, click Page Break Preview on the status bar or in the Workbook Views group on the View tab. In Page Break Preview, Excel displays watermarks, such as *Page 1*, indicating the area that will print on a specific page. Blue dashed lines indicate where the automatic page breaks occur, and solid blue lines indicate manual page breaks.

If the automatic page breaks occur in undesirable locations, you can adjust the page breaks. For example, if you have a worksheet listing sales data by date, the automatic page break might occur within a group of rows for one date, such as between two rows of data for 3/14/2016. To make all rows for that date appear together, you can either insert a page break above the first data row for that date or decrease the margins so that all 3/14/2015 transactions fit at the bottom of the page. To do this, drag a page break line to the desired location.

Manual Page Break: Do the following to set a manual break at a specific location:

STEP 2»

1. Click the cell that you want to be the first row and column on a new printed page. For example, click cell A50 if you want cell A50 to start a new page. If you click cell D50, you create a page for columns A through C, and then column D starts a new page.
2. Click the PAGE LAYOUT tab.
3. Click Breaks in the Page Setup group and select Insert Page Break. Excel displays a solid blue line in Page Break Preview or a dashed line in Normal view to indicate the manual page breaks you set. Figure 4.4 shows a worksheet with both automatic and manual page breaks.

Remove a Manual Page Break: To remove a manual page break, do the following:

1. Click a cell below a horizontal page break or a cell to the right of a vertical page break.
2. Click Breaks in the Page Setup group and select Remove Page Break.

Reset Page Breaks: To reset all page breaks back to the automatic page breaks, do the following:

1. Click Breaks in the Page Setup group.
2. Select Reset All Page Breaks.

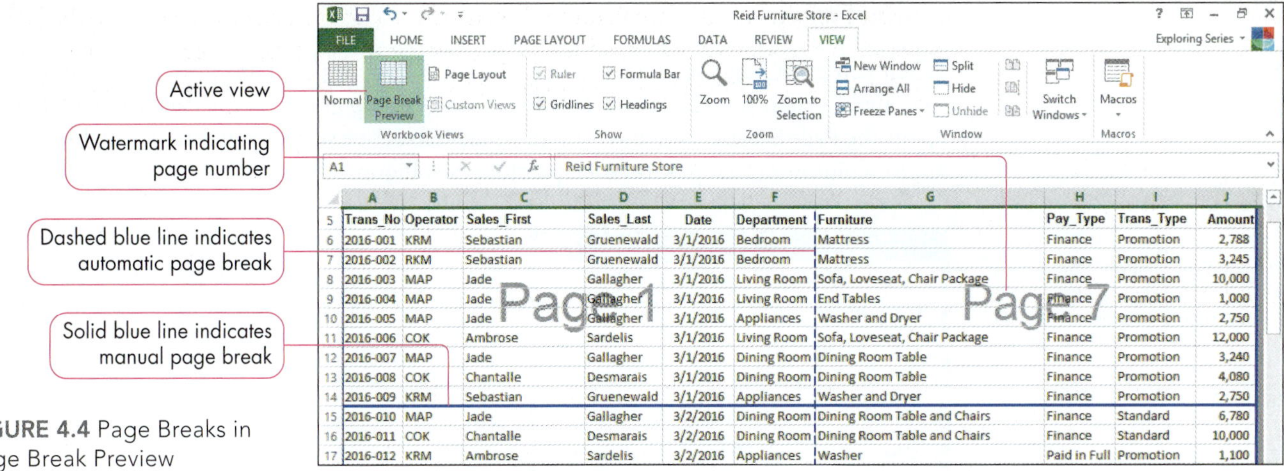

FIGURE 4.4 Page Breaks in Page Break Preview

Set and Clear a Print Area

The default Print settings send an entire dataset on the active worksheet to the printer. However, you might want to print only part of the worksheet data. If you display the worksheet in Page Break view, you can identify which page(s) you want to print. Then click the File tab and select Print. Type the number(s) of the page(s) you want to print. For example, to print page 2 only, type 2 in the Pages text box and in the *to* text box.

You can further restrict what is printed by setting the ***print area***, which is the range of cells that will print. For example, you might want to print only an input area or just the transactions that occurred on a particular date. To set a print area, do the following:

STEP 3»

1. Select the range you want to print.
2. Click the PAGE LAYOUT tab and click Print Area in the Page Setup group.
3. Select Set Print Area.

In Page Break Preview, the print area has a white background and solid blue border; the rest of the worksheet has a gray background (see Figure 4.5). In Normal view or Page Layout view, the print area is surrounded by thin gray lines.

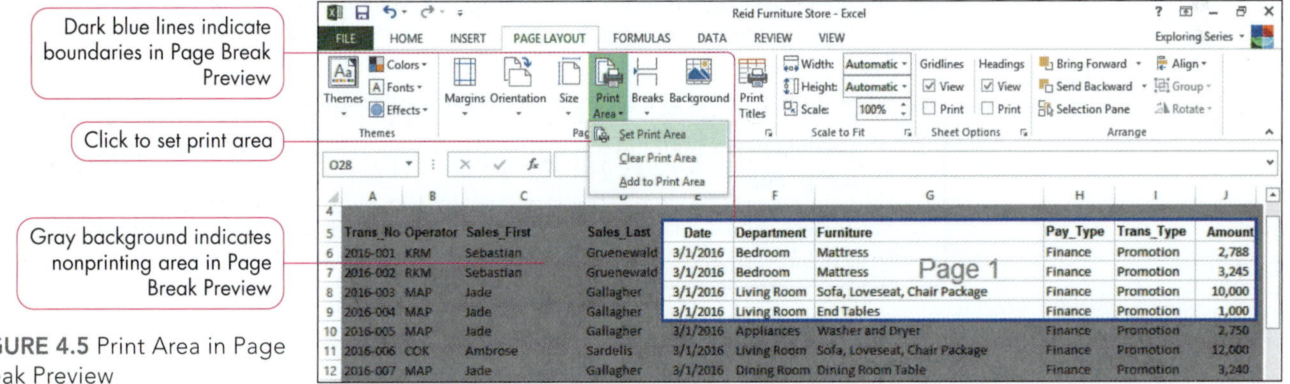

FIGURE 4.5 Print Area in Page Break Preview

To add print areas where each print area will print on a separate page, select the range you want to print, click Print Area, and then select *Add to Print Area*. To clear the print area, click Print Area in the Page Setup group and select Clear Print Area.

TIP Print a Selection

Another way to print part of a worksheet is to select the range you want to print. Click the File tab and click Print. Click the first arrow in the *Settings* section and select Print Selection.

Print Titles

When you print large datasets, it is helpful that every page contains descriptive column and row labels. When you click Print Titles in the Page Setup group on the Page Layout tab, Excel opens the Page Setup dialog box with the Sheet tab active so that you can select which row(s) and/or column(s) to repeat on each printout (see Figure 4.6).

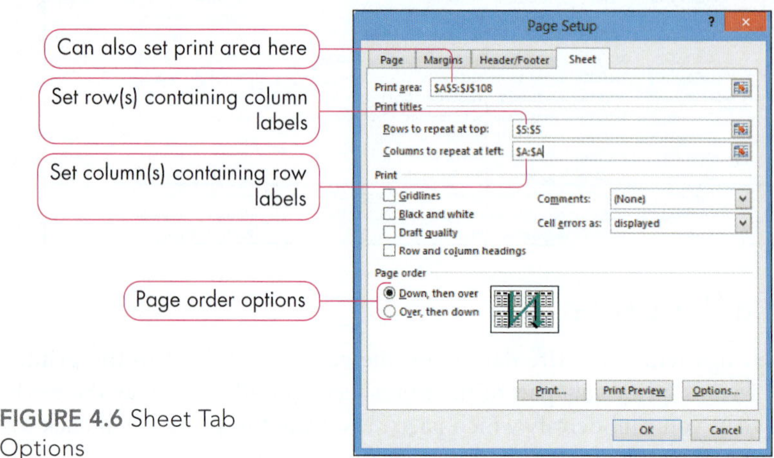

FIGURE 4.6 Sheet Tab Options

To print the column labels at the top of each page, select the row(s) that contain the labels or titles (such as row 5) in the *Rows to repeat at top* box to display $5:$5. To print the row labels at the left side of each page, select the column(s) that contain the labels or titles (such as column A) in the *Columns to repeat at left* box to display AA.

Control Print Page Order

Print order is the sequence in which the pages are printed. By default, the pages print in this order: top-left section, bottom-left section, top-right section, and bottom-right section. However, you might want to print the entire top portion of the worksheet before printing the bottom portion. To change the print order, open the Page Setup dialog box, click the Sheet tab, and then select the desired *Page order* option (see Figure 4.6).

1. What is the purpose of freezing panes in a worksheet? ***p. 267***
2. Why would you want to insert page breaks instead of using the automatic page breaks? ***p. 268***
3. What steps should you take to ensure that column labels display on each printed page of a large dataset? ***p. 270***

Hands-On Exercises

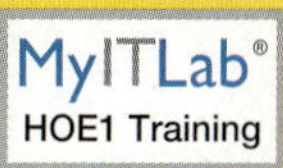

1 Large Datasets

You want to review the large dataset that shows the March 2016 transactions for Reid Furniture Store. You will need to view the data and adjust some page setup options so that you can print necessary labels on each page.

Skills covered: Freeze Rows and Columns • Manage Page Breaks • Set and Clear a Print Area • Print Titles

STEP 1 » FREEZE ROWS AND COLUMNS

Before printing the March 2016 transaction dataset, you want to view the data. The dataset contains more rows than will display onscreen at the same time. You decide to freeze the column and row labels to stay onscreen as you scroll through the transactions. Refer to Figure 4.7 as you complete Step 1.

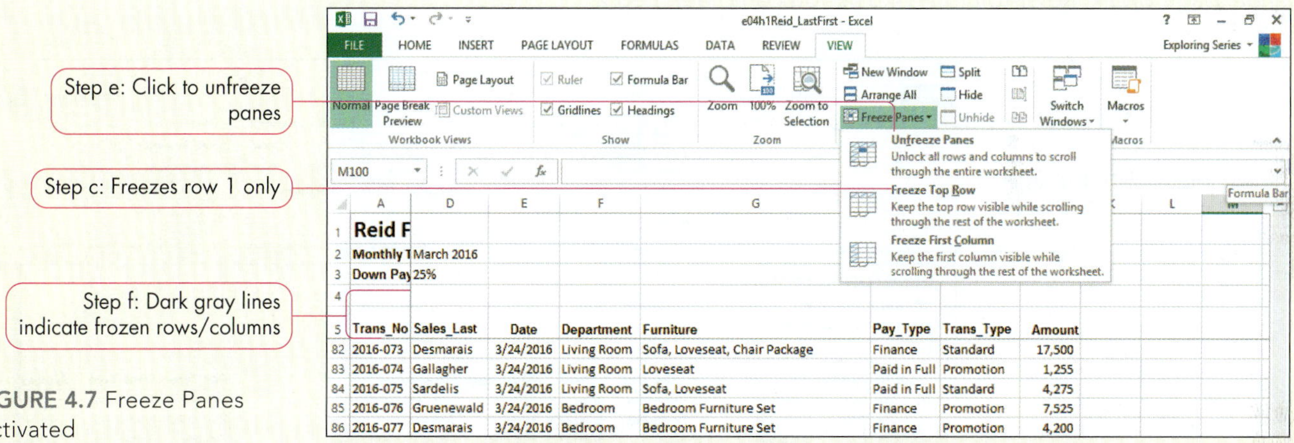

FIGURE 4.7 Freeze Panes Activated

a. Open *e04h1Reid* and save it as **e04h1Reid_LastFirst**.

> **TROUBLESHOOTING:** If you make any major mistakes in this exercise, you can close the file, open *e04h1Reid* again, and then start this exercise over.

The workbook contains three worksheets: March Data (for Hands-On Exercises 1–3), March Totals (for Hands-On Exercise 4), and March Range (for Hands-On Exercise 5).

b. Press **Page Down** four times to scroll through the dataset. Then press **Ctrl+Home** to go back to the top of the worksheet.

   After you press Page Down, the column labels in row 5 scroll off the screen, making it challenging to remember what type of data are in some columns.

c. Click the **VIEW tab**, click **Freeze Panes** in the Window group, and then select **Freeze Top Row**.

   A dark gray horizontal line displays between rows 1 and 2.

d. Press **Page Down** to scroll down through the worksheet.

   As rows scroll off the top of the Excel window, the first row remains frozen onscreen. The title by itself is not helpful; you need to freeze the column labels as well.

e. Click **Freeze Panes** in the Window group and select **Unfreeze Panes**.

f. Click **cell B6**, the cell below the row and one column to the right of what you want to freeze. Click **Freeze Panes** in the Window group and select **Freeze Panes.**

Excel displays a vertical line between columns A and B, indicating that column A is frozen, and a horizontal line between rows 5 and 6, indicating the first five rows are frozen.

g. Press **Ctrl+G**, type **M100** in the **Reference box** of the Go To dialog box, and then click **OK** to make cell M100 the active cell. Save the workbook.

Rows 6 through 81 and columns B and C are not visible because they scrolled off the screen.

TROUBLESHOOTING: Your screen may differ from Figure 4.7 due to different Windows resolution settings. If necessary, continue scrolling right and down until you see columns and rows scrolling offscreen.

STEP 2 » MANAGE PAGE BREAKS

You plan to print the dataset so that you and Vicki Reid can discuss the transactions in your weekly meeting. Because the large dataset will not fit on one page, you want to see where the automatic page breaks are and then insert a manual page break. Refer to Figure 4.8 as you complete Step 2.

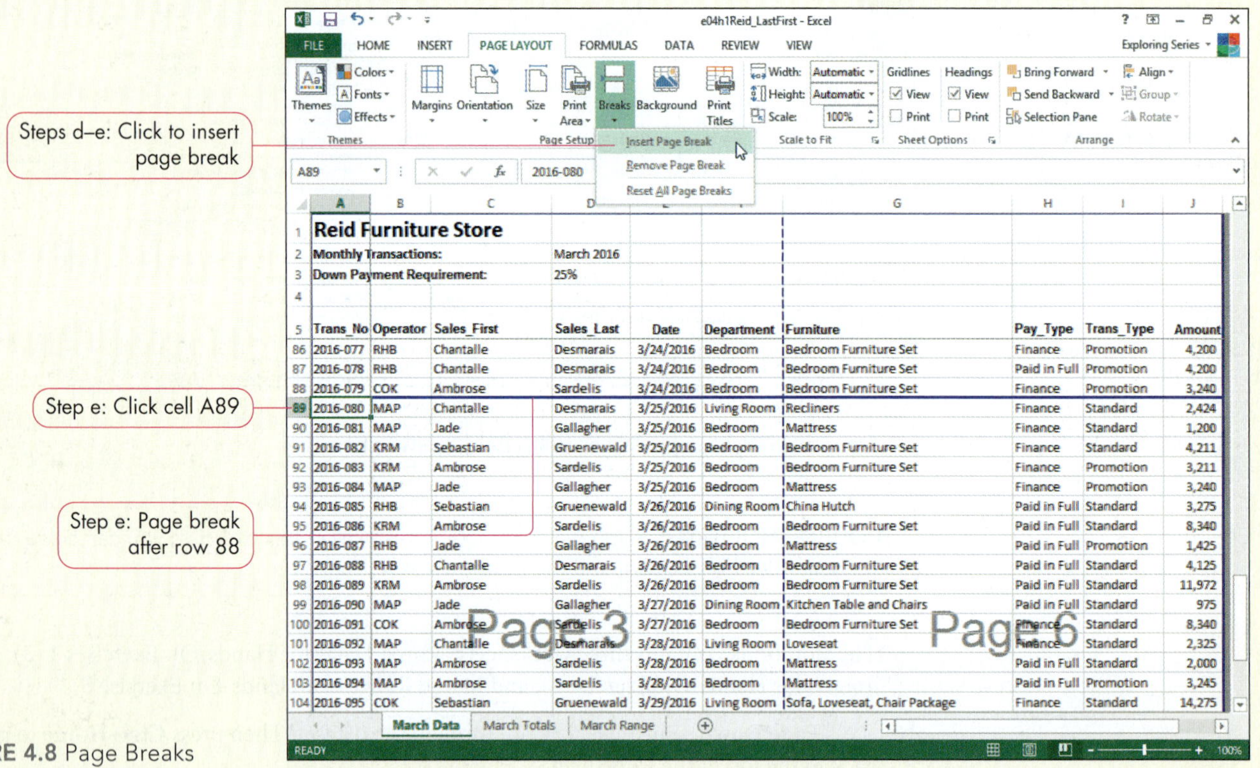

FIGURE 4.8 Page Breaks

a. Press **Ctrl+Home** to move to **cell B6**, the first cell in the unfrozen area. Click the **VIEW tab**, if necessary, and click **Page Break Preview** in the Workbook Views group or on the status bar.

Excel displays blue dashed lines to indicate the automatic page breaks.

b. Scroll down until you see row 44 below the frozen column labels.

The automatic horizontal page break is between rows 46 and 47 (or between rows 45 and 46). You do not want transactions for a particular day to span between printed pages, so you need to move the page break up to keep all 3/13/2016 transactions together.

c. Click **cell A45**, the first cell containing 3/13/2016 data and the cell to start the top of the second page.

d. Click the **PAGE LAYOUT tab**, click **Breaks** in the Page Setup group, and then select **Insert Page Break**.

You inserted a page break between rows 44 and 45 so that the 3/13/2016 transactions will be on one page.

e. Click **cell A89**, click **Breaks** in the Page Setup group, and then select **Insert Page Break**. Save the workbook.

You inserted a page break between rows 88 and 89 to keep the 3/25/2016 transactions on the same page.

Using the Mouse Pointer to Move Page Breaks

To use the mouse pointer to adjust a page break, position the mouse pointer on the page break line to see the two-headed arrow and drag the line to where you want the page break to occur.

STEP 3 » SET AND CLEAR A PRINT AREA

You want to focus on the transactions for only March 1, 2016. To avoid printing more data than you need, you will set the print area to print transactions for only that day. Refer to Figure 4.9 as you complete Step 3.

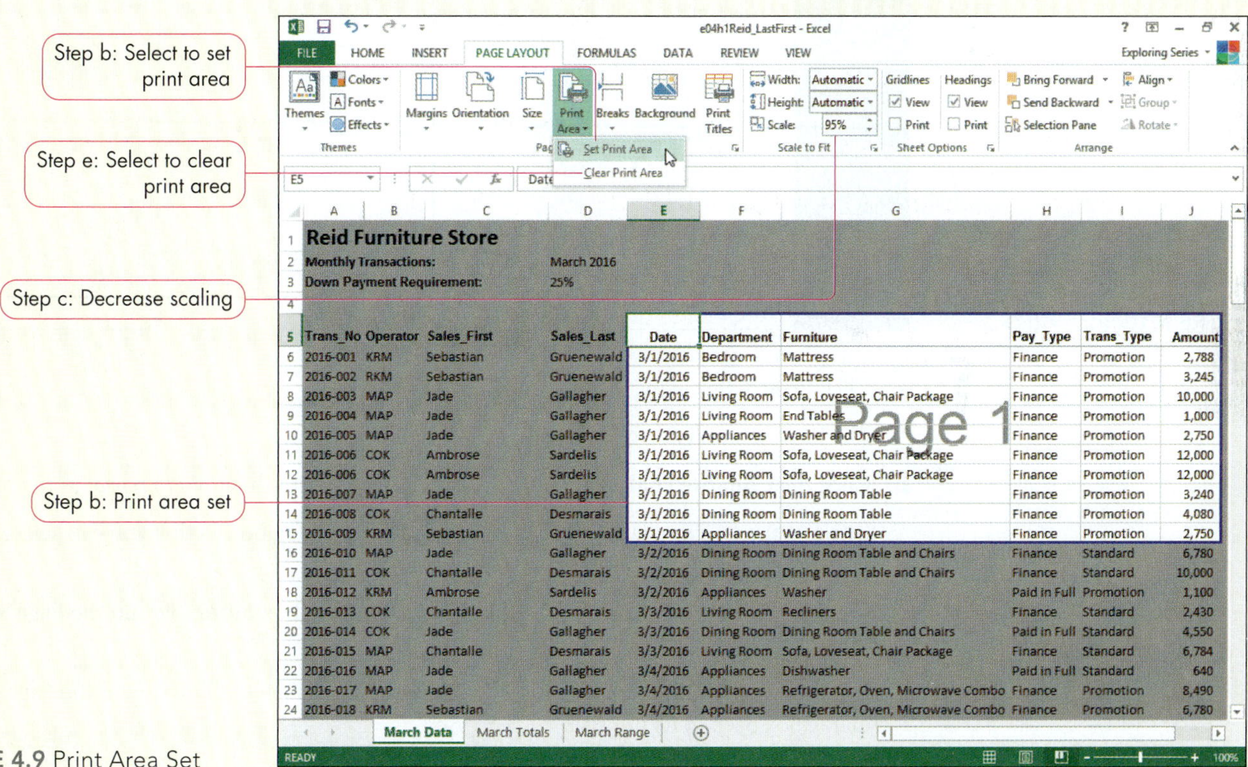

FIGURE 4.9 Print Area Set

a. Scroll up to see the first row of March data. Select the **range E5:J15**, the range of data for March 1, 2016.

b. Click the **PAGE LAYOUT tab**, if necessary, click **Print Area** in the Page Setup group, and then select **Set Print Area**.

Excel displays the print area with a solid blue border. A dotted blue line displays between columns I and J, indicating an automatic page break. The rest of the worksheet displays with a gray background.

c. Click **cell E5** and click the **Scale arrow** down one time in the *Scale to Fit* group.

The selected print area will print on one page.

d. Press **Ctrl+P** to see that only the print area will print. Press **Esc**.

e. Click **Print Area** in the Page Setup group and select **Clear Print Area**. Save the workbook.

STEP 4 » PRINT TITLES

Only the first page will print both row and column labels. Pages 2 and 3 will print the remaining row labels, Page 4 will print the remaining column labels, and Pages 5 and 6 will not print either label. You want to make sure the column and row labels print on all pages. To do this, you will print titles. Refer to Figure 4.10 as you complete Step 4.

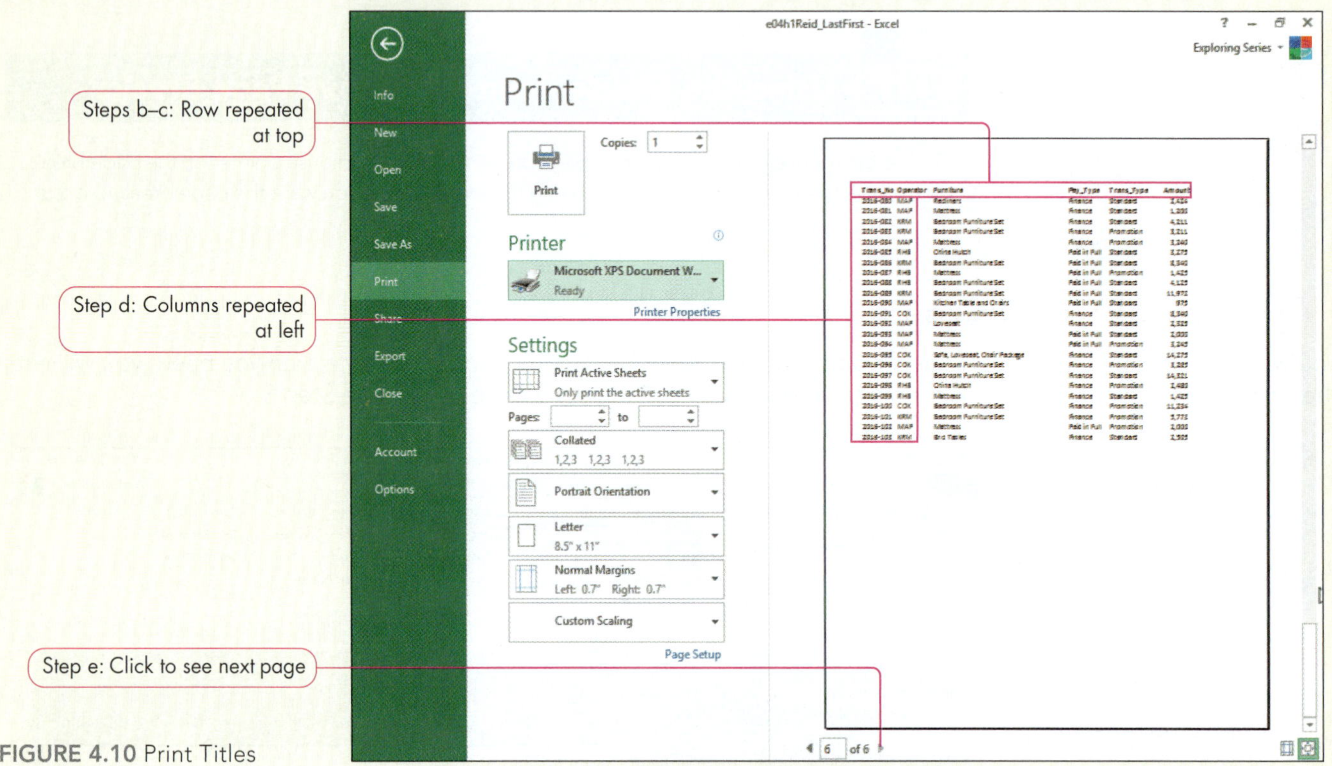

FIGURE 4.10 Print Titles

a. Click **Print Titles** in the Page Setup group.

   The Page Setup dialog box opens, displaying the Sheet tab.

b. Click the **Collapse Dialog box button** on the right side of the *Rows to repeat at top* box.

   Clicking the *Collapse Dialog box* button reduces the dialog box so that you can select a range in the worksheet easily.

c. Click the **row 5 heading** and click the **Collapse Dialog box button** within the Page Setup: Rows to repeat at top dialog box.

   You selected the fifth row, which contains the column labels, and expanded the Page Setup dialog box back to its full size.

d. Click in the **Columns to repeat at left box**, type **A:B**, and then click **Print Preview**.

e. Click **Next Page** at the bottom of the Microsoft Office Backstage view. Click **Next Page** until the sixth page displays.

   Figure 4.10 shows a preview of the sixth page. The column labels and the first two columns appear on all pages.

f. Click the **Back arrow** in the top-left corner of the Microsoft Office Backstage view.

g. Save the workbook. Keep the workbook onscreen if you plan to continue with the next Hands-On Exercise. If not, close the workbook and exit Excel.

Excel Tables

All organizations maintain lists of data. Businesses maintain inventory lists, educational institutions maintain lists of students and faculty, and governmental entities maintain lists of contracts. Although more complicated related data should be stored in a database-management program, such as Access, you can maintain structured lists in Excel tables. A ***table*** is a structured range that contains related data organized in such a way as to facilitate data management and analysis. Although you can manage and analyze a range of data, a table provides many advantages over a range of data:

- Column headings remain onscreen without having to use Freeze Panes.
- Filter arrows are available for efficient sorting and filtering.
- Table styles easily format table rows and columns with complementary fill colors.
- Calculated columns where the formulas copy down the columns automatically are available to create and edit.
- Calculated total row enables the user to implement a variety of summary functions.
- Structured references can be used instead of cell references in formulas.
- Table data can export to a SharePoint list.

In this section, you will learn table terminology and rules for structuring data. You will create a table from existing data, manage records and fields, and remove duplicates. Then you will apply a table style to format the table.

Designing and Creating Tables

A table is a group of related data organized in a series of rows and columns that is managed independently from any other data on the worksheet. Each column represents a ***field***, which is an individual piece of data, such as last names or quantities sold. Each field should represent the smallest possible unit of data. For example, instead of a Name field, separate name data into First Name and Last Name fields. Instead of one large address field, separate address data into Street Address, City, State, and ZIP Code fields. Separating data into the smallest units possible enables you to manipulate the data in a variety of ways for output. Each row in a table represents a ***record***, which is a collection of related data about one entity. For example, all data related to one particular transaction form a record in the Reid Department Store worksheet.

You should plan the structure before creating a table. The more thoroughly you plan, the fewer changes you will have to make to the table after you create it. To help plan your table, follow these guidelines:

- Enter field (column) names on the top row.
- Keep field names short, descriptive, and unique. No two field names should be identical.
- Format the field names so that they stand out from the data.
- Enter data for each record on a row below the field names.
- Do not leave blank rows between records or between the field names and the first record.
- Delete any blank columns between fields in the dataset.
- Make sure each record has something unique, such as a transaction number or ID.
- Insert at least one blank row and one blank column between the table and other data, such as the main titles. When you need multiple tables in one workbook, a best practice is to place each table on a separate worksheet.

Create a Table

STEP 1

When your worksheet data are structured correctly, you can easily create a table. To create a table from existing data, do the following:

1. Click within the existing range of data.
2. Click the INSERT tab and click Table in the Tables group. The Create Table dialog box opens (see Figure 4.11), prompting you to enter the range of data.
    - If Excel does not correctly predict the range, select the range for the *Where is the data for your table?* box.
    - If the existing range contains column labels, select the *My table has headers* check box.
3. Click OK to create the table.

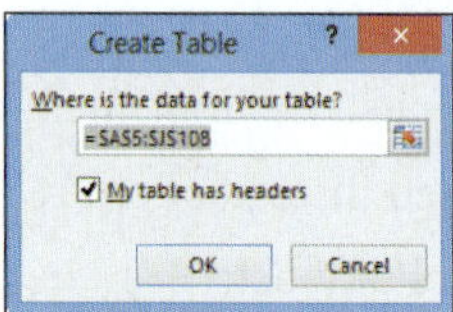

FIGURE 4.11 Create Table Dialog Box

Quick Analysis Table Creation

You can also create a table by selecting a range, clicking the Quick Analysis button, clicking TABLES (see Figure 4.12) in the Quick Analysis gallery, and then clicking Table. While Quick Analysis is efficient for tasks such as creating a chart, it may take more time to create a table because you have to select the entire range first. Some people find that it is faster to create a table from the Insert tab.

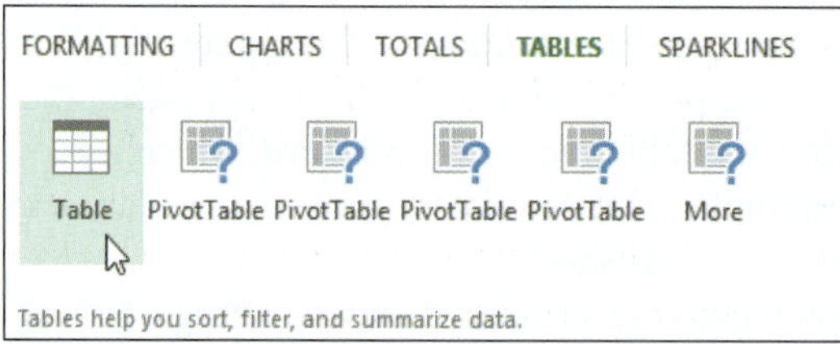

FIGURE 4.12 Quick Analysis Gallery

After you create a table, the Table Tools Design tab displays. Excel applies the default Table Style Medium 2 style to the table, and each cell in the header row has arrows, also called *filtering arrows* or *filtering buttons* in Excel Help (see Figure 4.13). This book uses the term *filter arrows* for consistency. Excel assigns a name to each table, such as Table 1. You can change the table name by clicking in the Table Name box in the Properties group, typing a new name using the same rules you applied when assigning range names, and then pressing Enter.

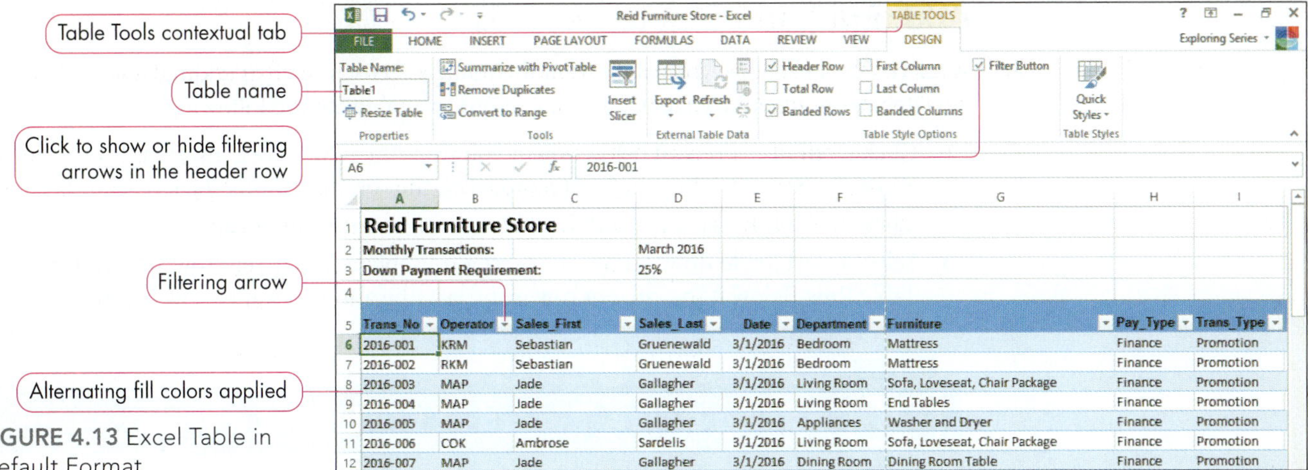

FIGURE 4.13 Excel Table in Default Format

Instead of converting a range to a table, you can create a table structure first and add data to it later. Select an empty range and follow the previously listed steps to create the range for the table. The default column headings are Column1, Column2, and so on. Click each default column heading and type a descriptive label. Then enter the data into each row of the newly created table.

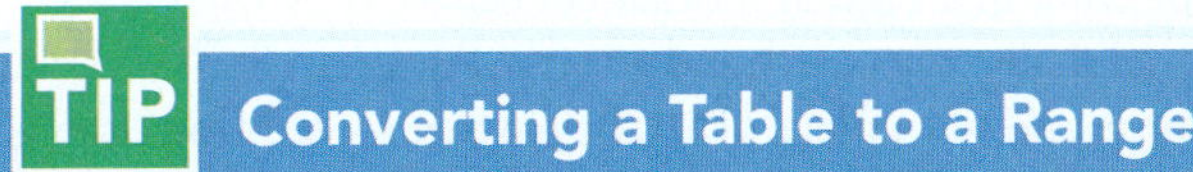

To convert a table back to a range, click within the table range, click the Table Tools Design tab, click *Convert to Range* in the Tools group, and then click Yes in the message box asking, *Do you want to convert the table to a normal range?*

Add and Delete Fields

STEP 2» After creating a table, you might want to add a new field. For example, you might want to add a field for product numbers to the Reid Furniture Store transaction table. To insert a field:

1. Click in any data cell (but not the cell containing the field name) in a field that will be to the right of the new field. For example, to insert a new field between the fields in columns A and B, click any cell in column B.
2. Click the HOME tab and click the Insert arrow in the Cells group.
3. Select *Insert Table Columns to the Left*.

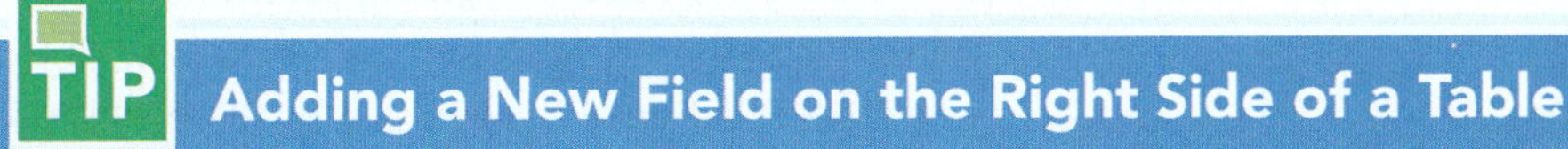

If you want to add a field at the end of the right side of a table, click in the cell to the right of the last field name and type a label. Excel will extend the table to include that field and will format the cell as a field name.

You can also delete a field if you no longer need any data for that particular field. Although deleting records and fields is easy, you must make sure not to delete data erroneously. If you accidentally delete data, click Undo immediately. To delete a field, do the following:

1. Click a cell in the field that you want to delete.
2. Click the Delete arrow in the Cells group on the HOME tab.
3. Select Delete Table Columns.

Add, Edit, and Delete Records

STEP 3»

After you create a table, you might want to add new records, such as adding a new client or a new item to an inventory table. To add a record to a table, do the following:

1. Click a cell in the record below which you want the new record inserted. If you want to add a new record below the last record, click the row containing the last record.
2. Click the HOME tab and click the Insert arrow in the Cells group.
3. Select Insert Table Rows Above to insert a row above the current row, or select Insert Table Row Below if the current row is the last one and you want a row below it.

TIP Adding a New Record at the End of a Table

You can also add a record to the end of a table by clicking in the row immediately below the table and typing. Excel will extend the table to include that row as a record in the table and will apply consistent formatting.

You might need to change data for a record. For example, when a client moves, you need to change the client's address and phone number. You edit data in a table the same way you edit data in a regular worksheet cell.

Finally, you can delete records. For example, if you maintain an inventory of artwork in your house and sell a piece of art, delete that record from the table. To delete a record from the table:

1. Click a cell in the record that you want to delete.
2. Click the HOME tab and click the Delete arrow in the Cells group.
3. Select Delete Table Rows.

Remove Duplicate Rows

STEP 4»

A table might contain duplicate records, which can give false results when totaling or performing other calculations on the dataset. For a small table, you might be able to detect duplicate records by scanning the data. For large tables, it is more difficult to identify duplicate records by simply scanning the table with the eye. To remove duplicate records, do the following:

1. Click within the table and click the DESIGN tab.
2. Click Remove Duplicates in the Tools group to display the Remove Duplicates dialog box (see Figure 4.14).
3. Click Select All to set the criteria to find a duplicate for every field in the record and click OK. If you select individual column(s), Excel looks for duplicates in the specific column(s) only and deletes all but one record of the duplicated data. Excel will display a message box informing you of how many duplicate rows it removed.

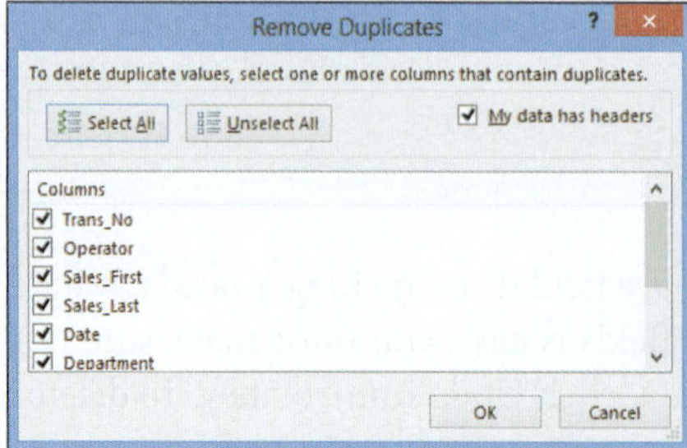

FIGURE 4.14 Remove Duplicates Dialog Box

TIP **Data Tab to Delete Duplicates**

You can also click the Data tab and click Remove Duplicates in the Data Tools group to open the Remove Duplicates dialog box.

Applying a Table Style

STEP 5 Excel applies a table style when you create a table. ***Table styles*** control the fill color of the header row (the row containing field names) and rows of records. In addition, table styles specify bold and border lines. You can change the table style to a color scheme that complements your organization's color scheme or to emphasize data the header rows or columns. Click Quick Styles in the Table Styles group to display the Table Styles gallery (see Figure 4.15). To see how a table style will format your table using Live Preview, position the pointer over a style in the Table Styles gallery. After you identify a style you want, click it to apply it to the table.

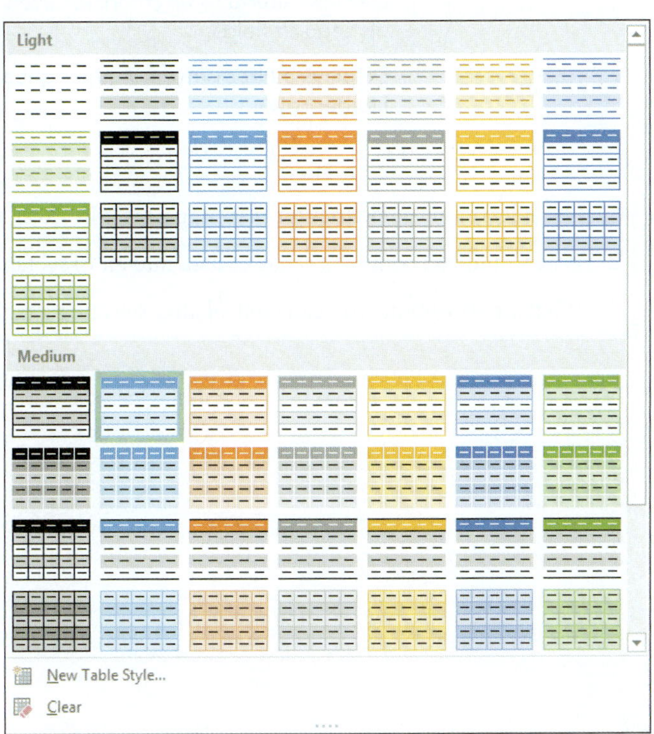

FIGURE 4.15 Table Styles Gallery

After you select a table style, you can control what the style formats. The Table Style Options group contains check boxes to select specific format actions in a table. Table 4.2 lists the options and the effect of each check box. Avoid overformatting the table. It is not good to apply so many formatting effects that the message you want to present with the data is obscured or lost.

TABLE 4.2 Table Style Options

Check Box	Action
Header Row	Displays the header row (field names) when checked; removes field names when not checked. Header Row formatting takes priority over column formats.
Total Row	Displays a total row when selected. Total Row formatting takes priority over column formats.
First Column	Applies a different format to the first column so that the row headings stand out. First Column formatting takes priority over Banded Rows formatting.
Last Column	Applies a different format to the last column so that the last column of data stands out; effective for aggregated data, such as grand totals per row. Last Column formatting takes priority over Banded Rows formatting.
Banded Rows	Displays alternate fill colors for even and odd rows to help distinguish records.
Banded Columns	Displays alternate fill colors for even and odd columns to help distinguish fields.
Filter Button	Displays a filter button on the right side of each heading in the header row.

1. List at least four guidelines for planning a table in Excel. ***p. 275***
2. Why would you convert a range of data into an Excel table? ***p. 275***
3. What are six options you can control after selecting a table style? ***p. 279***

Hands-On Exercises

2 Excel Tables

You want to convert the March data to a table. As you review the table, you will delete the unnecessary Operator field, add two new fields, insert a missing furniture sale transaction, and remove duplicate transactions. Finally, you will enhance the table appearance by applying a table style.

Skills covered: Create a Table • Add and Delete Fields • Add Records • Remove Duplicate Rows • Apply a Table Style

STEP 1 》 CREATE A TABLE

Although the Reid Furniture Store's March transaction data are organized in an Excel worksheet, you know that you will have additional functionality if you convert the range to a table. Refer to Figure 4.16 as you complete Step 1.

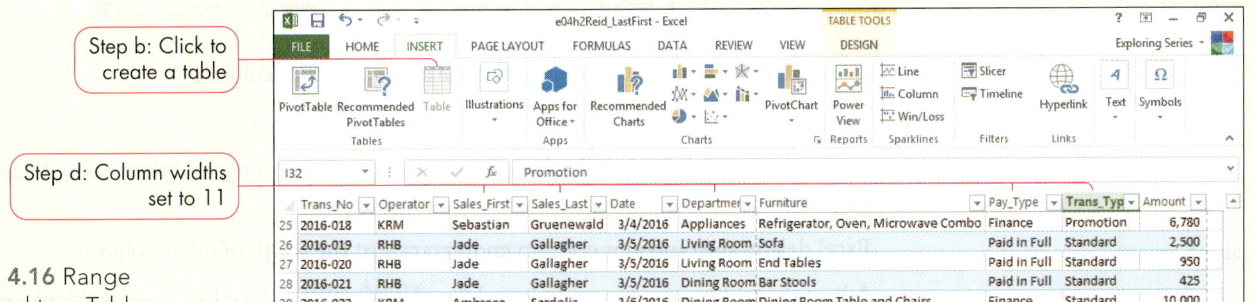

FIGURE 4.16 Range Converted to a Table

a. Open *e04h1Reid_LastFirst* if you closed it at the end of Hands-On Exercise 1 and save it as **e04h2Reid_LastFirst**, changing *h1* to *h2*. Click **Normal** on the status bar.

b. Click in any cell within the transactional data, click the **INSERT tab**, and then click **Table** in the Tables group.

   The Create Table dialog box opens. The *Where is the data for your table?* box displays =$A$5:$I$112. Keep the *My table has headers* check box selected so that the headings on the fifth row become the field names for the table.

c. Click **OK** and click **cell A5**.

   Excel creates a table from the data range and displays the DESIGN tab, filter arrows, and alternating fill colors for the records. The columns widen to fit the field names, although the wrap text option is still applied to those cells.

d. Set column width to **11** for the Sales_First, Sales_Last, Department, Pay_Type, and Trans_Type fields.

e. Unfreeze the panes and scroll through the table. Save the workbook.

   With a regular range of data, column labels scroll off the top of the screen if you do not freeze panes. When you scroll within a table, the table's header row remains onscreen by moving up to where the Excel column (letter) headings usually display (see Figure 4.16).

Filtering Data

Filtering is the process of specifying conditions to display only those records that meet certain conditions. For example, you might want to filter the data to show transactions for only a particular sales representative. To filter records by a particular field, click the filter arrow for that field. The list displays each unique label, value, or date contained in the column. Deselect the (Select All) check box and click the check box for each value you want to include in the filtered results.

Often you will need to apply more than one filter to display the needed records. You can filter more than one field. Each additional filter is based on the current filtered data and further reduces a data subset. To apply multiple filters, click each field's filter arrow and select the values to include in the filtered data results.

TIP Copying Before Filtering Data

Often, you need to show different filters applied to the same dataset. You can copy the worksheet and filter the data on the copied worksheet to preserve the original dataset.

Apply Text Filters

STEP 3

When you apply a filter to a text field, the filter menu displays each unique text item. You can select one or more text items from the list. For example, select Gallagher to show only her records. To display records for both Gallagher and Sardelis, deselect the (Select All) check mark and click the Gallagher and Sardelis check boxes. You can also select Text Filters to see a submenu of additional options, such as *Begins With*, to select all records for which the name begins with the letter G, for example.

Figure 4.23 shows the Sales_Last filter menu with two names selected. Excel displays records for these two reps only. The records for the other sales reps are hidden but not deleted. The filter arrow displays a filter icon, indicating which field is filtered. Excel displays the row numbers in blue, indicating that you applied a filter. The missing row numbers indicate hidden rows of data. When you remove the filter, all the records display again.

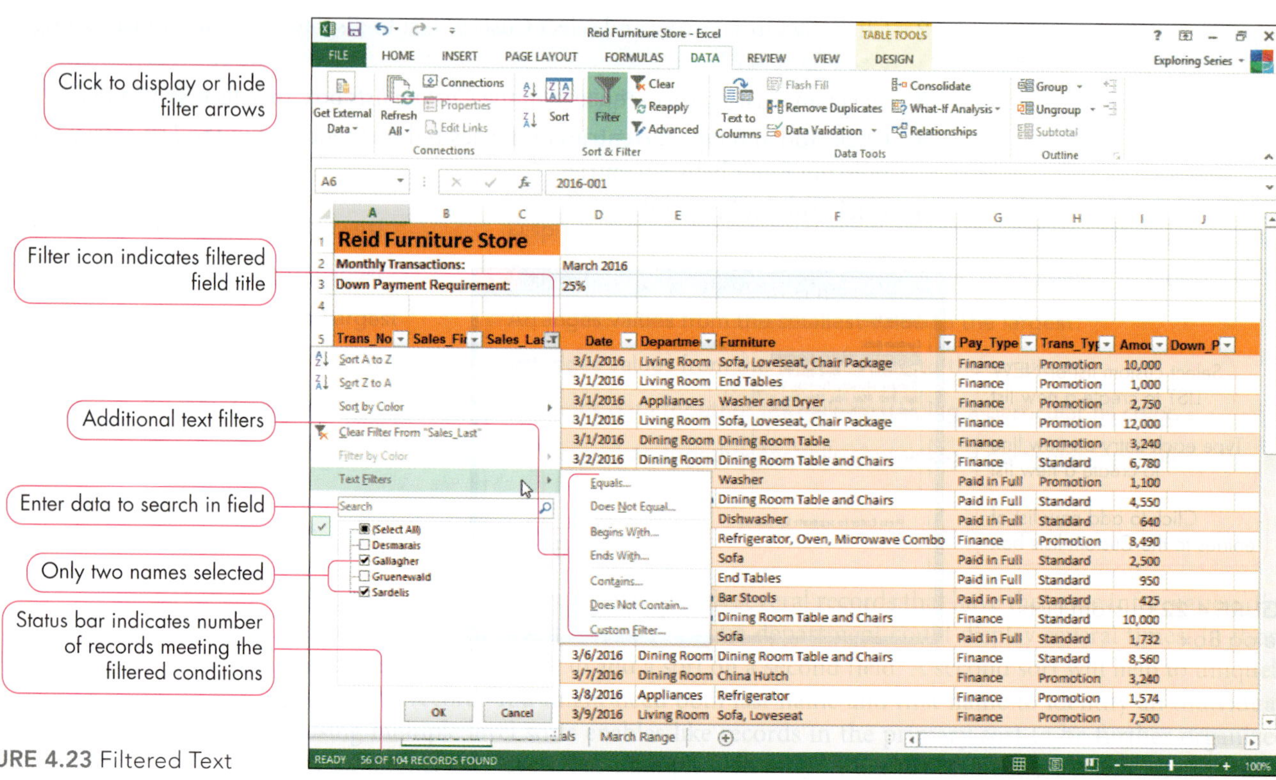

FIGURE 4.23 Filtered Text

Filter Arrows

Click the Filter Button check box in the Table Style Options group on the Design tab to display or hide the filter arrows. For a range of data instead of a table, click Filter in the Sort & Filter group on the Data tab to display or hide the filter arrows.

Apply Number Filters

STEP 4 When you filter a field of numbers, you can select specific numbers. You might want to filter numbers by a range, such as numbers greater than $5,000 or numbers between $4,000 and $5,000. The submenu enables you to set a variety of number filters. In Figure 4.24, the amounts are filtered to show only those that are above the average amount. In this situation, Excel calculates the average amount as $4,512. Only records above that amount display.

If the field contains a large number of unique entries, you can click in the Search box and then type a value, text label, or date. Doing so narrows the visible list so that you do not have to scroll through the entire list. For example, if you enter $7, the list will display only values that start with $7.

Click check box(es) for particular value(s)

Selected number filter

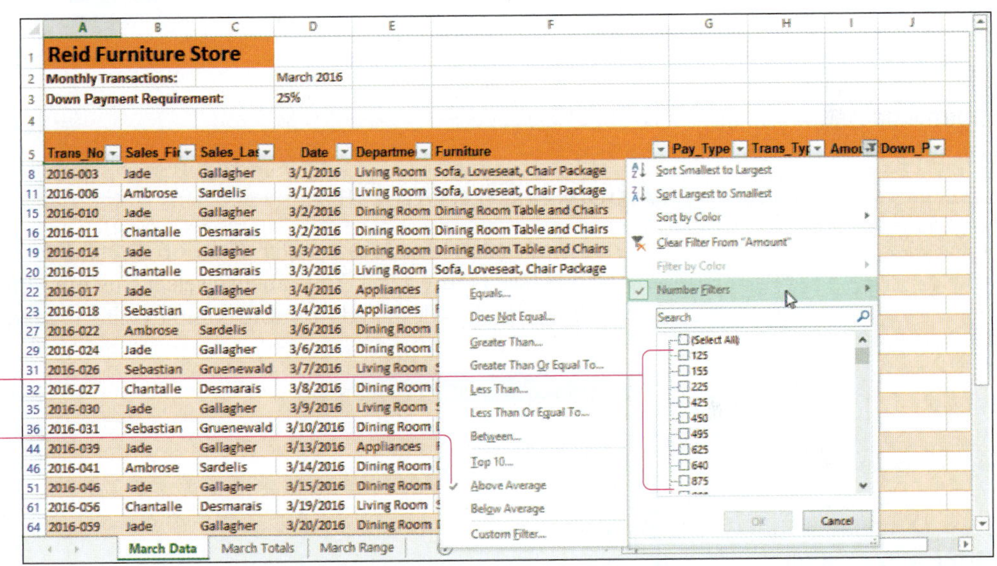

FIGURE 4.24 Filtered Numbers

The Top 10 option enables you to specify the top records. Although the option name is Top 10, you can specify the number or percentage of records to display. For example, you can filter the list to display only the top five or the bottom 7%. Figure 4.25 shows the Top 10 AutoFilter dialog box. Click the first arrow to select either Top or Bottom, click the spin arrows to indicate a value, and then click the last arrow to select either Items or Percent.

Top 10 AutoFilter
Show
Top
10
Items
OK
Cancel

FIGURE 4.25 Top 10 AutoFilter Dialog Box

Apply Date Filters

STEP 5» When you filter a field of dates, you can select specific dates or a date range, such as dates after 3/15/2016 or dates between 3/1/2016 and 3/7/2016. The submenu enables you to set a variety of date filters. For more specific date options, point to Date Filters, point to *All Dates in the Period*, and then select a period, such as Quarter 2 or October. Figure 4.26 shows the Date Filter menu.

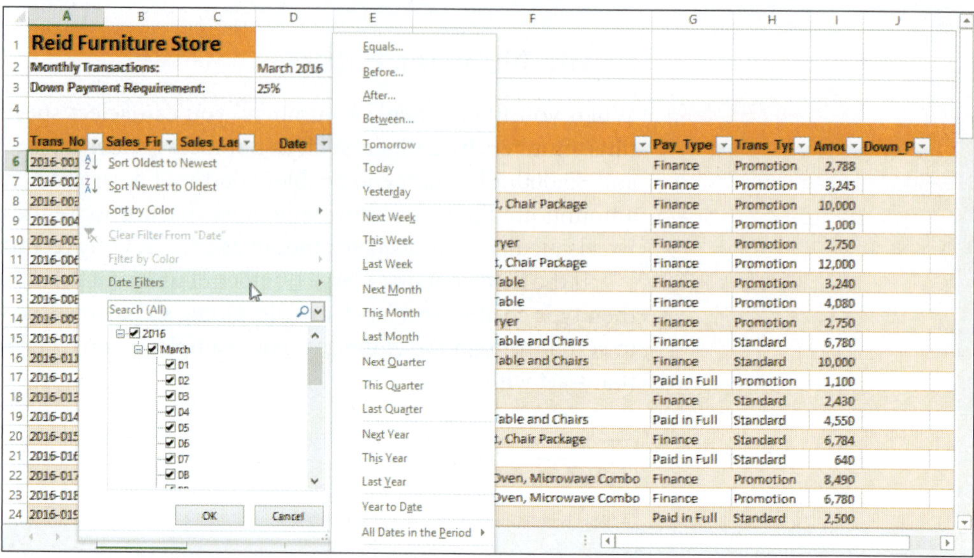

FIGURE 4.26 Filtered Dates

Apply a Custom Filter

If you select options such as *Greater Than* or *Before*, Excel displays the Custom AutoFilter dialog box (see Figure 4.27). You can also select Custom Filter from the menu to display this dialog box, which is designed for more complex filtering requirements.

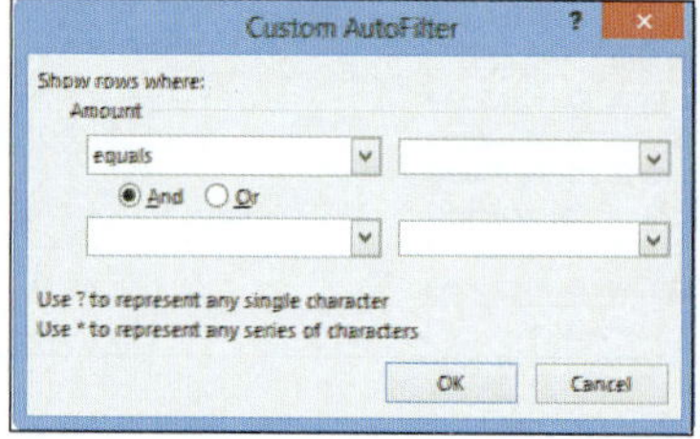

FIGURE 4.27 Custom AutoFilter Dialog Box

The dialog box indicates the column being filtered. To set the filters, click the arrows to select the comparison type, such as equals or contains. Click the arrow on the right to select a specific text, value, or date entry, or type the data yourself. For ranges of dates or values, click And, and then specify the comparison operator and value or date for the next condition row. For text, click Or. For example, if you want both Gallagher and Desmarais, you must select Or because each data entry contains either Gallagher or Desmarais but not both at the same time.

You can use wildcards to represent characters. For example, to select all states starting with New, type *New* * in the second box to obtain results such as New York or New Mexico. The asterisk (*) represents any number of characters. If you want a wildcard for only a single character, type the question mark (?).

Clear Filters

You can remove the filters from one or more fields to expand the dataset again. To remove only one filter and keep the other filters, click the filter arrow for the field from which you wish to clear the filter and select Clear Filter From.

To remove all filters and display all records in a dataset, do one of the following:

- Click Filter in the Sort & Filter group on the DATA tab.
- Click Sort & Filter in the Editing group on the HOME tab and select Filter.

1. What is the purpose of sorting data in a table? ***p. 286***
2. What are two ways to arrange (sort) dates? ***p. 286***
3. List at least five ways you can filter numbers. ***p. 289***
4. Assume you are filtering a list and want to display records for people who live in Boston or New York. What settings do you enter in the Custom AutoFilter dialog box for that field? ***p. 290***

Hands-On Exercises

3 Table Manipulation

You want to start analyzing the March 2016 transactions for Reid Furniture Store by sorting and filtering data in a variety of ways to help you understand the transactions better.

Skills covered: Sort One Field • Sort Multiple Fields • Apply Text Filters • Apply a Number Filter • Apply a Date Filter

STEP 1 » SORT ONE FIELD

First, you want to compare the number of transactions by sales rep, so you will sort the data by the Rep_Last field. After reviewing the transactions by sales reps, you want to arrange the transactions from the one with the largest purchase first to the smallest purchase last. Refer to Figure 4.28 as you complete Step 1.

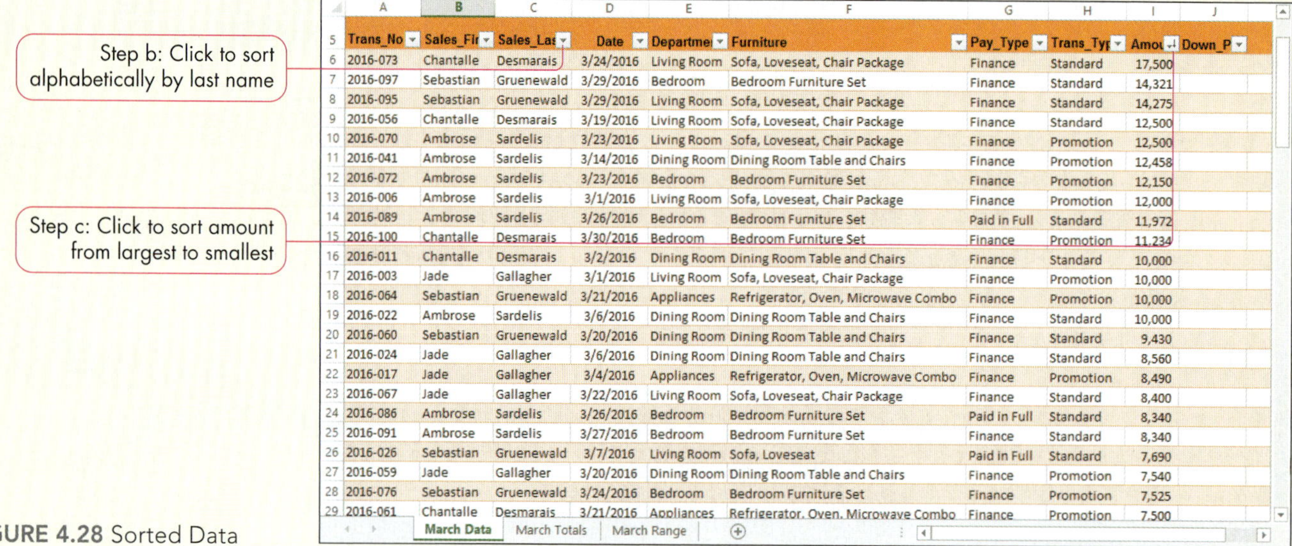

	A	B	C	D	E	F	G	H	I	J
5	Trans_No	Sales_Fir	Sales_Las	Date	Departme	Furniture	Pay_Type	Trans_Typ	Amou	Down_P
6	2016-073	Chantalle	Desmarais	3/24/2016	Living Room	Sofa, Loveseat, Chair Package	Finance	Standard	17,500	
7	2016-097	Sebastian	Gruenewald	3/29/2016	Bedroom	Bedroom Furniture Set	Finance	Standard	14,321	
8	2016-095	Sebastian	Gruenewald	3/29/2016	Living Room	Sofa, Loveseat, Chair Package	Finance	Standard	14,275	
9	2016-056	Chantalle	Desmarais	3/19/2016	Living Room	Sofa, Loveseat, Chair Package	Finance	Standard	12,500	
10	2016-070	Ambrose	Sardelis	3/23/2016	Living Room	Sofa, Loveseat, Chair Package	Finance	Promotion	12,500	
11	2016-041	Ambrose	Sardelis	3/14/2016	Dining Room	Dining Room Table and Chairs	Finance	Promotion	12,458	
12	2016-072	Ambrose	Sardelis	3/23/2016	Bedroom	Bedroom Furniture Set	Finance	Promotion	12,150	
13	2016-006	Ambrose	Sardelis	3/1/2016	Living Room	Sofa, Loveseat, Chair Package	Finance	Promotion	12,000	
14	2016-089	Ambrose	Sardelis	3/26/2016	Bedroom	Bedroom Furniture Set	Paid in Full	Standard	11,972	
15	2016-100	Chantalle	Desmarais	3/30/2016	Bedroom	Bedroom Furniture Set	Finance	Promotion	11,234	
16	2016-011	Chantalle	Desmarais	3/2/2016	Dining Room	Dining Room Table and Chairs	Finance	Standard	10,000	
17	2016-003	Jade	Gallagher	3/1/2016	Living Room	Sofa, Loveseat, Chair Package	Finance	Promotion	10,000	
18	2016-064	Sebastian	Gruenewald	3/21/2016	Appliances	Refrigerator, Oven, Microwave Combo	Finance	Promotion	10,000	
19	2016-022	Ambrose	Sardelis	3/6/2016	Dining Room	Dining Room Table and Chairs	Finance	Standard	10,000	
20	2016-060	Sebastian	Gruenewald	3/20/2016	Dining Room	Dining Room Table and Chairs	Finance	Standard	9,430	
21	2016-024	Jade	Gallagher	3/6/2016	Dining Room	Dining Room Table and Chairs	Finance	Standard	8,560	
22	2016-017	Jade	Gallagher	3/4/2016	Appliances	Refrigerator, Oven, Microwave Combo	Finance	Promotion	8,490	
23	2016-067	Jade	Gallagher	3/22/2016	Living Room	Sofa, Loveseat, Chair Package	Finance	Standard	8,400	
24	2016-086	Ambrose	Sardelis	3/26/2016	Bedroom	Bedroom Furniture Set	Paid in Full	Standard	8,340	
25	2016-091	Ambrose	Sardelis	3/27/2016	Bedroom	Bedroom Furniture Set	Finance	Standard	8,340	
26	2016-026	Sebastian	Gruenewald	3/7/2016	Living Room	Sofa, Loveseat	Paid in Full	Standard	7,690	
27	2016-059	Jade	Gallagher	3/20/2016	Dining Room	Dining Room Table and Chairs	Finance	Promotion	7,540	
28	2016-076	Sebastian	Gruenewald	3/24/2016	Bedroom	Bedroom Furniture Set	Finance	Promotion	7,525	
29	2016-061	Chantalle	Desmarais	3/21/2016	Appliances	Refrigerator, Oven, Microwave Combo	Finance	Promotion	7,500	

FIGURE 4.28 Sorted Data

a. Open *e04h2Reid_LastFirst* if you closed it at the end of Hands-On Exercise 2. Save it as **e04h3Reid_LastFirst**, changing *h2* to *h3*.

b. Click the **Sales_Last filter arrow** and select **Sort A to Z.**

Excel arranges the transactions in alphabetical order by last name, starting with Desmarais. Within each sales rep, records display in their original sequence by transaction number. If you scan the records, you can see that Gallagher completed the most sales transactions in March. The up arrow icon on the Sales_Last filter arrow indicates records are sorted in alphabetical order by that field.

Name Sorts

Always check the data to determine how many levels of sorting you need to apply. If your table contains several people with the same last name but different first names, you would first sort by the Last Name field, then sort by First Name field. All the people with the last name Desmarais would be grouped together and further sorted by first name, such as Amanda and then Bradley.

c. Click the **Amount filter arrow** and select **Sort Largest to Smallest**. Save the workbook.

The records are no longer sorted by Sales_Last. When you sort by another field, Excel arranges the data for that field. In this case, Excel arranges the transactions from the one with the largest amount to the smallest amount, indicated by the down arrow icon in the Amount filter arrow.

STEP 2 » SORT MULTIPLE FIELDS

You want to review the transactions by payment type (financed or paid in full). Within each payment type, you want to further compare the transaction type (promotion or standard). Finally, you want to compare costs within the sorted records by displaying the highest costs first. You will use the Sort dialog box to perform a three-level sort. Refer to Figure 4.29 as you complete Step 2.

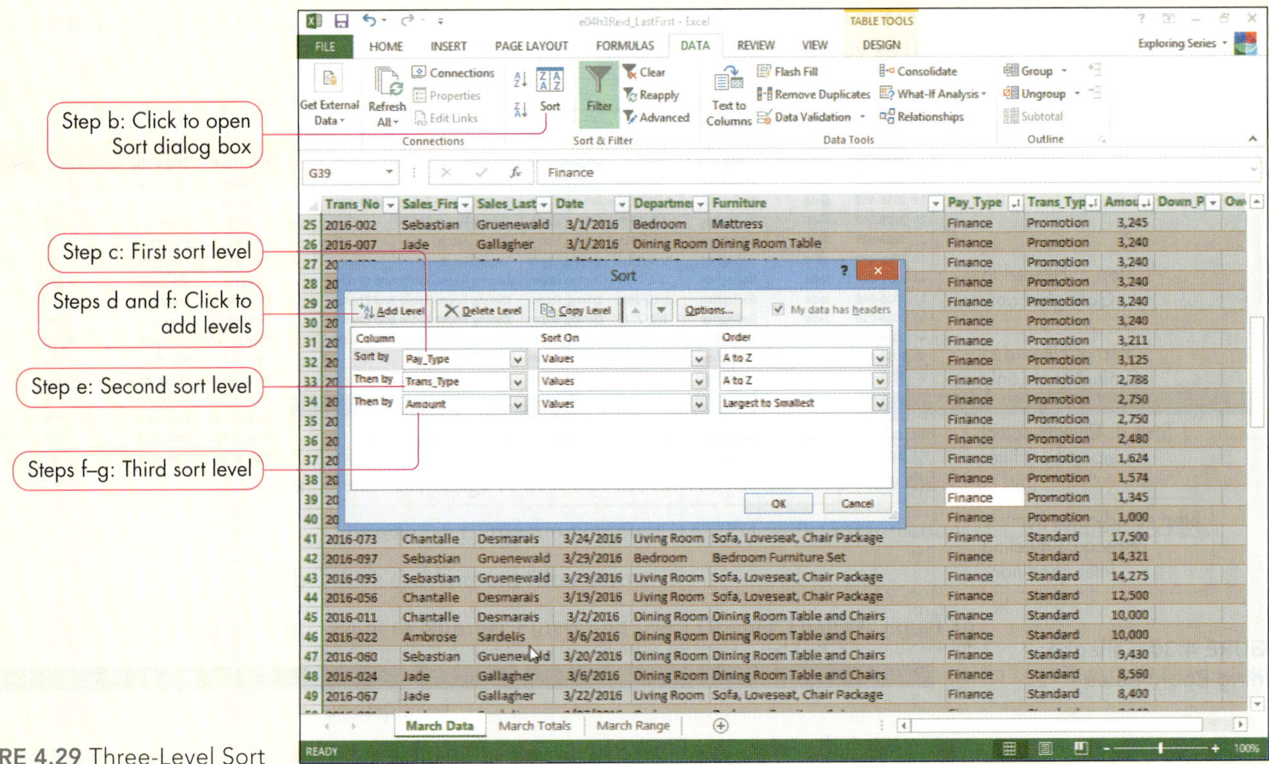

FIGURE 4.29 Three-Level Sort

a. Click inside the table and click the **DATA tab**.

Both the DATA and HOME tabs contain commands to open the Sort dialog box.

b. Click **Sort** in the Sort & Filter group to open the Sort dialog box.

c. Click the **Sort by arrow** and select **Pay_Type**. Click the **Order arrow** and select **A to Z**.

You start by specifying the column for the primary sort. In this case, you want to sort the records first by the Payment Type column.

d. Click **Add Level**.

The Sort dialog box adds the *Then by* row, which adds a secondary sort.

e. Click the **Then by arrow** and select **Trans_Type**.

The default order is A to Z, which will sort in alphabetical order by Trans_Type. Excel will first sort the records by the Pay_Type (Finance or Paid in Full). Within each Pay_Type, Excel will further sort records by Trans_Type (Promotion or Standard).

f. Click **Add Level** to add another *Then by* row. Click the second **Then by arrow** and select **Amount**.

are field names. This structured formula that includes references, such as table numbers, is called a *fully qualified structured reference.* When you build formulas *within* a table, you can use either unqualified or fully qualified structured references. If you need to use table data in a formula *outside* the table boundaries, you must use fully qualified structured references.

Add a Total Row

At times, aggregating data provides more meaningful quantitative interpretation than individual values. For regular ranges of data, you use basic statistical functions, such as SUM, AVERAGE, MIN, and MAX, to provide meaning for a dataset. An Excel table provides the advantage of being able to display a total row automatically without creating the aggregate function yourself. A ***total row*** displays below the last row of records in an Excel table and enables you to display summary statistics, such as a sum of values displayed in a column.

To display and use the total row:

STEP 2

1. Click the DESIGN tab.
2. Click Total Row in the Table Style Options group. Excel displays the total row below the last record in the table. Excel displays *Total* in the first column of the total row. Excel either sums or counts data for the last field, depending on the type of data stored in that field. If the last field consists of values, Excel sums the values. If the last field is text, Excel counts the number of records.
3. Click a cell in the total row, click that cell's total row arrow, and then select the function results that you desire. To add a summary statistic to another column, click in the empty cell for that field in the total row and click the arrow to select the desired function. Select None to remove the function.

Figure 4.34 shows the active total row with totals applied to the Amount, Down_Pay, and Owed fields. A list of functions displays to change the function for the last field.

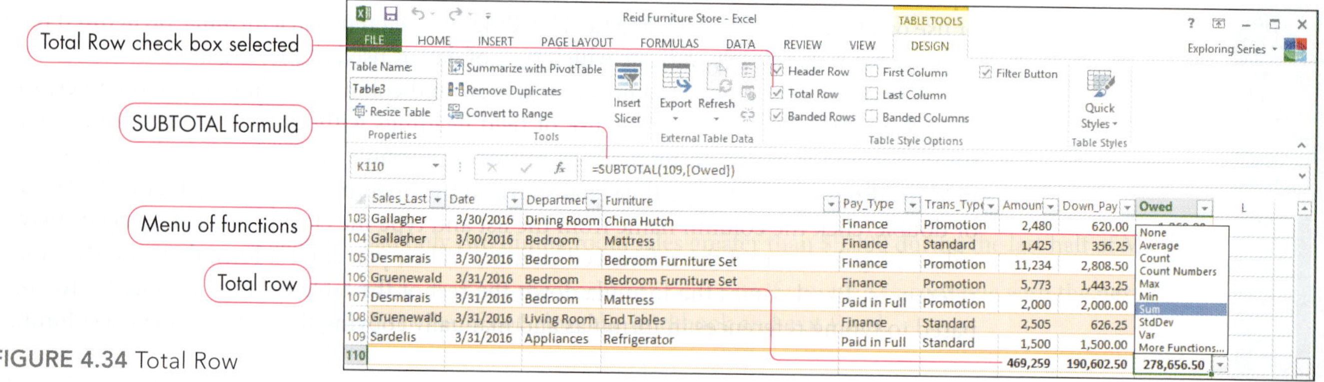

FIGURE 4.34 Total Row

Filtering Data and Subtotals

If you filter the data and display the total row, the SUBTOTAL function's 109 argument ensures that only the displayed data are summed; data for hidden rows are not calculated in the aggregate function.

The calculations on the total row use the SUBTOTAL function. The ***SUBTOTAL function*** calculates an aggregate value, such as totals or averages, for values in a range or database. If you click in a calculated total row cell, the SUBTOTAL function displays in the Formula Bar. The function for the total row looks like this: =SUBTOTAL(function_num,ref1). The function_num argument is a number that represents a function (see Table 4.4). The ref1 argument indicates the range of values to calculate. The SUBTOTAL function to total the values in the Owed field would be =SUBTOTAL(109,[Owed]), where the number 109 represents the SUM function, and [Owed] represents the Owed field. A benefit of the SUBTOTAL function is that it subtotals data for filtered records, so you have an accurate total for the visible records.

=SUBTOTAL(function_num,ref1,...)

TABLE 4.4 SUBTOTAL Function Numbers

Function	Database Number	Table Number
AVERAGE	1	101
COUNT	2	102
COUNTA	3	103
MAX	4	104
MIN	5	105
PRODUCT	6	106
STDEV	7	107
STDEVP	8	108
SUM	9	109
VAR	10	110
VARP	11	111

1. What is a structured reference? What is the general format for including a field name in a formula? Give an example. ***p. 297***
2. What are the benefits of displaying a total row and selecting functions instead of adding functions yourself below a table? ***p. 298***

Hands-On Exercises

4 Table Aggregation

You further analyze the March 2016 transactions for Reid Furniture Store: You want to calculate the required down payment amount and how much customers owe for their purchases. Finally, you will convert the table back to a range.

Skills covered: Create Structured References in Formulas • Add a Total Row • Convert a Table to a Range

STEP 1 » CREATE STRUCTURED REFERENCES IN FORMULAS

To continue reviewing the March transactions, you need to calculate the required down payment for customers who financed their purchases. The required down payment is located above the table data so that you can change that value if needed. In addition, you want to calculate how much customers owe on their purchases if they did not pay in full. You will use structured formulas to perform these calculations. Refer to Figure 4.35 as you complete Step 1.

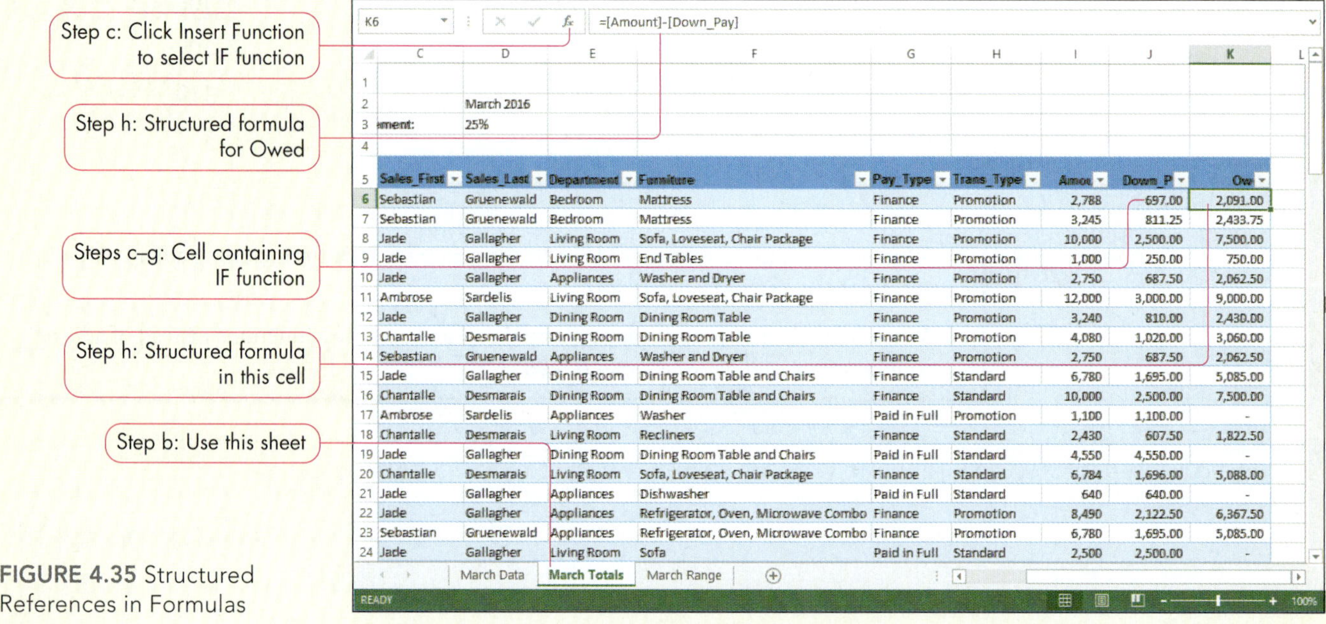

	Sales_First	Sales_Last	Department	Furniture	Pay_Type	Trans_Type	Amou	Down_P	Ow
6	Sebastian	Gruenewald	Bedroom	Mattress	Finance	Promotion	2,788	697.00	2,091.00
7	Sebastian	Gruenewald	Bedroom	Mattress	Finance	Promotion	3,245	811.25	2,433.75
8	Jade	Gallagher	Living Room	Sofa, Loveseat, Chair Package	Finance	Promotion	10,000	2,500.00	7,500.00
9	Jade	Gallagher	Living Room	End Tables	Finance	Promotion	1,000	250.00	750.00
10	Jade	Gallagher	Appliances	Washer and Dryer	Finance	Promotion	2,750	687.50	2,062.50
11	Ambrose	Sardelis	Living Room	Sofa, Loveseat, Chair Package	Finance	Promotion	12,000	3,000.00	9,000.00
12	Jade	Gallagher	Dining Room	Dining Room Table	Finance	Promotion	3,240	810.00	2,430.00
13	Chantalle	Desmarais	Dining Room	Dining Room Table	Finance	Promotion	4,080	1,020.00	3,060.00
14	Sebastian	Gruenewald	Appliances	Washer and Dryer	Finance	Promotion	2,750	687.50	2,062.50
15	Jade	Gallagher	Dining Room	Dining Room Table and Chairs	Finance	Standard	6,780	1,695.00	5,085.00
16	Chantalle	Desmarais	Dining Room	Dining Room Table and Chairs	Finance	Standard	10,000	2,500.00	7,500.00
17	Ambrose	Sardelis	Appliances	Washer	Paid in Full	Promotion	1,100	1,100.00	-
18	Chantalle	Desmarais	Living Room	Recliners	Finance	Standard	2,430	607.50	1,822.50
19	Jade	Gallagher	Dining Room	Dining Room Table and Chairs	Paid in Full	Standard	4,550	4,550.00	-
20	Chantalle	Desmarais	Living Room	Sofa, Loveseat, Chair Package	Finance	Standard	6,784	1,696.00	5,088.00
21	Jade	Gallagher	Appliances	Dishwasher	Paid in Full	Standard	640	640.00	-
22	Jade	Gallagher	Appliances	Refrigerator, Oven, Microwave Combo	Finance	Promotion	8,490	2,122.50	6,367.50
23	Sebastian	Gruenewald	Appliances	Refrigerator, Oven, Microwave Combo	Finance	Promotion	6,780	1,695.00	5,085.00
24	Jade	Gallagher	Living Room	Sofa	Paid in Full	Standard	2,500	2,500.00	-

FIGURE 4.35 Structured References in Formulas

a. Open *e04h3Reid_LastFirst* if you closed it at the end of Hands-On Exercise 3. Save it as **e04h4Reid_LastFirst**, changing *h3* to *h4*.

b. Click the **March Totals worksheet tab** and make **cell J6** the active cell.

   To preserve the integrity of the sorting and filtering in case your instructor wants to verify your work, you will continue with an identical dataset on another worksheet.

c. Click **Insert Function** to open the Insert Function dialog box, select **IF** in the **Select a function list**, and then click **OK**.

d. Type **[Pay_Type]="Paid in Full"** in the **Logical_test box**.

   The logical test evaluates whether a customer paid in full, indicated in the Pay_Type field. Remember to type the brackets around the column label.

e. Type **[Amount]** in the **Value_if_true box**.

   If a customer pays in full, the down payment is the full amount.

f. Type **[Amount]*$D$3** in the **Value_if_false box.**

If a customer does not pay in full, he or she must pay a required down payment. You use [Amount] to refer to the Amount field in the table. Enclose the field labels in brackets. The amount is multiplied by the absolute reference to D3, the cell containing the required down payment percentage. Make this cell reference absolute so that it does not change when Excel copies the formula down the Down_Pay column.

g. Click **OK** to enter the formula.

The formula looks like this in the Formula Bar: =IF([Pay_Type]= "Paid in Full",[Amount],[Amount]*$D$3). Because you are entering formulas in a table, Excel copies the formula down the column automatically. The first customer must pay a $697 down payment (25% of $2,788). The columns in the current worksheet have been formatted as Comma Style for you.

> **TROUBLESHOOTING:** If the results seem incorrect, check your function. Errors will result if you do not enclose the field names in brackets, if you have misspelled a field name, if you omit the quotation marks around *Paid in Full*, and so on. Correct any errors.

h. Click **cell K6**. Type the formula =**[Amount]**–**[Down_Pay]** and press **Enter**. Save the workbook.

The formula calculates how much customers owe if they finance their purchases. Excel copies the formula down the column.

STEP 2 » ADD A TOTAL ROW

You want to see the monthly totals for the Amount, Down_Pay, and Owed columns. Instead of entering SUM functions yourself, you will add a total row. Refer to Figure 4.36 as you complete Step 2.

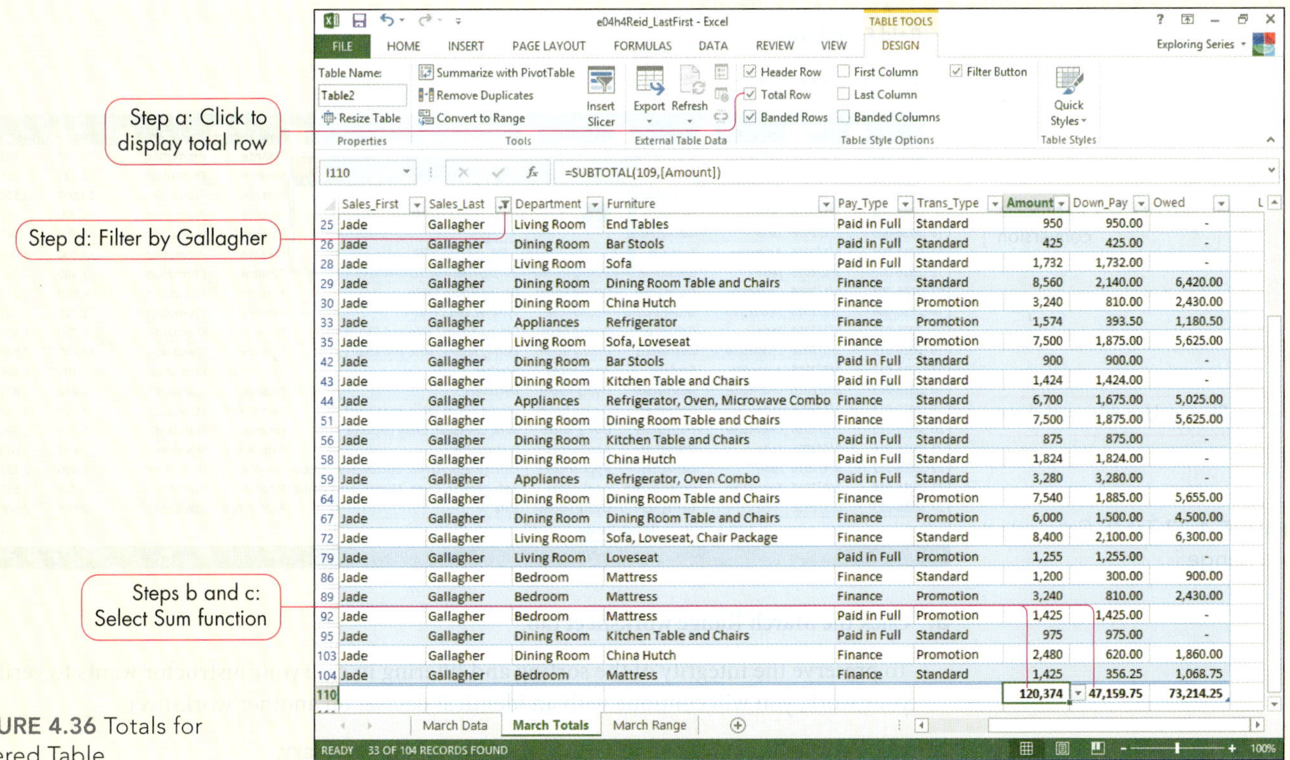

FIGURE 4.36 Totals for Filtered Table

Conditional Formatting

You use table styles, or a variety of font, alignment, and number formats on the Home tab, to format a worksheet. You can also apply special formatting to cells that contain particular values or text using conditional formatting. ***Conditional formatting*** applies special formatting to highlight or emphasize cells that meet specific conditions. For example, a sales manager might want to highlight cells containing the top 10 sales amounts, or a professor might want to highlight test scores that fall below the average. You can also apply conditional formatting to point out data for a specific date or duplicate values in a range.

In this section, you will learn about the five conditional formatting categories and how to apply conditional formatting to a range of values based on a condition you set.

Applying Conditional Formatting

Conditional formatting helps you and your audience understand a dataset better because it adds a visual element to the cells. The term is called *conditional* because the formatting occurs when a condition is met. This is similar logic to the IF function you have used. Remember with an IF function, you create a logical test that is evaluated. If the logical or conditional test is true, the function produces one result. If the logical or conditional test is false, the function produces another result. With conditional formatting, if the condition is true, Excel formats the cell automatically based on that condition. If the condition is false, Excel does not format the cell. If you change a value in a conditionally formatted cell, Excel examines the new value to see if it should apply the conditional format.

Apply Conditional Formatting with the Quick Analysis Tool

When you select a range and click the Quick Analysis button, the FORMATTING options display in the Quick Analysis gallery. Position the mouse over a thumbnail to see how it will affect the selected range (see Figure 4.38). You can also apply conditional formatting by clicking Conditional Formatting in the Styles group on the Home tab.

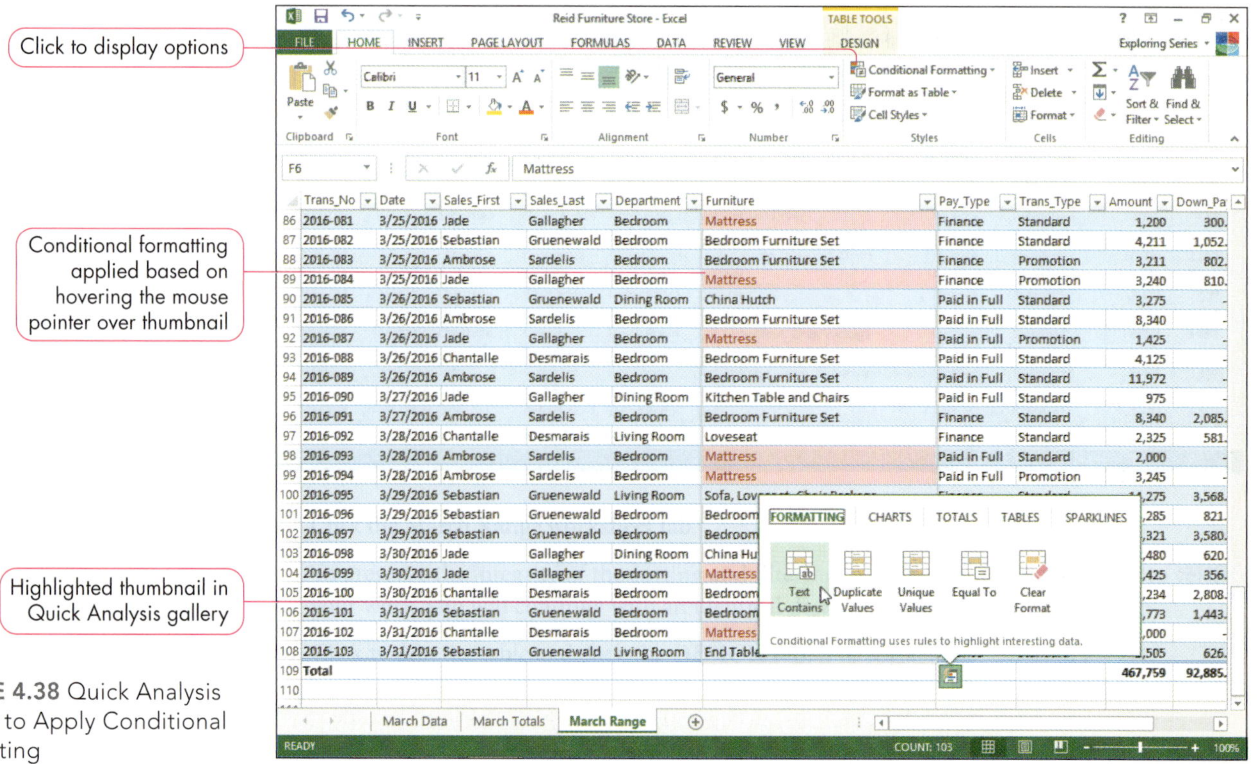

FIGURE 4.38 Quick Analysis Gallery to Apply Conditional Formatting

Table 4.5 describes the conditional formatting options in the Quick Analysis gallery.

TABLE 4.5 Conditional Formatting Options in Quick Analysis Gallery

Options	Description
Text Contains	Formats cells that contain the text in the first selected cell. In Figure 4.38, the first selected cell contains Mattress. If a cell contains Mattress and Springs, Excel would format that cell also because it *contains* Mattress.
Duplicate Values	Formats cells that are duplicated in the selected range.
Unique Values	Formats cells that are unique; that is, no other cell in the selected range contains the same data.
Equal To	Formats cells that are exactly like the data contained in the first selected cell.
Clear Format	Removes the conditional formatting from the selected range.

Table 4.6 lists and describes a number of different conditional formats that you can apply if you want more specific rules.

TABLE 4.6 Conditional Formatting Options

Options	Description
Highlight Cells Rules	Highlights cells with a fill color, font color, or border (such as Light Red Fill with Dark Red Text) if values are greater than, less than, between two values, equal to a value, or duplicate values; text that contains particular characters; or dates when a date meets a particular condition, such as *In the last 7 days*.
Top/Bottom Rules	Formats cells with values in the top 10 items, top 10%, bottom 10 items, bottom 10%, above average, or below average. You can change the exact values to format the top or bottom items or percentages, such as top 5 or bottom 15%.
Data Bars	Applies a gradient or solid fill bar in which the width of the bar represents the current cell's value compared to other cells' values.
Color Scales	Formats different cells with different colors, assigning one color to the lowest group of values and another color to the highest group of values, with gradient colors to other values.
Icon Sets	Inserts an icon from an icon palette in each cell to indicate values compared to each other.

To apply a conditional format, select the cells for which you want to apply a conditional format, click the Home tab, click Conditional Formatting in the Styles group, and then select the conditional formatting category you want to apply.

Apply the Highlight Cells Rules

STEP 1» The Highlight Cells Rules category enables you to apply a highlight to cells that meet a condition, such as a value greater than a particular value. This option contains predefined combinations of fill colors, font colors, and/or borders. This category is useful because it helps you identify and format automatically values of interest. For example, a weather tracker who developed a worksheet containing the temperatures for each day of a month might want to apply a conditional format to cells that contain temperatures between 70 and 75 degrees. To apply this conditional formatting, she would select Highlight Cells Rules and then select

Between. In the Between dialog box (see Figure 4.39), the weather tracker would type 70 in the *Format cells that are BETWEEN* box and 75 in the *and* box, select the type of conditional formatting, such as *Light Red Fill with Dark Red Text*, and then click OK to apply the formats.

FIGURE 4.39 Between Dialog Box

Figure 4.40 shows two columns of data that contain conditional formats. The Department column is conditionally formatted to highlight text with a Light Red Fill with Dark Red Text for cells that contain *Living Room*, and the Amount column is conditionally formatted to highlight with Red Border values between $5,000 and $10,000.

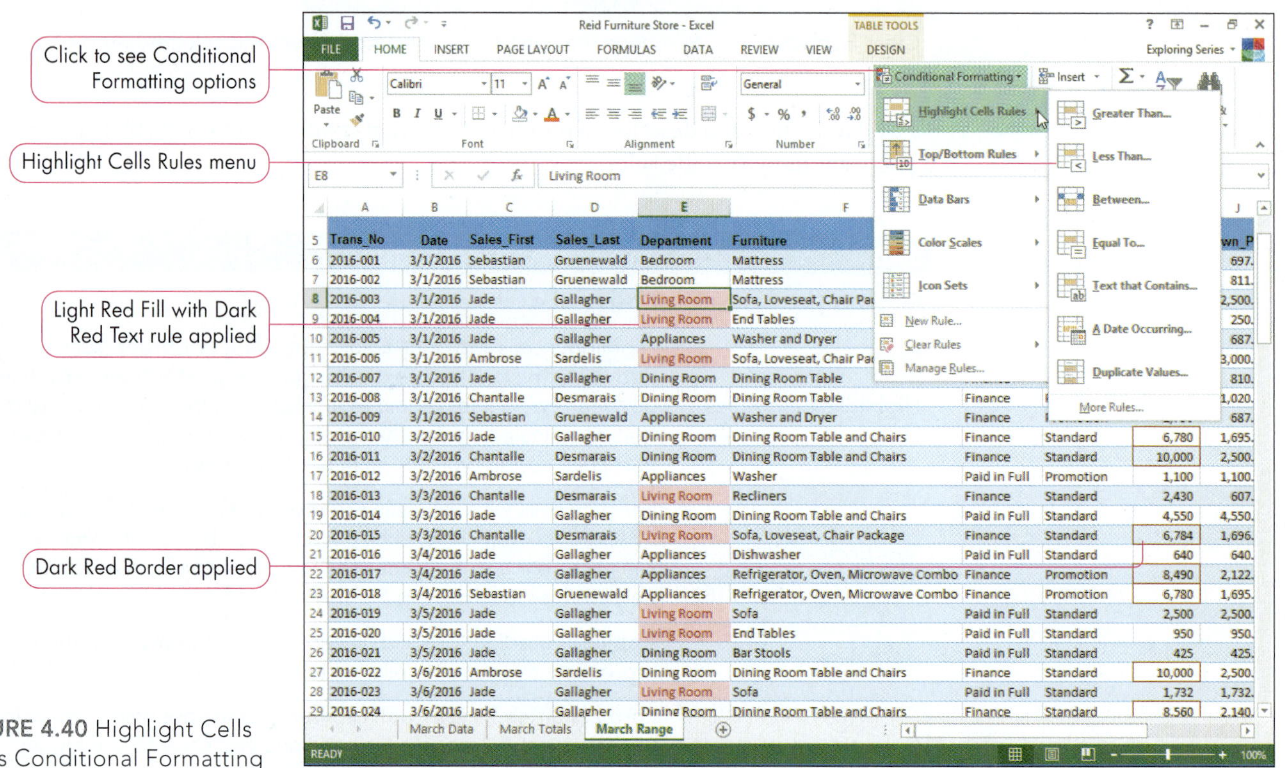

FIGURE 4.40 Highlight Cells Rules Conditional Formatting

Specify Top/Bottom Rules

STEP 2»

You might be interested in identifying the top five sales to reward the sales associates, or want to identify the bottom 15% of automobile dealers so that you can close underperforming locations. The Top/Bottom Rules category enables you to specify the top or bottom number, top or bottom percentage, or values that are above or below the average value in that range. In Figure 4.41, the Amount column is conditionally formatted to highlight the top five amounts. (Some rows are hidden so that all top five values display in the figure.) Although the menu option is Top 10 Items, you can specify the exact number of items to format.

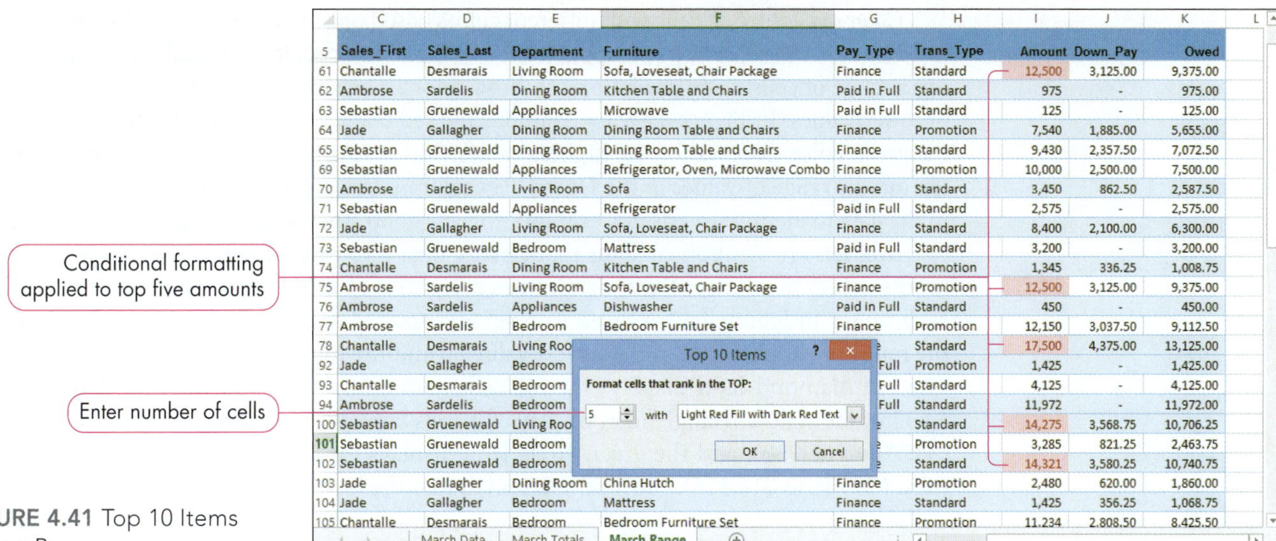

FIGURE 4.41 Top 10 Items Dialog Box

Display Data Bars, Color Scales, and Icon Sets

STEP 3

Data bars indicate the value of a cell relative to other cells (see Figure 4.42). The width of the data bar represents the value in a cell, with a wider bar representing a higher value and a narrower bar a lower value. Use data bar conditional formatting to identify high and low values. Excel locates the largest value and displays the widest data bar in that cell. Excel then finds the smallest value and displays the smallest data bar in that cell. Excel sizes the data bars for the remaining cells based on their values relative to the high and low values in the column. If you change the values, Excel updates the data bar widths. Excel uses the same color for each data bar, but each bar differs in size based on the value in the respective cells.

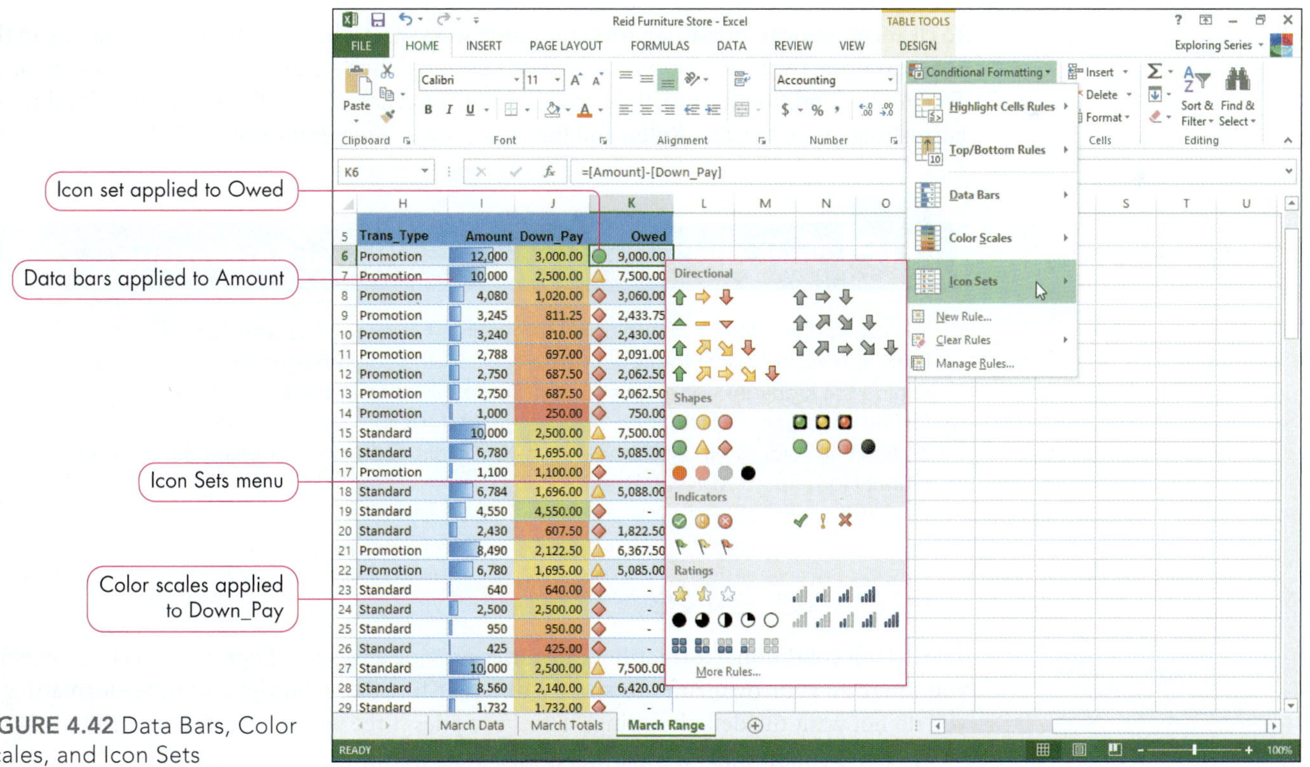

FIGURE 4.42 Data Bars, Color Scales, and Icon Sets

Color scales format cells with different colors based on the relative value of a cell compared to other selected cells. You can apply a two- or three-color scale. This scale assists in comparing a range of cells using gradations of those colors. The shade of the color represents higher or lower values. In Figure 4.42, for example, the red color scales display for the lowest values, the green color displays for the highest values, and gradients of yellow and orange represent the middle range of values in the Down_Pay column. Use color scales to understand variation in the data to identify trends, for example, to view good stock returns and weak stock returns.

Icon sets are symbols or signs that classify data into three, four, or five categories, based on the values in a range. Excel determines categories of value ranges and assigns an icon to each range. In Figure 4.42, a three-icon set was applied to the Owed column. Excel divided the range of values between the lowest value $0 and the highest value of $13,125 into thirds. The red diamond icon displays for the cells containing values in the lowest third ($0 to $4,375), the yellow triangle icon displays for cells containing the values in the middle third ($4,376 to $8,750), and the green circle icon displays for cells containing values in the top third ($8,751 to $13,125). Most purchases fall into the lowest third.

Don't Overdo It!

Although conditional formatting helps identify trends, you should use this feature wisely. Apply conditional formatting when you want to emphasize important data. When you decide to apply conditional formatting, think about which category is best to highlight the data. Sometimes simple highlighting will suffice when you want to point out data meeting a particular condition; other times, you might want to apply data bars to point out relative differences among values. Finally, do not apply conditional formatting to too many columns.

Clear Rules

To clear conditional formatting from the entire worksheet, click Conditional Formatting in the Styles group on the Home tab, point to Clear Rules, and then select *Clear Rules from Entire Sheet.* To remove conditional formatting from a range of cells, select cells. Then click Conditional Formatting, point to Clear Rules, and then select *Clear Rules from Selected Cells.*

Sort and Filter Using Conditional Formatting

You can sort and filter by conditional formatting. For example, if you applied the Highlight Cells Rules conditional formatting, you can sort the column by color so that all cells containing the highlight appear first or last. To do this, display the filter arrows, click the arrow for the conditionally formatted column you wish to sort, point to Sort by Color, and then click the fill color or No Fill in the *Sort by Cell Color* area. If you applied the Icon Sets conditional formatting, you can filter by icon.

Creating a New Rule

The default conditional formatting categories provide a variety of options. Excel also enables you to create your own rules to specify different fill colors, borders, or other formatting if you do not want the default settings. Excel provides three ways to create a new rule:

- Click Conditional Formatting in the Styles group and select New Rule.
- Click Conditional Formatting in the Styles group, select Manage Rules to open the Conditional Formatting Rules Manager dialog box, and then click New Rule.
- Click Conditional Formatting in the Styles group, select a rule category such as Highlight Cells Rules, and then select More Rules.

The New Formatting Rule dialog box opens (see Figure 4.43) so that you can define your new conditional formatting rule. First, select a rule type, such as *Format all cells based on their values*. The *Edit the Rule Description* section changes, based on the rule type you select. With the default rule type selected, you can specify the format style (2-Color Scale, 3-Color Scale, Data Bar, or Icon Sets). You can then specify the minimum and maximum values, the fill colors for color sets or data bars, or the icons for icon sets. After you edit the rule description, click OK to save your new conditional format.

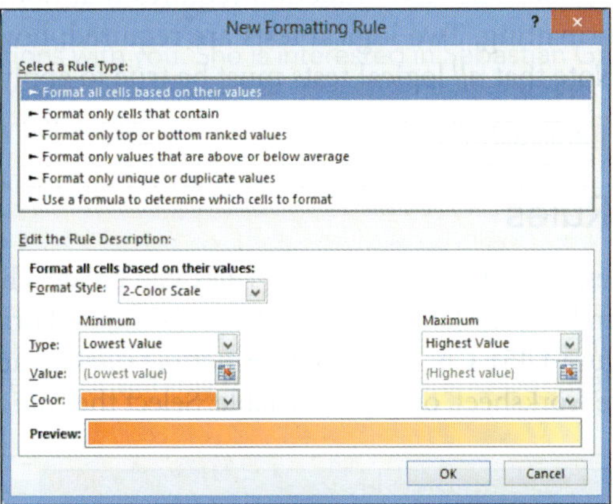

FIGURE 4.43 New Formatting Rule Dialog Box

If you select any rule type except the *Format all cells based on their values* rule, the dialog box contains a Format button. When you click Format, the Format Cells dialog box opens so that you can specify number, font, border, and fill formats to apply to your rule.

TIP Format Only Cells That Contain

This option provides a wide array of things you can format: values, text, dates, blanks, no blanks, errors, or no errors. Formatting blanks is helpful to see where you are missing data, and formatting cells containing errors helps you find those errors quickly.

Use Formulas in Conditional Formatting

STEP 4

If you need to create a complex conditional formatting rule, you can select a rule that uses a formula to format cells. For example, you might want to format merchandise amounts of financed items *and* amounts that are $10,000 or more. Figure 4.44 shows the Edit Formatting Rule dialog box and the corresponding conditional formatting applied to cells.

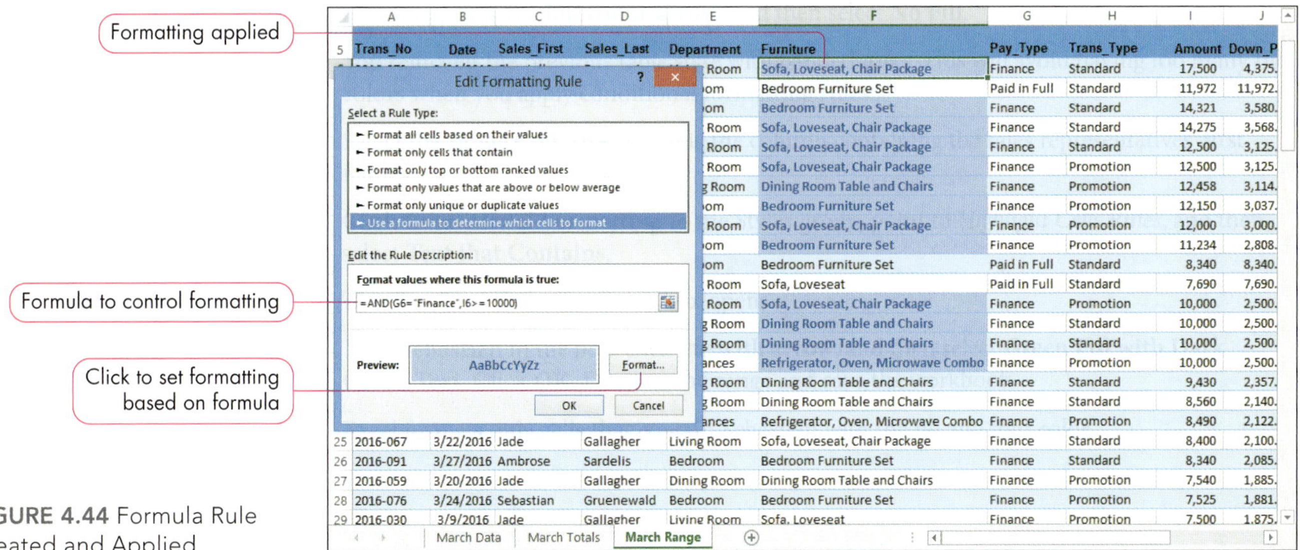

FIGURE 4.44 Formula Rule Created and Applied

Source total arrow, and then select **None**. Click **cell H358**, the *Replacement Value total* cell, click the **Replacement Value total arrow**, and then select **Sum**.

o. Prepare the Retired worksheet for printing by doing the following:
- Set **0.2"** left and right page margins.
- Select the **range E1:I358**, click the **PAGE LAYOUT tab**, click **Print Area** in the Page Setup group, and then select **Set Print Area**.
- Click **Print Titles** in the Page Setup group, click the **Rows to repeat at top Collapse Dialog box button**, click the **row 1 header**, and then click the **Collapse Dialog box button**. Click **OK**.
- Click the **VIEW tab** and click **Page Break Preview** in the Workbook Views group. Decrease the top margin to avoid having only one or two records print on the last page.

p. Create a footer with your name on the left side, the sheet name code in the center, and the file name code on the right side of each worksheet.

q. Save and close the workbook, and submit based on your instructor's directions.

2 Dentist Association Donation List

The Midwest Regional Dentist Association is planning its annual meeting in Lincoln, Nebraska, this spring. Several members donated items for door prizes at the closing general session. You will organize the list of donations and format it to highlight particular data for your supervisor, who is on the conference board of directors. This exercise follows the same set of skills as used in Hands-On Exercises 2–5 in the chapter. Refer to Figure 4.51 as you complete this exercise.

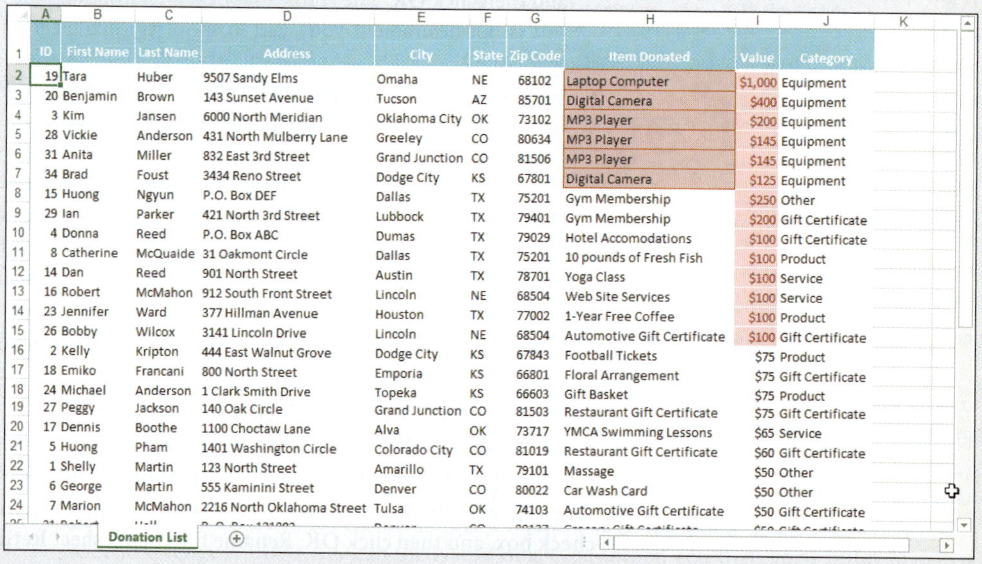

	A	B	C	D	E	F	G	H	I	J	K
1	ID	First Name	Last Name	Address	City	State	Zip Code	Item Donated	Value	Category	
2	19	Tara	Huber	9507 Sandy Elms	Omaha	NE	68102	Laptop Computer	$1,000	Equipment	
3	20	Benjamin	Brown	143 Sunset Avenue	Tucson	AZ	85701	Digital Camera	$400	Equipment	
4	3	Kim	Jansen	6000 North Meridian	Oklahoma City	OK	73102	MP3 Player	$200	Equipment	
5	28	Vickie	Anderson	431 North Mulberry Lane	Greeley	CO	80634	MP3 Player	$145	Equipment	
6	31	Anita	Miller	832 East 3rd Street	Grand Junction	CO	81506	MP3 Player	$145	Equipment	
7	34	Brad	Foust	3434 Reno Street	Dodge City	KS	67801	Digital Camera	$125	Equipment	
8	15	Huong	Ngyun	P.O. Box DEF	Dallas	TX	75201	Gym Membership	$250	Other	
9	29	Ian	Parker	421 North 3rd Street	Lubbock	TX	79401	Gym Membership	$200	Gift Certificate	
10	4	Donna	Reed	P.O. Box ABC	Dumas	TX	79029	Hotel Accomodations	$100	Gift Certificate	
11	8	Catherine	McQuaide	31 Oakmont Circle	Dallas	TX	75201	10 pounds of Fresh Fish	$100	Product	
12	14	Dan	Reed	901 North Street	Austin	TX	78701	Yoga Class	$100	Service	
13	16	Robert	McMahon	912 South Front Street	Lincoln	NE	68504	Web Site Services	$100	Service	
14	23	Jennifer	Ward	377 Hillman Avenue	Houston	TX	77002	1-Year Free Coffee	$100	Product	
15	26	Bobby	Wilcox	3141 Lincoln Drive	Lincoln	NE	68504	Automotive Gift Certificate	$100	Gift Certificate	
16	2	Kelly	Kripton	444 East Walnut Grove	Dodge City	KS	67843	Football Tickets	$75	Product	
17	18	Emiko	Francani	800 North Street	Emporia	KS	66801	Floral Arrangement	$75	Gift Certificate	
18	24	Michael	Anderson	1 Clark Smith Drive	Topeka	KS	66603	Gift Basket	$75	Product	
19	27	Peggy	Jackson	140 Oak Circle	Grand Junction	CO	81503	Restaurant Gift Certificate	$75	Gift Certificate	
20	17	Dennis	Boothe	1100 Choctaw Lane	Alva	OK	73717	YMCA Swimming Lessons	$65	Service	
21	5	Huong	Pham	1401 Washington Circle	Colorado City	CO	81019	Restaurant Gift Certificate	$60	Gift Certificate	
22	1	Shelly	Martin	123 North Street	Amarillo	TX	79101	Massage	$50	Other	
23	6	George	Martin	555 Kaminini Street	Denver	CO	80022	Car Wash Card	$50	Other	
24	7	Marion	McMahon	2216 North Oklahoma Street	Tulsa	OK	74103	Automotive Gift Certificate	$50	Gift Certificate	

Donation List

FIGURE 4.51 Donation List

a. Open *e04p2Donate* and save it as **e04p2Donate_LastFirst**.

b. Click the **DESIGN tab**, click **Remove Duplicates** in the Tools group, and then click **OK**. Click **OK** in the message box that tells you that Excel removed three duplicate records.

c. Click **Convert to Range** in the Tools group and click **Yes** in the message box.

d. Select the **range A2:J35**, click the **HOME tab**, click the **Fill Color arrow** in the Font group, and then select **No Fill** to remove the table fill colors.

e. Select the **range I2:I35**. Click **Conditional Formatting** in the Styles group, point to *Highlight Cells Rules*, and then select **Greater Than**. Type **99** in the **Format cells that are GREATER THAN box** and click **OK**.

f. Select **cells H2:H35**. Create a custom conditional format by doing the following:
  - Click **Conditional Formatting** in the Styles group and select **New Rule**.
  - Click **Use a formula to determine which cells to format.**
  - Type **=(J2="Equipment")** in the **Format values where this formula is true box**. The basic condition is testing to see if the contents of cell J2 equal the word *Equipment*. You type *Equipment* in quotation marks because you are comparing text instead of a value.
  - Click **Format**, click the **Fill tab** if necessary, and then click **Red, Accent 2, Lighter 60%** (sixth background color on the second row below the first horizontal line).
  - Click the **Border tab**, click the **Color arrow**, click **Dark Red**, and then click **Outline.**
  - Click **OK** in each dialog box.

DISCOVER 

g. Click in the table to deselect the range. Click **Sort & Filter** in the Editing group and select **Custom Sort**. The dialog box may contain existing sort conditions for the State and City fields, which you will replace. Set the following sort conditions:
  - Click the **Sort by arrow** and select **Item Donated**. Click the **Sort On arrow** and select **Cell Color**. Click the **Order arrow** and select the **RGB(146, 205, 220) fill color**. The fill color displays for the Order.
  - Click the **Then by arrow** and select **Value**. Click the **Order arrow** and select **Largest to Smallest**.
  - Click **OK.**

h. Select **Landscape orientation**, set appropriate margins, and then adjust column widths so that all the data will print on one page. Do not decrease the scaling.

i. Create a footer with your name on the left side, the sheet name code in the center, and the file name code on the right side.

j. Save and close the workbook, and submit based on your instructor's directions.

FIGUR

PivotTable Basics

Analyzing large amounts of data is important for making solid decisions. Entering data is the easy part; retrieving data in a structured, meaningful way is more challenging. ***Data mining*** is the process of analyzing large volumes of data, using advanced statistical techniques, and identifying trends and patterns in the data. Managers use data-mining techniques to address a variety of questions, such as the following:

- What snack foods do customers purchase most when purchasing Pepsi® products?
- What age group from what geographic region downloads the most top 10 songs from iTunes?
- What hotel chain and rental car combinations are most popular among Delta Air Lines passengers flying into Salt Lake City?

Questions similar to those above help organizations prepare their marketing plans to capitalize on consumer spending patterns. The more you know about your customer demographics, the better you can focus your strategic plans to increase market share.

A ***PivotTable*** is a powerful, interactive data-mining feature that enables you to summarize and analyze data, especially helpful when working with large datasets. An advantage of using a PivotTable is that you can group data into one or more categories and perform a variety of calculations without altering the original dataset. The most important benefit of a PivotTable is that it is dynamic. You can easily and quickly *pivot*, or rearrange, data to analyze them from different viewpoints, such as expanding or collapsing details, organizing and grouping data differently, and switching row and column categories. Viewing the PivotTable from different perspectives helps you more easily identify trends and patterns among the variables in the data that might not be obvious from looking at the data from only one viewpoint.

In this section, you will learn how to create a PivotTable by organizing data into columns and rows to aggregate data.

Creating a PivotTable

Before you create a PivotTable, ensure the data source is well structured. Applying the rules for good table design is a start: Use meaningful column labels, ensure data accuracy, and avoid blank rows and columns in the dataset. To consolidate and aggregate data, at least one column must have duplicate values, such as the same city, state, or department name for several records. You then use these columns of duplicate values to create categories for organizing and summarizing data. Another column must have numeric values that can be aggregated to produce quantitative summaries, such as averages or sums.

Create a PivotTable from the Quick Analysis Gallery

You can create a PivotTable from the Quick Analysis gallery. A benefit of this method is that Excel displays recommended PivotTables based on the data. To create a PivotTable using Quick Analysis, do the following:

STEP 1 »

1. Select the entire dataset, including the field names (column labels).
2. Click the Quick Analysis button in the bottom-right corner of the selected range.
3. Click TABLES in the Quick Analysis gallery.
4. Position the mouse pointer over the PivotTable thumbnails to see a preview of the different recommended PivotTables (see Figure 5.9).
5. Click the PivotTable thumbnail to create the desired PivotTable.

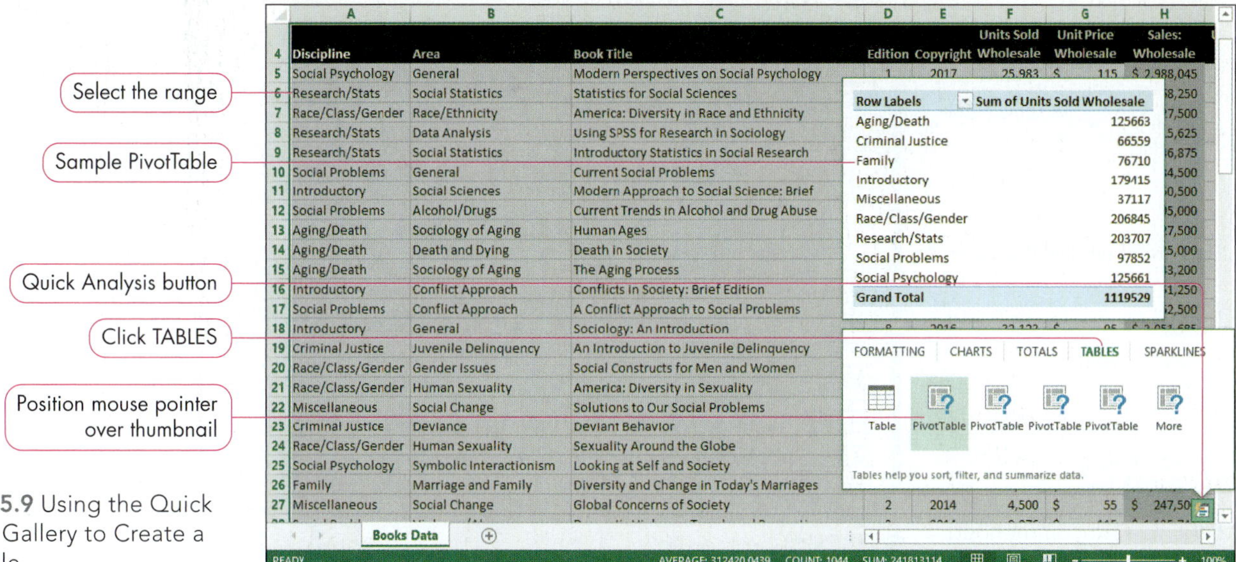

FIGURE 5.9 Using the Quick Analysis Gallery to Create a PivotTable

TIP PivotTable or Subtotals?

At first glance, PivotTables are similar to subtotals because they both produce subtotals, but PivotTables are more robust. PivotTables provide more flexibility than subtotals provide. If you need complex subtotals cross-referenced by two or more categories with filtering and other specifications, create a PivotTable.

Create a PivotTable from the Ribbon

You can also create a PivotTable by using commands on the Ribbon. The Insert tab contains PivotTable and Recommended PivotTables commands. If you click PivotTable, Excel displays the Create PivotTable dialog box so that you can create a blank PivotTable from scratch. However, if you click Recommended PivotTables, Excel displays a dialog box so that you can select from a gallery of PivotTables. This option is similar to using the Quick Analysis gallery. To create a recommended PivotTable using the Ribbon, do the following:

1. Click inside the dataset (the range of cells or table).
2. Click the INSERT tab and click Recommended PivotTables in the Tables group to open the Recommended PivotTables dialog box (see Figure 5.10).
3. Click a thumbnail in the gallery on the left side of the dialog box to see a preview of the PivotTable on the right side.
4. Click OK to create the desired PivotTable.

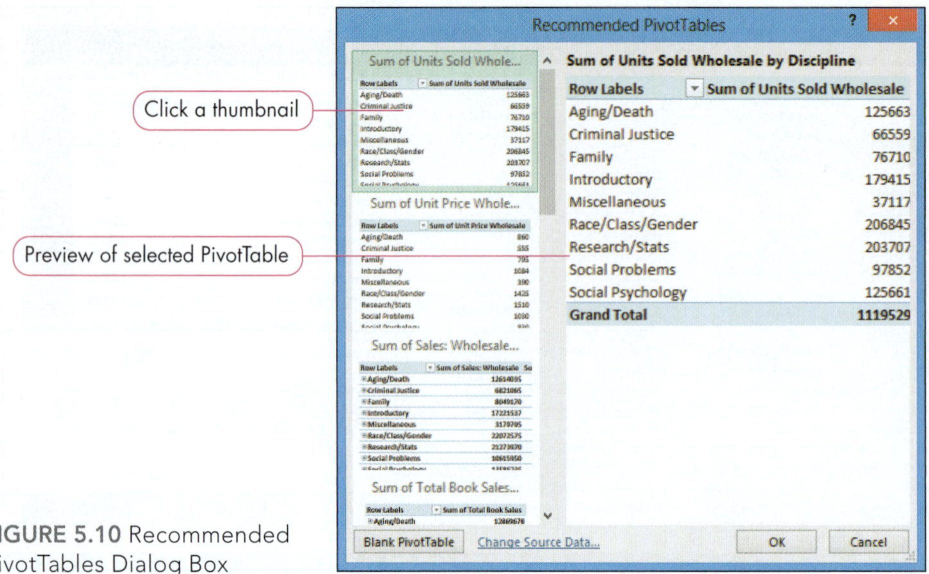

FIGURE 5.10 Recommended PivotTables Dialog Box

After you use the Recommended PivotTables dialog box or the Quick Analysis gallery, Excel creates a PivotTable on a new worksheet (see Figure 5.11). The ROWS area contains the category names of the summarized data. For example, each discipline, such as Family, is listed in only one row, regardless of how many times each category name appears in the original dataset.

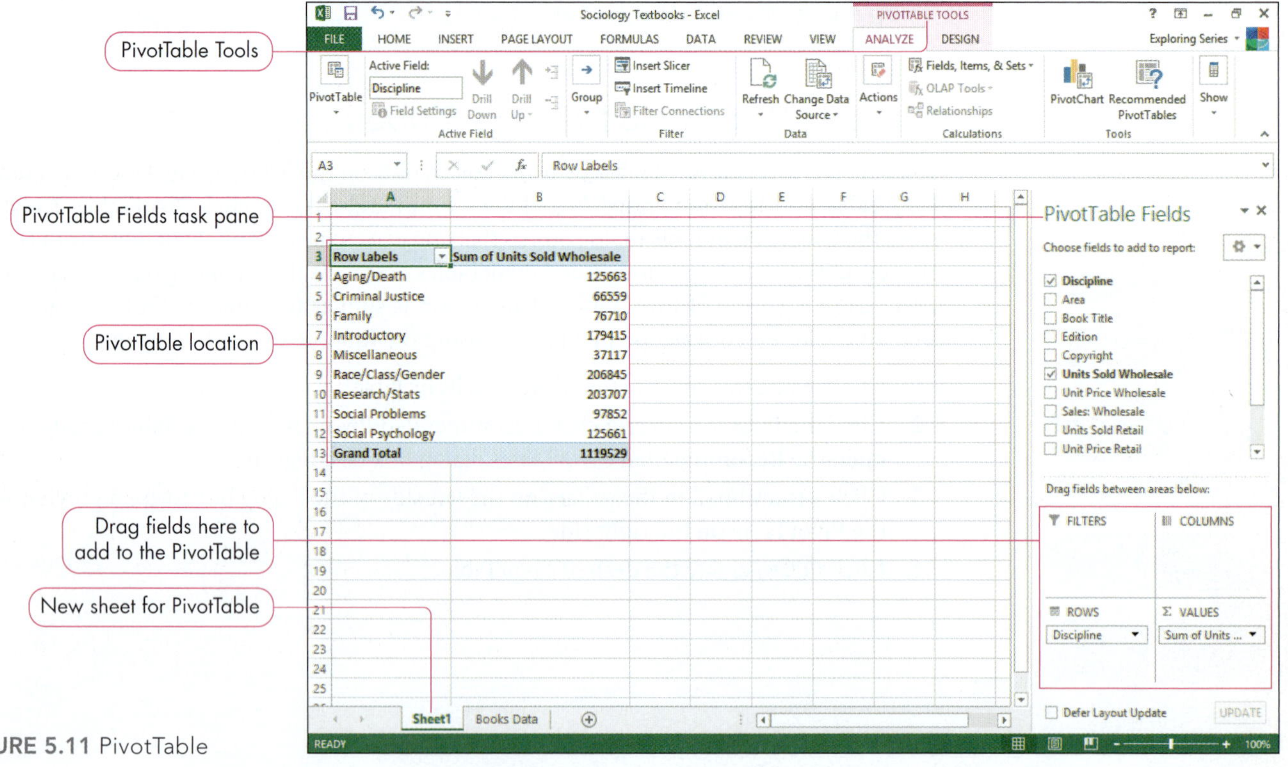

FIGURE 5.11 PivotTable

The PivotTable Fields task pane displays on the right side, and the PivotTable Tools Analyze and Design contextual tabs appear on the Ribbon. If you click outside the PivotTable, the contextual tabs and the task pane disappear. Click within the PivotTable to display these elements again.

TIP PivotTable Fields Task Pane

If the PivotTable Fields task pane does not appear when you click inside a PivotTable, click the Show arrow on the Analyze tab, and then click Field List. This command is a toggle, so you can click it to show or hide task pane.

The ***PivotTable Fields task pane*** contains two sections. The *Choose fields to add to report* section lists all the fields or column labels from the original data source. You can click either drag a field to an area in the bottom of the task pane or click the check box to add the field to the PivotTable. Use the *Drag fields between areas below* section to arrange fields in one of the four PivotTable areas. Table 5.3 describes the areas of a PivotTable.

TABLE 5.3 Areas of a PivotTable

Area	Description
Filters Area	Filters the data to display results based on particular conditions you set.
Columns Area	Subdivides data into one or more additional categories.
Rows Area	Organizes and groups data into categories on the left side. Each group name occupies a single row.
Values Area	Displays summary statistics, such as totals or averages.

Modifying a PivotTable

After you create a PivotTable, you might want to modify it to see the data from a different perspective. For example, you might want to add fields to the rows, values, and columns areas of the PivotTable. In addition, you might want to collapse the PivotTable to show fewer details or expand it to show more details.

Add Rows

You can add fields to provide a more detailed analysis. For example, you might want to organize data by discipline by adding the Discipline field to the ROWS area in the PivotTable Fields task pane. To add a field as a row, do one of the following:

STEP 2

- Click the field's check box in the *Choose fields to add to report* section. Excel adds the field to a PivotTable area based on the type of data stored in the field. If the field contains text, Excel usually places that field in the ROWS area.
- Drag the field from the *Choose fields to add to report* section and drop it in the ROWS area.
- Right-click the field name in the *Choose fields to add to report* section and select *Add to Row Labels.*

Add Values

A PivotTable has meaning when you include quantitative fields, such as quantities and monetary values, to aggregate the data. For example, you might want to display the total wholesale sales for each discipline and area. To add values, do one of the following:

- Click the field's check box in the *Choose fields to add to report* section. Excel makes it the value aggregate, such as *Sum of Sales.*

Creating a Calculated Field

You can create a ***calculated field***, which is a user-defined field that does not exist in the original dataset. It derives its values based on performing calculations on other original dataset values. For example, you can create a calculated field that converts totals to percentages for easier relative comparison among categories, or you might want to create a calculated field that determines what the number of units a 10% increase in units sold for the upcoming year would be. To create a calculated field, do the following:

STEP 3

1. Select a cell within the PivotTable.
2. Click the PIVOTTABLE TOOLS ANALYZE tab.
3. Click Fields, Items, & Sets in the Calculations group and select Calculated Field to display the Insert Calculated Field dialog box (see Figure 5.24).

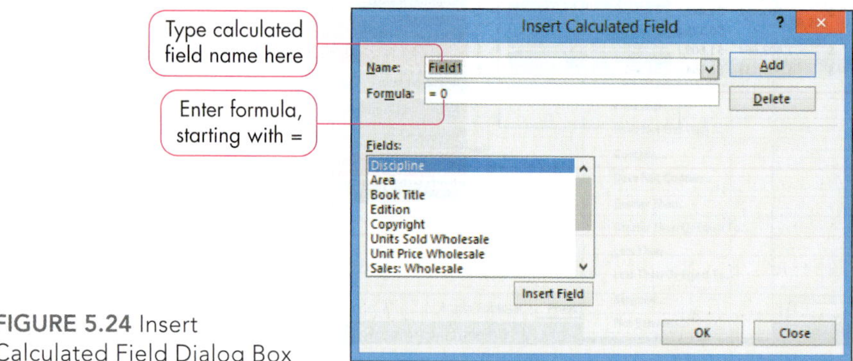

FIGURE 5.24 Insert Calculated Field Dialog Box

Type a descriptive label for the calculated field in the Name box. Build a formula starting with the equal sign (=). Instead of using cell references, insert the field names and other operands. For example ='Total Book Sales'*.1 calculates a 10% royalty amount on the total book sales. Click OK to insert the calculated field in the PivotTable. Format the numerical values in the calculated field column as needed.

Show Values as a Specific Calculation Result

In addition to creating calculated fields, you can apply built-in custom calculations that display relationships between values in rows and columns in the PivotTable. For example, you can show each value as a percentage of the grand total or each value's percentage of the row total. To display values in relation to others, do the following:

STEP 4

1. Click the field in the VALUES area of the task pane and select Value Field Settings (or click within the field in the PivotTable and click Field Settings in the Active Field group on the ANALYZE tab).
2. Click the Show Values As tab within the Value Field Settings dialog box.
3. Click the *Show values as* arrow and select the desired calculation type. Table 5.6 lists and describes some of the calculation options.
4. Click Number Format to set number formats, click OK to close the Format Cells dialog box, and then click OK to close the Value Field Settings dialog box.

TABLE 5.6 Calculation Options	
Option	**Description**
% of Grand Total	Displays each value as a percentage of the grand total.
% of Column Total	Displays each value as a percentage of the respective column total. The values in each column total 100%.
% of Row Total	Displays each value as a percentage of the respective row total. The values in each row total 100%.
% of Parent Row Total	Displays values as: (value for the item) / (value for the parent item on rows).
Running Total	Displays values as running totals.
Rank Smallest to Largest	Displays the rank of values in a specific field where 1 represents the smallest value.
Rank Largest to Smallest	Displays the rank of values in a specific field where 1 represents the largest value.

1. What is the purpose of applying a filter to a PivotTable? How do you apply a main filter and additional filters? ***p. 349***
2. What is a slicer? What do the three different colors indicate in a slicer? ***p. 350***
3. When would you create a calculated field in a PivotTable? ***p. 352***

Hands-On Exercises

3 PivotTable Options

The PivotTable you created has been beneficial for you to review sales data by discipline for each copyright year. In addition, you have used the PivotTable to compare grand total sales among disciplines and grand totals by copyright year. Now you want to extend your analysis. You will calculate author royalties from the sales and impose filters to focus your attention on each analysis.

Skills covered: Set Filters • Insert and Customize a Slicer • Create a Calculated Field • Show Values as Calculations

STEP 1 » SET FILTERS

The level of success of the first two editions especially determines the likelihood of approving subsequent revisions and editions. To display aggregated sales for these editions, you need to set a filter to remove the other editions from being included in the calculated sales data. After you review the first- and second-edition data, you will enable additional filters to review books published in the past two years. Refer to Figure 5.25 as you complete Step 1.

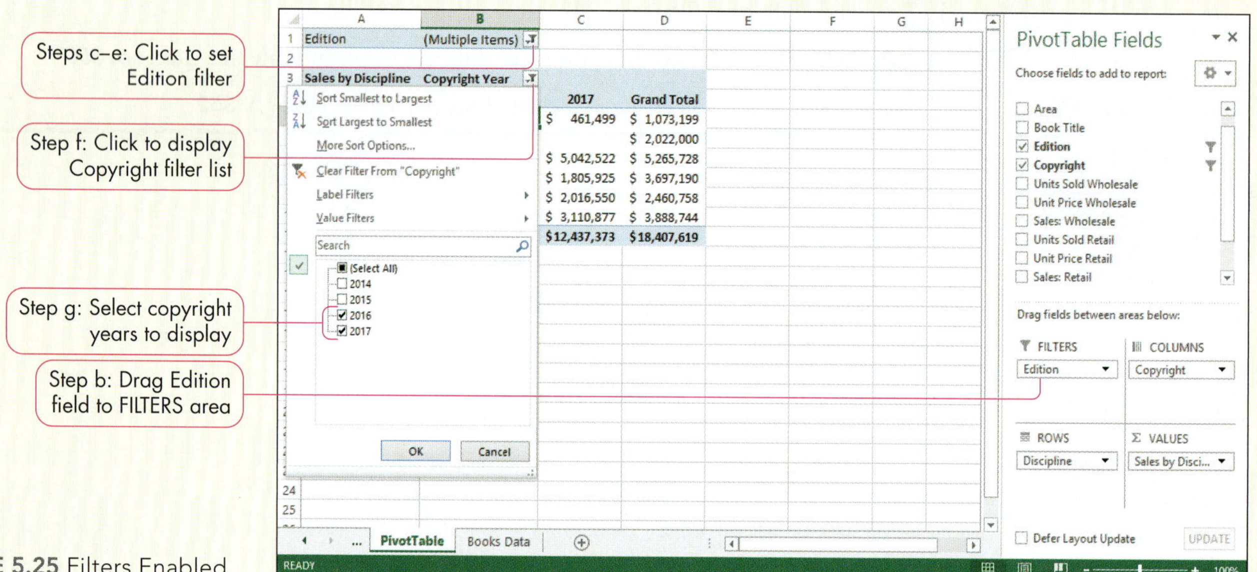

FIGURE 5.25 Filters Enabled

a. Open *e05h2Sociology_LastFirst* if you closed it at the end of Hands-On Exercise 2 and save it as **e05h3Sociology_LastFirst**, changing *h2* to *h3*.

> **TROUBLESHOOTING:** Click in the PivotTable to display the PivotTable Field task pane if necessary.

b. Make sure the PivotTable worksheet tab is active and drag the **Edition field** from the *Choose fields to add to report* section to the FILTERS area.

You can now filter the PivotTable based on the Edition field. Cell A1 displays the field name, and cell B1 displays (All) and the filter arrow.

c. Click the **Edition filter arrow** in **cell B1** and click the **Select Multiple Items check box**.

The list displays a check box for each item.

d. Click the **(All) check box** to deselect it.

e. Click the **1** and **2 check boxes** and click **OK**.

The summary statistics reflect sales data for only first- and second-edition publications. The filter arrow changes to a funnel icon in cell B1.

f. Click the **Copyright Year filter arrow** in **cell B3** and click the **(Select All) check box** to deselect it.

g. Click the **2016** and **2017 check boxes** and click **OK**.

Excel filters out data for years that do not meet the condition you set. The filter arrow changes to a funnel icon in cell B3.

h. Save the workbook.

STEP 2 » INSERT AND CUSTOMIZE A SLICER

You might distribute the workbook to colleagues who are not as skilled in Excel as you are. To help them set their own filters, you insert slicers. Refer to Figure 5.26 as you complete Step 2.

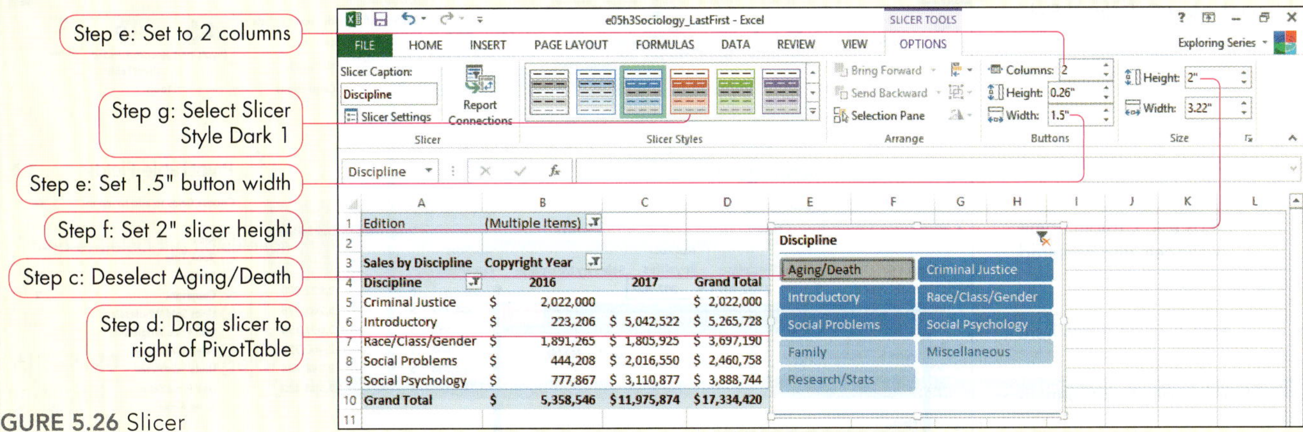

FIGURE 5.26 Slicer

a. Click **Insert Slicer** in the Filter group on the ANALYZE tab.

The Insert Slicers dialog box opens, listing each field name.

b. Click **Discipline** and click **OK**.

Excel inserts the Discipline slicer in the worksheet. Six slicer buttons are blue, indicating that those disciplines are selected. The grayed-out buttons at the bottom of the slicer indicate those disciplines are not applicable based on other engaged filters you set (first and second editions and 2016 and 2017 copyright years).

c. Press and hold **Ctrl** as you click **Aging/Death** in the Discipline slicer.

This deselects the Aging/Death discipline.

> **TROUBLESHOOTING:** Because several disciplines are selected, if you click Aging/Death instead of pressing Ctrl as you click it, you set Aging/Death as the only discipline. The others are filtered out. If this happens, immediately click Undo and repeat step c.

d. Drag the slicer to the right side of the PivotTable.

You moved the slicer so that it does not cover up data in the PivotTable.

e. Change the **Columns value** to **2** in the Buttons group on the SLICER TOOLS OPTIONS tab. Change the button **Width** to **1.5"** in the Buttons group.

The slicer now displays buttons in two columns. You changed the width of the buttons to 1.5" to display the full discipline names within the buttons.

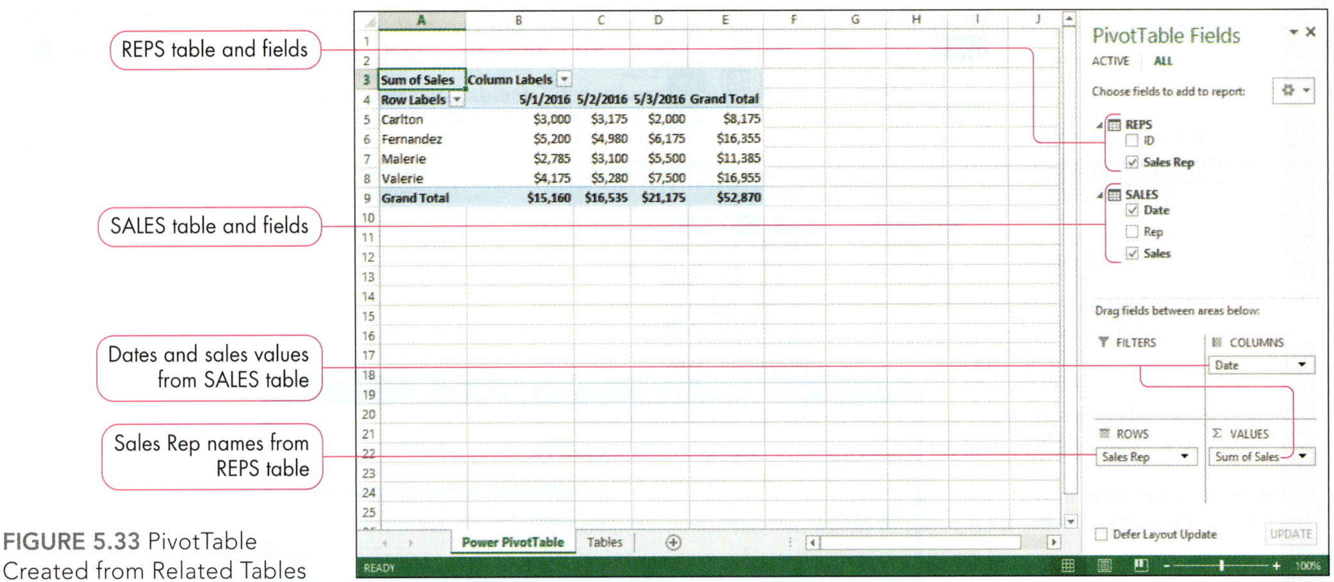

FIGURE 5.33 PivotTable Created from Related Tables

More Information on Power PivotTables

Look up the topic *What's new in PowerPivot in Excel 2013* to learn more about the PowerPivot functionality and how to create PivotTables from related tables. The Help menu also informs you which versions of Microsoft Office 2013 contain this feature and how you can enable it.

Creating a PivotChart

Charts display data visually. This visual representation may help you and your audience understand the data better than merely presenting the data in a spreadsheet. Although PivotTables help reduce the amount of data to analyze, PivotTables can be overwhelming. Another way to display a PivotTable's aggregated data is through a PivotChart. A ***PivotChart*** is an interactive graphical representation of the data in a PivotTable. A PivotChart presents the consolidated data visually.

A PivotChart is associated with a PivotTable. When you change the position of a field in either the PivotTable or the PivotChart, the corresponding object changes as well. To create a PivotChart, do the following:

STEP 2»

1. Click inside the PivotTable.
2. Click the ANALYZE tab and click PivotChart in the Tools group.

Excel creates a PivotChart based on the current PivotTable settings—row labels, column labels, values, and filters. The PivotChart contains elements that enable you to set filters. The ROWS area changes to AXIS (CATEGORY) and the COLUMNS area changes to LEGEND (SERIES) when you select the PivotChart (see Figure 5.34).

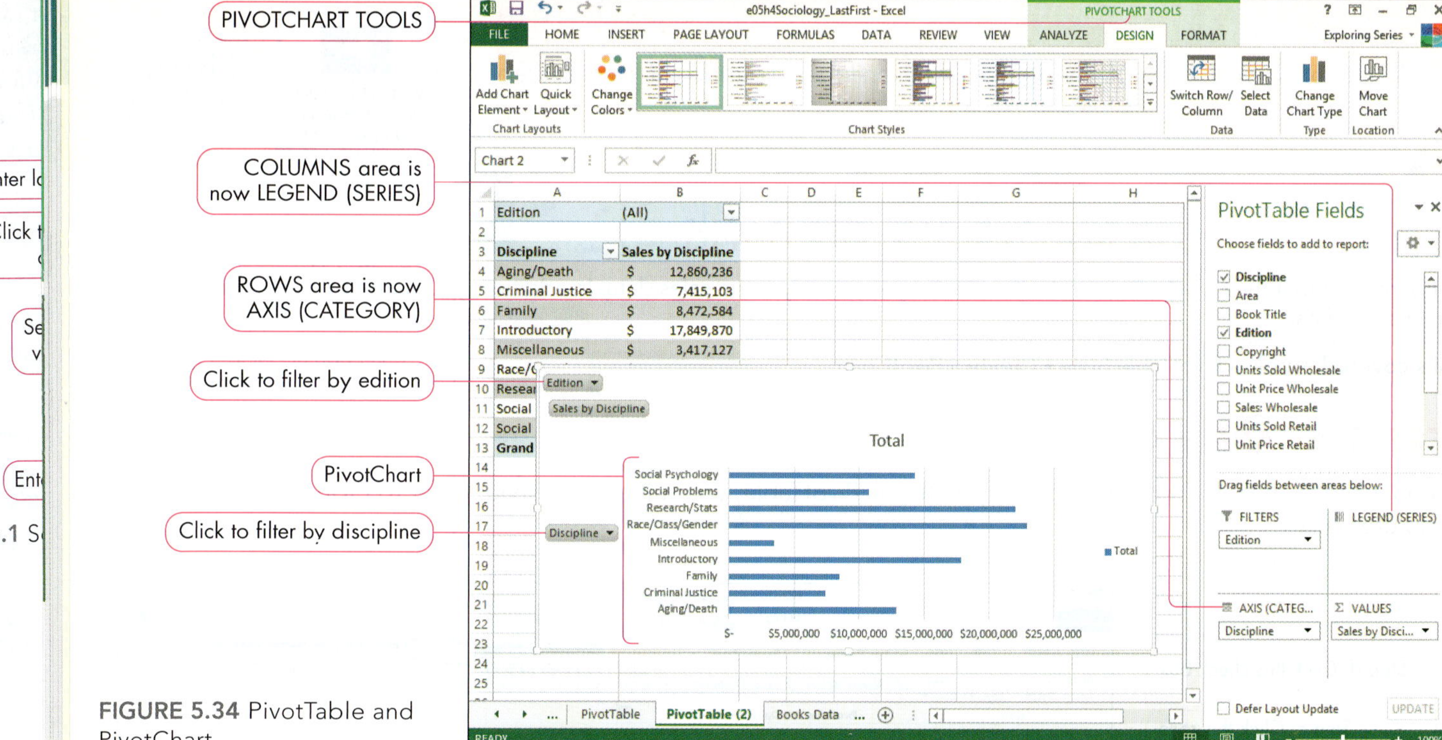

FIGURE 5.34 PivotTable and PivotChart

Although Excel creates the PivotChart based on the current PivotTable settings, you can change the settings using the PivotTable Field List. Click the FILTERS arrow and select values to filter the chart. Click the AXIS (CATEGORY) arrows to sort or filter the categories and subcategories in rows. Click the LEGEND (SERIES) to filter the chart representation based on the values. Changes you make to the PivotChart also affect the corresponding PivotTable. For example, if you apply a filter to the PivotChart, Excel also filters the PivotTable.

The Chart Tools Analyze tab contains the same options that you used to customize a PivotTable. In addition, the Actions group contains the Move Chart option so that you can move a PivotChart to a different worksheet.

The Chart Tools Design tab contains options to add a chart element, apply a layout, change colors, and apply a chart style. In addition, you can switch the data between the category axis and the legend, select the data used to create the chart, change the chart type, and move the chart to a different worksheet.

You can further customize PivotChart elements the same way you can customize regular charts—display data labels, change the fill color for a data series, display axis titles, and so forth. Use Help to learn more about customizing PivotCharts.

Quick Concepts

1. What types of specific elements can you select to be controlled by PivotTable styles? ***p. 359***
2. What must be done to create a PivotTable from more than one table? ***p. 360***
3. What replaces the ROWS and COLUMNS in the task pane when you create a PivotChart? ***p. 362***

For example, assume you want to compare the effect of different interest rates on the monthly payment, the total amount repaid, and the total interest paid. As shown in Figure 6.2, you need to set up three columns to show the calculated results. The first formula reference for monthly payment (=B12) goes in cell E3. To compare the effects of substitution values on other results, the second formula reference for total repaid (=B13) goes in cell F3, and the third formula reference for total interest paid (=B14) goes in cell G3.

Complete the Results

STEP 3» It is important that you enter the substitution values and formula references in the correct locations. This sets the left and top boundaries of the soon-to-be-completed data table. To complete the one-variable data table, do the following:

1. Select the data table boundaries, starting in the blank cell in the top-left corner of the data table. Drag down and to the right, if there is more than one column, to select the last blank cell at the intersection of the last substitution value and the last formula reference.
2. Click the DATA tab, click What-If Analysis in the Data Tools group, and then select Data Table to open the Data Table dialog box (see Figure 6.2).
3. Enter the cell reference of the cell containing the original variable for which you are substituting values. If you listed the substitution values in a row, enter the original variable cell reference in the *Row input cell* box. If you listed the substitution values in a column, enter the original variable cell reference in the *Column input cell* box. In Figure 6.2, for example, click cell B4—the original interest rate variable—in the *Column input cell* box because you entered the substitution interest rates in a column. Note that the cell reference is automatically made absolute so that Excel always refers to the original input cell as it performs calculations in the data table.
4. Click OK.

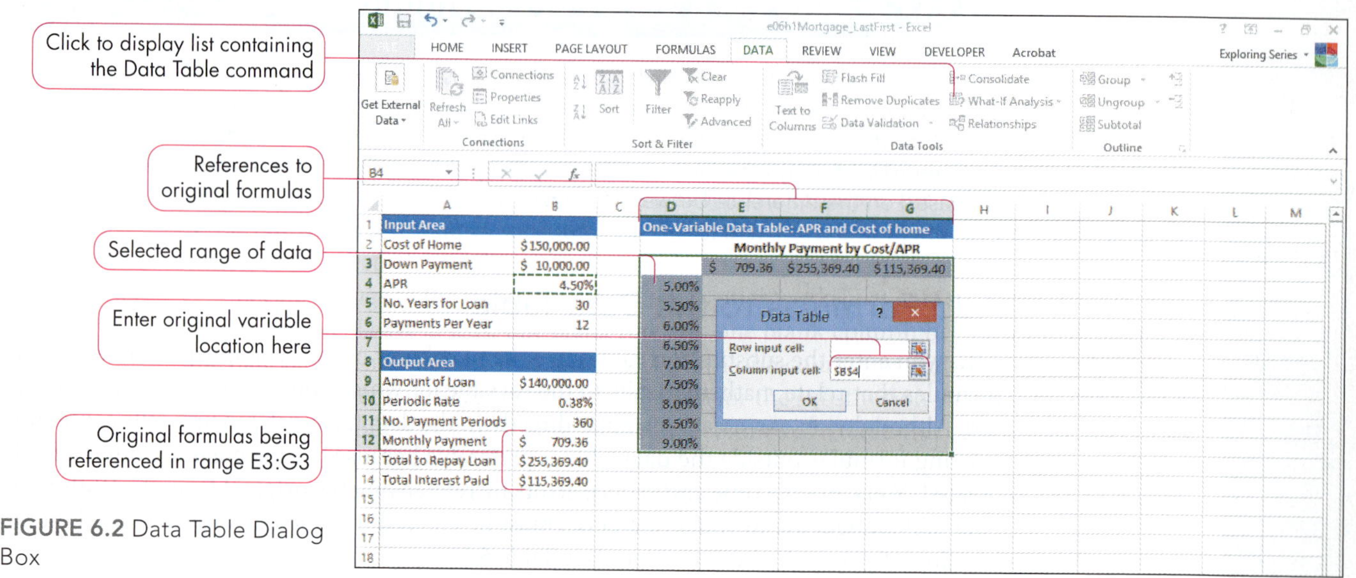

FIGURE 6.2 Data Table Dialog Box

When you create the one-variable data table, Excel uses the substitution values individually to replace the original variable's value, which is then used in the formulas to produce the results in the body of the data table. In Figure 6.3, the data table shows the substitution values of different interest rates, whereas the formulas produce the monthly payments (column E), total payments (column F), and total interest paid (column G) for the respective interest rates.

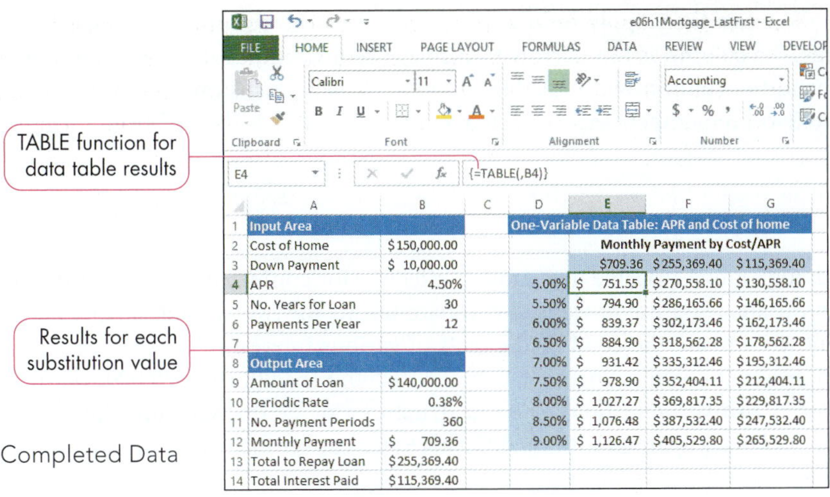

FIGURE 6.3 Completed Data Table

Format the Data Table

After creating the data table, you should format the values with Accounting Number Format. To reduce confusion, you should also create custom formats to disguise the formula references as column labels. To create custom formats, do the following:

1. Click in the cell containing a formula reference in the data table.
2. Click the Number Dialog Box Launcher in the Number group on the HOME tab to open the Format Cells dialog box with the Number tab active.
3. Click Custom in the Category list, scroll up in the Type list, and then select General in the list.
4. Select General in the Type box above the Type list and type what you want to appear as a column heading. Enter the text within quotation marks, such as "Payment," and click OK. Note that you must include the word to be displayed within quotation marks or the custom format will not display properly (see Figure 6.4).
5. Click OK.

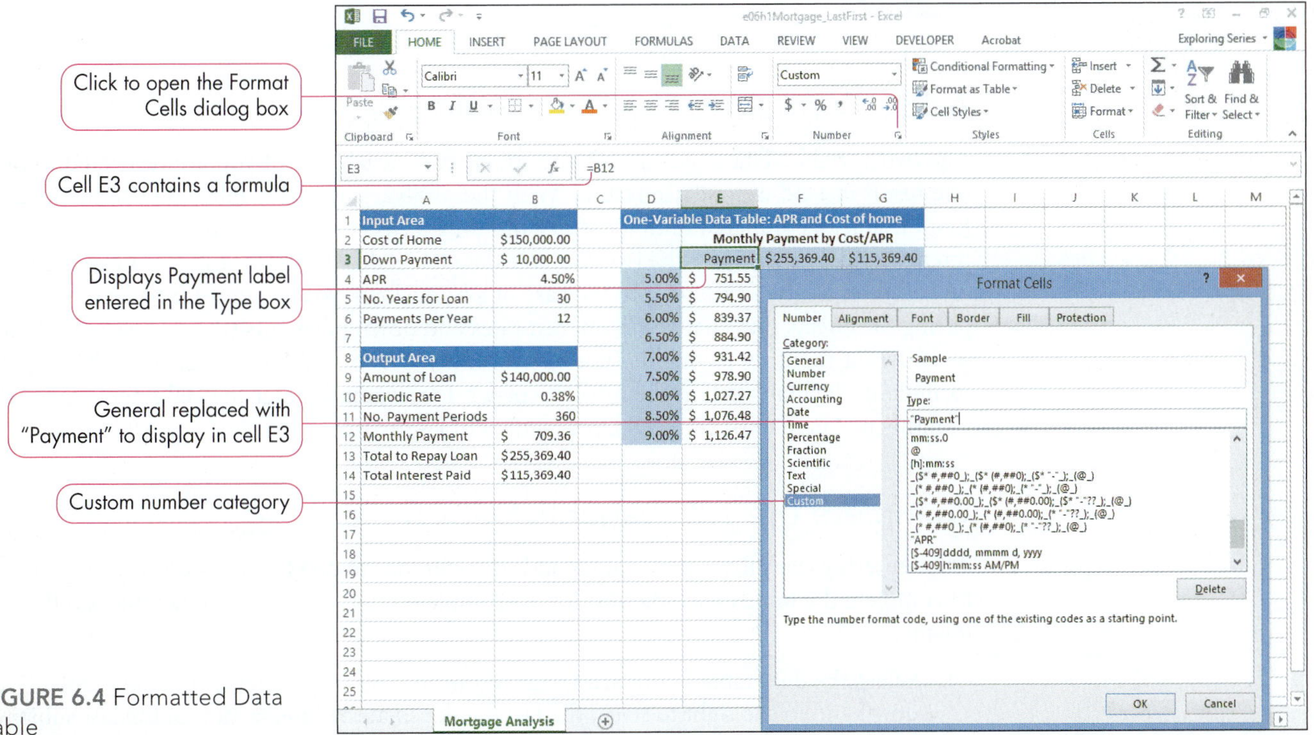

FIGURE 6.4 Formatted Data Table

You can then apply bold and centering to the column headings. If you see pound signs, the column is too narrow to display the text, indicating you need to wrap the text or expand the column width. Although you are using a custom number format that displays text, Excel remembers that the actual contents are values derived from formulas.

Creating a Two-Variable Data Table

Although a one-variable data table is effective for comparing results for different values for one variable, you might want to compare results for two variables. For example, you might want to compare the combined effects of various interest rates (such as 5%, 5.5%, and 6%) and different down payments (such as $10,000, $15,000, and $20,000) on the monthly payment. A ***two-variable data table*** is a structured range that contains different values for *two variables* to compare how these differing values affect the results for one calculated value.

Set Up the Substitution Values for Two Variables

STEP 4

Create the two-variable data table separate from regular worksheet data, similar to the method used for a one-variable data table. For a two-variable data table, you use the top row for one variable's substitution values and the first column for the other variable's substitution values. Figure 6.5 shows substitution interest rates in the first column (range D4:D12) and substitution down payments in the first row (range E3:G3).

Formula for one result

Down payment variable substitution values

Top-left cell contains formula for one result

Interest rate variable substitution values

D3 =B12

	A	B	C	D	E	F	G
1	Input Area			Two-Variable Data Table: APR and Down Payment			
2	Cost of Home	$150,000.00		Monthly Payment			
3	Down Payment	$ 10,000.00		$709.36	$10,000.00	$15,000.00	$ 20,000.00
4	APR	4.50%		5.00%			
5	No. Years for Loan	30		5.50%			
6	Payments Per Year	12		6.00%			
7				6.50%			
8	Output Area			7.00%			
9	Amount of Loan	$140,000.00		7.50%			
10	Periodic Rate	0.38%		8.00%			
11	No. Payment Periods	360		8.50%			
12	Monthly Payment	$ 709.36		9.00%			
13	Total to Repay Loan	$255,369.40					
14	Total Interest Paid	$115,369.40					

FIGURE 6.5 Substitution Values and Formula for a Two-Variable Data Table

Add a Formula to the Data Table

The two-variable data table enables you to use two variables, but you are restricted to only one result instead of multiple results. With the one-variable data table, you use the interest rate variable to compare multiple results: monthly payment, total to repay the loan, and total interest paid. However, for the two-variable data table, decide which result you want to focus on based on the two variables. In the case of a home loan, you might want to focus on comparing the effects that changes in interest rates and down payments (the two variables) have on different monthly payments (the result). Enter the formula or reference to the original formula in the blank cell in the top-left corner. For example, enter the cell reference for the monthly payment (=B12) in cell D3 as shown in Figure 6.5.

Complete the Two-Variable Data Table

STEP 5

After entering the substitution values and the reference to one formula result, you are ready to complete the table to see the results. To complete the two-variable data table, do the following:

1. Select the data table boundaries, starting in the top-left corner of the data table. Drag down and to the right to select the last blank cell at the intersection of the last substitution value for both the column and the row.

2. Click the DATA tab, click What-If Analysis in the Data Tools group, and then select Data Table. The Data Table dialog box opens.
3. Enter the cell that contains the original value for the substitution values in the first row in the *Row input cell* box. Enter the cell that contains the original value for the substitution values in the first column in the *Column input cell* box. For example, the original row (down payment) variable value is stored in cell B3, and the original column (APR) variable value is stored in cell B4.
4. Click OK.

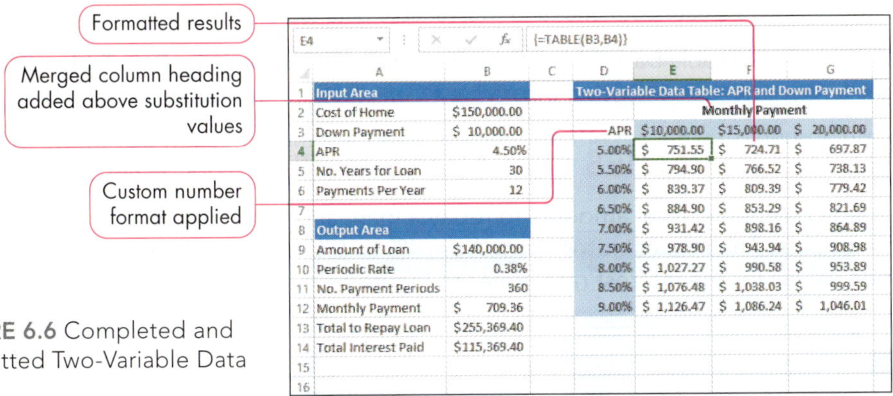

	A	B	C	D	E	F	G
1	Input Area			Two-Variable Data Table: APR and Down Payment			
2	Cost of Home	$150,000.00			Monthly Payment		
3	Down Payment	$ 10,000.00		APR	$10,000.00	$15,000.00	$ 20,000.00
4	APR	4.50%		5.00%	$ 751.55	$ 724.71	$ 697.87
5	No. Years for Loan	30		5.50%	$ 794.90	$ 766.52	$ 738.13
6	Payments Per Year	12		6.00%	$ 839.37	$ 809.39	$ 779.42
7				6.50%	$ 884.90	$ 853.29	$ 821.69
8	Output Area			7.00%	$ 931.42	$ 898.16	$ 864.89
9	Amount of Loan	$140,000.00		7.50%	$ 978.90	$ 943.94	$ 908.98
10	Periodic Rate	0.38%		8.00%	$ 1,027.27	$ 990.58	$ 953.89
11	No. Payment Periods	360		8.50%	$ 1,076.48	$ 1,038.03	$ 999.59
12	Monthly Payment	$ 709.36		9.00%	$ 1,126.47	$ 1,086.24	$ 1,046.01
13	Total to Repay Loan	$255,369.40					
14	Total Interest Paid	$115,369.40					
15							
16							

FIGURE 6.6 Completed and Formatted Two-Variable Data Table

After you complete the data table, to reduce confusion, you should format the results by applying a custom number format to the formula cell to appear as a heading and add a merged heading above the row substitution values (see Figure 6.6).

1. What is the first step to creating a one-variable data table? ***p. 378***
2. Why is it preferable to reference formula cells outside of a one-variable data table versus entering the formula manually? ***p. 379***
3. What is the difference between a one- and two-variable data table? ***p. 382***

Using Scenario Manager

You may want to compare several variables and their combined effects on multiple calculated results. This type of analysis involves identifying and setting up ***scenarios***, which are detailed sets of values that represent different possible situations. Business managers often create a best-case scenario, worst-case scenario, and most likely scenario to compare outcomes. For example, a best-case scenario could reflect an increase in units sold and lower production costs. A worst-case scenario could reflect fewer units sold and higher production costs.

Scenario Manager is a what-if analysis tool that enables you to define and manage up to 32 scenarios to compare their effects on calculated results. You can perform more sophisticated what-if analyses with Scenario Manager than with data tables with the increased number of variables and results. The Scenario Manager dialog box (see Figure 6.13) enables you to create, edit, and delete scenario names. Each scenario represents different sets of what-if conditions to assess the outcome of spreadsheet models. Each scenario is stored under its own name and defines cells whose values change from scenario to scenario.

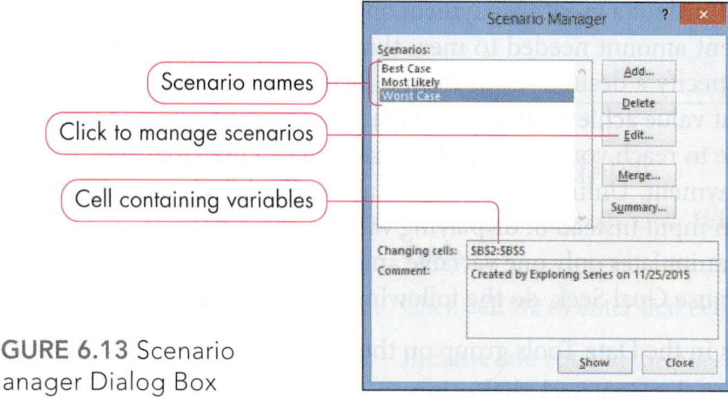

FIGURE 6.13 Scenario Manager Dialog Box

TIP Scenarios on Different Worksheets

When you create scenarios, Excel maintains those scenarios on the worksheet that was active when you created them. You can create scenarios for each worksheet in a workbook. The Scenario Manager dialog box displays only those scenarios you have created on the active worksheet.

Create and Edit Scenarios

STEP 2

Before you start the Scenario Manager, identify cells that contain the variables you want to change or manipulate. For example, in evaluating home loans, you might want to manipulate the values for these variables: cost, down payment, interest rate, and the duration of the loan. You enter the cell references for these variables as the changing cells because you change the values to compare the results. After identifying the variables you want to change, identify one or more cells containing formulas that generate results you want to compare. Note these formulas must directly impact the change cell. To create a scenario, do the following:

1. Click What-If Analysis in the Data Tools group on the DATA tab.
2. Select Scenario Manager to open the Scenario Manager dialog box.
3. Click Add to open the Add Scenario dialog box (see Figure 6.14).
4. Enter a meaningful name in the *Scenario name* box.
5. Enter the input cells for the scenario in the *Changing cells* box. These are the cells containing variable values that Scenario Manager will adjust or change. The changing cells must be identical cell references across all scenarios.

6. Click in the Comment box. Excel enters the name of the person who created the scenarios in the Comment box; however, you can change the name and enter additional descriptions and rationales for the scenarios.
7. Click OK to open the Scenario Values dialog box (see Figure 6.15), which lists the changing cell references that you specified in the previous dialog box. In each respective box, type the value you want to use for that particular scenario.

STEP 3»

8. Click Add to add another scenario and specify its values. After you enter values for the last scenario, click OK to return to the Scenario Manager dialog box.

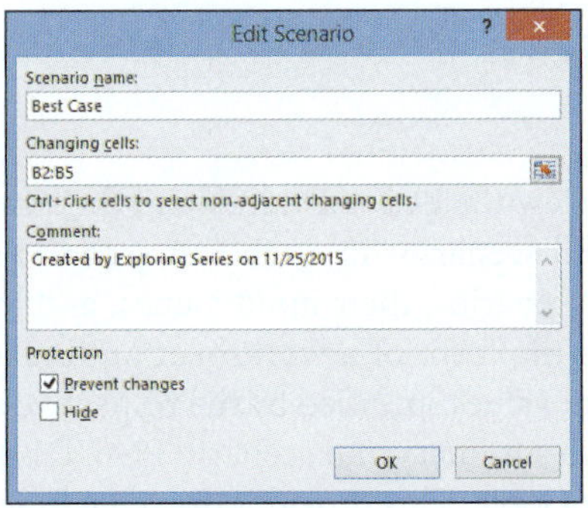

FIGURE 6.14 Add Scenario Dialog Box

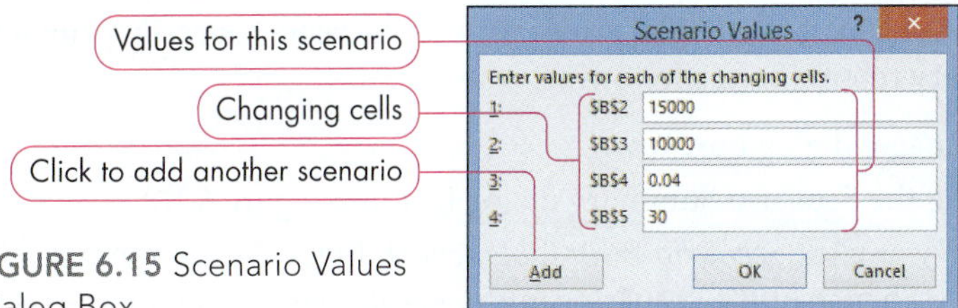

FIGURE 6.15 Scenario Values Dialog Box

TIP Range Names

To help you know what data to enter for the changing cells, you might want to assign a range name to the variable cells before using Scenario Manager. If you do this, the range names, rather than the cell references, appear in the Scenario Values dialog box.

If you need to modify the parameters of a scenario, such as the name or input values, open the Scenario Manager dialog box, select the scenario you want to modify in the Scenarios list, and then click Edit. The Edit Scenario dialog box opens so that you can change the values. Click OK after making the necessary changes.

If you have scenarios in several worksheets or workbooks, you can combine them. Click Merge in the Scenario Manager dialog box to open the Merge Scenarios dialog box. Select the workbook and worksheet and click OK. Use Help to learn more about merging scenarios.

View Scenarios

After you create the scenarios, you can view each of them. To view your scenarios, click What-If Analysis in the Data Tools group on the Data tab, select Scenario Manager, select the name of the scenario you want to view in the Scenarios list, and then click Show. Excel places the defined values in the respective changing cells and displays the results.

Generating Scenario Summary Reports

Updated Scenario Reports

Unlike one- and two-variable data tables that update results if you change other values in the input area, scenario reports do not update. If you change other values or assumptions, or if you add, edit, or delete scenarios, you will have to generate a new scenario report. To avoid this problem, do your best to double-check the scenarios to ensure they are perfect before you generate a scenario summary report.

Although you can view the defined values and their results individually, you will probably want to compare all scenarios in a table. A ***scenario summary report*** is an organized structured table of the scenarios, their input values, and their respective results. The summary report appears in the form of a worksheet outline and enables you to compare the results based on different values specified by the respective scenarios. Excel can produce two types of reports: scenario summary and scenario PivotTable report. PivotTable reports summarize the data in a pivot table. This provides the same functionality as any other pivot table. Scenario summary reports display the results of each scenario in a new worksheet. The data reported in the summary are formatted without gridlines, and the report is easily printable. To create a scenario summary report, do the following:

1. Open the Scenario Manager dialog box.
2. Click Summary to open the Scenario Summary dialog box (see Figure 6.16).
3. Click *Scenario summary* or click *Scenario PivotTable report*. Enter the reference for the cell(s) whose values change in the scenarios in the *Result cells* box. Drag to select a range of adjacent results cells, or press Ctrl as you click cells in nonadjacent ranges. For example, in Figure 6.16, the result cells are monthly payment (B12) and total interest (B14).
4. Click OK. Excel creates the Scenario Summary on a new worksheet (see Figure 6.17).

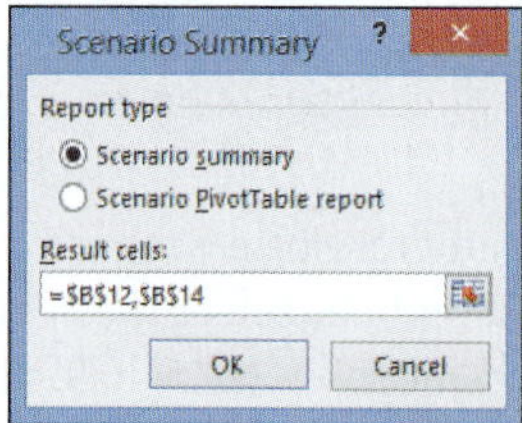

FIGURE 6.16 Scenario Summary Dialog Box

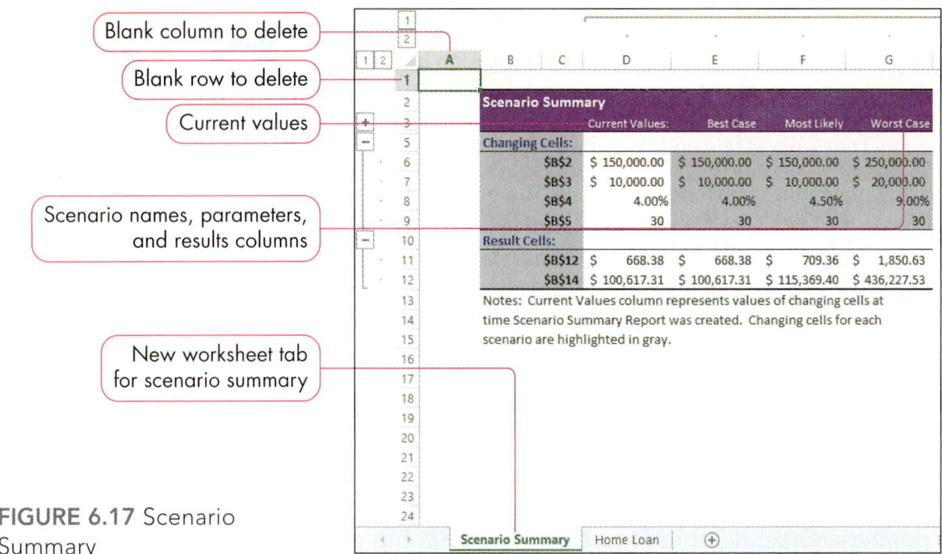

FIGURE 6.17 Scenario Summary

The scenario summary contains a column listing the changing and result cell references, current values and result values, and a column of values and results for each defined scenario. This organized structure helps you compare the results as you analyze the scenarios. You should modify the structure and format the data for a more professional look. Typically, you should do the following:

- Delete the blank row 1 and the blank column A.
- Delete the Current Values column if it duplicates a defined scenario or if you do not want that data.
- Replace cell reference labels with descriptive labels in the first column.
- Delete the explanatory paragraph below the table and replace it with a narrative analysis relevant to the data.

Quick Concepts

1. What is the difference between Goal Seek and Scenario Manager? ***p. 390***
2. What is the difference between a scenario summary report and a PivotTable report? ***p. 392***
3. Will scenario summary reports automatically update when variables are changed? ***p. 392***

Solver

Add-ins are programs that can be added to Excel to provide enhanced functionality. ***Solver*** is an add-in application that searches for the best or optimum solution to a problem by manipulating the values for several variables within restrictions that you impose. You can use Solver to create optimization models. ***Optimization models*** find the highest, lowest, or exact value for one particular result by adjusting values for selected variables. Solver is one of the most sophisticated what-if analysis tools, and people use Solver in a variety of situations and industries. For example, a cellular phone manufacturing facility can use Solver to maximize the number of phones made or minimize the number of labor hours required while conforming to other production specifications. A financial planner might use Solver to help a family adjust its expenses to stay within its monthly income.

In this section, you will learn how to load the Solver add-in. Then, you will use Solver to set a target, select changing cells, and create constraints.

Loading the Solver Add-In

STEP 1 » Because other companies create the add-ins, they are not active by default. You must load the Solver add-in before you can use it. To load Solver, do the following:

1. Click the FILE tab and select Options.
2. Click Add-Ins to see a list of active and inactive add-in applications. The Active Application Add-ins list displays currently enabled add-ins, and the Inactive Application Add-ins list displays add-ins that are not currently enabled.
3. Click the Manage arrow, select Excel Add-ins, and then click Go to open the Add-Ins dialog box (see Figure 6.21).
4. Click the Solver Add-in check box in the *Add-Ins available* list and click OK.

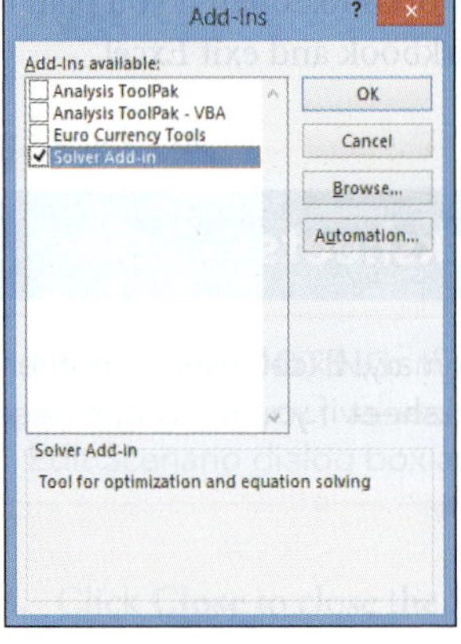

FIGURE 6.21 Add-Ins Dialog Box

When you load Solver, Excel displays Solver in the Analysis group on the Data tab (see Figure 6.22), where it remains until you remove the Solver add-in. However, if you are in a campus computer lab that resets software settings when you log off, you will have to load Solver again each time you log into the lab's network.

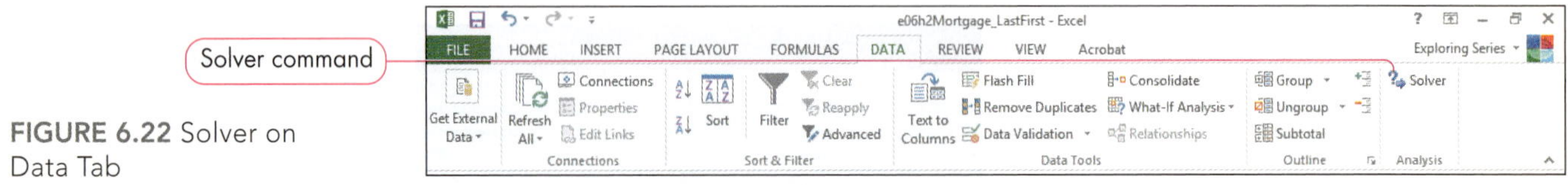

FIGURE 6.22 Solver on Data Tab

Solver

If you are working in a campus computer lab, your institution may prevent you from loading applications, such as Solver. Check with your instructor if your system in the lab prevents you from loading Solver.

Optimizing Results with Solver

Solver may be the best what-if analysis tool to solve complex linear and nonlinear problems. You can use it for complex equation solving and for constrained optimization where a set of constraints is specified and you want the outcome to be minimized or maximized. With Solver, you are able to change the values of several variables at once to achieve the desired result. For example, a business analyst might want to use Solver to maximize profits by changing selected variables while adhering to required limitations. Or a fulfillment company might want to determine the lowest shipping costs to transfer merchandise from a distribution center to retail stores.

Identify the Objective Cell and Changing Cells

STEP 2»

Before using Solver, review your spreadsheet as you specify the goal, identify one or more variables that can change to reach the desired goal, and determine the limitations of the model. You will use these data to specify three parameters in Solver: objective cell, changing cells, and constraints.

The ***objective cell*** specifies the cell that contains a formula that produces a value that you want to optimize (that is, maximize, minimize, or set to a value) by manipulating values of one or more variables. The formula in the objective cell relates directly or indirectly to the changing cells and constraints. Using the mortgage case study as an example, the objective cell is B14 (the cell containing the total interest paid formula), and your goal is to minimize the total interest.

The ***changing variable cells*** are the cells containing variables whose values change within the constraints until the objective cell reaches its optimum value. The changing variable cells typically contain values, not formulas, but these cells have a mathematical relationship to the formula in the objective. In the home loan example, the changing variable cells are B3 (down payment) and B5 (number of years). You can select up to 200 changing variable cells. To specify the objective and changing cells, do the following:

1. Click Solver in the Analysis group on the Data tab to open the Solver Parameters dialog box (see Figure 6.23).
2. Enter the cell containing the formula for which you want to optimize its value in the Set Objective box.
3. Click an option in the *To* section to specify what type of value you need to find for the target cell. Click Max to maximize the value, Min to find the lowest value, or Value Of, and then specify the value in the Value Of box.
4. Enter the cell references that contain variables in the By Changing Variable Cells box. These are the variables that you want to change to reach the objective.

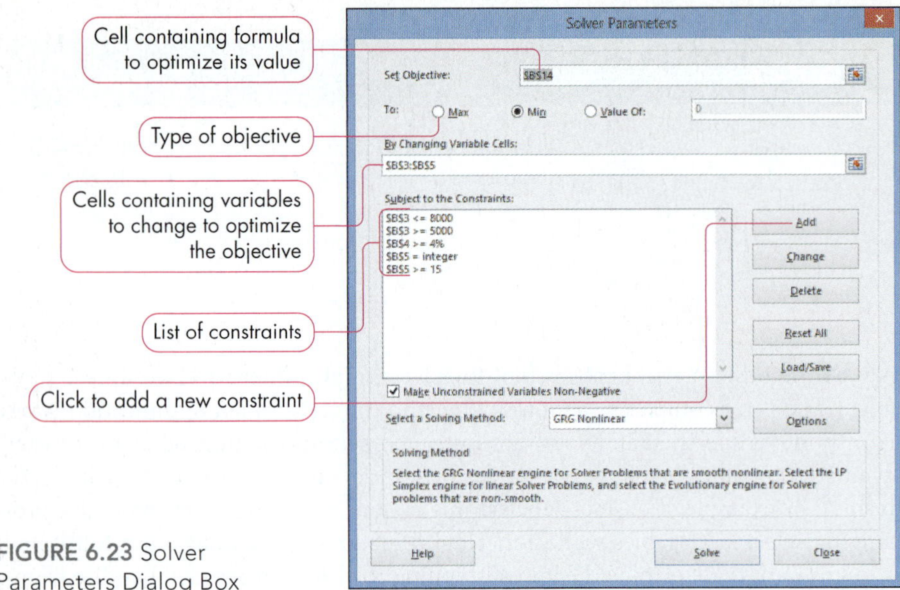

FIGURE 6.23 Solver Parameters Dialog Box

Define the Constraints

STEP 3

The ***constraints*** specify the restrictions or limitations imposed on a spreadsheet model as Solver determines the optimum value for the objective cell. Rules govern every business model, based on historical requirements, physical limitations, and other decisions. Probably the most challenging process in using Solver is identifying all legitimate limitations. You may identify limitations through conversations with your supervisor, by reading policy statements, gathering information in meetings, and so on. Even after you enter data into Solver and run a report, you may gain knowledge of other limitations that you must build into the model. Using the home loan example, a constraint might be that the down payment must be between $5,000 and $8,000.

To add constraints to the Solver, do the following inside the Solver Parameters dialog box:

1. Click Add to the right of the *Subject to the Constraints* list to open the Add Constraint dialog box.
2. Enter the cell reference, the operator to test the cell references, and the constraint the cell needs to match (see Figure 6.24). The cell reference contains a variable whose value you want to constrain or restrict to a particular value or range. The operator defines the relationship between the variable and the constraint. For example, cell B3 (the down payment) is restricted to being less than or equal to $8,000. Solver will not allow the cost to be higher than this value.
3. Click OK to add the constraint and return to the Solver Parameters dialog box, or click Add to add the constraint and create another constraint.

TIP Integer Constraint

One of the constraint operators is integer. This constraint requires the changing variable cell to be an integer, or whole number. For example, a manufacturing plant does not produce partial units such as 135.62 units, and a department store does not sell 18.32 shirts. To ensure that Solver produces realistic results, you should create integer constraints for these types of quantities. In Figure 6.23, the constraint $B$5 = integer limits the number of years for the loan to be a whole number.

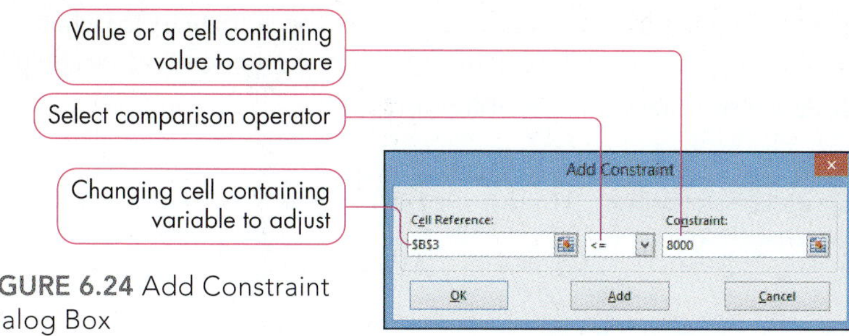

FIGURE 6.24 Add Constraint Dialog Box

To modify a constraint's definition, select the constraint in the *Subject to the Constraints* list and click Change. Make changes in the Change Constraint dialog box and click OK to update the definition. If you no longer need a constraint, select it in the *Subject to the Constraints* list and click Delete. Be careful when using Delete; Solver does not prompt you to confirm the deletion. Solver deletes the selected constraint immediately, and you cannot restore the deleted constraint.

TIP Greater-Than-Zero Constraint

Another often-overlooked constraint is the requirement that the value of a variable cell be greater than or equal to zero. Physically, it makes no sense to produce a negative number of products in any category. Mathematically, however, a negative value in a changing variable cell may produce a higher value for the objective cell. By default, the Make Unconstrained Variables Non-Negative check box is selected to ensure variable values are greater than or equal to zero. If you want to allow the lower end of a variable's value to be a negative value, you can create a constraint such as B2>=−100. That constraint takes priority over the Make Unconstrained Variables Non-Negative check box.

Create a Solver Report

STEP 4» After defining the objective, changing variable cells, and constraints, select a solving method. Solver uses the selected solving method to determine which type of algorithms it executes to reach the objective. The Solver add-in for Excel 2013 contains these solving methods: GRG Nonlinear, Simplex LP, and Evolutionary. Look up *Solver* in Help to link to a specific set of descriptions of these methods. You can also review additional information and download additional add-ins on www.solver.com. For the purposes of this chapter, accept the default option, GRG Nonlinear.

You are now ready to use Solver to find a solution to the problem. Solver uses an iterative process of using different combinations of values in the changing variable cells to identify the optimum value for the objective cell. It starts with the current values and adjusts those values in accordance with the constraints. Once it finds the best solution, given the parameters you set, it identifies the values for the changing variable cells and shows you the optimum value in the objective value. If Solver cannot determine an optimum value, it does not enable you to generate summary reports. To create a Solver report, do the following:

1. Click Solve in the Solver Parameters dialog box. When Solver completes the iterative process, the Solver Results dialog box appears (see Figure 6.25). If it finds a solution, the Reports list displays available report types. If Solver cannot reach an optimal solution, no reports are available. Solutions are unattainable if a logic error exists or if the constraints do not allow sufficient elasticity to achieve a result. For example, a constraint between 10 and 11 may not allow sufficient flexibility, or a constraint greater than 20 but also less than 10 is illogical. If this happens, check each constraint for range constraints or errors in logic.
2. Click Keep Solver Solution to keep the changed objective and variable values, or click Restore Original Values to return to the original values in the worksheet. If you keep the changed values, Excel makes those changes to the actual worksheet. Do this if you are comfortable with those changes. If you want to maintain the original values, you should restore the original values.

3. Select a report from the Reports list. Generating a report is appropriate to see what changes Solver made while preserving the original values in the worksheet from Step 2.
4. Click OK to generate the summary on a separate worksheet.

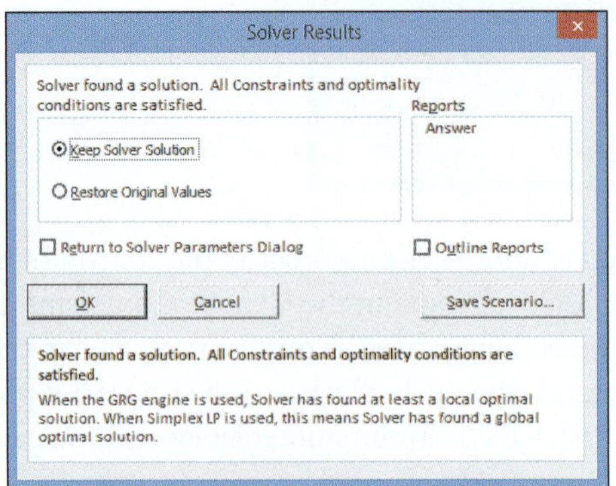

FIGURE 6.25 Solver Results Dialog Box

Solver creates a new worksheet for the Solver summary report containing four major sections (see Figure 6.26). The first section displays information about the Solver report. Specifically, it displays the report type, file name and worksheet containing the dataset, date and time the report was generated, Solver Engine details, and Solver Options that were set at the time the report was generated.

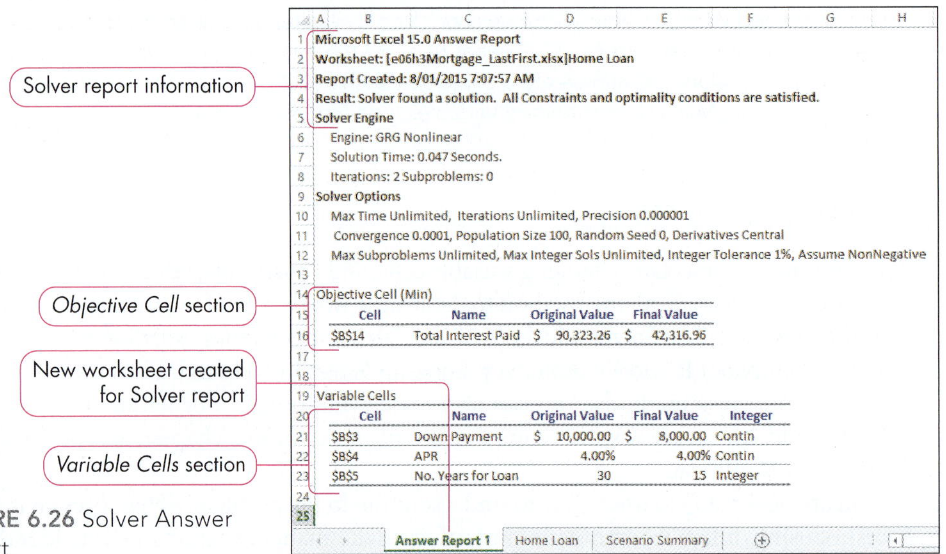

FIGURE 6.26 Solver Answer Report

The remaining sections of the report help you analyze the results. The section displays the objective cell information. Specifically, this section shows the original and final objective cell values. For example, using the original worksheet values, the original total interest paid in cell B14 was $100,617.31. The final minimized total interest paid is $47,064.23.

The third section displays the variable cells. Specifically, it displays the cell references, the variable cell names, original values, and final values. For example, the original down payment was $10,000, and the final value is $8,000.

The final section lists the constraints. Specifically, it displays the cell reference, description, new cell value, formula, status, and slack for each defined constraint. In this case, the down payment slack ($3,000) is the difference between the lower constraint ($5,000) and the final value ($8,000). The Status column indicates Binding or Not Binding. A ***binding constraint*** is a rule that Solver has to enforce to reach the objective value. That is, the value hits the maximum allowable value for a less-than-or-equal-to, minimum allowable value for a greater-than-or-equal-to, equal to, or integer constraint. For example, $B$3<=8000 is a binding constraint. That is, the down payment was raised to its maximum limit of $8,000 to identify the optimal least amount of total interest paid. If this constraint had not been set, Solver could have identified a higher down payment to obtain a lower value for the objective cell. A ***nonbinding constraint*** is one that does not restrict the target value that Solver finds. For example, $B$3>=5000 is nonbinding. Solver did not have to stop at a lowest down payment of $3,000 to reach the optimal total interest paid value.

If you change any of the Solver parameters—objective cell, changing variable cells, or constraints—you need to generate another report. Solver does not update the report automatically. Each time you generate a report, Solver creates another new worksheet with names like Answer Report 1, Answer Report 2, and so on. Delete any reports you no longer need to minimize the file size of your workbook.

Save Scenario

If you want to save the solution parameters to use in Scenario Manager, click Save Scenario in the Solver Results dialog box and type a name for the scenario in the *Scenario name* box.

Configure Solver

You can closely monitor the trial solutions prior to reaching the final solution. Solver is a mathematical modeling operation, and you can determine solutions using the associated mathematics. However, stepping through Solver enables you to view the steps Solver performs. To step through trial solutions, do the following:

1. Click Options in the Solver Parameters dialog box to open the Options dialog box.
2. Select the Show Iteration Results check box to see the values of each trial solution and click OK.
3. Click Solve in the Solver Parameters dialog box.
4. When the Show Trial Solution dialog box appears, either:
    - Click Stop to stop the process and open the Solver Results dialog box, or
    - Click Continue to continue the process and display the next trial solution.

You can also use the Options dialog box to customize Solver further. Because Solver uses an iterative approach, you can specify the number of iterations to try, how much time to take to solve the problem, and how precise the answer should be (i.e., accuracy to what number of decimal places), among other settings.

Save and Restore a Solver Model

When you use Solver, Excel keeps track of your settings and saves only the most recent Solver settings. In some cases, you may want to save the parameters of a model so that you can apply them again in the future. Saving a Solver model is helpful if the original data source might change and you want to compare results by generating multiple Solver answer reports. When you save a Solver model, you save the objective value, the changing variable cells, and the constraints.

Saving a Solver model places the information in a small block of cells on a worksheet. The number of cells required to save the Solver model is dependent on the number of constraints in the model. To save Solver settings, do the following:

1. Click Load/Save in the Solver Parameters dialog box.
2. Click in the worksheet where the first cell is to be placed. Make sure the worksheet has sufficient empty cells so the Solver information does not overwrite Excel data.
3. Click Save to return to the Solver Parameters dialog box.

g. Set a constraint to ensure the trip charge does not exceed $50.00.

h. Set a constraint to ensure hourly rate does not drop below $30.00

i. Create an Answer Report to outline your findings.

j. After solving, answer the questions in the Q&A section.

3 College Budget

You are beginning your freshman year of college. Prior to leaving for school, you worked a summer job and were able to save $1,500 for expenses such as books, supplies, and a university parking pass. After arriving on campus, you discovered your computer was out of date, and you need to purchase a newer model. Your books cost $700, a mini fridge for your room costs $250.00, and you are estimating your parking pass will cost $350.00. After researching pricing for newer computers, you determine a new computer will cost $750.00. Your parents have agreed to give you the additional money required to purchase the computer; however, they will only do so if you send them an Excel workbook outlining your expenses and the amount of money that they must contribute to the purchase. You have decided to create this document and then share the file with your parents through your family's SkyDrive account.

Student 1:

a. Open Excel and create a blank document. Save this document as **e06m3CollegeBudget_LastFirst**.

b. Click in **cell A1** and type item **Description**. Press **Tab** and type **Expense** in **cell B1**.

c. Click in **cell A2**, type the name of your first expense—for example, **Parking Pass**—and then enter the corresponding cost in **cell B2.**

d. Continue entering your expenses in **cells A3:B3** for books and in **cell A4:B4** for the mini fridge. Type **Total expenses** in cell **A5** and enter a SUM function in **cell B5** to total your expenses.

e. Highlight **cells A5:B5** and apply the **Bad style** from the styles group located in the HOME tab of the Ribbon.

f. Click **cell D1**, type **Summer Savings**, and then type **1500** in **cell D2**. Then complete the following tasks:

- Type **Savings after expenses** in **cell A6**.
- Type **Computer cost** in **cell A7**.
- Type **Parental contribution** in **cell A8**.
- Type **Deficit** in **cell A9**.
- Type **750** in **cell B7**.
- Type **0** in **cell B8**.

g. Click in **cell B9** and enter the following formula: **=B7-B6-B8**. This calculates the financial deficit after the computer has been purchased. The goal is for this cell to have a value of zero after your parents' contribution.

h. Use Goal Seek to set the deficit to **0** by changing your parents' contribution amount.

i. Format the worksheet with the font and color of your choice. Apply **Currency format** to all numbers.

j. Save the workbook to SkyDrive.

Student 2:

k. Open the worksheet and review the proposed budget.

l. Based on the budget, navigate to www.amazon.com and research the going rates on a college size mini fridge. If you are able to locate a better price, update the dollar amount and upload back to sky drive.

Beyond the Classroom

Too Cold to Snow

Have you ever wondered whether it could be too cold to snow? Actually, it is much more likely to snow if the temperature is close to freezing than if it is much below. The reason is because the air gets too dry to snow. As the air gets colder, it holds less water vapor for making snow. This explains why Nashville, Tennessee, typically gets more snowfall each year than frigid Barrow, Alaska! Because snow in northern Alaska does not melt as quickly as snow in Nashville, the area appears to get more snow.

You are a high school science teacher preparing a lesson on the effect of temperature and water vapor on snowfall. The dew point is the temperature at which water vapor condenses and forms into liquid or frozen precipitation, and the wet bulb temperature is the lowest temperature that can be reached by the evaporation of water only. Typically, the greater the difference between wet bulb and air temperatures, the drier the air. Because drier air is less likely to produce snow, you will use the wet bulb temperature to approximate the dryness of the air and the potential for snow. Use the Internet to find the temperature and dew point of Nashville on January 6 of the current year and develop an estimate of the wet bulb temperature.

Open *e06b2Snow* and save it as **e06b2Snow_LastFirst**. Use Scenario Manager to create a Most Likely and Least Likely projection of wet bulb temperature for Nashville. The Most Likely statistics are those that you identified for January 6. The Least Likely statistics are a temperature of 18° and a dew point of 5°. Wet bulb temperature is calculated by subtracting dew point from temperature and dividing the result by 3. Edit the summary as specified in the *Generating Scenario Summary Reports* section in the chapter. Insert a text box and write an analysis about your results. Create a footer with your name, the sheet name code, and the file name code. Save and close the workbook, and submit it based on your instructor's directions.

Mining Company

You work for an investment corporation that is considering purchasing a coal mine. One of your colleagues developed a spreadsheet model and started a what-if analysis using Solver. Unfortunately, Solver is unable to solve the problem given the parameters entered. You need to identify and correct the errors and then generate an answer report. Open *e06b3Mining* and save it as **e06b3Mining_LastFirst**. Make sure that Solver is loaded. If not, load the Solver add-in. The objective is to maximize the rate of return by the end of the fifth year. The investment firm is considering paying between $20 and $25 million for the mine with an anticipated 1 to 1.5 million tons sold in the first year. Research indicates the price per ton to be between $12.35 and $14.50 initially. The price-per-ton increase should range from 0.5% to 1.25%. Before you run the Solver report, change the number of iterations to 1,500 in the Solver Options dialog box. Insert notes to describe the parameter errors, correct the errors, and run a Solver answer report. Create a footer with your name, the sheet name code, and the file name code on the report. Adjust the left and right margins on the Answer Report 1 worksheet so that the data can print on one page. Deselect the options that print gridlines and headings on the Forecast worksheet. Save and close the workbook, and submit it based on your instructor's directions.

a. Load the Solver add-in if it is not already loaded.

b. Set the objective to calculate the highest balance possible.

c. Use the number of attendees and the ticket price per person as changing variable cells.

d. Look at the *Limitations* section of the spreadsheet model.

e. Set a constraint for the number of attendees.

f. Set constraints for the ticket price per person.

g. Set an appropriate integer constraint.

h. Set a constraint that ensures the valet parking expense is less than or equal to the product of the number of parking stalls and the valet price per vehicle.

i. Solve the problem, but keep the original values in the Budget worksheet. Generate the Answer Report. If you get an internal memory error message, remove Solver as an add-in, close the workbook, open the workbook, add Solver in again, and finish using Solver.

j. Answer questions 10 through 13 on the Q&A worksheet. Apply **landscape orientation** to the Q&A worksheet. Save the workbook.

k. Create a footer on all four worksheets with your name on the left side, the sheet name code in the center, and the file name code on the right side.

l. Save and close the workbook, and submit it based on your instructor's directions.

Excel

Specialized Functions

CHAPTER 7

Logical, Lookup, Databases, and Finances

Yuri Arcurs/Shutterstock

OBJECTIVES AFTER YOU READ THIS CHAPTER, YOU WILL BE ABLE TO:

CASE STUDY | Transpayne Filtration

You are an assistant accountant in the Human Resources (HR) Department for Transpayne Filtration, a company that sells water filtration systems to residential customers. Transpayne has locations in Atlanta, Boston, and Chicago, with a manager at each location who oversees several account representatives. You have an Excel workbook that contains names, locations, titles, hire dates, and salaries for the 20 managers and account representatives. To prepare for your upcoming salary analyses, you downloaded salary data from the corporate database into the workbook.

The HR manager wants you to perform several tasks based on locations and job titles. You will use logical functions to calculate annual bonus amounts and database functions to help analyze the data. Finally, you will review financial aspects of automobiles purchased for each manager.

Logical and Lookup Functions

Logical functions enable you to test conditions to determine if the condition is true or false. You have used the IF function, which is the most popular logical function, to perform different actions based on whether the logical test is true or false. Lookup and reference functions are valuable when you need to look up a value contained elsewhere in a workbook. For example, the VLOOKUP and HLOOKUP functions enable you to take an identified value, such as the number of months for a certificate of deposit (CD) to mature, look up that value in a vertical or horizontal lookup table, and then obtain a related value, such as the annual percentage rate (APR). Excel contains additional logical and lookup functions to perform more complex calculations and analyses.

In this section, you will learn how to create a nested logical function using the IF function. In addition, you will learn how to use the MATCH and INDEX lookup functions.

Creating a Nested Logical Function

The IF function contains three arguments: logical_test, Value_if_true, and Value_if_false. You can enter formulas within both the Value_if_true and Value_if_false arguments to perform calculations. For situations with multiple outcomes based on conditions, you can nest IF functions within the Value_if_true and Value_if_false arguments. A nested function is a function that is embedded within an argument of another function. Excel permits up to 64 IF statements in one formula.

Nested IF Within an IF Function

STEP 1 »

Figure 7.1 illustrates three bonus rates based on employee hire date. If a representative was hired before 1/1/2005, the rep receives 9% of her or his total salary as a bonus. If a representative was hired between 1/1/2005 and 1/1/2010, the rep earns a 5% bonus. Lastly, anyone hired after 1/1/2010 receives a 3% bonus.

Bonus rate date criteria

Percentage rate used based on date criteria

Dates evaluated by the IF statement

	A	B	C	D	E	F	G	H	I	J
1	Employee ID	4070	Criteria:	Title	Quick Search Results:	Account Rep		Bonus Amount	Date	Percent
2								Hired before	1/1/2005	9%
3	–				Manager Salary Threshold	$ 70,000.00		Hired on or before	1/1/2010	5%
4								Hired after	1/1/2010	3%
5			Transpayne Sales Rep Salary Information							
6	Employee ID	Name	Location	Title	Hire Date	Salary	Bonus Amount	Raise Status		
7	3824	Adams	Atlanta	Manager	10/14/2002	$ 68,750	$ 6,187.50	Due for raise		
8	4955	Akmatalieva	Chicago	Account Rep	11/3/2013	$ 49,575	$ 1,487.25	NA		
9	2521	Barnes	Boston	Account Rep	6/14/2009	$ 46,000	$ 2,300.00	NA		
10	4453	Crandell	Boston	Manager	3/9/2004	$ 75,800	$ 6,822.00	NA		
11	2967	Deberard	Chicago	Account Rep	12/4/2009	$ 46,795	$ 2,339.75	NA		
12	2645	Doering	Atlanta	Account Rep	6/5/2009	$ 43,750	$ 2,187.50	NA		
13	1268	Forgan	Atlanta	Account Rep	9/3/2010	$ 45,250	$ 1,357.50	NA		
14	4458	Franklin	Atlanta	Account Rep	7/19/2009	$ 47,240	$ 2,362.00	NA		
15	1370	Garbett	Atlanta	Account Rep	9/18/2009	$ 47,835	$ 2,391.75	NA		
16	2848	Gomez	Boston	Account Rep	10/15/2011	$ 46,725	$ 1,401.75	NA		
17	3996	Hartvigsen	Boston	Account Rep	2/18/2010	$ 45,000	$ 1,350.00	NA		
18	4070	Keone	Chicago	Account Rep	4/3/2010	$ 45,125	$ 1,353.75	NA		
19	3099	Laing	Chicago	Manager	1/17/2006	$ 65,500	$ 3,275.00	Due for raise		
20	2698	Lenz	Atlanta	Account Rep	4/15/2007	$ 49,750	$ 2,487.50	NA		
21	2611	Nitz	Chicago	Account Rep	8/15/2012	$ 41,000	$ 1,230.00	NA		
22										

FIGURE 7.1 Nested IF Function Results

Figure 7.2 illustrates the process as a flowchart. Diamonds are logical_test arguments and rectangles are Value_if_true and Value_if_false arguments. The second IF function is stored in the outer Value_if_false argument. Figure 7.3 illustrates the process with cell references.

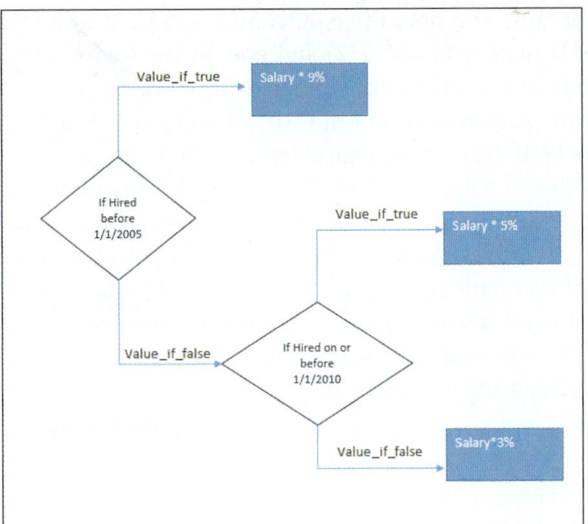

FIGURE 7.2 Nested IF Function Flowchart

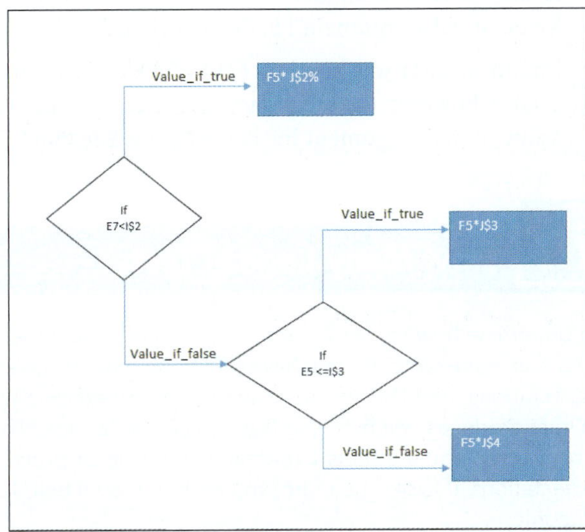

FIGURE 7.3 Nested IF Function Flowchart with Cell References

Figure 7.4 shows the nested IF function as the argument in the Value_if_false box in the Function Arguments dialog box. The function uses relative cell references for the hire date (cell E7) so that the cell reference will change to the next sales rep's hire date when you copy the formula down the column. The formula uses mixed references for the date thresholds (I$2 and I$3) and for the bonus percentages (J$2, J$3, and J$4) so that the references will point to the same rows when you copy the formulas down the column. You could use absolute instead of mixed references, such as $J$4, but doing so creates a longer formula and makes it a little more difficult to read. In the Formula Bar, the nested IF statement looks like this:

=IF(E5<J$7, F5*K$7,IF(E5<=J$8,F5*K$8,F5*K$9))

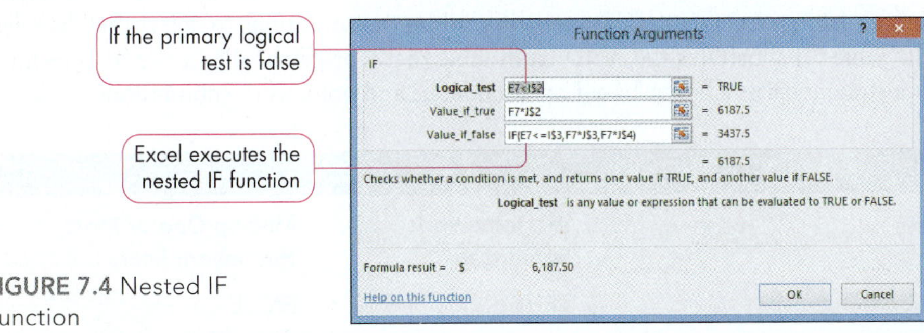

FIGURE 7.4 Nested IF Function

Because you have three outcomes, you need to have two logical tests: one for the primary IF statement (E7<I$2) and one for the nested IF statement (E7<=I$3). The primary logical test evaluates a rep's hire date in cell E7 against the first hire date cutoff stored in cell I2. If the primary logical test is true, Excel multiplies the salary in cell F7 by the rate stored in cell J2. If the primary logical test (E7<I$2) is false, Excel executes the nested IF function in the Value_if_false argument. The nested IF function then evaluates its logical test (E7<=I$3) to determine if the hire date meets the second bonus cutoff level. If that logical test is true, Excel multiplies the salary by the second bonus rate stored in cell J3. If that logical test is false, Excel multiples the salary by the third bonus rate stored in cell J4. You do not need a third logical test to execute the remaining outcome.

The following statements explain how the bonus is calculated for the individual representatives using the nested IF function:

- Employee 3824 was hired on 10/14/2002. In this situation, the logical test (E7<I$2) is true. This causes Excel to execute the Value_if_true argument J2*F$7, which is $68,750 * 9%.
- Employee 4955 was hired on 11/3/2013. In this situation, the logical test (E8<I$2) is false, as is the secondary logical test (E8<=I$3). This causes Excel to execute the Value_if_false argument F8*J$4, which is $49,575 * 3%.
- Employee 2521 was hired on 6/14/2009. In this situation, the logical test (E9<I$2) is false; however, the secondary logical test is true. This causes Excel to execute the Value_if_true argument F9*J$2, which is $46,000 * 5%.

How Many Logical Tests?

To determine how many logical tests you need, count the number of outcomes and subtract one. For example, if you have three outcomes (such as Exceeds Expectations, Meets Expectations, and Below Expectations), you need only two logical tests. The first logical test produces one outcome (Exceeds Expectations). The nested logical test produces a second outcome (Meets Expectations) if true or produces the third outcome (Below Expectations) if false. Therefore, you do not need a third logical test to produce the third outcome.

Nest AND, OR, and NOT Functions

STEP 2» At times, you might need to evaluate *multiple* conditions *at the same time* to determine the result. For example, you might want to evaluate all employees that make less than $50,000 and who are managers for an equity-based salary increase. Excel contains three additional functions to determine whether certain conditions are true or false. These functions are AND, OR, and NOT. You can use these functions individually (which has limited usefulness) or nest them inside another function, such as inside an IF statement (which can increase the capabilities of the function).

The ***AND function*** accepts two or more logical tests and displays TRUE if *all* conditions are true or FALSE if *any* of the conditions are false. You can test up to 255 conditions. Programmers often create truth tables to help analyze the conditions to determine the overall result. Table 7.1 illustrates the AND truth table that a professor might use to determine whether a student earns a bonus based on attendance and homework submissions.

TABLE 7.1 AND Truth Table

	All Homework Submitted	Missing One or More Homework Scores
Perfect Attendance	TRUE	FALSE
Absent 1 or More Days	FALSE	FALSE

The bonus is awarded (TRUE) only when a student has perfect attendance *and* has completed all homework assignments, as shown in column D in Figure 7.5. Only Zach had perfect attendance and completed all assignments. All other combinations of attendance and homework submissions result in FALSE. Although Bill had perfect attendance, he missed one assignment, so he does not get the bonus.

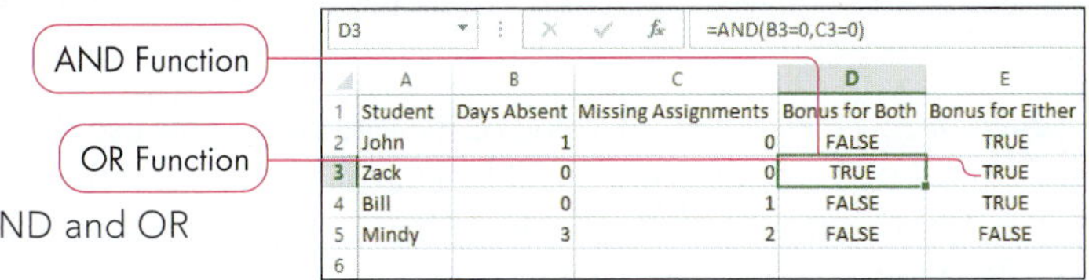

	A	B	C	D	E
1	Student	Days Absent	Missing Assignments	Bonus for Both	Bonus for Either
2	John	1	0	FALSE	TRUE
3	Zack	0	0	TRUE	TRUE
4	Bill	0	1	FALSE	TRUE
5	Mindy	3	2	FALSE	FALSE
6					

FIGURE 7.5 AND and OR Function

=AND(logical1,logical2)

You can nest the AND function inside the logical_test argument of an IF function to test to see if multiple conditions are met. For example, =IF(AND(B2=0,C2=0),10,0) where B2 contains the number of days absent, C2 contains the number of homework assignments missed, 10 represents the number of bonus points if both conditions are met, and 0 represents that no bonus points are awarded if either condition is false.

TIP AND Results

If the logical argument contains text or empty cells, those values are ignored. If no values exist in the logical argument, the AND function returns the #VALUE! error.

The ***OR function*** also accepts two or more conditions and returns TRUE if any of the conditions are true. It returns FALSE only if all conditions are false. You can test up to 255 conditions. Table 7.2 illustrates the OR truth table that a professor might use to determine whether a student earns a bonus based on attendance and homework submissions.

TABLE 7.2 OR Truth Table

	All Homework Submitted	**Missing One or More Homework Scores**
Perfect Attendance	TRUE	TRUE
Absent 1 or More Days	TRUE	FALSE

In column E in Figure 7.5, the bonus is awarded (TRUE) when the student had either perfect attendance *or* if the student completed all assignments. The only time the student does not earn a bonus is if the student is absent one or more days and is also missing one or more homework scores. Mindy was the only student who did not earn the bonus using the OR condition. See Table 7.3 for more detail on the differences between AND and OR functions.

=OR(logical1,logical2)

Table 7.3 displays the differences between AND and OR functions.

TABLE 7.3 AND vs. OR				
	All conditions are true	At least one condition is true	At least one condition is false	All conditions are false
AND	TRUE	FALSE	FALSE	FALSE
OR	TRUE	TRUE	TRUE	FALSE

The ***NOT function*** reverses the truth value of its argument. You use the NOT function when you want to make sure a value is not equal to a particular value. If the logical argument is false, the NOT function returns TRUE, and if the logical argument is true, the NOT function returns FALSE. Unlike the AND and OR functions that require two or more logical arguments, the NOT function contains only one logical argument.

=NOT(logical)

Using MATCH and INDEX Lookup Functions

You have used the VLOOKUP and HLOOKUP functions to look up a value, compare it to a lookup table, and then return a result from the lookup table. Two other lookup functions that are helpful when the order of data is not conducive to VLOOKUP or HLOOKUP are MATCH and INDEX. Figure 7.6 demonstrates the MATCH, INDEX, and nested functions.

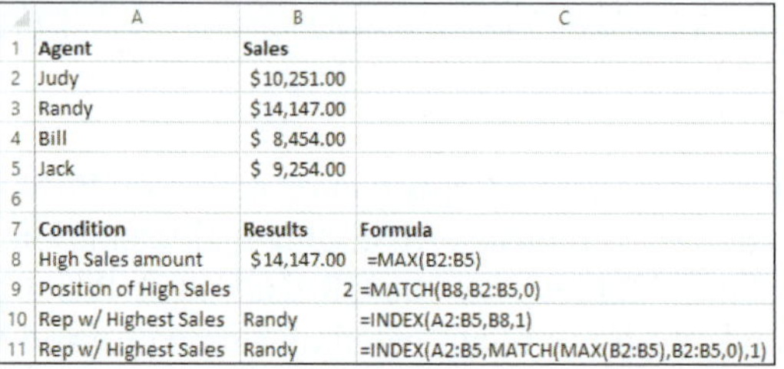

	A	B	C
1	Agent	Sales	
2	Judy	$10,251.00	
3	Randy	$14,147.00	
4	Bill	$ 8,454.00	
5	Jack	$ 9,254.00	
6			
7	Condition	Results	Formula
8	High Sales amount	$14,147.00	=MAX(B2:B5)
9	Position of High Sales	2	=MATCH(B8,B2:B5,0)
10	Rep w/ Highest Sales	Randy	=INDEX(A2:B5,B8,1)
11	Rep w/ Highest Sales	Randy	=INDEX(A2:B5,MATCH(MAX(B2:B5),B2:B5,0),1)

FIGURE 7.6 MATCH, INDEX, and Nested Functions

Use the MATCH Function

The ***MATCH function*** returns the position of a value in a list. Think of it like a reverse phone number lookup. Instead of using directory assistance to look up a person's phone number, it would be like using the phone number to look up the person. You should use the MATCH function, not the VLOOKUP function, when you have the value, such as $14,147, but want to identify its row position within a list, such as third row. Whereas the MATCH function is often nested inside other functions, you should understand how it works on its own. The MATCH function contains three arguments: lookup_value, lookup_array, and match_type. In Figure 7.6, the MATCH function in cell B9 returns 2, the position of $14,147 within the sales range. The following list explains the arguments of the MATCH function.

=MATCH(lookup_value,lookup_array,[match_type])

- **Lookup_value.** The lookup_value argument is the value that you want to find in the array or list. It can be a value, label, logical value, or cell reference that contains one of these items. In Figure 7.6, the lookup_value argument for the MATCH function in cell B9 refers to the cell containing the MAX function: B8.
- **Lookup_array.** This argument is a range of contiguous cells that contain potential lookup values. In Figure 7.6, the lookup_array argument for the MATCH function in cell B9 is the range of cells containing the sales values: B2:B5.

- **Match_type.** This argument is 1, 0, or -1 to indicate which value to return. Use 1 to find the largest value that is less than or equal to the lookup_value when the values in the lookup_array are arranged in ascending order. Use -1 to find the smallest value that is greater than or equal to the lookup_value when the values in the lookup_array are in descending order. Use 0 to find the first value that is identical to the lookup_value when the values in the lookup_array have no particular order. In Figure 7.6, the match_type is 0 to find an exact match of the highest sales amount.

Use the Index Function

The ***INDEX function*** returns a value or the reference to a value within a range based on X and Y coordinates. So, for example, it will return the value in the intersection of a specific row and column such as the 3rd value in the 2nd column of a worksheet. When you select this function, the Select Arguments dialog box opens so that you can select an array form or a reference form. The array form is the more commonly used option. It displays the value of an element in a table based on either a row or column number.

=INDEX(array,row_num,[column_num])

- **Array.** This argument is one or more ranges. In Figure 7.6, the array argument in the INDEX function in cell B10 is the range containing the agents and their respective sales: A2:B5.
- **Row_num.** This argument identifies the row number within the array range. In the INDEX function in cell B10 in Figure 7.6, the row_num argument is B9, the cell containing the MATCH function results. Recall that the MATCH function in cell B8 determined the position of the highest sales amount from the list of Sales values in cells B2:B5. Therefore, the INDEX function refers to cell B10, which then uses the second row of the array in the range A2:B5.
- **Column_num.** This argument identifies the column within the reference that contains the value you want. In Figure 7.6, the column_num is 1 to identify the first column within the range A2:B5. The first column contains the agent names. So, after the MATCH function identifies the row (2) containing the highest sales value ($14,147.00), the column_num argument (1) identifies the name (Randy) in the first column that corresponds to the highest sales value.

The array in the range A2:B5 contains more than one row and column; therefore, row_num and column_num arguments were required. If an array contains only one row, the column_num is required, and if the array contains only one column, the row_num is required.

INDEX Function in Reference Form

The reference form displays the cell reference of a row and column intersection. The syntax for the reference form is =INDEX(reference,row_num,[column_num],[area_num]). Use Help to learn about the arguments and to see an example of its usage.

You can reduce the number of cells containing functions by nesting the MATCH function inside the INDEX function. For example, cell B11 in Figure 7.6 contains a nested MAX function inside the MATCH function, which is then nested inside the INDEX function to identify which sales rep had the highest amount of sales.

Nest Functions in Other Functions

STEP 3 You can use the Insert Function and Function Arguments dialog boxes to insert functions as arguments for another function instead of typing the entire nested function directly in the Formula Bar. For example, to create =INDEX(A2:B5,MATCH(MAX(B2:B5),B2:B5,0),1) in dialog boxes, do the following:

1. Click Insert Function, select the outer function, such as INDEX, and then click OK to display the Function Arguments dialog box.
2. Click in the argument box where the nested function is needed, click the Name Box arrow on the Formula Bar, and then select the desired function from the list of recently used functions, or select More Functions from the Name Box drop-down list, select the function, such as MATCH, in the Insert Function dialog box, and then click OK to open the Function Arguments dialog box for the nested function.
3. Enter the arguments for the nested function. Click in the outer function's name—INDEX—in the Formula Bar to display the Function Arguments dialog box for the outer function again.
4. Continue entering or nesting other arguments. When the entire function is complete, click OK in the outer function's Function Arguments dialog box.

Quick Concepts

1. What is the difference between a single IF statement and a nested IF statement? ***p. 422***
2. In what situation would you use an AND function over a nested IF statement? ***p. 424***
3. What is the benefit of nesting the MATCH function inside the INDEX function? ***p. 427***

Hands-On Exercises

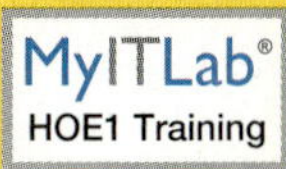

1 Logical and Lookup Functions

As the Transpayne accounting assistant, you have been asked to identify underpaid account representatives to bring their salaries up to a new minimum standard within the corporation. In addition, you want to calculate annual bonus amounts based on hire date as well as create a quick search lookup field to allow for instant access to individual information.

Skills covered: Create a Nested IF Function • Nest an AND Function Inside an IF Function • Create a Lookup Field Using INDEX and MATCH Functions

STEP 1 » CREATE A NESTED IF FUNCTION

Your first task is to calculate the annual bonus amount for each employee. The company uses a tiered bonus system that awards a specific percentage of salary based on hire date. Employees hired before 1/1/2005 receive 9%. Employees hired on or before 1/1/2010 receive 5%, and employees that were hired after 1/1/2010 receive 3%. You plan to use a nested IF function to calculate each employee's bonus. You will then use the fill handle to replace the function in the rest of the column. Refer to Figure 7.7 as you complete Step 1.

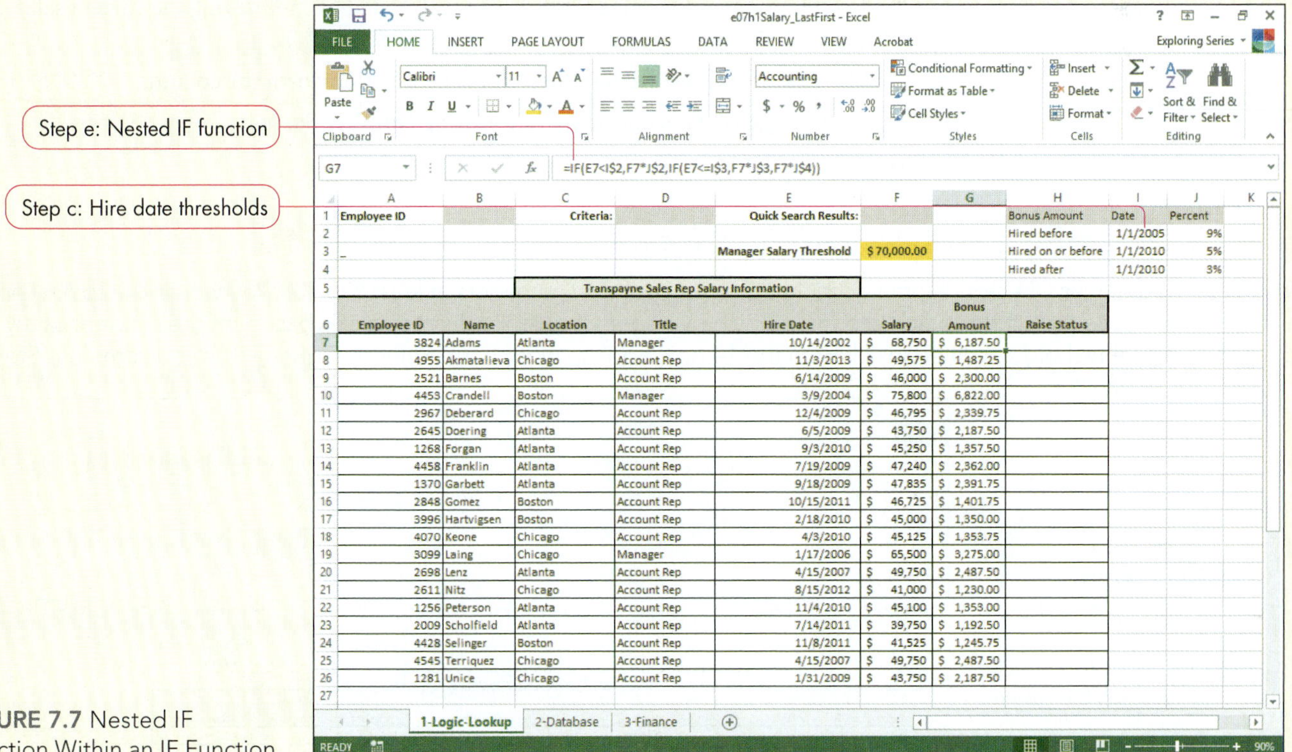

Employee ID	Name	Location	Title	Hire Date	Salary	Bonus Amount	Raise Status
3824	Adams	Atlanta	Manager	10/14/2002	$ 68,750	$ 6,187.50	
4955	Akmatalieva	Chicago	Account Rep	11/3/2013	$ 49,575	$ 1,487.25	
2521	Barnes	Boston	Account Rep	6/14/2009	$ 46,000	$ 2,300.00	
4453	Crandell	Boston	Manager	3/9/2004	$ 75,800	$ 6,822.00	
2967	Deberard	Chicago	Account Rep	12/4/2009	$ 46,795	$ 2,339.75	
2645	Doering	Atlanta	Account Rep	6/5/2009	$ 43,750	$ 2,187.50	
1268	Forgan	Atlanta	Account Rep	9/3/2010	$ 45,250	$ 1,357.50	
4458	Franklin	Atlanta	Account Rep	7/19/2009	$ 47,240	$ 2,362.00	
1370	Garbett	Atlanta	Account Rep	9/18/2009	$ 47,835	$ 2,391.75	
2848	Gomez	Boston	Account Rep	10/15/2011	$ 46,725	$ 1,401.75	
3996	Hartvigsen	Boston	Account Rep	2/18/2010	$ 45,000	$ 1,350.00	
4070	Keone	Chicago	Account Rep	4/3/2010	$ 45,125	$ 1,353.75	
3099	Laing	Chicago	Manager	1/17/2006	$ 65,500	$ 3,275.00	
2698	Lenz	Atlanta	Account Rep	4/15/2007	$ 49,750	$ 2,487.50	
2611	Nitz	Chicago	Account Rep	8/15/2012	$ 41,000	$ 1,230.00	
1256	Peterson	Atlanta	Account Rep	11/4/2010	$ 45,100	$ 1,353.00	
2009	Scholfield	Atlanta	Account Rep	7/14/2011	$ 39,750	$ 1,192.50	
4428	Selinger	Boston	Account Rep	11/8/2011	$ 41,525	$ 1,245.75	
4545	Terriquez	Chicago	Account Rep	4/15/2007	$ 49,750	$ 2,487.50	
1281	Unice	Chicago	Account Rep	1/31/2009	$ 43,750	$ 2,187.50	

FIGURE 7.7 Nested IF Function Within an IF Function

a. Open *e07h1Salary* and save it as **e07h1Salary_LastFirst**. Click the **1-Logic-Lookup worksheet tab**.

> **TROUBLESHOOTING:** If you make any major mistakes in this exercise, you can close the file, open *e07h1Salary* again, and then start this exercise over.

b. Click **cell G7**, click the **FORMULAS tab** if necessary, click **Logical** in the Function Library group, and then select **IF**.

c. Type **E7<I$2** in the **Logical_test box**.

The logical test compares the hire date to the first bonus threshold, 1/1/2005. Because you will copy the formula down the column and want to make sure the reference to the employee's hire date changes, use a relative cell reference to cell E7. To ensure that the reference to the date threshold remains constant, use a mixed cell reference to cell I$2. You could use an absolute reference, but because you are copying the formula down, the column letter I will remain the same. Using a mixed reference keeps the formula shorter and easier to read.

d. Type **F7*J$2** in the **Value_if_true box**.

This will multiply the salary by the bonus percentage if the logical test provided is true. If the logical test is not true, it will move on to the next argument created in step e.

e. Type **IF(E7<=I$3,F7*J$3,F7*J$4)** in the **Value_if_false box**.

By entering an IF statement in the Value_if_false box, you have created a nested function that evaluates the second threshold, 1/1/2010 (cell I3). If the hire date does not fall within the first or second thresholds defined by the primary and secondary logical tests, it will then by default trigger the Value_if_false, (F7*J$4). This will calculate the bonus based on the lowest bonus amount, 3% (cell J4). Use relative cell references for the employee's hire date (cell E7), because it should change when you copy the formula down the column. Use a mixed (or an absolute) reference for the threshold date (cell I$3) to ensure it does not change as you copy the formula down the column. Again, using mixed references keeps the formula shorter and easier to read than absolute references, but both produce the same results.

f. Click **OK** in the Function Arguments dialog box.

The function returns the value 6,188. This is calculated by multiplying the current salary, $68,750 (cell F7), by the bonus percentage rate of 9% (cell J2).

g. Double-click the **cell G7 fill handle** to copy the function down the column.

h. Select the **range G7:G26** and apply **Accounting Number Format**.

i. Save the workbook.

STEP 2 ≫ NEST AN AND FUNCTION INSIDE AN IF FUNCTION

The Human Resources Director recommends that the company pay managers at least $70,000. You would like to nest an AND function inside an IF function to determine which managers should receive pay raises based on their current salary level. The salary threshold is located in cell F3 in the 1-Logic-Lookup worksheet. Refer to Figure 7.8 as you complete Step 2.

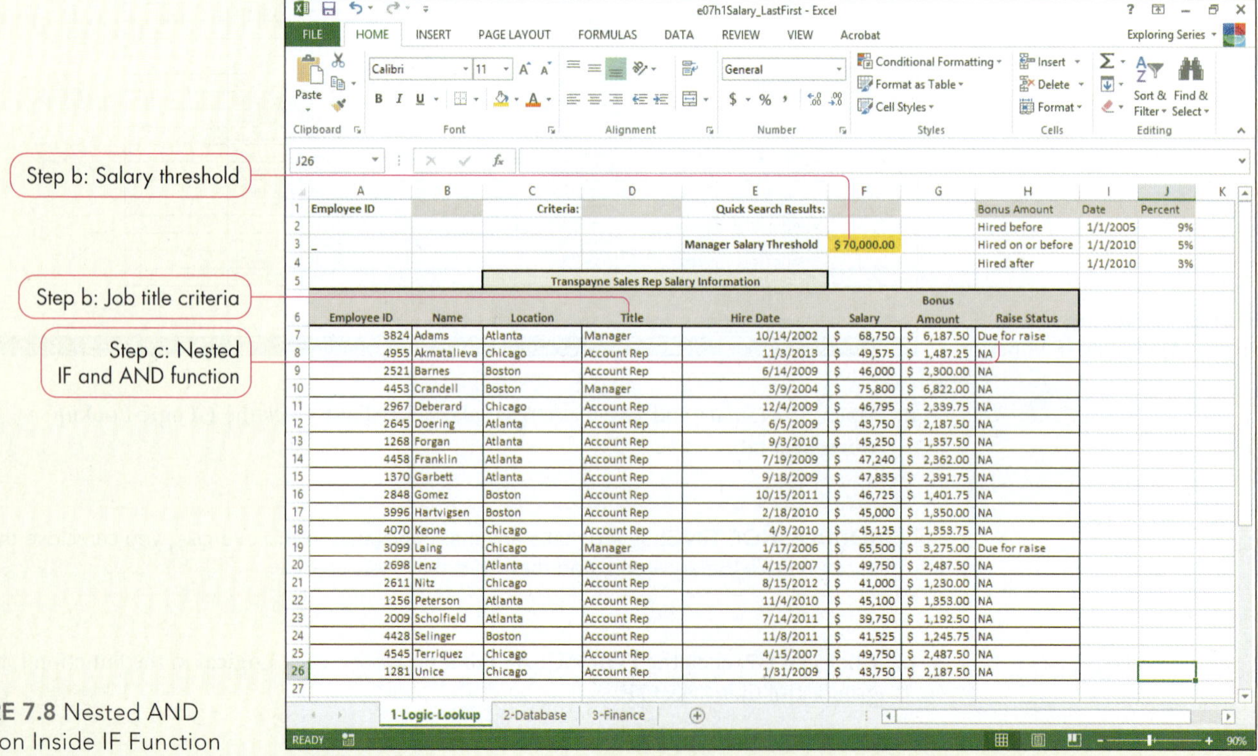

Employee ID	Name	Location	Title	Hire Date	Salary	Bonus Amount	Raise Status
3824	Adams	Atlanta	Manager	10/14/2002	$ 68,750	$ 6,187.50	Due for raise
4955	Akmatalieva	Chicago	Account Rep	11/3/2013	$ 49,575	$ 1,487.25	NA
2521	Barnes	Boston	Account Rep	6/14/2009	$ 46,000	$ 2,300.00	NA
4453	Crandell	Boston	Manager	3/9/2004	$ 75,800	$ 6,822.00	NA
2967	Deberard	Chicago	Account Rep	12/4/2009	$ 46,795	$ 2,339.75	NA
2645	Doering	Atlanta	Account Rep	6/5/2009	$ 43,750	$ 2,187.50	NA
1268	Forgan	Atlanta	Account Rep	9/3/2010	$ 45,250	$ 1,357.50	NA
4458	Franklin	Atlanta	Account Rep	7/19/2009	$ 47,240	$ 2,362.00	NA
1370	Garbett	Atlanta	Account Rep	9/18/2009	$ 47,835	$ 2,391.75	NA
2848	Gomez	Boston	Account Rep	10/15/2011	$ 46,725	$ 1,401.75	NA
3996	Hartvigsen	Boston	Account Rep	2/18/2010	$ 45,000	$ 1,350.00	NA
4070	Keone	Chicago	Account Rep	4/3/2010	$ 45,125	$ 1,353.75	NA
3099	Laing	Chicago	Manager	1/17/2006	$ 65,500	$ 3,275.00	Due for raise
2698	Lenz	Atlanta	Account Rep	4/15/2007	$ 49,750	$ 2,487.50	NA
2611	Nitz	Chicago	Account Rep	8/15/2012	$ 41,000	$ 1,230.00	NA
1256	Peterson	Atlanta	Account Rep	11/4/2010	$ 45,100	$ 1,353.00	NA
2009	Scholfield	Atlanta	Account Rep	7/14/2011	$ 39,750	$ 1,192.50	NA
4428	Selinger	Boston	Account Rep	11/8/2011	$ 41,525	$ 1,245.75	NA
4545	Terriquez	Chicago	Account Rep	4/15/2007	$ 49,750	$ 2,487.50	NA
1281	Unice	Chicago	Account Rep	1/31/2009	$ 43,750	$ 2,187.50	NA

FIGURE 7.8 Nested AND Function Inside IF Function

a. Click **cell H7**, click the **FORMULAS tab**, click **Logical** in the Function Library group, and then select **IF**.

b. Type **AND(D7="manager",F7<F$3)** in the **Logical_test box**.

Using the AND function nested in the logical test of the IF statement gives you the ability to add multiple arguments. In this scenario, you have the criteria if the employee is a manager (D7="manager" and makes less than $70,000 (F7<F$3).

c. Type **"Due for raise"** in the **Value_if_true box**.

If both conditions specified in the AND function are true, the employee is eligible for a raise. You use a mixed reference in cell F3 to ensure that row number 3 does not change when you copy the formula down the column.

d. Type **"NA"** in the **Value_if_false box**.

> **TROUBLESHOOTING:** Do not make cells D7 or F7 absolute or mixed. If you do, the function will use the incorrect values and return the first person's salary of $68,750, in the range H7:H26.

e. Click **OK**, double-click the **cell H7 fill handle** to copy the formula down the column, and then save the workbook.

The function now evaluates the employee's title and salary. If both arguments in the AND function are true, then *Due for raise* is displayed; if not, *NA* is displayed.

STEP 3 ›› CREATE A LOOKUP FIELD USING INDEX AND MATCH FUNCTIONS

You want to provide a simple search feature so that users can enter an employee number in cell B1 and then display employee title information in cell F1. For example, if Employee ID 4070 is entered in cell B1, cell F1 displays "Account Rep." Refer to Figure 7.9 as you complete Step 3.

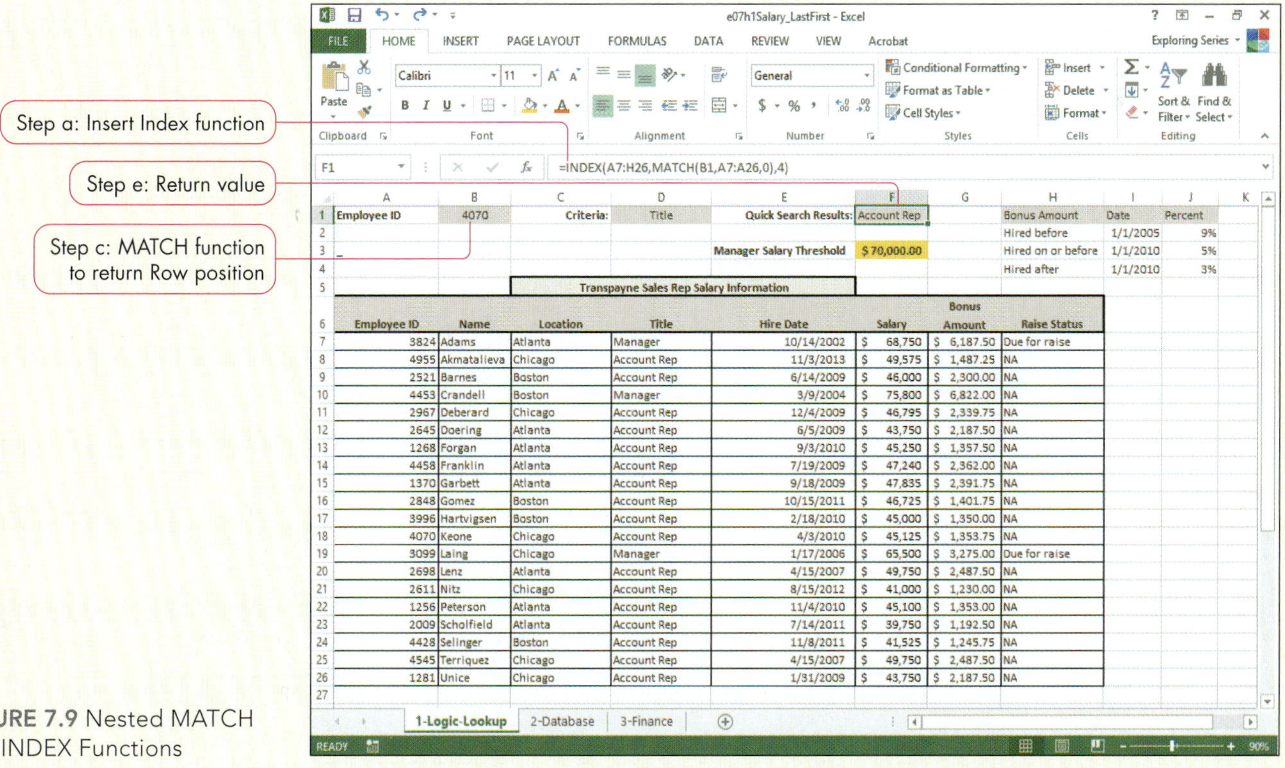

FIGURE 7.9 Nested MATCH and INDEX Functions

a. Click **cell F1**, click **Lookup & Reference** in the Function Library group, and then select **INDEX**. Choose **array, row_num, column_num** from the Select Arguments dialog box and click **OK**.

b. Select **range A7:H26** in the Array box.

   This defines the data pool from which Excel will pull information.

c. Type **MATCH(B1,A7:A26,0)** in the **Row_num box**.

   If you nest the MATCH function in the Row_num box of the index function, Excel will look up the position of the employee number in cell B1 within the range A7:A26 and return the relative position, which for employee 4070 is 12. Currently, the function returns #N/A because cell B1 is blank.

d. Type 4 in the **Column_num box**. Click **OK**.

   If you enter the number 4 in the Column_num box, the function returns information from the fourth column in the data set.

e. Type **4070** in **cell B1**.

   Cell F1 now displays the current position of employee 4070. It does this by matching the Employee ID in column A to the Title in column D.

f. Save and leave the workbook open if you plan to continue with Hands-On Exercise 2. If not, save and close the workbook, and exit Excel.

Database Filtering and Functions

Databases are prevalent in most organizations today to store and manipulate data, such as inventory details about automobiles at a particular dealership or financial transaction details for your credit card. Whereas Microsoft Access is more appropriate for relational database modeling, people often use Excel for basic database storage and manipulation. You have some experience in using Excel tables to perform basic database tasks, such as sorting and filtering data. However, you may need to perform more advanced filtering or calculations.

In this section, you will learn how to use advanced filtering techniques and insert database functions. Specifically, you will define a criteria range and extract data that meet certain criteria. Then you will insert the DSUM and DAVERAGE functions to calculate results based on filtered data.

Using Advanced Filtering

Data become more useful in decision making when you reduce the records to a subset of data that meets specific conditions. For example, a manager might want to identify account reps who earn more than $30,000 in Chicago. The manager can use the filter arrows to filter the table data by job title, salary, and location, and Excel will filter the original dataset by hiding records that do not meet the conditions. Sometimes, however, it may be important to keep the original dataset visible and create a copy of only those records that meet these conditions in another location of the worksheet. To do so, the manager can use advanced filtering techniques.

Define a Criteria Range

STEP 1» Before you apply advanced filtering techniques, you must define a criteria range. A ***criteria range*** is a separate range of cells—often several rows above or below the table—that specifies the conditions used to filter the table. A criteria range must contain at least two rows and one column. The first row contains the column labels as they appear in the table, and the second row contains the conditions (e.g., values) for filtering the table. Figure 7.10 shows the original table, criteria range, and copy of records that meet the conditions.

Criteria set on the second row of the criteria range

Original data

Labels on the first row of the criteria range

Copy of records meeting criteria

6	Employee ID	Name	Location	Title	Salary	Bonus Amount	Raise Status
7	3824	Adams	Atlanta	Manager	$ 68,750	$ 6,187.50	Due for raise
8	4955	Akmatalieva	Chicago	Account Rep	$ 49,575	$ 1,487.25	NA
9	2521	Barnes	Boston	Account Rep	$ 46,000	$ 2,300.00	NA
10	4453	Crandell	Boston	Manager	$ 75,800	$ 6,822.00	NA
11	2967	Deberard	Chicago	Account Rep	$ 46,795	$ 2,339.75	NA
12	2645	Doering	Atlanta	Account Rep	$ 43,750	$ 2,187.50	NA
13	1268	Forgan	Atlanta	Account Rep	$ 45,250	$ 1,357.50	NA
14	4458	Franklin	Atlanta	Account Rep	$ 47,240	$ 2,362.00	NA
15	1370	Garbett	Atlanta	Account Rep	$ 47,835	$ 2,391.75	NA
16	2848	Gomez	Boston	Account Rep	$ 46,725	$ 1,401.75	NA
17	3996	Hartvigsen	Boston	Account Rep	$ 45,000	$ 1,350.00	NA
18	4070	Keone	Chicago	Account Rep	$ 45,125	$ 1,353.75	NA
19	3099	Laing	Chicago	Manager	$ 65,500	$ 3,275.00	Due for raise
20							
21							
22	Employee ID	Name	Location	Title	Salary		
23			Chicago	Account Rep	>30000		
24							
25	Employee ID	Name	Location	Title	Salary		
26	4955	Akmatalieva	Chicago	Account Rep	$ 49,575		
27	2967	Deberard	Chicago	Account Rep	$ 46,795		
28	4070	Keone	Chicago	Account Rep	$ 45,125		
29	2611	Nitz	Chicago	Account Rep	$ 41,000		
30	4545	Terriquez	Chicago	Account Rep	$ 49,750		

FIGURE 7.10 Data, Criteria Range, and Output

Because you want to display records that meet all three conditions, you enter the conditions on the second row of the criteria range, immediately below their respective labels: Chicago below Location, Account Rep below Title, and >30000 below Salary. By default, Excel looks for an exact match. If you want to avoid an exact match for values, enter relational operators. For example, entering >30000 sets the condition for salaries that are greater than $30,000. You can use <, >, <=, >=, and <> relational operators, similar to using relational operators in the logical_test argument of an IF function. Excel copies only the records that meet all three conditions. Therefore, Adams earning $68,750 from Atlanta is excluded because Adams is a manager, not an account rep, and is not from Chicago. You can set an OR condition in the criteria range. For example, you want to display (a) Chicago account reps who earn more than $30,000 *or* (b) Atlanta account reps regardless of salary. Figure 7.11 shows the conditions in the criteria range. Notice that the criteria range contains three rows: column labels on the first row, the first set of conditions on the second row, and the second set of conditions on the third row. Each column of conditions sets an AND condition; that is, each criterion must be met. Each additional row sets an OR condition.

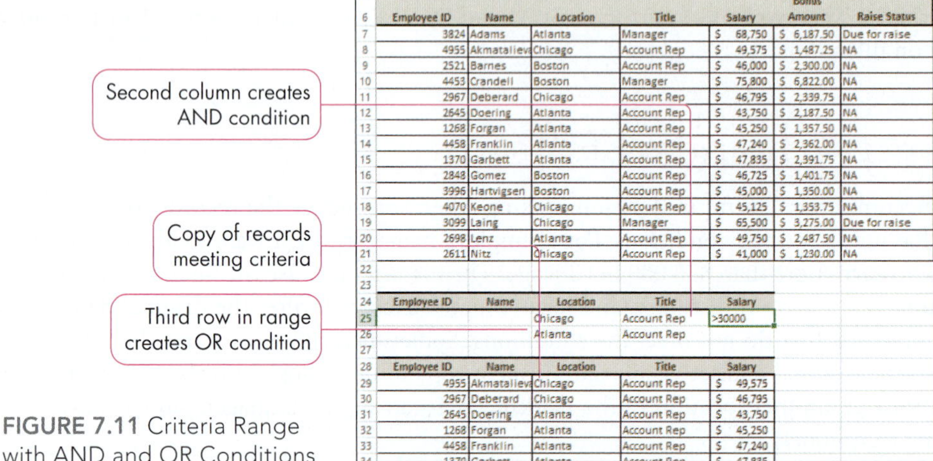

6	Employee ID	Name	Location	Title	Salary	Bonus Amount	Raise Status
7	3824	Adams	Atlanta	Manager	$ 68,750	$ 6,187.50	Due for raise
8	4955	Akmatalieva	Chicago	Account Rep	$ 49,575	$ 1,487.25	NA
9	2521	Barnes	Boston	Account Rep	$ 46,000	$ 2,300.00	NA
10	4453	Crandell	Boston	Manager	$ 75,800	$ 6,822.00	NA
11	2967	Deberard	Chicago	Account Rep	$ 46,795	$ 2,339.75	NA
12	2645	Doering	Atlanta	Account Rep	$ 43,750	$ 2,187.50	NA
13	1268	Forgan	Atlanta	Account Rep	$ 45,250	$ 1,357.50	NA
14	4458	Franklin	Atlanta	Account Rep	$ 47,240	$ 2,362.00	NA
15	1370	Garbett	Atlanta	Account Rep	$ 47,835	$ 2,391.75	NA
16	2848	Gomez	Boston	Account Rep	$ 46,725	$ 1,401.75	NA
17	3996	Hartvigsen	Boston	Account Rep	$ 45,000	$ 1,350.00	NA
18	4070	Keone	Chicago	Account Rep	$ 45,125	$ 1,353.75	NA
19	3099	Laing	Chicago	Manager	$ 65,500	$ 3,275.00	Due for raise
20	2698	Lenz	Atlanta	Account Rep	$ 49,750	$ 2,487.50	NA
21	2611	Nitz	Chicago	Account Rep	$ 41,000	$ 1,230.00	NA

24	Employee ID	Name	Location	Title	Salary
25			Chicago	Account Rep	>30000
26			Atlanta	Account Rep	

28	Employee ID	Name	Location	Title	Salary
29	4955	Akmatalieva	Chicago	Account Rep	$ 49,575
30	2967	Deberard	Chicago	Account Rep	$ 46,795
31	2645	Doering	Atlanta	Account Rep	$ 43,750
32	1268	Forgan	Atlanta	Account Rep	$ 45,250
33	4458	Franklin	Atlanta	Account Rep	$ 47,240

FIGURE 7.11 Criteria Range with AND and OR Conditions

TIP Using = and <>

Using equal (=) and unequal (<>) symbols with the criteria values selects records with empty and nonempty fields, respectively. An equal with nothing after it will return all records with no entry in the designated column. An unequal (<>) with nothing after it will select all records with an entry in the column. An empty cell in the criteria range returns every record in the list.

Apply the Advanced Filter

STEP 2» After you create the criteria range, you are ready to apply the advanced filter using the Advanced Filter dialog box. This dialog box enables you to filter the table in place or copy the selected records to another area in the worksheet, specify the list range, specify the criteria range, or display unique records only. To apply the advanced filter, do the following:

1. Click a cell in the data table.
2. Click Advanced in the Sort & Filter group on the DATA tab.
3. Click the desired action: *Filter the list, in-place* to filter the range by hiding rows that do not match your criteria or *Copy to another location* if you want to copy the rows that match your criteria instead of filtering the original dataset.
4. Make sure the *List range* displays the range containing the original dataset, including the column headings.
5. Enter the criteria range, including the criteria labels, in the *Criteria range* box. To perform the advanced filter for the OR condition in Figure 7.11, you must select all three rows of the criteria range: the column labels, the row containing the criteria for Chicago account reps earning more than $30,000, and the row containing criteria for Atlanta account reps.

6. Specify the *Copy to* range if you selected *Copy to another location* in Step 3. Notice that you enter only the starting row. Excel will copy the column labels and fill in the rows below the heading with the records that meet the conditions you set. Make sure the *Copy to* range contains sufficient empty rows to accommodate the copied records. If you do not include enough rows, Excel will replace existing data with the copied records. Click OK.

Figure 7.12 shows the Advanced Filter dialog box with settings to produce the advanced filter shown in Figure 7.11.

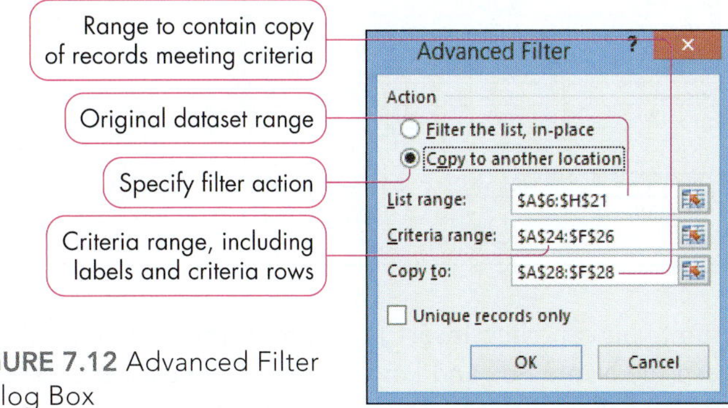

FIGURE 7.12 Advanced Filter Dialog Box

Auto Range Names

When you use the Advanced Filter dialog box, Excel assigns the range name *Criteria* to the criteria range and *Extract* to the output range.

Manipulating Data with Database Functions

Database functions analyze data for selected records only in a database table. These functions are similar to statistical functions (SUM, AVERAGE, MAX, MIN, COUNT) except that database functions are exclusively used for database tables; these functions affect only records that satisfy the specified criteria. Data not meeting the specified criteria are filtered out. All database functions use a criteria range that defines the filter parameters. Using range names can simplify the construction of database functions.

Database functions have three arguments: database, field, and criteria.

- **Database.** The database argument is the entire table, including column labels and all data, on which the function operates. The database reference may be represented by a range name. In Figure 7.13, the Database argument is A6:H21.
- **Field.** The field argument is the database column that contains the values operated on by the function. You can enter the name of the column label in quotation marks, such as "Salary," or you can enter the number that represents the location of that column within the table. For example, if the Salary column is the fifth column in the table, you can enter a 5 for the field argument. You can also enter a cell reference, for example, F6, as shown in Figure 7.13.
- **Criteria.** The criteria argument defines the conditions to be met by the function. This range must contain at least one column label and a cell below the label that specifies the condition. The criteria argument may include more than one column with conditions for each column label, indicated by a range such as A24:F25 or a range name.

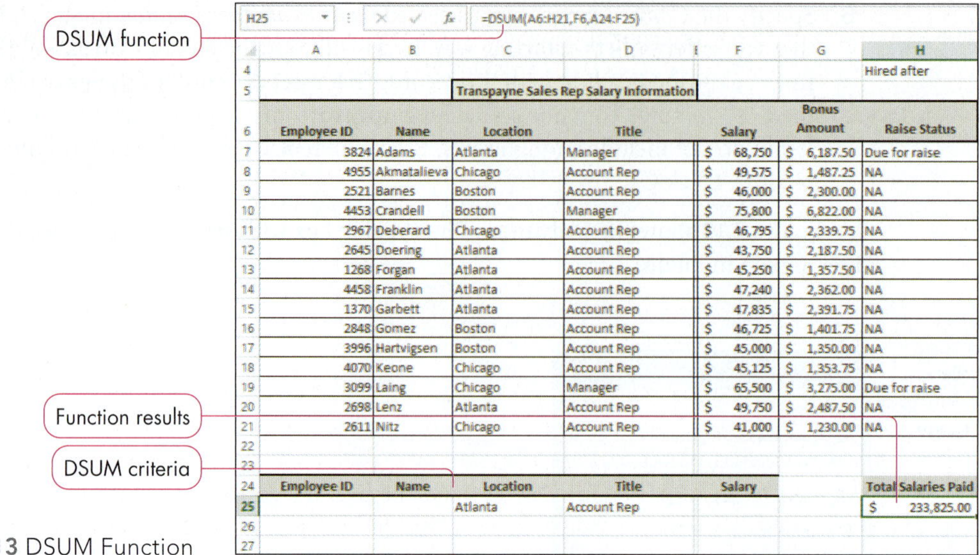

	A	B	C	D	F	G	H
4							Hired after
5			Transpayne Sales Rep Salary Information				
6	Employee ID	Name	Location	Title	Salary	Bonus Amount	Raise Status
7	3824	Adams	Atlanta	Manager	$ 68,750	$ 6,187.50	Due for raise
8	4955	Akmatalieva	Chicago	Account Rep	$ 49,575	$ 1,487.25	NA
9	2521	Barnes	Boston	Account Rep	$ 46,000	$ 2,300.00	NA
10	4453	Crandell	Boston	Manager	$ 75,800	$ 6,822.00	NA
11	2967	Deberard	Chicago	Account Rep	$ 46,795	$ 2,339.75	NA
12	2645	Doering	Atlanta	Account Rep	$ 43,750	$ 2,187.50	NA
13	1268	Forgan	Atlanta	Account Rep	$ 45,250	$ 1,357.50	NA
14	4458	Franklin	Atlanta	Account Rep	$ 47,240	$ 2,362.00	NA
15	1370	Garbett	Atlanta	Account Rep	$ 47,835	$ 2,391.75	NA
16	2848	Gomez	Boston	Account Rep	$ 46,725	$ 1,401.75	NA
17	3996	Hartvigsen	Boston	Account Rep	$ 45,000	$ 1,350.00	NA
18	4070	Keone	Chicago	Account Rep	$ 45,125	$ 1,353.75	NA
19	3099	Laing	Chicago	Manager	$ 65,500	$ 3,275.00	Due for raise
20	2698	Lenz	Atlanta	Account Rep	$ 49,750	$ 2,487.50	NA
21	2611	Nitz	Chicago	Account Rep	$ 41,000	$ 1,230.00	NA
22							
23							
24	Employee ID	Name	Location	Title	Salary		Total Salaries Paid
25			Atlanta	Account Rep			$ 233,825.00
26							
27							

FIGURE 7.13 DSUM Function

To insert a database function, you can click Insert Function in the Function Library group or Insert Function between the Name Box and Formula Bar. Then click the *Or select a category* arrow, select Database, and then click the desired database function in the *Select a function* list.

Using Formula AutoComplete

Alternatively, to begin using a database function, you can type =D in a cell. Excel displays the Formula AutoComplete list, showing a list of functions that start with the letter D. Select the appropriate database function from the list.

Use DSUM and DAVERAGE Functions

STEP 3»

The ***DSUM function*** adds the values in a numeric database column based on conditions you specify in a criteria range. In Figure 7.13, the criteria range sets conditions for Boston and account rep. You then use the criteria range to calculate the total salaries for records meeting those two conditions.

=DSUM(database,field,criteria)

The DSUM function is shorter and easier to read than other conditional summary functions, but you must create a criteria range to complete the conditions first. Note that the criteria argument does not need to include the entire database range A6:H21; it only needs to include the column labels and conditions such as A24:F25.

The ***DAVERAGE function*** determines the arithmetic mean, or average, of numeric entries in a database column that match conditions you specify. For example, you might want to determine the average salary of account reps in Boston using =DAVERAGE(A6:H21, "Salary",A24:F25).

=DAVERAGE(database,field,criteria)

TIP Division by Zero—#DIV/0—and How to Avoid It

The DAVERAGE function displays a division-by-zero error message if no records meet the specified criteria. You can hide the error message by nesting the DAVERAGE function inside the IFERROR function, which detects the error: =IFERROR(DAVERAGE(A6:H21, "Salary",A24:F25),"No Records Match the Criteria").

Identify Values with DMAX and DMIN

STEP 4» The ***DMAX function*** identifies the highest value in a database column that matches conditions you specify. For example, you can use the DMAX function to determine the highest salary ($49,750) of account reps in Boston. The ***DMIN function*** identifies the lowest value ($43,750) in a database column that matches conditions you specify. For example, you can use the DMIN function to determine the lowest salary for account reps in Boston.

=DMAX(database,field,criteria)

=DMIN(database,field,criteria)

Identify the Total Number with DCOUNT

STEP 5» The ***DCOUNT function*** counts the cells that contain numbers in a database column that match conditions you specify. For example, you can use the DCOUNT function to count the number of account reps in Boston, which is four. However, if one of the records is missing a value, DCOUNT excludes that record from being counted. If after completing the DCOUNT, you decide you would like to change the match conditions, you can do so by altering the information entered in the criteria area. To count records containing an empty cell, use DCOUNTA instead.

=DCOUNT(database,field,criteria)

=DCOUNTA(database,field,criteria)

TIP Additional Database Functions

Excel contains additional database functions, such as DSTDEV to calculate the sample population standard deviation for values in a database column and DVAR to estimate the sample population variance for values in a database column when specified conditions are met.

1. Why would you use advanced filtering over basic filtering? ***p. 433***
2. What are the benefits of database functions? ***p. 435***
3. Why would you use a database function over advanced filtering? ***p. 435***

Hands-On Exercises

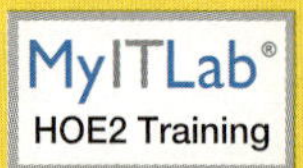

2 Database Filtering and Functions

Other assistant accountants want to be able to enter criteria to see a list of records that meet the conditions they specify. In addition, these assistants then want to calculate summary statistics based on the filtered results.

Skills covered: Create Criteria and Output Ranges • Perform an Advanced Filter • Insert a DAVERAGE Function • Use DMIN, DMAX, and DCOUNT Functions • Change the Filter Criteria

STEP 1 » CREATE CRITERIA AND OUTPUT RANGES

You want to set up the workbook with a criteria range and an output range. This will enable other assistant accountants to enter criteria of their choosing to filter the list of salary data. Refer to Figure 7.14 as you complete Step 1.

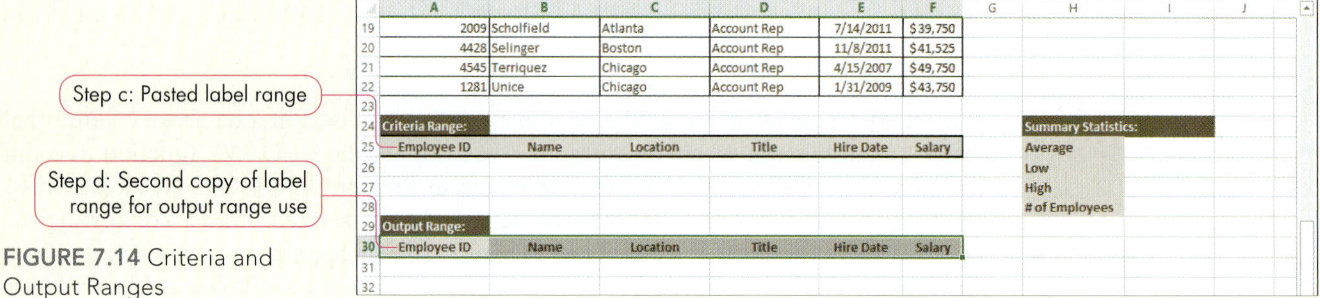

Step c: Pasted label range
Step d: Second copy of label range for output range use
2009 Scholfield Atlanta Account Rep 7/14/2011 $39,750
4428 Selinger Boston Account Rep 11/8/2011 $41,525
4545 Terriquez Chicago Account Rep 4/15/2007 $49,750
1281 Unice Chicago Account Rep 1/31/2009 $43,750
Criteria Range:
Employee ID Name Location Title Hire Date Salary
Output Range:
Employee ID Name Location Title Hire Date Salary
Summary Statistics:
Average
Low
High
# of Employees

FIGURE 7.14 Criteria and Output Ranges

a. Open *e07h1Salary_LastFirst* and save it as **e07h2Salary_LastFirst**, replacing *h1* with *h2*. Click the **2-Database worksheet tab**.

b. Select the **range A2:F2** and copy the range.

c. Paste the data in **cell A25**.

d. Click **cell A30**, paste another copy of the data, and then press **Esc**. Save the workbook.

You copied the original column labels and pasted them in the range A25:F25, the area for the Criteria Range, and another copy of the headings for the Output Range in cells A30:F30.

STEP 2 » PERFORM AN ADVANCED FILTER

You are ready to enter conditions to restrict the output list to Account Reps in Boston. Refer to Figure 7.15 as you complete Step 2.

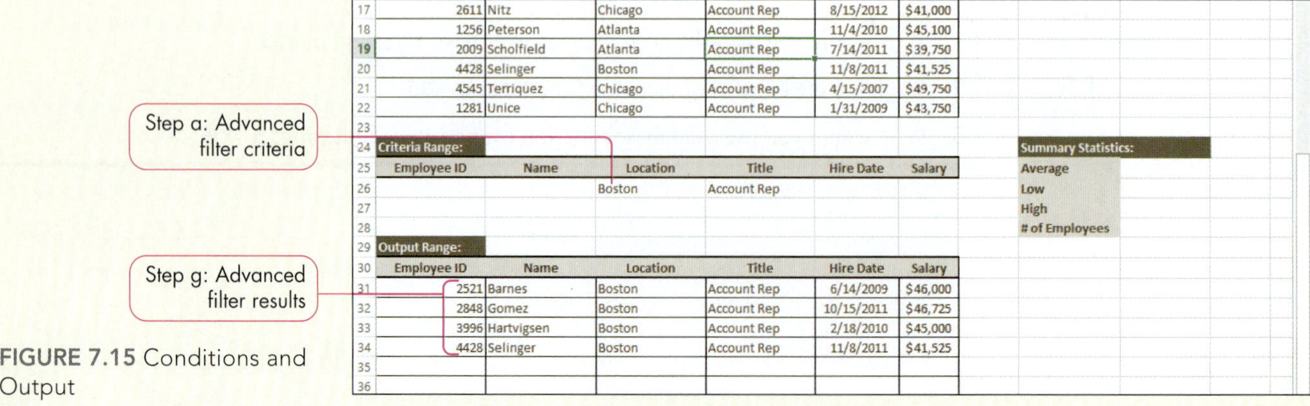

FIGURE 7.15 Conditions and Output

a. Type **Boston** in **cell C26** and type **Account Rep** in **cell D26**.

You entered the conditions on the first row below the labels in the criteria range. Because you entered both conditions on the same row, you created an AND condition. Both conditions must be met in order to display employee data in the output range.

b. Click in **cell D19** (or any cell within the dataset).

c. Click the **DATA tab** and click **Advanced** in the Sort & Filter group.

The Advanced Filter dialog box opens so that you can specify the desired filter action, the list, the criteria range, and other details.

d. Click **Copy to another location.**

e. Click in the **List range box** and select the **range A2:F22.**

f. Click in the **Criteria range box** and select the **range A25:F26.**

You selected the labels and the row containing the conditions for the criteria range.

g. Click in the **Copy to box**, select the **range A30:F30**, and then click **OK.**

Make sure you select only the labels for the output range.

h. Scroll down to see the output records. Save the workbook.

Four employees are account reps in Boston.

STEP 3 » INSERT A DAVERAGE FUNCTION

Regardless of the criteria entered in the criteria range A25:F26, you want to calculate the average salary for the records that meet those conditions. You will insert a DAVERAGE function to perform the calculation. Refer to Figure 7.16 as you complete Step 3.

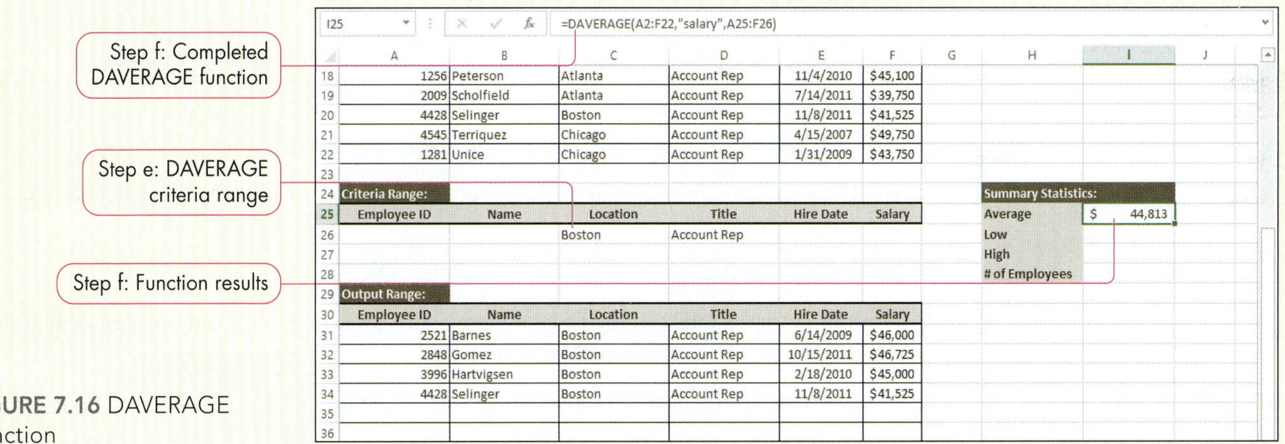

FIGURE 7.16 DAVERAGE Function

a. Click **cell I25** and click **Insert Function** in the Function Library group on the FORMULAS tab.

b. Click the **Or select a category arrow**, select **Database**, select **DAVERAGE** in the *Select a function* list if necessary, and then click **OK.**

c. Select the **range A2:F22** to enter that range in the Database box.

The database argument must include the column labels and original dataset.

d. Click in the **Field box** and type **Salary.**

Excel enters the quotation marks for you within the dialog box. If you want, you can enter the field name in quotation marks yourself, or you can enter the column number (6) of the column that contains the data you wish to average.

TROUBLESHOOTING: If you type the function instead of using the dialog box, make sure you type the double quotation marks (") around text. Otherwise, Excel will display an error message.

e. Click in the **Criteria box** and select the **range A25:F26**.

   Excel might display *Criteria* instead of the range in the Criteria box.

f. Click **OK**. Save the workbook.

   The average salary of account reps in Boston is $44,813.

STEP 4 ›› USE DMIN, DMAX, AND DCOUNT FUNCTIONS

The other accounting assistants would like to see the lowest and highest salaries based on the database conditions. In addition, you want to insert the DCOUNT function to count the number of records that meet the specified conditions. Refer to Figure 7.17 as you complete Step 4.

	A	B	C	D	E	F	G	H	I	J
16	2698	Lenz	Atlanta	Account Rep	4/15/2007	$49,750				
17	2611	Nitz	Chicago	Account Rep	8/15/2012	$41,000				
18	1256	Peterson	Atlanta	Account Rep	11/4/2010	$45,100				
19	2009	Scholfield	Atlanta	Account Rep	7/14/2011	$39,750				
20	4428	Selinger	Boston	Account Rep	11/8/2011	$41,525				
21	4545	Terriquez	Chicago	Account Rep	4/15/2007	$49,750				
22	1281	Unice	Chicago	Account Rep	1/31/2009	$43,750				
23										
24	Criteria Range:							Summary Statistics:		
25	Employee ID	Name	Location	Title	Hire Date	Salary		Average	$ 44,813	
26			Boston	Account Rep				Low	$ 41,525	
27								High	$ 46,725	
28								# of Employees	4	
29	Output Range:									
30	Employee ID	Name	Location	Title	Hire Date	Salary				
31	2521	Barnes	Boston	Account Rep	6/14/2009	$46,000				
32	2848	Gomez	Boston	Account Rep	10/15/2011	$46,725				
33	3996	Hartvigsen	Boston	Account Rep	2/18/2010	$45,000				
34	4428	Selinger	Boston	Account Rep	11/8/2011	$41,525				
35										
36										

FIGURE 7.17 DMIN, DMAX, DCOUNT Functions

a. Click **cell I26** and click **Insert Function** in the Function Library group.

   The Database functions should be listed because that was the last function category you selected.

b. Select **DMIN** in the *Select a function* list and click **OK**.

c. Select the **range A2:F22** in the Database box, select the **cell F2** in Field box, select the **range A25:F26** in the Criteria box, and then click **OK**.

   The lowest salary for account reps in Boston is $41,525.

d. Click **cell I27** and click **Insert Function** in the Function Library group. Select **DMAX** in the *Select a function* list and click **OK**.

e. Select the **range A2:F22** in the Database box, select the **cell F2** in Field box, select the **range A25:F26** in the Criteria box, and then click **OK.**

   The highest salary for account reps in Boston is $46,725.

f. Type **=DCOUNT(A2:F22,"Salary",A25:F26)** in **cell I28**. Save the workbook.

   The company has four account reps in the Boston location.

STEP 5 » CHANGE THE FILTER CRITERIA

You want to change the criteria to see the managers' salary data. Refer to Figure 7.18 as you complete Step 5.

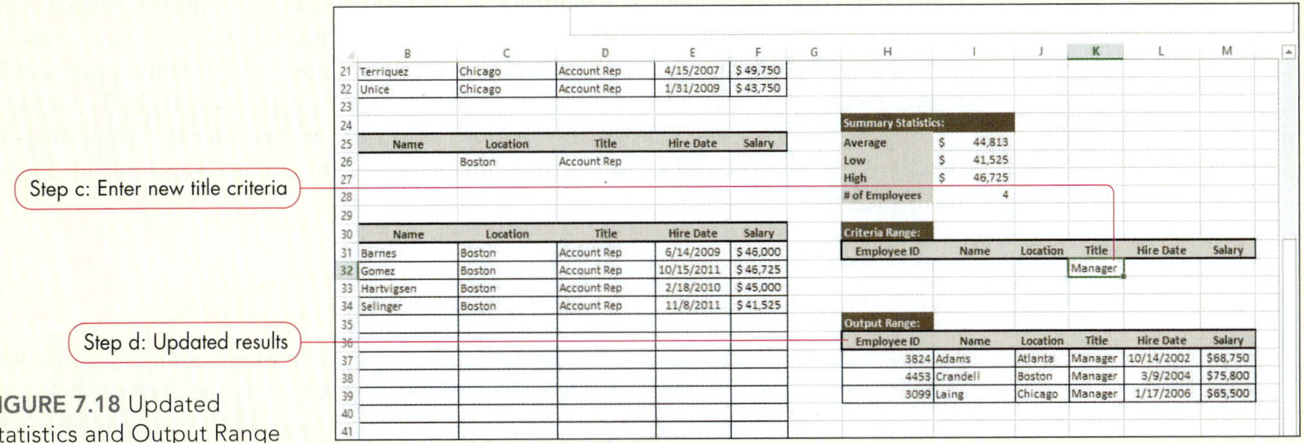

FIGURE 7.18 Updated Statistics and Output Range

a. Copy the data in the **range A24:F26** and paste the copied data in **cell H30**.

b. Delete the contents in **cells J32** and **K32**.

c. Type **Manager** in **cell K32** and press **Enter**.

d. Copy **cell A29** and paste it in **cell H35**.

e. Click anywhere in the original dataset. Repeat Steps 2c through f using the **data range A2:F22**, the **criteria range H31:M32**, and **copy to range H36:M36**.

   Excel updates the filtered list in the output range.

f. Save the workbook. Keep the workbook onscreen if you plan to continue with Hands-On Exercise 3. If not, close the workbook and exit Excel.

Financial Functions

Excel's financial functions are helpful for business financial analysts and for you in your personal financial management. Knowing what different financial functions can calculate and how to use them will benefit you as you plan retirement savings, identify best rates to obtain your financial goals, and evaluate how future values of different investments compare with today's values.

In this section, you will learn how to prepare a loan amortization table using financial functions. In addition, you will apply other financial functions to help you complete investment analyses.

Creating a Loan Amortization Table

STEP 2» You used the PMT function to calculate the monthly payment for an automobile or house loan with a fixed interest rate (such as 5.75% APR) for a specified period of time (such as 30 years). Although knowing the monthly payment is helpful to analyze a potential loan, you might want to know how much of that payment contains interest and how much actually goes toward paying off the loan balance. Interest is not identical for every month of the loan. Interest is calculated on the balance of the loan. As you continue making monthly payments, the loan balance continually decreases; therefore, the amount of interest decreases and the principal increases each month. Because your monthly payments are constant throughout the life of the loan, with each payment, more of the payment goes toward paying off the loan. To see the interest and principal portions of each monthly payment and the reduction in the loan amount, you can create a ***loan amortization table***, which is a schedule that calculates the interest, principal repayment, and remaining balance.

Figure 7.19 shows the top and bottom portions of an amortization schedule (rows 22:51 are hidden) for an automobile loan of $30,000 with an APR of 5.25% for a four-year loan with a monthly payment of $694.28, rounded to the nearest penny. The borrower pays a total of $33,325.51 (48 payments of $694.28). These payments equal the principal of $30,000 plus $3,325.51 in interest over the life of the loan.

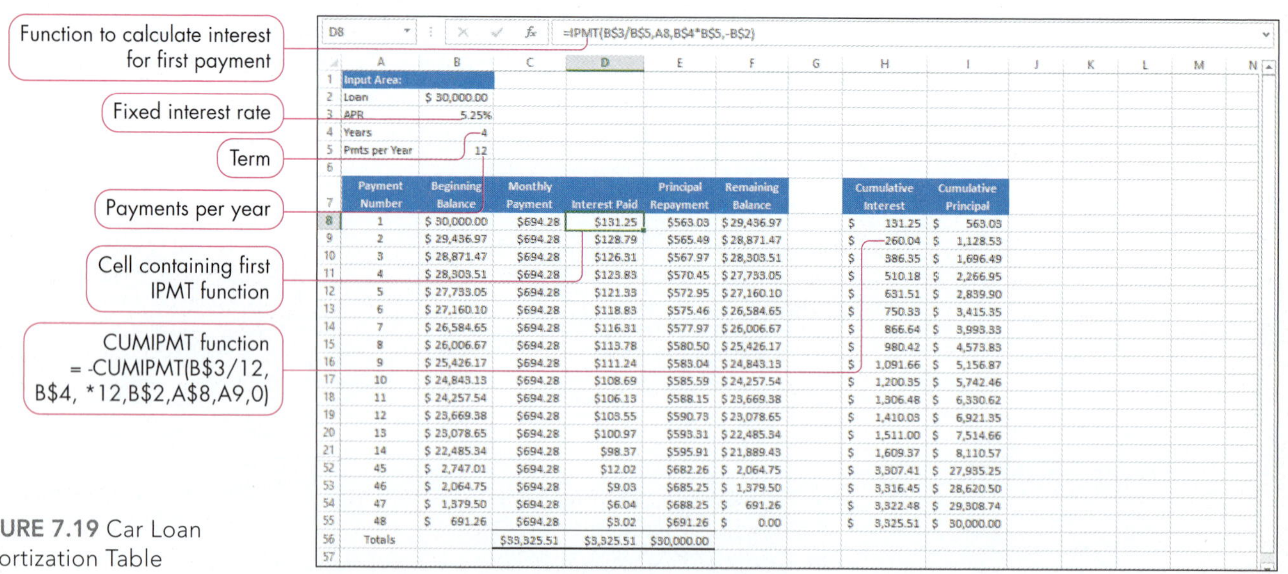

	A	B
1	Input Area:	
2	Loan	$ 30,000.00
3	APR	5.25%
4	Years	4
5	Pmts per Year	12

7	Payment Number	Beginning Balance	Monthly Payment	Interest Paid	Principal Repayment	Remaining Balance	Cumulative Interest	Cumulative Principal
8	1	$ 30,000.00	$694.28	$131.25	$563.03	$ 29,436.97	$ 131.25	$ 563.03
9	2	$ 29,436.97	$694.28	$128.79	$565.49	$ 28,871.47	$ 260.04	$ 1,128.53
10	3	$ 28,871.47	$694.28	$126.31	$567.97	$ 28,303.51	$ 386.35	$ 1,696.49
11	4	$ 28,303.51	$694.28	$123.83	$570.45	$ 27,733.05	$ 510.18	$ 2,266.95
12	5	$ 27,733.05	$694.28	$121.33	$572.95	$ 27,160.10	$ 631.51	$ 2,839.90
13	6	$ 27,160.10	$694.28	$118.83	$575.46	$ 26,584.65	$ 750.33	$ 3,415.35
14	7	$ 26,584.65	$694.28	$116.31	$577.97	$ 26,006.67	$ 866.64	$ 3,993.33
15	8	$ 26,006.67	$694.28	$113.78	$580.50	$ 25,426.17	$ 980.42	$ 4,573.83
16	9	$ 25,426.17	$694.28	$111.24	$583.04	$ 24,843.13	$ 1,091.66	$ 5,156.87
17	10	$ 24,843.13	$694.28	$108.69	$585.59	$ 24,257.54	$ 1,200.35	$ 5,742.46
18	11	$ 24,257.54	$694.28	$106.13	$588.15	$ 23,669.38	$ 1,306.48	$ 6,330.62
19	12	$ 23,669.38	$694.28	$103.55	$590.73	$ 23,078.65	$ 1,410.03	$ 6,921.35
20	13	$ 23,078.65	$694.28	$100.97	$593.31	$ 22,485.34	$ 1,511.00	$ 7,514.66
21	14	$ 22,485.34	$694.28	$98.37	$595.91	$ 21,889.43	$ 1,609.37	$ 8,110.57
52	45	$ 2,747.01	$694.28	$12.02	$682.26	$ 2,064.75	$ 3,307.41	$ 27,935.25
53	46	$ 2,064.75	$694.28	$9.03	$685.25	$ 1,379.50	$ 3,316.45	$ 28,620.50
54	47	$ 1,379.50	$694.28	$6.04	$688.25	$ 691.26	$ 3,322.48	$ 29,308.74
55	48	$ 691.26	$694.28	$3.02	$691.26	$ 0.00	$ 3,325.51	$ 30,000.00
56	Totals		$33,325.51	$3,325.51	$30,000.00			

FIGURE 7.19 Car Loan Amortization Table

Perform Internal Calculations

The body of the worksheet shows how principal and interest comprise each payment. The balance of the loan at the beginning of the first period is $30,000. The monthly payment includes interest and principal repayment. The interest for the first month ($131.25) is calculated on the beginning balance for the period, which is the original loan amount ($30,000) for the first payment at a monthly interest rate (5.25%/12).

The principal repayment is the amount of the monthly payment that is left over after deducting the monthly interest. For the first payment, the principal repayment is $563.03 ($694.28 – $131.25).

The remaining balance is the difference between the previous remaining balance and the principal repayment. For the first month, subtract the principal repayment from the original loan amount ($30,000 – $563.03).

The interest for the second month ($128.79) is less than interest for the previous period because the remaining balance to start that period is less ($29,436.97 * 5.25%/12). As each month's beginning balance decreases, so does the monthly interest. The principal repayment is higher for the second month because the interest is less than for the first month.

Extra Principal Payment

Many homebuyers choose a 30-year mortgage to keep the monthly payment low but opt to pay extra toward the principal each month to reduce the length of the mortgage and the total interest paid. This reduction in interest can be substantial. For example, paying an extra $100 a month on a 30-year, $350,000 mortgage with an interest rate of 3.24% APR can save more than $40,000 in interest over the life of the mortgage and pay off the mortgage before its original payoff date.

Calculate Interest and Principal Payments with IPMT and PPMT Functions

The financial category contains additional functions to calculate results for loan payments: IPMT and PPMT. You can use these functions in isolation or within the body of a loan amortization table if the table does not allow additional principal payments. If your loan amortization enables users to pay additional principal, these functions will not provide accurate results.

The ***IPMT function*** calculates the periodic interest for a specified payment period on a loan or an investment given a fixed interest rate, term, and periodic payments. In Figure 7.19, you use the IPMT function to calculate the interest payment for each period (for example, the calculation for interest for the first period is: =IPMT(B$3/B$5,A8,B$4*B$5,-B$2)). A benefit of the IPMT function is that you can use it to identify the interest for any given payment without having to create a loan amortization table. The IPMT function has four required arguments and two optional arguments:

=IPMT(rate,per,nper,pv,[fv],[type])

- **Rate.** The rate argument is the periodic interest rate. If the APR is 5.25% (cell B3) and monthly payments are made, the rate is 5.25%/12 (B3/12), or 0.438%.
- **Per.** The per argument is the specific payment or investment period to use to calculate the interest where the first payment period is 1. It is best to include a payment number column as in Figure 7.19. You can use a relative cell reference to avoid having raw numbers in the argument.
- **Nper.** The nper argument represents the total number of payment or investment periods. With a four-year loan consisting of monthly payments, the nper is 48. You should perform the calculation using the input cells, such as $B$4*$B$5, in the nper argument instead of typing the value 48 in case the number of years or number of payments per year changes.
- **Pv.** The pv argument represents the present value of the loan or investment. Enter a minus sign in front of the cell reference to avoid having a negative interest payment returned. In this example, pv would be –B$2.

- **Fv.** The optional fv argument represents the future value of the loan or investment. If you omit this argument, Excel defaults to 0. For loan payments, the balance should be zero after you pay off your loan.
- **Type.** The optional type argument represents the timing of the payments. Enter 0 if the payments are made at the end of the period, or enter 1 if the payments are made at the beginning of the period. If you omit this argument, Excel assumes a default of 0.

The ***PPMT function*** calculates the principal payment for a specified payment period on a loan or an investment given a fixed interest rate, term, and periodic payments. In Figure 7.19, you can use the PPMT function to calculate the principal repayment in column E. For example, cell E8 contains =PPMT(B$3/B$5,A8,B$4*B$5,-B$2). The first month's total payment of $694.28 includes $563.03 principal repayment. The PPMT function has the same four required arguments and two optional arguments as the IPMT function:

=PPMT(rate,per,nper,pv,[fv],[type])

Calculate Cumulative Interest and Principal Payments with CUMIPMT and CUMPRINC Functions

STEP 3 Although the IPMT function calculates the amount of interest paid in one particular loan payment, it does not determine the amount of interest paid over a specific number of payments. You can use the ***CUMIPMT function*** to calculate the cumulative interest throughout a loan amortization table. This function accumulates the interest paid between selected payments or throughout the entire loan. For the first payment, the cumulative interest is the same as the periodic interest. From that point on, you can calculate the cumulative interest, such as the sum of the interest paid for the first two periods, as shown in cell H9 in Figure 7.19. If you do not want to calculate a running total for the entire loan, you can specify the interest between two periods, such as between payment periods 5 and 10, to calculate the total interest paid for the second year of the loan. The CUMIPMT contains six arguments:

=CUMIPMT(rate,nper,pv,start_period,end_period,type)

The rate, nper, pv, and type arguments are the same arguments that you use in the IPMT and PPMT functions. The start_period argument specifies the first period you want to start accumulating the interest, and the end_period argument specifies the last payment period you want to include. In Figure 7.19, the first cumulative interest payment formula in cell G8 uses 1 for both the start_period and end_period arguments. From that point on, the start_period is still 1, but the end_period changes to reflect each payment period, using the payment numbers in column A.

STEP 4 You can use the ***CUMPRINC function*** to calculate the cumulative principal throughout a loan amortization table. This function accumulates the principal repayment between selected payments or throughout the entire loan. For the first payment, the cumulative principal paid is the same as the first principal repayment. From that point on, you can calculate the cumulative principal payment, such as the sum of the principal repayment paid for the first two periods, as shown in cell H9 in Figure 7.19. If you do not want to calculate a running total for the entire loan, you can specify the principal repayment between two periods, such as between payment periods 5 and 10, to calculate the total principal repaid for the second year of the loan. The CUMPRINC contains six arguments:

=CUMPRINC(rate,nper,pv,start_period,end_period,type)

Performing Other Financial Calculations

In addition to using financial functions to calculate monthly payments on a loan and to build a loan amortization table, you might want to make other investment-related calculations. For example, you can calculate present or future values, rates, and number of payment periods. Figure 7.20 illustrates the results of several financial functions.

	A	B	C	D	E	F
1	Present Value			Number of Periods		
2	Lump Sum	$ 1,000,000.00		Loan	$ 30,000.00	
3	Present Value	$1,246,221.03	$1,246,221.03	APR	5.25%	
4	Per Year	$ 100,000.00		Number of Periods in Year	12	
5	No. of Years	20		Monthly Payment	694.28	
6	Rate	5%		Number of Periods	48.0001	48.0001
7						
8	Future Value			Rate		
9	Yearly Contributions	3000		Loan	30000	
10	No. of Years	40		Monthly Payment	694.28	
11	APR	7%		Number of Periods in Year	12	
12	Future Value	$598,905.34	$598,905.34	Years	4	
13	Total Contributed	120000		Periodic Rate	0.44%	0.44%
14	Interest	$ 478,905.34		APR	5.25%	
15						
16	Net Present Value					
17	Invest End of Year	3000				
18	Yearly Income	1200				
19	Rate	3%				
20	Net Present Value	$382.85	$382.85			

FIGURE 7.20 Financial Functions

Calculate Present and Future Values

STEP 1

The ***PV function*** calculates the total present (i.e., current) value of a series of payments that will be made in the future. This function illustrates the time value of money in which the value of $1 today is worth more than the value of $1 received at some time in the future, given that you can invest today's $1 to earn interest in the future. For example, you might want to use the PV function to compare a lump-sum payment versus annual payments if you win the lottery to see which is better: receiving $100,000 per year for the next 20 years or $1 million now. The PV function has three required arguments (rate, nper, and pmt) and two optional arguments (fv and type). The rate, nper, and type arguments have the same definitions as in other financial functions. The pmt argument is the fixed periodic payment. The fv argument represents the future value of the investment. If you do not know the payment, you must enter a value for the fv argument. In Figure 7.20, cell B3 contains the PV function. The yearly payments of $100,000 invested at 5% yield a higher present value ($1,246,221.03) than the $1 million lump-sum payment.

```
=PV(rate,nper,pmt,[fv],[type])
```

The ***FV function*** calculates the future value of an investment, given a fixed interest rate, term, and periodic payment. You can use the FV function to determine how much an individual retirement account (IRA) would be worth at a future date. The FV function has three required arguments (rate, nper, and pmt) and two optional arguments (pv and type). If you omit the pmt argument, you must enter a value for the pv argument.

```
=FV(rate,nper,pmt,[pv],[type])
```

Assume that you plan to contribute $3,000 a year to an IRA for 40 years and that you expect the IRA to earn 7% interest annually. The future value of that investment—the amount you will have at age 65— would be $598,905.34! In Figure 7.20, cell B12 contains the FV function. You would have contributed $120,000 ($3,000 a year for 40 years). The extra $478,905.34 results from compound interest you will earn over the life of your $120,000 investment!

The ***NPV function*** calculates the net present value of an investment, given a fixed discount rate (rate of return) and a set of given cash inflows. Specifically, it considers periodic future income and payments. The NPV and PV functions are very similar in concept. The difference is that the PV function requires equal payments at the end of a payment period, whereas the NPV function can have unequal but constant payments. The NPV function contains two required arguments (rate and value1) and additional optional arguments (such as value2). If an investment returns a positive net present value, the investment is profitable. If an investment returns a negative net present value, the investment will lose money.

```
=NPV(rate,value1,value2,)
```

- **Rate.** The rate argument is the discount rate for one period. It is also called the rate of return or the percentage return on your investment. If an investment pays 12% per year and each period is one month, the rate is 1%.

the squared deviations divided by the amount of the sample (n – 1). While calculating standard deviation and variance mathematically may seem daunting, in Excel the functions are no more complicated than using a SUM function.

```
=STDEV.S(number1,number2)
```

```
=VAR.S(number1,number2)
```

The STDEV.S and VAR.S functions return values for a data sample rather than a population; however, Excel does contain functions to calculate population variation as well, as described in Table 8.3 and as displayed in syntax below.

```
=STDEV.P(number1,number2)
```

```
=VAR.P(number1,number2)
```

Use the CORREL Function

STEP 2》

The ***CORREL function***, short for correlation coefficient, helps determine the strength of a relationship between two variables. When used to compare datasets, the function will return a value between –1 and 1. The closer the value is to 1, the stronger the relationship. For example, Figure 8.9 depicts the strength of the relationship between salary and credit score. Cell D3 contains a calculated correlation of .913135908. This would indicate a strong correlation between salary and a high credit score.

The input variables for the CORREL function are entered in arrays.

```
=CORREL(Array1,Array2)
```

To use the CORREL function to calculate correlation, complete the steps below.

1. Click a cell.
2. Click the FORMULAS tab on the Ribbon and choose More Functions – Statistical – CORREL.
3. Select the range for the first data array.
4. Select the range for the second data array.
5. Click OK.

D3 =CORREL(A2:A8,B2:B8)

	A	B	C	D
1	Salary	Credit Score		
2	$ 40,000.00	450		Correlation
3	$ 50,000.00	450		0.913135908
4	$ 60,000.00	550		
5	$ 70,000.00	475		
6	$ 80,000.00	625		
7	$ 90,000.00	785		
8	$100,000.00	787		
9				

FIGURE 8.9 CORREL Function

Calculate Frequency Distribution

STEP 3》

The ***FREQUENCY function*** is a descriptive static function in Excel that determines the frequency distribution of a dataset. The frequency distribution is a meaningful descriptive tool because it determines how often a set of numbers appears within a dataset. For example, you may want to determine how many student GPAs fall within a specific range. FREQUENCY could determine how many students earned As, Bs, and Cs. Using the FREQUENCY function is somewhat unique because it returns a vertical array of data based on data bins that you determine. For example, in Figure 8.10, the FREQUENCY function returns the number of occurrences of each salary in the dataset as determined by quartiles. In this scenario, there are 12 occurrences of the salary that are less than or equal to $39,203.50.

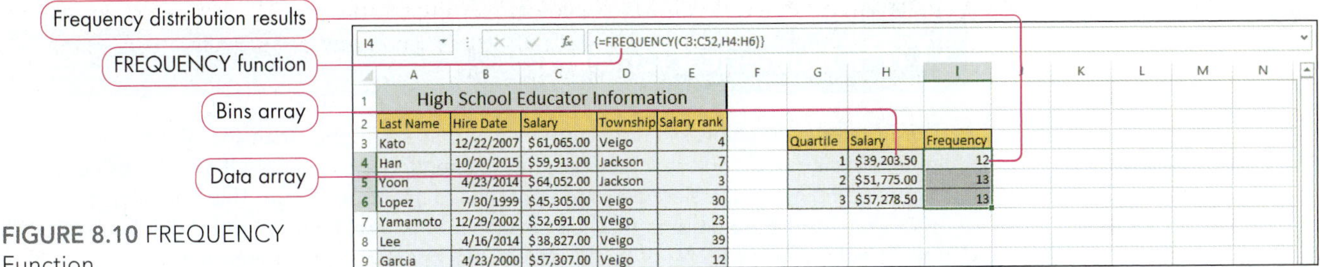

FIGURE 8.10 FREQUENCY Function

As shown in Figure 8.11, the FREQUENCY function requires two input variables, the data_array and the bins_array.

FREQUENCY function

Data array

Bin array

I4 =FREQUENCY(C3:C52,H4:H6)

High School Educator Information				
Last Name	Hire Date	Salary	Township	Salary rank
Kato	12/22/2007	$61,065.00	Veigo	4
Han	10/20/2015	$59,913.00	Jackson	7
Yoon	4/23/2014	$64,052.00	Jackson	3
Lopez	7/30/1999	$45,305.00	Veigo	30
Yamamoto	12/29/2002	$52,691.00	Veigo	23
Lee	4/16/2014	$38,827.00	Veigo	39
Garcia	4/23/2000	$57,307.00	Veigo	12
Thomas	10/2/2002	$48,384.00	Acorn	28
Gao	7/16/2006	$37,575.00	Jackson	41
Cruz	8/6/2011	$60,913.00	Veigo	6
Cruz	9/11/2006	$58,134.00	Acorn	9
Ortiz	8/16/2005	$57,394.00	Jackson	11
Rodriguez	8/4/2008	$43,815.00	Veigo	32
Ma	1/21/2010	$36,288.00	Jackson	42
Young	5/4/2010	$50,920.00	Veigo	26
Jhadav	8/3/2006	$55,953.00	Veigo	14
Jayaraman	10/14/2003	$64,261.00	Acorn	2
Sanchez	5/30/2009	$34,301.00	Acorn	47
Li	5/30/1999	$55,257.00	Veigo	18
He	1/17/2002	$44,450.00	Acorn	31
Mehta	1/13/2014	$35,259.00	Jackson	44
Hamade	8/17/2003	$58,478.00	Jackson	8
Bhatnagar	11/30/2011	$35,015.00	Jackson	45

Quartile	Salary	Frequency
1	$39,203.50	=FREQUENCY(C3:C52,H4:H6)
2	$51,775.00	
3	$57,278.50	

FIGURE 8.11 Frequency Function Input Variables

=FREQUENCY(Data_array,Bins_array)

- **Data_Array.** The data_array is the range of cells that contain the values that are being evaluated for frequency of occurrence. In Figure 8.11, the Data_Array C3:C52 is being evaluated to determine how many salaries fall within the first, second, or third quartile.
- **Bins_Array.** The bins_array is a predefined set of numerical values that are used to organize and count the data. In Figure 8.11, the range H4:H6 displays the quartile values that will be used to determine frequency of occurrence within the Data_Array.

Unlike other Excel functions, you do not simply type the FREQUENCY function in a cell and press Enter. Instead, you must first select the cells in which you want to put the FREQUENCY function, type the formula, and then press Ctrl+Shift+Enter. If you simply press Enter, then FREQUENCY will only calculate the frequency of the data that fall in the first cell bins_array. To use the FREQUENCY function, do the following:

1. Select a range to output results.
2. Type =FREQUENCY and press Tab.
3. Select the data_array.
4. Select the bins_array.
5. Press Ctrl+Shift+Enter.

Numerical Outliers

The frequency function will not return values that are higher than the highest number in the bins_array. If you are interested in documenting the numbers that fall outside the predefined bins_array, select one additional cell to the return range. This cell will populate with a count of the numbers that fall outside the highest number in the bins_array. For example, in Figure 8.12, there are 12 salaries that are outside the third quartile.

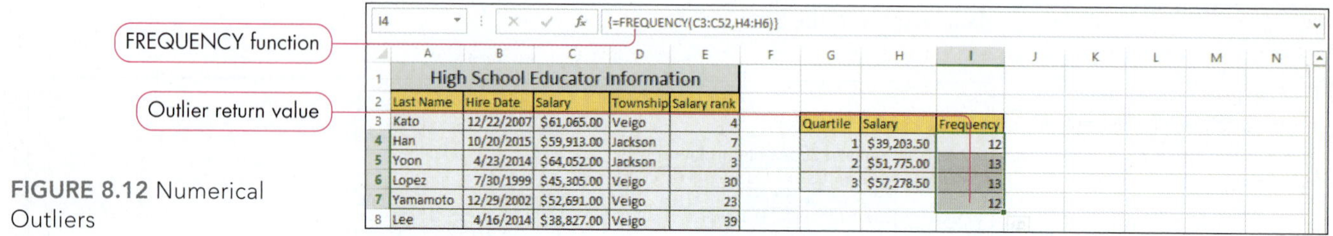

	A	B	C	D	E	F	G	H	I
1	High School Educator Information								
2	Last Name	Hire Date	Salary	Township	Salary rank				
3	Kato	12/22/2007	$61,065.00	Veigo	4		Quartile	Salary	Frequency
4	Han	10/20/2015	$59,913.00	Jackson	7		1	$39,203.50	12
5	Yoon	4/23/2014	$64,052.00	Jackson	3		2	$51,775.00	13
6	Lopez	7/30/1999	$45,305.00	Veigo	30		3	$57,278.50	13
7	Yamamoto	12/29/2002	$52,691.00	Veigo	23				12
8	Lee	4/16/2014	$38,827.00	Veigo	39				

FIGURE 8.12 Numerical Outliers

***Quick* Concepts**

1. When would you use STDEV.S instead of STDEV.P? ***pp. 479–480***
2. Why would you use FREQUENCY instead of COUNTIF? ***p. 480***
3. What is keyboard command to complete the FREQUENCY function if working with an array of data? ***p. 481***

Hands-On Exercises

2 Descriptive Statistical Functions

As the superintendent, you have been tasked with evaluating student performance. You have decided to base your assessment on standardized test scores and total attendance. You would also like to test the correlation between test scores and attendance. You plan to base your calculations on a sample of 50 students from the district.

Skills covered: Calculate Standard Deviation and Variance • Calculate Correlation Coefficient • Determine Frequency Distribution

STEP 1 »» CALCULATE STANDARD DEVIATION AND VARIANCE

The sample you have collected contains scores as well as attendance information of sixth- through eighth-grade students across the district. You will calculate the standard deviation of the test scores within the sample. Refer to Figure 8.13 as you complete Step 1.

H9 =STDEV.S(C4:C53)

6-8 Test Scores				
Student ID	Test Score	Township	School #	Days Absent
1075	725	Acorn	24	2
1912	325	Acorn	24	10
4196	648	Acorn	24	6
4483	750	Acorn	24	0
6237	585	Acorn	24	2
6284	325	Acorn	24	9
6285	707	Acorn	24	1
6312	684	Acorn	24	2
6353	407	Acorn	24	10
6747	501	Acorn	26	6
6778	282	Acorn	26	5
7025	596	Acorn	26	2
7284	789	Acorn	26	9
7486	621	Acorn	26	0
7717	600	Acorn	26	1
7788	406	Acorn	26	3
8362	234	Acorn	26	6
8843	650	Acorn	26	0
9573	532	Acorn	26	3
9849	550	Acorn	26	0
1625	417	Jackson	55	3
2309	524	Jackson	55	3

Max Test Score	Sample Size	Average
800	50	517

Standard Deviation	Variance	Correlation
181	32803	

Days Absent	Frequency
0	
5	
10	

Step c: Standard deviation of test scores

Step e: Variance of test scores

FIGURE 8.13 Calculate Standard Deviation and Variance

a. Open *e08h1Assessment_LastFirst*, click the **Test Scores worksheet**, and then save it as **e08h2TestScores_LastFirst**.

b. Click **cell H9**, click the **FORMULAS tab** if necessary, click **More Functions** in the Function Library group, select **Statistical**, and then click **STDEV.S**.

   STDEV.S is being used because the data is a random sample of 50 test scores. If every test score were included in the dataset, STDEV.P would be used.

c. Select the **range C4:C53** and click **OK**. Then with **cell H9** still selected, click the **Decrease Decimal button** in the Number group on the HOME tab until no decimal points are displayed.

   The standard deviation for the sample is 181. Therefore, assuming the distribution is normal, about 66% of students will receive a test score between 336 and 698. This is calculated by adding the standard deviation, 181, to the average test score of 517 to determine the high end of the range and subtracting 181 from 517 to determine the low end of the range.

d. Click **cell I9**, click the **FORMULAS tab** if necessary, click **More Functions** in the Function Library group, click **Statistical**, and then select **VAR.S**.

Open and Arrange Windows

You might want to see the contents of two worksheets in the same workbook at the same time. For example, you might want to compare the Qtr1 and Qtr2 worksheets simultaneously. Instead of clicking back and forth between worksheet tabs, you can open another window of the same workbook, and then display different worksheets within each window.

Open Another Window. To open another window of the current workbook, click the View tab, and then click New Window in the Window group. Excel opens another window of the workbook. The title bar adds *:1* to the original workbook view and *:2* to the second window. Although only one window appears maximized, both windows are open. There is no limit to the number of windows that can be opened.

Arrange the Windows. To see all windows of the same workbook, click Arrange All in the Window group. Select one of the options from the Arrange Windows dialog box (see Figure 9.4). You can display windows in a tiled arrangement, horizontally, vertically, or in a cascaded view. If you have other workbooks open when you click Arrange All, Excel includes those workbook windows. To display windows for the current workbook only, click the *Windows of active workbook* check box.

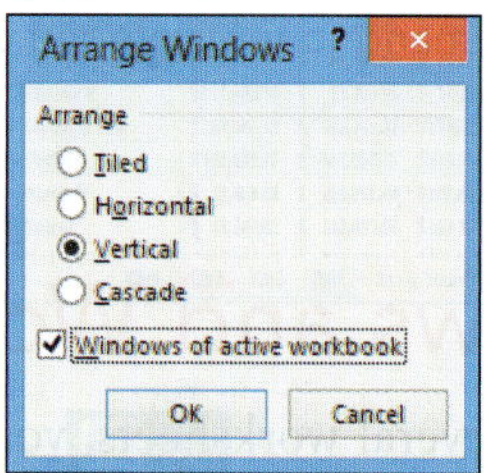

FIGURE 9.4 Arrange Windows Dialog Box

Split a Window

When you work with very large, complex worksheets, you may need to view different sections at the same time. For example, you may need to look at input data on rows 5 and 6 and see how changing the data affects overall results on row 150. To see these different worksheet sections at the same time, split the worksheet window. ***Splitting*** is the process of dividing a worksheet window into two or four resizable panes so you can view separate parts of a worksheet at the same time (see Figure 9.5). All panes are part of the one worksheet. Any changes you make to one pane affect the entire worksheet.

To divide a worksheet into panes, click Split in the Window group on the View tab. Depending on which cell is the active cell, Excel splits the worksheet into two or four panes with ***split bars***—vertical and horizontal lines that frame the panes—above and to the left of the active cell. If the active cell is in row 1, the worksheet appears in two *vertical* panes. If the active cell is in column A, the worksheet appears in two *horizontal* panes. If the active cell is cell A1 or any cell besides in the first row or first column, the worksheet appears in four panes.

Once the window is split, you can further customize the display by dragging the horizontal or vertical line that appears. Drag the vertical split bar to divide the worksheet into left and right (vertical) panes. Drag the horizontal split bar to divide the worksheet into upper and lower (horizontal) panes. While the active cell will be mirrored across all split panes, you can scroll each pane to the desired range you wish to see.

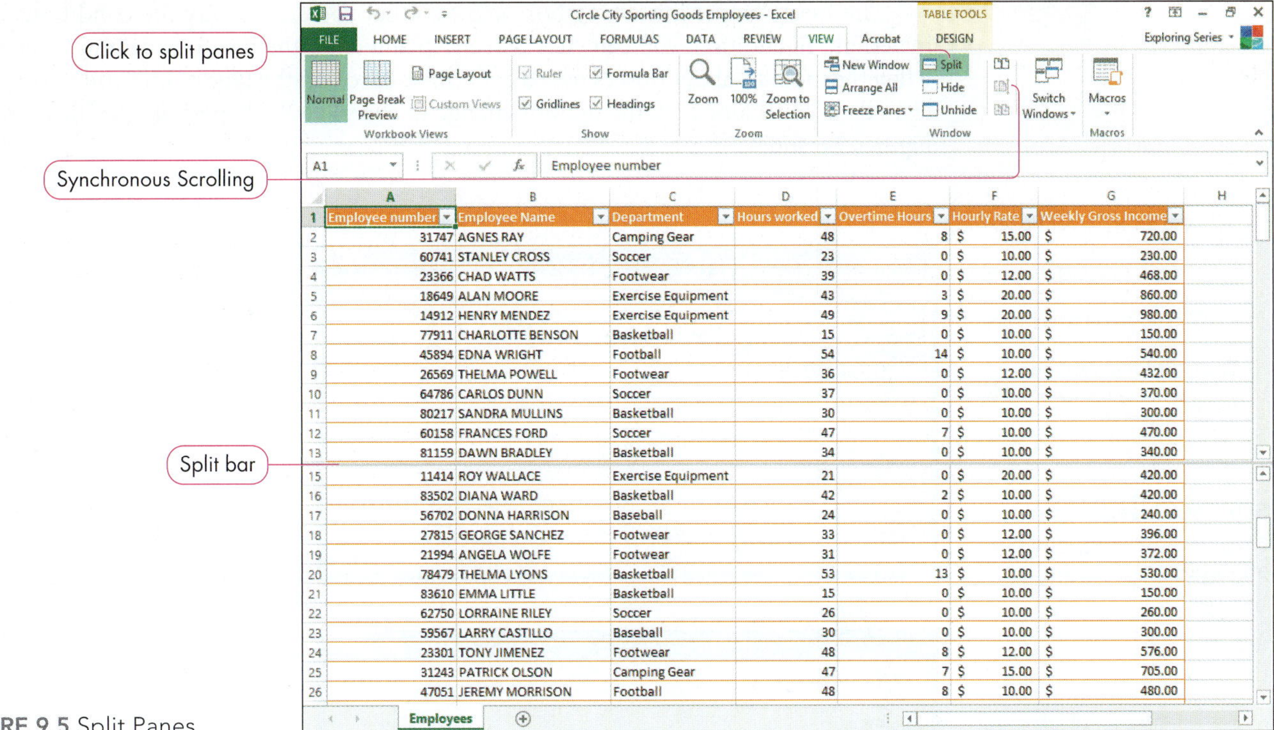

	A	B	C	D	E	F	G
1	Employee number	Employee Name	Department	Hours worked	Overtime Hours	Hourly Rate	Weekly Gross Income
2	31747	AGNES RAY	Camping Gear	48	8	$ 15.00	$ 720.00
3	60741	STANLEY CROSS	Soccer	23	0	$ 10.00	$ 230.00
4	23366	CHAD WATTS	Footwear	39	0	$ 12.00	$ 468.00
5	18649	ALAN MOORE	Exercise Equipment	43	3	$ 20.00	$ 860.00
6	14912	HENRY MENDEZ	Exercise Equipment	49	9	$ 20.00	$ 980.00
7	77911	CHARLOTTE BENSON	Basketball	15	0	$ 10.00	$ 150.00
8	45894	EDNA WRIGHT	Football	54	14	$ 10.00	$ 540.00
9	26569	THELMA POWELL	Footwear	36	0	$ 12.00	$ 432.00
10	64786	CARLOS DUNN	Soccer	37	0	$ 10.00	$ 370.00
11	80217	SANDRA MULLINS	Basketball	30	0	$ 10.00	$ 300.00
12	60158	FRANCES FORD	Soccer	47	7	$ 10.00	$ 470.00
13	81159	DAWN BRADLEY	Basketball	34	0	$ 10.00	$ 340.00
15	11414	ROY WALLACE	Exercise Equipment	21	0	$ 20.00	$ 420.00
16	83502	DIANA WARD	Basketball	42	2	$ 10.00	$ 420.00
17	56702	DONNA HARRISON	Baseball	24	0	$ 10.00	$ 240.00
18	27815	GEORGE SANCHEZ	Footwear	33	0	$ 12.00	$ 396.00
19	21994	ANGELA WOLFE	Footwear	31	0	$ 12.00	$ 372.00
20	78479	THELMA LYONS	Basketball	53	13	$ 10.00	$ 530.00
21	83610	EMMA LITTLE	Basketball	15	0	$ 10.00	$ 150.00
22	62750	LORRAINE RILEY	Soccer	26	0	$ 10.00	$ 260.00
23	59567	LARRY CASTILLO	Baseball	30	0	$ 10.00	$ 300.00
24	23301	TONY JIMENEZ	Footwear	48	8	$ 12.00	$ 576.00
25	31243	PATRICK OLSON	Camping Gear	47	7	$ 15.00	$ 705.00
26	47051	JEREMY MORRISON	Football	48	8	$ 10.00	$ 480.00

FIGURE 9.5 Split Panes

To remove panes, click Split in the Window group, or double-click the split bar, or drag a vertical split bar to the left or right edge of the worksheet window or a horizontal split bar to the top or bottom of the worksheet window.

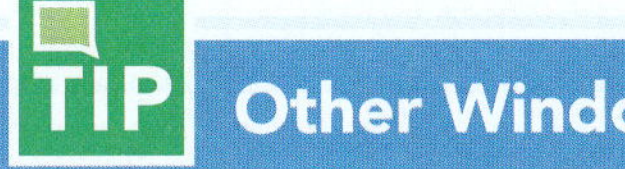

TIP Other Window Settings

The Window group on the View tab contains options to enable you to view two worksheet windows side by side and synchronize the scrolling for both windows or enable separate scrolling. If you have adjusted the window sizes, you can reset the open worksheet windows to share the screen equally. In addition, you can hide a worksheet if you do not want to display it, or you can display a previously hidden worksheet window. However, you cannot use the Freeze Panes settings and split bars at the same time.

Inserting Hyperlinks

STEP 3

When you create a workbook that has multiple worksheets, you might want to include a documentation worksheet that is similar to a table of contents. On the documentation worksheet, enter labels to describe each worksheet, and then create hyperlinks to the respective worksheets. A ***hyperlink***, or link, is an electronic marker that, when clicked, connects to another location in the same or a different worksheet, another file, a Web page, or an e-mail. To create a hyperlink, click the cell that will contain the hyperlink or select an object, such as an image, that you want to use as the hyperlink, and then do one of the following:

1. Click the INSERT tab and click Hyperlink in the Links group.
2. Right-click the cell or object and select Hyperlink.
3. Click a cell or object and press Ctrl+K.

The Insert Hyperlink dialog box opens so that you can specify the conditions of the hyperlink. In addition, you can click ScreenTip and enter the text to appear as a ScreenTip when the mouse pointer hovers over a hyperlink. Based on the type of link you select on the left side of the dialog box, the options change to complete the hyperlink specifications (see Figures 9.6 and 9.7).

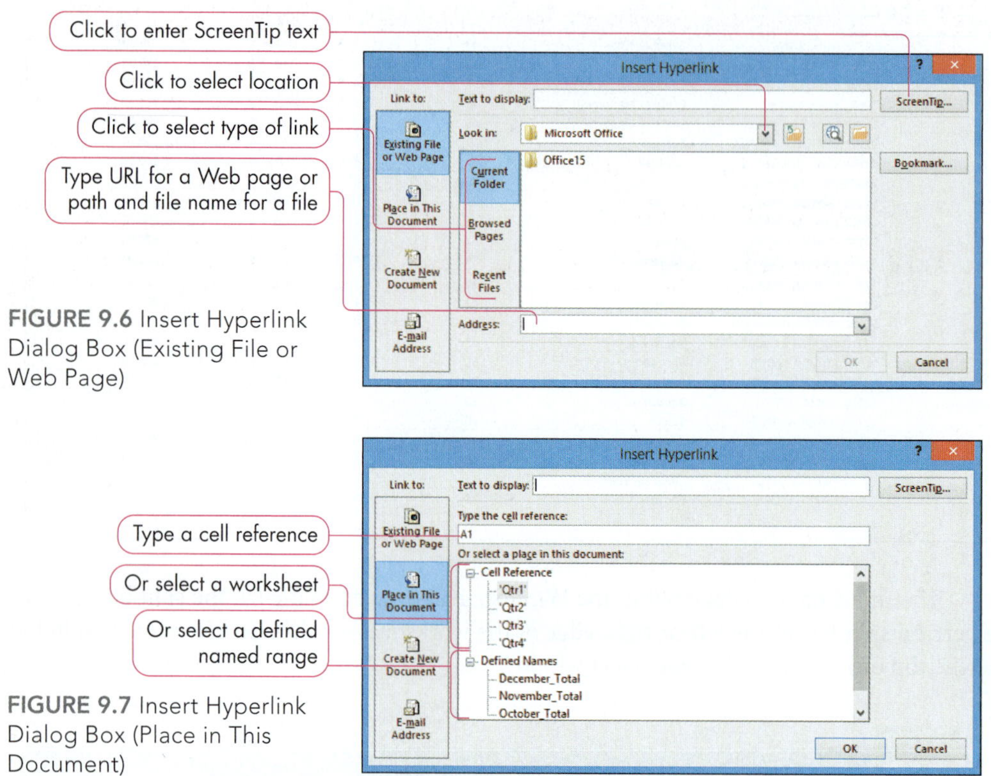

FIGURE 9.6 Insert Hyperlink Dialog Box (Existing File or Web Page)

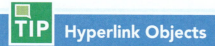

FIGURE 9.7 Insert Hyperlink Dialog Box (Place in This Document)

TIP Hyperlink Objects

You have the ability to add hyperlinks to more than just text. You have the ability to add links to inserted images and objects as well.

Workbook hyperlinks are similar to Web page hyperlinks. Textual hyperlinks appear blue with a blue underline. When you position the mouse pointer over a hyperlink, the pointer looks like a hand, and Excel displays a default ScreenTip indicating where the link will take you or the custom ScreenTip if you created one in the Set Hyperlink ScreenTip dialog box (see Figure 9.8). Click the link to jump to the link's destination. After you click a hyperlink, the color changes to purple so that you can distinguish between links you have clicked and links you have not clicked. The hyperlink color changes back to blue after a period of time.

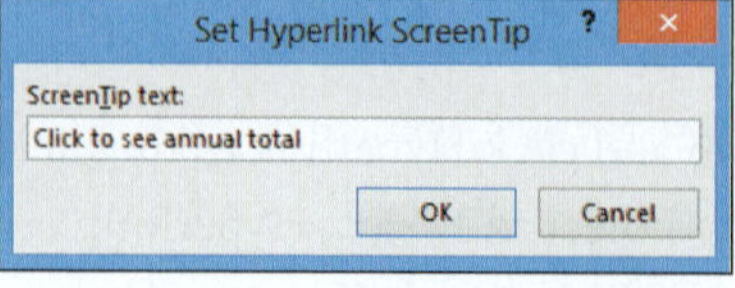

FIGURE 9.8 Set Hyperlink ScreenTip Dialog Box

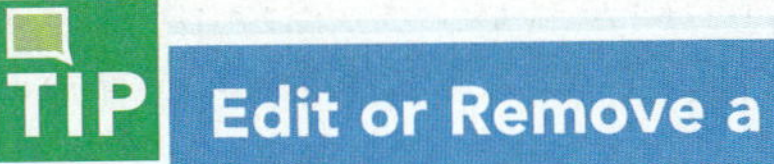

Edit or Remove a Hyperlink

To modify a hyperlink, right-click it, and then select Edit Hyperlink to open the Edit Hyperlink dialog box, which is similar to the Insert Hyperlink dialog box. Make the desired changes and click OK. To remove a hyperlink, right-click it and select Remove Hyperlink. This action removes the hyperlink but does not delete the cell contents or object.

1. What are the benefits of grouping worksheets? ***p. 506***
2. What are the benefits of using Split window? ***p. 510***
3. Besides linking inside a worksheet, where else can hyperlinks lead the user? ***p. 511***

Hands-On Exercises

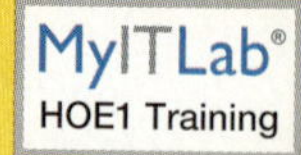

1 Multiple Worksheets

After reviewing last year's fiscal data, you need to improve the appearance of the worksheets for Circle City Sporting Goods. You need to enter a missing heading on the summary worksheet and enter formulas across the quarterly worksheets. To save time, you will group the worksheets to perform tasks to all grouped worksheets at the same time. After you complete the quarterly worksheets, you will insert hyperlinks from the yearly worksheet to the quarterly worksheets.

Skills covered: Group and Fill Across Worksheets • Enter and Format Data Across Worksheets • Insert Hyperlinks • Open and Arrange Worksheets

STEP 1 » GROUP AND FILL ACROSS WORKSHEETS

You noticed that the main title and the row headings are displayed only in the Qtr1 worksheet in the Indianapolis workbook. You need to fill in the title and row headings for the other three quarterly and the yearly worksheets. Refer to Figure 9.9 as you complete Step 1.

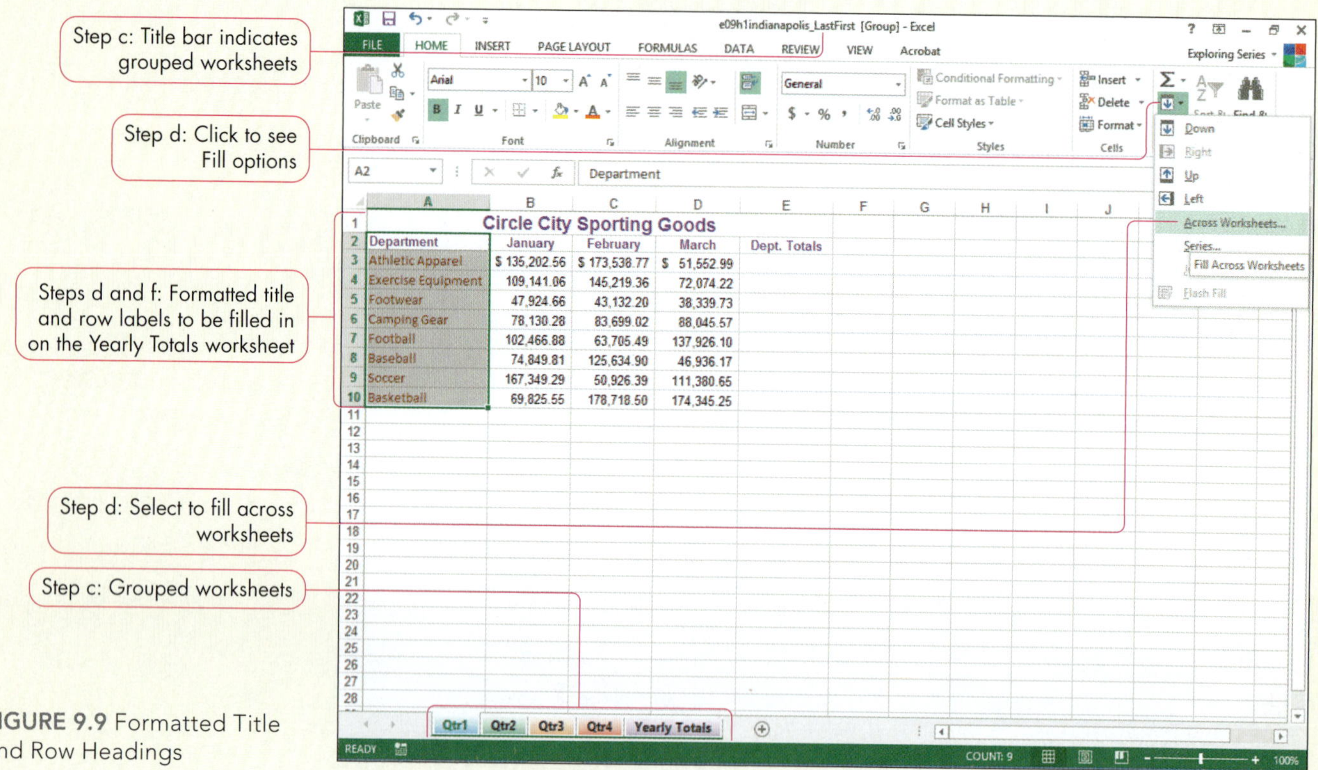

FIGURE 9.9 Formatted Title and Row Headings

a. Open *e09h1Indianapolis* and save it as **e09h1Indianapolis_LastFirst**.

> **TROUBLESHOOTING:** If you make any major mistakes in this exercise, you can close the file, open *e09h1Indianapolis* again, and then start this exercise over.

b. Click the **Qtr1 worksheet tab** and click each worksheet tab to see the differences.

   The Qtr1 worksheet contains a title and row labels, whereas the Qtr2, Qtr3, and Qtr4 worksheets are missing the title, row labels, and number formatting. The Yearly Totals worksheet is empty.

c. Click the **Qtr1 worksheet tab**, press and hold **Shift**, and then click the **Yearly Totals worksheet tab**.

You grouped all worksheets together. Anything you do now affects all grouped worksheets. The title bar displays *[Group]* after the file name.

d. Click **cell A1** in the Qtr1 worksheet to select it, click **Fill** in the Editing group on the HOME tab, and then select **Across Worksheets**.

The Fill Across Worksheets dialog box opens so that you can select what to fill from the active worksheet to the other grouped worksheets. The default option is All, which will fill in both the content and the formatting.

e. Click **OK**.

Excel fills in the formatted title from the Qtr1 worksheet to the other worksheets.

f. Select the **range A2:A10** on the Qtr1 worksheet, click **Fill** in the Editing group on the HOME tab, select **Across Worksheets**, and then click **OK**.

> **TROUBLESHOOTING:** Do not select the range A1:D9 to fill across worksheets. If you do, you will overwrite the other worksheet data with the January, February, and March labels and data. If this happens, click Undo to restore data in the other worksheets.

g. Right-click the **Yearly Totals worksheet tab** and select **Ungroup Sheets**. Click each worksheet to review the results. Save the workbook once review is complete.

You ungrouped the worksheets. Now all grouped worksheets contain the formatted title and row labels that were copied across worksheets.

STEP 2 » ENTER AND FORMAT DATA ACROSS WORKSHEETS

You need to regroup the worksheets so that you can increase the width of column A. In addition, you want to insert monthly and department totals for the quarterly worksheets. Refer to Figure 9.10 as you complete Step 2.

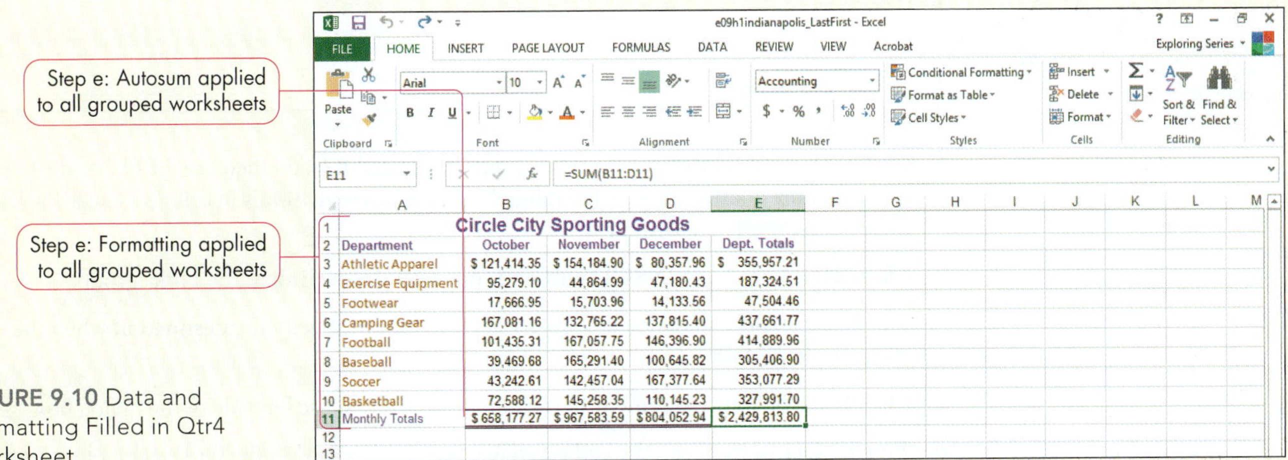

FIGURE 9.10 Data and Formatting Filled in Qtr4 Worksheet

a. Right-click the **Yearly Totals worksheet tab** and select **Select All Sheets**.

b. Click **cell A2**, click **Format** in the Cells group, select **Column Width**, type **18** in the **Column width box**, and then click **OK**.

You set the column width to 18 for the first column in the grouped worksheets, ensuring that column A's width is identical among the worksheets.

c. Right-click the **Qtr1 worksheet tab** and select **Ungroup Sheets**.

d. Press and hold **Shift** and click the **Qtr4 worksheet tab**.

You have to ungroup sheets and group only the four quarterly worksheets to perform the next few steps.

e. Do the following to the grouped quarterly worksheets:

- Select the **range B3:E11** and click **AutoSum** in the Editing group to insert department totals in column E and monthly totals in row 11.
- Apply **Accounting Number Format** to the **ranges B3:E3** and **B11:E11** to display $ and commas for the first and total rows.
- Type **Monthly Totals** in **cell A11**. Apply bold, increase indent, and **Purple font color**.
- Type **Dept. Totals** in **cell E2**. Use Format Painter to copy the formats from **cell D2** to **cell E2**.
- Select the **range B11:E11**, click the **Border arrow** in the Font group, and then select **Top and Double Bottom Border**.

You applied the Top and Double Bottom Border style to the monthly totals to conform to standard accounting formatting practices.

f. Right-click the **Qtr4 worksheet tab**, select **Ungroup Sheets**, click each quarterly worksheet tab to ensure the formats were applied to each worksheet, and then save the workbook.

STEP 3 » INSERT HYPERLINKS

You want to insert hyperlinks on the Yearly Totals worksheet so that you can click a hyperlink to jump back to the respective quarterly worksheet quickly. Refer to Figure 9.11 as you complete Step 3.

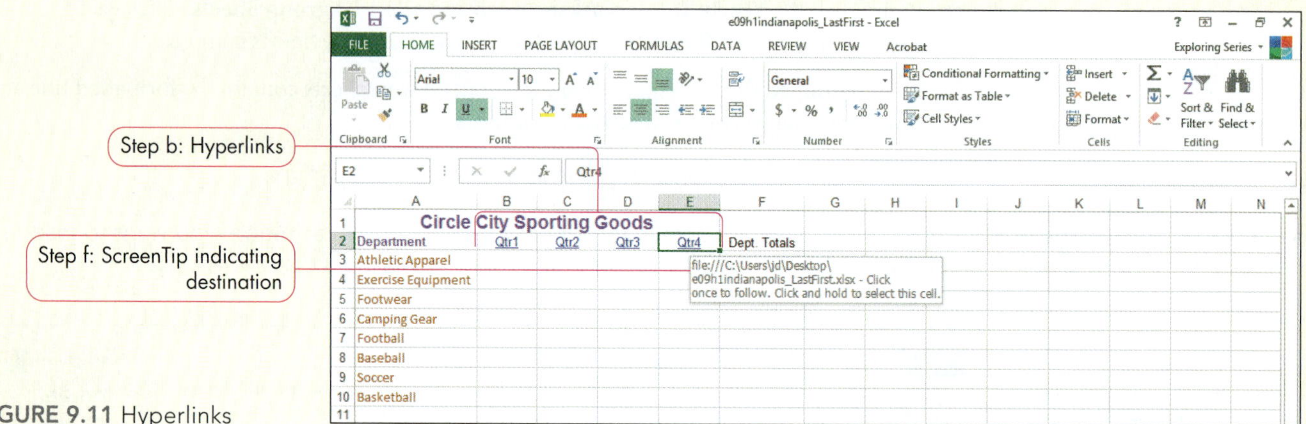

FIGURE 9.11 Hyperlinks

a. Click the **Yearly Totals worksheet tab**, type **Qtr1** in **cell B2**, and then use the fill handle to fill in the remaining quarter labels in the **range C2:E2**. Type **Dept. Totals** in **cell F2**. Center the labels. Increase the width of column F to **12**.

b. Click **cell B2**, click the **INSERT tab**, and then click **Hyperlink** in the Links group.

The Insert Hyperlink dialog box opens so that you can specify the destination when the user clicks the hyperlink.

c. Click **Place in This Document** in the *Link to* section on the left side of the dialog box.

d. Type **E2:E11** in the **Type the cell reference box**, click **'Qtr1'** in the **Or select a place in this document list**, and then click **OK**.

You created a hyperlink to the range E2:E11 in the Qtr1 worksheet. Note that if you do not specify a reference cell for the link it will default to cell A1.

e. Create the following hyperlinks by adapting steps b through d:

- **Cell C2**: Create a hyperlink to the **range E2:E11** in the Qtr2 worksheet.
- **Cell D2**: Create a hyperlink to the **range E2:E11** in the Qtr3 worksheet.
- **Cell E2**: Create a hyperlink to the **range E2:E11** in the Qtr4 worksheet.

f. Position the mouse pointer over cell E2.

The ScreenTip informs you where the hyperlink's destination is (see Figure 9.11). The path and file name shown on your screen will differ from those shown in the figure. If you had created a ScreenTip in the Insert Hyperlink dialog box, that text would appear instead of the destination.

g. Click the hyperlink in **cell E2**.

The hyperlink jumps to the destination: the range E2:E11 in the Qtr4 worksheet.

h. Click the **Yearly Totals worksheet tab** and click the other hyperlinks to ensure they work. When you are done, click the **Yearly Totals worksheet tab** and save the workbook.

> **TROUBLESHOOTING:** If a hyperlink does not jump to the correct range and worksheet, right-click the cell containing the wrong hyperlink, click Edit Hyperlink, and then edit the hyperlink in the Edit Hyperlink dialog box.

STEP 4 » OPEN AND ARRANGE WORKSHEETS

You want to see the four quarterly sales data worksheets at the same time. To do this, you need to open additional windows of the workbook, and then arrange them. Refer to Figure 9.12 as you complete Step 4.

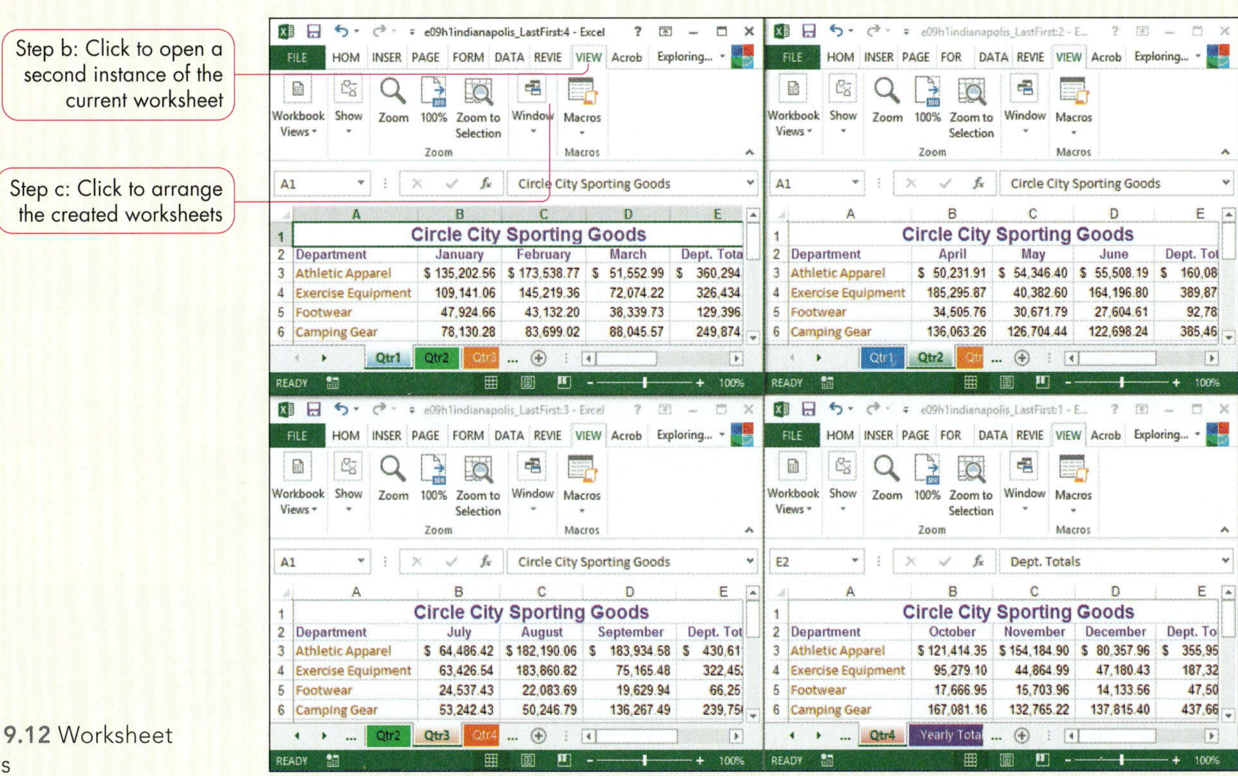

FIGURE 9.12 Worksheet Windows

a. Click the **VIEW tab** and click **New Window** in the Window group.

You opened another window of the same workbook. The title bar displays the same file name with *:2* at the end of the name.

b. Click **New Window** on the **VIEW tab** in the Window group twice.

Two new windows open with :3 and :4 at the end of each file name. You now have four windows open.

c. Click **Arrange All** in the Window group on the VIEW tab.

The Arrange Windows dialog box opens so you can specify how you want to arrange the open worksheet windows.

d. Click **Tiled**, if necessary, click the **Windows of active workbook check box**, and then click **OK**.

   Clicking the *Windows of active workbook* check box ensures that the windows display for the active workbook. If you have other workbooks open, those windows do not display.

   Excel arranges the four windows of the same workbook. Currently, all the windows display the Yearly Totals worksheet, but you will display a different worksheet in each window.

e. Click the **Qtr1 worksheet tab** twice in the top-left window, click the **Qtr2 worksheet tab** twice in the top-right window, click the **Qtr3 worksheet tab** twice in the bottom-left window, and click the **Qtr4 worksheet tab** twice in the bottom-right window.

f. Save the workbook. Close three of the four windows. Keep the workbook open if you plan to continue with Hands-On Exercise 2. If not, close the workbook and exit Excel.

3-D Formulas and Linked Workbooks

Excel workbooks often contain data from different time periods, geographic regions, or products. For example, a workbook might contain a worksheet to store data for each week in a month, data for each location of a chain of department stores, or data for sales of each type of automobile produced by one manufacturer. While you have experience creating formulas and functions to perform calculations within one worksheet, you need to be able to consolidate, or combine, data from multiple worksheets into one. For example, you might want to consolidate sales data from all of your department store locations into one worksheet for the year.

Additional data analysis occurs over time. To avoid overloading a workbook with detailed sales data for several years, you might have detailed sales data in individual worksheets in one workbook for a specific year. You then might want to determine the average yearly sales for the past 10 years.

In this section, you will create a 3-D formula to consolidate data from several worksheets. In addition, you will learn how to link data from several workbooks to one workbook.

Inserting a 3-D Formula

STEP 1》 You have referenced other cells in the same worksheet. For example, when you created a one-variable data table, you entered a reference, such as =B12, to display the contents of a formula in cell B12 instead of performing the calculation again in the one-variable data table. At times, you need to consolidate data from multiple worksheets into one worksheet. For example, you might want to create a yearly budget by consolidating values from monthly worksheets, or you might want to calculate average daily occupancy rates for a hospital from detailed weekly occupancy worksheets. When you create formulas that involve reference cells on different worksheets, you include worksheet references. A ***3-D reference,*** is a pointer to a cell in another worksheet, such as October!E3, which references cell E3 in the October worksheet. An exclamation point separates the worksheet name and the cell reference. If the value in cell E3 in the October worksheet changes, you do not have to edit the value in another worksheet; the reference does that for you automatically.

'Worksheet Name'!RangeOfCells

You can use worksheet references in formulas. For example, a formula that adds the values of cell E3 in the October, November, and December worksheets looks like this: =October!E3+November!E3+December!E3. If a worksheet name contains words separated by a space such as *October Sales*, single quotation marks surround the worksheet name, such as ='October Sales'!E3+'November Sales'!E3+'December Sales'!E3.

CamelCase Notation

CamelCase notation is a file naming convention that eliminates spaces and capitalizes compound words—for example, OctoberSales.xlsx versus October sales.xlsx. By using a naming convention such as CamelCase, you can reduce some of the complexity of a 3-D formula by eliminating the need for single quotation marks.

STEP 2》 Entering this type of formula manually or by using the semi-selection process is time-consuming to ensure you click every worksheet and every cell within the respective worksheets. When individual worksheets have an identical structure (i.e., totals for the Jewelry Department are in cell E7 in each quarterly worksheet), you can improve your efficiency in creating formulas by using a ***3-D formula***, which is a formula or function that refers to the same cell or range in multiple worksheets. The term *3-D formula* comes from having a reference with three dimensions: worksheet name, column letter, and row number. It is a convenient way to reference several identically structured worksheets in which the cells in each worksheet contain the same type of data, such as when you consolidate sales information from different branches into the Summary worksheet. For example, =SUM('Qtr1:Qtr4'!E3) is a 3-D formula that adds the values in cell E3 in each worksheet, starting in the Qtr1 worksheet and ending in the Qtr4 worksheet, including worksheets between those two. You can type a 3-D reference directly into a cell formula or function, but using the semi-selection method is more efficient. To create a 3-D formula, do the following:

1. Click the cell in which you will enter the 3-D formula.
2. Type =, type the name of the function, such as SUM, and then type an opening parenthesis.
3. Click the first worksheet tab, such as Qtr1.
4. Press and hold Shift as you click the last worksheet tab for adjacent worksheets, or press and hold Ctrl as you click nonadjacent worksheet tabs.
5. Click the cell or select the range that contains the value(s) you want to use in the function argument and press Enter. Figure 9.13 shows the process of creating a 3-D formula before you press Enter.

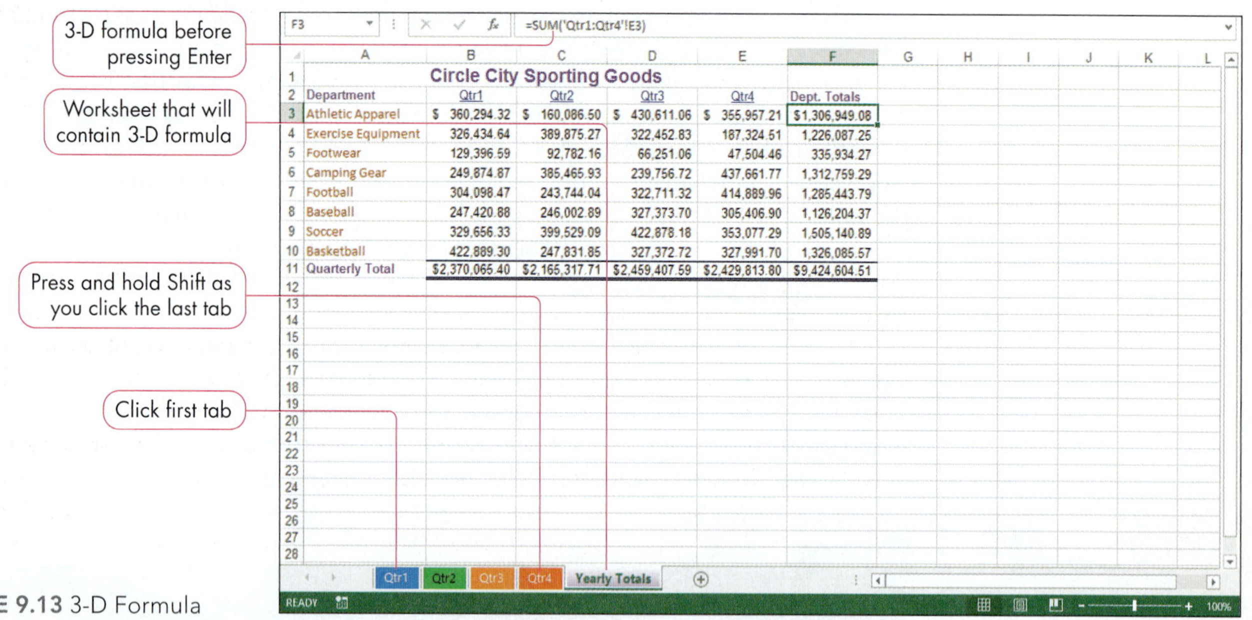

	A	B	C	D	E	F
1	Circle City Sporting Goods					
2	Department	Qtr1	Qtr2	Qtr3	Qtr4	Dept. Totals
3	Athletic Apparel	$ 360,294.32	$ 160,086.50	$ 430,611.06	$ 355,957.21	$1,306,949.08
4	Exercise Equipment	326,434.64	389,875.27	322,452.83	187,324.51	1,226,087.25
5	Footwear	129,396.59	92,782.16	66,251.06	47,504.46	335,934.27
6	Camping Gear	249,874.87	385,465.93	239,756.72	437,661.77	1,312,759.29
7	Football	304,098.47	243,744.04	322,711.32	414,889.96	1,285,443.79
8	Baseball	247,420.88	246,002.89	327,373.70	305,406.90	1,126,204.37
9	Soccer	329,656.33	399,529.09	422,878.18	353,077.29	1,505,140.89
10	Basketball	422,889.30	247,831.85	327,372.72	327,991.70	1,326,085.57
11	Quarterly Total	$2,370,065.40	$2,165,317.71	$2,459,407.59	$2,429,813.80	$9,424,604.51

FIGURE 9.13 3-D Formula

=SUM('First Worksheet:Last Worksheet'!RangeOfCells)

You can use a variety of functions for 3-D formulas. Some of these functions include SUM, AVERAGE, COUNT, MIN, and MAX. You can create 3-D formulas using some standard deviation and variance functions. Other functions, such as PMT, VLOOKUP, and COUNTIF, do not work with 3-D formulas.

TIP **3-D Formula Advantages**

When you have a function such as =SUM(B1:B5) and insert a new fourth row, Excel modifies the SUM function to include the new row: =SUM(B1:B6). Similarly, if you insert or copy a worksheet between the beginning and ending worksheet references, the 3-D formula automatically includes those worksheet data points in the calculation. If you move a worksheet out of the range, Excel excludes that worksheet's values from the 3-D formula calculations. Finally, if you move or delete an endpoint worksheet, Excel adjusts the 3-D formula for you.

Linking Workbooks

Workbook linking is another way of consolidating data. When you link workbooks, you consolidate the data from several workbooks into another workbook. ***Linking*** is the process of creating external cell references from worksheets in one workbook to cells on a worksheet in another workbook. For example, you might have three workbooks—Indianapolis, Bloomington, and South Bend—one for each store location. Each store manager maintains a workbook to record sales by department—such as exercise equipment, footwear, and camping gear—for a particular time period. As district manager, you want to consolidate the data from each workbook into one workbook. Instead of reentering the data, you can create links from specific cells of data in the individual workbooks to your active workbook.

Before creating links, identify the source and destination files. A ***source file*** is one that contains original data that you need elsewhere. For example, the individual department store workbooks—Indianapolis, Bloomington, and South Bend—are source files. The ***destination file*** is a file containing a pointer to receive data from the source files—that is, the target file that needs the data. When you link workbooks, you create a connection between the source and destination files. If data change in the source file, the destination file's data update also. Linking ensures that the destination file always contains the most up-to-date data.

Create an External Reference

STEP 3» When you create a link between source and destination files, you establish an external reference or pointer to one or more cells in another workbook. The external reference is similar to the worksheet reference that you created for 3-D formulas. However, an external reference must include the workbook name to identify which workbook contains the linked worksheet and cell reference. For example, to create a link to cell E3 in the Qtr3 worksheet in the Indianapolis file, type =[Indianapolis.xlsx]Qtr3!E3. You must type the workbook name, including the file name extension, between brackets, such as [Indianapolis.xlsx]. After the closing bracket, type the worksheet name, such as Qtr3, followed by an exclamation mark and the cell reference, such as E3. Table 9.2 lists additional rules to follow when entering external references.

[WorkbookName]WorksheetName!RangeOfCells

TABLE 9.2 External References

Situation	Rule	Example
Workbook and worksheet names do not contain spaces; source and destination files are in the same folder.	Type brackets around the workbook name and an exclamation mark between the worksheet name and range.	[Indianapolis.xlsx]Qtr3!A1
Workbook or worksheet name contains spaces; source and destination files are in the same folder.	Type single quotation marks on the left side of the opening bracket and the right side of the worksheet name.	'[South Bend.xlsx]Qtr3'!A1
Worksheet name contains spaces; source and destination files are in the same folder.	Type single quotation marks on the left side of the opening bracket and the right side of the worksheet name.	'[Bloomington.xlsx]Qtr 3 Sales'!A1
Source workbook is in a different folder than the destination workbook.	Type a single quotation mark, and then the full path—drive letter and folder name—before the opening bracket and a single quotation mark after the worksheet name.	'C:\Data[Indianapolis.xlsx] Sheet1'!A1

Excel displays formulas with external references in two ways, depending on whether the source workbook is open or closed. When the source is open, the external reference shows the file name, worksheet, and cell reference. When the source workbook is closed, the external reference shows the full path name in the Formula Bar. By default, Excel creates absolute cell references in the external reference. However, you can edit the external reference to create a relative or mixed cell reference. To create an external reference between cells in different workbooks:

1. Open the destination workbook and all source workbooks.
2. Select the cell or cells to hold the external reference.
3. Type =. If you want to perform calculations or functions on the external references, type the operator or function.
4. Switch to the source workbook and click the worksheet that contains the cells to which you want to link.
5. Select the cells you want to link to and press Enter.

Drive and Folder Reference

Excel updates an external reference regardless of whether the source workbook is open. The source workbooks must be in the same folder location as when you created the link to update the destination workbook. If the location of the workbooks changes, as may happen if you copy the workbooks to a different folder, click Edit Links in the Connections group on the Data tab.

Manage and Update Linked Workbooks

If you create an external reference when both the source and destination files are open, changes you make to the source file occur in the destination file as well. However, if the destination file is closed when you change data in the source file, the destination file does not automatically update to match the source file. Excel does not update linked data in a destination workbook automatically to protect the workbook against malicious activity, such as viruses.

When you open the destination file the first time, Excel displays the Security Warning Message Bar between the Ribbon and Formula Bar with the message *Automatic updates of links has been disabled.* If you are confident that the source files contain safe data, enable the links in the destination file. Click Enable Content to update the links and save the workbook. The next time you open the destination file, Excel displays a message box that prompts the user to update, do not update, or select help. Click Update to update the links. Figure 9.14 has been contrived to show you both ways of updating links.

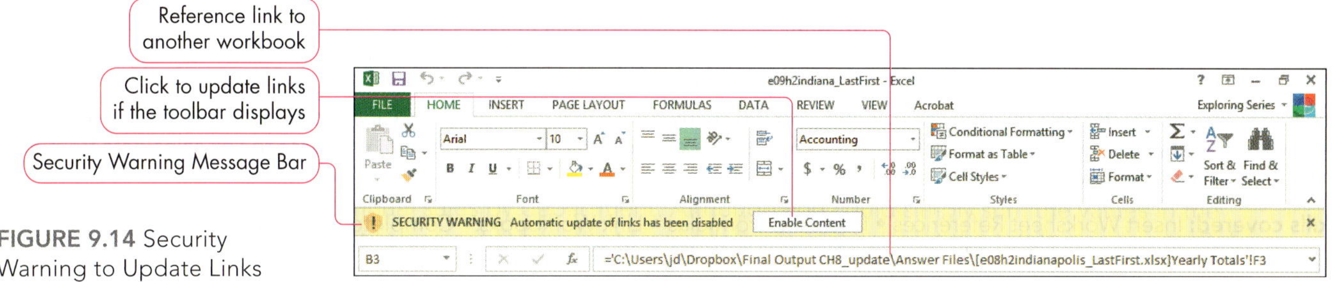

FIGURE 9.14 Security Warning to Update Links

External references identify the workbook names and locations. If you rename or move the source workbook, you must ensure that the external reference in the destination file matches the name of the new source workbook. Otherwise, when you open a destination file that contains external links that cannot be updated, Excel displays an error message, *This workbook contains one or more links that cannot be updated.* Click Edit Links to display the Edit Links dialog box and modify the source links (see Figure 9.15).

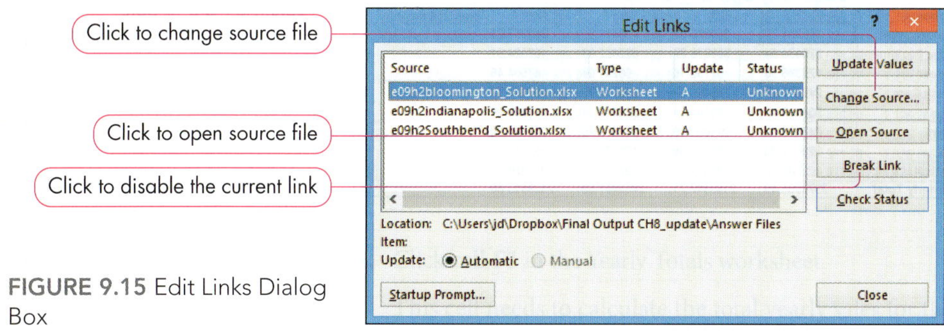

FIGURE 9.15 Edit Links Dialog Box

The Status column displays OK if the external reference link to the source file still works. If a problem exists, the Status column indicates the type of error, such as *Error: Source not found.* Click the source that contains an error and click Change Source to find and select the renamed or moved source file.

Quick Concepts

1. What is a 3-D formula? ***p. 520***
2. What are the benefits of 3-D formulas? ***p. 520***
3. How do you create an external reference? ***pp. 521–522***

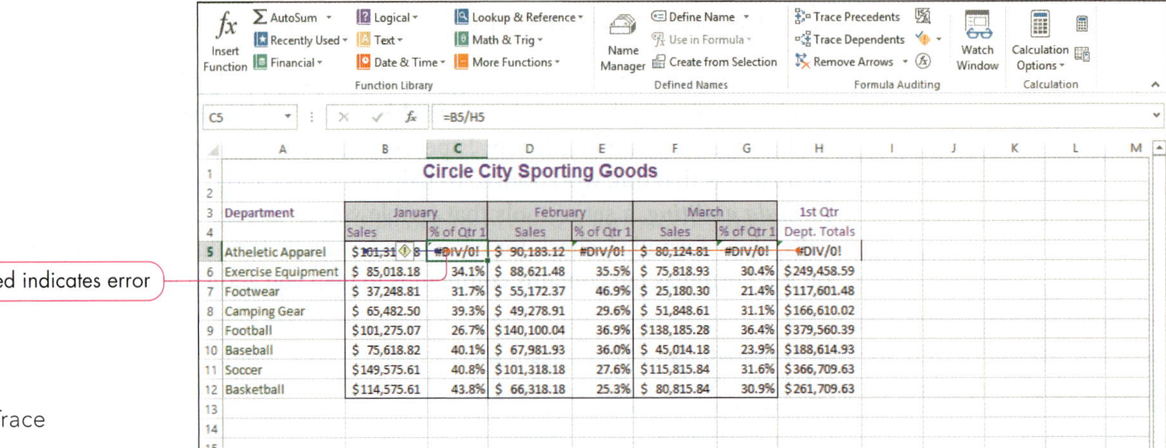

	Circle City Sporting Goods						
Department	January		February		March		1st Qtr
	Sales	% of Qtr 1	Sales	% of Qtr 1	Sales	% of Qtr 1	Dept. Totals
Atheletic Apparel	[illegible]	#DIV/0!	$ 90,183.12	#DIV/0!	$ 80,124.81	#DIV/0!	#DIV/0!
Exercise Equipment	$ 85,018.18	34.1%	$ 88,621.48	35.5%	$ 75,818.93	30.4%	$249,458.59
Footwear	$ 37,248.81	31.7%	$ 55,172.37	46.9%	$ 25,180.30	21.4%	$117,601.48
Camping Gear	$ 65,482.50	39.3%	$ 49,278.91	29.6%	$ 51,848.61	31.1%	$166,610.02
Football	$101,275.07	26.7%	$140,100.04	36.9%	$138,185.28	36.4%	$379,560.39
Baseball	$ 75,618.82	40.1%	$ 67,981.93	36.0%	$ 45,014.18	23.9%	$188,614.93
Soccer	$149,575.61	40.8%	$101,318.18	27.6%	$115,815.84	31.6%	$366,709.63
Basketball	$114,575.61	43.8%	$ 66,318.18	25.3%	$ 80,815.84	30.9%	$261,709.63

FIGURE 9.21 Trace Precedents

Remove Tracer Arrows

Click Remove Arrows in the Formula Auditing group on the Formulas tab to remove all tracer arrows, or click the Remove Arrows arrow and select Remove Arrows, Remove Precedent Arrows, or Remove Dependent Arrows.

Check For and Repair Errors

STEP 2

When the tracing of precedents or dependents shows errors in formulas, or if you want to check for errors that have occurred in formulas anywhere in a worksheet, you can use Error Checking in the Formula Auditing group. When Excel identifies an error, the Error Checking dialog box opens (see Figure 9.22) and identifies the cell containing an error and describes the error.

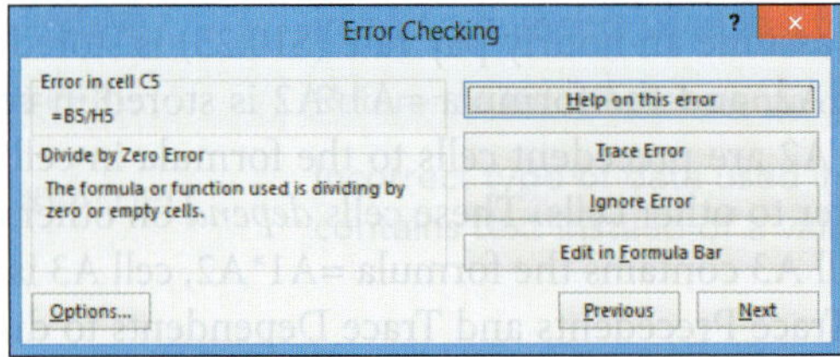

FIGURE 9.22 Error Checking Dialog Box

Click *Help on this error* to see a description of the error. Click Show Calculation Steps to open the Evaluate Formula dialog box (see Figure 9.23), which provides an evaluation of the formula and shows which part of the evaluation will result in an error. Clicking Ignore Error either moves to the next error or indicates that Error Checking is complete. When you click *Edit in Formula Bar*, you can correct the formula in the Formula Bar.

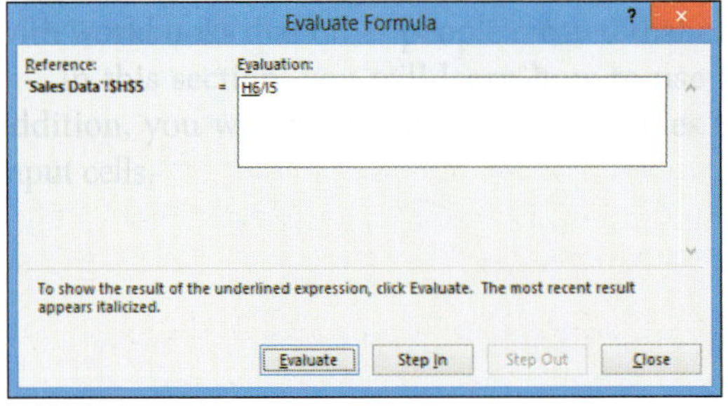

FIGURE 9.23 Evaluate Formula Dialog Box

Evaluate a Formula

Using nested formulas can make it difficult to understand the formula evaluation. Understanding how a nested formula calculates is hard because intermediate calculations and logical tests exist. You can use the Evaluate Formula dialog box to view different parts of a nested formula and evaluate each part. To use the Evaluate Formula dialog box, do the following:

1. Select the cell you want to evaluate.
2. Click Evaluate Formula in the Formula Auditing group to see the Evaluate Formula dialog box (see Figure 9.23).
3. Click Evaluate to examine the value of the reference that is underlined.
4. If the underlined part of the formula is a reference to another formula, click Step In to display the other formula in the Evaluation box.
5. Click Step Out to return to the previous cell and formula.
6. Continue until you have evaluated the entire formula and click Close.

Use the IFERROR Function to Detect Errors

If you create a workbook for others to use, you should anticipate errors the users will introduce so that you can provide a way to identify and correct those errors. The ***IFERROR function*** is a logical function that checks a cell to determine if that cell contains an error or if a formula will result in an error. If no error exists, the IFERROR function returns the value of the formula. The *value* argument contains the value being checked for an error, and the *value_if_error* argument is the value to return if the formula evaluates to an error. IFERROR detects the following types of errors: #N/A, #VALUE!, #REF!, #DIV/0!, #NUM!, #NAME?, and #NULL, although the output does not indicate the type of error.

Typically, you use a text string enclosed in quotation marks to return an error message. For example, if you divide the contents of cells in row 2 by cell B1 and anticipate that a #DIV/0! error might occur when copying the formula, you can use =IFERROR(A2/B1,"You cannot divide by zero. Change the value of cell B1 to a value higher than 0.").

=IFERROR(value,value_if_error)

Information Functions

The Information functions contain additional functions you can use for error checking. Of particular interest are the ERROR.TYPE and ISERROR functions. Use Help to learn how to incorporate these functions in error-checking tasks.

Setting Up a Watch Window

STEP 3»

When you are working with a worksheet containing a large dataset, formulas in cells that are not visible can be "watched" using the Watch Window. You do not need to keep scrolling to different parts of the worksheet if you are using a Watch Window. The ***Watch Window*** enables you to create a small window so you can conveniently inspect, audit, or confirm formula calculations involving cells not immediately visible on the screen. You can double-click a cell in the Watch Window to jump to that cell quickly. To add cells to the Watch Window, do the following:

1. Click Watch Window in the Formula Auditing group.
2. Click Add Watch in the Watch Window toolbar.
3. Select the cells to watch in the Add Watch dialog box and click Add. The Watch Window shows the cells and formulas you selected to watch (see Figure 9.24).

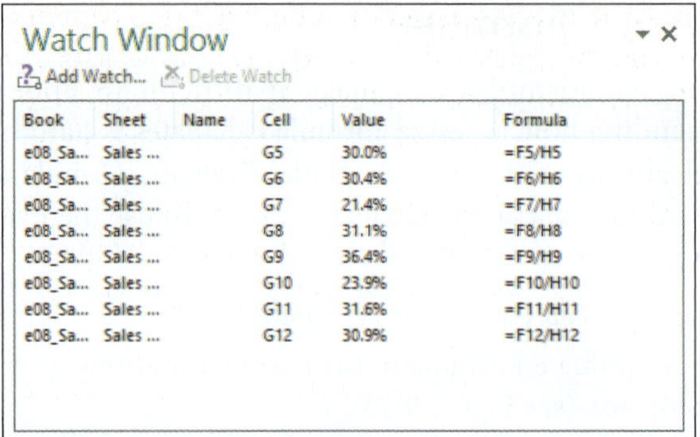

FIGURE 9.24 Watch Window

Changes to Watched Cells

Any time you make a change to the watched cell(s), the Watch Window shows you the current value of the watched cell(s).

Validating Data

STEP 4» ***Data validation*** enables you to control the data that can be entered into a cell. It warns and prevents people from entering "wrong" data in a cell, or it can provide a list of valid data from which to choose. Data validation enables you to specify and correct the kind of data that can be entered, specify an input message alerting users when they click a cell that only specific types of data can be entered in that cell, and specify error messages that appear when others persist and attempt to enter incorrect data. To set up a data validation rule, click the cell for which the rule will be applied, and then click Data Validation in the Data Tools group on the Data tab.

Specify Data Validation Criteria

In the Data Validation dialog box, use the Settings tab to specify the ***validation criteria***—the rules that dictate the type of data that can be entered in a cell. Click the Allow arrow to specify what type of data you will allow the user to enter, such as a whole number, a value that is part of a specific list, or a date that is within a particular date range. For example, if you specify whole number and the user attempts to enter a decimal, Excel displays an error message. You can also specify that the data must be between two values and specify the minimum and maximum values permitted. Figure 9.25 shows a validation rule in which the cell contents must be (a) a whole number and (b) between a minimum and maximum value, which are stored respectively in cells G5 and G6.

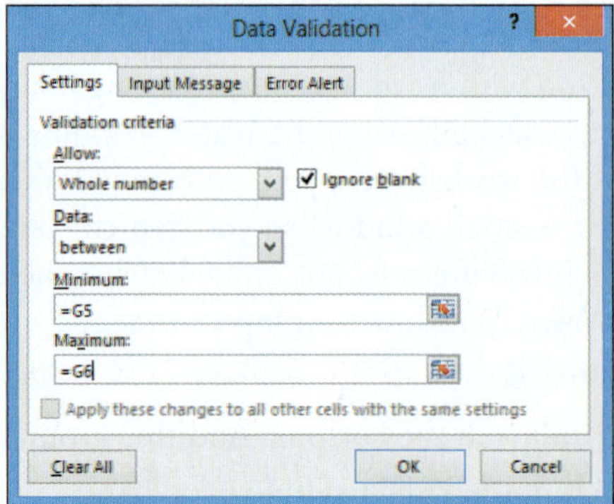

FIGURE 9.25 Data Validation Settings Tab: Criteria

To make data entry easier or to limit items to certain defined items and thereby be more accurate, you can create a list of valid entries from data contained in cells. When you create a list, Excel displays an arrow in the cell. The user clicks the arrow, and then selects the desired entry. The user cannot enter invalid data. To create a list, do the following:

1. Create a list of valid entries in a single column or row without blank cells.
2. Click the cell for which you want to create a validation rule.
3. Click the DATA tab and select Validation in the Data Tools group to show the Data Validation dialog box.
4. Click the Settings tab, click the Allow arrow, and then select List.
5. Enter a reference to the list in the Source box (see Figure 9.26).
6. Make sure that the *In-cell dropdown* check box is selected and that the *Ignore blank* check box is clear and click OK.

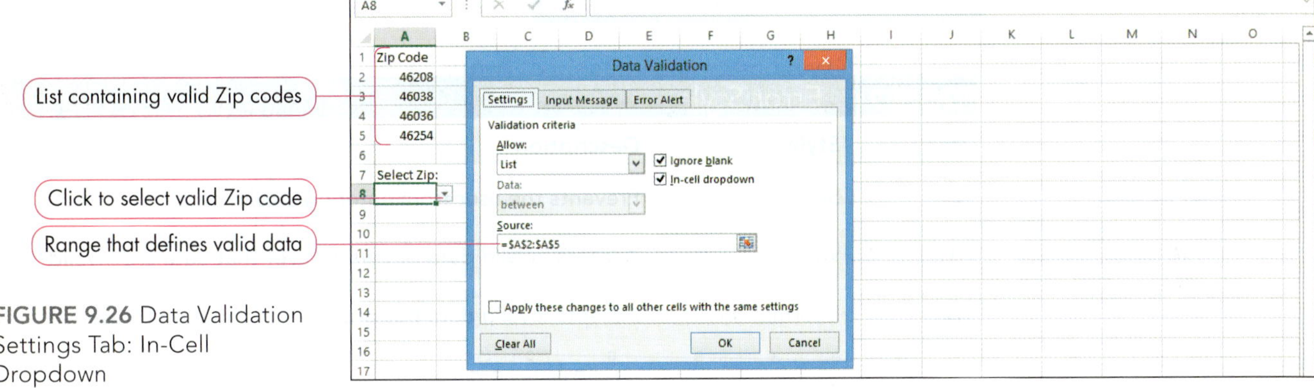

FIGURE 9.26 Data Validation Settings Tab: In-Cell Dropdown

Create an Input Message

STEP 5

Input messages are descriptive text or instructions for data entry that can be entered in the Data Validation dialog box. You add input messages to cells, and Excel displays these messages when a user moves to a cell that has a data-entry restriction. Input messages consist of two parts: a title and an input message (see Figure 9.27). These messages should describe the data validation and explain or show how to enter data correctly. For example, an input message might be *Enter hire date in the form: mm/dd/yyyy* or *Enter Employee name: last name, first name.*

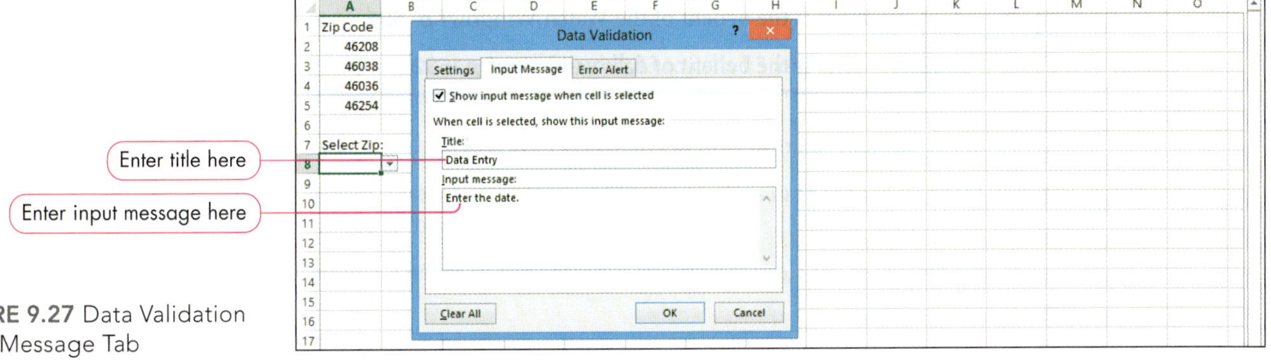

FIGURE 9.27 Data Validation Input Message Tab

Create an Error Alert

Sometimes, no matter how descriptive you are with an input message, users will attempt to enter invalid data in a cell. Instead of using Excel's default error message, you can create an ***error alert***, a message that displays when a user enters invalid data in a cell that has a validation rule applied to it. To create an error alert, specify the style, title, and error message on the Error Alert tab (see Figure 9.28). The error alert message should be polite and clearly

g. Adapt steps e and f to hide the Jan, Feb, and Mar worksheets in *e09p1South_LastFirst*.

h. Click **Switch Windows** in the Window group and select *e09p1Quarter1_LastFirst*.

i. Click **Arrange All** in the Window group, click the **Windows of active workbook check box** to deselect it if necessary, and then click **OK** in the dialog box.

j. Add links by doing the following:
- Click **cell B4** in the Quarter1 worksheet. Type =, display *e09p1Downtown_LastFirst*, click **cell B4** in the DowntownQtr1 worksheet, and then press **Ctrl+Enter**. Edit the formula to change *$B$4* to **B4**. Copy the formula down the Downtown column.
- Click **cell C4** in the Quarter1 worksheet. Type =, display *e09p1South_LastFirst*, click **cell B4** in the Qtr1 worksheet, and then press **Ctrl+Enter**. Edit the formula to change *$B$4* to **B4**. Copy the formula down the South column.
- Click **cell D4** in the Quarter1 worksheet. Type =, display *e09p1North_LastFirst*, click **cell B4** in the Qtr1 worksheet, and then press **Ctrl+Enter**. Edit the formula to change *$B$4* to **B4**. Copy the formula down the North column.
- Format the monetary values with **Accounting Number Format** with zero decimal places in the Quarter1 worksheet.

k. Click **cell B3** in the Quarter1 worksheet, click the **INSERT tab**, click **Hyperlink** in the Links group, scroll through the list of files, select *e09p1Downtown_LastFirst.xlsx*, and then click **OK**.

l. Adapt step k to create hyperlinks in **cells C3 and C4** to their respective files.

m. Create a footer with your name on the left side, the sheet name code in the center, and the file name code on the right side of the Quarter1 worksheet.

n. Save and close the workbooks, and submit based on your instructor's directions.

2 Retirement Planning

An associate created a worksheet to help people plan retirement based on a set of annual contributions to a retirement account. A user indicates the age to start contributions, projected retirement age, the number of years in retirement, and the rate of return expected to earn on the money when the user retires. The worksheet determines the total amount the user will have contributed, the amount the user will have accumulated, and the value of the monthly retirement amount. However, the worksheet contains errors. You will use the auditing tools to identify and correct errors. Then you will specify validation rules to ensure users enter valid data. This exercise follows the same set of skills as used in Hands-On Exercise 3 in the chapter. Refer to Figure 9.34 as you complete this exercise.

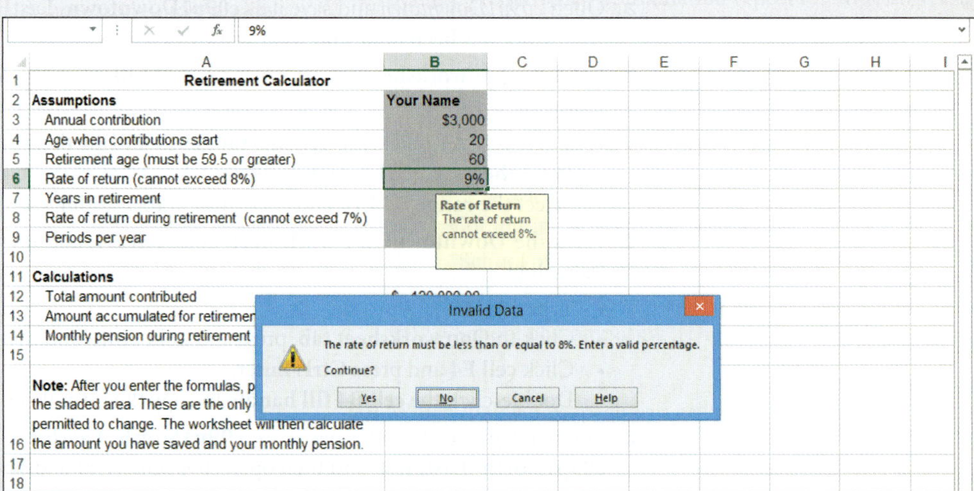

FIGURE 9.34 Retirement Planning

a. Open *e09p2Retire* and save it as **e09p2Retire_LastFirst**.

b. Click **cell B14**, click the **FORMULAS tab**, and then click **Trace Precedents** in the Formula Auditing group.

c. Click the **Error Checking arrow** in the Formula Auditing group and select **Error Checking.**

d. Click **Show Calculation Steps** in the Error Checking dialog box. The Evaluate Formula dialog box opens, showing the formula and stating that the next evaluation will result in an error. Click **Evaluate** to see the error replace the argument in the function: #DIV/0!. Click **Step In** to see the value and click **Step Out** to return to the evaluation. Repeat the Step In and Step Out process and click **Close.** Click **Next** in the Error Checking dialog box and click **OK** in the message box. Find the *0* in **cell B9** and change it to **12.**

e. Click **Remove Arrows** in the Formula Auditing group to remove the precedents arrow.

f. Click **Watch Window** in the Formula Auditing group and click **Add Watch.** Move the dialog boxes so that you can see the data, select the **range B12:B14**, and then click **Add.**

g. Create a data validation rule to ensure the retirement age is greater than 59.5 by doing the following:
   - Click **cell B5**, click the **DATA tab**, and then click **Data Validation** in the Data Tools group.
   - Click the **Settings tab**, click the **Allow arrow**, and then select **Decimal.**
   - Click the **Data arrow** and select **greater than or equal to.**
   - Type **59.5** in the **Minimum box.**
   - Click the **Input Message tab** and type **Retirement Age** in the **Title box.**
   - Type **Federal law does not permit payout prior to 59.5.** in the **Input message box.**
   - Click the **Error Alert tab**, click the **Style arrow**, and then select **Warning.**
   - Type **Invalid Data** in the **Title box**, type **Age must be greater than 59.5.** in the **Error message box**, and then click **OK.**

h. Adapt step g to create a validation rule for **cell B6** to ensure the rate of return will not exceed 8%. Include appropriate titles and messages.

i. Adapt step g to create a validation rule for **cell B8** to ensure the rate of return during retirement will not exceed 7%. Include appropriate titles and messages.

j. Type **50** in **cell B5.** Click **No** when the error message displays, change the value to **60**, and then press **Enter.**

k. Type **8.5%** in **cell B6.** Click **No** when the error message displays, change the value to **8%**, and then press **Enter.**

l. Type **7.5%** in **cell B8.** Click **No** when the error message displays, change the value to **7%**, and then press **Enter.** Close the Watch Window.

m. Create a footer with your name on the left side, the sheet name code in the center, and the file name code on the right side.

n. Save and close the workbook, and submit it based on your instructor's directions.

Managing Connections

When you import data using the options in the Get External Data group, Excel creates a link to the original data source so that you can update the data quickly in Excel. After you create the initial connection, you might want to view or modify the connection. The Connections group on the Data tab contains options to manage your external data connections.

Refresh Connections

Data on a Web page or data in an external database may change periodically. Although you created a connection to the external data within Excel, the data in the database or on a Web page may have changed. For example, if you created a connection to a Web page containing hourly weather, the weather may have changed after you created the connection. To ensure that the Excel data are current, you need to ***refresh*** the connections to the original external data source periodically. Do one of the following to refresh data:

STEP 5

- Click Refresh All in the Connections group to refresh all connections in the active workbook.
- Click the Refresh All arrow in the Connections group and select Refresh to update data for the range containing the active cell.
- Right-click in a range of data and select Refresh to update that data only.

The status bar will briefly display *Running background query...(Click here to cancel)* if you are refreshing a Web query.

Display Connections

To display a list of all connections in a workbook, click Connections in the Connections group to display the Workbook Connections dialog box (see Figure 10.10). To see where a specific connection is located, select the connection name in the top portion of the dialog box and click *Click here to see where the selected connections are used.* The dialog box shows the sheet name, connection name, and range in the worksheet.

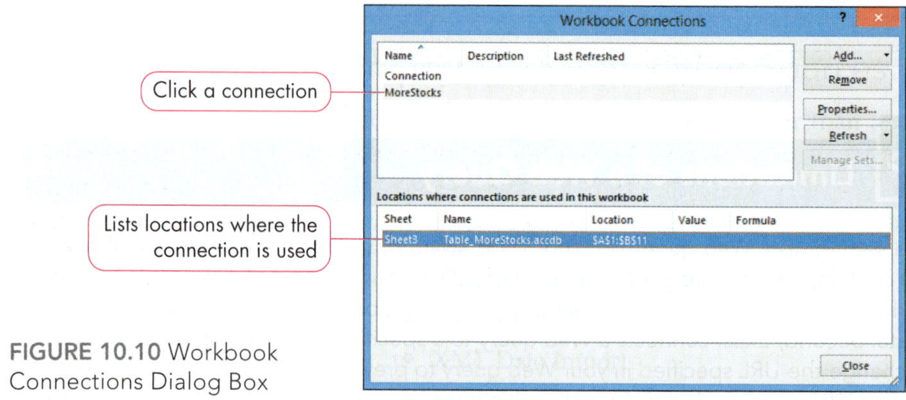

FIGURE 10.10 Workbook Connections Dialog Box

You can remove a connection if you no longer want to link the data to the external data source. After you disconnect the data in Excel from the external data source, you will not be able to refresh the data. To remove a connection, do the following:

1. Select it in the Workbook Connections dialog box.
2. Click Remove.
3. Click OK in the warning message box and click Close in the Workbook Connections dialog box.

Set Connection Properties

Data range properties are settings that control how imported data in cells connect to their source data. These properties also specify how the data display in Excel, how often the data are refreshed, and what happens if the number of rows in the data range changes based upon the current data in the external data source. To display the properties, do one of the following:

- Click Properties in the Connections group.
- Click the Refresh All arrow and select Connection Properties.
- Click Connections in the Connections group and click Properties.

When you click Properties in the Connections group, the External Data Range Properties dialog box displays (see Figure 10.11). This dialog box looks slightly different based on the type of external data you imported and based on which option you use to display the dialog box. For example, the dialog box has fewer options for a connection to an Access database table than it does for a Web query.

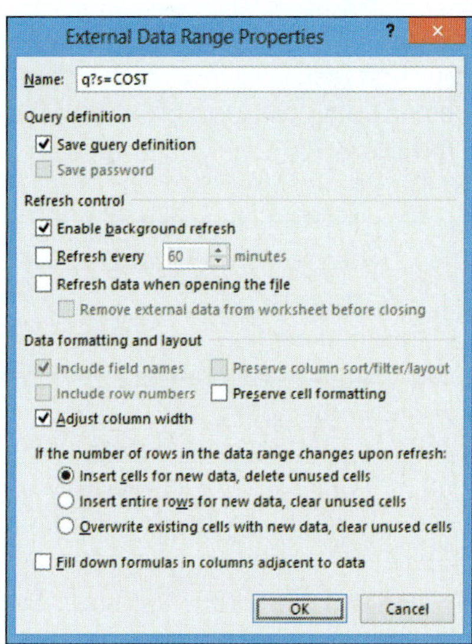

FIGURE 10.11 External Data Range Properties Dialog Box

1. What is the purpose of delimiters in a text file? Name two common text file delimiters. ***pp. 554–555***
2. What is the difference in opening a text file directly in Excel and using the Get External Data option to import text file data? ***p. 557***
3. What is the purpose in creating a Web query? Give two examples of Web pages for which it would make sense to create a Web query. ***pp. 558–559***

Hands-On Exercises

1 External Data

Angie e-mailed a list of 10 companies for you to research. In addition, you want to include a list of 10 other companies that is stored in an Access database table for her further consideration. You will research five companies on each list and then create a Web query to a specific company's historical stock information. Each day, you will need to refresh the connection to import the most up-to-date data into your worksheet.

Skills covered: Import a Text File • Import an Access Database Table • Create Web Queries for Multiple Stocks • Create a Web Query for Historical Stock Data • Maintain Connections

STEP 1 » IMPORT A TEXT FILE

Angie created her list of companies in Notepad, so your first task is to import the data into Excel. You do not need to create a connection to the text file because Angie does not plan to update the text file, so you will simply open the file directly from the Open dialog box in Excel. Refer to Figure 10.12 as you complete Step 1.

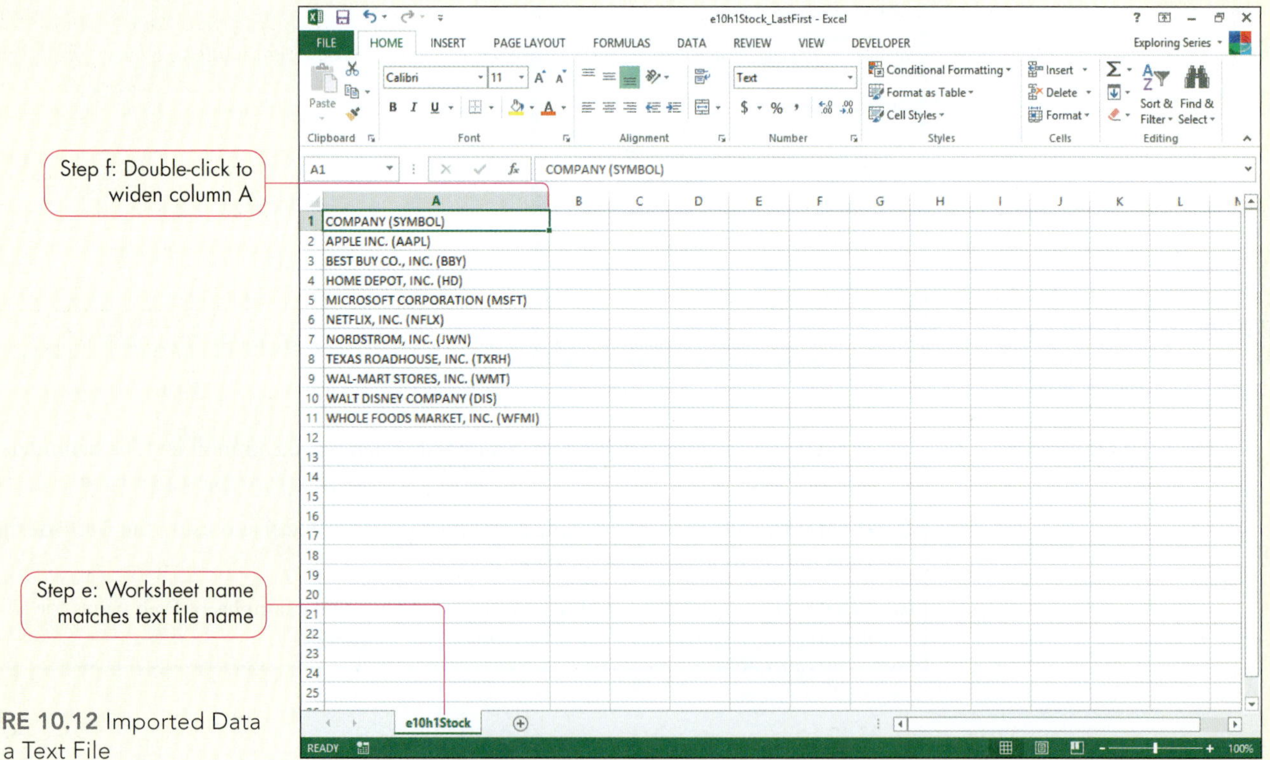

FIGURE 10.12 Imported Data from a Text File

a. Start Excel, click **Open Other Workbooks** in the bottom-left corner of the start window, and then double-click **Computer** to display the Open dialog box.

b. Click the **File Type arrow** that currently displays *All Excel Files*, select **Text Files**, select *e10h1Stock*, and then click **Open**.

   The Text Import Wizard dialog box opens. Accept the defaults: Delimited and 1 as *Start at row number*.

c. Click the **My data has headers check box** and click **Next**.

The *Text Import Wizard – Step 2 of 3* dialog box contains options to specify the type of delimiter(s) contained in the text file. This text file does not contain delimiters. You could use the opening parenthesis as a delimiter, but you will use text functions in Hands-On Exercise 2 to separate the company names from the stock symbols.

> **TROUBLESHOOTING**: If you select Space as a delimiter, you will import company names into separate columns. For example, the text *Home Depot, Inc.*, will appear in three separate cells. You cannot use the comma as a delimiter for a similar reason: Home Depot will appear in one cell and Inc. will appear in a separate cell.

d. Deselect all check boxes in the *Delimiters* section and click **Next**.

The *Text Import Wizard – Step 3 of 3* dialog box lets you select each column and specify its data type.

e. Click **Text** in the *Column data format* section and click **Finish**.

Excel imports the data from the text file into the first column of the worksheet. The worksheet name matches the name of the text file: *e10h1Stock*.

f. Double-click between the column A and B headings to widen column A.

g. Click the **FILE tab**, click **Save As**, double-click **Computer**, type **e10h1stock_LastFirst** in the **File name box**, click the **Save as type arrow**, select **Excel Workbook**, and then click **Save**.

STEP 2 » IMPORT AN ACCESS DATABASE TABLE

You created an Access database table that contains additional company names and their stock symbols. You want to import that into the Excel workbook so that you will be able to analyze more stock options for Angie. Refer to Figure 10.13 as you complete Step 2.

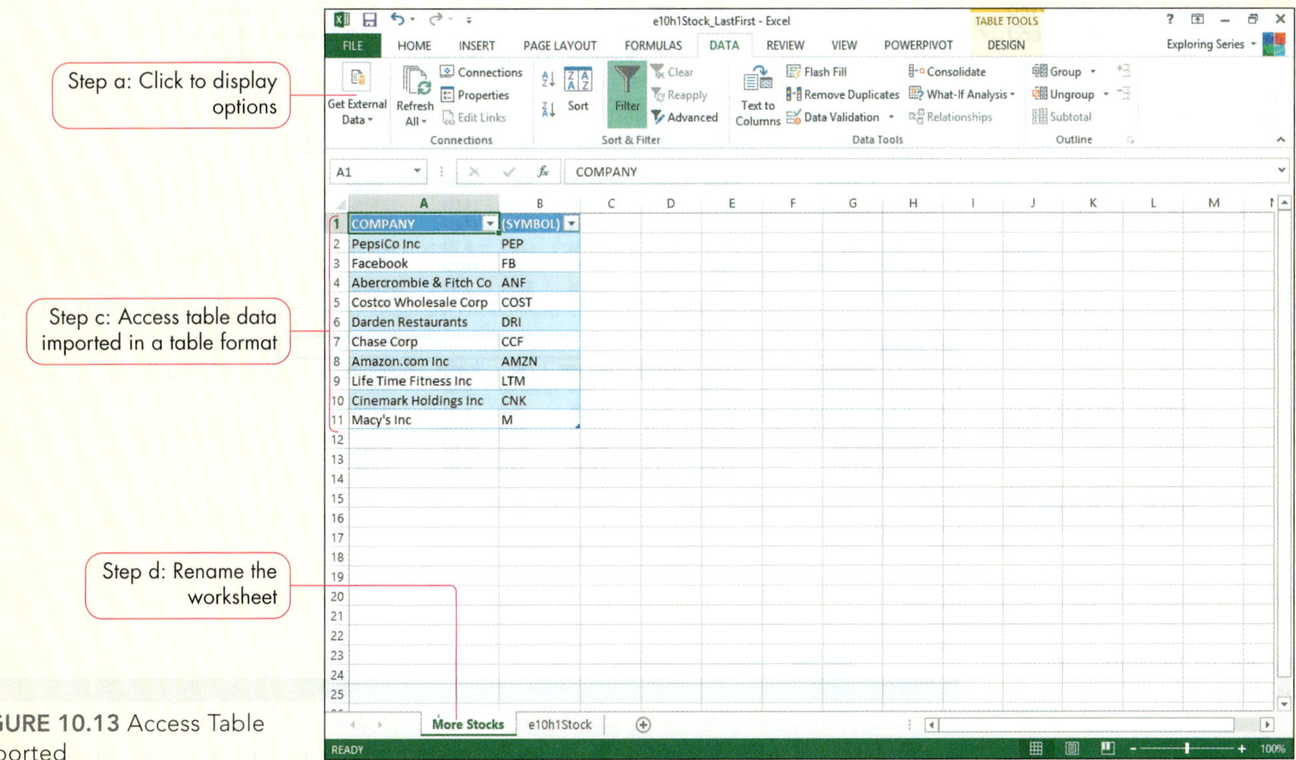

FIGURE 10.13 Access Table Imported

a. Click **cell D1**.

b. Click **Text** in the Function Library group and select **SUBSTITUTE**.

The Function Arguments dialog box opens so that you can specify the arguments for the SUBSTITUTE function.

c. Click **cell B1** to enter it in the Text box.

d. Press **Tab** and type) in the **Old_text box**.

e. Press **Tab** and type "" in the **New_text box**.

You are replacing the closing parenthesis with a null or empty string, indicated by the two double quotation marks.

> **TROUBLESHOOTING**: If you attempt to leave the New_text argument blank, an error will occur.

f. Click **OK** and double-click the **cell D1 fill handle** to copy the formula down the column. Save the workbook.

STEP 4 » USE FLASH FILL

While you have been using text functions, you want to experiment with using Flash Fill on the company names and stock symbols. Refer to Figure 10.24 as you complete Step 4.

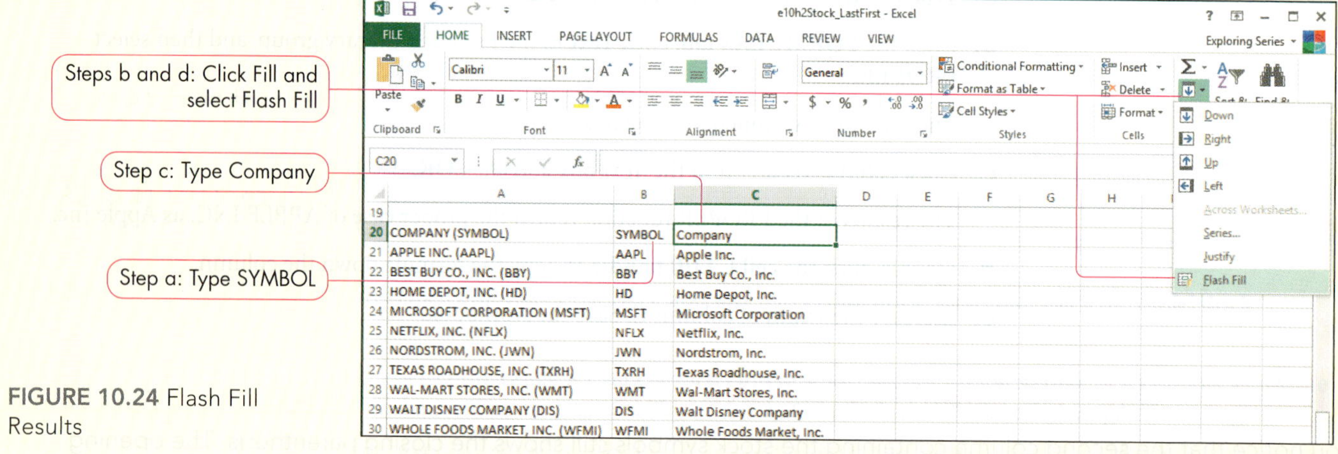

FIGURE 10.24 Flash Fill Results

a. Type **SYMBOL** in **cell B20** and press **Ctrl+Enter**.

b. Click the **HOME tab**, click **Fill** in the Editing group, and then select **Flash Fill**.

Excel detects that you entered SYMBOL without the parentheses and was able to use that data entry to fill in the stock symbols without parentheses.

c. Type **Company** in **cell C20** and press **Ctrl+Enter**.

d. Click **Fill** in the Editing group and select **Flash Fill** to fill in the company names in proper case. Widen column C so that the company names fit within the column.

e. Save the workbook. Keep the workbook open if you plan to continue with Hands-On Exercise 3. If not, close the workbook and exit Excel.

XML

Organizations run a variety of applications on different hardware and operating systems. Individuals access the same data from different cities or countries, using laptops, desktops, smartphones, and other mobile devices. The hardware and software vary greatly, but they share a common element: They access and manipulate data. Faced with the challenge of creating data that people can use on these various systems, the World Wide Web Consortium (W3C) developed a solution to standardize file formats using eXtensible Markup Language.

eXtensible Markup Language (XML) is an industry standard for structuring data across applications, operating systems, and hardware. It enables data to be sent and retrieved between otherwise incompatible systems. XML describes the structure of data but not the appearance or formatting. Individual users, rather than a central authority, create the XML elements.

In this section, you will learn how to interpret XML tags and how to import XML data into an Excel worksheet.

Understanding XML Syntax

You are probably asking: What is markup language and what makes it extensible? Why is it flexible? Consider the following example:

```
3bedrooms/2bathrooms–$1,000permonth–(305)555-1234
```

You probably recognize the text as an advertisement for an apartment. Although you recognize the advertisement, the computer needs a method to interpret it. Using XML, the advertisement would appear as this, with no space between the tags and the data:

```
<Apartment>
    <Bedrooms>3</Bedrooms>
    <Bathrooms>2</Bathrooms>
    <Rent>$1,000</Rent>
    <Telephone>(305) 555-1234</Telephone>
</Apartment>
```

The data have been marked up with various tags (enclosed in angled brackets) to give it structure. A ***tag*** is a user-defined marker that identifies the beginning or ending of a piece of data in an XML document. Various tags are nested within one another; for example, the Bedrooms, Bathrooms, Rent, and Telephone tags are nested within the Apartment tag. The tags are relatively obvious and can be read by any XML-compliant application for further processing. The XML document does not contain any information about *how* to display the data; XML *describes* the data itself rather than the formatting of the data.

HTML uses a finite set of predefined tags, such as <b></b> and <i></i> for bold and italic, respectively. XML, however, is much more general because it has an infinite number of tags that are defined as necessary in different applications. In other words, XML is ***extensible***, meaning it can be expanded as necessary to include additional data, such as adding elements for the apartment number.

Figure 10.25 displays an XML document that was created in Notepad. The XML declaration in the first line specifies the XML version and the character encoding used in the document. The question mark and angled brackets are part of the optional ***XML declaration***, which specifies the XML version and character encoding used. The document also contains a comment in the second line to identify the author. The indentation throughout the document makes it easier to read but is not required.

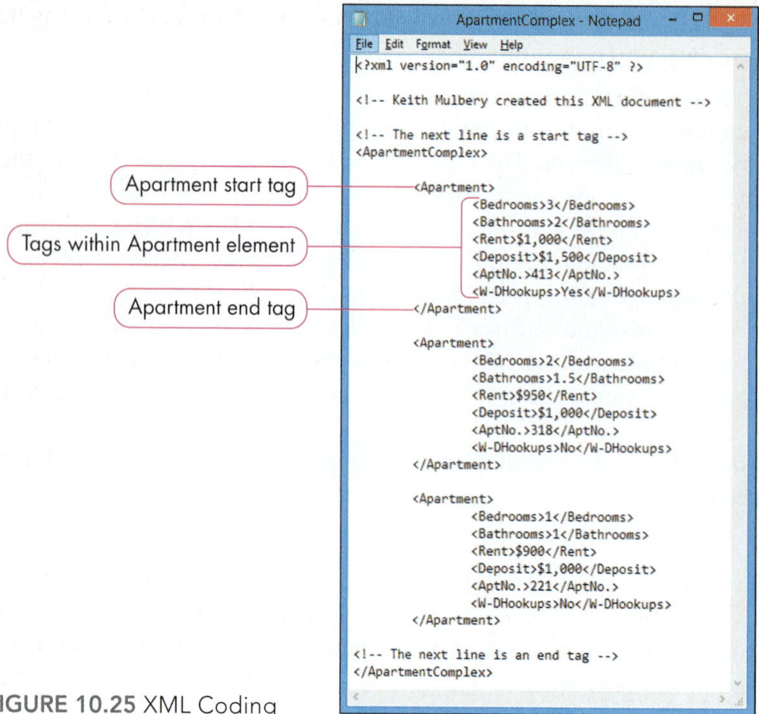

FIGURE 10.25 XML Coding

- An XML document is divided into elements. Each ***element*** contains a start tag, an end tag, and the associated data. The ***start tag*** contains the name of the element, such as Rent. The ***end tag*** contains the name of the element preceded by a slash, such as /Rent.
- XML tags are case sensitive. In Figure 10.25, <Rent> and </Rent> use the same case. However, <Rent> $1,000 </rent> would be incorrect because the start and end tags are not the same case.
- XML elements can be nested to any depth, but each inner element (or child) must be entirely contained within the outer element (or parent). For example, the Bedrooms and Rent elements are nested within the Apartment element.
- Indenting indicates the hierarchy structure. For example, elements for a particular month are indented one or two levels so that the start <Month> and end </Month> tags stand out. The outer element tags are aligned for readability.
- An XML comment is optional data that provide explanatory information about the coding. An XML comment starts with <!-- and ends with -->.

Creating an XML Document

Typically, people use Notepad, or any text editor, to create an XML document, switch to a Web browser, such as Internet Explorer, to view the XML document, and then switch back to Notepad to make any changes.

Importing XML Data into Excel

Excel is designed to analyze and manipulate data, but the source of that data is irrelevant. Data may originate within a worksheet, be imported from an Access table or query, come from a text file, or come from an XML document. Like a text file, an XML document can be opened directly from the Open dialog box or imported with a connection to the original document. To open an XML file, do the following:

1. Display the Open dialog box.
2. Click the File Type arrow and select XML Files.
3. Select the XML file you want and click Open. The Open XML dialog box opens (see Figure 10.26).
4. Select the option that describes how you want to open the file and click OK. If the Microsoft Excel message box appears stating *The specified XML source does not refer to a schema. Excel will create a schema based on the XML source data.* Click OK.

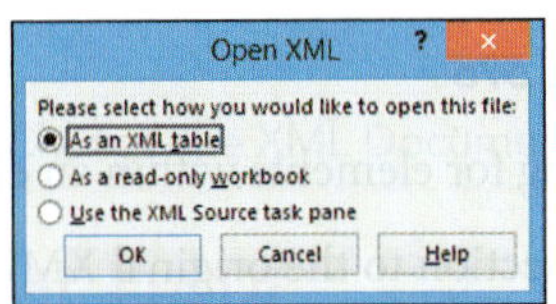

FIGURE 10.26 Open XML Dialog Box

The *As an XML table* default option opens the XML file as a table with each element as a column label or field. Excel imports all records from the source file without any connection to the original XML document. If the original XML document is changed, those changes will not be updated in the Excel workbook. You may have to format some imported XML data. For example, if you import the XML data shown in Figure 10.25, the monetary values import as text. You will then have to apply a number format to use the data as values.

If you select the *Use the XML Source task pane* option, Excel opens a new workbook and displays the XML Source task pane on the right side (see Figure 10.27). The data do not import by default. To map XML elements to worksheet cells and import data, do the following:

1. Drag an element to the desired cell in the worksheet. You do not have to use all XML elements, and you can drag them in any sequence. Notice the different sequence and the omission of the W-DHookups element.
2. Right-click a cell in the XML area and select XML.
3. Select Import, find the XML file containing the data you want to import, and then click OK. Excel imports the data that match the elements and sequence you specified.

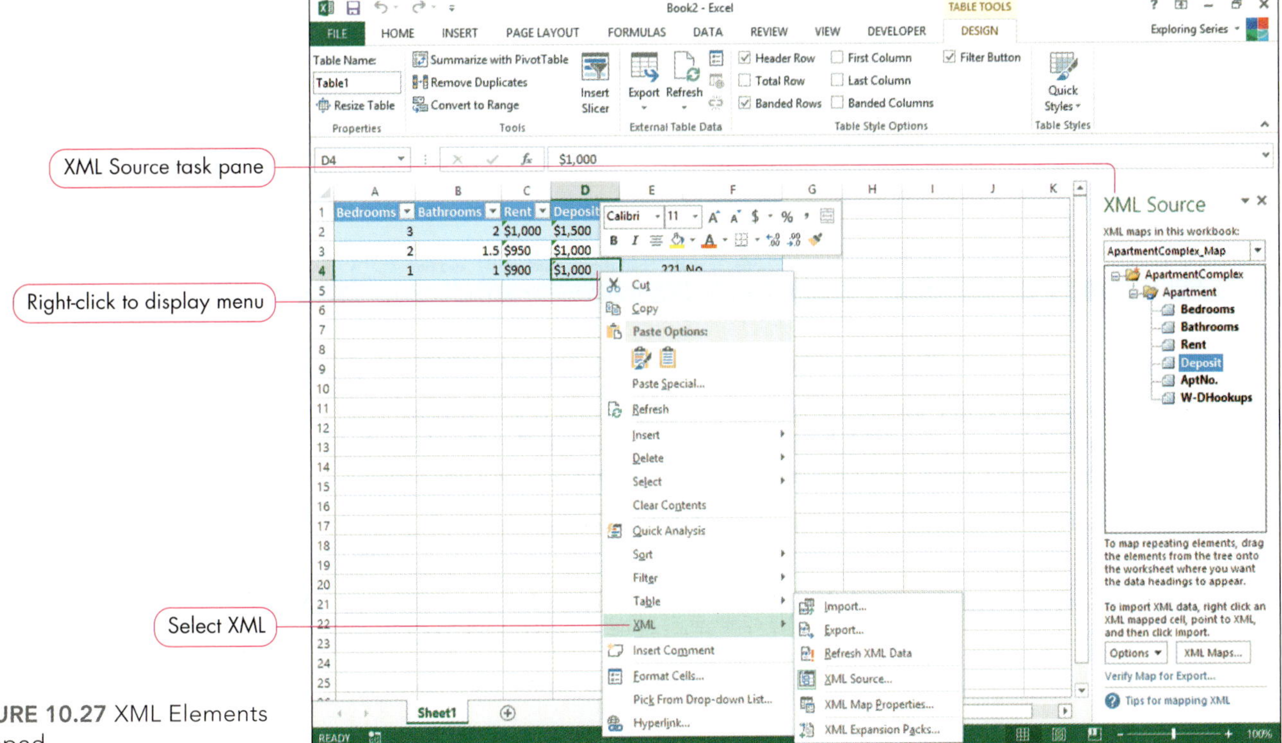

FIGURE 10.27 XML Elements Mapped

	A	B	C	D	E	F
1	FIRST	LAST	NAMES	E-MAIL ADDRESS	ALTERNATE E-EMAIL ADDRESS	
2	FRANK	BAILEY	Bailey, Frank	frank_bailey@ourcompany.com	frank.bailey@ourcompany.com	
3	RENA	BERKOWICZ	Berkowicz, Rena	rena_berkowicz@ourcompany.com	rena.berkowicz@ourcompany.com	
4	HEATHER	BOND	Bond, Heather	heather_bond@ourcompany.com	heather.bond@ourcompany.com	
5	JEFF	BOROW	Borow, Jeff	jeff_borow@ourcompany.com	jeff.borow@ourcompany.com	
6	ZEV	BOROW	Borow, Zev	zev_borow@ourcompany.com	zev.borow@ourcompany.com	
7	ARIEL	BOROW	Borow, Ariel	ariel_borow@ourcompany.com	ariel.borow@ourcompany.com	
8	LARRY	BRAGG	Bragg, Larry	larry_bragg@ourcompany.com	larry.bragg@ourcompany.com	
9	HARRY	BUNTING	Bunting, Harry	harry_bunting@ourcompany.com	harry.bunting@ourcompany.com	
10	JEFF	COTTRELL	Cottrell, Jeff	jeff_cottrell@ourcompany.com	jeff.cottrell@ourcompany.com	

FIGURE 10.32 Names and E-Mail Addresses

a. Open the Open dialog box in Excel, click the **File Type arrow**, select **Text Files**, select *e10p2Names*, and then click **Open**.

b. Do the following in the Text Import Wizard dialog box:
   - Click the **My data has headers check box** and click **Next**.
   - Deselect all check boxes in the *Delimiters* section and click **Next**.
   - Click **Text** in the *Column data format* section and click **Finish**.

c. Click the **FILE tab**, select **Save As**, type **e10p2Names_LastFirst** in the **File name box**, click the **Save as type arrow**, select **Excel Workbook**, and then click **Save**.

d. Convert the data into two columns by doing the following:
   - Click the **column A header**, click the **DATA tab**, and then click **Text to Columns** in the Data Tools group to open the *Convert Text to Columns Wizard* dialog box.
   - Make sure *Delimited* is selected and click **Next**.
   - Select the **Space check box**, deselect the other check boxes, and then click **Next**.
   - Click **Text**, click the **General column** in the *Data preview* section, and then click **Text**.
   - Click **Finish** and widen columns A and B.

e. Combine names and convert the text to proper case by doing the following:
   - Click **cell C1**, type **Last, First**, and then press **Ctrl+Enter**.
   - Click the **HOME tab**, click **Fill** in the Editing group, and then select **Flash Fill** to fill the names down the column. Widen column C.

f. Click **cell D2**, type **=LOWER(CONCATENATE(A2,"_",B2,"@ourcompany.com"))**, and then press **Ctrl+Enter**. Copy the formula down the column and widen column D.

g. Click **cell E2**, type **=SUBSTITUTE(D2,"_",".")**, and then press **Ctrl+Enter**. Copy the formula down the column and widen column E.

h. Type **NAMES** in **cell C1**, **E-MAIL ADDRESS** in **cell D1**, and **ALTERNATE E-MAIL ADDRESS** in **cell E1**. Bold and center the labels on the first row.

i. Select **Landscape orientation**, set **0.3"** left and right margins, and then set titles to repeat the first row.

j. Create a footer with your name on the left side, the sheet name code in the center, and the file name code on the right side for each worksheet.

k. Save and close the workbook, and submit based on your instructor's directions.

3 Years on the Job

You manage a local bank in Kansas City. Employee retention is a concern. You are considering providing incentives to employees who have worked for the bank for more than five years. The HR director provided a list of employees and dates they were hired in an XML document. You will import the data into Excel and create a formula to calculate the number of years each employee has worked. In addition, you will count the number of employees by years on the job and to apply a conditional format for employees who have worked more than five years. This exercise follows the same set of skills as used in Hands-On Exercise 3 in the chapter. Refer to Figure 10.33 as you complete this exercise.

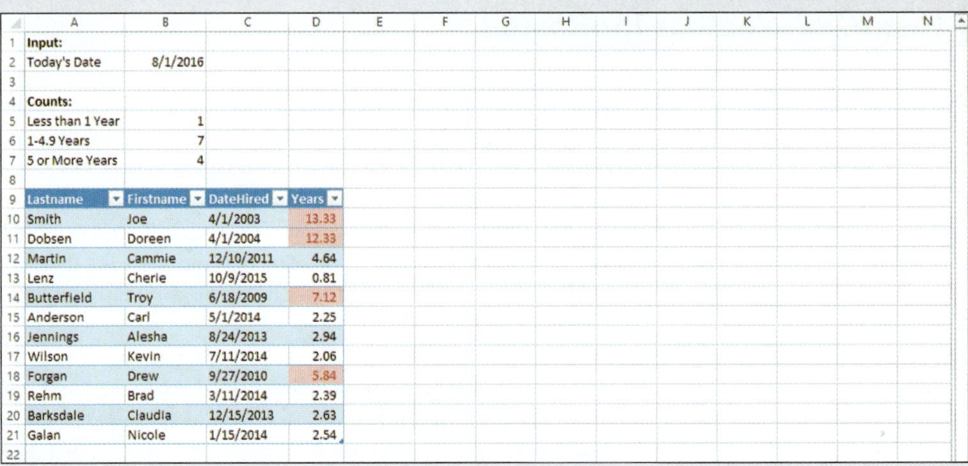

	A	B	C	D
1	**Input:**			
2	Today's Date	8/1/2016		
3				
4	**Counts:**			
5	Less than 1 Year	1		
6	1-4.9 Years	7		
7	5 or More Years	4		
8				
9	Lastname	Firstname	DateHired	Years
10	Smith	Joe	4/1/2003	13.33
11	Dobsen	Doreen	4/1/2004	12.33
12	Martin	Cammie	12/10/2011	4.64
13	Lenz	Cherie	10/9/2015	0.81
14	Butterfield	Troy	6/18/2009	7.12
15	Anderson	Carl	5/1/2014	2.25
16	Jennings	Alesha	8/24/2013	2.94
17	Wilson	Kevin	7/11/2014	2.06
18	Forgan	Drew	9/27/2010	5.84
19	Rehm	Brad	3/11/2014	2.39
20	Barksdale	Claudia	12/15/2013	2.63
21	Galan	Nicole	1/15/2014	2.54
22				

FIGURE 10.33 Employee List

a. Copy *e10p3People.xml* and rename the copied file as **e10p3People_LastFirst.xml**.

b. Open *e10p3Employees* in Excel and save it as **e10p3Employees_LastFirst**.

c. Import the XML data by doing the following:
   - Click the **DATA tab**, click **Get External Data** if needed, and then click **From Other Sources**.
   - Select **From XML Data Import**, select *e10p3People_LastFirst.xml*, and then click **Open**.
   - Click **OK** in the Microsoft Excel message box.
   - Type **A9** in the **XML table in existing worksheet box** and click **OK**.

d. Type **Years** in **cell D9**.

e. Calculate and conditionally format the number of years by doing the following:
   - Type **=YEARFRAC(C10,B$2)** in **cell D10** and press **Ctrl+Enter**.
   - Select the **range D10:D21** and apply the **Comma Style**.
   - Click **Conditional Formatting** in the Styles group on the HOME tab, point to *Highlight Cells Rules*, select **Greater Than**, type **4.99** in the **Greater Than dialog box**, and then click **OK**.

f. Enter functions to count the number of employees by year by doing the following:
   - Type **=COUNTIF(D10:D21,"<1")** in **cell B5**.
   - Type **=COUNTIFS(D10:D21,">=1",D10:D21,"<5")** in **cell B6**.
   - Type **=COUNTIF(D10:D21,">=5")** in **cell B7**.

g. Double-click between the column A and B column headings to increase the width of column A.

h. Save the workbook. Open *e10p3People_LastFirst.xml* in Notepad. Change Cheri Lenz's hire date to **10/9/2015**. Change Drew Forgan's hire date to **9/27/2010**. Be careful not to delete any XML tags. Press **Ctrl+S** to save the XML document and close it.

i. Click the **DATA tab** and click **Refresh All** in the Connections group. If warning messages appear, click **OK** in each message box and save the workbook. Adjust the width of column A.

j. Create a footer with your name on the left side, the sheet name code in the center, and the file name code on the right side of the worksheet.

k. Save and close the workbook, and submit based on your instructor's directions.

Mid-Level Exercises

1 Historical Weather for Boston

You own a tour company that provides historical tours and activities for vacationers in Boston, Massachusetts. In addition, you want to develop more off-season activities for the colder months. You want to develop a flexible plan to change your offerings based on the day's weather. You track three months of weather at a time. You want weather statistics to compare to your sales for the period to be able to see the weather correlation and fine-tune your product offerings. In the past, you created a Web query to a weather Web site; however, you realized that you can't select the table within the New Web Query dialog box. Therefore, you will copy and paste the data from the Web site into your Excel worksheet. (Although the Web page has a link for a comma-delimited file, the headings will not import into one row in Excel.)

a. Open *e10m1Weather* and save it as **e10m1Weather_LastFirst**.

b. Copy the URL in **cell C2** into the Address box of a Web browser. Select the starting and ending dates to extract the past full three months of data. Scroll down to the Observations table. Drag to select starting with the column labels through the end of the table, press **Ctrl+C**, click **cell A5** in the Raw Data sheet, and then click **Paste**.

c. Set **6.1** column widths for columns A:S, bold the headings on rows 5 and 6, and then apply **Align Right** for the headings on row 6. Apply **Bottom Border** for row 5.

d. Click **cell V7** and create a nested function that displays *sunny* for any day that does not have an event observation and repeats events if listed. Nest the IF statement in a function that displays the results in uppercase letters. After you copy the function down the column, delete functions on heading rows between months. Type **Weather** in **cell V6** and adjust the width for this column.

e. Display the Statistics sheet. In the **range B4:D10**, create functions to display the appropriate results for the number of days by event using data from the Raw Data sheet. Use the * wildcard to count multiple-event days respectively. For example, if the weather is *RAIN, THUNDERSTORM*, make sure the function counts that day for both Rain and Thunderstorm.

f. Insert functions to calculate the average temperatures and precipitation statistics in the **range B11:D16**. Use mixed cell references to enable efficient copying and slight editing of formulas as you copy them. Apply **Comma Style** with the appropriate number of decimal points to the results.

g. Use a formula that replaces the Month 1, Month 2, and Month 3 column labels in the Statistics worksheet with the name of the months in the Raw Data worksheet. Horizontally center the column labels.

h. Use the Raw Data worksheet to create three line charts—one per month—to plot the daily high, average, and low temperatures. Place each line chart on a separate sheet, and name the sheets appropriately, such as **November Temps**. Add an appropriate chart title to each chart.

i. Create a footer for all worksheets with your name on the left side, the sheet name code in the center, and the file name code on the right side.

j. Save and close the workbook, and submit based on your instructor's directions.

2 Animal Shelter

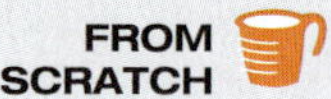

You manage a small animal shelter in Dayton, Ohio. Your assistant created an XML document that lists some of the recent small animals that your shelter took in. In particular, the XML document lists the animal type (such as cat); the age, sex, name, color, and date the animal was brought in; and the date the animal was adopted. You want to manage the data in an Excel worksheet, so you will create a link to the original data source in case they change.

a. Use Windows to copy the *e10m2Animals.xml* file and rename the copied file **e10m2Animals_LastFirst.xml**.

b. Start a new workbook and save it as **e10m2Animals_LastFirst**.

c. Import the XML document *e10m2Animals_LastFirst.xml* into Sheet1 of the workbook. Rename Sheet1 **Animals**.

DISCOVER 

d. Create a PivotTable from the imported data, placing the animal type and sex as row labels and counting names as values. Use the adoption date as a report filter and set a filter to show those animals that have *not* been adopted. Rename the PivotTable worksheet **PivotTable**. Delete the blank worksheets.

e. Open *e10m2Animals_LastFirst.xml* in Notepad. Edit the XML document by adding **3/25/2016** for the adoption date for Paws the cat. Edit Fido's data by entering his age: **6 months**. Edit Twerpy's color as **Orange**. Edit Misty's adoption date of **3/31/2016**. Save the XML file and close Notepad.

f. Display the Animals worksheet in Excel and refresh the connection. Display the PivotTable worksheet and refresh the PivotTable.

g. Display the PivotTable worksheet, type labels **Most Available Animals**, **Most Adopted Animals**, and **Cat Gender Most Adopted** in the **range A15:A17**. Type answers to these questions in the **range B15:B17**.

h. Display the Animals worksheet and type **Name, Type** as a column label in **cell H2**. In **cell H3**, type **Paws, Cat**. Use Flash Fill to complete the rest of the data entry in this column.

i. Create a footer with your name on the left side, the sheet name code in the center, and the file name code on the right side of each worksheet.

j. Save and close the workbook, and submit based on your instructor's directions.

3 Favorite Movies

It is interesting to find out what people's favorite movies are. Work with a classmate to create an Access database table of favorite movies that you can import into an Excel workbook.

a. Create a blank Access database named **e10m3Movies_LastFirst.accdb**.

b. Create a table with these fields: Movie Title, Genre, Rating, Year Released, Lead Actor, and Lead Actress. Save the table as Favorite Movies_Last First.

c. Enter 10 records in the table, one for each of your favorite 10 movies.

d. Close the Access database and upload it to a SkyDrive where you give your team member privileges to read and write files.

e. Download your team member's Access file and rename it by adding your last name after his or her name in the file name.

f. Start a new Excel workbook and save it as **e10m3Movies_LastFirst.xlsx**.

g. Import your team member's Access database table into your Excel workbook.

h. Create a footer with your name on the left side, the sheet name code in the center, and the file name code on the right side of the worksheet. Save the workbook.

i. Open the Access database file *e10m3Movies_LastFirstLastFirst.accdb.*

j. Add five of your favorite movies to the list. Make sure they do not duplicate any existing data. Sort the table in alphabetical order by movie title. Close the database.

k. Refresh the connection in Excel so that the data are updated to match the changes you made to the database.

l. Upload your completed files to the SkyDrive account so that your team member can access your files to see what movies you added.

Beyond the Classroom

Text Functions vs. Flash Fill

RESEARCH CASE 

After learning about text functions and Flash Fill in Excel, you speculate that you can use *always* use Flash Fill instead of using text functions. Open *e10b2TextFlash* and save it as **e10b2TextFlash_LastFirst**. The first column contains invoice numbers, such as 20151201, which represent the year (2015), the month (12 for December), and the invoice within that month (01).

Research the text functions that were not covered in Hands-On Exercise 2 and use text functions to separate the invoices to display the year, month, and invoice number in the range B4:D16. Answer the question by typing your responses in the range A19:E21. Use Flash Fill to complete data in the range H4:J16. Answer the question by typing your responses in the range H19:J21.

Create a footer with your name on the left side, the sheet name code in the center, and the file name code on the right side of the worksheet. Save and close the workbook, and submit based on your instructor's directions.

Personal Book Library

Your friend Jeromy wants to create a list of books in his personal home library. His brother created an XML document containing data for a few of Jeromy's books. Unfortunately, the document contains errors. Use Windows to copy *e10b3Books.xml* and rename the copied file **e10b3Books_LastFirst.xml**. Open the XML document in Notepad. Identify the errors. Insert XML-style comments that describe the errors. XML-style comments begin with <!-- and end with -->. Also, insert comments on style issues, although these issues are not programming errors. Fix the errors and style issues and save the XML document. Import the XML document into a new Excel workbook and name the workbook **e10b3Books_LastFirst** in the Excel Workbook format. Rename Sheet1 **Book List** and delete the extra worksheets. Create a footer with your name on the left side, the sheet name code in the center, and the file name code on the right side of the worksheet. Save and close the workbook, and submit based on your instructor's directions.

Sexual Harassment

SOFT SKILLS CASE 

Use a Web browser to read information about sexual harassment and then locate a table that provides statistics on sexual harassment or sexual harassment charges in the United States. Copy the URL. Start a new workbook named **e10b4Harassment_LastFirst**. Create a Web query using the URL you found. Select the option to preserve HTML formatting and import the data. Below the imported data, type a source line and paste the URL. In the next cell, type the date you retrieved this information. Create a footer with your name on the left side, the sheet name code in the center, and the file name code on the right side of the worksheet. Save and close the workbook, and submit based on your instructor's directions.

Capstone Exercise

Whisenhunt Enterprises is located in Oklahoma City. Denise Petrillo and Omar Vincent travel frequently for business. To help plan for flight delays, you will create a workbook that provides airline data with up-to-date arrival and departure information from the Will Rogers World Airport.

Import Text

You need to import airline data (airline names, codes, and URLs) from a tab-delimited file created by one of your colleagues. In addition, you need to separate the airline name from its code.

a. Use Windows to copy the *e10c1Airlines.txt*. Rename the copied file as **e10c1Airlines_LastFirst.txt**.

b. Open *e10c1Departures* and save it as **e10c1Departures_LastFirst**.

c. Display the Airline Codes worksheet. Create a link to *e10c1Airlines_LastFirst.txt*, a tab-delimited file. Select the option that the text file has headers.

d. Edit *e10c1Airlines_LastFirst.txt* in Notepad. Type **Frontier**, **F9**, and **FF5** in alphabetical order, pressing **Tab** between columns. Save and close the text file.

e. Refresh the connection to the text file.

Obtain Data from a Web Site

You want to copy data from the Will Rogers World Airport Web site. You can't create a Web query because Excel is not able to recognize the departures data as a table.

a. Use a Web browser to go to **http://flyokc.com/**, click **Departing**, and then click **Search**.

b. Copy and paste the departure data in the Departures worksheet in Excel.

Insert Text and Logic Functions

You want to use functions to extract data from the Departures worksheet to the Filtered List worksheet. For the first column, you want to insert a function to look up the airline code. For the second column, you want to combine the airline code with the flight number. For the third column, you want to display the city name in title case. For the fourth column, you want to display the time and then format it. For the last column, you want to display the status in title case.

a. Create a table using the **range A1:E51** on the Filtered List worksheet.

b. Click **cell A2**. Use a VLOOKUP function to look up the airline in the Departures worksheet, compare it to the airline table in the Airline Codes worksheet, and return the IATA code for that airline. For example, United will display as UA.

c. Click **cell B2**. Use a text function to combine the airline code from the previous step with a space and the flight number on the respective row in the Departures worksheet.

d. Click **cell C2**. Use a text function to display the cities from the Departures worksheet in the desired format, such as Houston.

e. Click **cell D2**. Enter a formula to repeat the time from the Departures worksheet. Format the entire column with the **Time format**, such as 1:30 PM.

f. Click **cell E2**. Enter a text function that returns the status in title case, such as On Time.

g. Set a filter for both Houston airports with a status of **On Time**.

Import XML Data

Another employee created an XML file containing city names and airport codes. You want to connect to this XML file. After importing the XML file, you realize one major airport is missing and an airport code is incorrect for another airport.

a. Use Windows to copy *e10c1Airports.xml*. Rename the copied file **e10c1Airports_LastFirst.xml**.

b. Create a connection to the *e10c1Airports_LastFirst.xml* file in the Airports worksheet.

c. Open *e10c1Airports_LastFirst.xml* in Notepad. Copy the first Airport element and paste the copy above the original first airport element. Edit the data by typing **Atlanta** and **ATL** within the proper tags.

d. Change the Chicago airport code to **ORD**.

e. Save the XML file and close it.

f. Refresh the XML connection only.

Finalize the Workbook

You are ready to finalize the workbook.

a. Create a footer with your name on the left side, the sheet name code in the center, and the file name code on the right side of each worksheet. Delete any extra worksheets.

b. Save and close the workbook, and submit based on your instructor's directions.

Excel

Collaboration and Workbook Distribution

CHAPTER 11

Sharing Data with Others

Yuri Arcurs/Shutterstock

OBJECTIVES

AFTER YOU READ THIS CHAPTER, YOU WILL BE ABLE TO:

CASE STUDY | Marching Band Senior Dinner

You are a senior member of your school's marching band. As a senior gift, you would like to organize a fundraiser to help the band purchase new uniforms. To raise the required funds, you are going to organize a dinner with music provided by the senior members of the band. Each dinner ticket is $100, but you plan to provide a few complimentary tickets to current benefactors of the program. The dinner is held in the university ballroom. The university waives the standard room rental fee, but the Facilities Department charges for table and chair rentals, linen cleaning, and cleanup. A grocery store donates the food ingredients, and a decorator prepares and donates a variety of decorations. Additional expenses include beverages, flowers, table decorations, and various publicity costs.

As the event coordinator, you developed a worksheet that contains an input section for the number of tables, chairs, complimentary tickets, and ticket price. In addition, you itemized revenue, donations, expenses, and net income. To ensure the budget is accurate and complete, you will share the workbook with other students to get their feedback using collaborative tools. After updating the workbook, you will check for issues, protect the workbook from unauthorized modification, save the workbook in several formats, and distribute the final workbook to other people who have a vested interest in the success of the event.

Customization and Personalization

When you move into a new apartment, you want to add your personal touches to it by decorating it to suit your style. Similarly, you might want to personalize Excel to suit your needs. You can customize Excel through the Excel Options dialog box. Think of the Excel Options dialog box as the control center that manages the behavior and settings of Excel—the color scheme, formula rules, automatic corrections, AutoComplete rules, and which items display onscreen. Previously, you used the Excel Options dialog box to load the Solver and Analysis ToolPak add-in applications.

In addition to customizing the Excel program itself, you might want to personalize workbooks that you create. For example, you might want to insert your name as the workbook author or add your company name to the workbook. Adding these attributes to your workbooks gives you the credit for the work you do in an organization.

In this section, you will customize Microsoft Office using your name as the user name. In addition, you will view and add properties to characterize a workbook.

Customizing Excel

The Excel Options dialog box contains a variety of settings that control how Excel behaves. Table 11.1 lists the options categories and some key options that you can customize.

TABLE 11.1 Excel Options Categories

Category	Description	Some Options
General	Controls general Excel options	Interface options, such as the color scheme. Defaults for new workbooks, such as font and number of sheets. Personalization: User name and the newly added customizable office backgrounds.
Formulas	Controls formula calculations, performance, and error handling	Workbook calculation Formula AutoComplete Error checking rules
Proofing	Controls corrections and formatting	AutoCorrect Spelling
Save	Controls how workbooks are saved	File format AutoRecover rules
Language	Specifies language preferences	Editing languages ScreenTip language
Advanced	Controls advanced settings	Editing options Cut, copy, and paste Display settings Formula settings
Customize Ribbon	Enables users to customize the Ribbon	Commands, tabs, and groups Reset Import/Export
Quick Access Toolbar	Enables users to customize the Quick Access Toolbar	Commands Reset Import/Export
Add-Ins	Manages add-in programs	Active and inactive add-ins
Trust Center	Keeps documents safe	Protecting your privacy Security and more Microsoft Excel Trust Center

When you create an Excel workbook, a Word document, or a PowerPoint presentation, the respective program identifies the default user information to code the files. The user name indicates who authored a particular document. You should personalize your copy of Microsoft Office so that the files will automatically indicate that you authored or edited the file. Because people share files with each other on a network or via e-mail within an organization, it is important to know who created or edited a particular file. For example, you want to add your name as the author of the Marching Band Senior Dinner workbook so that others will know that you created the budget. To personalize Microsoft Office, do the following:

1. Click the FILE tab to access the Backstage view.
2. Click Options to open the Excel Options dialog box, which shows the General options for working with Excel (see Figure 11.1).
3. Type your name in the User name box in the *Personalize your copy of Microsoft Office* section. (In Microsoft Word, PowerPoint, or Access, you can also enter your first and last initials in the Initials box.) Click OK.

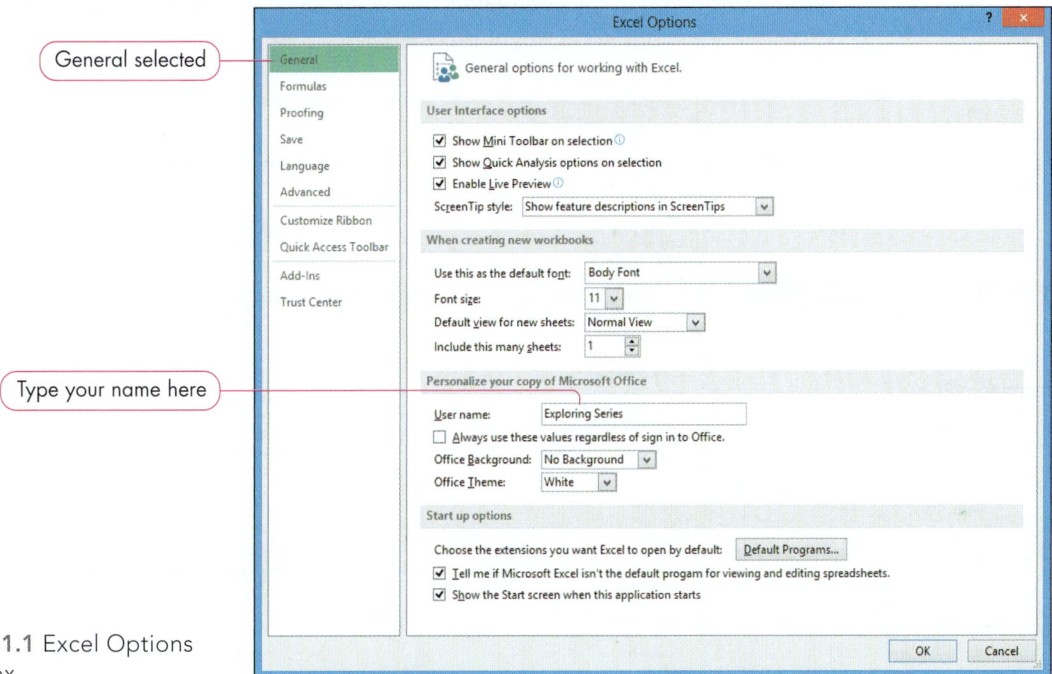

FIGURE 11.1 Excel Options Dialog Box

TIP Common Personalization

Entering your user name and initials in one Microsoft Office program stores that information in the other Microsoft Office programs. On a private computer, changes you make become the default. If you are in a computer lab, however, the lab settings may delete your preferences when you log out.

Customize the Ribbon

When you load an add-in such as Solver, Excel adds a command automatically to a tab on the Ribbon. In addition, if you install software, such as Adobe Acrobat, you might see an Add-Ins tab with commands that interact with those programs. You can customize the Ribbon by creating new tabs and groups, adding and removing commands, and resetting the Ribbon. People customize the Ribbon when they use particular commands frequently, but they do not want to click several original tabs to execute a command. By creating a custom tab with frequently used commands, they can use one tab to do most of their work. To create a new custom tab with commands, do the following:

1. Click the FILE tab, click Options, and then click Customize Ribbon (see Figure 11.2).
2. Click New Tab. Excel adds *New Tab (Custom)* with *New Group (Custom)* to the Main Tabs list.
3. Click New Tab (Custom) in the Main Tabs list, click Rename, type a name in the *Display name* box in the Rename dialog box, and then click OK. The tab now has a unique name. Use Help to learn how to hide a tab or change the order of tabs. Use the same process to rename New Group (Custom).
4. Click New Group to add another new group on the custom tab.
5. Click New Group (Custom) in the Main Tabs list, click Rename, type a name in the *Display name* box in the Rename dialog box, and then click OK. The group now has a unique name. Repeat this process to rename all new groups you add to the tab. Use Help to learn how to change the order of groups on a tab.
6. Click a group name, select a category from the *Choose commands from* drop down list, select a command in the commands list on the left side, and then click Add.
7. Click OK after adding commands to each new group.

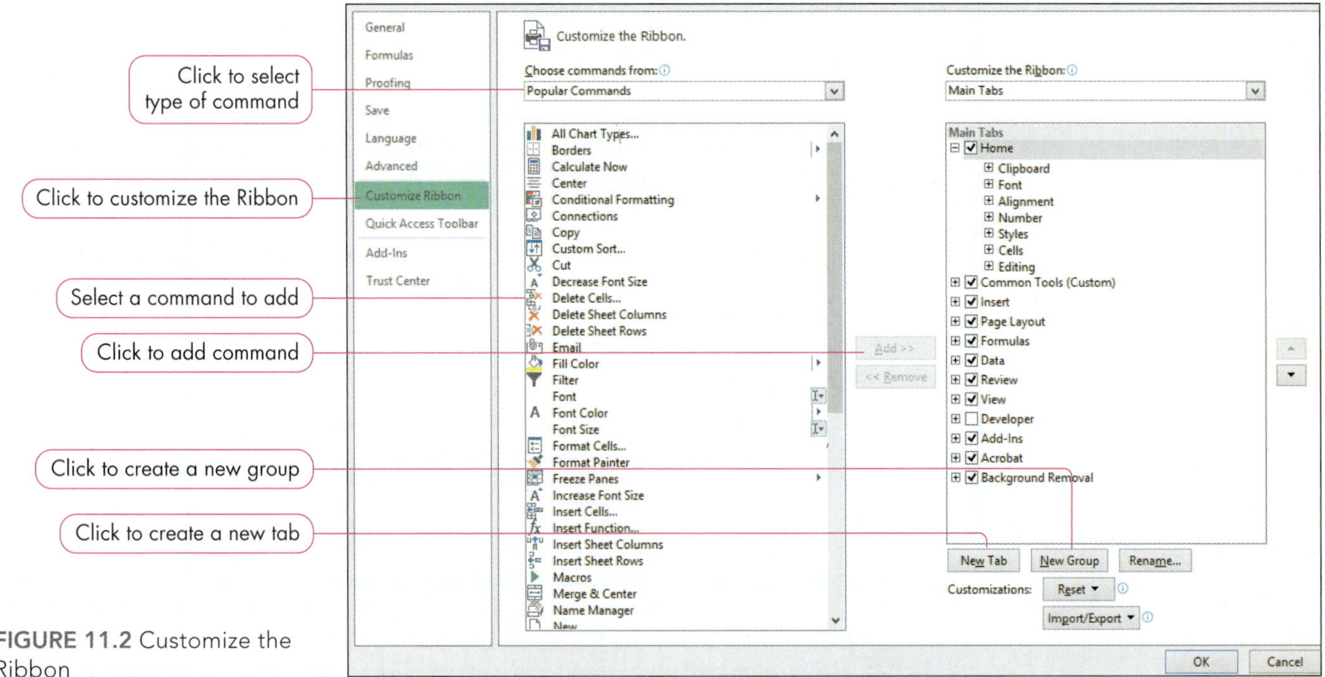

FIGURE 11.2 Customize the Ribbon

Reset the Ribbon

You can reset customizations if you no longer need them. To reset changes made to an original tab, select the tab in the Main Tabs list, click Reset, and then select *Reset only selected Ribbon tab*. To remove all customizations and return to the original settings, including new tabs created and Quick Access Toolbar customizations, click Reset, select *Reset all customizations*, and then click Yes. To remove a custom tab, right-click it in the dialog box and select Remove.

Customize the Quick Access Toolbar

By default, the Quick Access Toolbar contains three commands: Save, Undo, and Redo. You can customize the Quick Access Toolbar to add any frequently used commands. To customize the Quick Access Toolbar, do the following:

1. Click Customize Quick Access Toolbar, the arrow to the right of the Quick Access Toolbar, and select More Commands. Alternatively, click the FILE tab, click Options, and then click Quick Access Toolbar. The list of commands is similar to those for customizing the Ribbon.
2. Do one of the following to customize the Quick Access Toolbar:
   - Choose a command group from the *Choose commands from* drop down menu. Click a command in the list on the left and click Add to add a command to the Quick Access Toolbar.
   - Click a command in the right list and click Remove to remove it from the Quick Access Toolbar.
   - Click Reset and select *Reset only Quick Access Toolbar* to reset it to the default settings.
   - Use Help to learn how to change the order of commands or group commands by adding a separator.
3. Click OK.

Import and Export Settings

After customizing the Quick Access Toolbar or Ribbon, you can share the custom settings with other people. Click Import/Export, select *Export all customizations*, enter a file name in the File Save dialog box, and then click Save. The file is saved as an Exported Office UI File format. To import the customizations file on another computer, click Import/Export, select *Import customization file*, select the file in the File Open dialog box, and then click Open.

Changing Properties

STEP 1» When you create or edit a file, ***metadata*** (data that describe other data) or ***document properties*** are attached to that file. Document properties that describe or identify a file include details such as the author's name, title, subject, company, creation date, revision date, and keywords. Including document properties for your workbooks helps you organize your files. In addition, you can perform a search to find files that contain particular properties. For example, you can use Windows to perform a search for all files authored by a coworker or all files that contain *marching band* as keywords.

STEP 2» On the File tab, click Info, if necessary, to display the properties for the current workbook (see Figure 11.3). You can enter or edit standard properties, such as Title, Categories, and Author, by positioning the mouse pointer over the respective property, clicking, and typing the information. You are not able to change automatically updated properties directly, such as Size, Last Modified, and Last Printed. These properties change based on when you last perform an action, such as saving the workbook. When you save the workbook, the document properties are saved as part of the workbook too.

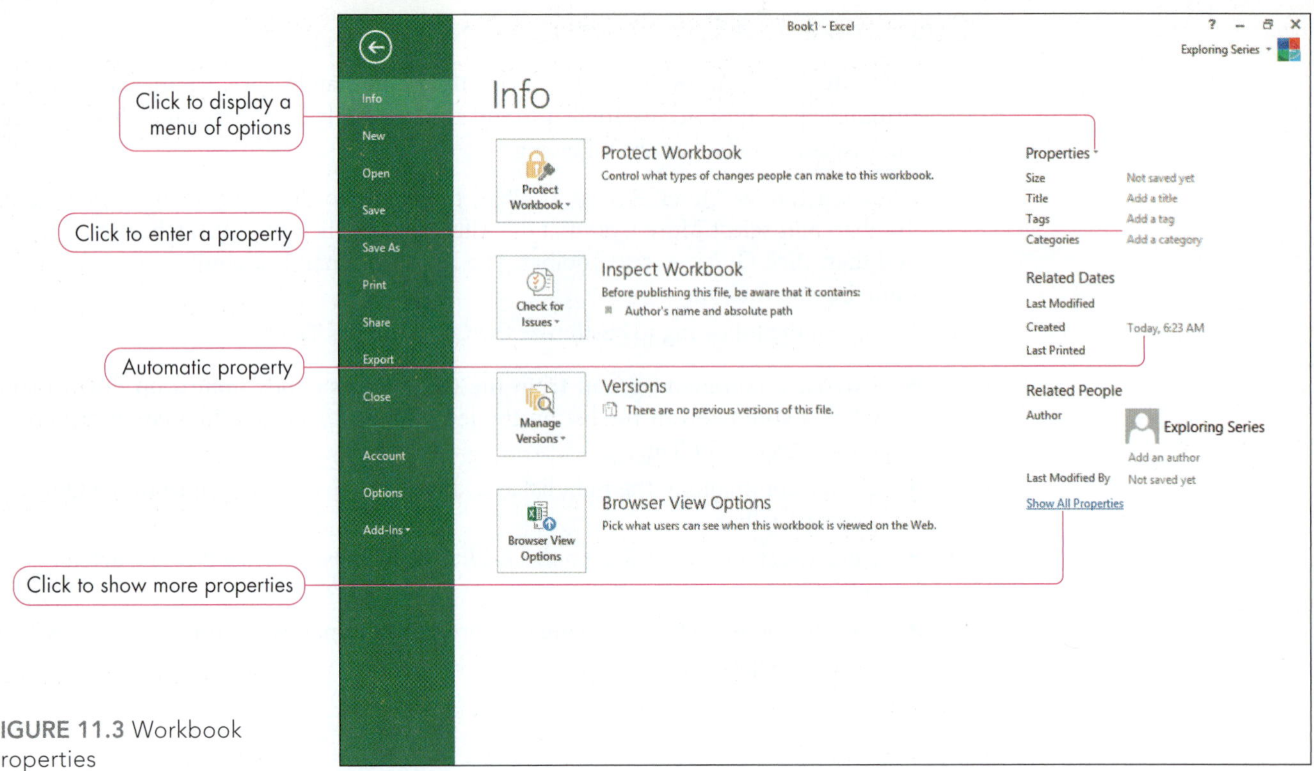

FIGURE 11.3 Workbook Properties

To view workbook properties, do the following. Click the File tab on the Ribbon to access the Backstage view. Click the Show All Properties link in the bottom-right corner to display additional properties, such as Company and Manager. When you display all the properties, the link changes to Show Fewer Properties. You can click Show Fewer Properties to display the original shortened list of properties again.

Use the Properties Dialog Box

The Properties dialog box provides more details than the property list. To display the Properties dialog box, click Properties on the right side of the Backstage view and select Advanced Properties. The dialog box name reflects the current workbook name, such as Marching Band Senior Dinner Properties (see Figure 11.4).

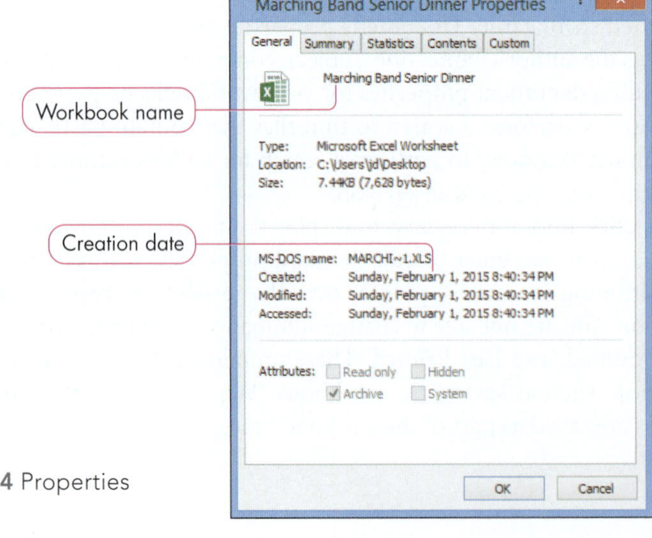

FIGURE 11.4 Properties Dialog Box

The dialog box contains five tabs to organize various properties:

STEP 3

- **General.** Displays the file name, file type, location, size, creation date, modification date, and last accessed date. In addition, it indicates the attributes, such as Read only or Hidden. General properties are created automatically and cannot be changed directly by the user.
- **Summary.** Displays properties the user can enter and change, such as title, subject, author, manager, company, category, keywords, and comments. Keywords are helpful to add as document properties because they help describe the document, and you can use keywords to search for files that contain particular keywords, such as when you enter keywords to conduct an Internet search.
- **Statistics.** Includes creation, modified, accessed, and printed dates. Also displays the author who last saved the file, revision number, and total editing time, if tracked.
- **Contents.** Displays the worksheet names contained in the workbook.
- **Custom.** Enables the user to create and maintain custom properties for the current workbook, such as Department, Project, and Purpose.

Show the Document Panel

STEP 4

You can display the Document Panel above the workbook so that you can view and edit properties while reviewing the workbook data. To do this:

1. Click the FILE tab, click Info, if necessary, and then click Properties.
2. Select Show Document Panel.
3. The Document Panel enables you to enter the Author, Title, Subject, Keywords, Category, Status, and Comments properties.
4. To remove the Document Panel, click the Close (X) button in the top-right corner of the Document Panel.

1. Why would you add custom tabs to the Ribbon? ***p. 595***
2. How do you add your author information to a Document's Properties? ***p. 595***
3. How do you show the Document Panel? ***p. 599***

Hands-On Exercises

1 Customization and Personalization

You want to personalize Microsoft Office on your computer so that your name will appear in the Author property on new files you create in any Microsoft Office 2013 program. In addition, you want to add some properties to the Marching Band Senior Dinner workbook.

Skills covered: Enter a User Name • Display and Add Properties • Add Advanced Properties • Display the Document Panel

STEP 1 » ENTER A USER NAME

Before working on the Marching Band Senior Dinner workbook, you want to enter your name as the user name for Microsoft Office 2013 on your computer.

a. Open *e11h1Dinner* and save it as **e11h1Dinner_LastFirst**.

> **TROUBLESHOOTING:** If you make any major mistakes in this exercise, you can close the file, open *e11h1Dinner* again, and then start this exercise over.

b. Click the **FILE tab** and click **Options**.

The Excel Options dialog box opens. General is the default category on the left side.

c. Select any existing text in the **User name box**, type your name, and then click **OK**. Save the workbook.

STEP 2 » DISPLAY AND ADD PROPERTIES

You want to display the document properties for the Marching Band Senior Dinner workbook. Because the workbook was created before you entered your name as the user name, you want to edit the Author property. In addition, you want to enter information about the Senior Dinner in the Title property. Refer to Figure 11.5 as you complete Step 2.

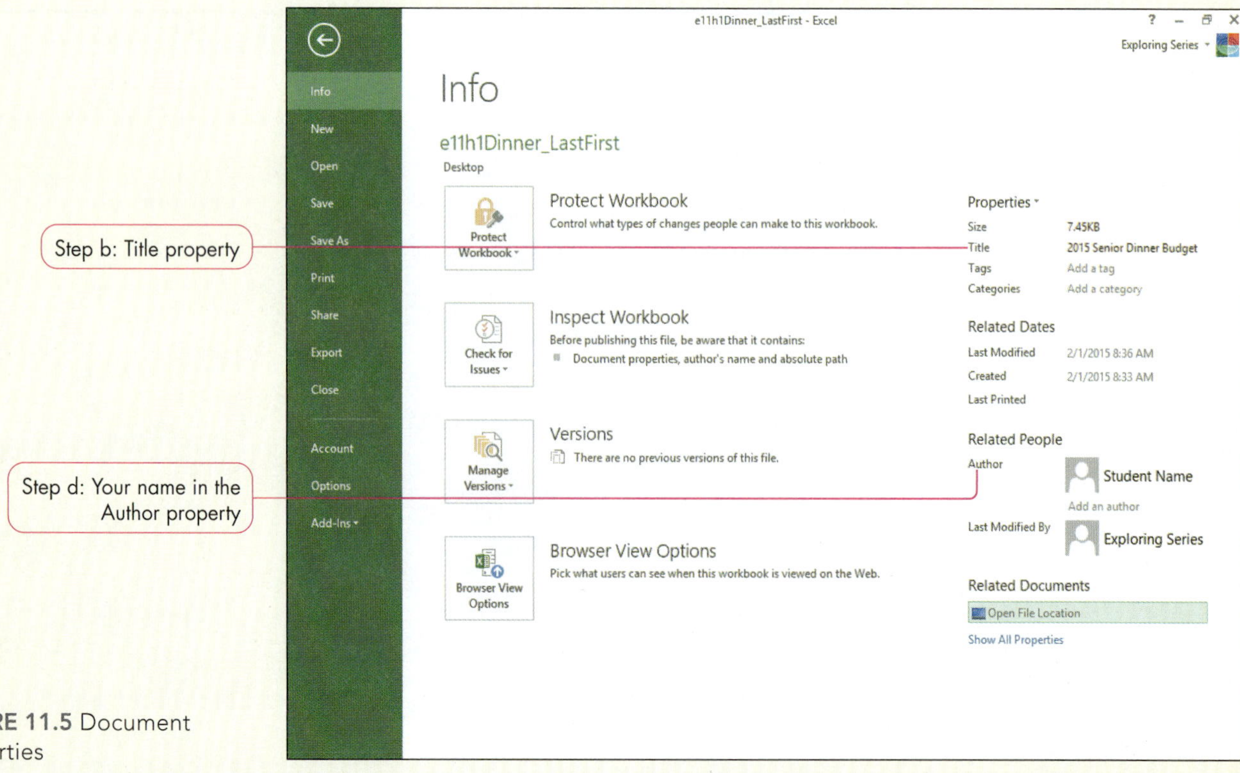

FIGURE 11.5 Document Properties

a. Click the **FILE tab**.

b. Click **Add a title** that displays next to the Title property, type **2015 Senior Dinner Budget**, and then press **Enter**.

The Title property displays the text you entered.

c. Right-click **Exploring Series**, the currently listed Author property, and select **Edit Property**.

The *Edit person* dialog box opens.

d. Select the text in the **Enter names or e-mail addresses box**, type your name, and then click **OK**.

e. Click the back arrow to exit the Backstage view and save the workbook.

STEP 3 » ADD ADVANCED PROPERTIES

You want to add some additional properties to the workbook. Specifically, you want to enter Chef Dan as the manager. In addition, you want to enter keywords, such as donations, ticket prices, and expenses. Refer to Figure 11.6 as you complete Step 3.

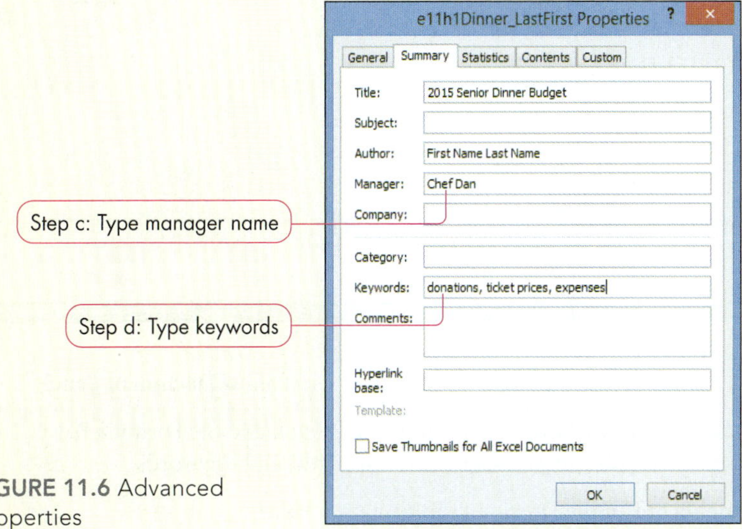

FIGURE 11.6 Advanced Properties

a. Click the **FILE tab**, if necessary, click **Info**, click **Properties**, and then select **Advanced Properties**.

The Properties dialog box for the current workbook opens.

b. Click the **Summary tab**, if necessary.

c. Click in the **Manager box** and type **Chef Dan**.

d. Click in the **Keywords box** and type **donations, ticket prices, expenses**.

e. Click **OK**, click the back arrow to leave the Backstage view, and then save the workbook.

STEP 4 ›› DISPLAY THE DOCUMENT PANEL

You want to look at the Senior Dinner worksheet data as you decide which additional properties to enter. To see the worksheet data and properties at the same time, you will display the Document Information Panel. Refer to Figure 11.7 as you complete Step 4.

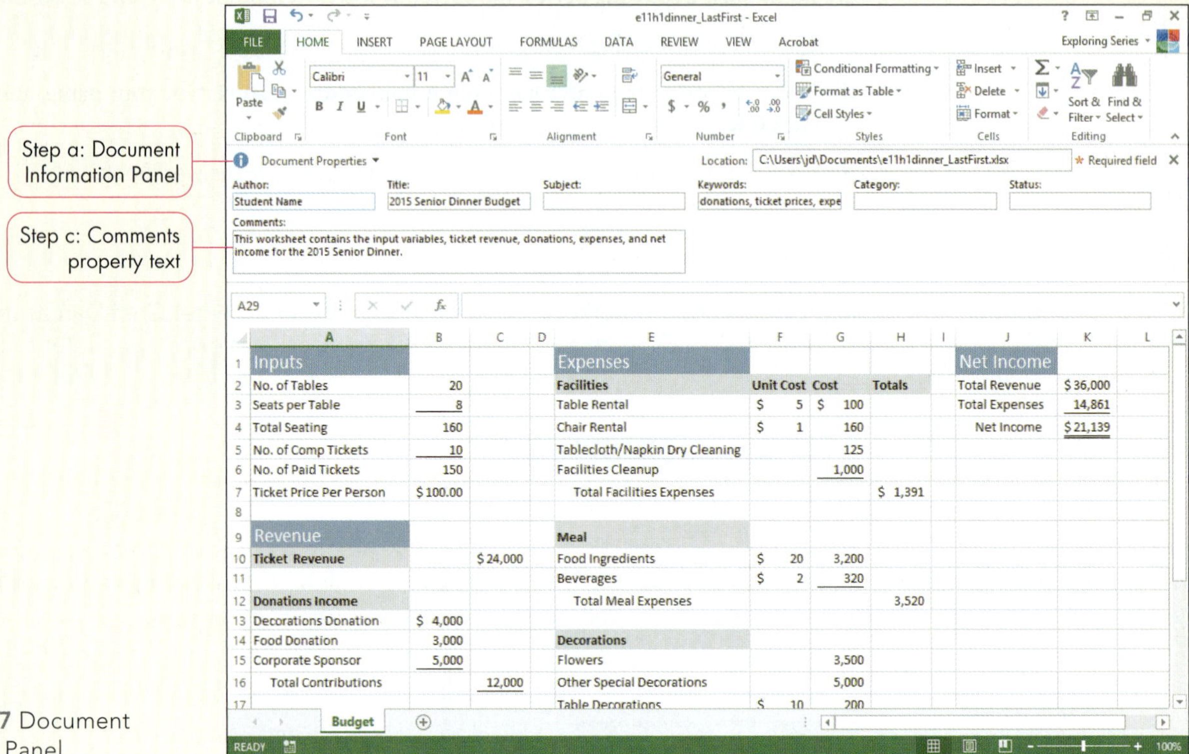

FIGURE 11.7 Document Information Panel

a. Click the **FILE tab**, if necessary, click **Properties**, and then select **Show Document Panel.**

The Document Information Panel displays between the Ribbon and the Formula Bar. It displays properties you have already set, such as Author, Title, and Keywords.

b. Click in the **Comments box** in the Document Information Panel.

c. Type **This worksheet contains the input variables, ticket revenue, donations, expenses, and net income for the 2015 Senior Dinner.**

d. Click **Close the Document Information Panel** in the top-right corner of the Document Information Panel and save the workbook.

You saved the comments along with the other properties.

e. Keep Excel open if you plan to continue with Hands-On Exercise 2. If not, exit Excel.

Collaboration

Collaboration is the process by which two or more individuals work together to achieve an outcome or goal by using software technology and features to share and edit the contents of a file. Often, the contents of a complex workbook result from the collaborative efforts of a team of people. Team members work together to plan, develop spreadsheets, conduct quantitative research, enter data, and analyze the results. For example, you are working with a team of students to prepare and finalize the Senior Dinner workbook. Together, your team obtains cost estimates, facilities expenses, meal expenses, decorations, publicity, projected donations, and revenue from ticket sales to prepare the budget worksheet.

You can share workbooks with other people and merge their workbooks into one workbook. In addition, Excel includes two key features that facilitate the collaborative process: comments and track changes. These features enable you and your team members to provide feedback and identify each other's suggested changes in a workbook.

In this section, you will learn how to share workbooks with others, compare and merge workbooks, and insert and edit comments. In addition, you will learn how to track changes made by team members and how to accept or reject their suggestions.

Sharing and Merging Workbooks

STEP 2»

One way to collaborate on a workbook is to create a shared workbook. In Excel, a ***shared workbook*** is a file that is designated as shareable and is stored on a network that is accessible to multiple people who can edit the workbook at the same time. Users can see changes made by other users. The person who creates the workbook and designates it as a shared workbook is the owner. The owner controls user access and resolves any conflicting changes made. To share a workbook, do the following:

1. Click the REVIEW tab and click Share Workbook in the Changes group to open the Share Workbook dialog box.
2. Click the *Allow changes by more than one user at the same time* check box and click the Advanced tab (see Figure 11.8) to specify the settings that control the shared workbook.
3. Specify how long, if at all, you want to keep a history of the changes made in the *Track changes* section.
4. Specify how often to update changes in the *Update changes* section.
5. Select one of the settings in the *Conflicting changes between users* section and click OK. Click OK if a message box opens informing you that the workbook will be saved.

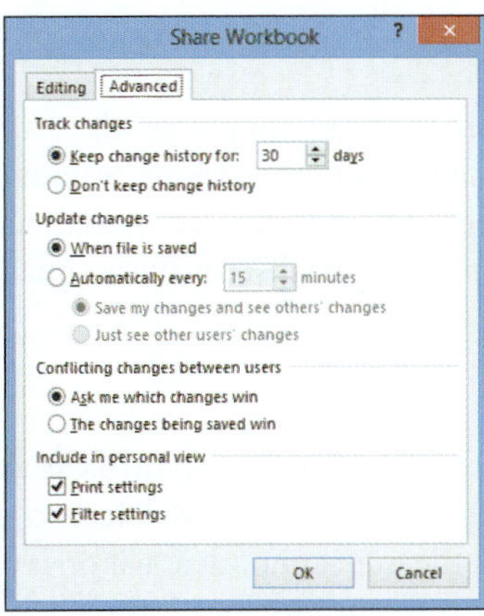

FIGURE 11.8 Share Workbook Dialog Box

After sharing a workbook on a network, you might want to know who is currently working on it. Click Share Workbook in the Changes group on the Review tab and then click the Editing tab. The *Who has this workbook open now* list displays names of people who have the workbook open (see Figure 11.9).

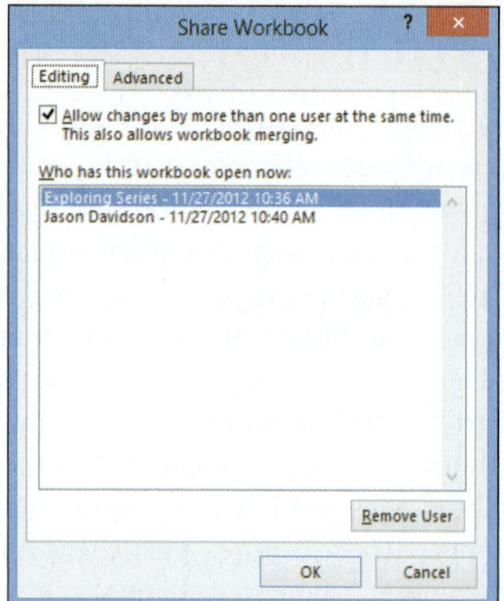

FIGURE 11.9 Share Workbook Dialog Box: Editing Tab

Shared Workbook Limitations

While sharing workbooks is a powerful collaboration tool, it does have limitations. Workbooks that contain tables may not be shared. Furthermore, the maximum number of users that can access the file at once is 256.

Understand Conflicts and Network Issues

Conflicts can arise when several users are working with shared workbooks. If multiple users attempt to change the same cell at the same time, a Resolve Conflicts dialog box opens for the second user (see Figure 11.10). The change is resolved based on the settings you select in the Share Workbook dialog box. When several people on a network share a workbook and make changes to it, the last person to make changes decides which changes to accept. This becomes a problematic situation when the last person is the least knowledgeable about Excel or the contents of a particular workbook.

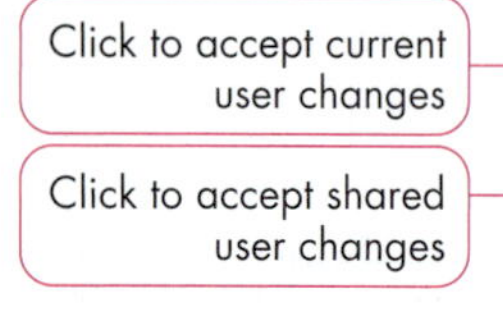

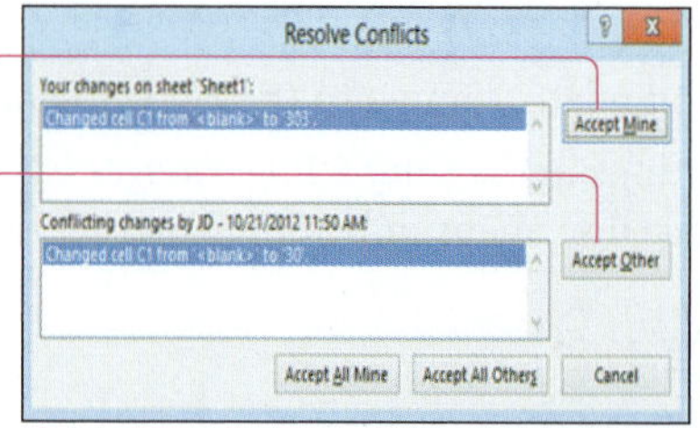

FIGURE 11.10 Resolve Conflicts Dialog Box

Issues with network permission also may arise when storing and using files on a network. The network permissions control who has rights to open and modify files. Furthermore, workbooks that have not been designated as shareable may still be able to be modified by various users. The next two paragraphs discuss these situations.

Network Permissions

A network drive may be set to Read-Only for some users and as Owner for other users. People who have Owner rights can open, save, delete, and modify files. People who have Read-Only rights can open a file but cannot delete it or save changes back to that location; however, they can save changes to another location such as their own hard drive or a flash drive. If you open a workbook from a network location of which you are not an owner, the title bar displays [Read-Only] after the file name.

Nonshareable Workbook

A workbook may be stored on a network that you can access, but the workbook might not be designated as a shared workbook. If another user has the workbook open and you try to open it, the *File in Use* dialog box will appear. Click Read Only to open the file in Read-Only mode, or click Notify to open the workbook in Read-Only mode and be notified when the workbook is no longer being used, or click Cancel to not open the workbook at this time. If you click Notify, the File Now Available dialog box opens when the other user closes the workbook.

Compare and Merge Workbooks

STEP 3» When you share a workbook with others, you might want to see what each person changed in the workbook instead of allowing immediate changes to the original workbook. You can use the *Compare and Merge Workbooks* command to combine the shared workbooks into one workbook so that you can compare the changes to decide which ones to keep. The *Compare and Merge* command works only with copies of a shared workbook; it does not work on workbooks that have not been designated as shared.

Each user must save a copy of the shared workbook with a unique name, such as *Senior Dinner Stephen* and *Senior Dinner Cheryl*, so that these names differ from the original file name. These files must be stored in the same folder that contains the shared workbook.

The *Compare and Merge* command is not on the Ribbon by default. However, you can add the command to either the Ribbon or the Quick Access Toolbar. To add the command to the Quick Access Toolbar, do the following:

1. Click Customize Quick Access toolbar on the right side of the Quick Access Toolbar and select More Commands. Alternatively, click the tab, click Options, and then click Quick Access Toolbar on the left side of the Excel Options dialog box.
2. Click the *Choose commands from* arrow and select *Commands Not in the Ribbon.*
3. Scroll through the list and click *Compare and Merge Workbooks.*
4. Click Add and click OK.

The *Compare and Merge Workbooks* command looks like a green circle on the Quick Access Toolbar when you open a shared workbook (see Figure 11.11). It appears dimmed when you work with regular workbooks.

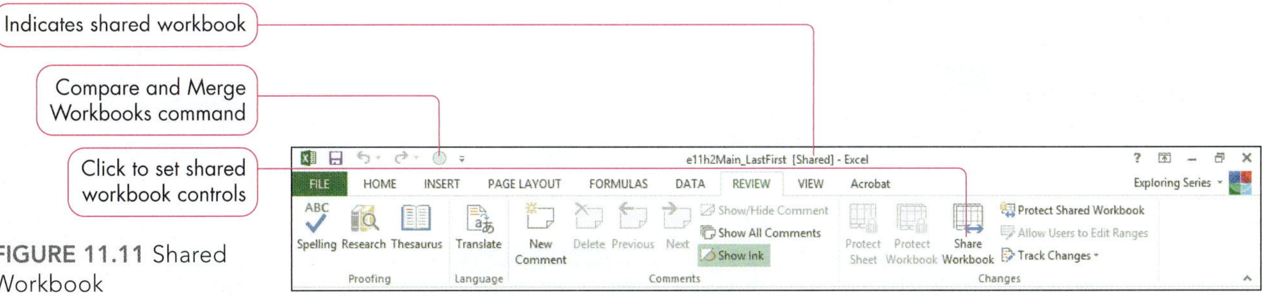

FIGURE 11.11 Shared Workbook

STEP 4» After adding the *Compare and Merge Workbooks* command to the Quick Access Toolbar, you can use it to merge copies of a shared workbook. To merge the workbooks, do the following:

1. Open the original shared workbook.
2. Click *Compare and Merge Workbooks* on the Quick Access Toolbar.
3. Click OK if the message box *This action will now save the workbook. Do you want to continue?* displays. The *Select Files to Merge Into Current Workbook* dialog box opens.
4. Click the file you want to merge. To select multiple files, press and hold Ctrl as you click the files. Click OK.

Changes are indicated by different color borders and top-left triangles, representing the different users who made changes to the shared workbook (see Figure 11.12).

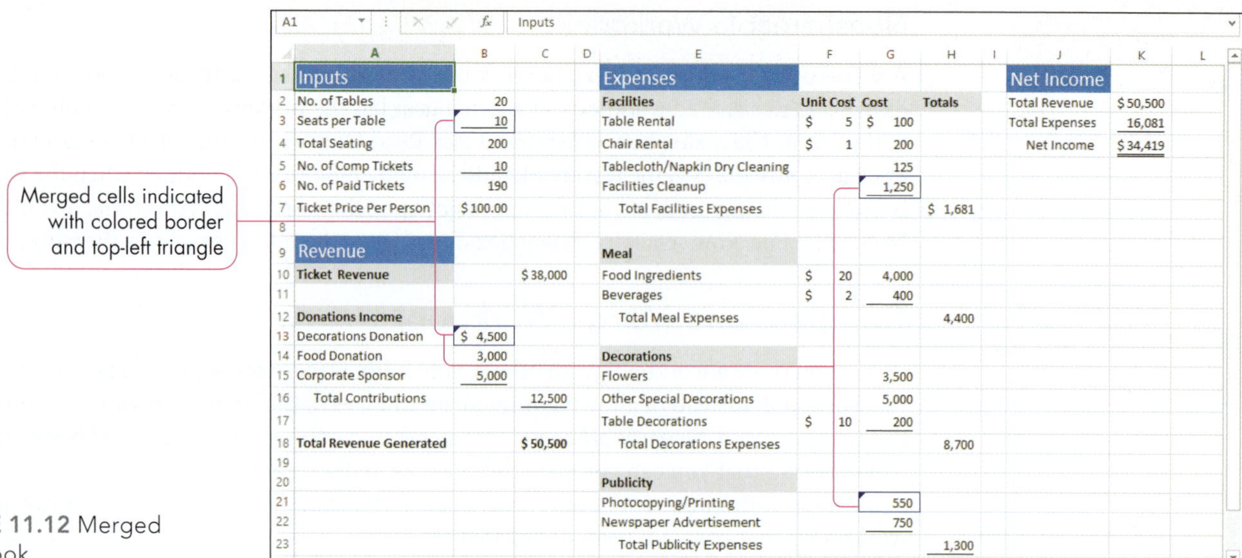

FIGURE 11.12 Merged Workbook

Inserting Comments

You can insert notes to yourself or make suggestions to another team member by inserting comments into a cell. A ***comment*** is a note or annotation to ask a question or provide a suggestion to another person about content in a worksheet cell. Comments help document a worksheet by providing additional information or clarification of the data, formula results, or labels. For example, in the Senior Dinner workbook, you want to insert the comment in cell C18 regarding income. To insert a comment for a particular cell, do the following:

1. Click the cell in which you want to insert the comment.
2. Click the REVIEW tab and click New Comment in the Comments group or right-click the cell and select Insert Comment. A red triangle, known as a ***comment indicator***, appears in the top-right corner of a cell containing a comment. A comment box appears, showing the default user name in bold.
3. Type the text that you want to appear in the comment box and click outside the comment box (see Figure 11.13).

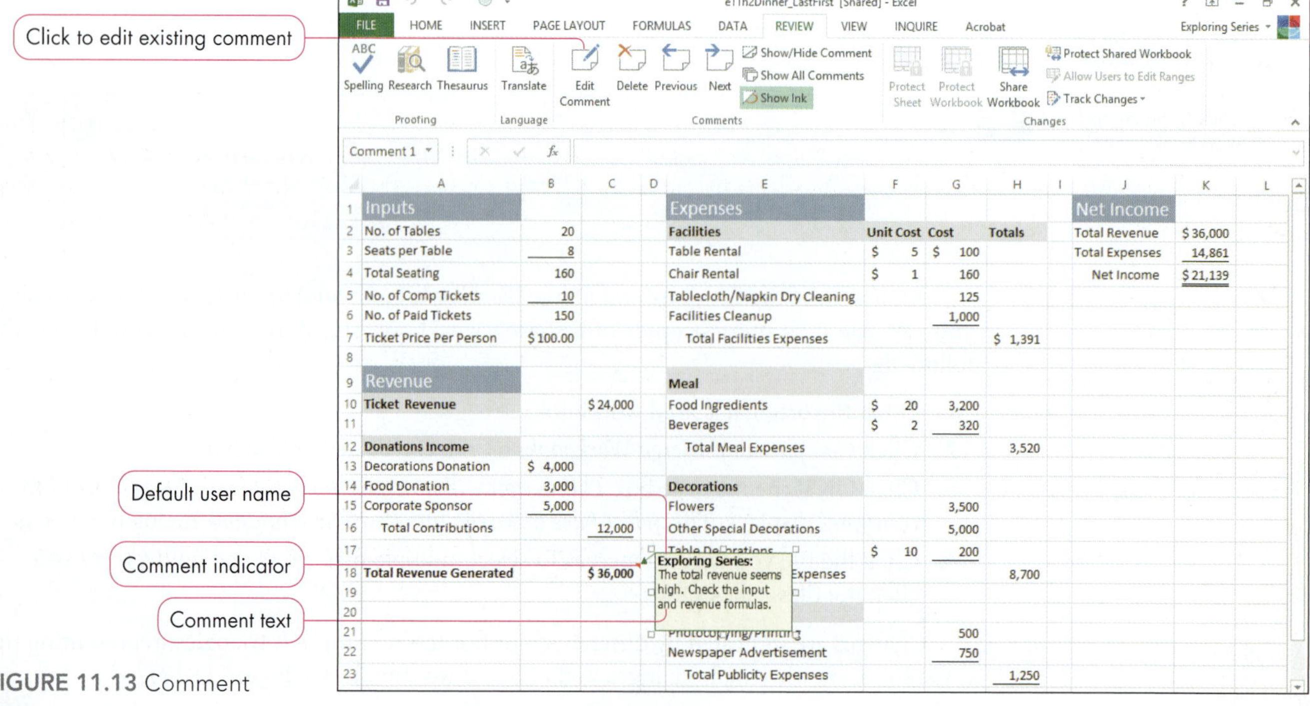

FIGURE 11.13 Comment

Show and Hide Comments

When you click outside the comment box, it closes, but the comment indicator remains in the cell. Position the mouse pointer over that cell to display the comment again. The comment in that cell remains onscreen until the cell selector is moved. Other comments remain hidden unless you show them. Table 11.2 lists steps to show and hide comments onscreen.

TABLE 11.2 Show and Hide Comments

Action	Ribbon Method	Shortcut Method
Show a comment	1. Click the cell containing the comment. 2. Click Show/Hide Comment in the Comments group on the Review tab.	1. Right-click the cell containing the comment. 2. Select Show/Hide Comments.
Hide a comment	1. Click the cell containing the comment. 2. Click Show/Hide Comment in the Comments group.	1. Right-click the cell containing the comment. 2. Select Hide Comment.
Display or hide all comments in the entire workbook	1. Click Show All Comments in the Comments group.	Not applicable

Click Previous in the Comments group on the Review tab to go to the cell containing the previous comment, or click Next to go to the next comment. When you click these commands, Excel goes to the respective cell and displays the comment box.

Comment Box

If the comment box obstructs the view of a cell you would like to see, it can be repositioned by clicking the outer edge of the comment box and dragging to a new location. You can also drag a selection handle on the outer edge of a comment box to increase or decrease its size.

Edit and Delete Comments

STEP 1》 You may need to edit the comment text if information changes. You might have originally inserted a general comment such as *Some decorations will be donated.* A few days later, another team member identifies a supply store called Party America that is willing to donate some decorations. Therefore, you can edit the comment to display *Party America will provide $500 worth of decorations.* To edit a comment, do the following:

1. Click the cell that contains the comment you want to edit.
2. Click the REVIEW tab. Click Edit Comment in the Comments group or right-click the cell and select Edit Comment.
3. Edit the comment text.
4. Format the comment text, if desired. Select the comment text, right-click the selected text, select Format Comment, select formats in the Format Comment dialog box, and then click OK. Alternatively, select comment text and apply font attributes, such as bold and font size, from the Font group on the HOME tab.
5. Click outside the comment box when you are done.

You can delete a comment if you no longer need it. To delete a comment, do the following:

1. Click the cell that contains the comment you want to delete.
2. Click the REVIEW tab and click Delete in the Comments group, or right-click the cell and select Delete Comment. Excel immediately deletes the comment without providing a warning. If you need to restore the comment, immediately click Undo on the Quick Access Toolbar.

Removing All Comments

To remove all comments at the same time, press Ctrl+G to display the Go To dialog box, click Special, make sure Comments is selected, and then click OK. This selects all cells containing comments in the current worksheet. Click the Home tab, click Clear in the Editing group, and then select Clear Comments.

Print Comments

When you print a worksheet, comments do not print by default. The Sheet tab in the Page Setup dialog box contains two options for printing comments. The default Comments setting is (None). If you choose *As displayed on sheet*, the visible comment boxes appear where they are located onscreen. Hidden comments do not print. Choose *At end of sheet* to print the comments on a separate page (see Figure 11.14). This printout includes the cell reference and the comment text for each comment on the active worksheet, even if the comments are hidden.

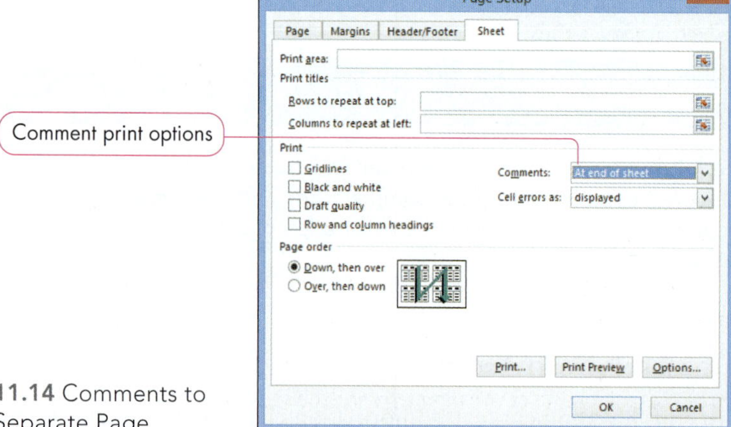

FIGURE 11.14 Comments to Print on Separate Page

Tracking Changes

Although comments are helpful for posing questions or suggestions, you may want to create a log that identifies changes you and other people make in a workbook. ***Track Changes*** is a feature that records particular changes made in a workbook. It tracks changes to cell contents, row and column insertions and deletions, and copied and moved data. With several team members contributing to the Senior Dinner workbook, you can activate Change Tracking to see who makes what change, such as changing the value of the price per person from \$75 to \$100.

Excel does not track all changes. For example, it does not track formatting changes such as applying bold or Accounting Number Format or adjusting column width or row height. Because Excel does not track these types of changes, keep a copy of the original workbook. You can compare the original workbook to the workbook your team members changed to see if they made any formatting changes.

To activate the Change Tracking feature, do the following:

1. Click the REVIEW tab.
2. Click Track Changes in the Changes group and select Highlight Changes. The Highlight Changes dialog box opens.
3. Click the *Track changes while editing. This also shares your workbook* check box. The remaining options are now available (see Figure 11.15).
4. Click OK. If prompted, enter the name of the workbook and click Save.

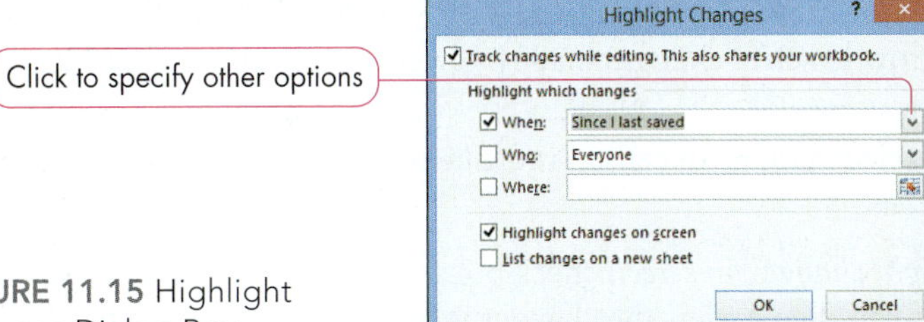

FIGURE 11.15 Highlight Changes Dialog Box

You can track changes only in a shared workbook. When you activate Track Changes, [Shared] appears on the right side of the file name on the title bar. Shared workbooks are often stored on a network server so that several people can simultaneously edit the workbook. However, you can track changes in a workbook stored on a local hard drive or external storage device.

A small triangle appears in the top left corner when an edit is made and Track Changes is enabled. When you position the mouse pointer on that cell, a yellow message box similar to a comment box displays the name of the person who made the change, the date and time the change was made, and the type of change made.

When you share a workbook or activate Change Tracking, some Excel features are disabled, indicated by dimmed commands on the Ribbon. You cannot do the following tasks when you turn on Change Tracking:

- Merge cells together or split merged cells into several cells.
- Add or change conditional formats.
- Format a range as an Excel table.
- Delete, protect, or unprotect worksheets.
- Change the tab color for worksheets.
- Create or change charts, PivotTables, PivotCharts, shapes, pictures, objects, and hyperlinks.
- Apply, change, or remove passwords.
- Import or link external data, display connections, or edit links.
- Add, modify, or remove data validation rules.
- Create, edit, delete, or view scenarios.
- Group, ungroup, or subtotal tables.
- Edit a macro, insert controls, and assign a macro to a control.

TIP Turning Off Change Tracking

After reviewing the changes, you can turn off Change Tracking by clicking Track Changes in the Changes group, selecting Highlight Changes, deselecting the *Track changes while editing* check box in the Highlight Changes dialog box, and then clicking OK. If you turn off Change Tracking, the workbook is no longer shared, the history of changes made is lost, and other users who are sharing the workbook will not be able to save the changes they have made.

Highlight Changes

STEP 5»

When changes are made with Change Tracking on, each cell changed contains a colored triangle in the top-left corner. If you close the workbook and open it again, the triangles indicating changes are hidden. To display the triangles, do the following:

1. Click Track Changes in the Changes group on the REVIEW tab.
2. Select Highlight Changes.
3. Select which changes to highlight:
    - Click the When arrow to select *Since I last saved*, *All*, *Not yet reviewed*, or *Since date*.
    - Click the Who arrow to select changes made by Everyone, Everyone but Me, you, or another person.
    - Click Where and select a range of cells to indicate whether changes are made to those respective cells.

    By default, the *Highlight changes on screen* check box is selected to ensure that changes display onscreen. You can then review the changes in any sequence by positioning the mouse pointer over the cells containing blue triangles. Click *List changes on a new sheet* to create a list of changes made on a new worksheet.
4. Click OK.

Accept and Reject Changes

STEP 6»

You can view changes in sequence through a dialog box that enables you to accept or reject changes. When you accept a change, the change is no longer indicated by the colored triangle; the change is accepted as part of the worksheet. When you reject a change, the suggested change is removed from the worksheet. For example, if someone made a change by deleting a row and you reject that change, the row is restored. To accept and reject changes, do the following:

1. Click Track Changes in the Changes group on the REVIEW tab. If you have not saved the workbook, you will be prompted to do so.
2. Select Accept/Reject Changes. The *Select Changes to Accept or Reject* dialog box opens (see Figure 11.16).
3. Click the check boxes for the type of changes to accept and reject and specify their settings. Click OK. The *Accept or Reject Changes* dialog box opens (see Figure 11.17), displaying the change number, who made the change, and what the person changed.
4. Click Accept to accept the change, click Reject to reject that change and move to the next change, click Accept All to accept all changes made, or click Reject All to reject all changes made. The dialog box closes automatically after all changes have been either accepted or rejected.

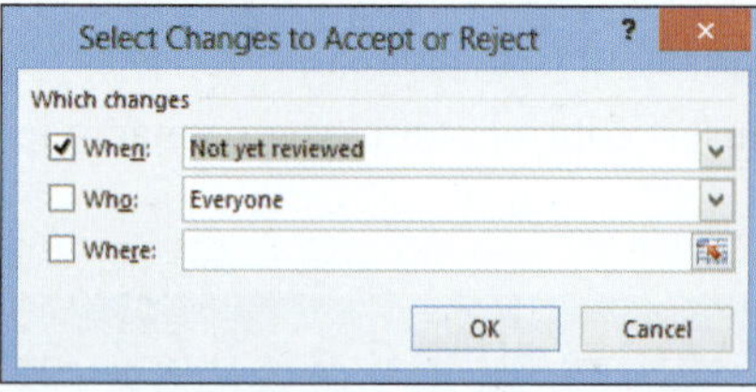

FIGURE 11.16 Select Changes to Accept or Reject Dialog Box

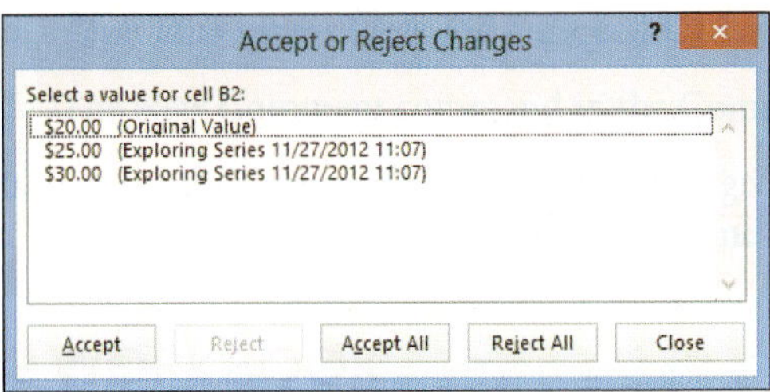

FIGURE 11.17 Accept or Reject Changes Dialog Box

Before accepting or rejecting changes, you might want to create a list of changes in a ***history worksheet***. Within the Highlight Changes dialog box, click *List changes on a new sheet*. When you click OK, Excel creates a History worksheet that lists the changes made to the workbook, such as value changes, inserted and deleted columns and rows, and some formula changes. Note that changes made to formulas that are dependent on other cells, also known as dependent values, are not listed. The log does not track font changes or hiding/unhiding columns or rows. Figure 11.18 shows a change log in a new worksheet named History. The change log shows the dates, times, new and original values, and other details about all the changes. The History worksheet is temporary; Excel removes it when you close the workbook.

Action Number	Date	Time	Who	Change	Sheet	Range	New Value	Old Value	Action Type	Losing Action
1	11/27/2012	11:07 AM	Exploring Series	Cell Change	Budget	B2	$25.00	$20.00		
2	11/27/2012	11:07 AM	Exploring Series	Cell Change	Budget	B2	$30.00	$25.00		
3	11/27/2012	11:13 AM	Exploring Series	Cell Change	Budget	B13	$5,000.00	$4,000.00		
4	11/27/2012	11:13 AM	Exploring Series	Cell Change	Budget	F10	$15.00	$20.00		
5	11/27/2012	11:13 AM	Exploring Series	Cell Change	Budget	F3	$10.00	$5.00		
6	11/27/2012	11:14 AM	Exploring Series	Cell Change	Budget	B2	$25.00	$30.00		
7	11/27/2012	11:14 AM	Exploring Series	Cell Change	Budget	B13	$4,500.00	$5,000.00		
8	11/27/2012	11:14 AM	Exploring Series	Cell Change	Budget	F10	$20.00	$15.00		
9	11/27/2012	11:14 AM	Exploring Series	Cell Change	Budget	F3	$15.00	$10.00		

FIGURE 11.18 Change Log

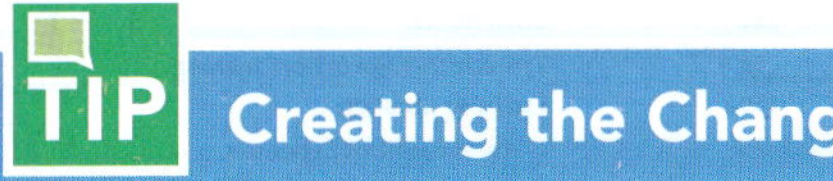

TIP Creating the Change Log

The History worksheet is deleted when you save a workbook; however, you can copy and paste the values into a new worksheet that will remain when the workbook is saved.

Quick Concepts

1. Why do you insert a comment? ***p. 606***
2. How do you edit or delete a comment? ***p. 607***
3. What are the benefits of Track Changes? ***p. 608***

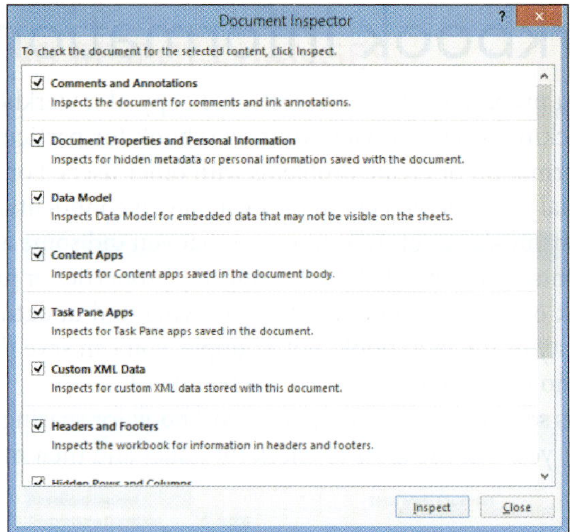

FIGURE 11.24 Document Inspector

Check Accessibility

Many organizations provide electronic documents for the public to download from Web sites or as e-mail attachments. With a diverse audience of people using technology today, you should ensure your documents are accessible by everyone. The ***Accessibility Checker*** reviews your files for potential issues that could hinder the ability of users who access your public files and then alerts you to these issues so that you can address them. The Accessibility Checker identifies the following types of issues, among other issues:

- Has alt text been assigned to objects so that the object is described when the pointer hovers over it?
- Do tables contain header rows?
- Do tables contain merged cells?
- Do hyperlinks contain meaningful text as ScreenTips?

Accessibility Checker provides three types of feedback for each issue:

- **Error.** Content that creates extreme difficulty or impossibility for persons with disabilities to view correctly.
- **Warning.** Content that is difficult for users to comprehend.
- **Tip.** Content that is understandable but could be presented or organized differently to maximize comprehension.

STEP 2 ›

To use the Accessibility Checker, do the following:

1. Click the FILE tab and click Info.
2. Click *Check for Issues* and select Check Accessibility. The Accessibility Checker task pane opens on the right side of the worksheet window, showing the results.
3. Click a listed issue to see feedback in the Additional Information window. This window tells you why you should fix the problem and how to fix it.

Check Compatibility

When you provide an Excel workbook for others to use, they may have an older version of Excel on their computers. Because each new version of Excel contains new features, you may be using features that are not compatible with previous versions. For example, you may be using a conditional formatting feature or an updated function, such as the newly added Web functions, that was not available in previous Excel versions. You can use ***Compatibility Checker*** to check the workbook contents to see what data and features are not compatible with previous versions. To use Compatibility Checker, do the following:

1. Click the FILE tab and click Info.
2. Click *Check for Issues* and select Check Compatibility. The Microsoft Excel - Compatibility Checker dialog box opens, showing a list of issues (see Figure 11.25). You have the option to check compatibility against Excel 97-2003, 2007, and 2010. By default, all three options are selected.
3. Click the *Check compatibility when saving this workbook* check box if you want to check compatibility every time you save the workbook. Leave the check box blank if you do not want to check the workbook automatically upon saving.
4. Click *Copy to New Sheet* to create a report on a separate worksheet that lists the issues.
5. Click OK after reviewing the issues so that you can address them in the workbook.

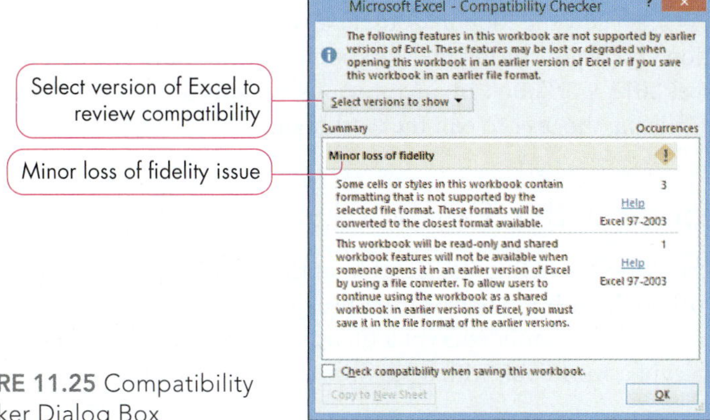

FIGURE 11.25 Compatibility Checker Dialog Box

Unsupported Features

Look up *Check file compatibility with earlier versions* in Help to find out about Excel 2013 features that are not supported in earlier versions. This Help topic provides details about significant loss of functionality, what it means, and what to do to solve the problem.

Protecting a Workbook

You can protect a workbook to ensure the integrity of its contents. Workbook protection includes marking the workbook as final with an easy-to-remove read-only mode and inserting a digital signature that ensures the workbook's integrity and that it has not been changed since it was signed electronically. The type of protection you add depends on the level of security you need to place on the workbook contents.

Mark a Workbook as Final

STEP 4 › After completing a workbook, you may want to communicate that it is a final version of the workbook. The *Mark as Final* command communicates that it is a final version and makes the file read-only. Excel prevents users from typing in and editing the workbook, displays a *Marked as Final* icon to the right of Ready on the status bar, and sets the Status document property as Final. If a workbook is shared, you cannot mark it as final; you must first remove the sharing attribute. To mark a workbook as final, do the following:

1. Click the FILE tab and click Info.
2. Click Protect Workbook and select *Mark as Final*. A warning message box appears, stating *This workbook will be marked as final and then saved.*

3. Click OK. If you have note saved the file, you will be prompted to do so. Excel then displays an information message box (see Figure 11.26).
4. Click OK. The Permissions area of the Backstage view displays *This workbook has been marked as final to discourage editing.*

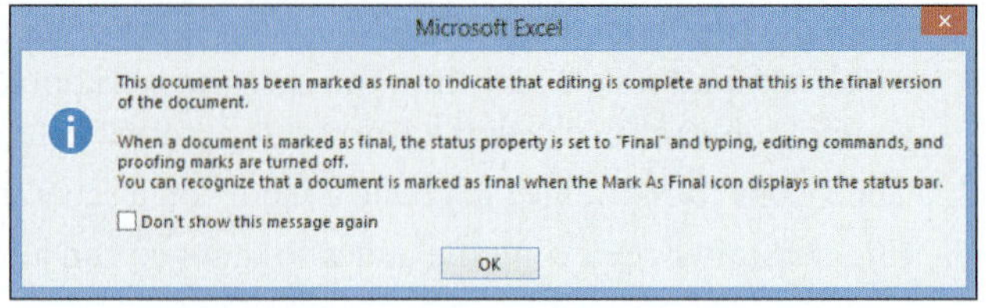

FIGURE 11.26 *Mark as Final* Verification Box

The Message Bar appears below the Ribbon. A user can click Edit Anyway to remove the marked-as-final indication and begin editing the workbook. Furthermore, if a person opens the marked-as-final Excel 2013 workbook in any previous version of Excel, the read-only attribute is removed, permitting the user to edit the workbook.

Encrypt a Workbook with a Password

You can protect a workbook by restricting its access to authorized people only. To do this, you can encrypt the workbook with a password the user is required to enter in order to open the workbook. However, you cannot encrypt a file with a password if you have already marked it as final. To encrypt a workbook with a password, do the following:

1. Click the FILE tab and click Info.
2. Click Protect Workbook and select *Encrypt with Password*. The Encrypt Document dialog box opens (see Figure 11.27) so that you can enter a password in the Password box. If you forget the password, you cannot recover the workbook.
3. Type a password and click OK to display the Confirm Password dialog box. Type the same password in the *Reenter password* box and click OK. The Permissions area of the Backstage view displays *A password is required to open this workbook.*

FIGURE 11.27 Encrypt Document Dialog Box

When you attempt to open a password-protected workbook, the Password dialog box opens. Enter the password and click OK.

Problems with Forgotten Passwords

You should make a note of passwords you use for saving files. If you forget a password, you will not be able to open the file.

Add a Digital Signature

A ***digital signature*** is an electronic, encrypted notation that stamps a document to authenticate the contents, confirms that a particular person authorized it, and marks the workbook as final. Use a digital signature to ensure that a workbook is authentic and that the content has not been changed since the signature was added. Your digital signature is valid until you make changes and resave the file. For example, an auditor might add a digital signature to a company's year-end financial statements to authenticate that no changes have been made after the audit.

To digitally sign a workbook, you must obtain a certificate from a certified authority who can verify your signature. If you review the links at the Microsoft Office Marketplace Web site, you can choose a signature service. This is similar to having your signature notarized. Digital signatures may be either visible or invisible.

An invisible digital signature means that a signature is not added as a graphic object in the workbook. The digital signature is an electronic tag or attribute added to the workbook. For more information on creating a digital signature through a third-party certificate authority, complete the following steps:

1. Click the FILE tab and click Info.
2. Click Protect Workbook and select *Add a Digital Signature*. If you have not saved the file, you will be prompted to do so. The Microsoft Excel message box appears. Click Signature Services from the Office Marketplace to find a service to issue a digital ID for you, or click OK to continue.

Add a Signature Line

Instead of creating an invisible digital signature, you may want to include a signature line. A ***signature line*** is similar to a signature line in a printed document, such as a contract or legal document. In Microsoft Office 2013, an author can create a signature line to request someone type a signature, select an image containing a signature, or write a signature using a tablet PC. When the person electronically signs the document, Microsoft Office adds a digital signature indicating the time signed as a means to authenticate the person's identity. In addition, Microsoft Office designates the file as read-only and displays the Marked as Final Message Bar. To create a signature line, do the following:

STEP 3»

1. Click the INSERT tab and click Signature Line in the Text group. If the Microsoft Excel message box opens, click OK. The Signature Setup dialog box opens (see Figure 11.28).
2. Enter information in the appropriate boxes and click OK.
3. Repeat the process to create additional signature lines in the same workbook.

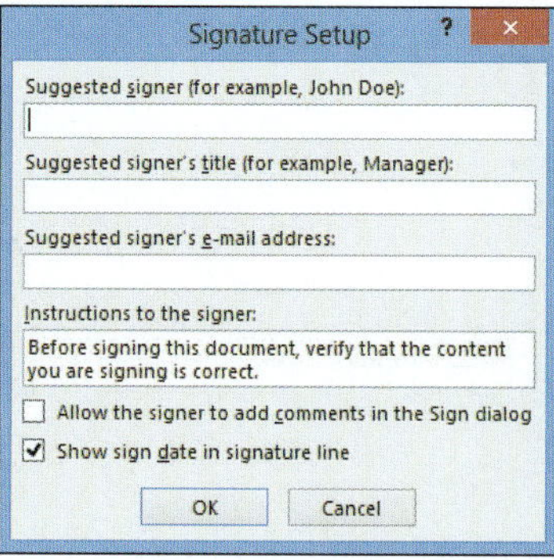

FIGURE 11.28 Signature Setup Dialog Box

When you save the workbook and open it again, the Signatures Message Bar appears, stating *This document needs to be signed.* Note, you only receive this message after closing and reopening the workbook. Click View Signatures to complete the process. To sign the document, do the following:

1. Right-click the signature line and select Sign. If the Microsoft Excel message box opens, click OK.

2. Add your signature using one of the following methods:
   - Type your name next to the X if you want a printed version of your signature.
   - Click Select Image on the right side of the dialog box, find and select an image file of your signature in the Select Signature Image dialog box, and then click Select.
   - Use the inking feature on a tablet PC to add a handwritten signature.
3. Click Sign.

   The Signatures button, which looks like a red ribbon, appears on the status bar.

1. What is the functionality of the Document Inspector? ***p. 617***
2. Why is it important to check compatibility? ***p. 618***
3. How do you edit a workbook that has been marked as final? ***p. 620***

Hands-On Exercises

3 Workbook Information

To prepare your Senior Dinner budget workbook to share the updates with other students, chefs, and donors, you need to check for and resolve issues. Then you will mark the budget as being final and add a digital signature.

Skills covered: Use the Document Inspector • Check Accessibility and Compatibility • Add a Signature Line • Mark as Final

STEP 1 » USE THE DOCUMENT INSPECTOR

Your budget may contain some items that you do not want to appear in the workbook you distribute to others. In particular, you want to make sure all comments are removed. Refer to Figure 11.29 as you complete Step 1.

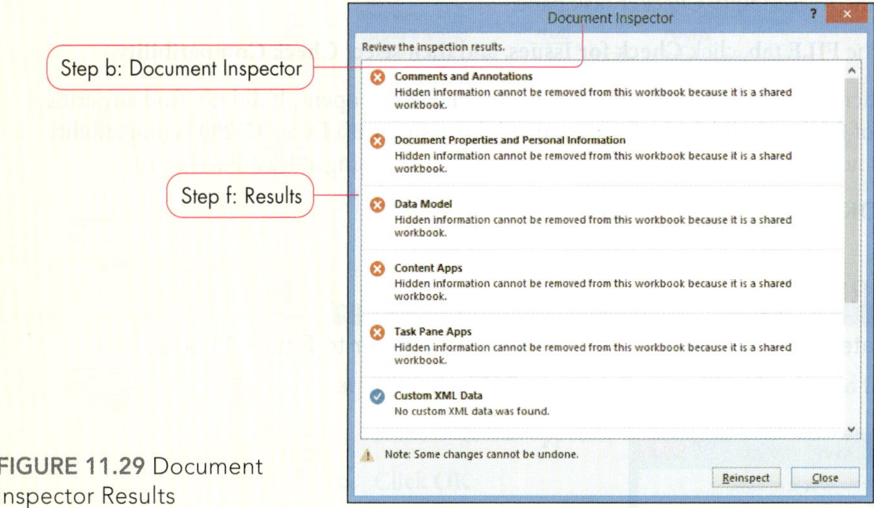

FIGURE 11.29 Document Inspector Results

a. Open *e11h2Main_LastFirst* and save it as **e11h3Main_LastFirst**.

> **TROUBLESHOOTING:** If you closed and reopened *e11h2Main_LastFirst*, make sure the file is still shareable, as indicated by [Shared] on the title bar. If not, complete the process to share the workbook again that was detailed in Hands-On Exercise 2, Step 2.

b. Click the **FILE tab**, click **Info** if necessary, click **Check for Issues**, and then select **Inspect Document**.

   The Document Inspector dialog box opens.

c. Ensure all the check boxes are selected and click **Inspect**.

   The Document Inspector results indicate that some hidden information cannot be removed because the workbook is shared.

d. Click **Close** to close the Document Inspector and click the back arrow to return to the spreadsheet.

e. Click the **REVIEW tab**, click **Share Workbook** in the Changes group, deselect the **Allow changes by more than one user at the same time check box**, and then click **OK**. Click **Yes** when a message box opens.

Workbook Distribution

Some people prefer different formats for files they receive. While you are primarily working in Excel 2013, you might need to save a file in other formats for the convenience of other users. Excel provides the means for you to change the file type and create different types of files from your Excel 2013 workbooks. If you do not provide data in a file format your recipients can manipulate, the data are useless to them. After saving a workbook, you are ready to distribute it. Excel provides a variety of distribution methods so that you can provide others with easy access to your workbooks, whether that is as an e-mail attachment or uploaded to a server.

In this section, you will learn how to save a workbook in different file formats and how to send the workbook to others electronically.

Saving a Workbook in Different Formats

When you save a workbook in Excel 2013, you save the workbook in the default 2013 file format, which ends with the .xlsx extension. Excel 2010 and 2007 also save files in the .xlsx format. However, previous versions of Excel saved workbooks with the .xls extension. The primary reasons that the .xlsx file format is better than the .xls format are that the .xlsx files are smaller in size because the .xlsx format uses a built-in compression feature, and content images and macros are stored separately to enable increased probability of data recovery if a file becomes corrupted. In addition, any Office version beginning with 2007 uses XML (eXtensible Markup Language), a standardized way of tagging data so that programs can automatically extract data from workbooks.

Although you use the default .xlsx file format when you save most Excel 2013 workbooks, you might need to save a workbook in another format. Excel enables you to save workbooks in many different formats. Table 11.3 lists and describes some of the most commonly used file formats.

TABLE 11.3 File Formats

Format	Extension	Description
Excel Workbook	.xlsx	Default Office Excel 2007–2013 XML-based file format.
Excel 97-2003 Workbook	.xls	Binary file format used for Excel 97-2003 workbooks.
OpenDocument Spreadsheet	.ods	Format for spreadsheet applications such as Google Docs and OpenOffice.
Excel Template	.xltx	The default Office Excel 2007–2013 file format for an Excel template.
Excel Macro-Enabled Workbook	.xlsm	XML-based and macro-enabled format for Excel 2007–2013.
Excel Binary Workbook	.xlsb	Binary file format for Excel 2007–2013.
Text (Tab delimited)	.txt	Tab-delimited format so that the file contents can be used with other Microsoft Windows programs. Uses the tab character as a delimiter to separate data into columns. Saves only the active worksheet.
CSV (Comma delimited)	.csv	Comma-delimited text file for use with other Windows programs. Uses the comma as a delimiter to separate data into columns. Saves only the active worksheet.
Formatted Text (Space delimited)	.prn	Lotus space-delimited format. Saves only the active worksheet.
Portable Document Format	.pdf	File format that preserves formatting and prevents changes.

TIP **Change File Type**

As an alternative method to change the file format, you can choose Change File Type from the Export menu in the Backstage area. This will list all export options and corresponding details.

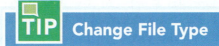

Save a Workbook for Previous Excel Versions

More people are upgrading from Excel 2007 or Excel 2010 to Excel 2013. However, some people will continue to use previous versions of Excel. You can open a workbook saved in Excel 2003 format within Excel 2013 and save it in the .xlsx format. However, Excel 2013 workbooks are not by default backward compatible with Excel 2003 and previous versions. If you need to send a workbook to someone who is using a previous version of Excel, you can save the workbook in the Excel 97-2003 Workbook format (.xls) by following these steps:

1. Click the FILE tab and click Export.
2. Click Change File Type, located on the left side of the Export menu. The Backstage view displays a third column of File Types (see Figure 11.32).
3. Select Excel 97-2003 Workbook in the *Change File type* list.
4. Navigate to the folder in which you want to store the file and type an appropriate name in the *File name* box.
5. Click Save in the Save As dialog box to save the workbook.

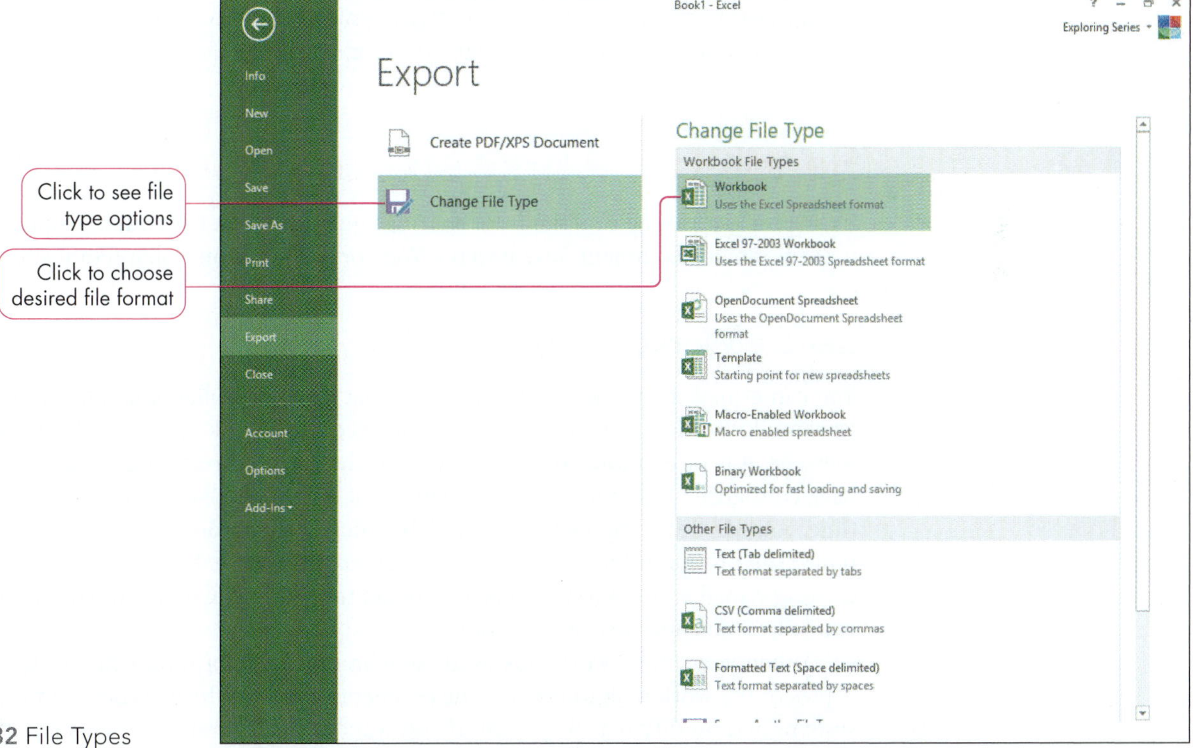

FIGURE 11.32 File Types

Save a Workbook as a PDF File

STEP 1

Sometimes you may want to save an Excel workbook so those who do not have Excel can display and print the file. The most common and best way to enable non–Excel users to display and print Excel workbooks is to save the Excel file in ***Portable Document Format (PDF)***, a standard file format that preserves the formatted data, including images, as originally intended in the source program and ensures that other people cannot edit the original data or see proprietary formulas. People can view PDF files correctly on various computer systems and platforms, even if the user does not have the source program. Saving a workbook as a PDF file saves the formatting that you used in an Excel workbook and enables non-Windows users to display and print the file because Adobe Systems Incorporated designed PDF as a universal file format. To save a file in the PDF format, do the following:

1. Click the FILE tab and click Export.
2. Click Create PDF/XPS Document in the *Export* section. The Backstage view displays a third column of *Create a PDF/XPS Document*.
3. Click Create PDF/XPS in the third column to open the *Publish as PDF or XPS* dialog box.
4. Click the *Save as type* arrow and select PDF if it is not already selected.
5. Navigate to the folder in which you want to store the file and type an appropriate name in the *File name* box. If you want to see how the file looks in PDF format after publishing it, click the *Open file after publishing* check box.
6. Click Options to open the Options dialog box. Select appropriate settings, such as the page range, and click OK.
7. Click Publish in the *Publish as PDF or XPS* dialog box to save the workbook in PDF format.

Print to PDF

If you have Adobe Acrobat (not just Adobe Reader) or other third-party applications that create PDF files installed, you can create a file through the Print options. Click the File tab, click Print, click the Printer arrow, select Adobe PDF, and then click Print. You will be prompted to enter a file name for the PDF file.

Sending a Workbook to Others

Excel provides multiple methods for sharing your workbook with other people. You can send it as an e-mail attachment, save it to the Web, or publish it on a SharePoint site.

Send a Workbook by E-Mail

You can e-mail the workbook to others so that they can collaborate on the contents of the workbook. While it is possible to send an Excel workbook as an attachment to an e-mail message, it is often more convenient to send the e-mail directly from Excel, as long as you have configured Outlook as your e-mail client. When you start Outlook 2013 for the first time, you will be prompted to complete the Microsoft Outlook 2013 Startup Wizard to configure the program. Follow the prompts, enter the required information to connect your existing e-mail account to Outlook, download the Outlook Connector (if prompted), restart your computer, and then start Outlook.

When you send a workbook as an attachment, keep in mind you are sending separate copies of the workbook to others. The recipients can save the workbook on their computer systems and modify it as they wish. If you want to incorporate their changes, the recipients will need to e-mail their modified copy back to you so that you can compare and merge the workbook with yours. To send an Excel workbook as an attachment by e-mail, do the following:

1. Click the FILE tab and click Share.
2. Click the E-mail icon in the *Share* section. The Backstage view displays a third column; click *Send as Attachment*.

3. Click *Send as Attachment* or another send option. If a dialog box opens to prompt you to enter your Windows Live ID credentials, enter your credentials.
4. Enter your information in the *E-mail address* and Password boxes and click OK. The workbook file name appears in the Attached box (see Figure 11.33).
5. Type the recipient's e-mail address in the To box.
6. Change the default subject line to an appropriate title.
7. Compose a message that informs the recipient of the workbook attachment and what you want the recipient to do with the workbook.
8. Click Send to send the e-mail message with the attached Excel workbook.

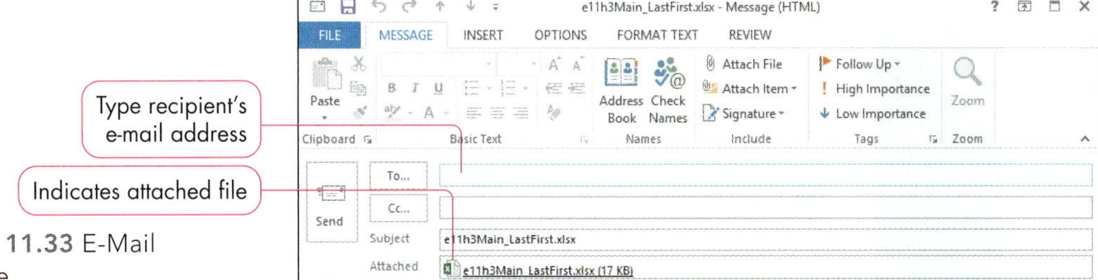

FIGURE 11.33 E-Mail Interface

TIP Sending an Attached Workbook Without Outlook

If Outlook is not installed as your default e-mail client, you may not be able to use the Send Using E-mail options to start the e-mail program and attach the workbook. Instead, you should close the workbook, open your e-mail client, and then click the Attach button or command in that window to send the workbook as an e-mail attachment.

Save to the Web

STEP 2

You probably find yourself needing files when you are away from your base computer. For example, you might save your homework for your Excel class on your home computer, but then you need to work on it between classes on campus. However, you might not want to carry a flash drive or external drive with you. You can save a workbook to your Windows Live SkyDrive. ***SkyDrive*** is a central storage location in which you can save and access files via an Internet connection. Saving to SkyDrive is an effective way to access your files from any device that has an Internet connection, including your smartphone or tablet (see Figure 11.34).

TIP Accessing Windows Live Account

When Microsoft Office 2013 is installed, you are required to create or sign in with an existing Windows Live account. This allows you to access SkyDrive without additional logins. If you attempt to access your SkyDrive account remotely, you will need to enter your user name and password. If you forget your SkyDrive password it can be reset at the following URL: https://account.live.com/ResetPassword.

You can create folders on SkyDrive just as you create folders on your computer's hard drive or on a flash drive. Furthermore, you can give other people access to a particular folder and the files it contains so that they can view and edit documents. This approach may be preferable to sending an e-mail attachment and then consolidating changes from multiple

Key Terms Matching

Match the key terms with their definitions. Write the key term number by the appropriate numbered definition.

- **a.** Accessibility Checker
- **b.** Collaboration
- **c.** Comment
- **d.** Comment indicator
- **e.** Compatibility Checker
- **f.** Digital signature
- **g.** Document Inspector
- **h.** Document property
- **i.** History worksheet
- **j.** Metadata
- **k.** Portable Document Format (PDF)
- **l.** Shared workbook
- **m.** Signature line
- **n.** SkyDrive
- **o.** Track Changes

1. _______ A central storage location where you can save and access files via Internet connection. **p. 629**

2. _______ Enables a person to type or insert a visible digital signature to authenticate the workbook. **p. 621**

3. _______ A universal file format that preserves a document's original data and formatting for multiplatform use. **p. 627**

4. _______ An electronic notation in a document to authenticate the contents. **p. 620**

5. _______ Detects issues that could hinder a user's ability to use a workbook. **p. 618**

6. _______ Detects data and features that are not compatible with previous versions of Excel. **p. 618**

7. _______ Lists particular types of changes made to a workbook. **p. 611**

8. _______ Detects hidden and personal data in a workbook to remove. **p. 617**

9. _______ A colored triangle in the top-right corner of a cell to indicate that the cell contains comments. **p. 606**

10. _______ Records certain types of changes made in a workbook. **p. 608**

11. _______ Occurs when multiple people work together to achieve a common goal by using technology to edit the contents of a file. **p. 603**

12. _______ A file that enables multiple users to make changes at the same time. **p. 603**

13. _______ An attribute, such as an author's name or keyword, that describes a file. **p. 597**

14. _______ A notation attached to a cell to pose a question or provide commentary. **p. 606**

15. _______ Pieces of data, such as a keyword, that describe other data, such as the contents of a file. **p. 597**

Multiple Choice

1. Which statement about comments in Excel is true?
   (a) Comments remain onscreen in the right margin area.
   (b) Position the mouse pointer over the cell containing a comment indicator to display a comment box.
   (c) After you insert a comment, Excel prevents you from changing it.
   (d) Comment boxes display the date and time that the user inserted the comment in the worksheet.

2. Which document property cannot be changed within the Backstage view?
   (a) Author
   (b) Title
   (c) Categories
   (d) Last Modified date

3. What is the default file format for a basic Excel 2013 file?
   (a) .xls
   (b) .pdf
   (c) .xlsx
   (d) .csv

4. Which tool detects issues that could hinder a user's ability to use a workbook?
   (a) Accessibility Checker
   (b) Compatibility Checker
   (c) Change tracker
   (d) Document Inspector

5. The Track Changes feature does not detect what type of change?
   (a) Changing a value of a number from 10 to 25
   (b) Inserting a new row above row 18
   (c) Deleting text within a label
   (d) Applying Percent Style for the range B4:B10

6. A workbook that has been marked as final:
   (a) Opens in Read-Only mode.
   (b) Is password protected to make any changes.
   (c) Displays a nonstop, flashing Message Bar that the workbook is final.
   (d) Must contain a digital signature.

7. The _______ tool detects particular properties, such as Author, and removes those properties from a file that you plan to distribute.
   (a) Compatibility Checker
   (b) Document Inspector
   (c) Advanced Properties
   (d) Accessibility Checker

8. If you want to save a file in a format that preserves worksheet formatting, prevents changes, and ensures that the document looks the same on most computers, save the workbook in the _______ file format.
   (a) .csv
   (b) Excel template
   (c) Excel 97-2003 workbook
   (d) .pdf

9. If you want to save a workbook to a highly secure central location to enable efficient collaboration:
   (a) Send the workbook as an e-mail attachment.
   (b) Save the workbook to a SharePoint site or to a shared SkyDrive folder.
   (c) Save the workbook to a regular Web site.
   (d) Backup the workbook to an external hard drive.

10. You can do all of the following *except* _______ for both customizing the Ribbon and customizing the Quick Access Toolbar.
    (a) Add a command
    (b) Reset the customizations
    (c) Print
    (d) Import and export customizations

l. Create a Windows Live account if you do not already have one. Create a folder on your SkyDrive and name it **Exploring**. Enter your instructor's e-mail address so that you can share that folder with your instructor.

m. Save the workbook to the Exploring folder on your SkyDrive.

n. Save and close the workbook, and submit based on your instructor's directions.

2 Ribbon Customization

COLLABORATION CASE

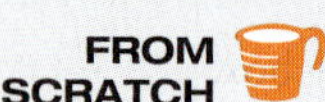

You and a coworker have been assigned to a team that manages financial sheets that must be merged and then e-mailed to management. To synchronize your efforts, you have decided to customize your Office Ribbon and then share the settings with your fellow team members. In addition, you will insert before and after screenshots into a Word document and change document properties.

Student 1

a. Start a new workbook and save it as **e11m2Custom_LastFirst**.

b. Make sure your name is the user name in the Excel Options dialog box.

c. Display the Document Panel, add the following document properties, and then close the Document Panel:
- Author: your name
- Title: **Excel 2013 Custom Ribbon**
- Keywords: **Excel, customization, Ribbon, groups, commands**

d. Click the **FILE tab**, select **Options**, and then click **Customize Ribbon**.

e. Click **New Tab** from the *Customize the Ribbon* section.

f. Click **Rename** and name the newly created tab **Group Project**.

g. Create a new group in the Group Project tab named **Common Functions** and do the following:
- Click **Choose commands from** and select **All Tabs**. Click **Review**, select **Changes**, and then add Share Workbook and Track Changes to the newly created Common Functions group.
- Click **Choose commands from** and select **Commands Not in the Ribbon**. Select **Compare and Merge Workbook** and click **Add** to add the option to the Common Functions Group.

h. Click the **Import/Export menu** and select **Export all customizations**. Save the file as **e11m2CustomSet_LastFirst**.

Student 2

i. Open Excel, create a new workbook, click the **FILE tab**, and then click **Options**. Click **Customize Ribbon**.

j. Click **Import/Export** and select **Import customization file**.

k. Import the file *e11m2CustomSet_LastFirst.exportedUI*. Click **Yes** when prompted to replace all existing Ribbon and Quick Access Toolbar customizations. Then display the newly customized tab.

l. Open Microsoft Word and create a new document.

m. Click the **INSERT tab** on the Ribbon and insert a screen shot of your Excel application with the newly added customizations.

n. Save the document as **e11m2ScreenCapture_LastFirst**. Save the document and close Word.

Beyond the Classroom

Cell Phone Plans

RESEARCH CASE 

You and a classmate want to compare individual cell phone plans for three cell phone companies. Open *e11b2CellPhone* and save it as **e11b2CellPhone_LastFirst**. Make sure your name is the user name in Excel Options. Research individual plans in your city. Use the following parameters: 450 anytime minutes, unlimited texting, and a data plan to use the Internet. Enter the cost details in the worksheet. Enter number of weekend minutes used, and enter a formula to calculate the total monthly costs, not including taxes and fees. Save the workbook and send as an e-mail attachment to a classmate. Have that classmate do the same for you.

You and your classmate should save the received workbook with your name, turn on Track Changes, make some changes, and insert comments. Then e-mail the workbooks back to each other and save the updated workbook as **e11b2CellPhone2_LastFirst**. Accept and reject changes as necessary, turn off the shared workbook, and then mark the workbook as final. Close the workbook and submit all files based on your instructor's directions.

Passenger Car Ratings

DISASTER RECOVERY 

You work as an analyst for an independent automobile rating company that provides statistics to consumers. You prepared a worksheet containing the test results of five 2015 mid-sized passenger car models. Open *e11b3Autos* and save it as **e11b3Autos_LastFirst**. Make sure your name is the user name in Excel Options. Insert a comment in the cell that indicates the top-ranked car. Insert a footer with your name on the left side, the sheet name code in the center, and the file name code on the right side. Insert a signature line with your name and job title below the worksheet data. Close the workbook and make a copy of it in File Explorer. Open the copied workbook. Use Compatibility Checker to see what features are not compatible with previous versions. Create a memo in Word that includes a full screenshot of the Compatibility Checker's results. Explain how you plan to handle each warning. Save the Word document as **e11b3AutosMemo_LastFirst**. Make appropriate changes in the workbook and save it in Excel 97-2003 Workbook format as **e11b3Autos2_LastFirst**. Submit the three files based on your instructor's directions.

Workplace Etiquette

SOFT SKILLS CASE 

You have recently been hired at CBK Financial, a wealth management company located in Atlanta. CBK has strict etiquette for managing and distributing Excel workbooks. They require each document to be checked for compatibility, free of all personal information, and digitally signed.

Open the file *e11b4Etiquette*. Save the file as **e11b4Etiquette_LastFirst**. Review the document for errors, and after you are satisfied that it is free of anomalies, use the Document Inspector to delete any personal information. Next check the document for ignoring any minor or major issues with any version prior to Excel 2007. Add a digital signature approving the document. Save the workbook and send as an e-mail attachment to a classmate. Have that classmate do the same for you. Close the workbook and submit all files based on your instructor's directions.

Templates, Themes, and Styles

Designing the perfect workbook can be time consuming. By now, you know you have to plan the layout before you enter data to minimize data-entry changes later. You decide what column and row labels are needed to describe the data, where to place the labels, and how to format the labels. In addition, you enter and format quantitative data, such as applying Accounting Number Format and decreasing the number of decimal places. The longer you work for the same department or organization, the more you will notice that you create the same types of workbooks. Excel has the right tools to improve your productivity in developing consistently formatted workbooks. Some of these tools include templates, themes, backgrounds, and styles.

In this section, you will select an Excel template. After opening the template, you will apply a theme, display a background, and apply cell styles.

Selecting a Template

STEP 1

A ***template*** is a partially completed document that you use as a model to create other documents that have the same structure and purpose. A template typically contains standard labels, formulas, and formatting but may contain little or no quantitative data. Templates help ensure consistency and standardization for similar workbooks, such as detailed sales reports for all 12 months of a year. When you start Excel, you are presented with a gallery of templates. If you are already working within a workbook, click the File tab and click New. The Backstage view displays a gallery of featured templates (see Figure 12.1). You can select from templates you have recently used, sample templates that were installed with the software, or templates you created, or download new templates. To create a workbook based on a template, do the following:

1. Click a sample template, such as *Travel expense report*.
2. A pop-up window will display a sample of the selected template (see Figure 12.2).
3. Click Create to load the template data as a new workbook.

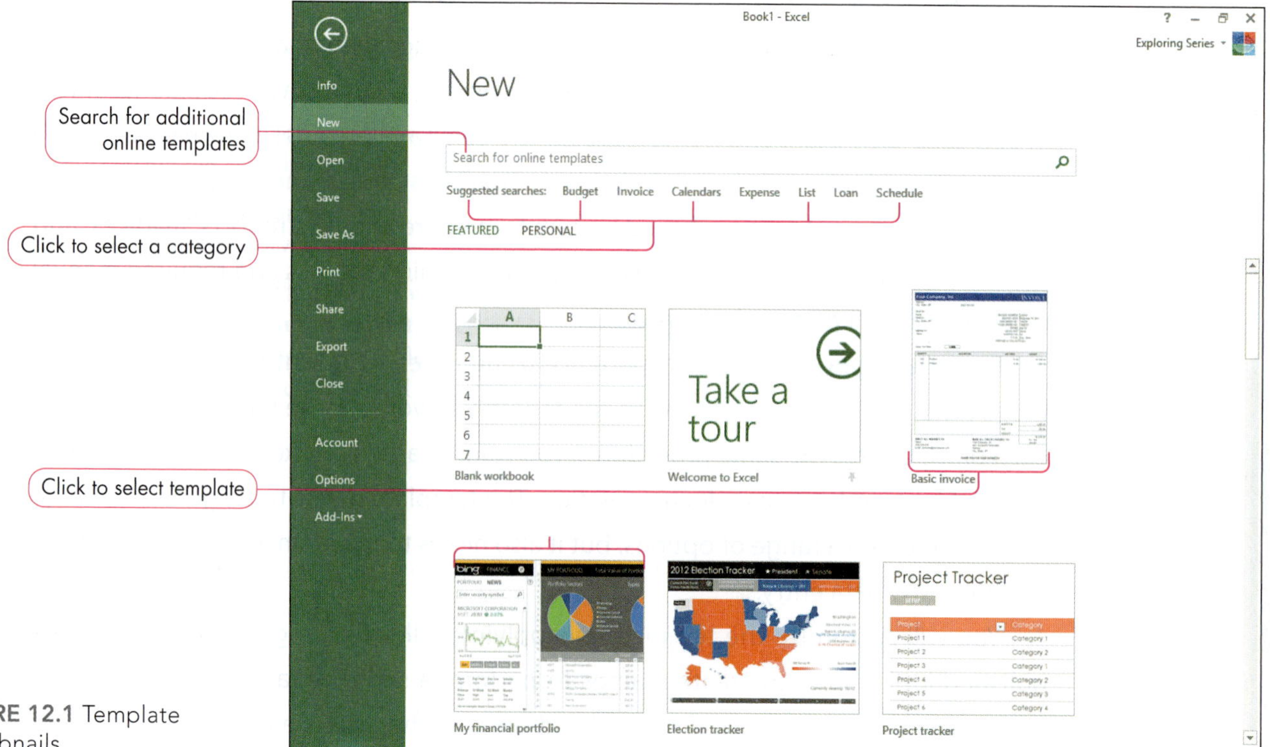

FIGURE 12.1 Template Thumbnails

The *Search for online templates* box allows you to search Office.com for a particular template by entering your search conditions and pressing Enter. Start searching, or you can select a template from a category, such as Budgets. These templates are created by Microsoft, a Microsoft partner, or a member of the Microsoft community. To download an Office.com template, do the following:

1. Click a template category, such as Expense. The Backstage view then displays thumbnails representing the various templates in that category.
2. Click the template thumbnail representing the template you want to download. A pop-up window displays information about the selected template, such as the template name and creator and the download size (see Figure 12.2).
3. Click Create. The Download Template message box displays briefly, after which the template is opened as a workbook in Excel.

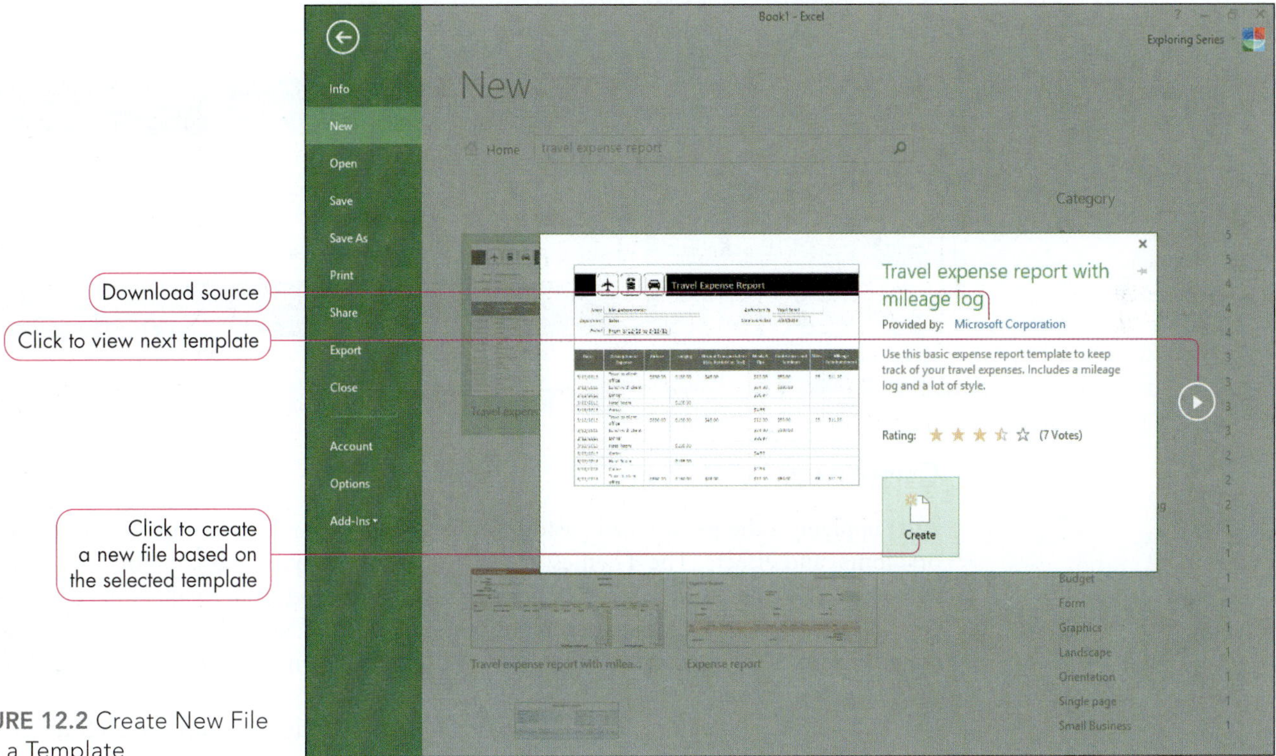

FIGURE 12.2 Create New File from a Template

Downloading the template does not save it to a storage location. You must save the workbook on a storage device. When you save a workbook from a downloaded template for the first time, the Save As dialog box defaults to SkyDrive in Windows 8; however, you can select another location in which to save the workbook.

Applying Themes and Backgrounds

STEP 2»

In addition to selecting a template, you might want to apply a theme or insert a background to create a consistent look with the workbooks you create. A ***theme*** is a collection of formats that include coordinating colors, fonts, and special effects to provide a stylish appearance. You can apply a theme to a workbook to give it a consistent look with other workbooks used in your department or organization. Most organizations have a style that encompasses particular fonts, colors, and a logo or trademark on corporate stationery, advertisements, and Web pages. You can use themes in Excel workbooks to match the corporate "look and feel." Some of the Excel theme names match theme names in other Office applications so that you can provide continuity and consistency in all of your documents. To apply a theme to all worksheets in a workbook, do the following:

1. Click the PAGE LAYOUT tab.
2. Click Themes in the Themes group. The Office theme is presented first; the other built-in themes are listed alphabetically in the Themes gallery (see Figure 12.3).
3. Position the pointer over each theme to display a Live Preview of how the theme would format existing data on the current worksheet.
4. Click a theme to make it active.

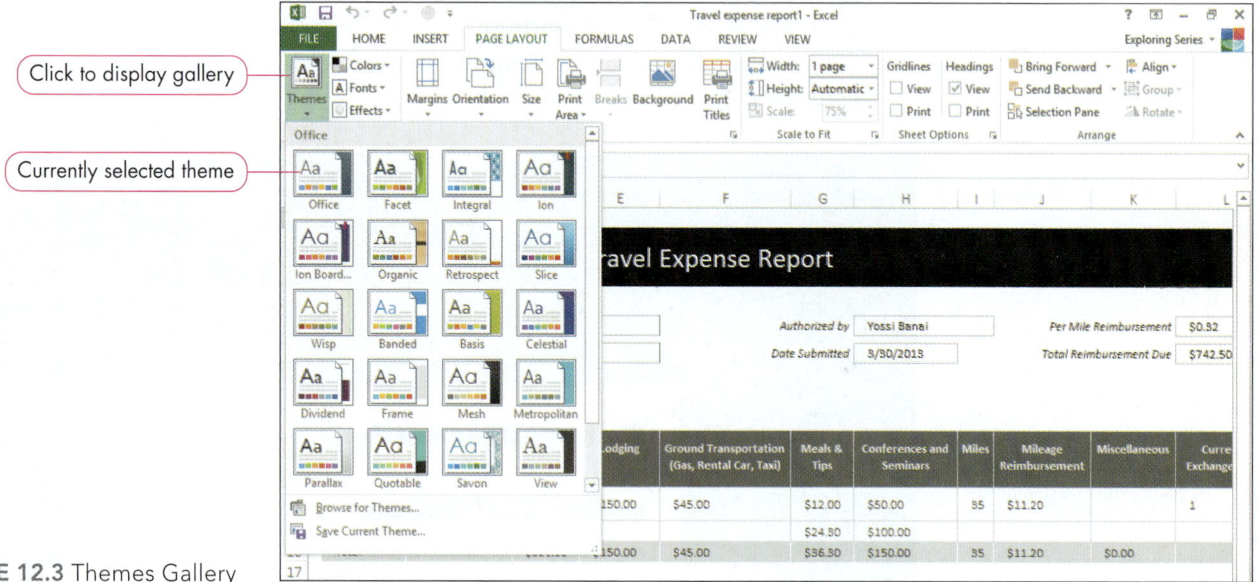

FIGURE 12.3 Themes Gallery

Customize a Theme

After applying a theme, you can customize the three elements that comprise the theme: colors, fonts, and effects. The Themes group on the Page Layout tab contains commands to customize your theme. When you click Colors, you can select from a gallery of colors, or you can select Customize Colors to define the text, background, accent, hyperlink, and followed hyperlink colors. If you create and name your own color theme, that theme name will appear in the *Custom* section of the Colors menu.

Theme fonts contain a coordinating heading and body text font for each theme. For example, the Office theme uses Calibri Light for headings and Calibri for cell entries. To select a theme font, click Fonts in the Themes group and select a theme font, or select Customize Fonts to define your own theme fonts.

Theme effects are special effects that control the design differences in objects, such as shapes, SmartArt, and object borders. To select a theme effect, click Effects in the Themes group, position the mouse pointer over an effect to see a Live Preview of how that effect will affect objects, and click the desired effect to apply it to your workbook.

Apply a Background

STEP 3»

Excel enables you to use graphics as the background of a worksheet. The effect is similar to placing a background on a Web page. A ***background*** is an image placed behind the worksheet data. For example, you might want to use the corporate logo as your background, or you might want a "Confidential" graphic image to remind onscreen viewers that the worksheet contains corporate trade secrets. (If you want an image to appear behind data on a printed worksheet, insert the image as a watermark in a header.) Be careful in selecting and using backgrounds, because the images can distract users from comprehending the quantitative data. A subtle, pale image is less likely to distract a workbook user than a bright, vividly colored image. To add a background to a worksheet, do the following:

1. Click Background in the Page Setup group on the PAGE LAYOUT tab to open the Insert Pictures dialog box.

2. Select the picture file, such as a jpeg or bitmap file, that you want to use as a background.
3. Click Insert.

The image, like background images in Web pages, is tiled across your worksheet (see Figure 12.4). The background image displays only in the worksheet onscreen; it does not print. Notice that Delete Background replaces Background in the Page Setup group after you insert a background for a specific worksheet.

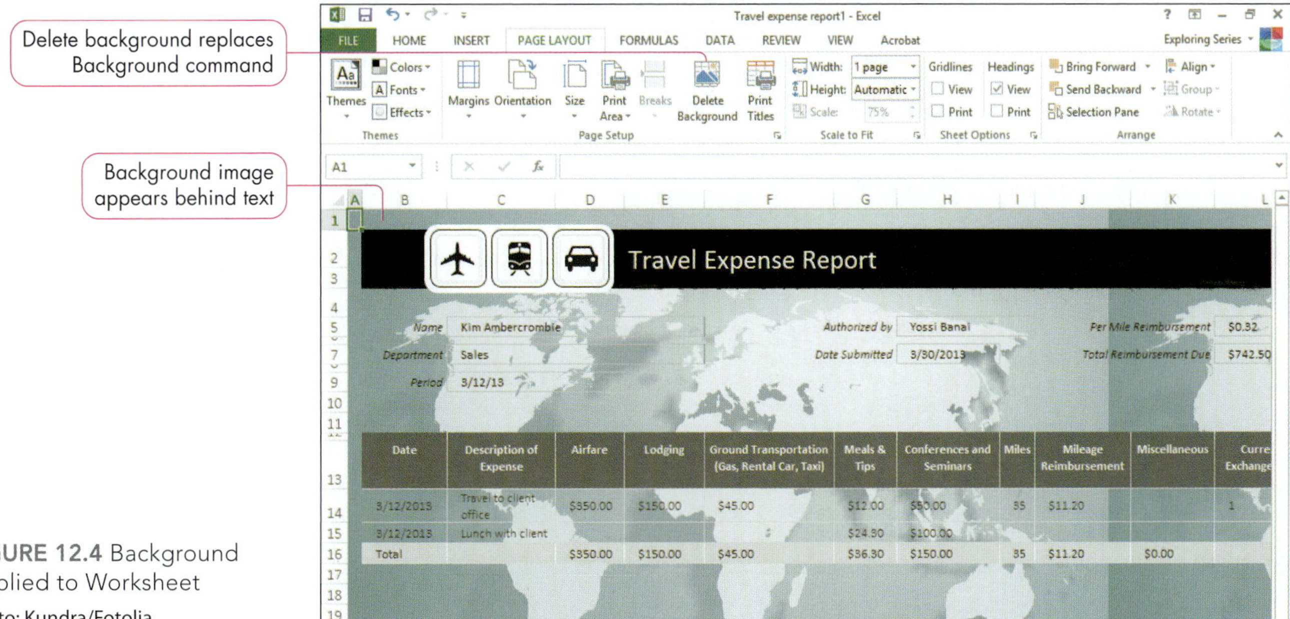

FIGURE 12.4 Background Applied to Worksheet
Photo: Kundra/Fotolia

TIP Background Visibility

You can turn off the gridlines to increase the visibility of the background image and the worksheet data. Click the Page Layout tab and deselect the Gridlines View check box in the Sheet Options group.

TIP Delete Background Image

To delete a background picture, click Delete Background in the Page Setup group on the Page Layout tab.

Applying Cell Styles

STEP 4

Different areas of a worksheet have different formatting. For example, titles may be centered in 16-pt size; column labels may be bold, centered, and dark blue font; and input cells may be formatted differently from output cells. A ***cell style*** is a collection of format settings based on the currently selected theme to provide a consistent appearance within a worksheet and among similar workbooks. Cell styles control the following formats:

- Font attributes, such as font and font size
- Borders and fill styles and colors
- Vertical and horizontal cell alignment

- Number formatting, such as Currency and number of decimal places
- Cell-protection settings

The currently selected theme controls cell styles. If you change the theme, Excel updates cells formatted by cell styles to reflect the new theme. For example, if you change from Facet theme to Integral, particular fill colors change from shades of green to blue. To apply a style to a cell or range of cells, do the following:

1. Click the HOME tab and click Cell Styles in the Styles group to display the Cell Styles gallery (see Figure 12.5).
2. Position the mouse pointer over a style name to see a Live Preview of how that style will affect the active cell.
3. Click a style to apply it to the active cell or range.

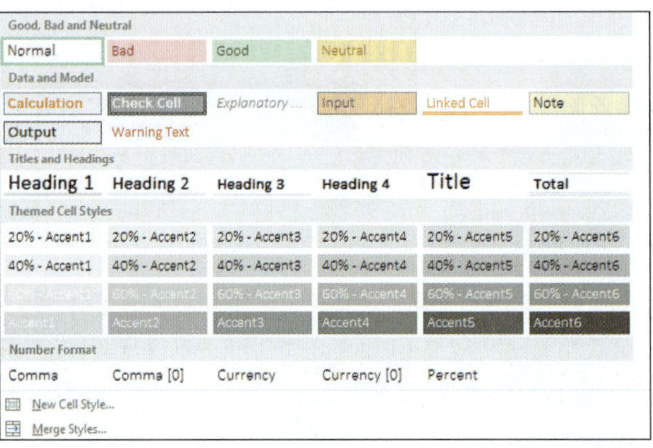

FIGURE 12.5 Cell Styles

The gallery contains the following five predefined cell categories:

- **Good, Bad, and Neutral:** Use to emphasize bad, good, or neutral results, or click Normal to reset a cell to its original default setting.
- **Data and Model:** Use to indicate special cell contents, such as a calculated result, input cell, output cell, or warning.
- **Titles and Headings:** Use to format titles and headings, such as column and row labels, for emphasis.
- **Themed Cell Styles:** Use Accent styles for visual emphasis. These cell styles are dependent on the currently selected theme.
- **Number Format:** Provide the same formatting as commands in the Number group on the Home tab.

Create Custom Cell Styles

You can create your own custom cell styles if the predefined cell styles do not meet your needs. For example, you might want to create custom cell styles that match the color, font, and design of your corporate logo or stationery to help brand your workbooks with the company image. After you create custom cell styles, you can apply them in multiple workbooks instead of formatting each workbook individually. To create a custom cell style do the following:

1. Click the cell that contains the desired formatting.
2. Click the HOME tab and click Cell Styles in the Styles group.
3. Select New Cell Style at the bottom of the gallery to open the Style dialog box (see Figure 12.6).
4. Type the name for your new style in the *Style name* box.

5. Click the check boxes to select the style options you want in the *Style Includes (By Example)* section. (If you are not creating a style using the active cell as an example, click Format to open the Format Cells dialog box and select the formats just as you would format an individual cell.)
6. Click OK to close the Style dialog box.

After you create a custom style, Excel displays another section, *Custom*, at the top of the Cell Styles gallery. This section lists the custom styles you create.

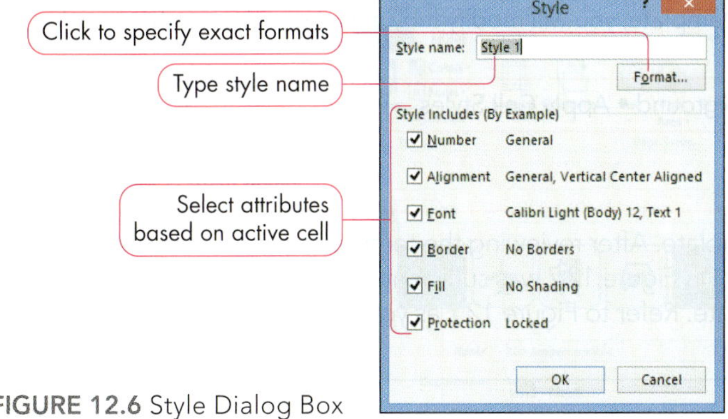

FIGURE 12.6 Style Dialog Box

Modify and Remove Custom Cell Styles

After you create and apply custom styles to worksheet cells, you might decide to change the format. For example, you might want to change the font size or fill color. The primary advantage to creating and applying styles is that you can modify the style, and Excel updates all cells for which you applied the style automatically. To modify a style, do the following:

1. Right-click the style in the *Custom* section of the Cell Styles palette.
2. Select Modify to open the Style dialog box.
3. Make the desired format changes and click OK.

If you no longer need a cell style, you can delete it. However, if you delete a cell style that has been applied to worksheet cells, Excel will remove all formatting from those cells. To delete a cell style, right-click the style name in the *Custom* section of the Cell Styles palette and select Delete. Excel does not ask for confirmation before deleting the style.

Use Styles in Other Workbooks

When you create your own cell styles, the styles are saved with the workbook in which you created the styles. However, you may want to apply those styles in other workbooks as well. To do this, open the workbook that contains the custom cell styles (the source) and open the workbook in which you want to apply those custom styles (the destination). In the destination workbook, click Cell Styles in the Styles group on the Home tab. Select Merge Styles at the bottom of the Cell Styles gallery to open the Merge Styles dialog box. In the *Merge styles from* list, select the name of the workbook that contains the styles you want and click OK. When you click Cell Styles again, the custom styles appear in the gallery.

1. What are the benefits of using templates? ***p. 644***
2. How do you print worksheets with background images? ***p. 646***
3. Why would you create a custom cell style? ***p. 648***

After you finalize your workbook, you need to save it. To save a workbook as a template, do the following:

1. Click the FILE tab and click Export.
2. Click Change File Type.
3. Click Template in the Change File Type scrollable list and click Save As at the bottom of the Backstage view to open the Save As dialog box. Notice that the *Save as type* is set to Excel Template.
4. Select the desired location, type a name in the *File name* box, and then click Save. **Note: This method does not default to the "correct" Template folder to provide easy access.**

To save the template so that it automatically is included in the Templates gallery, do the following:

1. From the Backstage view, click Save As and click Computer to open the Save As dialog box.
2. Click the *Save as type* arrow and select Excel Template. Excel then selects the C:\Users\username\Documents\CustomOfficeTemplates folder automatically.
3. Type a name in the *File name* box and click Save.

Templates Folder

Templates use a different file extension (.xltx) than Excel workbooks (.xlsx). In order for your template to appear in the Template gallery in the Backstage view, be sure to save it in the correct folder, C:\Users\username\Documents\CustomOfficeTemplates in Windows 8 and Windows 7. If you use File Explorer to find the Templates folder, you will need to display hidden folders to do so. If you save your custom templates in the correct location, you can use them to create new workbooks by clicking the File tab, clicking New, and then clicking Personal in the Templates gallery of the Backstage view. The New dialog box displays thumbnails and names for the templates you created.

Protecting a Cell, a Worksheet, and a Workbook

Most templates protect worksheets by enabling users to change only particular cells in a worksheet. For example, users are permitted to enter data in input cells, but they cannot change formulas or alter formatting or worksheet structure. In Hands-On Exercise 2, you will protect the formula cells in the Travel Expense Report template. This will prevent users from changing the formulas. Protecting worksheets prevents modification of formulas and text but enables you to change values in unprotected cells.

Lock and Unlock Cells

STEP 1 A ***locked cell*** is one that prevents users from editing the contents or formatting of that cell in a protected worksheet. By default, all cells are locked as indicated by the blue border around the padlock icon for the Lock Cell option on the Format menu in the Cells group on the Home tab. Locked cells are not enforced until you protect the worksheet. Locking or unlocking cells has no effect if the worksheet has not been protected. Before protecting the worksheet, you should unlock the cells that you want users to be able to edit. For example, you will unlock the Per Mile Reimbursement and Date Submitted cells in the Travel Expense Report template so that users can enter unique values. However, you will keep the cells containing formulas locked. To unlock input cells, do the following:

1. Select the cells in which you want users to be able to enter or edit data.
2. Click the HOME tab and click Format in the Cells group (see Figure 12.11). Note that Lock Cell is active by default.
3. Select Lock Cell in the *Protection* section to unlock the active cell or selected range of cells.

   To relock cells, repeat the above process.

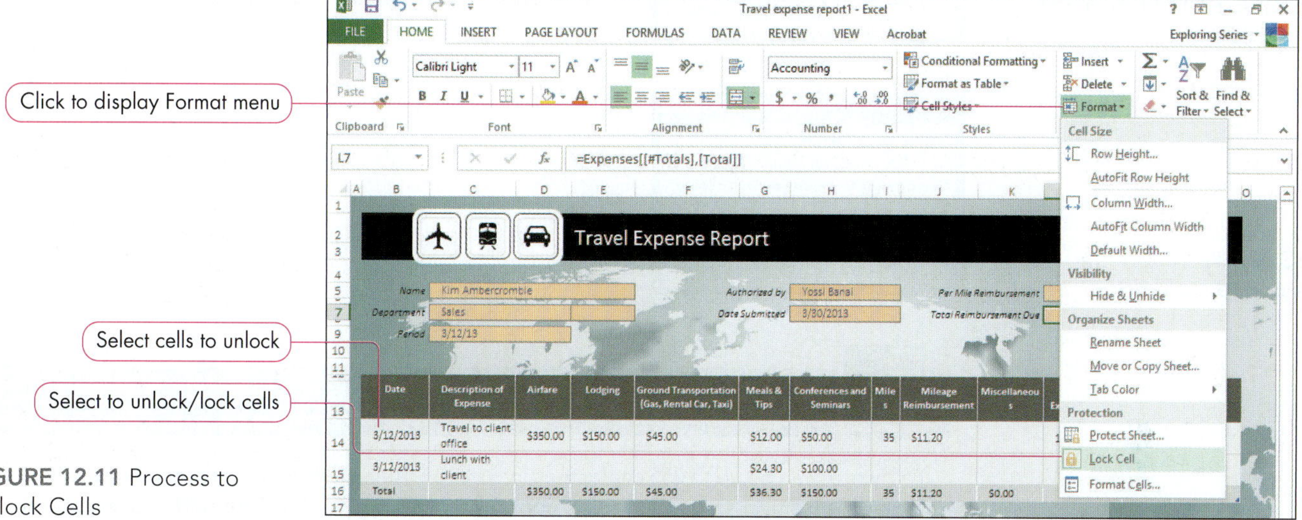

FIGURE 12.11 Process to Unlock Cells

TIP Using the Format Cells Dialog Box

Alternatively, after selecting a cell or range of cells to unlock, you can open the Format Cells dialog box, click the Protection tab, deselect the Locked check box, and then click OK.

Protect a Worksheet

STEP 2» After unlocking cells that you want the users to be able to modify, you are ready to protect the worksheet. When you protect a worksheet, you prevent users from altering the locked cells. During the process of protecting a worksheet, you can enter a password to ensure that only those who know the password can unprotect the worksheet. Protecting the template is typically the final step in the creation of a custom template because you need to enter standard labels, create formulas, and unprotect input cells first. If you protect the worksheet before finalizing the content, you will have to unprotect the worksheet, make content changes, and then protect the worksheet again. To protect a worksheet, do the following:

STEP 3»

1. Click the HOME tab and click Format in the Cells group.
2. Select Protect Sheet in the *Protection* section (or click Protect Sheet in the Changes group on the REVIEW tab) to open the Protect Sheet dialog box (see Figure 12.12).
3. Select the check boxes for actions you want users to be able to do in the *Allow all users of this worksheet to* list.
4. Type a password in the *Password to unprotect sheet* box and click OK. The Confirm Password dialog box opens (see Figure 12.13). Type the same password in the *Reenter password to proceed* box.
5. Read the caution statement and click OK.

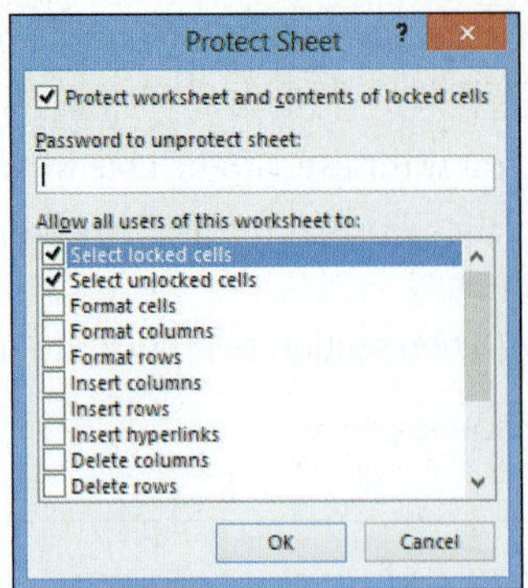

FIGURE 12.12 Protect Sheet Dialog Box

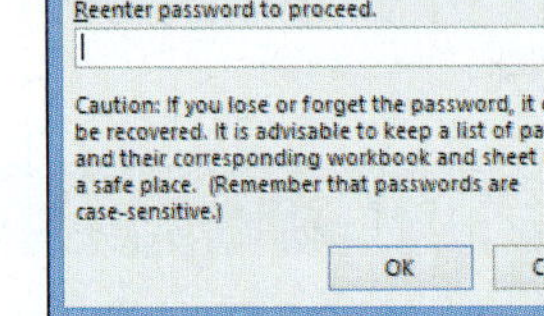

FIGURE 12.13 Confirm Password Dialog Box

Passwords

Passwords can be up to 255 characters, including letters, numbers, and symbols. Passwords are case sensitive, so *passWORD* is not the same as *Password*. Make sure you record your password in a secure location or select a password that you will always remember. If you forget the password, you will not be able to unprotect the worksheet.

After you protect a worksheet, most commands on the Ribbon are dimmed, indicating that they are not available. If someone tries to enter or change data in a locked cell on a protected workbook, Excel displays the warning message and instructs the user how to remove the protection (see Figure 12.14). To unprotect a worksheet, do the following:

1. Click Unprotect Sheet in the Changes group on the REVIEW tab, or click Format in the Cells group on the HOME tab and select Unprotect Sheet. The Unprotect Sheet dialog box opens.
2. Type the password in the Password box and click OK. The worksheet is then unprotected so that you can make changes.

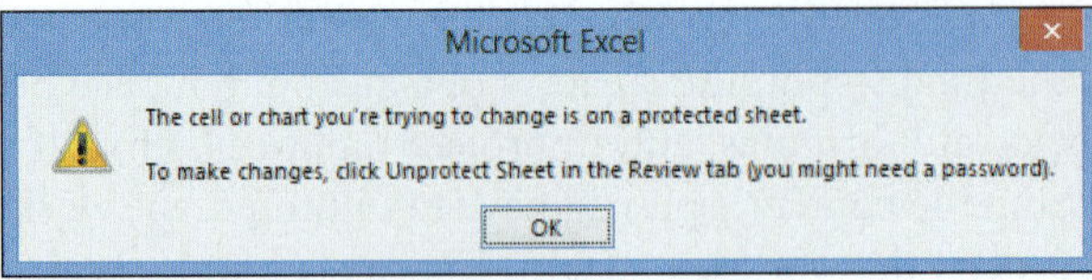

FIGURE 12.14 Warning Message

Protect a Workbook

Although locking cells and protecting a worksheet prevents unauthorized modifications, users might make unwanted changes to other parts of the workbook. You can prevent users from inserting, deleting, renaming, moving, copying, and hiding worksheets within the workbook by protecting the workbook with a password. Protecting an entire workbook does not disable the unlocked cells within a workbook; it merely prevents worksheet manipulation from occurring. That is, individual cells must still be unlocked even if a workbook is unprotected. To protect a workbook, do the following:

1. Click the REVIEW tab and click Protect Workbook in the Changes group. The Protect Structure and Windows dialog box opens (see Figure 12.15).
2. Click the check boxes for the desired action in the *Protect workbook for* section.
3. Type a password in the *Password (optional)* box and click OK. The Confirm Password dialog box opens.
4. Type the same password in the *Reenter password to proceed* box and click OK.

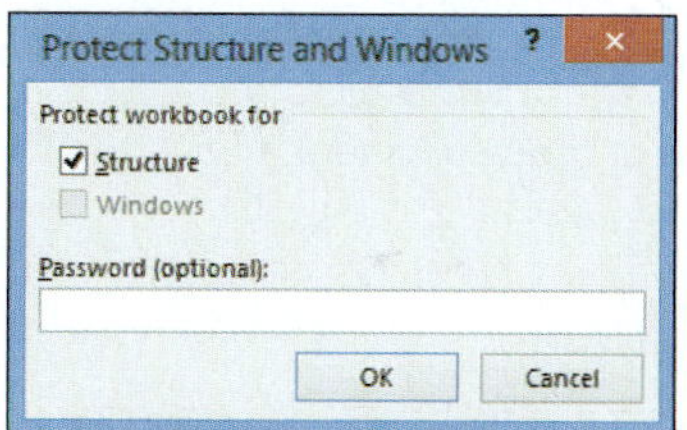

FIGURE 12.15 Protect Structure and Windows Dialog Box

TIP Unprotect a Workbook

To unprotect a workbook, click the Review tab, click Protect Workbook, type the password in the Password box in the Unprotect Workbook dialog box, and then click OK.

STEP 4» Once a workbook is completed and the appropriate cells are locked, the last step is to save the file as a template. Saving the file as a template not only stores the files as a template in the Custom Office Templates folder on your computer, it also displays the file as a personal template in the Backstage gallery. To save a workbook as a template, do the following:

STEP 5»

1. Click the FILE tab.
2. Click Save As, click Computer, and then click Browse.
3. Select Excel Template from the *Save as type* menu.
4. Click Save.

Quick Concepts

1. What is the default file extension for a template? *p. 654*
2. Where are templates saved in Windows 8? *p. 654*
3. Why would you protect a workbook? *p. 657*

Hands-On Exercises

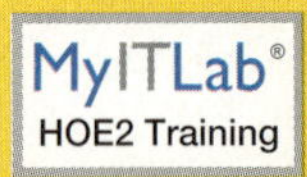

2 Custom Templates and Workbook Protection

After customizing the Travel Expense Report, you want to ensure consistency of use within the company by saving the workbook as a template. As the manager, you do not want your staff deleting formulas or other imperative sections of the expense form you have created. Your next set of steps will include protecting the workbook and then saving it as a template.

Skills covered: Unlock Input Cells • Delete Sample Values • Protect the Worksheet • Save the Workbook as a Template • Use the Template to Create a Sample Expense Report

STEP 1 » UNLOCK INPUT CELLS

Before protecting the worksheet, you will unlock input cells. You need to ensure the input cells are unlocked so that each employee can enter specific lodging, mileage, and miscellaneous costs. Refer to Figure 12.16 as you complete Step 1.

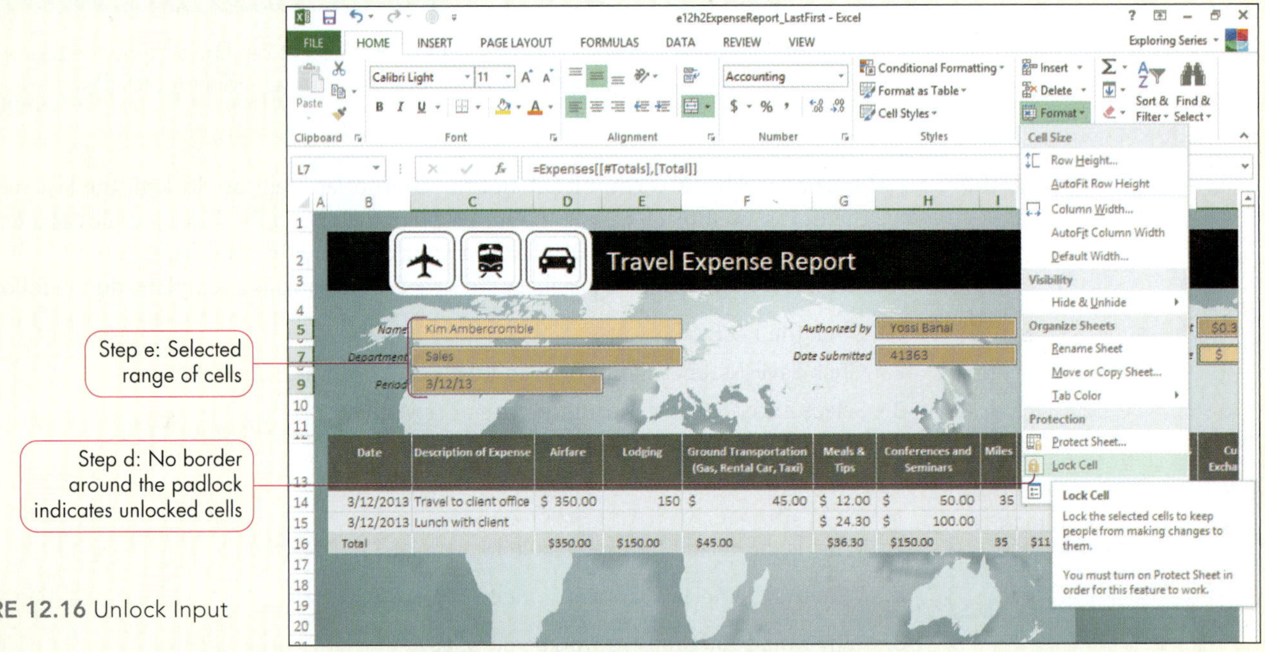

FIGURE 12.16 Unlock Input Cells

a. Open the *e12h1ExpenseReport_LastFirst* workbook and save it as **e12h2ExpenseReport_LastFirst**, changing *h1* to *h2*.

b. Select **cell C5**.

   This cell will be the input area for the name of the creator of the report.

c. Click the **HOME tab**, if necessary, and click **Format** in the Cells group.

   The Format menu opens.

d. Select **Lock Cell** in the *Protection* section.

The Lock Cell option does not change to Unlock Cell. However, when you unlock a cell, the Lock Cell command does not have a blue border around the padlock icon on the menu. The selected range of cells is unlocked and will remain unlocked when you protect the worksheet later.

e. Press **Ctrl** while selecting the following cells and range and repeat steps c and d to unlock the cells and range:

- **Cell C7**
- **Cell C9**
- **Cell H5**
- **Cell H7**
- **Cell L5**
- **Range B14:M15**

> **TROUBLESHOOTING**: If you unlock too many cells, select the cells that should be locked, click Format, and then select Lock Cell to lock them again.

f. Save the workbook.

STEP 2 » DELETE SAMPLE VALUES

Although you unlocked the input cells for Name, Department, Period, Authorized by, Date Submitted, Per Mile Reimbursement, and Total Reimbursement, you need to delete the sample values to create a ready-to-use empty form before you protect the worksheet and save it as a template. Refer to Figure 12.17 as you complete Step 2.

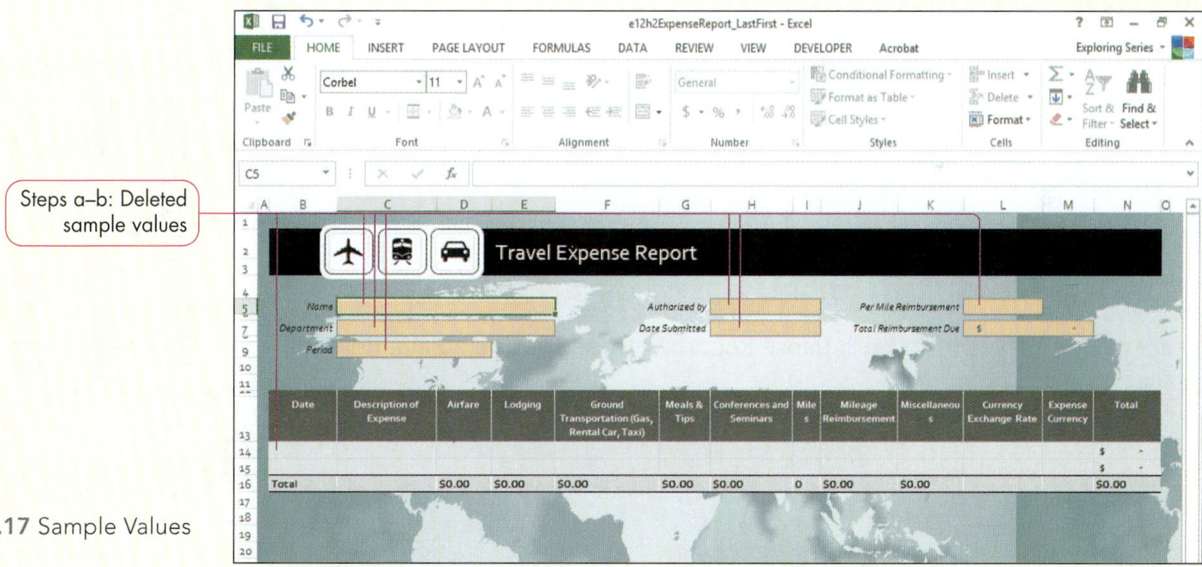

FIGURE 12.17 Sample Values Removed

a. Select **cell C5** and press **Delete**.

b. Delete the sample values in the following cells and range:

- **Cell C7**
- **Cell C9**
- **Cell H5**
- **Cell H7**
- **Cell L5**
- **Range B14:M15**

c. Save the workbook.

STEP 3 » PROTECT THE WORKSHEET

Now that you have unlocked input cells and deleted sample expense values, you are ready to protect the Expense Report worksheet. The other cells in the worksheet still have the Lock Cell property enabled. So, after you protect the worksheet, those cells will not be able to be modified.

a. Press **Ctrl+Home**.

b. Click **Format** in the Cells group and select **Protect Sheet**. If not already checked, check *Select locked cells* and *Select unlocked cells*.

   The Protect Sheet dialog box opens. The *Protect worksheet and contents of locked cells* check box is selected by default. In addition, the users are allowed to *Select locked cells* and *Select unlocked cells*. Although they can select locked cells, they will not be able to change those cells. Notice that users are not allowed to format data, insert columns or rows, or delete columns or rows.

c. Type **eXploring** in the **Password to unprotect sheet box**.

   Remember that passwords are case sensitive and that you must remember the password. If you forget it, you will not be able to unprotect the sheet.

d. Click **OK**.

   The Confirm Password dialog box opens with a caution.

e. Read the caution, type **eXploring** in the **Reenter password to proceed box**, and then click **OK**.

f. Click **cell N14** and try to type **1000**.

   Excel displays the warning box that the cell is protected with instructions on how to unprotect the worksheet.

> **TROUBLESHOOTING**: If you are allowed to enter the new value without the warning box, the cell is not locked. Click Undo to restore the formula, review Step 1, and then lock this cell.

g. Click **OK** to close the warning box and save the workbook.

STEP 4 » SAVE THE WORKBOOK AS A TEMPLATE

You are ready to save the Travel Expense Report workbook as a template. Refer to Figure 12.18 as you complete Step 4.

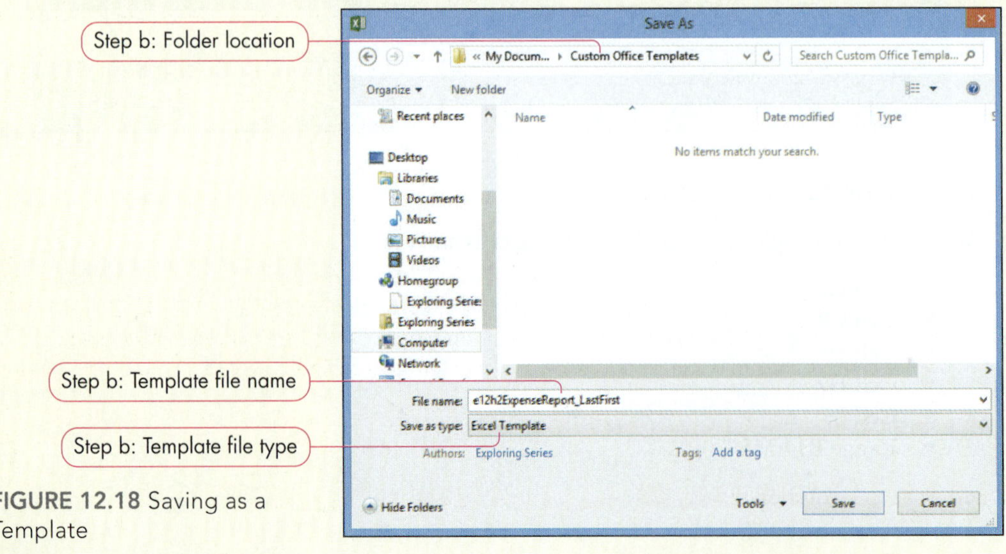

FIGURE 12.18 Saving as a Template

a. Click the **FILE tab**, click **Save As**, click **Browse**, and then click the **Save as type arrow**.

b. Select **Excel Template** and save the file to the default folder, Custom Office Templates, as **e12h2ExpenseReportTemplate_LastFirst**.

   The Save As dialog box opens, displaying the current workbook name and Excel Workbook as the default file type.

> **TROUBLESHOOTING**: When saving a template, Excel changes the file location to C:\Users\Username\My Documents\CustomOfficeTemplates. You may not have the ability to save a template to the hard drive of your school's computer lab, or your instructor may request you submit the file. To ensure you do not lose the template, be sure to change the save location to your student data folder. Note that if you do change the default location, the template will not display in the Personal template gallery and you will need to manually open the file from your student data folder to continue.

c. Click **Save**.

   This will save the workbook as a template and exit the backstage area.

d. Click the **FILE tab** and click **Close**.

STEP 5 » USE THE TEMPLATE TO CREATE A SAMPLE EXPENSE REPORT

Now that you have created a Travel Expense Report template, you are ready to enter data for one of your coworkers. Refer to Figure 12.19 as you complete Step 5.

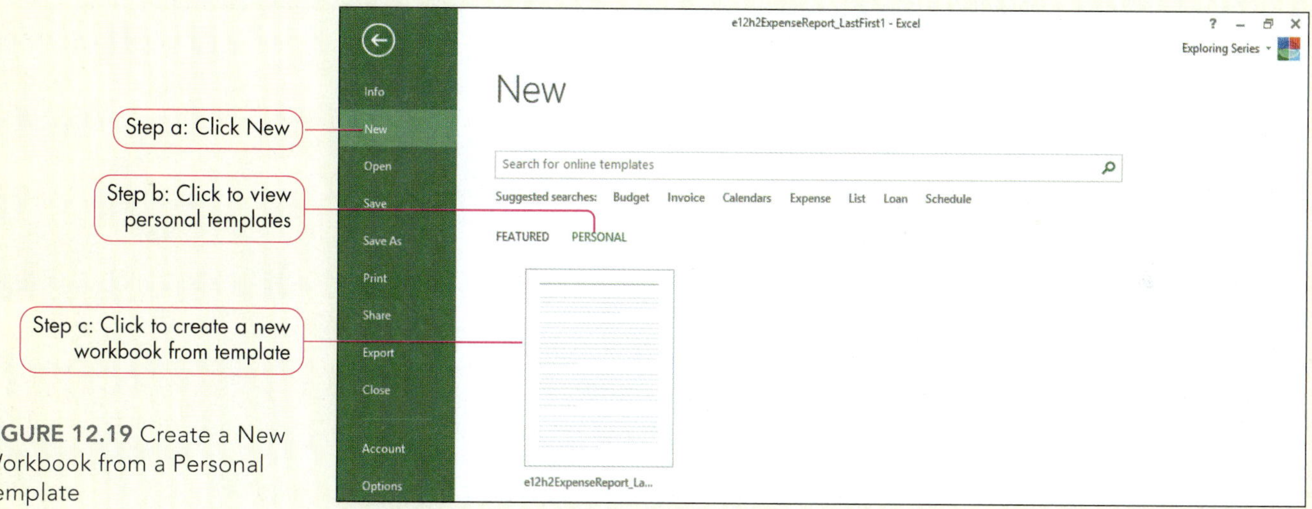

FIGURE 12.19 Create a New Workbook from a Personal Template

a. Click the **FILE tab** and click **New**.

   The Backstage view displays a gallery of available templates.

b. Click **PERSONAL** in the *gallery* section.

   This displays personal templates saved on your computer.

> **TROUBLESHOOTING**: If you were not able to save the template to the Custom Office Templates folder in Step 4, you will not see the template in the Personal template gallery. If this is the case, the file can be located by searching Recent Workbooks from the Open menu in the Backstage view.

c. Click *e12h2ExpenseReportTemplate_LastFirst* and click **OK**.

The template creates a new workbook based on the same file name but with a number appended to the end, such as *e12h2ExpenseReportTemplate_LastFirst1*.

d. Type **Your Name** in **cell C5**.

e. Type the following values in the appropriate cells:

Cell	Value
C7	Finance
H7	1/28/2015
L5	.35
B14	1/3/2015
C14	Sales Conference
D14	250.00
E14	125.00
F14	35.00

f. Press **Ctrl+Home** and save the workbook as **e12h2Sample_LastFirst** in the Excel Workbook file format. Close the workbook and submit based on your instructor's directions.

Macros

By now, you have used most of the tabs on the Ribbon to perform a variety of tasks. Often, you repeat the execution of the same commands as you develop and modify workbooks. Although the sequence to execute commands is easy, you lose productivity when you repeat the same procedures frequently. Previously, you learned how to apply styles and themes and how to create and use templates as models to develop similar workbooks. However, you can automate other routine tasks to increase your productivity. For example, think about how often you set a print range, adjust scaling, set margins, insert a standard header or footer, and specify other page setup options.

You can automate a series of routine or complex tasks by creating a macro. A ***macro*** is a set of instructions that execute a sequence of commands to automate repetitive or routine tasks. While the term *macro* often intimidates people, you should view macros as your personal assistants that do routine tasks for you! After you create a macro, you can execute the macro to perform all the tasks with minimal work on your part. When you run a macro, the macro executes all of the tasks the same way each time, and faster than you could execute the commands yourself, thus reducing errors while increasing efficiency.

The default Excel Workbook file format (.xlsx) cannot store macros. When you save a workbook containing macros, click the *Save as type* arrow in the Save As dialog box, and select one of the following file formats that support macros:

- Excel Macro-Enabled Workbook (.xlsm)
- Excel Binary Workbook (.xlsb)
- Excel Macro-Enabled Template (.xltm)

In this section, you will learn how to use the Macro Recorder to record a macro. You will also learn how to run a macro, edit a macro, create macro buttons, and review macro security issues.

Creating a Macro

Excel provides two methods for creating macros. You can use the Macro Recorder or type instructions using ***Visual Basic for Applications (VBA)***. VBA is a robust programming language that is the underlying code of all macros. While programmers use VBA to create macros, you do not have to be a programmer to write macros. It is relatively easy to use the ***Macro Recorder*** within Excel to record your commands, keystrokes, and mouse clicks to store Excel commands as VBA code within a workbook. Before you record a macro, keep the following points in mind:

- Remember that once you begin recording a macro, most actions you take are recorded in the macro. If you click something in error, you have to edit the code or undo the action to correct it.
- Practice the steps before you start recording the macro so that you will know the sequence in which to perform the steps when you record the macro.
- Ensure your macros are broad enough to apply to a variety of situations or an action you perform often for the workbook.
- Determine whether cell references should be relative, absolute, or mixed if you include cell references in the macro.

Use the Macro Recorder

You can access the Macro Recorder in a variety of ways: from the View tab, from the Developer tab, or from the status bar. The following list briefly describes what each method includes:

- The View tab contains the Macros group with the Macros command. You can click the Macros arrow to view macros, record a macro, or use relative references.

STEP 1

- The Developer tab, when displayed, provides more in-depth tools that workbook developers use. The Code group contains the same commands as the Macros arrow on the View tab, but it also includes commands to open the Visual Basic editor and set macro security.
- The status bar displays the Macro Recording button so that you can quickly click it to start and stop recording macros.

To display the Developer tab on the Ribbon, do the following:

1. Click the FILE tab and click Options to open the Excel Options dialog box.
2. Click Customize Ribbon on the left side to display the *Customize the Ribbon* options.
3. Click the Developer check box in the Main Tabs list to select it and click OK. Figure 12.20 shows the DEVELOPER tab.

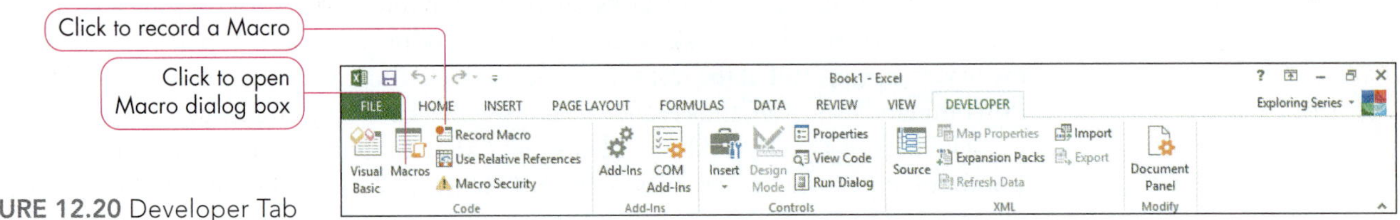

FIGURE 12.20 Developer Tab

Record a Macro

STEP 2

Recording a macro is relatively straightforward: You initiate the macro recording, perform a series of commands as you normally do, then stop the macro recording. Be careful and thorough when recording a macro to ensure that it performs the task it is designed to do and to avoid the need to edit the macro in the VBA Editor. Before recording a macro, you should practice it first and make sure you know the sequence of tasks you want to perform. After planning a macro, you are ready to record it. To record a macro, do the following:

1. Click the VIEW tab, click the Macros arrow in the Macros group, and then select Record Macro; or click the DEVELOPER tab and click Record Macro in the Code group; or click Macro Recording on the status bar. The Record Macro dialog box opens (see Figure 12.21 and Figure 12.22).
2. Type a name for the macro in the *Macro name* box. Macro names cannot include spaces or special characters and must start with a letter. Use CamelCasing (capitalize the first letter of each word but without a space), a programming naming convention, to increase readability of the macro name.
3. Assign a keyboard shortcut, if desired, for your macro in the *Shortcut key* box. Use caution, because many Ctrl+ shortcuts are already assigned in Excel. To be safe, it is best to use Ctrl+Shift+, such as Ctrl+Shift+C instead of Ctrl+C, because Ctrl+C is the existing keyboard shortcut for the Copy command.
4. Click the *Store macro in* arrow and select a storage location, such as This Workbook.
5. Type a description of the macro and its purpose in the Description box and click OK to start recording the macro.
6. Perform the commands that you want to record.
7. Click the VIEW tab, click Macros in the Macros group, and then select Stop Recording; or click the DEVELOPER tab and click Stop Recording in the Code group; or click Stop Recording on the status bar.

Adding to an Existing Macro

You cannot append a macro using the macro recorder. Additional steps can only be added using the VBA Editor; however, writing new programming code takes time to learn. Until you are comfortable adding a lot of commands to a macro, you can create a temporary macro, record the commands you need, and then copy the code in the VBA Editor and paste it in the appropriate location in the primary macro code.

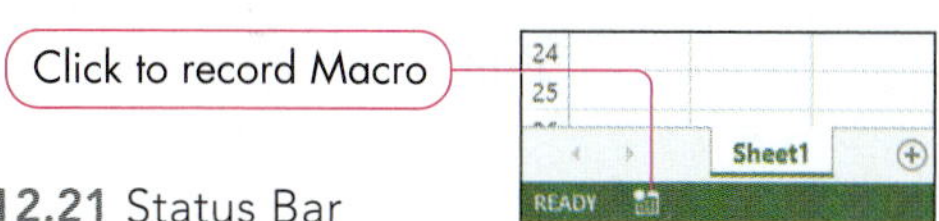

FIGURE 12.21 Status Bar

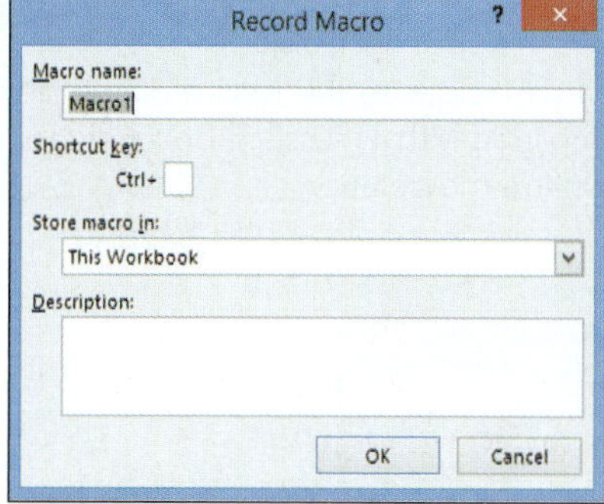

FIGURE 12.22 Record Macro Dialog Box

Record a Personal Macro Workbook

The default *Store macro in* setting is This Workbook. If you want to create a macro that is available in any Excel workbook, click the *Store macro in* arrow and select Personal Macro Workbook. This option creates Personal.xlsb, a hidden ***Personal Macro Workbook*** containing the macro in the C:\Users\Username\AppData\Roaming\Microsoft\Excel\XLStart folder within Windows 8 and Windows 7. Workbooks stored in the XLStart folder open automatically when you start Excel. When the Personal Macro workbook opens, the macros in it are available to any other open workbook.

Use Relative References

It is important to determine if your macro should use relative, absolute, or mixed references as you record the macro. By default, when you select cells when recording a macro, the macro records the cells as absolute references. When you run the macro, the macro executes commands on the absolute cells, regardless of which cell is the active cell when you run the macro. If you want flexibility in that commands are performed relative to the active cell when you run the macro, click the Macros arrow in the Macros group on the View tab and select Use Relative References *before* you perform the commands. Relative references look like this in the VBA Editor:

```
ActiveCell.Offset(3,-2).Range("A1").Select
```

This code moves the active cell down three rows and back to the left by two cells. If the active cell is D1 when you run the macro, the active cell becomes B4 (down three rows; to the left by two cells).

Run a Macro

STEP 3》 After you record a macro, you should run a test to see if it performs the commands as you had anticipated. When you run a macro, Excel performs the tasks in the sequence in which you recorded the steps. To run a macro, do the following:

1. Select the location where you will test the macro. It is recommended to test a macro in a new, blank workbook if you recorded it so that it is available for multiple workbooks. If you saved it to the current workbook only, insert a new worksheet to test the macro.
2. Click the VIEW tab, click the Macros arrow in the Macros group, and then select View Macros; or click the DEVELOPER tab and click Macros in the Code group. The Macro dialog box opens (see Figure 12.23).
3. Select the macro from the *Macro name* list and click Run.

TIP Delete a Macro

If you no longer need a macro, use the Macro dialog box to select the macro and click Delete. Excel will prompt you with a message box asking if you want to delete the selected Macro. Click Yes to confirm the deletion.

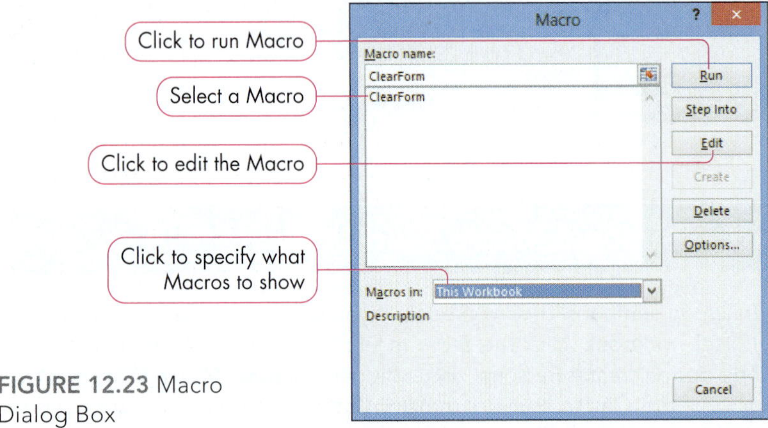

FIGURE 12.23 Macro Dialog Box

Creating Macro Buttons

STEP 4》 For the most part, it will be a rare macro that is so all-encompassing that it would rate a place on the Quick Access Toolbar. On the other hand, you may create a macro that is frequently used in a particular workbook. The easiest way to access frequently used macros within a workbook is to assign a macro to a button on a worksheet. That way, when you or other people use the workbook, it is easy to click the button to run the macro. To add a macro button to a worksheet, do the following:

1. Click the DEVELOPER tab, click Insert in the Controls group, and then click Button (Form Control) in the *Form Controls* section of the Insert gallery. See Figure 12.24.
2. Drag the crosshair pointer to draw the button on the worksheet. When you release the mouse button, the Assign Macro dialog box opens (see Figure 12.25).
3. Select the macro to assign to the button and click OK.
4. Right-click the button, select Edit Text, delete the default text, and then type a more descriptive name for the button.
5. Click the worksheet to complete the button.
6. Click a cell, if necessary, that should be the active cell when the macro runs and click the button to execute the macro assigned to the button.

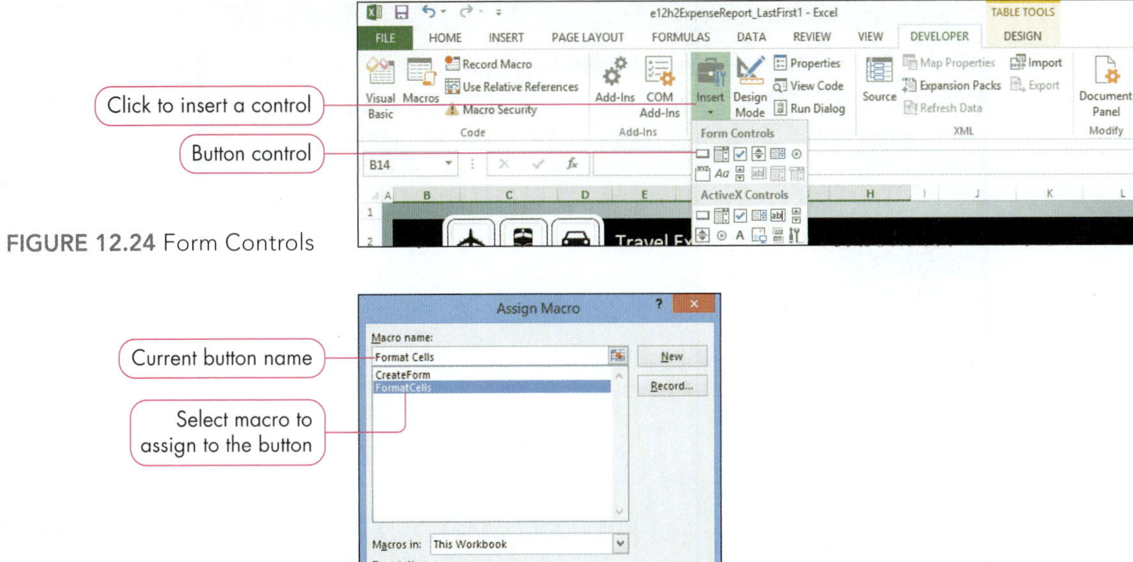

FIGURE 12.24 Form Controls

FIGURE 12.25 Assign Macro Dialog Box

TIP Other Controls

You can insert other controls in a worksheet such as images and artwork and then assign macros to them. For example, you can insert combo boxes, check boxes, and option buttons by clicking Insert in the Controls group on the Developer tab and selecting the desired control. Drag an area on the worksheet to draw the control, right-click the object, and then select Assign Macro to assign a macro action for that particular control.

Setting Macro Security

Macro security is a concern for anyone who uses files containing macros. A macro virus is nothing more than actions written in VBA set to perform malicious actions when run. The proliferation of macro viruses has made people more cautious about opening workbooks that contain macros. By default, Excel automatically disables the macros and displays a security warning that macros have been disabled (see Figure 12.26). Click Enable Content to use the workbook and run macros.

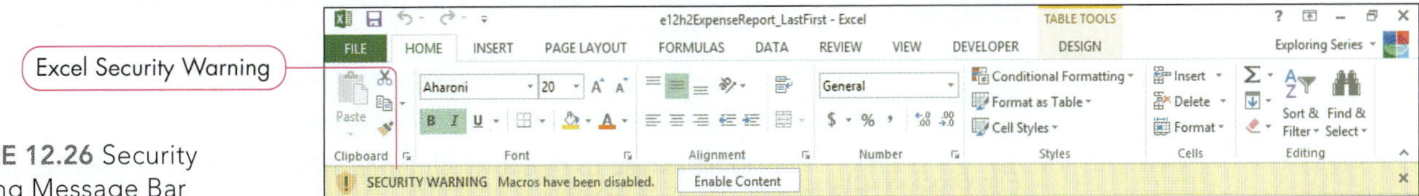

FIGURE 12.26 Security Warning Message Bar

You can use the Trust Center dialog box to change settings to make it easier to work with macros. The Trust Center can direct Excel to trust files in particular folders, trust workbooks created by a trusted publisher, and lower the security settings to allow macros. To open the Trust Center, do the following:

1. Click the FILE tab and click Options.
2. Click Trust Center on the left side of the Excel Options dialog box.
3. Click Trust Center Settings. The Trust Center dialog box displays the sections described in Table 12.1 on the left side of the dialog box (see Figure 12.27).

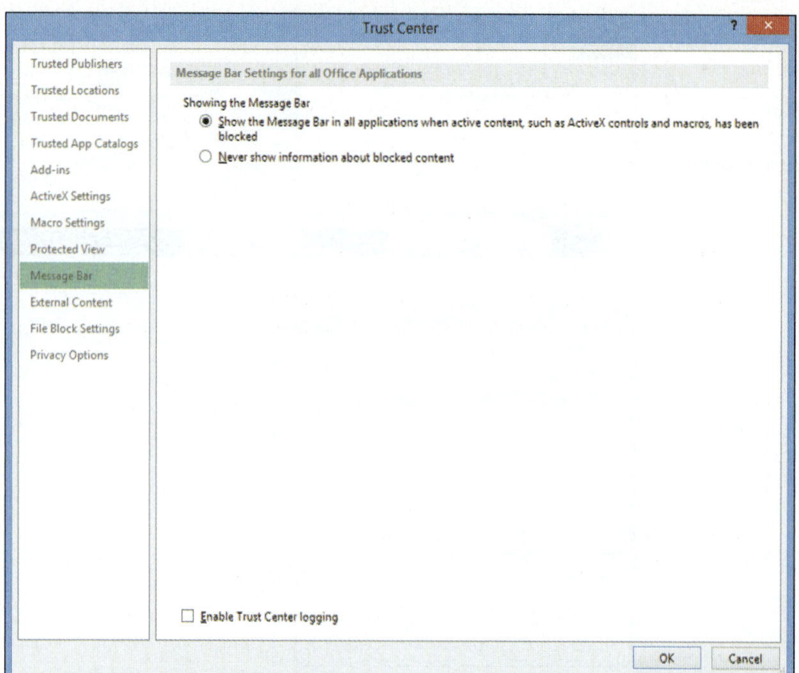

FIGURE 12.27 Trust Center Dialog Box

TABLE 12.1 Trust Center Options

Item	Description
Trusted Publishers	Directs Excel to trust digitally signed workbooks by certain creators.
Trusted Locations	Enables you to select places on your computer to store workbooks securely.
Trusted Documents	Enables you to trust network documents to open without Excel displaying any security warnings.
Trusted App Catalogs	Enables you to trust third-party Office Apps that run inside Excel.
Add-Ins	Enables you to specify which add-ins will be allowed to run given the desired level of security.
ActiveX Settings	Enables you to adjust how Excel deals with ActiveX controls.
Macro Settings	Enables you to specify how Excel deals with macros.
Protected View	Opens potentially dangerous files in a restricted mode but without any security warnings.
Message Bar	Enables you to specify when Excel shows the message bar when it blocks macros.
External Content	Enables you to specify how Excel deals with links to other workbooks and data from other sources.
File Block Settings	Enables you to select which types of files, such as macros, to open in Protected View or which file type to prevent saving a file in.
Privacy Options	Enables you to deal with nonmacro privacy issues.

Quick Concepts

1. What is the purpose of a macro? ***p. 663***
2. How are macros accessed after they have been recorded? ***p. 666***
3. What potential risks are associated with macros? ***p. 667***

Hands-On Exercises

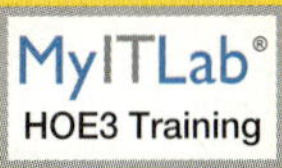

3 Macros

Because you want all employees to use the Travel Expense Report template to report expenditures each month, you want to create a macro to clear the form. In addition, you want to create a button to run the macro so that other users can easily clear the form if they do not know what a macro is or how to run it.

Skills covered: Display Developer Tab • Record a Macro • Run a Macro • Add a Macro Button

STEP 1 » DISPLAY DEVELOPER TAB

The average employee at your company does not use developer tools; therefore, they are not enabled on your workstation. You would like to display the Developer tab so that you can record the macro.

a. Open *e12h2ExpenseReportTemplate_LastFirst* and save it with the file name **e12h3ExpenseReportTemplate_LastFirst**, changing *h2* to *h3*.

   When you use Open or Recent to open a template, you open it as a template to edit. When you use New, you make a copy of the template as a workbook.

> **TROUBLESHOOTING**: If you do not see Templates in Recent Places, click Open and navigate to the local directory that contains your student files.

b. Click the **FILE tab** and click **Options** to open the Excel Options dialog box.

c. Click **Customize Ribbon**, click the **Developer check box** in the Main Tabs list, and then click **OK**.

   The Developer tab is added to the Ribbon.

STEP 2 » RECORD A MACRO

You do not want to assume the level of Excel expertise throughout your company; therefore, you want to craft a macro that will automate as much as possible. The macro you would like to create needs to automatically clear existing values and then display an instruction for users to enter specific data. Although the template is empty to start, users might open the template, save a workbook, and then want to use that workbook to prepare future months' reports. Therefore, you need the macro to clear cells even though the original template has no values. Refer to Figure 12.28 as you complete Step 2.

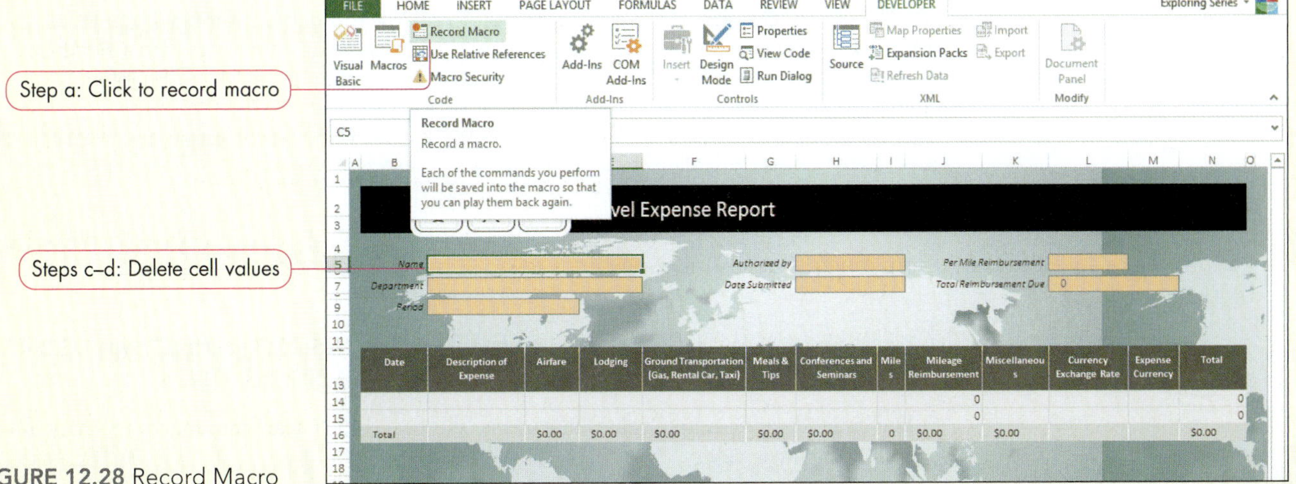

FIGURE 12.28 Record Macro

a. Click the **DEVELOPER tab** and click **Record Macro** in the Code group.

The Record Macro dialog box opens so that you can name and describe the macro.

b. Type **ClearForm** in the **Macro name box**, click in the **Description box**, type **This macro clears existing values in the current Travel Expense Report**, and then click **OK**.

> **TROUBLESHOOTING**: Read through steps c–g in advance before you proceed. Remember most actions taken in Excel are recorded by the macro recorder. Practice the steps below before activating the recorder. If you make a major mistake, delete the macro and repeat steps b through j.

c. Select **cell C5** and press **Delete**.

Even though the cells are empty now, they may contain values at some point. You want the macro to delete any values that might exist in this range.

d. Adapt step c for the following cells and ranges:

- **Cell C7**
- **Cell C9**
- **Cell H5**
- **Cell H7**
- **Cell L5**
- **Range B14:I15**
- **Range K14:M15**

You deleted ranges that might contain values after the user enters data into any workbooks created from the template. It is always good to plan for various possibilities in which data might be entered even if those ranges do not contain values now.

e. Press **Ctrl+G**, type **C5** in the **Reference box** of the Go To dialog box, and then click **OK**.

f. Type **Enter Name Here** in **cell C5** and press **Ctrl+Enter**.

Pressing Ctrl+Enter keeps cell C5 the active cell so that users can immediately enter the label when they open a workbook from the template.

g. Click **cell C7**, type **Enter Department Name**, and then press **Ctrl+Enter**.

h. Click **Stop Recording** in the Code group on the DEVELOPER tab.

i. Save the *e12h3ExpenseReportTemplate_LastFirst* template; click **No** when prompted that the workbook cannot be saved with the macro in it.

Excel opens the Save As dialog box so that you can select the file type.

j. Click the **Save as type arrow**, select **Excel Macro-Enabled Template**, and then click **Save**.

> **TROUBLESHOOTING**: Make sure you select Excel Macro-Enabled Template, not Excel Macro-Enabled Workbook, because you want the file saved as a template, not a workbook. Because the template contains macros, you must save it as an Excel Macro-Enabled Template, not just a template.

STEP 3 » RUN A MACRO

You want to make sure the ClearForm macro does what you want it to do. First, you will add some sample data and run the macro.

a. Type your name in **cell C5**, type **Finance** in **cell C7**, type **1/25/2015** in **cell H7**, type **1/5/2015** in **cell B14**, type **Sales Meeting** in **cell C14**, and then type **$75.00** in **cell G14**.

You entered some sample values in various cells to test the ClearForm macro to verify if it will delete those values.

b. Click the **DEVELOPER tab**, if necessary, and click **Macros** in the Code group.

The Macro dialog box opens and displays the ClearForm macro, which should be selected in the Macro name box.

c. Select **ClearForm**, if necessary, and click **Run**.

The ClearForm macro quickly goes through the worksheet, erasing the values in the specified ranges, goes to cells C5 and C7, enters descriptive labels, and then stops.

> **TROUBLESHOOTING**: If the macro does not delete sample values, delete the macro and rerecord it.

STEP 4 》 ADD A MACRO BUTTON

Your colleagues are probably not Excel experts and do not know how to run a macro. To make it easier to clear values from the form, you want to assign the ClearForm macro to a button. The users can then click the button to clear the form to use it for another month. Refer to Figure 12.29 as you complete Step 4.

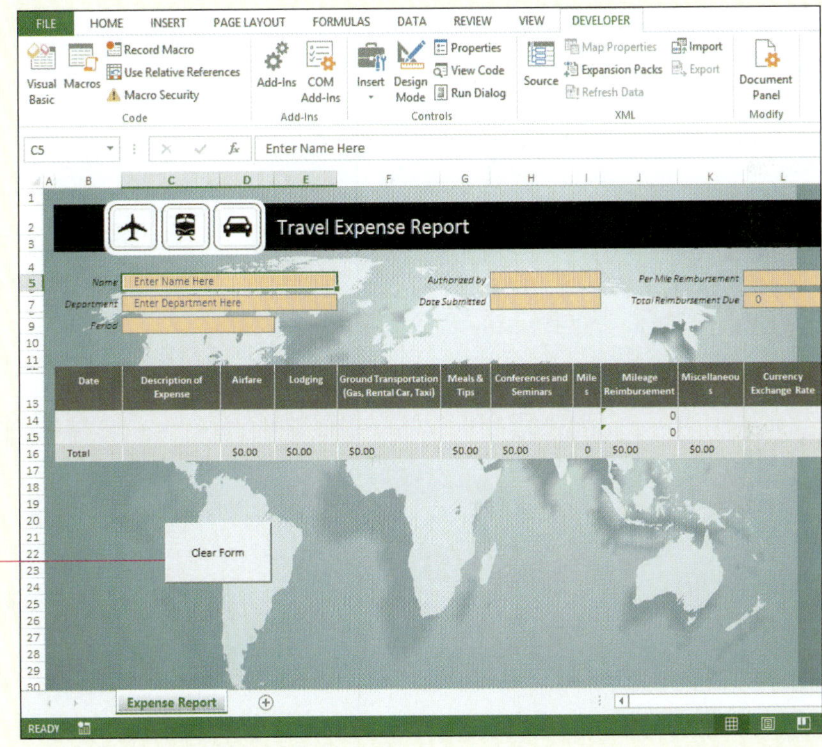

FIGURE 12.29 Macro Button

a. Click the **HOME tab**, click **Format** in the Cells group, select **Unprotect Sheet**, type **eXploring** in the **Password box** in the Unprotect Sheet dialog box, and then click **OK**.

You have to unprotect the worksheet before you can insert a macro button.

b. Click the **DEVELOPER tab**, click **Insert** in the Controls group, and then click **Button (Form Control)** in the *Form Controls* section of the gallery.

c. Click the top of **cell C20** and drag down and to the right to the bottom of **cell D23** to create the area where the button will be placed.

The Assign Macro dialog box opens.

d. Select **ClearForm** in the Macro name list and click **OK**.

This action assigns the ClearForm macro to the button. The button appears in cells C20:D23, is selected, and displays *Button 1*. You will provide descriptive text to appear on the button.

e. Right-click **Button 1** and select **Edit Text**. Select the **Button 1 text**, type **Clear Form**, and then click any cell on the worksheet outside the button.

   The button now shows *Clear Form*, which is more descriptive of the button's purpose than *Button 1*.

f. Right-click the **Expense Report worksheet tab**, select **Protect Sheet**, type **eXploring** in the **Password to protect sheet box**, click **OK**, type **eXploring** in the **Reenter password to proceed box**, and then click **OK**.

   You need to protect the worksheet after creating the macro button.

g. Type **6/1/2015** in cell **B14** and type **6/29/2015** in **cell B15** to enter sample data.

h. Click **Clear Form** in the worksheet.

   When you click Clear Form, Excel runs the ClearForm macro.

i. Save the Macro-Enabled Template. Keep the workbook open if you plan to continue with Hands-On Exercise 4. If not, close the workbook and exit Excel.

Visual Basic for Applications

As you perform commands while recording a macro, those commands are translated into programming code called Visual Basic for Applications (VBA). VBA is a robust programming language that can be used within various software packages to enhance and automate functionality. While many casual users will be able to complete required tasks using just the macro recorder, more advanced VBA macros can be created by authoring code directly into modules within the Visual Basic Editor. A ***module*** is a file in which macros are stored. The ***Visual Basic Editor*** is an application used to create, edit, execute, and debug Office application macros using programming code. These macros can then be used within a Macro-Enabled Workbook or Template. The two types of VBA macros are sub procedures and custom functions. ***Sub procedures***, which are also created when using the macro recorder, perform actions on a workbook, such as the ClearForm example earlier in the chapter. For example, you can create a sub procedure to insert the current date in a worksheet. Similar to the hundreds of built-in functions in Excel, custom functions have the ability to manipulate input variables and return a value.

Creating a Sub Procedure

STEP 1» The first step to creating a sub procedure is inserting a new module or editing data in an existing module within the VBA editor. To access the VBA Editor, press Alt+F11 on your keyboard. The left side of the VBA window contains the Project Explorer, which is similar in concept and appearance to the File Explorer except that it displays only open workbooks and/or other Visual Basic projects (see Figure 12.30).

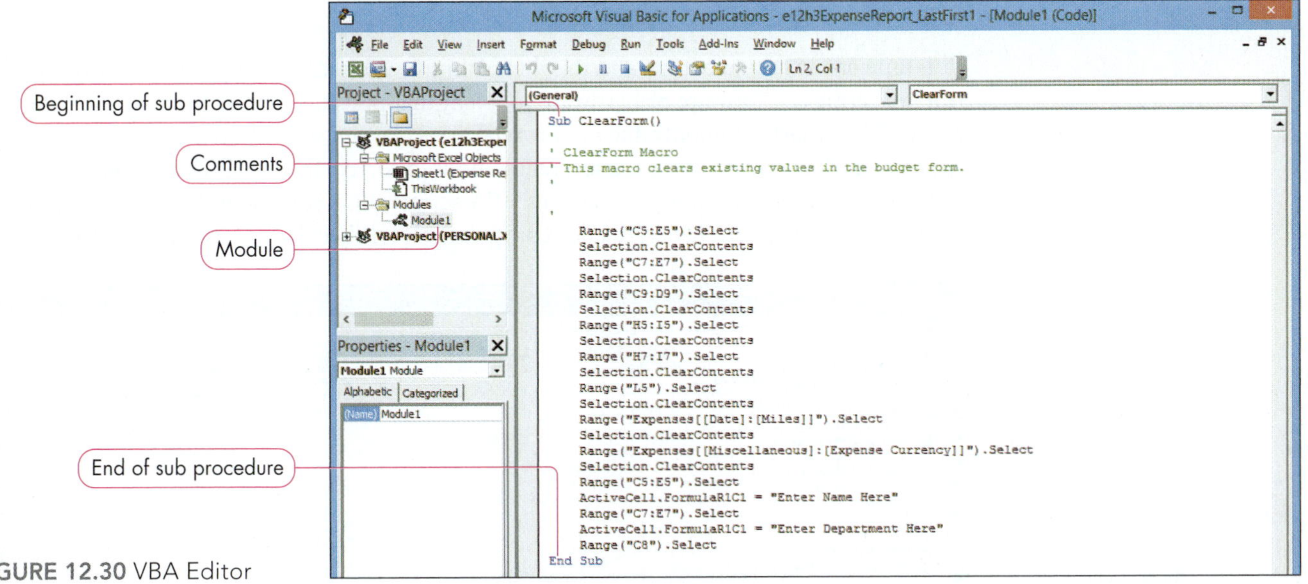

FIGURE 12.30 VBA Editor

The Visual Basic statements appear in the Code window on the right side. A Visual Basic module consists of at least one ***procedure***, which is a named sequence of statements stored in a macro. In this example, Module1 contains the ClearForm procedure, which is also the name of the macro created in Excel. Module1 is stored in the Travel Expense Report workbook.

A procedure or macro always begins and ends with the Sub and End Sub statements. The Sub statement contains the name of the macro, such as Sub ClearForm() in Figure 12.30. The End Sub statement is the last statement and indicates the end of the macro. Sub and End Sub are Visual Basic keywords and appear in blue. ***Keywords*** are special programming syntax that have special meaning with the programming language and must be used for their intended purposes.

Comments, which are indicated by an apostrophe and appear in green, provide information about the macro but do not affect its execution and are considered documentation. Comments can be entered manually or are inserted automatically by the macro recorder to document the macro name, its author, and shortcut key (if any). You can add, delete, or modify comments. To create a basic sub procedure that would enter a date into a cell, complete the following steps:

1. From the VBA Editor, select Module from the Insert menu.
2. Type *sub currentdate()* and press Enter.
3. Type *'This macro will insert the current date in cell H7.*
4. Type *range("H7") = date* and press Enter.
5. Type *range("H7").font.bold = true.*
6. Save and exit the Visual Basic Editor.

Table 12.2 explains some of the lines of code used to create the previous sub procedure. The first word, *range*, refers to an object. An ***object*** is a variable that contains both data and code and represents an element of Excel such as Range or Selection. A period follows the object name, and the next word is often a behavior or attribute, such as Select or ClearContents, that describes a behavior or action performed on the object.

TABLE 12.2 VBA Editor Code

Code	Explanation
range("H7")	Identifies the range H7
= date	Applies the current date to the cell
font.bold = true	Applies object property, setting the font to bold. To disable, change *true* to *false*.

Use VBA with Protected Worksheets

Run time errors can sometimes occur when running VBA scripts on protected worksheets. A ***run time error*** is a software or hardware problem that prevents a program from working correctly. This is most commonly due to a procedure such as *range("H7").font.bold = true*, attempting to alter a locked cell. There are several methods to correct this issue. The simplest, as shown in Figure 12.31, is to encase your current VBA script with a statement that will unprotect the worksheet, run the current script, and reprotect the worksheet before ending the procedure.

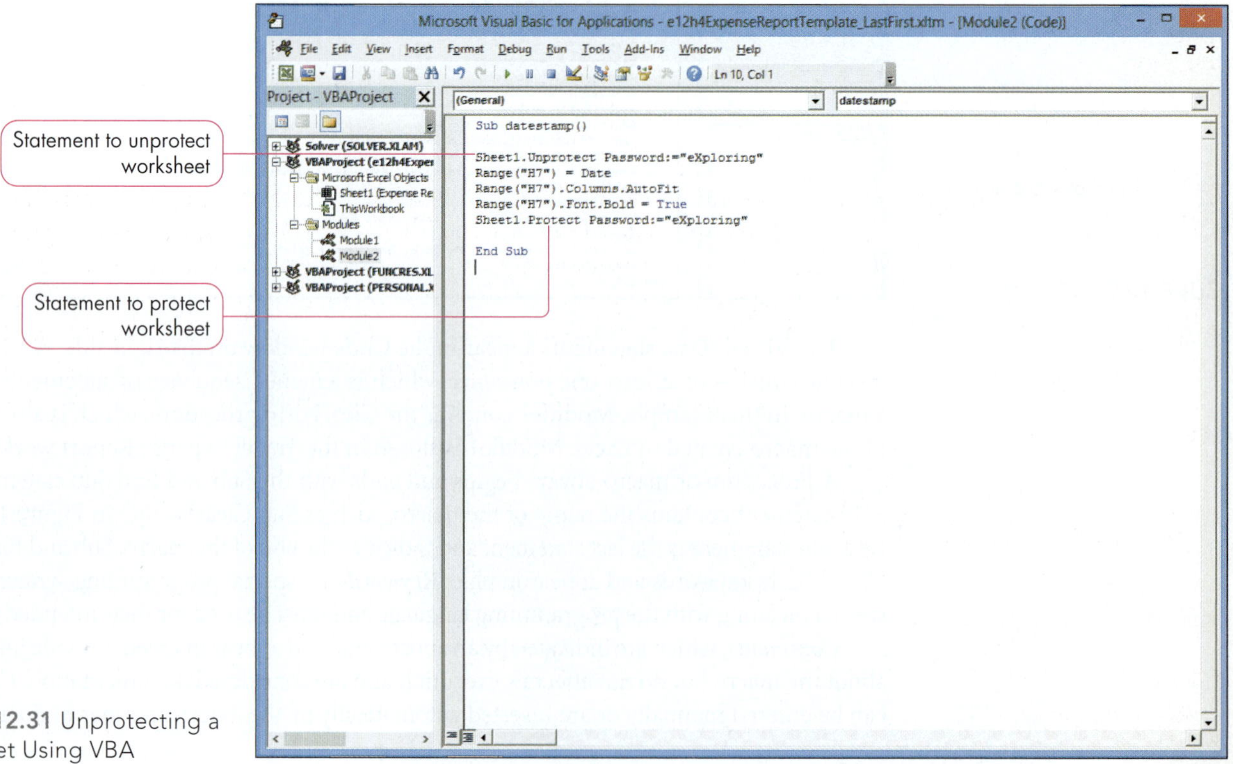

FIGURE 12.31 Unprotecting a Worksheet Using VBA

In the example given, cell H7 is formatted and the column size is altered. However, this will create a run time error because the worksheet is protected. The statement *Sheet1. Unprotect Password:= "eXploring"* unprotects the worksheet to allow the format changes to occur. The statement *Sheet1.Protect Password:= "eXploring"* then reprotects the worksheet.

Edit a Macro in the Visual Basic Editor

STEP 2

If you work with a workbook that has macros that were created by a coworker or you used the macro recorder, you can edit the existing macro using the Visual Basic Editor. For example, if you record a macro to apply bold, Arial font, 12-pt size, and Red font color, each command appears in a separate statement (see Figure 12.32). The two statements to apply bold and italic start with Selection.Font, indicating that a font attribute will be applied to the current selection. The statement continues with a period and behavior, such as *Bold = True,* indicating that bold is activated. If the sub procedure is turning off bold, the statement looks like this:

```
Selection.Font.Bold = False
```

The With statement enables you to perform multiple actions on the same object. All commands between the With and the corresponding End With statement are executed collectively. Although the font and font size were changed in the macro, the macro also indicates that other attributes, such as superscript and subscript, are turned off. You can delete those lines of code if you want.

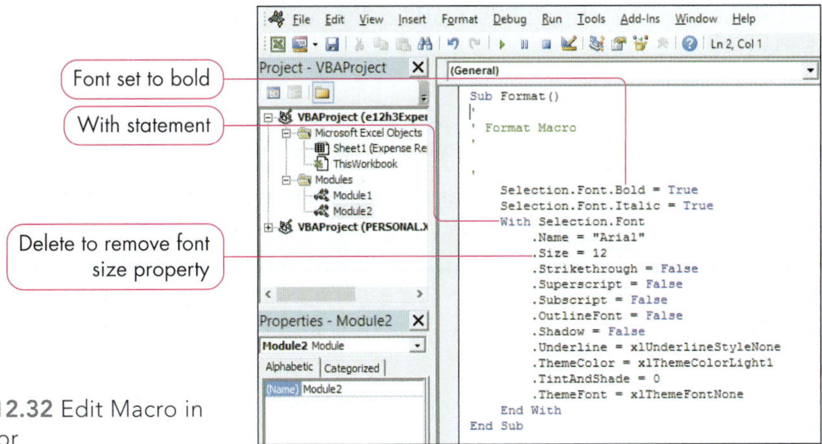

FIGURE 12.32 Edit Macro in VBA Editor

Creating a Custom Function

STEP 4

There are several hundred built-in functions in Excel that can perform tasks as simple as capitalizing the first letter of a word, such as the Proper function, or as complex as a multiconditional sum, as created with SumIFs. In the event that one of the numerous built-in functions does not meet your needs, you have the ability to create your own custom function using VBA. Custom functions are virtually limitless. However, like sub procedures, they are still saved in modules. This means that if they are not saved to a Personal Macro Workbook, they will only be available within the Macro-Enabled Workbook in which they were created.

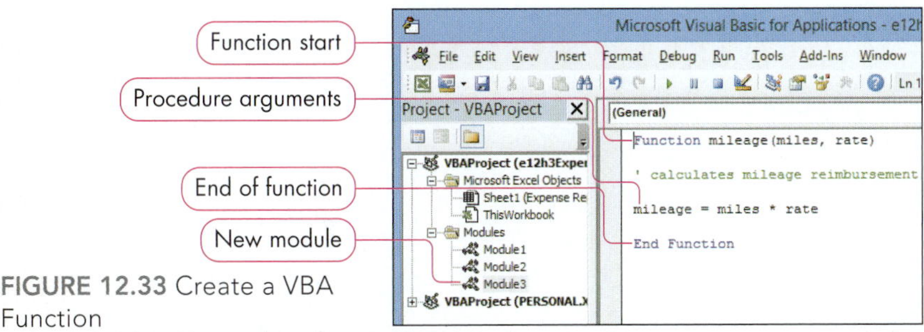

FIGURE 12.33 Create a VBA Function

When creating a custom function in VBA, you must start by creating a new module and typing *function* followed by the name of the function you are creating and the arguments that the function will use inside parentheses (see Figure 12.32).

After entering arguments on the next line, you have the ability to add comments in the same manner they were added to sub procedures. Your next step is to enter the statement that defines your function such as:

```
Mileage = miles * rate
```

After completing the statement, you end the function by typing End Function. However, this step should automatically be completed by the VBA editor.

Once a custom function is completed, it can be viewed within Excel under User Defined functions within the Insert Function command in the Function Library. Furthermore, you can access the function by simply typing = in the cell of your choice and the name of the function. This will allow you to use the custom function in the same manner as any of the built-in Excel functions. To create the VBA function described above, complete the following steps:

1. Press Alt+F11 to open the VBA Editor.
2. From the INSERT tab, select Module.
3. Type *Function mileage (rate, miles)* and press Enter.
4. Type *mileage = rate * miles.*
5. Type End Function.
6. Save the module and return to the workbook to access the newly created custom function.

1. When using Excel, why would you want to access the VBA editor? ***p. 673***
2. What are the two types of VBA macros that can be created in the VBA editor? ***p. 673***
3. Why would it be necessary to create a custom function? ***p. 675***

Hands-On Exercises

Watch the Video for this Hands-On Exercise!

MyITLab®
HOE4 Training

4 Visual Basic for Applications

You would like to automate as much of the Travel Expense Report as possible. Therefore, you will create a sub procedure assigned to a macro button to automatically insert the current date into the worksheet. You would also like to add an additional function that will allow the user to estimate mileage reimbursement prior to submission.

Skills covered: Create a Sub Procedure • Edit a Macro • Assign a Macro to an Image • Create a Custom Function

STEP 1 » CREATE A SUB PROCEDURE

Before you create the sub procedure, you will open the template you created in Hands-On Exercise 3 and save it as a template with another name to preserve the original template in case you make any mistakes.

a. Open the Macro-Enabled Template *e12h3ExpenseReportTemplate_LastFirst*, click **Enable Content** to activate the prior macro, and save it as **e12h4ExpenseReportTemplate_LastFirst**, changing *h3* to *h4*.

   When you use Open or Recent to open a template, you open it as a template to edit. When you use New, you make a copy of the template as a workbook.

b. Press **Alt+F11** on your keyboard to open the Visual Basic Editor.

c. Click the **Insert menu** and select **Module**.

d. Type ***sub datestamp ()*** on the first line of the newly created module and press **Enter**.

e. Type **Sheet1.Unprotect Password:= "eXploring"** and press **Enter**.

   This unprotects the workbook to allow the remaining changes to take place.

f. Type **range("H7") = date** and press **Enter**.

   This enters the current date.

g. Type **range("H7").columns.autofit** and press **Enter**.

   This sets the selected column to autofit, which will ensure proper display of the date.

h. Type **range("H7").Font.Bold = True**.

   This sets the newly entered date to bold.

i. Type **Sheet1.Protect Password:= "eXploring"** and press **Enter**.

j. Save the macro and press **F5** to test the newly created macro.

   When run, the newly created sub procedure unprotects the worksheet, adds and formats the current date, sets the column width to auto, and reprotects the document.

STEP 2 » EDIT A MACRO

After running the created sub procedure, you have decided that the newly inserted date should be italicized instead of bold. You will make this change in the VBA Editor by editing the bold property.

a. Press **Alt+F11** on your keyboard if the VBA Editor is not open.

   Excel opens the VBA Editor so that you can edit the macro programming language.

b. Click **module 2**, if it is not already selected, to display the sub procedure created in Step 1. Select the line **Range("H7").Font.Bold = True** and replace the word *Bold* with **Italic**.

   This edits the command to set the inserted date to italics instead of bold.

c. Save and exit the VBA Editor.

STEP 3 » ASSIGN A MACRO TO AN IMAGE

After creating the sub procedure to insert the current date in the worksheet, you would like to enhance the usability of the document by creating a calendar icon to activate the macro. Refer to Figure 12.34 as you complete Step 3.

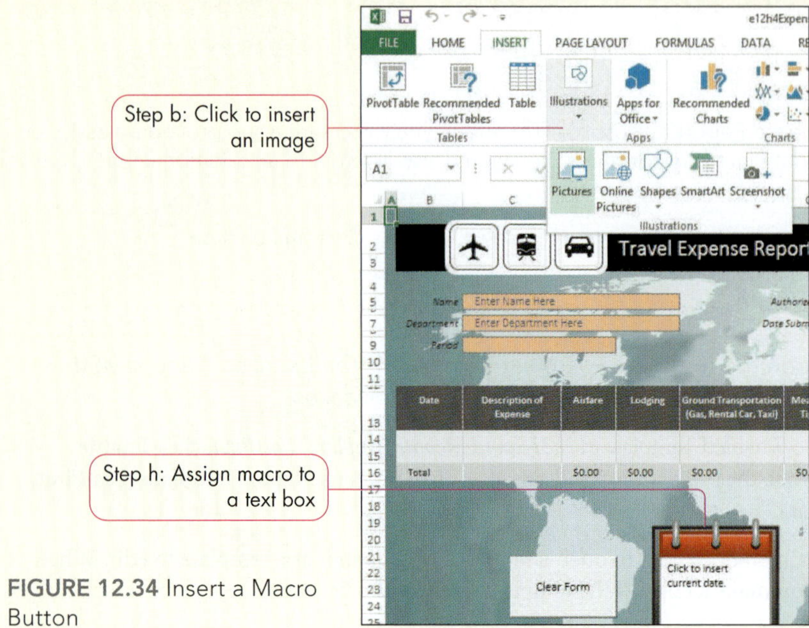

FIGURE 12.34 Insert a Macro Button

a. Right-click the **Expense Report worksheet tab**, select **Unprotect Sheet**, type **eXploring** in the **Password to unprotect sheet box**, and then click **OK**.

b. Click the **INSERT tab** and select **Pictures** from the Illustrations group.

c. Insert the image **e12h4Calendar.png** and position the image to the right of Clear Form.

d. Right-click the inserted image and click **Assign Macro**. Click the **datestamp macro**, Click **OK**.

e. Click the **INSERT tab**, if necessary, and click **Text Box** in the Text group.

f. Draw a text box inside the image inserted in step b.

g. Type **Click to insert current date** in the text box.

h. Right-click the text box and click **Assign Macro**. Click the **datestamp macro box.**

   You decided to assign the macro to both the inserted image and the text box to make sure that the macro activates no matter where the end user clicks on the image.

i. Click the newly created button to verify the current date. Once the date is verified, click **Clear Form** and save the template.

STEP 4 » CREATE A CUSTOM FUNCTION

Even though the Travel Expense Report has the ability to automatically calculate travel mileage reimbursement, you have decided to create a custom function to allow users to manually calculate their mileage reimbursement if they choose.

a. Press **Alt +F11** on your keyboard to open the Visual Basic Editor.

b. Click the **Insert menu** and select **Module**.

c. Type **function mileage(miles,rate)** on the first line of the newly created module and press **Enter**.

d. Type **This function will calculate mileage reimbursement**. Press **Enter**.

This will appear as a comment in the module. However, it will not impact the calculation of the function.

e. Type the statement **mileage = miles * rate** and press **Enter**.

f. Save and exit the VBA Editor.

This creates a custom function that can be used in a similar fashion to any built-in function within Excel.

g. Click **cell H21** and type **=mileage(32,0.75)**. This returns the value 24.

You entered 32 miles at the rate of $.75 per mile to test the newly created function.

h. Delete the contents of **cell H21**.

i. Right-click the **Expense Report worksheet tab**, select **Protect Sheet**, type **eXploring** in the **Password to protect sheet box**, click **OK**, type **eXploring** in the **Reenter password to proceed box**, and then click **OK**.

j. Save the workbook and submit based on your instructor's directions.

e. Create a macro that filters the database to show internal medicine doctors in Miami who are accep ing new patients by doing the following:

- Click the **DEVELOPER tab** if necessary and click **Record Macro** in the Code group to open th Record Macro dialog box.
- Type **MiamiInternalNew** in the **Macro name box**, type **Extracts a list of Miami doctors wh specialize in internal medicine and who are accepting new patients** in the **Description bo** and then click **OK**.
- Click the **Criteria Settings sheet tab**, select the **range A2:H2**, and then press **Delete** to dele any conditions that a user might enter to perform their own filter.
- Click **cell D2**, type **Miami**, click **cell E2**, type **Internal Medicine**, click **cell H2**, type **Yes**, an then press **Ctrl+Enter**.
- Click the **Output sheet tab** and click **cell B6** to place the active cell in the Extract range.
- Click the **DATA tab** and click **Advanced** in the Sort & Filter group to open the Advanced Filte dialog box.
- Click the **Copy to another location option**, type **Database** in the **List range box**, type **Criteri** in the **Criteria range box**, type **Extract** in the **Copy to box**, and then click **OK**.
- Press **Ctrl+Home** to position the active cell in **cell A1**.
- Click the **DEVELOPER tab** and click **Stop Recording** in the Code group. Save the workbook.

f. Create a macro that clears the criteria range and the output by doing the following:

- Click the **DEVELOPER tab** if necessary and click **Record Macro** in the Code group to open th Record Macro dialog box.
- Type **Clear** in the **Macro name box**, type **Clears the criteria range and the output** in th **Description box**, and then click **OK**.
- Click the **Criteria Settings sheet tab**, select the **range A2:H2**, and then press **Delete** to delet any existing conditions that might exist later.
- Click **cell A2**, type **-100** as a dummy value, and then press **Ctrl+Enter**.
- Click the **Output sheet tab** and click **cell B6** to place the active cell in the Extract range.
- Click the **DATA tab** and click **Advanced** in the Sort & Filter group to open the Advanced Filte dialog box.
- Click the **Copy to another location option**, type **Database** in the **List range box**, type **Criteria** in the **Criteria range box**, type **Extract** in the **Copy to box**, and then click **OK**.
- Press **Ctrl+Home** to position the active cell in **cell A1**.
- Click the **DEVELOPER tab** and click **Stop Recording** in the Code group.

g. Create a macro button and assign the Clear macro to it by doing the following:

- Click the **DEVELOPER tab** if necessary, click **Insert** in the Controls group, and then click **Button (Form Control)** in the *Form Controls* section.
- Click in **cell A2** and create a button that fills the range A2:B4. When you release the mouse button, the Assign Macro dialog box opens.
- Select **Clear** in the *Macro name* list and click **OK**. The button displays *Button 1*.
- Right-click the button, select **Edit Text**, select **Button 1**, type **Clear Output**, and then click in **cell A1**. Save the workbook.

h. Create a macro button and assign the PediatricsNew macro to it by doing the following:

- Click **Insert** in the Controls group and click **Button (Form Control)** in the *Form Controls* section.
- Drag to create a button on the right side of the Clear Output button. Make sure the second button is approximately the same height and width as the Clear Output button.
- Select **PediatricsNew** in the *Macro name* list and click **OK**. The button displays *Button 2*.
- Right-click the button, select **Edit Text**, select **Button 2**, type **Pediatrics Accepting New Patients**, and then click in **cell A1**. If you need to resize the button to display the button text, press **Ctrl** as you click the button to select it. Then resize the button as necessary. Save the workbook.

i. Adapt step h to create a macro button on the right side of the Pediatrics button and assign the MiamiInternalNew macro to it. Display the text **Miami Internal Medicine Accept New** and click in **cell A1**. Save the workbook.

j. Run the macros by doing the following:
   - Click **Pediatrics Accepting New Patients**. The Output sheet should display 18 records (see Figure 12.35).
   - Click **Miami Internal Medicine Accept New**. The Output sheet should display 4 records.
   - Click **Clear Output**.

k. Edit any macro that does not run correctly: Click the **DEVELOPER tab**, click **Macros** in the Code group, select the macro that contains errors, and then click **Edit**. Edit the code as necessary in the VBA Editor (see Figure 12.36), click **Save**, close the VBA Editor, and then run the macro again.

l. Create a footer with your name on the left side, the sheet name code in the center, and the file name code on the right side of all three worksheets.

m. Save and close the workbook, and submit based on your instructor's directions.

Mid-Level Exercises

1 Little League Statistics

You volunteered to coach for your community Little League program. You are working with the Pirates, a team of 10- to 12-year-olds who respond well to seeing their batting statistics. You created a workbook to record the Pirates' batting data and calculate their statistics. The recreation department manager is a friend of yours from high school and is impressed with your workbook. He wondered if you could make something similar for the other coaches when he saw how you were recording statistics.

a. Open *e12m1Pirates* and save it as **e12m1Pirates_LastFirst**.

b. Apply the **Title cell style** to **cell A1**, the **Heading 2 cell style** to the **range A2:R2**, the **Heading 4 cell style** to the **range A4:A20**, and **Output style** to the **range B3:R20**.

c. Apply the **Wood Type theme** and apply the **Red theme colors**.

d. Add *e12m1Pirate.jpg* as a background image for the worksheet.

e. Save the Excel workbook and save it as a template named **e12m1Baseball_LastFirst**.

f. Delete the background from the Statistics worksheet and insert *e12m1Baseball.jpg* as the background image for the template before distributing the template to the other teams.

g. Select the **Game 1 worksheet**, delete all players' names and batting information from the **range A3:M16**. Right-align the labels in the **range C2:M2**.

h. Unlock cells in **cell A1**, the **range A3:M16** of the Game 1 worksheet, and **cell A1** in the Statistics worksheet. Right-align the labels in the **range B2:R2** in the Statistics worksheet.

i. Set **0.2"** left and right margins on both worksheets. Set a width of **6.00** for columns B:H and J:O on the Statistics worksheet.

j. Create a footer with your name on the left side, the sheet name code in the center, and the file name code on the right side of both worksheets.

k. Protect all worksheets with a password of **eXploring**. Allow all users to format cells, columns, and rows.

l. Save and close the template.

m. Create a new workbook from the *e12m1Baseball_LastFirst* template and save the workbook as **e12m1Broncos_LastFirst**.

n. Edit the league name from *Pirates* to **Broncos** in **cell A1** of each worksheet and enter player names and data for 14 players in the Games 1 worksheet.

o. Save the workbook and submit based on your instructor's directions.

2 Jackson Municipal Airport

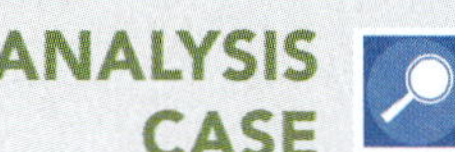

Hulett Enterprises is located in Jackson, Mississippi. In the past, you have created Web queries to find departure and arrival information for your supervisors, Denise Petrillo and Omar Vincent, who travel frequently for business meetings. Because of your Excel experience, other managers are interested in having you develop a workbook with this information they can use. You decide to create macros to update the Web queries, adjust formatting of the imported data, and then print the worksheets. Finally, you will assign the macros to macro buttons.

a. Open *e12m2Airport* and save it as **e12m2Airport_LastFirst** as an Excel Macro-Enabled Workbook file format.

b. Create a Web query in **cell A8** to **http://www.jmaa.com/JAN/FlightInfo_arr.asp** to the arrival schedule table on the Arrivals worksheet.

c. Create a Web query in **cell A8** to **http://www.jmaa.com/JAN/FlightInfo_arr.asp** to the departure schedule table on the Departures worksheet.

d. Apply **conditional formatting** to the Status column (the **range F9:F50**) to highlight DELAYED flights with **Light Red Fill with Dark Red Text formatting** on both worksheets.

DISCOVER 

e. Display the Arrivals worksheet and record a macro named **Update** to do the following:
   - Refresh all Web queries.
   - Bold the column labels on row **8**.
   - Set **cell A1** as the active cell.

f. Create a button on each worksheet in the **range A4:C6** that is assigned to the Update macro and displays *Refresh the List* on the button.

g. Click **Refresh the List** on each worksheet to ensure it works.

h. Create a footer with your name on the left side, the sheet name code in the center, and the file name code on the right side on each worksheet.

 i. Answer the questions on the Q&A worksheet.

j. Save and close the workbook, and submit based on your instructor's directions.

3 Fundraiser

OLLABORATION CASE 

You work for a regional philanthropic organization that helps raise money for underprivileged youth. To help meet an end-of-the-year fundraising goal, you have decided to deploy regional donation agents to help collect contributions. You would like to make a worksheet to help track donations. Once the worksheet is completed, you will share the file via e-mail with a collaborator in the region who will update the numbers.

Student 1:

a. Open *e12m3FundRaiser* and save it as **e12m3FundRaiser_LastFirst**.

b. Select **cell B2** and apply the **Heading 2 cell style**.

c. Select the **range B3:E10**, click the **HOME tab**, click **Format** and then unlock the cells.

d. Click **Format** and protect the worksheet using the password **eXploring**.

e. Click the **FILE tab** and select **Share** in the Backstage view.

f. Select **EMAIL** and choose **Send as Attachment**.

g. E-mail the worksheet to your collaborator.

Student 2:

h. Open the e-mail and the attachment and enter the following data:

Date	Name	Donation	Collector
12/20/2015	Smith	$350.00	
12/22/2015	Williams	$125.00	
12/23/2015	Wilky	$110.00	
12/23/2015	Barns	$500.00	

i. Type your name as the **collector** in column E.

j. Create a footer with your name on the left side, the sheet name code in the center, and the file name code on the right side on each worksheet.

k. Save and close the workbook, and submit based on your instructor's directions.

Beyond the Classroom

Trust Center

RESEARCH CASE

So far, you have worked with the default Trust Center settings. You want to learn more about the Trust Center. Open the Trust Center dialog box in Excel and display the Macro Settings options. Start Word and insert a screenshot of the default Macro Settings. Set a 3" shape height for the screenshot. Save the Word document as **e12b2Trust_LastFirst**. Compose a short explanation of the default Macro Settings option. Display the File Block Settings options and select the Excel 2007 and later Macro-Enabled Workbooks and Templates Open and Save check boxes. Insert a screenshot in your Word document and set a **3"** shape height. Click **OK** in each open dialog box.

In Excel, open *e12h3ExpenseReportTemplate_LastFirst.xltm*, the Macro-Enabled Template. In Word, explain what happens when you open this template and what happens when you try to run the macro by clicking **Clear Form**. Close the Macro-Enabled Template and deselect the check boxes you just selected in the File Block Settings. In the Word document, insert a footer with your name on the left side and a file name field on the right side. Save the document and submit based on your instructor's directions.

Real Estate Listings

DISASTER RECOVERY

You are a real estate analyst who works for Mountain View Realty in the North Utah County area. Your assistant, Joey, compiled a list of houses sold during the past few months in a Macro-Enabled Workbook. Joey created three macros: (1) a Clear macro to clear the existing Criteria Range and run the filter to empty the Output Range, (2) a CedarHills macro to set a criterion in the Criteria Range to filter the list for Cedar Hills only, and (3) a CityAgentCombo interactive macro with input boxes to prompt the user for the city and agent, enter those in respective cells, and run the advanced filter. In addition, Joey created three macro buttons, one to run each macro. However, the macros and buttons have errors. Open *e12b3RealEstate.xlsm* and save it as a Macro-Enabled Workbook named **e12b3RealEstate_LastFirst**. Find the errors in the macros, document the problems in the macro code using programming comments, and then fix the errors. Find and correct the macro button errors. Create a footer with your name on the left side, the sheet name code in the center, and the file name code on the right side of the Input-Output worksheet. Save and close the workbook, and submit based on your instructor's directions.

Interview Techniques

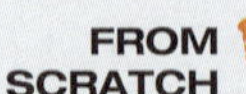

SOFT SKILLS CASE

FROM SCRATCH

Soon you will graduate from college and, in preparation for graduation, you will be participating in several job interviews. As part of your preparation, you would like to do research on interview techniques. Your next goal is to create an Excel worksheet to help rate your overall feelings toward your performance during each interview.

After completing your research, create a workbook named **e12b4Evaluation_LastFirst**. Name the worksheet **Interview Notes**. Type the heading **Company** in **cell A1**, **Position** in **cell B1**, **Date** in **cell C1**, and **Notes** in **cell D1**. Format the cells with the **Heading 2 cell style**. Highlight the **range A1:D1** and ensure the cells are locked. Your last step is to protect the worksheet, using the password **eXploring**. Create a footer with your name on the left side, the sheet name code in the center, and the file name code on the right side of the Input-Output worksheet. Save and close the workbook, and submit based on your instructor's directions.

Capstone Exercise

As the department head of the Information Systems Department at a university, you are responsible for developing the class teaching schedules for your faculty. You have a tentative Fall 2015 schedule developed in sequence, but you want to ensure that you are not double-booking classrooms or faculty. To help you review room and faculty schedules, you will need to sort the original list in various ways. In addition, you want to create a model to use as a template for future semesters and to share with other department heads.

Create a Template

You want to convert the existing Fall 2015 schedule into a template so that you can use it to develop future semester schedules. In addition, you want to apply cell styles to format the template.

a. Open *e12c1Schedule* and save it as **e12c1Schedule_LastFirst** in Macro-Enabled Template file format.

b. Apply the **Retrospect theme**.

c. Apply the **Heading 3 cell style** to the column labels in the **range A4:K4** in the Sequential worksheet.

d. Apply the **Aspect theme color**.

e. Save the template.

Create the RoomSort Macro

You will sort the table by room number to ensure you do not have any room conflicts, such as double-booking a room. To avoid having to create a custom sort each time you want to perform this sort, you will record the steps as a macro.

a. Record a macro named **RoomSort**.

b. Display the Room worksheet data, use the Name Box to select the **range A4:M100**, and then delete the selected range. (This process will delete any existing data to ensure empty cells before copying new data to this worksheet.)

c. Display the Sequential worksheet, use the Go To command to go to **cell A4**, and then press **Ctrl+Shift+End** to select the scheduling data. Copy the selected range and paste it starting in **cell A4** of the Room worksheet. Use the Go To command to go to **cell A4**.

d. Create a custom sort with these settings:
   - Sort by Room in alphabetical order.
   - Sort then by Days with a custom order by adding entries in this order: MWF, MW, M, W, TR, T, R, S.
   - Sort then by Start Time from earliest to latest.
   - Perform the sort.

e. Display the Sequential worksheet, use the Go To command to go to **cell A1**, and then stop recording the macro.

f. Save the file as a Macro-Enabled Template.

Create the FacultySort Macro

You want to sort the table by faculty, days, and times to ensure you do not have any scheduling conflicts, such as double-booking a faculty member with two classes at the same time. To avoid having to create a custom sort each time you want to perform this sort, you will record the steps as a macro.

a. Record a macro named **FacultySort**.

b. Display the Faculty worksheet data, use the Name Box to select the **range A4:M100**, and then delete the selected range. (This process will delete any existing data to ensure empty cells before copying new data to this worksheet.)

c. Display the Sequential worksheet, use the Go To command to go to **cell A4**, and then press **Ctrl+Shift+End** to select the scheduling data. Copy the selected range and paste it starting in **cell A4** of the Faculty worksheet. Use the Go To command to go to **cell A4**.

d. Create a custom sort with these settings:
   - Sort by Instructor in alphabetical order.
   - Sort then by Days with a custom order you created previously.
   - Sort then by Start Time from earliest to latest.
   - Perform the sort.

e. Display the Sequential worksheet, use the Go To command to go to **cell A1**, and then stop recording the macro. Save the Macro-Enabled Template.

Create Macro Buttons

To create a user-friendly interface for yourself and others who might use your Macro-Enabled Template, you will insert two macro buttons, one for each macro, on the Sequential worksheet.

a. Insert a button at the top of the worksheet and assign it to the RoomSort macro.

b. Edit the text that appears on the button to display appropriate text.

c. Create, place, and edit a button for the second macro.

d. Right-click each macro button and set **0.5**" height and **1.5**" width. Ensure all buttons are the same distance from the top of the worksheet and the same distance apart.

e. Save the Macro-Enabled Template.

Finalize the Template

You will save the current data as a Macro-Enabled Workbook to preserve the data. Then you will prepare the file to be a template without the data.

a. Save the workbook as **e12c1InfoSys_LastFirst** in the Excel Macro-Enabled Workbook file type.

Glossary

100% stacked column chart A chart type that places (stacks) data in one column per category, with each column the same height of 100%.

3-D formula A formula or function that refers to the same range in multiple worksheets, such as =SUM(January:December!C5).

3-D reference A pointer to a cell in another worksheet, such as =Sheet1!B15.

Absolute cell reference A designation that provides a permanent reference to a specific cell. When you copy a formula containing an absolute reference, the cell reference in the copied formula does not change, regardless of where you copy the formula. An absolute cell reference appears with a dollar sign before both the column letter and the row number, such as $B$4.

Access Relational database management software that enables you to record and link data, query databases, and create forms and reports.

Accessibility Checker A tool that detects issues that could hinder a user's ability to use a workbook.

Accounting Number Format A number format that displays $ on the left side of a cell and formats values with commas for the thousands separator and two decimal places.

Active cell The current cell in a worksheet. It is indicated by a dark green border onscreen.

Add-in A program that can be added to Excel to provide enhanced functionality.

Alignment Placement of data within cell boundaries.

Analysis ToolPak An add-in program that contains tools for performing complex statistical analysis, such as ANOVA, Correlation, and Histogram.

AND function A logical function that returns TRUE when all arguments are true and FALSE when at least one argument is false.

ANOVA ANOVA stands for Analysis of Variance and is a statistical tool that compares the means between two data samples to determine if they were derived from the same population.

Area chart A chart type that emphasizes magnitude of changes over time by filling in the space between lines with a color.

Argument A variable or constant input, such as a cell reference or value, needed to complete a function. The entire group of arguments for a function is enclosed in parentheses.

Auto Fill A feature that enables you to copy the contents of a cell or a range of cells or to continue a sequence by dragging the fill handle over an adjacent cell or range of cells.

AutoComplete A feature that searches for and automatically displays any other label in that column that matches the letters you typed.

AVERAGE function A statistical function that calculates the arithmetic mean, or average, of values in a range.

AVERAGEIF function A statistical function that calculates the average of values in a range when a specified condition is met.

AVERAGEIFS function A statistical function that returns the average (arithmetic mean) of all cells that meet multiple criteria.

Axis Category or incremental value labels to identify the measurements along the horizontal and vertical axes of a chart.

Axis title A label that describes either the category axis or the value axis. Provides clarity, particularly in describing the value axis.

Background An image that appears behind the worksheet data onscreen; it does not print.

Backstage view A component of Office 2013 that provides a concise collection of commands related to common file activities and provides information on an open file.

Backup A copy of a file or folder on another drive.

Bar chart A chart type that compares values across categories using horizontal bars. In a bar chart, the horizontal axis displays values and the vertical axis displays categories.

Binding constraint A constraint that Solver enforces to reach the target value.

Border A line that surrounds a cell or a range of cells to offset particular data from the rest of the data in a worksheet.

Breakpoint The lowest value for a specific category or series in a lookup table.

Bubble chart A chart type that shows relationships among three values by using bubbles to show a third dimension. The third dimension is indicated by the size of the bubble; the larger the bubble, the larger the value.

Calculated field A user-defined field that performs an arithmetic calculation based on other fields in a PivotTable.

CAPTCHA A scrambled code used with online forms to prevent mass sign-ups. It helps to ensure that an actual person is requesting the account.

Category axis The chart element that displays descriptive group names or labels, such as city names or departments, to identify data.

Category label Text that describes a collection of data points in a chart.

Cell The intersection of a column and row in a worksheet.

Cell address The unique identifier of a cell, starting with the column letter and then the row number, such as A9.

Cell style A set of formatting options applied to worksheet cells to produce a consistent appearance for similar cells within a worksheet.

Changing variable cell A cell containing a variable whose value changes until Solver optimizes the value in the objective cell.

Charms A toolbar for Windows 8 made up of five icons (Search, Share, Start, Devices, and Settings) that enables you to search for files and applications, share information with others within an application that is running, return to the Start screen, control devices that are connected to your computer, or modify various settings depending on which application is running when accessing the Setting icon.

Chart A visual representation of numerical data and helps reveal trends or patterns to help people make informed decisions.

Chart area A boundary that contains the entire chart and all of its elements, including the plot area, titles, legends, and labels.

Chart element A component of a chart that helps complete or clarify the chart.

Chart filter A setting that controls what data series are displayed or hidden in a chart.

Chart sheet A sheet within a workbook that contains a single chart and no spreadsheet data.

Chart style A collection of formatting that controls the color of the chart area, plot area, and data series.

Chart title The label that describes the entire chart. The title is usually placed at the top of the chart area.

Circular reference A situation that occurs when a formula contains a direct or an indirect reference to the cell containing the formula.

Clip art An electronic illustration that can be inserted into an Office project.

Clipboard An Office feature that temporarily holds selections that have been cut or copied and allows you to paste the selections.

Cloud storage A technology used to store files and to work with programs that are stored in a central location on the Internet.

Clustered column chart A type of chart that groups, or clusters, similar data into columns to compare values across columns.

Collaboration A process that occurs when multiple people work together to achieve a common goal by using technology to edit the contents of a file.

Color scale A conditional format that displays a particular color based on the relative value of the cell contents to the other selected cells.

Column chart A type of chart that displays data vertically in columns to compare values across different categories.

Column heading An alphabetical letter above a column in a worksheet.

Column index number The number of the column in the lookup table that contains the return values. Used as the third argument in a VLOOKUP or HLOOKUP function.

Column width The horizontal measurement of a column in a table or a worksheet. In Excel, it is measured by the number of characters or pixels.

Columns area The region in which to place a field that will display labels to organize data vertically in a PivotTable.

Combo chart A chart that combines two chart types, such as column and line, to plot different types of data, such as quantities and percentages.

Comma Style A number format that formats values with commas for the thousands separator and two decimal places.

Command A button or area within a group that you click to perform tasks.

Comma separated values (CSV) file A text file that uses commas to separate text into columns and a newline character to separate data into rows.

Comment (1) A notation attached to a cell to pose a question or provide commentary. (2) A line that documents programming code; starts with an apostrophe and appears in green in the VBA Editor.

Comment indicator A colored triangle in the top-right corner of a cell to indicate that the cell contains comments.

Compatibility Checker A tool that detects data and features that are not compatible with previous versions of Excel.

CONCATENATE function A text function that joins two or more text strings into one text string.

Conditional formatting A set of rules that applies specific formatting to highlight or emphasize cells that meet specifications.

Constraint A limitation that imposes restrictions on a spreadsheet model as Solver determines the optimum value for the objective cell.

Contextual tab A Ribbon tab that displays when an object, such as a picture or table, is selected. A contextual tab contains groups and commands specific to the selected object.

Copy The process of duplicating an item from the original location and place the copy in the Office Clipboard.

CORREL function A statistical function that calculates the correlation coefficient of two data series.

COUNT function A statistical function that tallies the number of cells in a range that contain values you can use in calculations, such as the numerical and date data, but excludes blank cells or text entries from the tally.

COUNTA function A statistical function that tallies the number of cells in a range that are not blank; that is, cells that contain data, whether a value, text, or a formula.

COUNTBLANK function A statistical function that tallies the number of cells in a range that are blank.

COUNTIF function A statistical function that counts the number of cells in a range when a specified condition is met.

COUNTIFS function A statistical function that applies criteria to cells across multiple ranges and counts the number of times all criteria are met.

Covariance Measure of how to sample sets of data vary simultaneously.

Criteria Range An area that is separate from the data table and specifies the conditions used to filter the table.

CUMIPMT A financial function that calculates cumulative interest for specified payment period.

CUMPRINC A financial function that calculates cumulative principal for specified payment periods.

Cut The process of removing an item from the original location and place it in the Office Clipboard.

Data bar A conditional format that displays horizontal gradient or solid fill indicating the cell's relative value compared to other selected cells.

Data label An identifier that shows the exact value of a data point on the value axis in a chart. Appears above or on a data point in a chart. May indicate percentage of a value to the whole on a pie chart.

Data mining The process of analyzing large volumes of data to identify patterns and trends.

Data point A numeric value that describes a single value in a chart or worksheet.

Data range property A setting that controls the format, refresh rate, and other characteristics of a connection to external data.

Data series A group of related data points that display in row(s) or column(s) in a worksheet.

Data table A grid that contains the data source values and labels to plot data in a chart. A data table may be placed below a chart or hidden from view.

Data validation A setting that requires that rules be followed in order to allow data to be entered in a cell.

Database function A function that analyzes data for selected records in a table.

DAVERAGE function A database function that averages values in a database column based on specified conditions.

DCOUNT function A database function that counts the cells that contain a number in a database column based on specified conditions.

Default Office settings that remain in effect unless you specify otherwise.

Delimiter A character, such as a comma or tab, used to separate data in a text file.

Dependent cell A cell containing a formula that is dependent on other cells to obtain its value.

Destination file A file that contains a pointer to the source file.

Dialog box A window that displays when a program requires interaction with you, such as inputting information, before completing a procedure. This window typically provides access to more precise, but less frequently used, commands.

Dialog Box Launcher An icon in a Ribbon group that you can click to open a related dialog box. It is not found in all groups.

Digital signature An electronic notation in a document to authenticate the contents.

DMAX function A database function that identifies the highest value in a database column based on specified conditions.

DMIN function A database function that identifies the lowest value in a database column based on specified conditions.

Document Inspector A tool that detects hidden and personal data in a workbook to remove.

Document property An attribute, such as an author's name or keyword, that describes a file.

Doughnut chart A chart type that displays values as percentages of the whole but may contain more than one data series.

DSUM function A database function that adds values in a database column based on specified conditions.

Element An XML component, including the start tag, an end tag, and the associated data.

Embed The process of importing external data into an application but not maintaining any connection to the original data source.

End tag An XML code that indicates the end of an element and contains the element's name preceded by a slash character, such as </Rent>.

Enhanced ScreenTip A feature that provides a brief summary of a command when you point to the command button.

Error alert A message that appears when the user enters invalid data in a cell containing a validation rule.

Error bar Visual that indicates the standard error amount, a percentage, or a standard deviation for a data point or marker.

Excel A software application used to organize records, financial transactions, and business information in the form of worksheets.

Exploded pie chart A chart type in which one or more pie slices are separated from the rest of the pie chart for emphasis.

Extensible Characteristics that indicate that XML can be expanded to include additional data.

eXtensible Markup Language (XML) A data-structuring standard that enables data to be shared across applications, operating systems, and hardware.

Field The smallest data element in a table, such as first name, last name, address, or phone number.

File Electronic data such as documents, databases, slide shows, worksheets, digital photographs, music, videos, and Web pages.

File Explorer A component of the Windows operating system that can be used to create and manage folders.

Fill color The background color that displays behind the data in a cell.

Fill handle A small square at the bottom-right corner of a cell used to copy cell contents or text or number patterns to adjacent cells.

Filtering The process of specifying conditions to display only those records that meet those conditions.

Filters area The region in which to place a field so that the user can then filter the data by that field in a PivotTable or PivotChart.

Find An Office feature that locates a word or phrase that you indicate in a document.

Fixed-width text file A text file that stores data in columns that have a specific number of characters designated for each column.

Flash Fill A feature that fills in data or values automatically based on one or two examples you enter using another part of data entered in a previous column in the dataset.

Folder A directory into which you place data files in order to organize them for easier retrieval.

Font A combination of typeface and type style.

Format Painter A command that copies the formatting of text from one location to another.

Formula A combination of cell references, operators, values, and/or functions used to perform a calculation. A formula starts with an equal sign (=).

Formula auditing Tools to enable you to detect and correct errors in formulas by identifying relationships among cells.

Formula AutoComplete A feature that displays a list of functions and defined names that match letters as you type a formula.

Formula Bar An element in Excel that appears below the Ribbon and to the right of the Insert Function command. It shows the contents of the active cell.

Freezing The process of keeping rows and/or columns visible onscreen at all times even when you scroll through a large dataset.

FREQUENCY function A statistical function that determines the number of occurrences of numerical values in a dataset based on predetermined bins.

Function A predefined computation that simplifies creating a complex calculation and produces a result based on inputs known as arguments.

Function ScreenTip A small pop-up description that displays the arguments for a function as you enter it directly in a cell.

FV function A financial function that calculates the future value of an investment given a fixed interest rate, a term, and periodic payments.

Gallery A set of selections that displays when you click a More button, or in some cases when you click a command, in a Ribbon group.

Goal Seek A tool that identifies the necessary input value to obtain a desired goal.

Gridline A horizontal or vertical line that extends from the horizontal or vertical axis through the plot area to guide the reader's eyes across the chart to identify values.

Group A subset of a tab that organizes similar tasks together; to combine two or more objects.

Grouping (1) The process of joining rows or columns of related data into a single entity so that groups can be collapsed or expanded for data analysis. (2) The process of selecting worksheets to perform the same action at the same time.

Histogram A tabular display of data frequencies organized into bins.

History worksheet A specially created worksheet through the Change Tracking feature that lists particular types of changes made to a workbook.

HLOOKUP function A lookup & reference function that looks up a value in a horizontal lookup table where the first row contains the values to compare with the lookup value.

Homegroup A Windows 8 feature that enables you to share resources on a home network.

Horizontal alignment The placement of cell data between the left and right cell margins in a worksheet.

Hyperlink An electronic marker to another location in a worksheet, workbook, file, Web page, or email.

Icon set A conditional format that displays an icon representing a value in the top third, quarter, or fifth based on values in the selected range.

IF function A logical function that evaluates a condition and returns one value if the condition is true and a different condition if the value is false.

IFERROR function A logical function that checks a value and returns the result if possible or an error message.

Importing The process of inserting data from one application or file into another.

Indent A format that positions cell contents to the right of the left cell margin to offset the data.

INDEX function A lookup & reference value or reference to a value within a range.

Input area A range of cells in a worksheet used to store and change the variables used in calculations.

Input message A description or instructions for data entry.

IPMT function A financial function that calculates periodic interest for a fixed-term, fixed-rate loan or investment.

Key Tip The letter or number for the associated keyboard shortcut that displays over features on the Ribbon or Quick Access Toolbar.

Keyword A special programming syntax used for a specific purpose that appears in blue in the VBA Editor.

Landscape An orientation for a displayed page or worksheet that is wider than it is tall.

Legend A key that identifies the color, gradient, picture, texture, or pattern assigned to each data series in a chart.

Library A collection of files from different locations that is displayed as a single unit.

Line chart A chart type that displays lines connecting data points to show trends over equal time periods, such as months, quarters, years, or decades.

Linking The process of connecting cells between worksheets.

Live Preview An Office feature that provides a preview of the results of a selection when you point to an option in a list or gallery. Using Live Preview, you can experiment with settings before making a final choice.

Loan amortization table A schedule showing monthly payments, interest per payment, amount toward paying off the loan, and the remaining balance for each payment.

Locked Cell A cell that prevents users from making changes to that cell in a protected worksheet.

Logic error An error that occurs when a formula adheres to syntax rules but produces inaccurate results.

Logical test An expression that evaluates to true or false; the first argument in an IF function.

Lookup table A range that contains data for the basis of the lookup and data to be retrieved. In a vertical lookup table, the first column contains a list of values to compare to the lookup value. In a horizontal lookup table, the first row contains a list of values to compare to the lookup value.

Lookup value The cell reference of the cell that contains the value to look up within a lookup table.

LOWER function A text function that converts all uppercase letters to lowercase.

Macro A set of instructions that tells Excel which commands to execute.

Macro Recorder A tool that records a series of commands in the sequence performed by a user and converts the commands into programming syntax.

Margin The area of blank space that displays to the left, right, top, and bottom of a document or worksheet.

MATCH function A lookup & reference function that identifies a searched item's position in a list.

MAX function A statistical function that finds the highest value in a range.

MEDIAN function A statistical function that finds the midpoint value, which is the value that one half of the values in a list are above or below.

Metadata Pieces of data, such as a keyword, that describe other data, such as the contents of a file.

Microsoft Office A productivity software suite including four primary software components, each one specializing in a particular type of output.

MIN function A statistical function that finds the lowest value in a range.

Mini toolbar The feature that provides access to common formatting commands, displayed when text is selected.

Mixed cell reference A designation that combines an absolute cell reference with a relative cell reference, such as $B4 or B$4.

Module A VBA module is a file that stores Sub procedures and Functions. Modules can be created and viewed in the VBA Editor.

Name Box An identifier that displays the address or the range name of the current cell in an Excel worksheet.

Navigation Pane A section of the File Explorer interface that provides ready access to computer resources, folders, files, and networked peripherals.

Nested function A function that contains another function embedded inside one or more of its arguments.

Newline character A character that designates the end of a line and starts data on a new line or row in a text file.

Nonadjacent range A collection of multiple ranges that are not positioned in a contiguous cluster in an Excel worksheet.

Nonbinding constraint A constraint that does not restrict the target value that Solver finds.

Normal view The default view of a document, worksheet, or presentation.

NOT function A logical function that returns TRUE if the argument is false and FALSE if the argument is true.

NOW function A date & time function that uses the computer's clock to display the current date and time in a cell.

Nper The number of payment periods over the life of a loan or investment; the second argument in the PMT function.

NPER function A financial function that calculates the number of periods for an investment or loan.

NPV function A financial function that calculates the net present value of an investment with periodic payments and a discount rate.

Number formats Predefined settings that control how values appear in cells.

Object A variable that contains both data and code and represents an element of Excel.

Objective cell The cell that contains the formula-based value that you want to maximize, minimize, or set to a value in Solver.

One-variable data table A data analysis tool that provides various results based on changing one variable.

Operating system Software that directs computer activities such as checking all components, managing system resources, and communicating with application software.

Optimization model A model that finds the highest, lowest, or exact value for one particular result by adjusting values for selected variables.

OR function A logical function that returns TRUE if any argument is true and returns FALSE if all arguments are false.

Order of operations (order of precedence) A set of rules that determines the sequence by which operations are calculated in an expression.

Outline A hierarchical structure of data organized so that groups can be expanded to show details or collapsed to show high-level structure.

Output area The range of cells in an Excel worksheet that contain formulas dependent on the values in the input area.

Page break An indication where data will start on another printed page. The software inserts automatic page breaks based on data, margins, and paper size. Users can insert additional page breaks.

Page Break Preview The display that shows the worksheet data and page breaks within the worksheet.

Page Layout view The display that shows the worksheet data, margins, headers, and footers.

Paste The process of placing a cut or copied item in another location.

Paste Options button An icon that displays in the bottom-right corner immediately after using the Paste command. It enables the user to apply different paste options.

Percent Style A number format that displays values as if they were multiplied by 100 and with the % symbol.

PERCENTILE.EXC function A statistical function that returns the percentile of a range excluding the 0 or 100% percentile.

PERCENTILE.INC function A statistical function that returns the percentile of a range including the 0 or 100% percentile.

PERCENTRANK.EXC function A statistical function that identifies a value's rank as a percentile, excluding 0 and 1, of a list of values.

PERCENTRANK.INC function A statistical function that identifies a value's rank as a percentile between 0 and 1 of a list of values.

Personal Macro Workbook A hidden workbook stored in the XL Start folder that contains macros and opens automatically when you start Excel.

Picture A graphic file that is retrieved from storage media or the Internet and placed in an Office project.

Pie chart A chart type that shows each data point in proportion to the whole data series as a slice in a circle. A pie chart depicts only one data series.

PivotChart A graphical representation of data in a PivotTable.

PivotTable An interactive organization of data that consolidates and aggregates data by categories that can be sorted, filtered, and calculated.

PivotTable Fields task pane A window that enables a user to specify what fields are used from a dataset and how to organize the data in columns, rows, values, and filters.

Plot area The region of a chart containing the graphical representation of the values in the data series.

PMT function A financial function in Excel that calculates the periodic loan payment.

Pointing The process of using the mouse pointer to select cells while building a formula. Also known as *semi-selection*.

Population A dataset that contains all the information you would like to evaluate.

Portable Document Format (PDF) A universal file format that preserves a document's original data and formatting for multiplatform use.

Portrait An orientation for a displayed page or worksheet that is taller than it is wide.

PowerPivot A PivotTable functionality in which two or more related tables can be used to extract data into a PivotTable.

PowerPoint A software application used to create dynamic presentations to inform groups and persuade audiences.

PPMT function A financial function that calculates the principal payment for a specified payment period given a fixed interest rate, term, and periodic payments.

Precedent cell A cell that is referenced by a formula in another cell.

Print area The range of cells within a worksheet that will print.

Print order The sequence in which the pages are printed.

Procedure A named sequence of statements that execute as one unit.

PROPER function A text function that capitalizes the first letter in a text string and any other letters in text that follow any character other than a letter.

Pv The present value of a loan or an annuity; the third argument in the PMT function and refers to the original amount of the loan.

PV function A financial function that calculates the present value of an investment.

Quartile A value used to divide a range of numbers into four equal groups.

QUARTILE.EXC function A statistical function that identifies the value at a specific quartile, exclusive of 0 and 4.

QUARTILE.INC function A statistical function that identifies the value at a specific quartile.

Quick Access Toolbar A component of Office 2013, located at the top-left corner of the Office window, that provides handy access to commonly executed tasks such as saving a file and undoing recent actions.

Quick Analysis A tool that provides a fast way to analyze a selected range of data by inserting basic calculations, creating charts, converting the data to a table, or applying conditional formatting or other analytical features.

Radar chart A chart type that compares aggregate values of three or more variables represented on axes starting from the same point.

Range A group of adjacent or contiguous cells in an Excel worksheet.

Range name A word or string of characters assigned to one or more cells. It can be up to 255 letters, characters, or numbers but must start with a letter or underscore and have no spaces or special symbols.

RANK.AVG function A statistical function that identifies the rank of a value, providing an average ranking for identical values.

RANK.EQ function A statistical function that identifies the rank of a value, omitting the next rank when tie values exist.

Rate The periodic interest rate; the percentage of interest paid for each payment period; the first argument in the PMT function.

RATE function A financial function that calculates the periodic rate for an investment or loan.

Record A group of related fields representing one entity, such as data for one person, place, event, or concept.

Refresh The process of updating data in Excel to match current data in the external data source.

Relationship A connection between two or more tables using a common field, such as an ID field.

Relative cell reference A designation that indicates a cell's relative location within the worksheet using the column letter and row number, such as B5. When a formula containing a relative cell reference is copied, the cell references in the copied formula change relative to the position of the copied formula.

Replace An Office feature that finds text and replaces it with a word or phrase that you indicate.

Ribbon The long bar of tabs, groups, and commands located just beneath the Title bar.

Row heading A number to the left side of a row in a worksheet.

Row height The vertical measurement of the row in a worksheet.

Rows area The region in which to place a field that will display labels to organize data horizontally in a PivotTable.

Run time error A software or hardware problem that prevents a program from working correctly.

Sample A smaller portion of the population that is easier to evaluate.

Scenario A set of values that represent a possible situation.

Scenario Manager A tool that enables you to define and manage scenarios to compare how they affect results.

Scenario summary report A worksheet that contains the scenarios, their input values, and their respective results from using Scenario Manager.

Semi-selection The process of using the mouse pointer to select cells while building a formula. Also known as *pointing*.

Shared workbook A file that enables multiple users to make changes at the same time.

Sheet tab A visual element that shows the name of a worksheet contained in the workbook.

Sheet tab navigation Visual elements that help you navigate to the first, previous, next, or last sheet within a workbook.

Shortcut menu A menu that provides choices related to the selection or area at which you right-click.

Signature line A visible digital signature to authenticate the workbook.

Sizing handles A series of faint dots on the outside border of a selected chart or object; enables the user to adjust the height and width of the chart or object.

SkyDrive A central storage location in which you can store, access, and share files via an Internet connection.

Slicer A window listing all items in a field so that the user can click button to filter data by that particular item or value.

Slicer caption The text or field name that appears as a header or title at the top of a slicer to identify the data in that field.

SmartArt A diagram that presents information visually to effectively communicate a message.

Snip The output of using the Snipping Tool.

Snipping Tool A Windows 8 accessory program that provides users the ability to capture an image of all (or part of) their computer's screen.

Solver An add-in application that manipulates variables based on constraints to find the optimal solution to a problem.

Sorting The process of listing records or text in a specific sequence, such as alphabetically by last name.

Source file A file that contains original data.

Sparkline A small line, column, or win/loss chart contained in a single cell to provide a simple visual illustrating one data series.

Split bar A vertical or horizontal line that frames panes in a worksheet and enables the user to resize the panes.

Splitting The process of dividing a worksheet window into resizable panes to enable viewing separate parts of a worksheet at the same time.

Spreadsheet An electronic file that contains a grid of columns and rows used to organize related data and to display results of calculations, enabling interpretation of quantitative data for decision making.

Stacked column chart A chart type that places stacks of data in segments on top of each other in one column, with each category in the data series represented by a different color.

Standard deviation A statistic that measures how far the data sample is spread around the mean.

Start screen The display that you see after you turn on your computer and respond to any username and password prompts.

Start tag An XML code that indicates the starting point for an element and contains the element's name, such as <Rent>.

Status bar A horizontal bar found at the bottom of the program window that contains information relative to the open file. It provides information about a selected command or an operation in progress.

Stock chart A chart type that shows fluctuations in stock changes, such as the high, low, and closing stock prices for a given company on a given day.

Structured reference A tag or use of a table element, such as a column label, as a reference in a formula. Column labels are enclosed in square brackets, such as [Amount], within the formula.

Sub Procedure Command lines written in the VBA Editor that have the ability to perform actions in Excel.

Subfolder A folder that is housed within another folder.

SUBSTITUTE function A text function that substitutes new text for old text in a text string.

Substitution value A value that replaces the original value of a variable in a data table.

Subtotal An aggregate calculation, such as SUM or AVERAGE, that applies for a subcategory of related data within a larger dataset.

SUBTOTAL function A math or trig function that calculates the total of values contained in two or more cells; the first argument in the function specifies which aggregate function applies to the values in the range specified by the second argument.

SUM function A statistical function that calculates the total of values contained in two or more cells.

SUMIF function A statistical function that calculates the total of a range of values when a specified condition is met.

SUMIFS function A statistical function that adds the cells in a range that meet multiple criteria.

Surface chart A chart type that displays trends using two dimensions on a continuous curve.

Syntax The rules that dictate the structure and components required to perform the necessary calculations in an equation or to evaluate expressions.

Syntax error An error that occurs when formula construction rules are violated.

Tab A component of the Ribbon that is designed to appear much like a tab on a file folder, with the active tab highlighted, that is used to organize groups by function.

Tab-delimited file A text file that uses tabs to separate data.

Table An object used to store and organize data in a series of records (rows) with each record made up of a number of fields (columns).

Table array The range that contains the body of the lookup table, excluding column labels. The first column must be in ascending order to find a value in a range, or it can be in any order to look up an exact value. It is the second argument within a VLOOKUP or HLOOKUP function.

Table style A named collection of color, font, and border design that can be applied to a table.

Tag A user-defined marker that identifies the beginning or ending of a piece of data in an XML document.

Template A predesigned workbook that incorporates formatting elements, such as themes and layouts, and may include content that can be modified. A template is used as a model to create similar workbooks.

Text Any combination of letters, numbers, symbols, and spaces not used in Excel calculations.

Text file A data file that contains letters, numbers, and symbols only; it does not contain formatting, sound, or video.

Theme A collection of design choices that includes colors, fonts, and special effects used to give a consistent look to a document, workbook, database form or report, or presentation.

Tile A colorful block on the Start screen that when clicked will launch a program, file, folder, or other Windows 8 app.

Title bar A component of Microsoft Office that identifies the current file name and the application in which you are working and includes control buttons that enable you to minimize, maximize, restore down, or close the application window.

TODAY function A date & time function that displays the current date in a cell.

Toggle The action of switching from one setting to another. Several Home tab tasks, such as Bold and Italic, are actually toggle commands.

Total row A table row that displays below the last row of records in an Excel table, or in Datasheet view of a table or query, and displays summary or aggregate statistics, such as a sum or an average.

Tracer arrow A colored line that indicates relationships between precedent and dependent cells.

Track Changes A collaboration feature that records certain types of changes made in a workbook.

Trendline A line that depicts trends or helps forecast future data in a chart. For example, if the plotted data includes 2005, 2010, and 2015, a trendline can help forecast values for 2020 and beyond.

Two-variable data table A data analysis tool that provides results based on changing two variables.

Ungrouping The process of deselecting worksheets that are grouped.

UPPER function A text function that converts text to uppercase letters.

User interface The screen display through which you communicate with the software.

Validation criteria Rules that dictate the data to enter in a cell.

Value A number that represents a quantity or a measurable amount.

Value axis The chart element that displays incremental numbers to identify approximate values, such as dollars or units, of data points in a chart.

Values area The range in which to place a field that will display aggregates, such as SUM, for categories of data in a PivotTable.

Variable A value that you can change to see how that change affects other values.

Variance A descriptive statistics tool that determines the summation of the squared deviations divided by the amount of the sample – 1.

Vertical alignment The position of data between the top and bottom cell margins.

View The way contents of a file appear onscreen.

View controls Icons on the right side of the status bar that enable you to change to Normal, Page Layout, or Page Break view to display the worksheet.

Visual Basic Editor The Office application used to create, edit, execute, and debug macros using programming language.

Visual Basic for Applications (VBA) The Office application used to create, edit, execute, and debug macros using programming language.

VLOOKUP function A lookup & reference function that looks up a value and returns a related result from the lookup table.

Watch Window A window that enables you to view formula calculations.

Web query A data connection that links an Excel worksheet to a particular data table on a Web page.

What-if analysis The process of changing variables to observe how changes affect calculated results.

Windows 8 A Microsoft operating system released in 2012 that can operate on touch-screen devices as well as laptops and desktops because it has been designed to accept multiple methods of input.

Windows 8 app An application specifically designed to run in the Start screen interface of Windows 8 that is either already installed and ready to use or can be downloaded from the Windows Store.

Word A word processing software application used to produce all sorts of documents, including memos, newsletters, forms, tables, and brochures.

Workbook A collection of one or more related worksheets contained within a single file.

Worksheet A single spreadsheet that typically contains descriptive labels, numeric values, formulas, functions, and graphical representations of data.

Worksheet reference A pointer to a cell in another worksheet.

Workspace file A document that specifies the window settings for a workbook.

Wrap text An Excel feature that makes data appear on multiple lines within a cell.

X Y (scatter) chart A chart type that shows a relationship between two variables using their X and Y coordinates. Excel plots one coordinate on the horizontal X-axis and the other variable on the vertical Y-axis. Scatter charts are often used to represent data in educational, scientific, and medical experiments.

X-axis A horizontal border that provides a frame of reference for measuring data horizontally on a chart.

XML declaration A statement that specifies the XML version and character encoding used in the XML document.

Y-axis A vertical border that provides a frame of reference for measuring data vertically on a chart.

Zoom control A control that enables you to increase or decrease the size of the worksheet data onscreen.

Zoom slider A horizontal bar on the far right side of the status bar that enables you to increase or decrease the size of file contents onscreen.

Index

B

C

E

F

O

P

Q

R

S